MILITARY AIRCRAFT MARKINGS 2002

Ian Allan abc

£1

Peter R. March &
Howard J. Curtis

Ian Allan

60th

ANNIVERSARY

Contents

Introduction	5
Acknowledgements	6
Abbreviations	7
A Guide to the Location of Operational Bases in the UK	10
British Military Aircraft Serials	12
British Military Aircraft Markings	13
Civil Registered Aircraft in UK Military Service	103
RAF Maintenance/Support Command Cross-reference	109
RN Landing Platform and Shore Station Code-letters	113
Ships' Numeric Code – Deck Letters Analysis	115
RN Code – Squadron – Base – Aircraft Cross-check	115
Royal Air Force Squadron Markings	116
University Air Squadrons/Air Experience Flights	120
Historic Aircraft in Overseas Markings	121
Irish Military Aircraft Markings	140
Overseas Military Aircraft Markings	141
US Military Aircraft Markings	184
UK-based USAF Aircraft	184
UK-based US Navy Aircraft	185
European-based USAF Aircraft	186
European-based US Navy/US Army Aircraft	188
US-based USAF Aircraft	192
US-based USN/USMC Aircraft	213
US-based US Coast Guard Aircraft	216
US Government Aircraft	216
Military Aviation Sites on the Internet	217

Photographs by Peter R. March (PRM) unless otherwise credited

This twenty-third edition published 2002

ISBN 0 7110 2846 X

Published by Ian Allan Publishing

an imprint of Ian Allan Publishing Ltd, Hersham, Surrey KT12 4RG.
Printed by Ian Allan Printing Ltd, Hersham, Surrey KT12 4RG

Code: 0203/F2

Front cover:
Lockheed C-130J Hercules C5 ZH889 of No 24 Squadron. *Andrew Brooks www.avcollect.com*

Back cover:
Panavia Tornado GR1 ZA447 of No XV Squadron, coded TA. *PRM*

3

The first of the RAF's four Globemasters, ZZ171, touching down at RAF Brize Norton. *PRM*

Introduction

This twenty-third annual edition of the *abc Military Aircraft Markings*, jointly edited by Peter R. March and Howard J Curtis, lists in alphabetical and numerical order all of the aircraft that carry a United Kingdom military serial, and **which are based, or might be seen, in the UK**. It also includes airworthy and current RAF/RN/Army aircraft that are based permanently or temporarily overseas. The term *aircraft* used here covers powered, manned aeroplanes, helicopters, airships and gliders. Included are all the current Royal Air Force, Royal Navy, Army Air Corps, Defence Procurement Agency, QinetiQ operated, manufacturers' test aircraft and civilian-owned aircraft with military markings.

Aircraft withdrawn from operational use but which are retained in the UK for ground training purposes or otherwise preserved by the Services and in the numerous museums and collections are listed. The serials of some incomplete aircraft have been included, such as the cockpit sections of machines displayed by the RAF, aircraft used by airfield fire sections and for service battle damage repair training (BDRT), together with significant parts of aircraft held by preservation groups and societies. Where only part of the aircraft fuselage remains the abbreviation <ff> for front fuselage/cockpit section or <rf> for rear fuselage is shown after the type. Many of these aircraft are allocated, and sometimes wear, a secondary identity, such as an RAF 'M' maintenance number. These numbers are listed against those aircraft to which they have been allocated.

A serial 'missing' from a sequence is either because it was never issued as it formed part of a 'black-out block' (a practice that has now ceased) or because the aircraft is written off, scrapped, sold abroad or allocated an alternative marking. Aircraft used as targets on MoD ranges to which access is restricted, and un-manned target drones, are generally omitted, as are UK military aircraft that have been permanently grounded and are based overseas and unlikely to return to Britain.

In the main, the serials listed are those markings presently displayed on the aircraft. Where an aircraft carries a false serial it is quoted in *italic type*. Very often these serials are carried by replicas, that are denoted by <R> after the type. The manufacturer and aircraft type are given, together with recent alternative, previous, secondary or civil identity shown in round brackets. Complete records of multiple previous identities are only included where space permits. The operating unit and its based location, along with any known unit and base code markings in square brackets, are given as accurately as possible. The unit markings are normally carried boldly on the sides of the fuselage or on the aircraft's fin. In the case of RAF and AAC machines currently in service, they are usually one or two letters or numbers, while the RN continues to use a well-established system of three-figure codes between 000 and 999 together with a fin letter code denoting the aircraft's operational base. RN squadrons, units and bases are allocated blocks of numbers from which individual aircraft codes are issued. To help identification of RN bases and landing platforms on ships, a list of tail-letter codes with their appropriate name, helicopter code number, ship pennant number and type of vessel, is included; as is a helicopter code number/ships' tail-letter code grid cross-reference.

Codes change, for example when aircraft move between units, and therefore the markings currently painted on a particular aircraft might not be those shown in this edition because of subsequent events. Aircraft currently under manufacture or not yet delivered to the Service, such as Westland WAH-64 Apaches at Yeovil, BAE Systems Hawks, Eurofighter Typhoons etc are listed under their allocated serial number. Likewise there are a number of newly built aircraft for overseas air arms that carry British serials for their UK and delivery flights. The four C-17 Globemasters leased from the US government unusually carry out-of-sequence serials ZZ171-ZZ174. Those airframes which may not appear in the next edition because of sale, accident, etc, have their fates, where known, given in italic type in the *locations* column.

The Irish Army Air Corps fleet is listed, together with the serials of other overseas air arms whose aircraft might be seen visiting the UK from time to time. The serial numbers are as usually presented on the individual machine or as they are normally identified. Where possible, the aircraft's base and operating unit have been shown.

USAF, US Army and US Navy aircraft based in the UK and in Western Europe, and types that regularly visit the UK from the USA, are each listed in separate sections by aircraft type. The serial number actually displayed on the aircraft is shown in full, with additional Fiscal Year (FY) or full serial information also provided. Where appropriate, details of the operating wing, squadron allocation and base are added. The USAF is, like the RAF, in a continuing period of change, resulting in the adoption of new unit titles, squadron and equipment changes and the closure of bases. Only details that concern changes effected by January 2002 are shown.

Veteran and vintage aircraft which carry overseas military markings but which are based in the UK or regularly visit from mainland Europe, have been separately listed showing their principal means of identification. The growing list of aircraft in government or military service, often under contract to private operating companies, that carry civil registrations has again been included, but in this edition at the end of the respective country.

With the use of the Internet now very well established as a rich source of information, the section listing a selection of military aviation 'world wide web' sites, has been further expanded and up-dated this year. Although only a few of these provide details of aircraft serials and markings, they do give interesting insights into air arms and their operating units, aircraft, museums and a broad range of associated topics.

Information shown is believed to be correct at 31 January 2002, and significant changes can be monitored through the monthly 'Military Markings' and 'Vintage Serials' columns in *Aircraft Illustrated* and for Internet up-dates the 'Airnet' column.

Acknowledgements

The compilers wish to thank the many people who have taken trouble to send comments, additions, deletions and other useful information following the publication of the previous edition of *abc Military Aircraft Markings*. In particular the following individuals: Mark Almond, David Apps, Bob Archer, Ash Bailey, Allan Barley, Nick Blacow, Nigel Burch, Phil Butler, Steve Buttriss, Tim Cheney, Barry Cooper, Dougie Couch, Antoin Daltun, John Davison, Ollie Dewey, Perry Dirkx, Al Duncan, Bob Dunn, Ben Dunnell, John Dyer, Tony Exelby, Ray Fitton, Wal Gandy, Edwin de Greeuw, Jerry Gunner, Dave Haines, Kevin Hall, Erik-Jan Hartman, David Hastings, Frank van Hemert, Alistair Henderson, Lee Howard, Tim Jones, Thomas Kaminski, Peter Kesselaar, Mark Kortvely, Iain Logan, Doug MacDonald, Dan March, Andy Marden, Bernard Martin, Gianfranco Mauri, Tom McGhee, Frank McMeiken, Tom Meikle, Julian Moody, Martyn Morgan, Coert Munk, Simon Munns, Peter Norris, Mike O'Leary, Steve Poole, Nigel Porembski, Martin Powell, Doug Pritchard, Nigel Pritchard, John Ross, Kev Slade, Rick Sleight, Philip Smith, Gary Stedman, Kev Storer, David Stretton, Martyn Swann, Tony Szulc, Mervyn Thomas, Andy Thomson, Lee Weston, Ian Woodcock, Mark Young.

This compilation has also relied heavily on the publications and aviation groups and societies as follows: Aerodata Quantum+, Air-Britain Information Exchange, Air-Britain Digest, Air-Britain News, Graham Gaff/East London Aviation Society, Military Aviation Review, Military Spotter's Forum, St Athan Aviation Group, SAAB Viggen E-mail group, Scramble, Wolverhampton Aviation Group and the World Wide Web.

PRM & HJC   January 2002

Abbreviations

AAC	Army Air Corps	CC	County Council
AACS	Airborne Air Control Squadron	CCF	Combined Cadet Force/Canadian Car & Foundry Company
AACTS	Airborne Air Control Training Squadron		
AAS	Aeromedical Airlift Squadron	CDE	Chemical Defence Establishment
ABS	Air Base Squadron	CEAM	Centre d'Expérimentation Aériennes
ACC	Air Combat Command		Militaires (Military Air Experimental
ACCGS	Air Cadets Central Gliding School		Centre)
ACCS	Airborne Command and Control Squadron	CEPA	Centre d'Expérimentation Pratique de
ACW	Airborne Control Wing		l'Aéronautique Navale
AD&StA	Aberdeen, Dundee & St Andrews	CEV	Centre d'Essais en Vol (Flight Test Centre)
AEF	Air Experience Flight	CFS	Central Flying School
AESS	Air Engineering & Survival School	CGMF	Central Glider Maintenance Flight
AEW	Airborne Early Warning	CIFAS	Centre d'Instruction des Forces
AF	Arméflyget (Army Air Battalion)		Aériennes Stratégiques (Air Strategic
AFB	Air Force Base		Training Centre)
AFD	Air Fleet Department	CinC	Commander in Chief
AFRC	Air Force Reserve Command	CinCLANT	Commander in Chief Atlantic
AFSC	Air Force Systems Command	CITac	Centre d'Instruction Tactique (Tactical
AFSK	Armeflygskolan (Army Flying School)		Training Centre)
AFWF	Advanced Fixed Wing Flight	Co	Company
AG	Airlift Group	Comp	Composite with
AGA	Academia General del Aire (General Air	CT	College of Technology
	Academy)	CTE	Central Training Establishment
AkG	Aufklärüngsgeschwader	CV	Chance-Vought
	(Reconnaissance Wing)	D-BA	Daimler-Benz Aerospace
AMC	Air Mobility Command	D-BD	Dassault-Breguet Dornier
AMD-BA	Avions Marcel Dassault-Breguet Aviation	D&G	Dumfries and Galloway
AMF	Aircraft Maintenance Flight	DARA	Defence Aviation Repair Agency
AMG	Aircraft Maintenance Group	DEODS	Defence Explosives Ordnance Disposal
AMIF	Aircraft Maintenance Instruction Flight		School
AMS	Air Movements School	DERA	Defence Evaluation and Research Agency
AMW	Air Mobility Wing	Det	Detachment
ANG	Air National Guard	DH	de Havilland
APS	Aircraft Preservation Society	DHC	de Havilland Canada
ARS	Air Refuelling Squadron	DHFS	Defence Helicopter Flying School
ARW	Air Refuelling Wing	DLMW	Dywizjon Lotniczy Marynarki Wojennej
ARWS	Advanced Rotary Wing Squadron	dlt	dopravni letka (Transport Squadron)
AS	Airlift Squadron/Air Squadron	DPA	Defence Procurement Agency
ASCW	Airborne Surveillance Control Wing	DTI	Department of Trade and Industry
ASF	Aircraft Servicing Flight	EA	Escadron Aérien (Air Squadron)
AS&RU	Aircraft Salvage and Repair Unit	EAC	Ecole de l'Aviation de Chasse (Fighter
ATC	Air Training Corps		Aviation School)
ATCC	Air Traffic Control Centre	EAP	European Aircraft Project
Avn	Aviation	EAT	Ecole de l'Aviation de Transport
Avn Co	Aviation Company		(Transport Aviation School)
AW	Airlift Wing/Armstrong Whitworth Aircraft	EC	Escadre de Chasse (Fighter Wing)
AWC	Air Warfare Centre	ECS	Electronic Countermeasures Squadron
BAC	British Aircraft Corporation	EDA	Escadre de Detection Aéroportée
BAe	British Aerospace PLC		(Air Detection Wing)
BAPC	British Aviation Preservation Council	EdC	Escadron de Convoyage
BATUS	British Army Training Unit Suffield	EDCA	Escadron de Détection et de Control
BBMF	Battle of Britain Memorial Flight		Aéroportée (Airborne Detection & Control
BDRF	Battle Damage Repair Flight		Sqn)
BDRT	Battle Damage Repair Training	EE	English Electric/Escadrille Electronique
Be	Beech	EET	Escadron Electronique Tactique (Tactical
Bf	Bayerische Flugzeugwerke		Electronics Flight)
BFWF	Basic Fixed Wing Flight	EH	Escadron d'Helicoptères (Helicopter Flight)
BG	Bomber Group	EHI	European Helicopter Industries
BGA	British Gliding & Soaring Association	EL	Escadre de Liaison (Liaison Wing)
bk	black (squadron colours and markings)	EMA	East Midlands Airport
bl	blue (squadron colours and markings)	EMVO	Elementaire Militaire Vlieg Opleiding
BNFL	British Nuclear Fuels Ltd		(Elementary Flying Training)
BnHATk	Helicopter Attack Battalion	ENOSA	Ecole des Navigateurs Operationales
BnHLn	Liaison Battalion		Systemes d'Armees (Navigation School)
BP	Boulton & Paul	EoN	Elliot's of Newbury
br	brown (squadron colours and markings)	EPAA	Ecole de Pilotage Elementaire de l'Armée
BS	Bomber Squadron		de l'Air (Air Force Elementary Flying
B-V	Boeing-Vertol		School)
BW	Bomber Wing	EPE	Ecole de Pilotage Elementaire
CAC	Commonwealth Aircraft Corporation		(Elementary Flying School)
CAM	College of Aviation Medicine	EPNER	Ecole du Personnel Navigant d'Essais et
CARG	Cotswold Aircraft Restoration Group		de Reception
CASA	Construcciones Aeronautics SA	EPTT	Exhibition, Production & Transportation
Cav	Cavalry		Team

ER	Escadre de Reconnaissance (Reconnaissance Wing)
ERS	Escadron de Reconnaissance Stratégique (Strategic Reconnaissance Squadron)
ERV	Escadre de Ravitaillement en Vol (Air Refuelling Wing)
ES	Escadrille de Servitude
Esc	Escuadron (Squadron)
Esk	Eskadrille (Squadron)
Eslla	Escuadrilla (Squadron)
Esq	Esquadra (Squadron)
ET	Escadre de Transport (Transport Squadron)
ETE	Escadron de Transport et Entrainment (Transport Training Squadron)
ETEC	Escadron de Transport d'Entrainement et de Calibration (Transport Training & Calibration Sqn)
ETL	Escadron de Transport Légère (Light Transport Squadron)
ETO	Escadron de Transition Operationnelle
ETOM	Escadron de Transport Outre Mer (Overseas Transport Squadron)
ETPS	Empire Test Pilots' School
ETS	Engineering Training School
FAA	Fleet Air Arm/Federal Aviation Administration
FACF	Forward Air Control Flight
FBS	Flugbereitschaftstaffel
FBW	Fly by wire
FC	Forskokcentralen (Flight Centre)
FE	Further Education
FETC	Fire and Emergency Training Centre
ff	Front fuselage
FG	Fighter Group
FH	Fairchild-Hiller
FI	Falkland Islands
FISt	Flieger Staffel (Flight Squadron)
Flt	Flight
FMA	Fabrica Militar de Aviones
FMT	Flotila Militara de Transport (Transport Regiment)
FMV	Forsvarets Materielwerk
FONA	Flag Officer Naval Aviation
FRADU	Fleet Requirements and Air Direction Unit
FRA	FR Aviation
FS	Fighter Squadron
FSAIU	Flight Safety & Accident Investigation Unit
FSCTE	Fire Services Central Training Establishment
FTS	Flying Training School
FTW	Flying Training Wing
Fw	Focke Wulf
FW	Fighter Wing/Foster Wickner
FWTS	Fixed Wing Test Squadron
FY	Fiscal Year
F3 OCU	Tornado F3 Operational Conversion Unit
GAL	General Aircraft Ltd
GAM	Groupe Aerien Mixte (Composite Air Group)
gd	gold (squadron colours and markings)
GD	General Dynamics
GHL	Groupe d'Helicopteres Legeres (Light Helicopter Group)
GI	Ground Instruction/Groupement d'Instruction (Instructional Group)
gn	green (squadron colours and markings)
GRD	Gruppe fur Rustunggdienste (Group for Service Preparation)
GT	Grupo de Transporte (Transport Wing)
GTT	Grupo de Transporte de Tropos (Troop Carrier Wing)
gy	grey (squadron colours and markings)
H&W	Hereford and Worcester
HAF	Historic Aircraft Flight
HC	Helicopter Combat Support Squadron
HF	Historic Flying Ltd

HFR	Heeresfliegerregiment (Army Air Regiment)
HFWS	Heeresflieger Waffenschule (Army Air Weapons School)
Hkp Div	Helikopterdivisionen (Helicopter Division)
HMA	Helicopter Maritime Attack
HMF	Harrier Maintenance Flight/Helicopter Maintenance Flight
HMS	Her Majesty's Ship
HOCU	Harrier OCU
HP	Handley-Page
HQ	Headquarters
HRO	Harcàszati Repülö Ezred
HS	Hawker Siddeley
HSF	Harrier Servicing Flight
IAF	Israeli Air Force
INTA	Instituto Nacional de Tecnica Aerospacial
IOW	Isle Of Wight
IWM	Imperial War Museum
JATE	Joint Air Transport Establishment
JbG	Jagdbombergeschwader (Fighter Bomber Wing)
JFACSTU	Joint Forward Air Control Students Training Unit
JG	Jagdgeschwader (Fighter Wing)
Kridlo	Wing
Letka	Squadron
LMAC	Lockheed Martin Aeronautics Co
ltBVr	letka Bitevnich Vrtulníkù (Attack Helicopter Squadron)
LTG	Lufttransportgeschwader (Air Transport Wing)
LTV	Ling-Temco-Vought
LVG	Luftwaffen Versorgungs Geschwader (Air Force Maintenance Wing)/Luft Verkehrs Gesellschaft
LZO	Letecky Zku ební Odbor (Aviation Test Department)
m	multi-coloured (squadron colours and markings)
MAPK	Mira Anachestisis Pantos Kerou (All Weather Interception Sqn)
MARPAT	Maritime Patrouillegroep (Maritime Patrol Group)
MASU	Mobile Aircraft Support Unit
MBB	Messerschmitt Bolkow-Blohm
MCAS	Marine Corps Air Station
McD	McDonnell Douglas
Med	Medical
MFG	Marine Flieger Geschwader (Naval Air Wing)
MH	Max Holste
MIB	Military Intelligence Battalion
MiG	Mikoyan — Gurevich
Mod	Modified
MR	Maritime Reconnaissance
MRF	Meteorological Research Flight
MS	Morane-Saulnier
MTM	Mira Taktikis Metaforon (Tactical Transport Sqn)
MU	Maintenance Unit
Mus'm	Museum
NA	North American
NACDS	Naval Air Command Driving School
NAEWF	NATO Airborne Early Warning Force
NAF	Naval Air Facility
NAS	Naval Air Station
NASU	Naval Air Support Unit
NATO	North Atlantic Treaty Organisation
NAWC	Naval Air Warfare Center
NAWC-AD	Naval Air Warfare Center Aircraft Division
NBC	Nuclear, Biological and Chemical
NE	North-East
NFATS	Naval Force Aircraft Test Squadron
NI	Northern Ireland
NMSU	Nimrod Major Servicing Unit
NYARC	North Yorks Aircraft Restoration Centre

OCU	Operational Conversion Unit
OEU	Operation Evaluation Unit
OFMC	Old Flying Machine Company
or	orange (squadron colours and markings)
OSAC	Operational Support Airlift Command
OVH Kmp	Observations-Helicopter Kompagni
PASF	Puma Aircraft Servicing Flight
PAT	Priority Air Transport Detachment
PBN	Pilatus Britten-Norman
PLM	Pulk Lotnictwa Mysliwskiego (Fighter Regiment)
pr	purple (squadron colours and markings)
PRU	Photographic Reconnaissance Unit
PVH Kmp	Panservaerns-Helicopter Kompagni
pzdlt	prùzkumná dopravni letka (Reconnaissance & Transport Squadron)
r	red (squadron colours and markings)
R	Replica
RAeS	Royal Aeronautical Society
RAF	Royal Aircraft Factory/Royal Air Force
RAFC	Royal Air Force College
RAFM	Royal Air Force Museum
RAFGSA	Royal Air Force Gliding and Soaring Association
RCAF	Royal Canadian Air Force
RE	Royal Engineers
Regt	Regiment
REME	Royal Electrical & Mechanical Engineers
rf	Rear fuselage
RJAF	Royal Jordanian Air Force
RM	Royal Marines
RMB	Royal Marines Base
RMC of S	Royal Military College of Science
RN	Royal Navy
RNAS	Royal Naval Air Station
RNAW	Royal Naval Aircraft Workshop
RNAY	Royal Naval Aircraft Yard
RNGSA	Royal Navy Gliding and Soaring Association
ROF	Royal Ordnance Factory
RQS	Rescue Squadron
R-R	Rolls-Royce
RS	Reid & Sigrist/Reconnaissance Squadron
RSV	Reparto Sperimentale Volo (Experimental Flight School)
RW	Reconnaissance Wing
SA	Scottish Aviation
Saab	Svenska Aeroplan Aktieboleg
SAH	School of Air Handling
SAL	Scottish Aviation Limited
SAOEU	Strike/Attack Operational Evaluation Unit
SAR	Search and Rescue
Saro	Saunders-Roe
SARTU	Search and Rescue Training Unit
SBoLK	Stíhacie Bombardovacie Letecké Kridlo (Fighter Bomber Air Wing)
SCW	Strategic Communications Wing
SEAE	School of Electrical & Aeronautical Engineering
SEPECAT	Société Européenne de Production de l'avion Ecole de Combat et d'Appui Tactique
SFDO	School of Flight Deck Operations
SHAPE	Supreme Headquarters Allied Forces Europe
si	silver (squadron colours and markings)
SIET	Section d'Instruction et d'Etude du Tir
SKTU	Sea King Training Unit
Skv	Skvadron (Squadron)
SLK	Stíhacie Kridlo (Fighter Air Wing)
slt	stíhací letka (Fighter Squadron)
SLV	School Licht Vliegwezen (Flying School)
Sm	Smaldeel (Squadron)
SNCAN	Société Nationale de Constructions Aéronautiques du Nord
SOES	Station Operations & Engineering Squadron
SOG	Special Operations Group
SOS	Special Operations Squadron
SoTT	School of Technical Training
SOW	Special Operations Wing
SPAD	Société Pour les Appareils Deperdussin
Sqn	Squadron
SSF	Station Servicing Flight
SWWAPS	Second World War Aircraft Preservation Society
TA	Territorial Army
TAP	Transporten Avio Polk (Air Transport Regiment)
T&EE	Test & Evaluation Establishment
TFC	The Fighter Collection
TGp	Test Groep
TIARA	Tornado Integrated Avionics Research Aircraft
tlt	taktická letka (Tactical Squadron)
TMF	Tornado Maintenance Flight
TMTS	Trade Management Training School
tpzlt	taktická a prùzkumná letka (Tactical & Reconnaissance Squadron)
TS	Test Squadron
TsAGI	Tsentral'ny Aerogidrodinamicheski Instut (Central Aero & Hydrodynamics Institute)
TsLw	Technische Schule der Luftwaffe (Luftwaffe Technical School)
TSW	Tactical Supply Wing
TW	Test Wing
UAS	University Air Squadron
Uberwg	Uberwachunggeschwader (Surveillance Wing)
UK	United Kingdom
UKAEA	United Kingdom Atomic Energy Authority
UNFICYP	United Nations' Forces in Cyprus
US	United States
USAF	United States Air Force
USAFE	United States Air Forces in Europe
USAREUR	US Army Europe
USCGS	US Coast Guard Station
USEUCOM	United States European Command
USMC	United States Marine Corps
USN	United States Navy
NWTSPM	United States Navy Test Pilots School
VAAC	Vectored thrust Advanced Aircraft flight Control
VFW	Vereinigte Flugtechnische Werke
VGS	Volunteer Gliding School
vlt	vycviková letka (Training Squadron)
VMGR	Marine Aerial Refuelling/Transport Squadron
VMGRT	Marine Aerial Refuelling/Transport Training Squadron
VQ	Fleet Air Reconnaissance Squadron
VR	Fleet Logistic Support Squadron
VS	Vickers-Supermarine
VSD	Vegyes Szàllitorepülö Dandàr (Aircraft Transport Brigade)
VSL	Vycvikové Stredisko Letectva (Flying Training Centre)
w	white (squadron colours and markings)
Wg	Wing
WHL	Westland Helicopters Ltd
WLT	Weapons Loading Training
WRS	Weather Reconnaissance Squadron
WS	Westland
WTD	Wehrtechnische Dienstelle (Technical Support Unit)
WW2	World War II
y	yellow (squadron colours and markings)
zDL	základna Dopravního Letectva (Air Transport Base)
ZmDK	Zmie an_ Dopravn_ Kridlo (Mixed Transport Wing)
zSL	základna kolního Letectva (Training Air Base)
zTL	základna Taktického Letectva (Tactical Air Base)
zVrL	základna Vrtulníkového Letectva (Helicopter Air Base)

9

A Guide to the Location of Operational Military Bases in the UK

This section is to assist the reader to locate the places in the United Kingdom where operational military aircraft are based. The term *aircraft* also includes helicopters and gliders.

The alphabetical order listing gives each location in relation to its county and to its nearest classified road(s) (*by* means adjoining; *of* means proximate to), together with its approximate direction and mileage from the centre of a nearby major town or city. Some civil airports are included where active military units are also based, but **excluded** are MoD sites with non-operational aircraft (eg *gate guardians*), the bases of privately-owned civil aircraft that wear military markings and museums.

User	Base name	County/Region	Location	Distance/direction from (town)
QinetiQ	Aberporth	Dyfed	N of A487	6m ENE of Cardigan
Army	Abingdon	Oxfordshire	W by B4017, W of A34	5m SSW of Oxford
RAF	Aldergrove/Belfast Airport	Co Antrim	W by A26	13m W of Belfast
RM	Arbroath	Angus	E of A933	2m NW of Arbroath
RAF/HCS	Barkston Heath	Lincolnshire	W by B6404, S of A153	5m NNE of Grantham
RAF	Benson	Oxfordshire	E by A423	1m NE of Wallingford
QinetiQ/ RAF	Boscombe Down	Wiltshire	S by A303, W of A338	6m N of Salisbury
RAF	Boulmer	Northumberland	E of B1339	4m E of Alnwick
RAF	Brize Norton	Oxfordshire	W of A4095	5m SW of Witney
Marshall	Cambridge Airport/ Teversham	Cambridgeshire	S by A1303	2m E of Cambridge
RM/RAF	Chivenor	Devon	S of A361	4m WNW of Barnstaple
RAF	Church Fenton	Yorkshire North	S of B1223	7m WNW of Selby
RAF	Colerne	Wiltshire	S of A420, E of Fosse Way	5m NE of Bath
RAF	Coltishall	Norfolk	W of B1150	9m NNE of Norwich
RAF	Coningsby	Lincolnshire	S of A153, W by B1192	10m NW of Boston
RAF	Cosford	Shropshire	W of A41, N of A464	9m WNW of Wolverhampton
RAF	Cottesmore	Rutland	W of A1, N of B668	9m NW of Stamford
RAF	Cranwell	Lincolnshire	N by A17, S by B1429	5m WNW of Sleaford
RN	Culdrose	Cornwall	E by A3083	1m SE of Helston
Army	Dishforth	Yorkshire North	E by A1	4m E of Ripon
USAF	Fairford	Gloucestershire	S of A417	9m ESE of Cirencester
RN	Fleetlands	Hampshire	E by A32	2m SE of Fareham
RAF	Glasgow Airport	Strathclyde	N by M8 jn 28	7m W of city
RAF	Halton	Buckinghamshire	N of A4011, S of B4544	4m ESE of Aylesbury
RAF	Henlow	Bedfordshire	E of A600, W of A6001	1m SW of Henlow
RAF	Honington	Suffolk	E of A134, W of A1088	6m S of Thetford
Army	Hullavington	Wiltshire	W of A429	1m N of M4 jn 17
RAF	Kenley	Greater London	W of A22	1m W of Warlingham
RAF	Kinloss	Grampian	E of B9011, N of B9089	3m NE of Forres
RAF	Kirknewton	Lothian	E by B7031, N by A70	8m SW of Edinburgh
USAF	Lakenheath	Suffolk	W by A1065	8m W of Thetford
RAF	Leeming	Yorkshire North	E by A1	5m SW of Northallerton
RAF	Leuchars	Fife	E of A919	7m SE of Dundee
RAF	Linton-on-Ouse	Yorkshire North	E of B6265	10m NW of York
QinetiQ	Llanbedr	Gwynedd	W of A496	7m NNW of Barmouth
RAF	Lossiemouth	Grampian	W of B9135, S of B9040	4m N of Elgin
RAF	Lyneham	Wiltshire	W of A3102, S of A420	10m WSW of Swindon
RAF	Marham	Norfolk	N by A1122	6m W of Swaffham
Army	Middle Wallop	Hampshire	S by A343	6m SW of Andover
USAF	Mildenhall	Suffolk	S by A1101	9m NNE of Newmarket
RAF	Northolt	Greater London	N by A40	3m E of M40 jn 1
RAF	Odiham	Hampshire	E of A32	2m S of M3 jn 5
RN	Predannack	Cornwall	W by A3083	7m S of Helston
RAF	St Athan	South Glamorgan	N of B4265	13m WSW of Cardiff
RAF	St Mawgan/Newquay	Cornwall	N of A3059	4m ENE of Newquay
RAF	Scampton	Lincolnshire	W by A15	6m N of Lincoln
RAF	Sealand	Flint	W by A550	6m WNW of Chester
RAF	Shawbury	Shropshire	W of B5063	7m NNE of Shrewsbury
RAF	Syerston	Nottinghamshire	W by A46	5m SW of Newark
RAF	Ternhill	Shropshire	SW by A41	3m SW of Market Drayton

User	Base name	County/Region	Location	Distance/direction from (town)
RAF/ Army	Topcliffe	Yorkshire North	E of A167, W of A168	3m SW of Thirsk
RAF	Valley	Gwynedd	S of A5 on Anglesey	5m SE of Holyhead
RAF	Waddington	Lincolnshire	E by A607, W by A15	5m S of Lincoln
Army/ RAF	Wattisham	Suffolk	N of B1078	5m SSW of Stowmarket
QinetiQ	West Freugh	Dumfries & Galloway	S by A757, W by A715	5m SE of Stranraer
RAF	Weston-on-the-Green	Oxfordshire	E by A43	9m N of Oxford
RAF	Wittering	Cambridgeshire	W by A1, N of A47	3m S of Stamford
RAF	Woodvale	Merseyside	W by A565	5m SSW of Southport
RAF	Wyton	Cambridgeshire	E of A141, N of B1090	3m NE of Huntingdon
RN	Yeovilton	Somerset	S by B3151, S of A303	5m N of Yeovil

Rolls-Royce-powered Eurofighter ZH588 flying with Spitfire XIX PL983. *PRM*

British Military Aircraft Serials

The Committee of Imperial Defence through its Air Committee introduced a standardised system of numbering aircraft in November 1912. The Air Department of the Admiralty was allocated the first batch 1-200 and used these to cover aircraft already in use and those on order. The Army was issued with the next block from 201-800, which included the number 304 which was given to the Cody Biplane now preserved in the Science Museum. By the outbreak of World War 1 the Royal Navy was on its second batch of serials 801-1600 and this system continued with alternating allocations between the Army and Navy until 1916 when number 10000, a Royal Flying Corps BE2C, was reached.

It was decided not to continue with five digit numbers but instead to start again from 1, prefixing RFC aircraft with the letter A and RNAS aircraft with the prefix N. The RFC allocations commenced with A1 an FE2D and before the end of the year had reached A9999 an Armstrong Whitworth FK8. The next group commenced with B1 and continued in logical sequence through the C, D, E and F prefixes. G was used on a limited basis to identify captured German aircraft, while H was the last block of wartime-ordered aircraft. To avoid confusion I was not used, so the new postwar machines were allocated serials in the J range. A further minor change was made in the serial numbering system in August 1929 when it was decided to maintain four numerals after the prefix letter, thus omitting numbers 1 to 999. The new K series therefore commenced at K1000, which was allocated to an AW Atlas.

The Naval N prefix was not used in such a logical way. Blocks of numbers were allocated for specific types of aircraft such as seaplanes or flying-boats. By the late 1920s the sequence had largely been used up and a new series using the prefix S was commenced. In 1930 separate naval allocations were stopped and subsequent serials were issued in the 'military' range which had by this time reached the K series. A further change in the pattern of allocations came in the L range. Commencing with L7272 numbers were issued in blocks with smaller blocks of serials between not used. These were known as blackout blocks. As M had already been used as a suffix for Maintenance Command instructional airframes it was not used as a prefix. Although N had previously been used for naval aircraft it was used again for serials allocated from 1937.

With the build-up to World War 2 the rate of allocations quickly accelerated and the prefix R was being used when war was declared. The letters O and Q were not allotted, and nor was S which had been used up to S1865 for naval aircraft before integration into the RAF series. By 1940 the serial Z9999 had been reached, as part of a blackout block, with the letters U and Y not used to avoid confusion. The option to recommence serial allocation at A1000 was not taken up; instead it was decided to use an alphabetical two-letter prefix with three numerals running from 100 to 999. Thus AA100 was allocated to a Blenheim IV.

This two-letter, three-numeral serial system which started in 1940 continues today. The letters C, I, O, Q, U and Y were, with the exception of NC, not used. For various reasons the following letter combinations were not issued: DA, DB, DH, EA, GA to GZ, HA, HT, JE, JH, JJ, KR to KT, MR, NW, NZ, SA to SK, SV, TN, TR and VE. The first postwar serials issued were in the VP range while the end of the WZs had been reached by the Korean War. The current new issues are in the latter part of the ZJ range and there are now no blackout blocks of unallocated serials. This being so, and at the current rate of issue, the Z range will last for many years. Occasionally an 'out-of-sequence' serial is issued to a manufacturer's prototype or development aircraft viz ZK101 and ZT800. However, a break in the established sequence has come with the four Boeing C-17 Globemasters leased from Boeing, that carry the serials ZZ171-ZZ174.

Note: Whilst every effort has been made to ensure the accuracy of this publication, no part of the contents has been obtained from official sources. The compilers will be pleased to receive comments, corrections and further information for inclusion in subsequent editions of *Military Aircraft Markings* and the monthly up-date of additions and amendments that is published in *Aircraft Illustrated*. Please send your information to Military Aircraft Markings, PO Box 46, Westbury-on-Trym, Bristol BS9 1TF; fax to 0117 968 3928 or e-mail to HJCurtis@ntlworld.com

British Military Aircraft Markings

A serial in *italics* denotes that it is not the genuine marking for that airframe.

Serial	Type (other identity) [code]	Owner/operator, location or fate	Notes
168	Sopwith Tabloid Scout <R> (G-BFDE)	RAF Museum, Hendon	
304	Cody Biplane (BAPC 62)	Science Museum, South Kensington	
687	RAF BE2b <R> (BAPC 181)	RAF Museum, Hendon	
1701	RAF BE2c <R> (BAPC 117)	Privately owned, Orpington	
2345	Vickers FB5 Gunbus <R> (G-ATVP)	RAF Museum, Hendon	
2699	RAF BE2c	Imperial War Museum, Lambeth	
2882	Vickers FB5 Gunbus <R> (BAPC 234)	Barton Aviation Heritage Society, Barton	
3066	Caudron GIII (G-AETA/9203M)	RAF Museum, Hendon	
5964	DH2 <R> (BAPC 112)	Museum of Army Flying, stored Middle Wallop	
5964	DH2 <R> (G-BFVH)	Privately owned, Withybush	
6232	RAF BE2c <R> (BAPC 41)	Yorkshire Air Museum, stored Elvington	
8359	Short 184 <ff>	FAA Museum, RNAS Yeovilton	
A301	Morane BB (frame)	RAF Museum Restoration Centre, Cosford	
A1325	RAF BE2e (G-BVGR)	Privately owned, Milden	
A1742	Bristol Scout D <R> (BAPC 38)	Privately owned, Solihull	
A4850	RAF SE5a <R> (BAPC 176)	Bygone Times Antique Warehouse, Ecclestone, Lancs	
A7317	Sopwith Pup <R> (BAPC 179)	Midland Air Museum, Coventry	
A8226	Sopwith 1_ Strutter <R> (G-BIDW)	RAF Museum, Hendon	
B895	RAF SE5a <R> (G-BUOD)	Privately owned, Kemble	
B1807	Sopwith Pup (G-EAVX) [A7]	Privately owned, Keynsham, Avon	
B2458	Sopwith 1F.1 Camel <R> (G-BPOB/F542) [R]	Privately owned, Booker	
B3459	Nieuport Scout 17/23 <R> (G-BWMJ) [21]	Privately owned, Fairoaks	
B6401	Sopwith 1F.1 Camel <R> (G-AWYY/C1701)	FAA Museum, RNAS Yeovilton	
B7270	Sopwith 1F.1 Camel <R> (G-BFCZ)	Brooklands Museum, Weybridge	
C1904	RAF SE5a <R> (G-PFAP) [Z]	Privately owned, Syerston	
C3011	Phoenix Currie Super Wot (G-SWOT) [S]	The Real Aeroplane Company, Breighton	
C3988	Sopwith 5F.1 Dolphin	RAF Museum, stored Wyton	
C4451	Avro 504J <R> (BAPC 210)	Southampton Hall of Aviation	
C4918	Bristol M1C <R> (G-BWJM)	The Shuttleworth Collection, Old Warden	
C4940	Bristol M1C <R>		
C4994	Bristol M1C <R> (G-BLWM)	RAF Museum, Hendon	
C9533	RAF SE5a <R> (G-BUWE) [M]	Privately owned, QinetiQ Boscombe Down	
D276	RAF SE5a <R> (BAPC 208) [A]	Prince's Mead Shopping Centre, Farnborough	
D3419	Sopwith 1F.1 Camel <R> (F1921/BAPC 59)	RAF Museum, Cosford	
D5329	Sopwith SF1 Dolphin	RAF Museum Restoration Centre, Cosford	
D5649	Airco DH9	Aero Vintage, Hatch	
D7560	Avro 504K	Science Museum, South Kensington	
D7889	Bristol F2b Fighter (G-AANM/BAPC 166)	Privately owned, Old Warden	
D8084	Bristol F2b Fighter (G-ACAA/F4516) [S]	The Fighter Collection, Duxford	
D8096	Bristol F2b Fighter (G-AEPH) [D]	The Shuttleworth Collection, Old Warden	
D8781	Avro 504K <R> (G-ECKE)	The Aircraft Restoration Company, Duxford	
E373	Avro 504K <R> (BAPC 178)	Privately owned,	
E449	Avro 504K (G-EBJE/9205M)	RAF Museum, Hendon	
E2466	Bristol F2b Fighter (BAPC 165) [I]	RAF Museum, Hendon	

Notes	Serial	Type (other identity) [code]	Owner/operator, location or fate
	E2581	Bristol F2b Fighter [13]	Imperial War Museum, Duxford
F141		RAF SE5a <R> (G-SEVA) [G]	Privately owned, QinetiQ Boscombe Down
F235		RAF SE5a <R> (G-BMDB) [B]	Privately owned, Boscombe Down
F760		SE5a Microlight <R> [A]	Privately owned, Redhill
F904		RAF SE5a (G-EBIA)	The Shuttleworth Collection, Old Warden
F938		RAF SE5a (G-EBIC/9208M)	RAF Museum, Hendon
F943		RAF SE5a <R> (G-BIHF) [S]	Museum of Army Flying, Middle Wallop
F943		RAF SE5a <R> (G-BKDT)	Yorkshire Air Museum, Elvington
F1010		Airco DH9A [C]	RAF Museum, Hendon
F3556		RAF RE8	Imperial War Museum, Duxford
F4013		Sopwith 1F.1 Camel <R>	Privately owned, Coventry
F5447		RAF SE5a <R> (G-BKER) [N]	Privately owned, Cumbernauld
F5459		RAF SE5a <R> (G-INNY) [Y]	Privately owned, Goodwood
F5475		RAF SE5a <R> (BAPC 250)	Brooklands Museum, Weybridge
F6314		Sopwith 1F.1 Camel (9206M) [B]	RAF Museum Restoration Centre, Cosford
F8010		RAF SE5a <R> (G-BDWJ) [Z]	Privately owned, Graveley
F8614		Vickers FB27A Vimy IV <R> (G-AWAU)	RAF Museum, Hendon
H1968		Avro 504K <R> (BAPC 42)	Yorkshire Air Museum, stored Elvington
H2311		Avro 504K (G-ABAA)	Gr Manchester Mus of Science & Industry
H3426		Hawker Hurricane <R> (BAPC 68)	Privately owned,
H5199		Avro 504K (BK892/3118M/ G-ACNB/G-ADEV)	The Shuttleworth Collection, Old Warden
J7326		DH53 Humming Bird (G-EBQP)	Privately owned, Audley End
J8067		Westland Pterodactyl 1a	Science Museum, South Kensington
J9941		Hawker Hart 2 (G-ABMR)	RAF Museum, Hendon
K1786		Hawker Tomtit (G-AFTA)	The Shuttleworth Collection, Old Warden
K1930		Hawker Fury <R> (G-BKBB/ OO-HFU)	Privately owned, Old Warden
K2050		Isaacs Fury II (G-ASCM)	Privately owned, Brize Norton
K2059		Isaacs Fury II (G-PFAR)	Privately owned, Dunkeswell
K2060		Isaacs Fury II (G-BKZM)	Privately owned, Haverfordwest
K2075		Isaacs Fury II (G-BEER)	Privately owned, Temple Bruer
K2227		Bristol 105 Bulldog IIA (G-ABBB)	RAF Museum, Hendon
K2567		DH82A Tiger Moth (DE306/7035M/ G-MOTH)	Privately owned, Tadlow
K2572		DH82A Tiger Moth (NM129/ G-AOZH)	Privately owned, Redhill
K2572		DH82A Tiger Moth <R>	The Aircraft Restoration Company, Duxford
K2587		DH82A Tiger Moth <R> (G-BJAP)	Privately owned, Shobdon
K3215		Avro 621 Tutor (G-AHSA)	The Shuttleworth Collection, Old Warden
K3661		Hawker Nimrod II (G-BURZ)	Aero Vintage, St Leonards-on-Sea
K3731		Isaacs Fury <R> (G-RODI)	Privately owned, Hailsham
K4259		DH82A Tiger Moth (G-ANMO) [71]	Privately owned, White Waltham
K4972		Hawker Hart Trainer IIA (1764M)	RAF Museum, Cosford
K5054		Supermarine Spitfire <R> (BAPC 190/*EN398*)	Privately owned, Sevenoaks, Kent
K5054		Supermarine Spitfire <R> (BAPC 214)	Tangmere Military Aviation Museum
K5054		Supermarine Spitfire <R> (G-BRDV)	Southampton Hall of Aviation
K5054		Supermarine Spitfire <R>	Kent Battle of Britain Museum, Hawkinge
K5414		Hawker Hind (G-AENP/BAPC 78) [XV]	The Shuttleworth Collection, Old Warden
K5600		Hawker Audax I (2015M/G-BVVI)	Aero Vintage, St Leonards-on-Sea
K5673		Isaacs Fury II (G-BZAS)	Bournemouth Aviation Museum
K5673		Hawker Fury I <R> (BAPC 249)	Brooklands Museum, Weybridge
K6035		Westland Wallace II (2361M)	RAF Museum, Hendon
K7271		Hawker Fury II <R> (BAPC 148)	Shropshire Wartime Aircraft Recovery Grp Mus, Sleap
K8042		Gloster Gladiator II (8372M)	RAF Museum, Hendon
K8203		Hawker Demon I (G-BTVE/2292M)	Demon Displays, Hatch
K8203		Isaacs Fury II (G-BWWN) [D]	Privately owned, Lower Upham
K9926		VS300 Spitfire I <R> (BAPC 217) [JH-C]	RAF Bentley Priory, on display
K9942		VS300 Spitfire I (8383M) [SD-D]	RAF Museum, Hendon
K9962		VS300 Spitfire I <R> [JH-C]	Privately owned, Greenford, W London

Serial	Type (other identity) [code]	Owner/operator, location or fate	Notes
L1070	VS300 Spitfire I <R> (BAPC 227) [XT-A]	Edinburgh airport, on display	
L1592	Hawker Hurricane I [KW-Z]	Science Museum, South Kensington	
L1679	Hawker Hurricane I <R> (BAPC 241) [JX-G]	Tangmere Military Aviation Museum	
L1710	Hawker Hurricane I <R> (BAPC 219) [AL-D]	RAF Biggin Hill, on display	
L2301	VS Walrus I (G-AIZG)	FAA Museum, RNAS Yeovilton	
L2940	Blackburn Skua I	FAA Museum, RNAS Yeovilton	
L5343	Fairey Battle I [VO-S]	RAF Museum, Hendon	
L6906	Miles M14A Magister I (G-AKKY/T9841/BAPC 44)	Museum of Berkshire Aviation, Woodley	
L8756	Bristol 149 Bolingbroke IVT (RCAF 10001) [XD-E]	RAF Museum, Hendon	
L8841	Bristol 149 Bolingbroke IVT (G-BPIV/R3821) [QY-C]	Repainted as R3821	
N248	Supermarine S6A (S1596)	Southampton Hall of Aviation	
N500	Sopwith LC-1T Triplane <R> (G-PENY/G-BWRA)	Privately owned, Dunkeswell/ RNAS Yeovilton	
N546	Wright Quadruplane 1 <R> (BAPC 164)	Southampton Hall of Aviation	
N1671	Boulton Paul P82 Defiant I (8370M) [EW-D]	RAF Museum, Hendon	
N1854	Fairey Fulmar II (G-AIBE)	FAA Museum, RNAS Yeovilton	
N2078	Sopwith Baby (8214/8215)	FAA Museum, RNAS Yeovilton	
N2532	Hawker Hurricane I <R> (BAPC ..) [GZ-H]	Kent Battle of Britain Museum, Hawkinge	
N2980	Vickers Wellington IA [R]	Brooklands Museum, Weybridge	
N3177	RAF BE2e <R>	Barton Aviation Heritage Society, Barton	
N3194	VS300 Spitfire I <R> (BAPC 220) [GR-Z]	RAF Biggin Hill, on display	
N3289	VS300 Spitfire I <R> (BAPC 65) [DW-K]	Kent Battle of Britain Museum, Hawkinge	
N3313	VS300 Spitfire I <R> (MH314/ BAPC 69) [KL-B]	Kent Battle of Britain Museum, Hawkinge	
N3317	VS361 Spitfire IX <R>	Privately owned, St Mawgan	
N3320	VS361 Spitfire IX <R>	Privately owned, Wellesbourne Mountford	
N3378	Boulton Paul P82 Defiant I	Boulton Paul Association, Wolverhampton	
N4389	Fairey Albacore (N4172) [4M]	FAA Museum, RNAS Yeovilton	
N4877	Avro 652A Anson I (G-AMDA) [VX-F]	Imperial War Museum, Duxford	
N5177	Sopwith 1_ Strutter <R>	Botany Bay Village, Chorley, Lancs	
N5182	Sopwith Pup <R> (G-APUP/ 9213M)	RAF Museum, Hendon	
N5195	Sopwith Pup (G-ABOX)	Museum of Army Flying, Middle Wallop	
N5492	Sopwith Triplane <R> (BAPC 111)	FAA Museum, RNAS Yeovilton	
N5628	Gloster Gladiator II	RAF Museum, Hendon	
N5903	Gloster Gladiator II (N2276/ G-GLAD) [H]	The Fighter Collection, Duxford	
N5912	Sopwith Triplane (8385M)	RAF Museum, Hendon	
N6181	Sopwith Pup (G-EBKY/N5180)	The Shuttleworth Collection, Old Warden	
N6290	Sopwith Triplane <R> (G-BOCK)	The Shuttleworth Collection, Old Warden	
N6452	Sopwith Pup <R> (G-BIAU)	FAA Museum, RNAS Yeovilton	
N6466	DH82A Tiger Moth (G-ANKZ)	Privately owned, Sywell	
N6537	DH82A Tiger Moth (G-AOHY)	AAC Historic Aircraft Flt, Middle Wallop	
N6720	DH82A Tiger Moth (G-BYTN/ 7014M) [RUO-B]	Privately owned, Hatch	
N6797	DH82A Tiger Moth (G-ANEH)	Privately owned, Goodwood	
N6812	Sopwith 2F.1 Camel	Imperial War Museum, Lambeth	
N6847	DH82A Tiger Moth (G-APAL)	Privately owned, Little Gransden	
N6965	DH82A Tiger Moth (G-AJTW) [FL-J] (wreck)	Privately owned, Tibenham	
N9191	DH82A Tiger Moth (G-ALND)	Privately owned, Abergavenny	
N9192	DH82A Tiger Moth (G-DHZF) [RCO-N]	Privately owned, Sywell	
N9389	DH82A Tiger Moth (G-ANJA)	Privately owned, Seething	
N9899	Supermarine Southampton I (fuselage)	RAF Museum, Hendon	
P1344	HP52 Hampden I (9175M) [PL-K]	RAF Museum Restoration Centre, Cosford	
P1344	HP52 Hampden I <rf> (parts Hereford L6012)	RAF Museum, Hendon	

P2617 – T6991

Notes	Serial	Type (other identity) [code]	Owner/operator, location or fate
	P2617	Hawker Hurricane I (8373M) [AF-A]	RAF Museum, Hendon
	P2793	Hawker Hurricane I <R> (BAPC 236) [SD-M]	Eden Camp Theme Park, Malton, North Yorkshire
	P2902	Hawker Hurricane I (G-ROBT) [DX-X]	Privately owned, Milden
	P2921	Hawker Hurricane I <R> (BAPC ..) [GZ-L]	Kent Battle of Britain Museum, Hawkinge
	P3059	Hawker Hurricane I <R> (BAPC 64) [SD-N]	Privately owned, Bassingbourn
	P3175	Hawker Hurricane I (wreck)	RAF Museum, Hendon
	P3208	Hawker Hurricane I <R> (BAPC 63/ L1592) [SD-T]	Kent Battle of Britain Museum, Hawkinge
	P3386	Hawker Hurricane I <R> (BAPC 218) [FT-A]	RAF Bentley Priory, on display
	P3395	Hawker Hurricane IV (KX829) [JX-B]	Millennium Discovery Centre, Birmingham
	P3554	Hawker Hurricane I (composite)	The Air Defence Collection, Salisbury
	P3717	Hawker Hurricane I (composite) (DR348)	Privately owned, Hinckley, Leics
	P3873	Hawker Hurricane I <R> [YO-H]	Yorkshire Air Museum, Elvington
	P4139	Fairey Swordfish II (HS618) [5H]	FAA Museum, RNAS Yeovilton
	P6382	Miles M14A Hawk Trainer 3 (G-AJRS) [C]	The Shuttleworth Collection, Old Warden
	P7350	VS329 Spitfire IIA (G-AWIJ) [XT-D]	RAF BBMF, Coningsby
	P7540	VS329 Spitfire IIA [DU-W]	Dumfries & Galloway Avn Mus, Dumfries
	P7966	VS329 Spitfire II <R> [D-B]	Manx Aviation & Military Museum, Ronaldsway
	P8140	VS329 Spitfire II <R> (P9390/ BAPC 71) [ZF-K]	Norfolk & Suffolk Avn Museum, Flixton
	P8448	VS329 Spitfire II <R> (BAPC 225) [UM-D]	RAF Cranwell, on display
	P9374	VS300 Spitfire IA (G-MKIA)	Privately owned, Isle of Wight
	P9444	VS300 Spitfire IA [RN-D]	Science Museum, South Kensington
	R1914	Miles M14A Magister (G-AHUJ)	Privately owned, Strathallan
	R3821	Bristol 149 Bolingbroke IVT (G-BPIV/Z5722) [UX-N]	The Aircraft Restoration Company, Duxford
	R4115	Hawker Hurricane I <R> [LE-X]	Imperial War Museum, Duxford
	R4118	Hawker Hurricane I (G-HUPW)	Privately owned, Sutton Courtenay
	R4959	DH82A Tiger Moth II (G-ARAZ) [59]	Privately owned, Temple Bruer
	R5136	DH82A Tiger Moth II (G-APAP)	The Aircraft Restoration Co, Duxford
	R5172	DH82A Tiger Moth II (G-AOIS) [FIJ-E]	Privately owned, Sherburn-in-Elmet
	R5250	DH82A Tiger Moth II (G-AODT)	Privately owned, Tibenham
	R5868	Avro 683 Lancaster I (7325M) [PO-S]	RAF Museum, Hendon
	R6690	VS300 Spitfire I <R> (BAPC 254) [PR-A]	Yorkshire Air Museum, Elvington
	R6915	VS300 Spitfire I	Imperial War Museum, Lambeth
	R9125	Westland Lysander III (8377M) [LX-L]	RAF Museum, Hendon
	R9371	HP59 Halifax II <ff>	Cotswold Aircraft Rest'n Grp, Innsworth
	S1287	Fairey Flycatcher <R> (G-BEYB)	FAA Museum, RNAS Yeovilton
	S1579	Hawker Nimrod I <R> (G-BBVO) [571]	Privately owned, Basingstoke
	S1581	Hawker Nimrod I (G-BWWK) [573]	The Fighter Collection, Duxford
	S1595	Supermarine S6B	Science Museum, South Kensington
	T5298	Bristol 156 Beaufighter I (4552M) <ff>	Midland Air Museum, Coventry
	T5424	DH82A Tiger Moth II (G-AJOA)	Privately owned, Chiseldon
	T5672	DH82A Tiger Moth II (G-ALRI)	Privately owned, Chalmington
	T5854	DH82A Tiger Moth II (G-ANKK)	Privately owned, Welshpool
	T5879	DH82A Tiger Moth II (G-AXBW) [RUC-W]	Privately owned, Frensham
	T6296	DH82A Tiger Moth II (8387M)	RAF Museum, Hendon
	T6313	DH82A Tiger Moth II (G-AHVU)	Privately owned, Liphook
	T6562	DH82A Tiger Moth II (G-ANTE)	Privately owned, Sywell
	T6818	DH82A Tiger Moth II (G-ANKT) [91]	The Shuttleworth Collection, Old Warden
	T6953	DH82A Tiger Moth II (G-ANNI)	Privately owned, Little Gransden
	T6991	DH82A Tiger Moth II (G-ANOR/ DE694)	Privately owned, Paddock Wood

Serial	Type (other identity) [code]	Owner/operator, location or fate	Notes
T7230	DH82A Tiger Moth II (G-AFVE)	Privately owned, Boscombe Down	
T7281	DH82A Tiger Moth II (G-ARTL)	Privately owned, Egton, nr Whitby	
T7404	DH82A Tiger Moth II (G-ANMV) [04]	Privately owned, Booker	
T7793	DH82A Tiger Moth II (G-ANKV)	Privately owned, Croydon, on display	
T7842	DH82A Tiger Moth II (G-AMTF)	Privately owned, Boughton, Suffolk	
T7909	DH82A Tiger Moth II (G-ANON)	Privately owned, Sherburn-in-Elmet	
T7997	DH82A Tiger Moth II (NL750/ G-AHUF)	Privately owned, Edburton	
T8191	DH82A Tiger Moth II (G-BWMK)	Privately owned, Welshpool	
T9707	Miles M14A Magister I (G-AKKR/ 8378M/T9708)	Museum of Army Flying, Middle Wallop	
T9738	Miles M14A Magister I (G-AKAT)	Privately owned, Breighton	
V1075	Miles M14A Magister I (G-AKPF)	Privately owned, stored Sandown	
V3388	Airspeed AS10 Oxford I (G-AHTW)	Imperial War Museum, Duxford	
V6028	Bristol 149 Bolingbroke IVT (G-MKIV) [GB-D] <rf>	The Aircraft Restoration Co, stored Duxford	
V6799	Hawker Hurricane I <R> (BAPC 72/V7767) [SD-X]	Gloucestershire Avn Coll, stored Gloucester	
V7350	Hawker Hurricane I (fuselage)	Brenzett Aeronautical Museum	
V7467	Hawker Hurricane I <R> (BAPC 223) [LE-D]	RAF Coltishall, on display	
V7467	Hawker Hurricane I <R>	Wonderland Pleasure Pk, Farnsfield, Notts	
V9367	Westland Lysander IIIA (G-AZWT) [MA-B]	The Shuttleworth Collection, Old Warden	
V9441	Westland Lysander IIIA (G-AZWT) [AR-A]	Repainted as V9367, Spring 2001	
V9673	Westland Lysander IIIA (V9300/ G-LIZY) [MA-J]	Imperial War Museum, Duxford	
V9723	Westland Lysander IIIA (2442/ OO-SOT) [MA-D]	SABENA Old Timers, Brussels, Belgium	
W1048	HP59 Halifax II (8465M) [TL-S]	RAF Museum, Hendon	
W2068	Avro 652A Anson I (VH-ASM) [68]	RAF Museum, Hendon	
W2718	VS Walrus I (G-RNLI)	Dick Melton Aviation, Great Yarmouth	
W4041	Gloster E28/39 [G]	Science Museum, South Kensington	
W4050	DH98 Mosquito	Mosquito Aircraft Museum, London Colney	
W5856	Fairey Swordfish II (G-BMGC) [A2A]	RN Historic Flight, Yeovilton	
W9385	DH87B Hornet Moth (G-ADND) [YG-L,3]	The Shuttleworth Collection, Old Warden	
X4590	VS300 Spitfire I (8384M) [PR-F]	RAF Museum, Hendon	
X7688	Bristol 156 Beaufighter I (3858M/ G-DINT)	Privately owned, Hatch	
Z2033	Fairey Firefly I (G-ASTL) [275]	FAA Museum, stored RNAS Yeovilton	
Z2315	Hawker Hurricane IIA [JU-E]	Imperial War Museum, Duxford	
Z2389	Hawker Hurricane IIA	Brooklands Museum, Weybridge	
Z5207	Hawker Hurricane IIB (G-BYDL)	Privately owned, Billingshurst	
Z5252	Hawker Hurricane IIB (G-BWHA/ Z5053) [GO-B]	Privately owned, Dursley, Glos	
Z7015	Hawker Sea Hurricane IB (G-BKTH) [7-L]	The Shuttleworth Collection, Old Warden	
Z7197	Percival P30 Proctor III (G-AKZN/ 8380M)	RAF Museum, Hendon	
Z7258	DH89A Dragon Rapide (NR786/ G-AHGD)	Privately owned, Membury (wreck)	
Z7381	Hawker Hurricane XIIA (G-HURI) [XR-T]	Historic Aircraft Collection, Duxford	
AA550	VS349 Spitfire VB <R> (BAPC 230/ AA908) [GE-P]	Eden Camp Theme Park, Malton, North Yorkshire	
AB130	VS349 Spitfire VA (parts)	Privately owned,	
AB910	VS349 Spitfire VB (G-AISU) [ZD-C]	RAF BBMF, Coningsby	
AD540	VS349 Spitfire VB (wreck)	Kennet Aviation, Cranfield	
AE436	HP52 Hampden I [PL-J] (parts)	Lincolnshire Avn Heritage Centre, E Kirkby	
AE977	Hawker Sea Hurricane X (G-TWTD) [LE–D]	Sold as N33TF, September 2001	
AL246	Grumman Martlet I	FAA Museum, RNAS Yeovilton	
AM561	Lockheed Hudson V (parts)	Cornwall Aero Park, Helston	

Notes	Serial	Type (other identity) [code]	Owner/operator, location or fate
	AP506	Cierva C30A (G-ACWM)	The Helicopter Museum, Weston-super-Mare
	AP507	Cierva C30A (G-ACWP) [KX-P]	Science Museum, South Kensington
	AR213	VS300 Spitfire IA (K9853/G-AIST) [PR-D]	Privately owned, Booker
	AR501	VS349 Spitfire LF VC (G-AWII/ AR4474) [NN-A]	The Shuttleworth Collection, Old Warden
	BB807	DH82A Tiger Moth (G-ADWO)	Southampton Hall of Aviation
BE417	Hawker Hurricane XIIB (G-HURR) [LK-A]	The Real Aeroplane Company, Breighton
BE421	Hawker Hurricane IIC <R> (BAPC 205) [XP-G]	RAF Museum, Hendon
	BL614	VS349 Spitfire VB (4354M) [ZD-F]	RAF Museum, Hendon
	BL655	VS349 Spitfire VB (wreck)	Lincolnshire Avn Heritage Centre, East Kirkby
BL924	VS349 Spitfire VB <R> (BAPC 242) [AZ-G]	Tangmere Military Aviation Museum
BM361	VS349 Spitfire VB <R> [XR-C]	RAF Lakenheath, on display
	BM597	VS349 Spitfire LF VB (5718M/ G-MKVB) [JH-C]	Historic Aircraft Collection, Duxford
BN230	Hawker Hurricane IIC (LF751/ 5466M) [FT-A]	RAF Manston, Memorial Pavilion
BR600	VS361 Spitfire IX <R> (BAPC 222) [SH-V]	RAF Uxbridge, on display
BR600	VS361 Spitfire IX <R> (fuselage)	Privately owned, Dunkeswell, derelict
	BW881	Hawker Hurricane XIIA (G-KAMM)	Privately owned, Milden
CB733	SA122 Bulldog (G-BCUV/G-112)	Privately owned, Old Sarum
DD931	Bristol 152 Beaufort VIII (9131M) [L]	RAF Museum, Hendon
	DE208	DH82A Tiger Moth II (G-AGYU)	Privately owned, Ronaldsway
	DE470	DH82A Tiger Moth II (G-ANMY)	Privately owned, Oaksey Park, Wilts
	DE623	DH82A Tiger Moth II (G-ANFI)	Privately owned, Cardiff
	DE673	DH82A Tiger Moth II (6948M/ G-ADNZ)	Privately owned, Swanton Morley
	DE992	DH82A Tiger Moth II (G-AXXV)	Privately owned, Upavon
DE998	DH82A Tiger Moth (comp G-APAO & G-APAP) [RC-T]	The Aircraft Restoration Company, Duxford
	DF112	DH82A Tiger Moth II (G-ANRM)	Privately owned, Clacton
	DF128	DH82A Tiger Moth II (G-AOJJ) [RCO-U]	Privately owned, White Waltham
	DF155	DH82A Tiger Moth II (G-ANFV)	Privately owned, Shempston Fm, Lossiemouth
	DF198	DH82A Tiger Moth II (G-BBRB)	Privately owned, Biggin Hill
	DG202	Gloster F9/40 (5758M) [G]	RAF Museum, Cosford
	DG590	Miles M2H Hawk Major (8379M/ G-ADMW)	RAF Museum Restoration Centre, Cosford
	DP872	Fairey Barracuda II (fuselage)	FAA Museum, stored Yeovilton
	DR613	Foster-Wikner GM1 Wicko (G-AFJB)	Privately owned, Southampton
	DV372	Avro 683 Lancaster I <ff>	Imperial War Museum, Lambeth
	EE416	Gloster Meteor F3 <ff>	Martin Baker Aircraft, Chalgrove
	EE425	Gloster Meteor F3 <ff>	Gloucestershire Avn Coll, stored Gloucester
	EE531	Gloster Meteor F4 (7090M)	Midland Air Museum, Coventry
	EE549	Gloster Meteor F4 (7008M) [A]	Tangmere Military Aviation Museum
	EF545	VS349 Spitfire VC <ff>	Privately owned, High Wycombe
	EJ693	Hawker Tempest V (N7027E) [SA-J]	Privately owned, Booker
	EJ922	Hawker Typhoon IB <ff>	Privately owned, Hawkinge
	EM720	DH82A Tiger Moth II (G-AXAN)	Privately owned, Little Gransden
	EM727	DH82A Tiger Moth II (G-AOXN)	Privately owned, Yeovil
	EN224	VS366 Spitfire F XII (G-FXII)	Privately owned, Newport Pagnell
EN343	VS365 Spitfire PR XI <R> (BAPC 226)	RAF Benson, on display
EN398	VS361 Spitfire F IX <R> (BAPC 184) [WO-A]	Shropshire Wartime Aircraft Recovery Grp Mus, Sleap
	EP120	VS349 Spitfire LF VB (5377M/ 8070M/G-LFVB) [AE-A]	The Fighter Collection, Duxford
	EX976	NA AT-6D Harvard III (FAP.1657)	FAA Museum, RNAS Yeovilton

Serial	Type (other identity) [code]	Owner/operator, location or fate	Notes
EZ259	NA AT-6D Harvard III (G-BMJW) <ff>	Privately owned, Wakefield, West Yorkshire	
FB226	Bonsall Mustang <R> (G-BDWM) [MT-A]	Privately owned, Gamston	
FE695	Noorduyn AT-16 Harvard IIB (G-BTXI) [94]	The Fighter Collection, Duxford	
FE905	Noorduyn AT-16 Harvard IIB (LN-BNM)	RAF Museum, Hendon	
FE992	Noorduyn AT-16 Harvard IIB (G-BDAM) [K-T]	Privately owned, Duxford	
FH153	Noorduyn AT-16 Harvard IIB (G-BBHK) [GW-A]	Privately owned, stored Cardiff	
FJ992	Boeing-Stearman PT-17 Kaydet (442/OO-JEH)	Privately owned, Wevelgem, Belgium	
FL586	Douglas C-47A Dakota C3 (G-DAKS) [D]	Privately owned, North Weald	
FM118	Avro 683 Lancaster B X <ff>	Privately owned, Gosport, Hants	
FR886	Piper L-4J Cub (G-BDMS)	Privately owned, Old Sarum	
FR887	Piper J-3C Cub 85 (G-BWEZ)	Privately owned, Cumbernauld	
FS628	Fairchild Argus 2 (43-14601/ G-AIZE)	RAF Museum, Cosford	
FS668	Noorduyn AT-16 Harvard IIB (PH-TBR)	Privately owned, The Netherlands	
FS728	Noorduyn AT-16 Harvard IIB (HB-RCP)	Privately owned, Gelnhausen, Germany	
FT323	NA AT-6D Harvard III (FAP 1513)	Air Engineering Services, Swansea	
FT391	Noorduyn AT-16 Harvard IIB (G-AZBN)	Privately owned, Goodwood	
FX301	NA AT-6D Harvard III (EX915/ G-JUDI) [FD-NQ]	Privately owned, Bryngwyn Bach, Clwyd	
FX360	Noorduyn AT-16 Harvard IIB (KF435)	Booker Aircraft Museum	
FX442	Noorduyn AT-16 Harvard IIB	Kent Battle of Britain Museum, Hawkinge	
FX760	Curtiss P-40N Kittyhawk IV (9150M) [GA-?]	RAF Museum, Hendon	
HB275	Beech C-45 Expeditor II (G-BKGM)	Privately owned, North Weald	
HB751	Fairchild Argus III (G-BCBL)	Privately owned, Little Gransden	
HH268	GAL48 Hotspur II (BAPC 261) [H]	Museum of Army Flying, AAC Middle Wallop	
HH379	GAL48 Hotspur II (BAPC 261)	*Repainted as HH268, November 2001*	
HJ711	DH98 Mosquito NF II [VI-C]	Night-Fighter Preservation Tm, Elvington	
HM354	Percival P34 Proctor III (G-ANPP)	Privately owned, Stansted	
HM503	Miles M12 Mohawk (G-AEKW)	RAF Museum, stored Wyton	
HM580	Cierva C-30A (G-ACUU) [KX-K]	Imperial War Museum, Duxford	
HS503	Fairey Swordfish IV (BAPC 108)	RAF Museum Restoration Centre, Cosford	
JG891	VS349 Spitfire LF VC (A58-178/ G-LFVC)	Historic Flying Ltd, Audley End	
JR505	Hawker Typhoon IB <ff>	Midland Air Museum, Coventry	
JV482	Grumman Wildcat V	Ulster Aviation Society, Langford Lodge	
JV579	Grumman FM-2 Wildcat (N4845V/ G-RUMW) [F]	The Fighter Collection, Duxford	
JV928	Consolidated PBY-5A Catalina (N423RS) [Y]	Super Catalina Restoration, Lee-on-Solent	
KB889	Avro 683 Lancaster B X (G-LANC) [NA-I]	Imperial War Museum, Duxford	
KB976	Avro 683 Lancaster B X (G-BCOH) (fuselage)	Privately owned, Sandtoft	
KB994	Avro 683 Lancaster B X (G-BVBP) <ff>	Privately owned, North Weald	
KD345	Goodyear FG-1D Corsair (88297/ G-FGID) [130-A]	The Fighter Collection, Duxford	
KD431	CV Corsair IV [E2-M]	FAA Museum, RNAS Yeovilton	
KE209	Grumman Hellcat II	FAA Museum, RNAS Yeovilton	
KE418	Hawker Tempest <rf>	RAF Museum, stored Wyton	
KF183	Noorduyn AT-16 Harvard IIB [3]	DPA/AFD, QinetiQ Boscombe Down	
KF435	Noorduyn AT-16 Harvard IIB <ff>	Privately owned, Swindon	
KF487	Noorduyn AT-16 Harvard IIB	The Aircraft Restoration Co, Duxford, spares use	
KF488	Noorduyn AT-16 Harvard IIB <ff>	Bournemouth Aviation Museum	
KF532	Noorduyn AT-16 Harvard IIB <ff>	Newark Air Museum, Winthorpe	

Notes	Serial	Type (other identity) [code]	Owner/operator, location or fate
	KF584	CCF T-6J Texan (FT239/G-BIWX/ G-RAIX) [RAI-X]	Privately owned, North Weald
	KG374	Douglas Dakota IV (KN645/8355M) [YS]	RAF Museum, Cosford
	KJ351	Airspeed AS58 Horsa II (TL659/ BAPC 80) [23]	Museum of Army Flying, Middle Wallop
	KK995	Sikorsky Hoverfly I [E]	RAF Museum, Hendon
	KL216	Republic P-47D Thunderbolt (45-49295/9212M) [RS-L]	RAF Museum, Cosford
	KN442	Douglas Dakota C4 (G-AMPZ)	Atlantic Airlines, Coventry
	KN448	Douglas Dakota C4 <ff>	Science Museum, South Kensington
	KN751	Consolidated Liberator C VI (IAF HE807) [F]	RAF Museum, Cosford
	KP208	Douglas Dakota IV [YS]	Airborne Forces Museum, Aldershot
	KZ191	Hawker Hurricane IV (frame only)	Privately owned, North Weald
	KZ321	Hawker Hurricane IV (G-HURY)	The Fighter Collection, stored Duxford (frame only)
	LA198	VS356 Spitfire F21 (7118M) [RAI-G]	Royal Scottish Mus'm of Flight, E Fortune
	LA226	VS356 Spitfire F21 (7119M)	RAF Museum Restoration Centre, Cosford
	LA255	VS356 Spitfire F21 (6490M) [JX-U]	RAF No 1 Sqn, Cottesmore (preserved)
	LB264	Taylorcraft Plus D (G-AIXA)	Privately owned, Loughborough
	LB294	Taylorcraft Plus D (G-AHWJ)	Museum of Army Flying, Whitchurch, Hants
	LB312	Taylorcraft Plus D (HH982/ G-AHXE)	Privately owned, Old Sarum
	LB367	Taylorcraft Plus D (G-AHGZ)	Privately owned, Duxford
	LB375	Taylorcraft Plus D (G-AHGW)	Privately owned, Edge Hill
	LF363	Hawker Hurricane IIC [US-C]	RAF BBMF, Coningsby
	LF738	Hawker Hurricane IIC (5405M) [UH-A]	RAF Museum, Cosford
	LF789	DH82 Queen Bee (K3584/ BAPC 186) [R2-K]	Mosquito Aircraft Museum, London Colney
	LF858	DH82 Queen Bee (G-BLUZ)	Privately owned, Rush Green
	LS326	Fairey Swordfish II (G-AJVH) [L2]	RN Historic Flight, Yeovilton
	LV907	HP59 Halifax III (HR792) [NP-F]	Yorkshire Air Museum, Elvington
	LZ551	DH100 Vampire	FAA Museum, RNAS Yeovilton
	LZ766	Percival P34 Proctor III (G-ALCK)	Imperial War Museum, Duxford
	MF628	Vickers Wellington T10 (9210M)	RAF Museum, Hendon
	MH434	VS361 Spitfire LF IXB (G-ASJV) [ZD-B]	The Old Flying Machine Company, Duxford
	MH486	VS361 Spitfire LF IX <R> (BAPC 206) [FF-A]	RAF Museum, Hendon
	MH777	VS361 Spitfire IX <R> (BAPC 221) [RF-N]	RAF Northolt, on display
	MJ147	VS361 Spitfire LF IX	Privately owned, Kent
	MJ627	VS509 Spitfire T9 (G-BMSB) [9G-P]	Privately owned, Coventry
	MJ751	VS361 Spitfire IX <R> (BAPC 209) [DU-V]	D-Day Museum, Shoreham Airport
	MJ832	VS361 Spitfire IX <R> (L1096/ BAPC 229) [DN-Y]	RAF Digby, on display
	MK178	VS361 Spitfire LF XVIE (TE311/ X4474/7241M) [LZ-V]	RAF BBMF, stored Coningsby
	MK356	VS361 Spitfire LF IXC (5690M) [2I-V]	RAF BBMF, Coningsby
	MK356	VS361 Spitfire LF IXC <R> [2I-V]	Kent Battle of Britain Museum, Hawkinge
	MK673	VS361 Spitfire LF XVIE (TB382/ X4277/7244M) [SK-E]	RAF BBMF, stored Coningsby
	MK805	VS361 Spitfire LF IX <R> [SH-B]	Privately owned, Lowestoft
	MK912	VS361 Spitfire LF IXE (G-BRRA) [SH-L]	Silver Victory Collection, Duxford
	ML407	VS509 Spitfire T9 (G-LFIX) [OU-V]	Privately owned, Duxford
	ML411	VS361 Spitfire LF IXE	Privately owned, Kent
	ML417	VS361 Spitfire LF IXE (G-BJSG) [2I-T]	The Fighter Collection, Duxford
	ML427	VS361 Spitfire IX (6457M) [HK-A]	Millennium Discovery Centre, Birmingham
	ML796	Short S25 Sunderland V	Imperial War Museum, Duxford
	ML824	Short S25 Sunderland V [NS-Z]	RAF Museum, Hendon
	MN235	Hawker Typhoon IB	RAF Museum, Hendon

Serial	Type (other identity) [code]	Owner/operator, location or fate	Notes
MP425	Airspeed AS10 Oxford I (G-AITB) [G]	RAF Museum, Hendon	
MS902	Miles M25 Martinet TT1 (TF-SHC)	Museum of Berkshire Aviation, Woodley	
MT197	Auster IV (G-ANHS)	Privately owned, Spanhoe	
MT438	Auster III (G-AREI)	Privately owned, Petersfield	
MT847	VS379 Spitfire FR XIVE (6960M) [AX-H]	Gr Manchester Mus of Science & Industry	
MT928	VS359 Spitfire HF VIIIC (G-BKMI/ MV154/AR654)[ZX-M]	Privately owned, Filton	
MV262	VS379 Spitfire FR XIV (G-CCVV)	Privately owned, Catfield	
MV268	VS379 Spitfire FR XIVE (MV293/ G-SPIT) [JE-J]	The Fighter Collection, Duxford	
MW401	Hawker Tempest II (IAF HA604/ G-PEST)	Privately owned, Hemswell, Lincs	
MW404	Hawker Tempest II (IAF HA557)	Privately owned	
MW758	Hawker Tempest II (IAF HA580)	Privately owned	
MW763	Hawker Tempest II (IAF HA586/ G-TEMT) [HF-A]	Privately owned, Hibaldstow, Lincs	
MW810	Hawker Tempest II (IAF HA591)	Privately owned, Hibaldstow, Lincs	
NF370	Fairey Swordfish III	Imperial War Museum, Duxford	
NF389	Fairey Swordfish III [D]	RN Historic Flight, Yeovilton	
NJ673	Auster 5D (G-AOCR)	Privately owned, Canterbury	
NJ695	Auster 4 (G-AJXV)	Privately owned, Newark	
NJ703	Auster 5 (G-AKPI)	Privately owned, Croft, Lincs	
NJ719	Auster 5 (TW385/G-ANFU)	Privately owned, Newcastle	
NL750	DH82A Tiger Moth II (T7997/ G-AOBH)	Privately owned, Thruxton	
NL846	DH82A Tiger Moth II (F-BGEQ)	Brooklands Museum, Weybridge	
NL985	DH82A Tiger Moth I (7015M/ G-BWIK)	Privately owned, Sywell	
NM181	DH82A Tiger Moth I (G-AZGZ)	Privately owned, Dunkeswell	
NP294	Percival P31 Proctor IV [TB-M]	Lincolnshire Avn Heritage Centre, E Kirkby	
NP303	Percival P31 Proctor IV (G-ANZJ)	Privately owned, Byfleet, Surrey	
NV778	Hawker Tempest TT5 (8386M)	RAF Museum Restoration Centre, Cosford	
NX534	Auster III (G-BUDL)	Privately owned, Netheravon	
NX611	Avro 683 Lancaster B VII (8375M/ G-ASXX) [DE-C,LE-C]	Lincolnshire Avn Heritage Centre, E Kirkby	
PA474	Avro 683 Lancaster B I [QR-M]	RAF BBMF, Coningsby	
PF179	HS Gnat T1 (XR541/8602M)	Privately owned	
PK624	VS356 Spitfire F22 (8072M) [RAU-T]	The Fighter Collection, Duxford	
PK664	VS356 Spitfire F22 (7759M) [V6-B]	RAF Museum Restoration Centre, Cosford	
PK683	VS356 Spitfire F24 (7150M)	Southampton Hall of Aviation	
PK724	VS356 Spitfire F24 (7288M)	RAF Museum, Hendon	
PL344	VS361 Spitfire LF IXE (G-IXCC) [Y2-P]	Sold to the USA, Spring 2001	
PL965	VS365 Spitfire PR XI (G-MKXI) [R]	Sold to the USA, September 2001	
PL983	VS365 Spitfire PR XI (G-PRXI)	Crashed Rouen, France, 4 June 2001	
PM631	VS390 Spitfire PR XIX [S]	RAF BBMF, Coningsby	
PM651	VS390 Spitfire PR XIX (7758M) [X]	RAF Museum Restoration Centre, Cosford	
PN323	HP Halifax VII <ff>	Imperial War Museum, Lambeth	
PP566	Fairey Firefly I (fuselage)	Currently not known	
PP972	VS358 Seafire LF IIIC (G-BUAR)	Flying A Services, Earls Colne	
PR536	Hawker Tempest II (IAF HA457) [OQ-H]	RAF Museum, Hendon	
PS853	VS390 Spitfire PR XIX (G-MXIX/ G-RRGN) [C]	Rolls-Royce, Filton	
PS915	VS390 Spitfire PR XIX (7548M/ 7711M) [UM-G]	RAF BBMF, Coningsby	
PT462	VS509 Spitfire T9 (G-CTIX/ N462JC) [SW-A]	Privately owned, Caernarfon/Duxford	
PV202	VS509 Spitfire T9 (G-TRIX) [5R-Q]	Historic Flying Ltd, Audley End (wreck)	
PZ865	Hawker Hurricane IIC (G-AMAU) [Q]	RAF BBMF, Coningsby	
RA848	Slingsby Cadet TX1	The Aeroplane Collection, stored Wigan	
RA854	Slingsby Cadet TX1	Privately owned, Wigan	
RA897	Slingsby Cadet TX1	Newark Air Museum, Winthorpe	
RD220	Bristol 156 Beaufighter TF X	Royal Scottish Mus'm of Flight, E Fortune	

RD253 – TJ707

Notes	Serial	Type (other identity) [code]	Owner/operator, location or fate
	RD253	Bristol 156 Beaufighter TF X (7931M)	RAF Museum, Hendon
	RF342	Avro 694 Lincoln B II (G-29-1/ G-APRJ)	Privately owned, Sandtoft
	RF398	Avro 694 Lincoln B II (8376M)	RAF Museum, Cosford
RG333		Miles M38 Messenger IIA (G-AIEK)	Privately owned, Felton, Bristol
	RH377	Miles M38 Messenger IIA (G-ALAH)	Privately owned, Stretton, Cheshire
	RH746	Bristol 164 Brigand TF1 (fuselage)	Bristol Aero Collection, Kemble
	RL962	DH89A Dominie II (G-AHED)	RAF Museum, stored Wyton
	RM221	Percival P31 Proctor IV (G-ANXR)	Privately owned, Biggin Hill
	RM689	VS379 Spitfire F XIV (G-ALGT) (remains)	Rolls-Royce, Derby
	RM694	VS379 Spitfire F XIV (6640M)	Privately owned, High Wycombe
	RM927	VS379 Spitfire F XIV	Privately owned, High Wycombe
	RN201	VS379 Spitfire FR XIV (SG-31/ SG-3/G-BSKP)	Historic Flying Ltd, Duxford
RN218		Isaacs Spitfire <R> (G-BBJI) [N]	Privately owned, Langham
	RR232	VS361 Spitfire HF IXC (G-BRSF)	Privately owned, Exeter
	RT486	Auster 5 (G-AJGJ) [PF-A]	Bournemouth Aviation Museum
	RT520	Auster 5 (G-ALYB)	Aeroventure, Doncaster
	RT610	Auster 5A-160 (G-AKWS)	Privately owned, Crowfield
	RW388	VS361 Spitfire LF XVIE (6946M) [U4-U]	Stoke-on-Trent City Museum, Hanley
	RW393	VS361 Spitfire LF XVIE (7293M) [XT-A]	RAF Museum, Cosford
	RX168	VS358 Seafire L IIIC (IAC 157/ G-BWEM)	Privately owned, Exeter
	SL611	VS361 Spitfire LF XVIE	Supermarine Aero Engineering, Stoke-on-Trent
	SL674	VS361 Spitfire LF IX (8392M) [RAS-H]	RAF Museum Restoration Centre, Cosford
	SM520	VS361 Spitfire LF IX (G-BXHZ)	Privately owned, Oxford
	SM832	VS379 Spitfire F XIVE (G-WWII/ F-AZSJ) [YB-A]	Privately owned, Dijon, France
	SM845	VS394 Spitfire FR XVIII (G-BUOS)	Silver Victory Collection, Duxford
	SX137	VS384 Seafire F XVII	FAA Museum, RNAS Yeovilton
	SX336	VS384 Seafire F XVII (G-BRMG)	Kennet Aviation, Cranfield
	TA122	DH98 Mosquito FB VI [UP-G]	Mosquito Aircraft Museum, London Colney
	TA634	DH98 Mosquito TT35 (G-AWJV) [8K-K]	Mosquito Aircraft Museum, London Colney
	TA639	DH98 Mosquito TT35 (7806M) [AZ-E]	RAF Museum, Cosford
	TA719	DH98 Mosquito TT35 (G-ASKC)	Imperial War Museum, Duxford
	TA805	VS361 Spitfire HF IX (G-PMNF)	Privately owned, Sandown
	TB252	VS361 Spitfire LF XVIE (G-XVIE) [GW-H]	Historic Flying Ltd, Audley End
	TB752	VS361 Spitfire LF XVIE (8086M) [KH-Z]	RAF Manston, Memorial Pavilion
	TD248	VS361 Spitfire LF XVIE (7246M/ G-OXVI) [D]	Silver Victory Collection, Duxford
	TD314	VS361 Spitfire LF IX (*N601DA*)	Privately owned, Norwich
	TE462	VS361 Spitfire LF XVIE (7243M)	Royal Scottish Mus'm of Flight, E Fortune
	TE517	VS361 Spitfire LF IXE (G-CCIX) [HL-K]	Privately owned, stored Booker
	TG263	Saro SR A1 (G-12-1) [P]	Southampton Hall of Aviation
	TG511	HP67 Hastings C1 (8554M)	RAF Museum, Cosford
	TG517	HP67 Hastings T5	Newark Air Museum, Winthorpe
	TG528	HP67 Hastings C1A	Imperial War Museum, Duxford
	TJ118	DH98 Mosquito TT35 <ff>	Mosquito Aircraft Museum, stored London Colney
	TJ138	DH98 Mosquito B35 (7607M) [VO-L]	RAF Museum, Hendon
TJ324		Auster 5 (G-APAH)	Privately owned, Cumbernauld
	TJ343	Auster 5 (G-AJXC)	Privately owned, stored Hook
TJ398		Auster AOP6 (BAPC 70)	Aircraft Pres'n Soc of Scotland, E Fortune
	TJ534	Auster 5 (G-AKSY)	Privately owned, Breighton
	TJ569	Auster 5 (G-AKOW)	Museum of Army Flying, Middle Wallop
	TJ672	Auster 5D (G-ANIJ) [TS-D]	Privately owned, Whitchurch, Hants
TJ704		Beagle A61 Terrier 2 (VW993/ G-ASCD) [JA]	Yorkshire Air Museum, Elvington
	TJ707	Auster 5 (frame)	Boscombe Down Museum

Serial	Type (other identity) [code]	Owner/operator, location or fate	Notes
TK718	GAL59 Hamilcar I	National Tank Museum, Bovington	
TK777	GAL59 Hamilcar I (fuselage)	Museum of Army Flying, Middle Wallop	
TL615	Airspeed AS58 Horsa II	Robertsbridge Aviation Society, Mayfield	
TS201	Slingsby Cadet TX1 (BGA852)	Royal Scottish Mus'm of Flight, E Fortune	
TS423	Douglas C-47A Dakota C3 (G-DAKS/N147DC) [A]	*Repainted as FL586*	
TS798	Avro 685 York C1 (G-AGNV)	RAF Museum, Cosford	
TV959	DH98 Mosquito T III [AF-V]	The Fighter Collection, stored Duxford	
TV959	DH98 Mosquito T III <R>	Privately owned, Heald Green, Cheshire	
TW439	Auster 5 (G-ANRP)	The Real Aeroplane Company, Breighton	
TW467	Auster 5 (G-ANIE) [ROD-F]	Privately owned, Bassingbourn	
TW511	Auster 5 (G-APAF)	Privately owned, Henstridge	
TW533	Beagle A61 Terrier 2 (G-ASAX)	Privately owned, Netherley, Grampian	
TW536	Auster AOP6 (7704M/G-BNGE) [TS-V]	Privately owned, Netheravon	
TW591	Auster 6A (G-ARIH) [N]	Privately owned, Abbots Bromley	
TW641	Beagle A61 Terrier 2 (G-ATDN)	Privately owned, Biggin Hill	
TX183	Avro 652A Anson C19 (G-BSMF)	*Sold to the UAE, April 2001*	
TX213	Avro 652A Anson C19 (G-AWRS)	North-East Aircraft Museum, Usworth	
TX214	Avro 652A Anson C19 (7817M)	RAF Museum, Cosford	
TX226	Avro 652A Anson C19 (7865M)	Air Atlantique Historic Flight, Coventry	
TX235	Avro 652A Anson C19	Air Atlantique Historic Flight, Coventry	
VF301	DH100 Vampire F1 (7060M) [RAL-G]	Midland Air Museum, Coventry	
VF512	Auster 6A (G-ARRX) [PF-M]	Privately owned, White Waltham	
VF516	Beagle A61 Terrier 2 (G-ASMZ) [T]	Privately owned, Bagby	
VF526	Auster 6A (G-ARXU) [T]	Privately owned, Netheravon	
VF548	Beagle A61 Terrier 1 (G-ASEG)	Privately owned, Dunkeswell	
VF560	Auster 6A (frame)	Aeroventure, Doncaster	
VF581	Beagle A61 Terrier 1 (G-ARSL)	Privately owned, Dunkeswell	
VF611	Beagle A61 Terrier 2 (G-ATBU)	Privately owned, Hucknall	
VH127	Fairey Firefly TT4 [200/R]	FAA Museum, RNAS Yeovilton	
VL348	Avro 652A Anson C19 (G-AVVO)	Newark Air Museum, Winthorpe	
VL349	Avro 652A Anson C19 (G-AWSA) [V7-Q]	Norfolk & Suffolk Avn Mus'm, Flixton	
VM325	Avro 652A Anson C19	Privately owned, stored Gloucester	
VM360	Avro 652A Anson C19 (G-APHV)	Royal Scottish Mus'm of Flight, E Fortune	
VM791	Slingsby Cadet TX3 (XA312/8876M)	RAF Manston History Museum	
VN148	Grunau Baby IIb (BAPC 33/BGA2400)	Privately owned, North Wales	
VN485	VS356 Spitfire F24 (7326M)	Imperial War Museum, Duxford	
VN799	EE Canberra T4 (WJ874)	RAF No 39(1 PRU) Sqn, Marham	
VP293	Avro 696 Shackleton T4 [A] <ff>	Avro Aircraft Heritage Society, Coventry	
VP519	Avro 652 Anson C19 (G-AVVR) <ff>	Privately owned, Wolverhampton	
VP952	DH104 Devon C2 (8820M)	RAF Museum, Cosford	
VP955	DH104 Devon C2 (G-DVON)	Privately owned, Kemble	
VP957	DH104 Devon C2 (8822M) <ff>	No 1137 Sqn ATC, Belfast	
VP975	DH104 Devon C2 [M]	Science Museum, Wroughton	
VP981	DH104 Devon C2 (G-DHDV)	Air Atlantique Historic Flight, Coventry	
VR137	Westland Wyvern TF1	FAA Museum, RNAS Yeovilton	
VR192	Percival P40 Prentice T1 (G-APIT)	SWWAPS, Lasham	
VR249	Percival P40 Prentice T1 (G-APIY) [FA-EL]	Newark Air Museum, Winthorpe	
VR259	Percival P40 Prentice T1 (G-APJB) [M]	Air Atlantique Historic Flight, Coventry	
VR930	Hawker Sea Fury FB11 (8382M) [110/O]	RN Historic Flight, Yeovilton	
VS356	Percival P40 Prentice T1 (G-AOLU)	Privately owned, Montrose	
VS562	Avro 652A Anson T21 (8012M)	Maes Artro Craft Village, Llanbedr	
VS610	Percival P40 Prentice T1 (G-AOKL) [K-L]	The Shuttleworth Collection, Old Warden	
VS623	Percival P40 Prentice T1 (G-AOKZ) [KQ-F]	Midland Air Museum, Coventry	
VT409	Fairey Firefly AS5 <rf>	North-East Aircraft Museum, stored Usworth	
VT812	DH100 Vampire F3 (7200M) [N]	RAF Museum, stored Wyton	
VT871	DH100 Vampire FB6 (J-1173/LZ551/G-DHXX) [G]	Source Classic Jet Flight, Bournemouth	
VT935	Boulton Paul P111A (VT769)	Midland Air Museum, Coventry	
VT987	Auster AOP6 (G-BKXP)	Aerobuild Ltd, Little Gransden, Cambs	

Notes	Serial	Type (other identity) [code]	Owner/operator, location or fate
	VV106	Supermarine 510 (7175M)	FAA Museum, stored RNAS Yeovilton
	VV217	DH100 Vampire FB5 (7323M)	North-East Aircraft Museum, stored Usworth
VV612		DH112 Venom FB50 (J-1523/ *WE402*/G-VENI)	Source Classic Jet Flight, Bournemouth
	VV901	Avro 652A Anson T21	Yorkshire Air Museum, Elvington
VW238		Hawker Fury FB10 (Iraqi AF 243/ *PR772*/G-BTTA)[107/Q]	*Sold as N103FD, January 2001*
	VW453	Gloster Meteor T7 (8703M) [Z]	RAF Innsworth, on display
	VW985	Auster AOP6 (G-ASEF)	Privately owned, Upper Arncott, Oxon
	VX118	Auster AOP6 (G-ASNB)	Vliegend Museum, Seppe, The Netherlands
VX147		Alon A2 Aircoupe (G-AVIL)	Privately owned, Monewdon
	VX185	EE Canberra B(I)8 (7631M) <ff>	Royal Scottish Mus'm of Flight, E Fortune
	VX250	DH103 Sea Hornet 21 [48] <rf>	Mosquito Aircraft Museum, London Colney
	VX272	Hawker P.1052 (7174M)	FAA Museum, stored RNAS Yeovilton
	VX275	Slingsby T21B Sedbergh TX1 (8884M/BGA 572)	RAF Museum Restoration Centre, Cosford
	VX461	DH100 Vampire FB5 (7646M)	RAF Museum, stored Wyton
	VX573	Vickers Valetta C2 (8389M)	RAF Museum, stored Cosford
	VX580	Vickers Valetta C2	Norfolk & Suffolk Avn Museum, Flixton
	VX595	WS51 Dragonfly HR1	FAA Museum, stored RNAS Yeovilton
	VX665	Hawker Sea Fury FB11 <rf>	RN Historic Flight, at BAE Systems Brough
	VX926	Auster T7 (G-ASKJ)	Privately owned, Little Gransden
	VZ345	Hawker Sea Fury T20S	RN Historic Flight, stored Yeovilton
	VZ467	Gloster Meteor F8 (G-METE)	*Sold as VH-MBX, June 2001*
	VZ477	Gloster Meteor F8 (7741M) <ff>	Midland Air Museum, Coventry
	VZ608	Gloster Meteor FR9	Newark Air Museum, Winthorpe
	VZ634	Gloster Meteor T7 (8657M)	Newark Air Museum, Winthorpe
	VZ638	Gloster Meteor T7 (G-JETM) [HF]	Gatwick Aviation Museum, Charlwood, Surrey
	VZ728	RS4 Desford Trainer (G-AGOS)	Snibston Discovery Park, stored Coalville
	VZ962	WS51 Dragonfly HR1 [904]	The Helicopter Museum, Weston-super-Mare
	WA473	VS Attacker F1 [102/J]	FAA Museum, RNAS Yeovilton
	WA576	Bristol 171 Sycamore 3 (7900M/ G-ALSS)	Dumfries & Galloway Avn Mus, Dumfries
	WA577	Bristol 171 Sycamore 3 (7718M/ G-ALST)	North-East Aircraft Museum, Usworth
	WA591	Gloster Meteor T7 (7917M/ G-BWMF) [W]	Meteor Flight, Yatesbury
	WA630	Gloster Meteor T7 [69] <ff>	Robertsbridge Aviation Society, Newhaven
	WA634	Gloster Meteor T7/8	RAF Museum, Cosford
	WA638	Gloster Meteor T7(mod)	Martin Baker Aircraft, Chalgrove
	WA662	Gloster Meteor T7	Aeroventure, Doncaster
WA829		Gloster Meteor F8 (WA984) [A]	Tangmere Military Aviation Museum
	WB188	Hawker Hunter F3 (7154M)	Tangmere Military Aviation Museum
WB188		Hawker Hunter GA11 (WV256/ G-BZPB)	Classic Jets (UK), Exeter (duck egg green)
WB188		Hawker Hunter GA11 (XF300/ G-BZPC)	Classic Jets (UK), Exeter (red)
	WB271	Fairey Firefly AS5 [204/R]	RN Historic Flight, RNAS Yeovilton
	WB440	Fairey Firefly AS6 <ff>	Privately owned, Newton-le-Willows
	WB491	Avro 706 Ashton 2 (TS897/ G-AJJW) <ff>	Avro Aircraft Heritage Society, BAE Systems Woodford
	WB556	DHC1 Chipmunk T10	RAFGSA, Bicester
	WB560	DHC1 Chipmunk T10 (comp WG403)	Aeroventure, stored Doncaster
	WB565	DHC1 Chipmunk T10 (G-PVET) [X]	Privately owned, Kemble
	WB569	DHC1 Chipmunk T10 (G-BYSJ) [R]	Privately owned, Duxford
	WB584	DHC1 Chipmunk T10 (7706M) <ff>	Royal Scottish Mus'm of Flight, E Fortune
	WB585	DHC1 Chipmunk T10 (G-AOSY) [M]	Privately owned, Blackbushe
	WB588	DHC1 Chipmunk T10 (G-AOTD) [D]	Privately owned, Biggin Hill
	WB615	DHC1 Chipmunk T10 (G-BXIA) [E]	Privately owned, Blackpool
	WB624	DHC1 Chipmunk T10 <ff>	Newark Air Museum, Winthorpe
	WB626	DHC1 Chipmunk T10 <ff>	Privately owned, Aylesbury
	WB627	DHC1 Chipmunk T10 (9248M) [N]	Dulwich College CCF
	WB645	DHC1 Chipmunk T10 (8218M)	RAFGSA, Bicester, spares use
	WB652	DHC1 Chipmunk T10 (G-CHPY) [V]	Privately owned, Cardiff
	WB654	DHC1 Chipmunk T10 (G-BXGO) [U]	Privately owned, Booker
	WB657	DHC1 Chipmunk T10 [908]	RN Historic Flight, Yeovilton

Serial	Type (other identity) [code]	Owner/operator, location or fate	Notes
WB660	DHC1 Chipmunk T10 (G-ARMB)	Privately owned, Shipdham	
WB670	DHC1 Chipmunk T10 (8361M) <ff>	Privately owned, Currie, Lothian	
WB671	DHC1 Chipmunk T10 (G-BWTG) [910]	Privately owned, Epse, The Netherlands	
WB685	DHC1 Chipmunk T10 (comp WP969/G-ATHC)	North-East Aircraft Museum, Usworth	
WB697	DHC1 Chipmunk T10 (G-BXCT) [95]	Privately owned, Wickenby	
WB702	DHC1 Chipmunk T10 (G-AOFE)	Privately owned, Goodwood	
WB703	DHC1 Chipmunk T10 (G-ARMC)	Privately owned, White Waltham	
WB711	DHC1 Chipmunk T10 (G-APPM)	Privately owned, Crowfield	
WB726	DHC1 Chipmunk T10 (G-AOSK) [E]	Privately owned, Audley End	
WB733	DHC1 Chipmunk T10 (comp WG422)	Aeroventure, Doncaster	
WB758	DHC1 Chipmunk T10 (7729M) [P]	Privately owned, Torbay	
WB763	DHC1 Chipmunk T10 (G-BBMR) [14]	Privately owned, Twyford, Bucks	
WB922	Slingsby T21B Sedbergh TX1 (BGA 4366)	Privately owned, Rufforth	
WB924	Slingsby T21B Sedbergh TX1 (BGA 3901)	Privately owned, Dunstable	
WB938	Slingsby T21B Sedbergh TX1	Privately owned, Halton	
WB943	Slingsby T21B Sedbergh TX1 (BGA 2941)	Privately owned, Rufforth	
WB969	Slingsby T21B Sedbergh TX1	Aeroventure, Doncaster	
WB971	Slingsby T21B Sedbergh TX1 (BGA 3324)	Privately owned, Tibenham	
WB975	Slingsby T21B Sedbergh TX1 (BGA 3288)	Privately owned, Drumshade, Fife	
WB981	Slingsby T21B Sedbergh TX1 (BGA 1218)	Privately owned, Aston Down	
WD286	DHC1 Chipmunk T10 (G-BBND)	Privately owned, Croydon, Cambs	
WD288	DHC1 Chipmunk T10 (G-AOSO) [38]	Privately owned, Charlton Park, Wilts	
WD292	DHC1 Chipmunk T10 (G-BCRX)	Privately owned, White Waltham	
WD293	DHC1 Chipmunk T10 (7645M) <ff>	No 210 Sqn ATC, Newport, Gwent	
WD305	DHC1 Chipmunk T10 (G-ARGG)	Privately owned, Meppershall	
WD310	DHC1 Chipmunk T10 (G-BWUN) [B]	Privately owned, Ringmer, E Sussex	
WD318	DHC1 Chipmunk T10 (8207M) <ff>	No 145 Sqn ATC, Timperley, Gr Manchester	
WD325	DHC1 Chipmunk T10 [N]	AAC Historic Aircraft Flight, Middle Wallop	
WD331	DHC1 Chipmunk T10 (G-BXDH) [J]	Privately owned, Kemble	
WD347	DHC1 Chipmunk T10 (G-BBRV)	Privately owned, Liverpool	
WD355	DHC1 Chipmunk T10 (WD335/G-CBAJ)	Privately owned, Solihull	
WD363	DHC1 Chipmunk T10 (G-BCIH) [5]	Privately owned, Andrewsfield	
WD370	DHC1 Chipmunk T10 <ff>	Privately owned, Brighton	
WD373	DHC1 Chipmunk T10 (G-BXDI) [12]	Privately owned, Gloucester	
WD377	DHC1 Chipmunk T10 <ff>	RAF Millom Museum, Haverigg	
WD379	DHC1 Chipmunk T10 (WB696/G-APLO) [K]	Privately owned, Jersey	
WD386	DHC1 Chipmunk T10 (comp WD377)	Dumfries & Galloway Avn Mus, Dumfries	
WD390	DHC1 Chipmunk T10 (G-BWNK) [68]	Privately owned, Breighton	
WD615	Gloster Meteor TT20 (WD646/8189M) [R]	RAF Manston History Museum	
WD686	Gloster Meteor NF11	Muckleburgh Collection, Weybourne	
WD790	Gloster Meteor NF11 (8743M) <ff>	North-East Aircraft Museum, Usworth	
WD889	Fairey Firefly AS5 <ff>	North-East Aircraft Museum, Usworth	
WD931	EE Canberra B2 <ff>	RAF Museum, stored Cosford	
WD935	EE Canberra B2 (8440M) <ff>	Privately owned, Stroud, Glos	
WD954	EE Canberra B2 <ff>	Privately owned, Golders Green	
WE113	EE Canberra B2 <ff>	Privately owned, Woodhurst, Cambridgeshire	
WE122	EE Canberra TT18 [845] <ff>	Blyth Valley Aviation Collection, Walpole, Suffolk	
WE139	EE Canberra PR3 (8369M)	RAF Museum, Hendon	
WE168	EE Canberra PR3 (8049M) <ff>	Privately owned, Colchester	

Notes	Serial	Type (other identity) [code]	Owner/operator, location or fate
	WE173	EE Canberra PR3 (8740M) <ff>	Robertsbridge Aviation Society, Mayfield
	WE188	EE Canberra T4	Solway Aviation Society, Carlisle
	WE192	EE Canberra T4 <ff>	Blyth Valley Aviation Collection, Walpole, Suffolk
	WE275	DH112 Venom FB50 (J-1601/ G-VIDI)	BAE Systems Hawarden, Fire Section
	WE569	Auster T7 (G-ASAJ)	Privately owned, Bassingbourn
	WE591	Auster T7 (G-ASAK) [Y]	Privately owned, Biggin Hill
	WE600	Auster T7 Antarctic (7602M)	RAF Museum, Cosford
	WE724	Hawker Sea Fury FB11 (VX653/ G-BUCM) [062]	The Fighter Collection, Duxford
	WE925	Gloster Meteor F8	Classic Jet Aircraft Group, Loughborough
	WE982	Slingsby T30B Prefect TX1 (8781M)	RAF Museum, stored Cosford
	WE990	Slingsby T30B Prefect TX1 (BGA 2583)	Privately owned, stored Beds
	WF118	Percival P57 Sea Prince T1 (G-DACA)	Gatwick Aviation Museum, Charlwood, Surrey
	WF122	Percival P57 Sea Prince T1 [575/CU]	Flambards Village Theme Park, Helston
	WF128	Percival P57 Sea Prince T1 (8611M)	Norfolk & Suffolk Avn Museum, Flixton
	WF137	Percival P57 Sea Prince C1	SWWAPS, Lasham
	WF145	Hawker Sea Hawk F1 <ff>	Privately owned, Welshpool
	WF225	Hawker Sea Hawk F1 [CU]	RNAS Culdrose, at main gate
	WF259	Hawker Sea Hawk F2 [171/A]	Royal Scottish Mus'm of Flight, E Fortune
	WF369	Vickers Varsity T1 [F]	Newark Air Museum, Winthorpe
	WF372	Vickers Varsity T1 [A]	Brooklands Museum, Weybridge
	WF376	Vickers Varsity T1	Bristol Airport Fire Section
	WF408	Vickers Varsity T1 (8395M)	Privately owned, East Grinstead
	WF410	Vickers Varsity T1 [F]	Brunel Technical College, Lulsgate
	WF643	Gloster Meteor F8 [X]	Norfolk & Suffolk Avn Museum, Flixton
	WF714	Gloster Meteor F8 (WK914)	Privately owned, stored Scampton
	WF784	Gloster Meteor T7 (7895M)	Gloucestershire Avn Coll, stored Gloucester
	WF825	Gloster Meteor T7 (8359M) [A]	Avon Air Museum, stored Malmesbury
	WF877	Gloster Meteor T7 (G-BPOA)	Privately owned, Kemble
	WF911	EE Canberra B2 [CO] <ff>	The Griffin Trust, Hooton Park, Cheshire
	WF922	EE Canberra PR3	Midland Air Museum, Coventry
	WG300	DHC1 Chipmunk T10 <ff>	RAFGSA, Bicester
	WG303	DHC1 Chipmunk T10 (8208M) <ff>	RAFGSA, Bicester
	WG307	DHC1 Chipmunk T10 (G-BCYJ)	Privately owned, Shempston Fm, Lossiemouth
	WG308	DHC1 Chipmunk T10 (G-BYHL) [71]	Privately owned, Newton
	WG316	DHC1 Chipmunk T10 (G-BCAH)	Privately owned, Shoreham
	WG321	DHC1 Chipmunk T10 (G-DHCC)	Privately owned, Wevelgem, Belgium
	WG348	DHC1 Chipmunk T10 (G-BBMV)	Privately owned, Sywell
	WG350	DHC1 Chipmunk T10 (G-BPAL)	Privately owned, Thruxton
	WG362	DHC1 Chipmunk T10 (8437M/ 8630M/*WX643*) <ff>	RAF Newton, instructional use
	WG407	DHC1 Chipmunk T10 (G-BWMX)	Privately owned, Shefford, Beds
	WG418	DHC1 Chipmunk T10 (8209M/ G-ATDY) <ff>	No 1940 Sqn ATC, Levenshulme, Gr Manchester
	WG419	DHC1 Chipmunk T10 (8206M) <ff>	No 1053 Sqn ATC, Armthorpe
	WG422	DHC1 Chipmunk T10 (8394M/ G-BFAX) [116]	Privately owned, Duxford
	WG432	DHC1 Chipmunk T10 [L]	Museum of Army Flying, Middle Wallop
	WG465	DHC1 Chipmunk T10 (G-BCEY)	Privately owned, White Waltham
	WG469	DHC1 Chipmunk T10 (G-BWJY) [72]	Privately owned, Newtownards
	WG471	DHC1 Chipmunk T10 (8210M) <ff>	No 301 Sqn ATC, Bury St Edmunds
	WG472	DHC1 Chipmunk T10 (G-AOTY)	Privately owned, Bryngwyn Bach, Clwyd
	WG477	DHC1 Chipmunk T10 (8362M/ G-ATDP) <ff>	No 281 Sqn ATC, Birkdale, Merseyside
	WG482	DHC1 Chipmunk T10 (VH-ZOT) [01]	Privately owned, Duxford
	WG483	DHC1 Chipmunk T10 (WG393/ VH-ZIT)	Privately owned, Duxford
	WG486	DHC1 Chipmunk T10 [G]	RAF BBMF, Coningsby

Serial	Type (other identity) [code]	Owner/operator, location or fate	Notes
WG498	Slingsby T21B Sedbergh TX1 (BGA 3245)	Privately owned, Aston Down	
WG511	Avro 696 Shackleton T4 (fuselage)	Flambards Village Theme Park, Helston	
WG718	WS51 Dragonfly HR3 [934]	Privately owned, Elvington	
WG719	WS51 Dragonfly HR5 (G-BRMA)	The Helicopter Museum, Weston-super-Mare	
WG724	WS51 Dragonfly HR5 [932]	North-East Aircraft Museum, Usworth	
WG751	WS51 Dragonfly HR5 [710/GJ]	World Naval Base, Chatham	
WG760	EE P1A (7755M)	RAF Museum, Cosford	
WG763	EE P1A (7816M)	Gr Manchester Mus of Science & Industry	
WG768	Short SB5 (8005M)	RAF Museum, Cosford	
WG774	BAC 221	Science Museum, at FAA Museum, RNAS Yeovilton	
WG777	Fairey FD2 (7986M)	RAF Museum, Cosford	
WG789	EE Canberra B2/6 <ff>	Privately owned, Mendlesham, Suffolk	
WH132	Gloster Meteor T7 (7906M) [J]	No 276 Sqn ATC, Chelmsford	
WH166	Gloster Meteor T7 (8052M) [A]	Privately owned, Birlingham, Worcs	
WH291	Gloster Meteor F8	SWWAPS, Lasham	
WH301	Gloster Meteor F8 (7930M) [T]	RAF Museum, Hendon	
WH364	Gloster Meteor F8 (8169M)	Meteor Flight, Yatesbury	
WH453	Gloster Meteor D16 [L]	DPA, stored QinetiQ Llanbedr	
WH646	EE Canberra T17A <ff>	Midland Air Museum, Coventry	
WH657	EE Canberra B2	Brenzett Aeronautical Museum	
WH665	EE Canberra T17 (8763M) [J]	BAE Systems Filton, Fire Section	
WH701	EE Canberra B2 (7659M) <ff>	No 2077 Sqn ATC, Talbot Green, S Wales	
WH725	EE Canberra B2	Imperial War Museum, Duxford	
WH734	EE Canberra B2(mod)	DPA, QinetiQ Llanbedr	
WH739	EE Canberra B2 <ff>	No 2475 Sqn ATC, Ammanford, Dyfed	
WH740	EE Canberra T17 (8762M) [K]	East Midlands Airport Aeropark	
WH773	EE Canberra PR7 (8696M)	Gatwick Aviation Museum, Charlwood, Surrey	
WH775	EE Canberra PR7 (8128M/8868M) <ff>	Privately owned, Welshpool	
WH779	EE Canberra PR7 <ff>	QinetiQ Farnborough	
WH779	EE Canberra PR7 [BP] <rf>	RAF, stored Shawbury	
WH780	EE Canberra T22 <rf>	Scrapped	
WH791	EE Canberra PR7 (8165M/8176M/ 8187M)	Newark Air Museum, Winthorpe	
WH797	EE Canberra T22 <rf>	RAF St Athan, Fire Section	
WH803	EE Canberra T22 <ff>	Privately owned,	
WH840	EE Canberra T4 (8350M)	Privately owned, Flixton	
WH846	EE Canberra T4	Yorkshire Air Museum, Elvington	
WH849	EE Canberra T4	RAF No 39(1 PRU) Sqn, Marham	
WH850	EE Canberra T4 <ff>	Barton Aviation Heritage Society, Barton	
WH863	EE Canberra T17 (8693M) [CP] <ff>	Newark Air Museum, Winthorpe	
WH876	EE Canberra B2(mod) <ff>	Boscombe Down Museum	
WH887	EE Canberra TT18 [847]	DPA, stored QinetiQ Llanbedr	
WH903	EE Canberra B2 <ff>	Yorkshire Air Museum, Elvington	
WH904	EE Canberra T19	Newark Air Museum, Winthorpe	
WH946	EE Canberra B6(mod) (8185M) <ff>	Privately owned, Tetney, Grimsby	
WH953	EE Canberra B6(mod) <ff>	Blyth Valley Aviation Collection, Walpole, Suffolk	
WH957	EE Canberra E15 (8869M) <ff>	Lincolnshire Avn Heritage Centre, East Kirkby	
WH960	EE Canberra B15 (8344M) <ff>	Privately owned, Nottingham	
WH964	EE Canberra E15 (8870M) <ff>	Privately owned, Southampton	
WH984	EE Canberra B15 (8101M) <ff>	RAF Sealand	
WH991	WS51 Dragonfly HR3	Privately owned, Elvington	
WJ231	Hawker Sea Fury FB11 (*WE726*) [115/O]	FAA Museum, Yeovilton	
WJ358	Auster AOP6 (G-ARYD)	Museum of Army Flying, Middle Wallop	
WJ565	EE Canberra T17 (8871M) <ff>	Privately owned	
WJ567	EE Canberra B2 <ff>	Privately owned, Houghton, Cambs	
WJ576	EE Canberra T17 <ff>	Boulton Paul Association, Wolverhampton	
WJ581	EE Canberra PR7 <ff>	Privately owned, Canterbury	
WJ603	EE Canberra B2 (8664M) <ff>		
WJ630	EE Canberra T17 [ED]		
WJ633	EE Canberra T17 [EF] <ff>	RAF Wyton	
WJ639	EE Canberra TT18 [39]	North-East Aircraft Museum, Usworth	

Notes	Serial	Type (other identity) [code]	Owner/operator, location or fate
	WJ640	EE Canberra B2 (8722M) <ff>	Pinewood Studios, Bucks
	WJ676	EE Canberra B2 (7796M) <ff>	NW Aviation Heritage, Hootonn Park
	WJ677	EE Canberra B2 <ff>	Privately owned, Redruth
	WJ680	EE Canberra TT18 (G-BURM) [CT]	*Sold to Australia, January 2002*
	WJ717	EE Canberra TT18 (9052M) <ff>	RAF St Athan, Fire Section
	WJ721	EE Canberra TT18 [21]	Dundonald Aviation Centre, Strathclyde
	WJ731	EE Canberra B2T [BK] <ff>	Privately owned, Dunstable
	WJ821	EE Canberra PR7 (8668M)	Army, Bassingbourn, on display
	WJ863	EE Canberra T4 <ff>	Cambridge Airport Fire Section
	WJ865	EE Canberra T4	Privately owned, Bromsgrove
	WJ866	EE Canberra T4 [AV]	RAF No 39(1 PRU) Sqn, Marham
	WJ872	EE Canberra T4 (8492M) <ff>	No 327 Sqn ATC, Kilmarnock
	WJ876	EE Canberra T4 <ff>	*Scrapped*
	WJ880	EE Canberra T4 (8491M) <ff>	Dumfries & Galloway Avn Mus, Dumfries
	WJ903	Vickers Varsity T1 <ff>	Aeroventure, Doncaster
	WJ945	Vickers Varsity T1 (G-BEDV) [21]	Imperial War Museum, Duxford
	WJ975	EE Canberra T19	Bomber County Aviation Museum, Hemswell
	WJ992	EE Canberra T4	Bournemouth Int'l Airport, Fire Section
	WK102	EE Canberra T17 (8780M) <ff>	Privately owned, Welshpool
	WK118	EE Canberra TT18 <ff>	Privately owned, Worcester
	WK122	EE Canberra TT18 <ff>	Phoenix Aviation, Bruntingthorpe
	WK124	EE Canberra TT18 (9093M) [CR]	MoD FSCTE, Manston
	WK126	EE Canberra TT18 (N2138J) [843]	Gloucestershire Avn Coll, stored Gloucester
	WK127	EE Canberra TT18 (8985M) <ff>	No 2484 Sqn ATC, Bassingbourn
	WK128	EE Canberra B2	DPA, QinetiQ Llanbedr
	WK146	EE Canberra B2 <ff>	Gatwick Aviation Museum, Charlwood, Surrey
	WK163	EE Canberra B2/6 (G-BVWC)	Air Atlantique Historic Flight, Coventry
	WK198	VS Swift F4 (7428M) (fuselage)	North-East Aircraft Museum, Usworth
	WK275	VS Swift F4	Privately owned, Upper Hill, nr Leominster
	WK277	VS Swift FR5 (7719M) [N]	Newark Air Museum, Winthorpe
	WK281	VS Swift FR5 (7712M) [S]	Tangmere Military Aviation Museum
	WK393	DH112 Venom FB1 <ff>	Aeroventure, Doncaster
	WK436	DH112 Venom FB50 (J-1614/ G-VENM)	Kennet Aviation, Cranfield
	WK511	DHC1 Chipmunk T10 (G-BVBT) [905]	Privately owned, Duxford
	WK512	DHC1 Chipmunk T10 (G-BXIM) [A]	Privately owned, Brize Norton
	WK517	DHC1 Chipmunk T10 (G-ULAS) [84]	Privately owned, Booker
	WK518	DHC1 Chipmunk T10 [K]	RAF BBMF, Coningsby
	WK522	DHC1 Chipmunk T10 (G-BCOU)	Privately owned, Duxford
	WK549	DHC1 Chipmunk T10 (G-BTWF)	Privately owned, Breighton
	WK570	DHC1 Chipmunk T10 (8211M) <ff>	No 424 Sqn ATC, Southampton Hall of Aviation
	WK576	DHC1 Chipmunk T10 (8357M) <ff>	No 1206 Sqn ATC, Lichfield
	WK584	DHC1 Chipmunk T10 (7556M) <ff>	No 216 Sqn ATC, Bawtry
	WK585	DHC1 Chipmunk T10 (G-BZGA)	The Aircraft Restoration Co, Duxford
	WK586	DHC1 Chipmunk T10 (G-BXGX) [V]	Privately owned, Shoreham
	WK590	DHC1 Chipmunk T10 (G-BWVZ) [69]	Privately owned, Spanhoe
	WK608	DHC1 Chipmunk T10 [906]	RN Historic Flight, Yeovilton
	WK609	DHC1 Chipmunk T10 (G-BXDN) [B]	Privately owned, Halton
	WK611	DHC1 Chipmunk T10 (G-ARWB)	Privately owned, Thruxton
	WK613	DHC1 Chipmunk T10 [P]	
	WK620	DHC1 Chipmunk T10 [T] (fuselage)	Privately owned, Twyford, Bucks
	WK622	DHC1 Chipmunk T10 (G-BCZH)	Privately owned, Horsford
	WK624	DHC1 Chipmunk T10 (G-BWHI)	The Aircraft Restoration Co, Duxford
	WK626	DHC1 Chipmunk T10 (8213M) <ff>	Aeroventure, stored Doncaster
	WK628	DHC1 Chipmunk T10 (G-BBMW)	Privately owned, Goodwood
	WK630	DHC1 Chipmunk T10 (G-BXDG) [11]	Privately owned, Swanton Morley
	WK633	DHC1 Chipmunk T10 (G-BXEC) [A]	Privately owned, Seething
	WK640	DHC1 Chipmunk T10 (G-BWUV) [C]	Privately owned, Bagby
	WK642	DHC1 Chipmunk T10 (G-BXDP) [94]	Privately owned, Kilrush, Eire
	WK654	Gloster Meteor F8 (8092M) [B]	City of Norwich Aviation Museum

Serial	Type (other identity) [code]	Owner/operator, location or fate	Notes
WK800	Gloster Meteor D16 [Z]	DPA, QinetiQ Llanbedr	
WK864	Gloster Meteor F8 (WL168/7750M) [C]	Yorkshire Air Museum, Elvington	
WK935	Gloster Meteor Prone Pilot (7869M)	RAF Museum, Cosford	
WK991	Gloster Meteor F8 (7825M)	Imperial War Museum, Duxford	
WL131	Gloster Meteor F8 (7751M) <ff>	Aeroventure, Doncaster	
WL181	Gloster Meteor F8 [X]	North-East Aircraft Museum, Usworth	
WL332	Gloster Meteor T7 [888]	Privately owned, Long Marston	
WL345	Gloster Meteor T7	St Leonard's Motors, Hollington, E Sussex	
WL349	Gloster Meteor T7 [Z]	Staverton, Glos, stored	
WL360	Gloster Meteor T7 (7920M) [G]	Meteor Flight, Yatesbury	
WL375	Gloster Meteor T7(mod)	Dumfries & Galloway Avn Mus, Dumfries	
WL405	Gloster Meteor T7	Meteor Flight, Yatesbury	
WL419	Gloster Meteor T7	Martin Baker Aircraft, Chalgrove	
WL505	DH100 Vampire FB9 (7705M/ G-FBIX)	De Havilland Aviation, Bridgend	
WL505	DH100 Vampire FB6 (J-1167/ *VZ304*/G-MKVI)	De Havilland Aviation, Swansea	
WL626	Vickers Varsity T1 (G-BHDD) [P]	East Midlands Airport Aeropark	
WL627	Vickers Varsity T1 (8488M) [D] <ff>	Privately owned, Preston, E Yorkshire	
WL679	Vickers Varsity T1 (9155M)	RAF Museum, Cosford	
WL732	BP P108 Sea Balliol T21	RAF Museum, Cosford	
WL795	Avro 696 Shackleton MR2C (8753M) [T]	RAF St Mawgan, on display	
WL798	Avro 696 Shackleton MR2C (8114M) <ff>	Privately owned, Elgin	
WL925	Slingsby T31B Cadet TX3 (WV925) <ff>	RAF No 633 VGS, Cosford	
WM145	AW Meteor NF11 <ff>	N Yorks Aircraft Recovery Centre, Chop Gate	
WM167	AW Meteor NF11 (G-LOSM)	Privately owned, Bournemouth	
WM267	Gloster Meteor NF11 <ff>	Blyth Valley Aviation Collection, Walpole, Suffolk	
WM292	AW Meteor TT20 [841]	FAA Museum, stored RNAS Yeovilton	
WM311	AW Meteor TT20 (WM224/8177M)	Privately owned, North Weald	
WM366	AW Meteor NF13 (4X-FNA) (comp VZ462)	SWWAPS, Lasham	
WM367	AW Meteor NF13 <ff>	Jet Avn Preservation Grp, Long Marston	
WM571	DH112 Sea Venom FAW21 [VL]	Southampton Hall of Aviation	
WM729	DH112 Vampire NF10 <ff>	Mosquito Aircraft Museum, London Colney	
WM913	Hawker Sea Hawk FB5 (8162M) [456/J]	Newark Air Museum, Winthorpe	
WM961	Hawker Sea Hawk FB5 [J]	Caernarfon Air World	
WM969	Hawker Sea Hawk FB5 [10/Z]	Imperial War Museum, Duxford	
WM993	Hawker Sea Hawk FB5 [034]	*Broken up*	
WN105	Hawker Sea Hawk FB3 (WF299/ 8164M)	Privately owned, Birlingham, Worcs	
WN108	Hawker Sea Hawk FB5 [033]	Ulster Aviation Society, Langford Lodge	
WN149	BP P108 Balliol T2	Boulton Paul Association, Wolverhampton	
WN411	Fairey Gannet AS1 (fuselage)	Privately owned, Southampton	
WN493	WS51 Dragonfly HR5	FAA Museum, RNAS Yeovilton	
WN499	WS51 Dragonfly HR5 [Y]	Caernarfon Air World	
WN516	BP P108 Balliol T2 <ff>	North-East Aircraft Museum, Usworth	
WN534	BP P108 Balliol T2 <ff>	Boulton Paul Association, Wolverhampton	
WN890	Hawker Hunter F2 <ff>	Aeroventure, Doncaster	
WN904	Hawker Hunter F2 (7544M) [3]	RE 39 Regt, Waterbeach, on display	
WN907	Hawker Hunter F2 (7416M) <ff>	Blyth Valley Aviation Collection, Walpole, Suffolk	
WN957	Hawker Hunter F5 <ff>	Privately owned, Llanbedr	
WP185	Hawker Hunter F5 (7583M)	Privately owned, Great Dunmow, Essex	
WP190	Hawker Hunter F5 (7582M/8473M/ *WP180*) [K]	Privately owned, Quedgeley, Glos.	
WP250	DH113 Vampire NF10 <ff>	Privately owned,	
WP255	DH113 Vampire NF10 <ff>	Aeroventure, Doncaster	
WP270	EoN Eton TX1 (8598M)	Gr Manchester Mus of Science & Industry, stored	
WP271	EoN Eton TX1	Privately owned, stored Keevil	
WP308	Percival P57 Sea Prince T1 (G-GACA) [572/CU]	Gatwick Aviation Museum, Charlwood, Surrey	

Notes	Serial	Type (other identity) [code]	Owner/operator, location or fate
	WP313	Percival P57 Sea Prince T1 [568/CU]	FAA Museum, stored RNAS Yeovilton
	WP314	Percival P57 Sea Prince T1 (8634M) [573/CU]	Privately owned, Carlisle Airport
	WP321	Percival P57 Sea Prince T1 (N7SY)	Bournemouth Aviation Museum
	WP515	EE Canberra B2 <ff>	Privately owned, Welshpool
	WP772	DHC1 Chipmunk T10 [Q] (wreck)	RAF Manston History Museum
	WP784	DHC1 Chipmunk T10 <ff>	Jet Avn Preservation Grp, Long Marston
	WP788	DHC1 Chipmunk T10 (G-BCHL)	Privately owned, Sleap
	WP790	DHC1 Chipmunk T10 (G-BBNC) [T]	Mosquito Aircraft Museum, London Colney
	WP795	DHC1 Chipmunk T10 (G-BVZZ) [901]	Privately owned, Lee-on-Solent
	WP800	DHC1 Chipmunk T10 (G-BCXN) [2]	Privately owned, Halton
	WP803	DHC1 Chipmunk T10 (G-HAPY) [G]	Privately owned, Booker
	WP805	DHC1 Chipmunk T10 (G-MAJR) [D]	Privately owned, Fareham
	WP808	DHC1 Chipmunk T10 (G-BDEU)	Privately owned, Binham
	WP809	DHC1 Chipmunk T10 (G-BVTX) [78]	Privately owned, Husbands Bosworth
	WP833	DHC1 Chipmunk T10 (G-BZDU) [H]	Privately owned, Duxford
	WP835	DHC1 Chipmunk T10 (D-ERTY)	Privately owned, The Netherlands
	WP839	DHC1 Chipmunk T10 (G-BZXE) [A]	Privately owned, Blackpool
	WP840	DHC1 Chipmunk T10 (G-BXDM) [9]	Privately owned, Halton
	WP843	DHC1 Chipmunk T10 (G-BDBP) [F]	*Sold as ZS-COX, August 2000*
	WP844	DHC1 Chipmunk T10 (G-BWOX) [85]	Privately owned, King's Coughton
	WP845	DHC1 Chipmunk T10 <ff>	Privately owned, Leicestershire
	WP856	DHC1 Chipmunk T10 (G-BVWP) [904]	Privately owned, Horsham
	WP857	DHC1 Chipmunk T10 (G-BDRJ) [24]	Privately owned, Elstree
	WP859	DHC1 Chipmunk T10 (G-BXCP) [E]	Privately owned, Eire
	WP860	DHC1 Chipmunk T10 (G-BXDA) [6]	Privately owned, Cumbernauld
	WP863	DHC1 Chipmunk T10 (8360M/ G-ATJI) <ff>	No 1011 Sqn ATC, QinetiQ Boscombe Down
	WP871	DHC1 Chipmunk T10 [W]	AAC, Middle Wallop, for display
	WP896	DHC1 Chipmunk T10 (G-BWVY) [M]	Privately owned, London
	WP901	DHC1 Chipmunk T10 (G-BWNT) [B]	Privately owned, East Midlands Airport
	WP903	DHC1 Chipmunk T10 (G-BCGC)	Privately owned, Shoreham
	WP907	DHC1 Chipmunk T10 <ff> (7970M)	Privately owned, Reading
	WP912	DHC1 Chipmunk T10 (8467M)	RAF Museum, Cosford
	WP921	DHC1 Chipmunk T10 (G-ATJJ) <ff>	Privately owned, Brooklands
	WP925	DHC1 Chipmunk T10 (G-BXHA) [C]	Privately owned, Camberley
	WP927	DHC1 Chipmunk T10 (8216M/ G-ATJK) <ff>	No 1343 Sqn ATC, Odiham
	WP928	DHC1 Chipmunk T10 (G-BXGM) [D]	Privately owned, Shoreham
	WP929	DHC1 Chipmunk T10 (G-BXCV) [F]	The Aircraft Restoration Company, Duxford
	WP930	DHC1 Chipmunk T10 (G-BXHF) [J]	Privately owned, Redhill
	WP962	DHC1 Chipmunk T10 [C]	RAF Museum, Hendon
	WP964	DHC1 Chipmunk T10 [Y]	AAC Historic Aircraft Flight, Middle Wallop
	WP971	DHC1 Chipmunk T10 (G-ATHD)	Privately owned, Denham
	WP978	DHC1 Chipmunk T10 (7467M) <ff>	Privately owned, Bournemouth
	WP983	DHC1 Chipmunk T10 (G-BXNN) [B]	Privately owned, Old Sarum
	WP984	DHC1 Chipmunk T10 (G-BWTO) [H]	Privately owned, Duxford
	WR360	DH112 Venom FB50 (J-1626/ G-DHSS)	Source Classic Jet Flight, Bournemouth
	WR410	DH112 Venom FB50 (J-1539/ G-DHUU/*WE410*)	Source Classic Jet Flight, Bournemouth
	WR410	DH112 Venom FB54 (J-1790/ G-BLKA) [N]	Source Classic Jet Flight, stored Bournemouth
	WR421	DH112 Venom FB50 (J-1611/ G-DHTT)	Source Classic Jet Flight, Bournemouth
	WR539	DH112 Venom FB4 (8399M) <ff>	Mosquito Aircraft Museum, London Colney
	WR960	Avro 696 Shackleton AEW2 (8772M)	Gr Manchester Mus of Science & Industry
	WR963	Avro 696 Shackleton AEW2	Air Atlantique Historic Flight, Coventry
	WR971	Avro 696 Shackleton MR3 (8119M) [Q]	Fenland & W Norfolk Aviation Museum, Wisbech

Serial	Type (other identity) [code]	Owner/operator, location or fate	Notes
WR974	Avro 696 Shackleton MR3 (8117M) [K]	Gatwick Aviation Museum, Charlwood, Surrey	
WR977	Avro 696 Shackleton MR3 (8186M) [B]	Newark Air Museum, Winthorpe	
WR982	Avro 696 Shackleton MR3 (8106M) [J]	Gatwick Aviation Museum, Charlwood, Surrey	
WR985	Avro 696 Shackleton MR3 (8103M) [H]	Privately owned, Long Marston	
WS103	Gloster Meteor T7 [709/VL]	FAA Museum, stored RNAS Yeovilton	
WS692	Gloster Meteor NF12 (7605M) [C]	Newark Air Museum, Winthorpe	
WS726	Gloster Meteor NF14 (7960M) [G]	No 1855 Sqn ATC, Royton, Gr Manchester	
WS739	Gloster Meteor NF14 (7961M)	Newark Air Museum, Winthorpe	
WS760	Gloster Meteor NF14 (7964M)	Meteor Flight, stored Yatesbury	
WS774	Gloster Meteor NF14 (7959M)	Privately owned, Quedgeley, Glos	
WS776	Gloster Meteor NF14 (7716M) [K]	Privately owned, Sandtoft	
WS788	Gloster Meteor NF14 (7967M) [Z]	Yorkshire Air Museum, Elvington	
WS792	Gloster Meteor NF14 (7965M) [K]	Brighouse Bay Caravan Park, Borgue, D&G	
WS807	Gloster Meteor NF14 (7973M) [N]	Gloucestershire Avn Coll, stored Gloucester	
WS832	Gloster Meteor NF14 [W]	Solway Aviation Society, Carlisle	
WS838	Gloster Meteor NF14	Midland Air Museum, Coventry	
WS843	Gloster Meteor NF14 (7937M) [Y]	RAF Museum, stored Cosford	
WT121	Douglas Skyraider AEW1 [415/CU]	FAA Museum, stored RNAS Yeovilton	
WT205	EE Canberra B15	RAF Manston History Museum	
WT308	EE Canberra B(I)6	RN, Predannack Fire School	
WT309	EE Canberra B(I)6 <ff>	Privately owned, Farnborough	
WT319	EE Canberra B(I)6 <ff>	Privately owned, Lavendon, Bucks	
WT333	EE Canberra B6(mod) (G-BVXC)	Privately owned, Bruntingthorpe	
WT339	EE Canberra B(I)8 (8198M)	RAF Barkston Heath Fire Section	
WT480	EE Canberra T4 [AT]	RAF, stored Shawbury	
WT482	EE Canberra T4 <ff>	Privately owned	
WT483	EE Canberra T4 [83]	Privately owned, Long Marston	
WT486	EE Canberra T4 (8102M) <ff>	Flight Experience Workshop, Belfast	
WT507	EE Canberra PR7 (8131M/8548M) [44] <ff>	No 384 Sqn ATC, Mansfield	
WT509	EE Canberra PR7 [BR]	RAF, stored Marham	
WT510	EE Canberra T22 <ff>	Privately owned, Stock, Essex	
WT519	EE Canberra PR7 [CH]	RAF Wyton, Fire Section	
WT520	EE Canberra PR7 (8094M/8184M) <ff>	No 967 Sqn ATC, Warton	
WT525	EE Canberra T22 <ff>	Privately owned, South Woodham Ferrers	
WT532	EE Canberra PR7 (8728M/8890M) <ff>	Bournemouth Aviation Museum	
WT534	EE Canberra PR7 (8549M) [43] <ff>	No 492 Sqn ATC, Shirley, W. Midlands	
WT536	EE Canberra PR7 (8063M) <ff>	Privately owned, Shirrell Heath, Hants	
WT537	EE Canberra PR7	BAE Systems Samlesbury, on display	
WT538	EE Canberra PR7 [CJ] <ff>	*Scrapped at St Athan, January 2001*	
WT555	Hawker Hunter F1 (7499M)		
WT569	Hawker Hunter F1 (7491M)	No 2117 Sqn ATC, Kenfig Hill, Mid-Glamorgan	
WT612	Hawker Hunter F1 (7496M)	RAF Henlow on display	
WT619	Hawker Hunter F1 (7525M)	Gr Manchester Mus of Science & Industry	
WT648	Hawker Hunter F1 (7530M) <ff>	Boscombe Down Museum	
WT651	Hawker Hunter F1 (7532M) [C]	Newark Air Museum, Winthorpe	
WT660	Hawker Hunter F1 (7421M) [C]	Highland Aircraft Preservation Society, Inverness	
WT680	Hawker Hunter F1 (7533M) [J]	No 1429 Sqn ATC, at QinetiQ Aberporth	
WT684	Hawker Hunter F1 (7422M) <ff>	Privately owned, Lavendon, Bucks	
WT694	Hawker Hunter F1 (7510M)	Caernarfon Air World	
WT711	Hawker Hunter GA11 (833/DD)	Air Atlantique, Coventry	
WT720	Hawker Hunter F51 (RDAF E-408/ 8565M) [B]	RAF Sealand, on display	
WT722	Hawker Hunter T8C (G-BWGN) [878/VL]	Classic Jets (UK), Exeter	
WT723	Hawker Hunter PR11 (G-PRII) [866/VL,3]	Privately owned, Exeter	
WT744	Hawker Hunter GA11 [868/VL]	South West Aviation Heritage, Eaglescott	
WT746	Hawker Hunter F4 (7770M) [A]	Dumfries & Galloway Avn Mus, Dumfries	

Notes	Serial	Type (other identity) [code]	Owner/operator, location or fate
	WT799	Hawker Hunter T8C [879]	Classic Jets (UK), Exeter
	WT804	Hawker Hunter GA11 [831/DD]	FETC, Moreton-in-Marsh, Glos
	WT806	Hawker Hunter GA11	Northbrook College, Shoreham Airport
	WT859	Supermarine 544 <ff>	Privately owned, Booker
	WT867	Slingsby T31B Cadet TX3	Privately owned, Eaglescott
	WT877	Slingsby T31B Cadet TX3	Boulton Paul Association, Wolverhampton
	WT898	Slingsby T31B Cadet TX3 (BGA 3284/BGA 4412)	Privately owned, Rufforth
	WT899	Slingsby T31B Cadet TX3	Privately owned, stored Swindon
	WT901	Slingsby T31B Cadet TX3	Privately owned, stored Rothwell, Northants
	WT902	Slingsby T31B Cadet TX3 (BGA 3147)	Privately owned, Lleweni Parc, Clwyd
	WT905	Slingsby T31B Cadet TX3	Privately owned
	WT908	Slingsby T31B Cadet TX3 (BGA 3487)	Privately owned, Dunstable
	WT910	Slingsby T31B Cadet TX3 (BGA 3953)	Privately owned, Challock
	WT933	Bristol 171 Sycamore 3 (G-ALSW/ 7709M)	Newark Air Museum, Winthorpe
	WV106	Douglas Skyraider AEW1 [427/C]	FAA Museum, stored Yeovilton
	WV198	Sikorsky S55 Whirlwind HAR21 (G-BJWY) [K]	Solway Aviation Society, Carlisle
	WV256	Hawker Hunter GA11 (G-BZPB) [862/VL]	Repainted as WB188, May 2001
	WV276	Hawker Hunter F4 (7847M) [D]	Privately owned, stored Scampton
	WV318	Hawker Hunter T7B (G-FFOX)	Delta Jets, Kemble
	WV322	Hawker Hunter T8C (G-BZSE/ 9096M) [Y]	Privately owned, Kemble
	WV332	Hawker Hunter F4 (7673M) <ff>	No 1254 Sqn ATC, Godalming
	WV372	Hawker Hunter T7 (G-BXFI) [R]	Privately owned, Kemble
	WV381	Hawker Hunter GA11 [732/VL] (fuselage)	UKAEA, Culham, Oxon
	WV382	Hawker Hunter GA11 [830/VL]	Jet Avn Preservation Grp, Long Marston
	WV383	Hawker Hunter T7	QinetiQ Farnborough, on display
	WV396	Hawker Hunter T8C (9249M) [91]	RAF Valley, at main gate
	WV483	Percival P56 Provost T1 (7693M) [N-E]	Privately owned
	WV493	Percival P56 Provost T1 (G-BDYG/ 7696M) [29]	Royal Scottish Mus'm of Flight, stored E Fortune
	WV499	Percival P56 Provost T1 (G-BZRF/ 7698M) [P-S]	Privately owned, Sandtoft
	WV562	Percival P56 Provost T1 (7606M) [P-C]	RAF Museum, Cosford
	WV605	Percival P56 Provost T1 [T-B]	Norfolk & Suffolk Avn Museum, Flixton
	WV606	Percival P56 Provost T1 (7622M) [P-B]	Newark Air Museum, Winthorpe
	WV679	Percival P56 Provost T1 (7615M) [O-J]	Wellesbourne Wartime Museum
	WV703	Percival P66 Pembroke C1 (8108M/G-IIIM)	Privately owned, Tattershall Thorpe
	WV705	Percival P66 Pembroke C1 <ff>	Southampton Hall of Aviation, stored
	WV740	Percival P66 Pembroke C1 (G-BNPH)	Privately owned, Jersey
	WV746	Percival P66 Pembroke C1 (8938M)	RAF Museum, Cosford
	WV753	Percival P66 Pembroke C1	Cardiff Int'l Airport Fire Section
	WV781	Bristol 171 Sycamore HR12 (G-ALTD/7839M)	Caernarfon Air World
	WV783	Bristol 171 Sycamore HR12 (G-ALSP/7841M)	RAF Museum Restoration Centre, Cosford
	WV787	EE Canberra B2/8 (8799M)	Newark Air Museum, Winthorpe
	WV795	Hawker Sea Hawk FGA6 (8151M)	Kennet Aviation, Cranfield
	WV797	Hawker Sea Hawk FGA6 (8155M) [491/J]	Midland Air Museum, Coventry
	WV798	Hawker Sea Hawk FGA6 [026/CU]	SWWAPS, Lasham
	WV838	Hawker Sea Hawk FGA4 <ff>	DARA Fleetlands Museum
	WV856	Hawker Sea Hawk FGA6 [163]	FAA Museum, RNAS Yeovilton
	WV903	Hawker Sea Hawk FGA4 (8153M) [128/C]	RN Historic Flight, stored Yeovilton
	WV908	Hawker Sea Hawk FGA6 (8154M) [188/A]	RN Historic Flight, Yeovilton

Serial	Type (other identity) [code]	Owner/operator, location or fate	Notes
WV910	Hawker Sea Hawk FGA6 <ff>	Boscombe Down Museum	
WV911	Hawker Sea Hawk FGA4 [115/C]	RN Historic Flight, Yeovilton	
WW138	DH112 Sea Venom FAW22 [227/Z]	FAA Museum, RNAS Yeovilton	
WW145	DH112 Sea Venom FAW22 [680/LM]	Royal Scottish Mus'm of Flight, E Fortune	
WW217	DH112 Sea Venom FAW22 [351]	Newark Air Museum, Winthorpe	
WW388	Percival P56 Provost T1 (7616M) [O-F]	Bomber County Aviation Museum, Hemswell	
WW421	Percival P56 Provost T1 (G-BZRE/ 7688M) [P-B]	Privately owned, Sandtoft	
WW442	Percival P56 Provost T1 (7618M) [N]	Gatwick Aviation Museum, Charlwood, Surrey	
WW444	Percival P56 Provost T1 [D]	Privately owned, Rugeley, Staffs	
WW447	Percival P56 Provost T1	Privately owned, Grazeley, Berks	
WW453	Percival P56 Provost T1 (G-TMKI) [W-S]	Privately owned, RNAS Yeovilton	
WW654	Hawker Hunter GA11 [834/DD]	Privately owned, Ford, W Sussex	
WX788	DH112 Venom NF3	Night-Fighter Preservation Team, Elvington	
WX853	DH112 Venom NF3 (7443M)	Mosquito Aircraft Museum, London Colney	
WX905	DH112 Venom NF3 (7458M)	Newark Air Museum, Winthorpe	
WZ425	DH115 Vampire T11	Privately owned, Birlingham, Worcs	
WZ450	DH115 Vampire T11 <ff>	Lashenden Air Warfare Museum, Headcorn	
WZ458	DH115 Vampire T11 (7728M) [31] <ff>	*Scrapped at Walpole*	
WZ464	DH115 Vampire T11 (N62430) [40]	Vintage Aircraft Team, Bruntingthorpe	
WZ507	DH115 Vampire T11 (G-VTII)	De Havilland Aviation, Swansea	
WZ515	DH115 Vampire T11 [60]	Solway Aviation Society, Carlisle	
WZ518	DH115 Vampire T11	North-East Aircraft Museum, Usworth	
WZ549	DH115 Vampire T11 (8118M) [F]	Ulster Aviation Society, Langford Lodge	
WZ553	DH115 Vampire T11 (G-DHYY) [40]	Source Classic Jet Flight, stored Bournemouth	
WZ557	DH115 Vampire T11	N Yorks Aircraft Recovery Centre, Chop Gate	
WZ572	DH115 Vampire T11 [65] <ff>	Privately owned, Southampton	
WZ581	DH115 Vampire T11 <ff>	The Vampire Collection, Hemel Hempstead	
WZ584	DH115 Vampire T11 (G-BZRC) [K]	Privately owned, Sandtoft	
WZ589	DH115 Vampire T11 [19]	Lashenden Air Warfare Museum, Headcorn	
WZ589	DH115 Vampire T55 (U-1230/ G-DHZZ)	Source Classic Jet Flight, Bournemouth	
WZ590	DH115 Vampire T11 [19]	Imperial War Museum, Duxford	
WZ608	DH115 Vampire T11 [56] <ff>	Privately owned,	
WZ620	DH115 Vampire T11 [68]	Avon Aviation Museum, Yatesbury	
WZ662	Auster AOP9 (G-BKVK)	Privately owned, Middle Wallop	
WZ706	Auster AOP9 (7851M/G-BURR)	Privately owned, Middle Wallop	
WZ711	Auster AOP9/Beagle E3 (G-AVHT)	Privately owned, Middle Wallop	
WZ721	Auster AOP9	Museum of Army Flying, Middle Wallop	
WZ724	Auster AOP9 (7432M)	AAC Middle Wallop, at main gate	
WZ729	Auster AOP9 (G-BXON)	Privately owned, Newark-on-Trent	
WZ736	Avro 707A (7868M)	Gr Manchester Mus of Science & Industry	
WZ744	Avro 707C (7932M)	RAF Museum, Cosford	
WZ753	Slingsby T38 Grasshopper TX1	Southampton Hall of Aviation	
WZ767	Slingsby T38 Grasshopper TX1	North-East Aircraft Museum, stored Usworth	
WZ768	Slingsby T38 Grasshopper TX1 (comp XK820)	Privately owned, Kirton-in-Lindsey, Lincs	
WZ769	Slingsby T38 Grasshopper TX1	Privately owned,	
WZ772	Slingsby T38 Grasshopper TX1	Museum of Army Flying, Middle Wallop	
WZ779	Slingsby T38 Grasshopper TX1	Privately owned, Old Sarum	
WZ784	Slingsby T38 Grasshopper TX1	Solway Aviation Society, Carlisle	
WZ791	Slingsby T38 Grasshopper TX1 (8944M)	RAF Museum, Hendon	
WZ792	Slingsby T38 Grasshopper TX1	Privately owned, Sproughton	
WZ793	Slingsby T38 Grasshopper TX1	Whitgift School, Croydon	
WZ796	Slingsby T38 Grasshopper TX1	Privately owned, stored Nympsfield, Glos	
WZ798	Slingsby T38 Grasshopper TX1	Bournemouth Aviation Museum	

Notes	Serial	Type (other identity) [code]	Owner/operator, location or fate
	WZ816	Slingsby T38 Grasshopper TX1 (BGA 3979)	Privately owned, Redhill
	WZ819	Slingsby T38 Grasshopper TX1 (BGA 3498)	Privately owned, Halton
	WZ820	Slingsby T38 Grasshopper TX1	Shoreham Airport, on display
	WZ822	Slingsby T38 Grasshopper TX1	Aeroventure, stored Doncaster
	WZ824	Slingsby T38 Grasshopper TX1	Privately owned, stored Strathaven, Strathclyde
	WZ825	Slingsby T38 Grasshopper TX1	
	WZ826	Vickers Valiant B(K)1 (XD826/ 7872M) <ff>	Privately owned, Foulness
	WZ827	Slingsby T38 Grasshopper TX1	RAFGSA, stored Bicester
	WZ828	Slingsby T38 Grasshopper TX1 (BGA 4421)	Privately owned, Bicester
	WZ831	Slingsby T38 Grasshopper TX1	Privately owned, stored Nympsfield, Glos
	WZ846	DHC1 Chipmunk T10 (G-BCSC/ 8439M)	No 1404 Sqn ATC, Chatham
	WZ847	DHC1 Chipmunk T10 (G-CPMK) [F]	Privately owned, Sleap
	WZ866	DHC1 Chipmunk T10 (8217M/ G-ATEB) <ff>	*Scrapped at Firbeck, March 1999*
	WZ868	DHC1 Chipmunk T10 (G-BCIW) [H]	Privately owned, Sandtoft
	WZ868	DHC1 Chipmunk T10 (WG322/ G-ARMF) [H]	Privately owned
	WZ869	DHC1 Chipmunk T10 (8019M) [R] <ff>	
	WZ872	DHC1 Chipmunk T10 (G-BZGB) [E]	Privately owned, Newcastle
	WZ876	DHC1 Chipmunk T10 (G-BBWN) <ff>	Privately owned, Yateley, Hants
	WZ879	DHC1 Chipmunk T10 (G-BWUT) [73]	Privately owned, Earls Colne
	WZ882	DHC1 Chipmunk T10 (G-BXGP) [K]	Privately owned, Eaglescott
	XA109	DH115 Sea Vampire T22	Royal Scottish Mus'm of Flight, E Fortune
	XA127	DH115 Sea Vampire T22 <ff>	FAA Museum, stored RNAS Yeovilton
	XA129	DH115 Sea Vampire T22	FAA Museum, stored RNAS Yeovilton
	XA225	Slingsby T38 Grasshopper TX1	Privately owned, Upavon
	XA228	Slingsby T38 Grasshopper TX1	Royal Scottish Mus'm of Flight, E Fortune
	XA230	Slingsby T38 Grasshopper TX1 (BGA 4098)	Privately owned, Henlow
	XA231	Slingsby T38 Grasshopper TX1 (8888M)	RAF Manston History Museum
	XA240	Slingsby T38 Grasshopper TX1 (BGA 4556)	Privately owned, Keevil
	XA241	Slingsby T38 Grasshopper TX1	Shuttleworth Collection, Old Warden
	XA243	Slingsby T38 Grasshopper TX1 (8886M)	Privately owned, Gransden Lodge, Cambs
	XA244	Slingsby T38 Grasshopper TX1	RAF, stored Cosford
	XA282	Slingsby T31B Cadet TX3	Caernarfon Air World
	XA286	Slingsby T31B Cadet TX3	Privately owned, stored Rufforth
	XA289	Slingsby T31B Cadet TX3	Privately owned, Eaglescott
	XA290	Slingsby T31B Cadet TX3	Privately owned, stored Rufforth
	XA293	Slingsby T31B Cadet TX3	Privately owned, Breighton
	XA302	Slingsby T31B Cadet TX3 (BGA3786)	Privately owned, Syerston
	XA459	Fairey Gannet ECM6 [E]	Privately owned, Lambourn, Berks
	XA460	Fairey Gannet ECM6 [768/BY]	Deeside College, Connah's Quay, Clwyd
	XA466	Fairey Gannet COD4 [777/LM]	FAA Museum, stored Yeovilton
	XA508	Fairey Gannet T2 [627/GN]	FAA Museum, at Midland Air Museum, Coventry
	XA564	Gloster Javelin FAW1 (7464M)	RAF Museum, Cosford
	XA634	Gloster Javelin FAW4 (7641M)	RAF Leeming, on display
	XA699	Gloster Javelin FAW5 (7809M)	Midland Air Museum, Coventry
	XA847	EE P1B (8371M)	Privately owned, Stowmarket, Suffolk
	XA862	WS55 Whirlwind HAR1 (G-AMJT) [9]	The Helicopter Museum, Weston-super-Mare
	XA864	WS55 Whirlwind HAR1	FAA Museum, stored Yeovilton
	XA870	WS55 Whirlwind HAR1	Flambards Village Theme Park, Helston
	XA880	DH104 Devon C2 (G-BVXR)	Privately owned, Kemble
	XA893	Avro 698 Vulcan B1 (8591M) <ff>	RAF Museum, Cosford
	XA903	Avro 698 Vulcan B1 <ff>	Privately owned, Wellesbourne Mountford
	XA917	HP80 Victor B1 (7827M) <ff>	Privately owned, Pitscottie, Fife

Serial	Type (other identity) [code]	Owner/operator, location or fate	Notes
XB259	Blackburn B101 Beverley C1 (G-AOAI)	Museum of Army Transport, Beverley	
XB261	Blackburn B101 Beverley C1 <ff>	Duxford Aviation Society, Duxford	
XB446	Grumman TBM-3 Avenger ECM6B	FAA Museum, Yeovilton	
XB480	Hiller HT1 [537]	FAA Museum, stored Yeovilton	
XB812	Canadair CL-13 Sabre F4 (9227M) [U]	RAF Museum, Hendon	
XD145	Saro SR53	RAF Museum, Cosford	
XD163	WS55 Whirlwind HAR10 (8645M)	The Helicopter Museum, Weston-super-Mare	
XD165	WS55 Whirlwind HAR10 (8673M) [B]	AAC Wattisham, instructional use	
XD215	VS Scimitar F1 <ff>	Privately owned, Cheltenham	
XD235	VS Scimitar F1 <ff>	Privately owned, Welshpool	
XD317	VS Scimitar F1 [112/R]	FAA Museum, RNAS Yeovilton	
XD332	VS Scimitar F1 [194/C]	Southampton Hall of Aviation	
XD377	DH115 Vampire T11 (8203M) <ff>	Aeroventure, stored Doncaster	
XD382	DH115 Vampire T11 (8033M)	Anchor Surplus, Ripley, Derbys	
XD425	DH115 Vampire T11 <ff>	RAF Millom Museum, Haverigg	
XD434	DH115 Vampire T11 [25]	Fenland & W Norfolk Aviation Museum, Wisbech	
XD445	DH115 Vampire T11	Bomber County Aviation Museum, Hemswell	
XD447	DH115 Vampire T11 [50]	Jet Avn Preservation Grp, Long Marston	
XD452	DH115 Vampire T11 (7990M) [66] <ff>	Vampire Support Team, RAF Sealand	
XD459	DH115 Vampire T11 [63] <ff>	East Midlands Airport Aeropark	
XD463	DH115 Vampire T11 (8023M)	Privately owned, Nottingham	
XD506	DH115 Vampire T11 (7983M)	Gloucestershire Avn Coll, stored Gloucester	
XD515	DH115 Vampire T11 (7998M/ XM515)	Privately owned, Rugeley, Staffs	
XD525	DH115 Vampire T11 (7882M) <ff>	Kinegar Camp, Hollywood, Northern Ireland	
XD528	DH115 Vampire T11 (8159M) <ff>	Gamston Aerodrome Fire Section	
XD534	DH115 Vampire T11 [41]	Military Aircraft Pres'n Grp, Barton	
XD536	DH115 Vampire T11 (7734M) [H]	Alleyn's School CCF, Northolt	
XD542	DH115 Vampire T11 (7604M) [N]	Montrose Air Station Museum	
XD547	DH115 Vampire T11 [Z] (composite)	Dumfries & Galloway Avn Mus, Dumfries	
XD593	DH115 Vampire T11 [50]	Newark Air Museum, Winthorpe	
XD595	DH115 Vampire T11 <ff>	Privately owned, Glentham, Lincs	
XD596	DH115 Vampire T11 (7939M)	Southampton Hall of Aviation	
XD599	DH115 Vampire T11 <ff>	Privately owned, Ingatstone, Essex	
XD602	DH115 Vampire T11 (7737M) (composite)	Privately owned, Wearside	
XD614	DH115 Vampire T11 (8124M) <ff>	*Really WZ572*	
XD616	DH115 Vampire T11 [56]	Mosquito Aircraft Museum, stored Gloucester	
XD622	DH115 Vampire T11 (8160M)	No 2214 Sqn ATC, Usworth	
XD624	DH115 Vampire T11 [O]	Macclesfield Technical College	
XD626	DH115 Vampire T11 [Q]	Midland Air Museum, Coventry	
XD674	Hunting Jet Provost T1 (7570M) [T]	RAF Museum, stored Cosford	
XD693	Hunting Jet Provost T1 (XM129/ G-AOBU) [Z-Q]	Kennet Aviation, Cranfield	
XD816	Vickers Valiant B(K)1 <ff>	Brooklands Museum, Weybridge	
XD818	Vickers Valiant B(K)1 (7894M)	RAF Museum, Hendon	
XD857	Vickers Valiant B(K)1 <ff>	RAF Manston History Museum	
XD875	Vickers Valiant B(K)1 <ff>	British Aviation Heritage, Bruntingthorpe	
XE317	Bristol 171 Sycamore HR14 (G-AMWO) [S-N]	Aeroventure, stored Doncaster	
XE327	Hawker Sea Hawk FGA6 [644/LH]	Privately owned, Bruntingthorpe	
XE339	Hawker Sea Hawk FGA6 (8156M) [149/E]	RN Historic Flight, stored Yeovilton	
XE340	Hawker Sea Hawk FGA6 [131/Z]	FAA Museum, at Montrose Air Station Museum	
XE368	Hawker Sea Hawk FGA6 [200/J]	Flambards Village Theme Park, Helston	
XE489	Hawker Sea Hawk FGA6 (G-JETH)	Gatwick Aviation Museum, Charlwood, Surrey	
XE521	Fairey Rotodyne Y (parts)	The Helicopter Museum, Weston-super-Mare	

Notes	Serial	Type (other identity) [code]	Owner/operator, location or fate
	XE584	Hawker Hunter FGA9 <ff>	Avro Aircraft Heritage Society, Woodford
	XE597	Hawker Hunter FGA9 (8874M) <ff>	FETC, Moreton-in-Marsh, Glos
	XE601	Hawker Hunter FGA9	Boscombe Down Museum
	XE606	Hawker Hunter F6A (XJ673/ 8841M)	RAF Cottesmore, preserved
	XE624	Hawker Hunter FGA9 (8875M) [G]	Army, Cawdor Barracks, Brawdy, on display
	XE627	Hawker Hunter F6A [T]	Imperial War Museum, Duxford
	XE643	Hawker Hunter FGA9 (8586M) <ff>	RAF EPTT, Aldergrove
	XE664	Hawker Hunter F4 <ff>	Gloucestershire Avn Coll, stored Gloucester
	XE665	Hawker Hunter T8C (G-BWGM) [876/VL]	Classic Jets (UK), Exeter
	XE668	Hawker Hunter GA11 [832/DD]	RN, Predannack Fire School
	XE670	Hawker Hunter F4 (7762M/8585M) <ff>	RAF Museum, Cosford
	XE683	Hawker Hunter F51 (RDAF E-409)	City of Norwich Aviation Museum
	XE685	Hawker Hunter GA11 (G-GAII) [861/VL]	Privately owned, Exeter
	XE689	Hawker Hunter GA11 (G-BWGK) [864/VL]	Classic Jets (UK) Exeter
	XE786	Slingsby T31B Cadet TX3	RAF, stored Arbroath
	XE793	Slingsby T31B Cadet TX3 (8666M)	Privately owned
	XE796	Slingsby T31B Cadet TX3	Privately owned, stored North Weald
	XE799	Slingsby T31B Cadet TX3 (8943M) [R]	RAFGSA, Syerston
	XE802	Slingsby T31B Cadet TX3	Privately owned, stored Cupar, Fife
	XE807	Slingsby T31B Cadet TX3 (BGA3545)	Privately owned, Halesland
	XE849	DH115 Vampire T11 (7928M) [V3]	Privately owned, Shobdon
	XE852	DH115 Vampire T11 [H]	No 2247 Sqn ATC, Hawarden
	XE855	DH115 Vampire T11	Midland Air Museum, Coventry
	XE856	DH115 Vampire T11 (G-DUSK)	Privately owned, Henlow
	XE864	DH115 Vampire T11(comp XD435) <ff>	Privately owned, Ingatstone, Essex
	XE872	DH115 Vampire T11 [62]	Midland Air Museum, Coventry
	XE874	DH115 Vampire T11 (8582M)	Montrose Air Station Museum
	XE897	DH115 Vampire T11 (XD403)	Privately owned, Errol, Tayside
	XE897	DH115 Vampire T55 (U-1214/ G-DHVV)	Source Classic Jet Flight, Bournemouth
	XE920	DH115 Vampire T11 (8196M/ G-VMPR) [A]	The Jet Fighter Experience, Swansea
	XE921	DH115 Vampire T11 [64] <ff>	Privately owned, Welshpool
	XE935	DH115 Vampire T11	Aeroventure, Doncaster
	XE946	DH115 Vampire T11 (7473M) <ff>	RAF Cranwell Aviation Heritage Centre
	XE956	DH115 Vampire T11 (G-OBLN)	De Havilland Aviation, Bridgend
	XE979	DH115 Vampire T11 [54]	Privately owned, Birlingham, Worcs
	XE982	DH115 Vampire T11 (7564M) [01]	Privately owned, Dunkeswell
	XE985	DH115 Vampire T11 (WZ476)	De Havilland Aviation, Swansea
	XE993	DH115 Vampire T11 (8161M)	Privately owned, Cosford
	XE995	DH115 Vampire T11 [53]	Privately owned, High Halden, Kent
	XE998	DH115 Vampire T11 (U-1215)	Privately owned, Farnborough
	XF113	VS Swift F7 [19] <ff>	Boscombe Down Museum
	XF114	VS Swift F7 (G-SWIF)	Privately owned, Scampton
	XF300	Hawker Hunter GA11 (G-BZPC) [860/VL]	Repainted as WB188, June 2001
	XF303	Hawker Hunter F58A (J-4105/ G-BWOU) [105,A]	The Old Flying Machine Company, Scampton
	XF314	Hawker Hunter F51 (RDAF E-412) [N]	Privately owned, Booker
	XF321	Hawker Hunter T7	Classic Jets (UK), Exeter (spares use)
	XF324	Hawker Hunter F51 (RDAF E-427) [D]	British Aviation Heritage, Bruntingthorpe
	XF358	Hawker Hunter T8C [870/VL]	QinetiQ, stored Boscombe Down
	XF368	Hawker Hunter GA11 (G-BZRH) [863/VL]	Sold to South Africa, 17 June 2001
	XF375	Hawker Hunter F6A (8736M/ G-BUEZ) [05]	The Old Flying Machine Co, Duxford
	XF382	Hawker Hunter F6A [15]	Midland Air Museum, Coventry
	XF383	Hawker Hunter F6 (8706M) <ff>	Privately owned, Kidlington
	XF418	Hawker Hunter F51 (RDAF E-430)	Gatwick Aviation Museum, Charlwood, Surrey

Serial	Type (other identity) [code]	Owner/operator, location or fate	Notes
XF509	Hawker Hunter F6 (8708M)	Humbrol Paints, Marfleet, E Yorkshire	
XF515	Hawker Hunter F6A (8830M/ G-KAXF) [R]	Kennet Aviation, Cranfield	
XF516	Hawker Hunter F6A (8685M/ G-BVVC) [19]	Classic Jets (UK), Exeter	
XF519	Hawker Hunter FGA9 (8677M/ 8738M/9183M) (comp XJ695) [J]	MoD FSCTE, Manston	
XF522	Hawker Hunter F6 <ff>	No 1365 Sqn ATC, Aylesbury	
XF526	Hawker Hunter F6 (8679M) [78/E]	Privately owned, Birlingham, Worcs	
XF527	Hawker Hunter F6 (8680M)	RAF Halton, on display	
XF545	Percival P56 Provost T1 (7957M) [O-K]	Privately owned, Thatcham	
XF597	Percival P56 Provost T1 (G-BKFW) [AH]	Privately owned, Thatcham	
XF603	Percival P56 Provost T1 (G-KAPW)	The Shuttleworth Collection, Old Warden	
XF690	Percival P56 Provost T1 (8041M/ G-MOOS)	Kennet Aviation, Cranfield	
XF708	Avro 716 Shackleton MR3 (203/C]	Imperial War Museum, Duxford	
XF785	Bristol 173 (7648M/G-ALBN)	Bristol Aero Collection, Kemble	
XF836	Percival P56 Provost T1 (8043M/ G-AWRY) [JG]	Privately owned, Thatcham	
XF844	Percival P56 Provost T1 [70]	British Aviation Heritage, Bruntingthorpe	
XF877	Percival P56 Provost T1 (G-AWVF) [JX]	Privately owned, Sandown	
XF926	Bristol 188 (8368M)	RAF Museum, Cosford	
XF967	Hawker Hunter T8C (9186M/ G-BZRI) [T]	*Sold to South Africa, 17 June 2001*	
XF994	Hawker Hunter T8C [873/VL]	Boscombe Down Museum	
XF995	Hawker Hunter T8B (G-BZSF/ 9237M) [K]	Delta Jets, Kemble	
XG154	Hawker Hunter FGA9 (8863M) [54]	RAF Museum, Hendon	
XG160	Hawker Hunter F6A (8831M/ G-BWAF)	Bournemouth Aviation Museum	
XG164	Hawker Hunter F6 (8681M)	Privately owned, Wellington, Somerset	
XG172	Hawker Hunter F6A (8832M) [A]	City of Norwich Aviation Museum	
XG190	Hawker Hunter F51 (RDAF E-425) [C]	Midland Air Museum, Coventry	
XG193	Hawker Hunter FGA9 (XG297) (comp with WT741)	Bomber County Aviation Museum, Hemswell	
XG195	Hawker Hunter FGA9 <ff>	Shropshire Wartime Aircraft Recovery Grp Mus, Sleap	
XG196	Hawker Hunter F6A (8702M) [31]	Army, Mytchett, Surrey, on display	
XG209	Hawker Hunter F6 (8709M) <ff>	Privately owned, Chelmsford	
XG210	Hawker Hunter F6	Privately owned, Beck Row, Suffolk	
XG225	Hawker Hunter F6A (8713M) [S]	RAF Cosford on display	
XG226	Hawker Hunter F6A (8800M) [28] <ff>	No 1242 Sqn ATC, Faversham, Kent	
XG252	Hawker Hunter FGA9 (8840M) [U]	Privately owned, Bosbury, Hereford	
XG254	Hawker Hunter FGA9 (8881M)	Privately owned, Clacton	
XG274	Hawker Hunter F6 (8710M) [71]	Privately owned, Newmarket	
XG290	Hawker Hunter F6 (8711M) <ff>	Boscombe Down Museum	
XG297	Hawker Hunter FGA9 <ff>	Privately owned, Worksop	
XG325	EE Lightning F1 <ff>	No 1476 Sqn ATC, Southend	
XG329	EE Lightning F1 (8050M)	Privately owned, Flixton	
XG331	EE Lightning F1 <ff>	Gloucestershire Avn Coll, stored Gloucester	
XG337	EE Lightning F1 (8056M) [M]	RAF Museum, Cosford	
XG452	Bristol 192 Belvedere HC1 (7997M/G-BRMB)	The Helicopter Museum, Weston-super-Mare	
XG454	Bristol 192 Belvedere HC1 (8366M)	Gr Manchester Mus of Science & Industry	
XG462	Bristol 192 Belvedere HC1 <ff>	The Helicopter Museum, stored Weston-super-Mare	
XG474	Bristol 192 Belvedere HC1 (8367M) [O]	RAF Museum, Hendon	
XG502	Bristol 171 Sycamore HR14	Museum of Army Flying, Middle Wallop	
XG506	Bristol 171 Sycamore HR14 (7852M) <ff>	Privately owned, South Kirby	
XG518	Bristol 171 Sycamore HR14 (8009M) [S-E]	Norfolk & Suffolk Avn Museum, Flixton	
XG523	Bristol 171 Sycamore HR14 <ff> [K]	Norfolk & Suffolk Avn Museum, Flixton	
XG544	Bristol 171 Sycamore HR14	Privately owned,	

Notes	Serial	Type (other identity) [code]	Owner/operator, location or fate
	XG547	Bristol 171 Sycamore HR14 (G-HAPR) [S-T]	The Helicopter Museum, Weston-super-Mare
	XG571	WS55 Whirlwind HAR3 [752/PO]	FAA Museum, RNAS Yeovilton
	XG577	WS55 Whirlwind HAR3 (9050M)	RAF Leconfield Crash Rescue Training
	XG588	WS55 Whirlwind HAR3 (G-BAMH/ VR-BEP)	East Midlands Airport Aeropark
	XG594	WS55 Whirlwind HAS7 [517/PO]	FAA Museum, at R. Scottish Mus'm of Flt, E Fortune
	XG596	WS55 Whirlwind HAS7 [66]	The Helicopter Museum, Weston-super-Mare
	XG597	WS55 Whirlwind HAS7	Scrapped at Siddal, W Yorks
	XG613	DH112 Sea Venom FAW21	Imperial War Museum, Duxford
	XG629	DH112 Sea Venom FAW22	Privately owned, Stone, Staffs
	XG680	DH112 Sea Venom FAW22 [438]	North-East Aircraft Museum, Usworth
	XG691	DH112 Sea Venom FAW22 [93/J]	Gloucestershire Avn Coll, stored Gloucester
	XG692	DH112 Sea Venom FAW22 [668/LM]	Privately owned, Stockport
	XG730	DH112 Sea Venom FAW22 [499/A]	Mosquito Aircraft Museum, London Colney
	XG736	DH112 Sea Venom FAW22	Ulster Aviation Society, Newtownards
	XG737	DH112 Sea Venom FAW22 [220/Z]	Jet Avn Preservation Grp, stored Long Marston
	XG743	DH115 Sea Vampire T22 [597/LM]	Imperial War Museum, Duxford
XG775	DH115 Vampire T55 (U-1219/ G-DHWW) [VL]	Source Classic Jet Flight, Bournemouth
	XG797	Fairey Gannet ECM6 [277]	Imperial War Museum, Duxford
	XG831	Fairey Gannet ECM6 [396]	Flambards Village Theme Park, Helston
	XG882	Fairey Gannet T5 (8754M) [771/LM]	Privately owned, Errol, Tayside
	XG883	Fairey Gannet T5 [773/BY]	FAA Museum, at Museum of Berkshire Aviation, Woodley
	XG900	Short SC1	Science Museum, South Kensington
	XG905	Short SC1	Ulster Folk & Transpt Mus, Holywood, Co Down
	XH131	EE Canberra PR9 [AA]	RAF No 39(1 PRU) Sqn, Marham
	XH134	EE Canberra PR9 [AB]	RAF No 39(1 PRU) Sqn, Marham
	XH135	EE Canberra PR9 [AC]	RAF No 39(1 PRU) Sqn, Marham
	XH136	EE Canberra PR9 (8782M) <ff>	Phoenix Aviation, Bruntingthorpe
	XH165	EE Canberra PR9 <ff>	Blyth Valley Aviation Collection, Walpole
	XH168	EE Canberra PR9 [AD]	RAF No 39(1 PRU) Sqn, Marham
	XH169	EE Canberra PR9	RAF No 39(1 PRU) Sqn, Marham
	XH170	EE Canberra PR9 (8739M)	RAF Wyton, on display
	XH171	EE Canberra PR9 (8746M) [U]	RAF Museum, Cosford
	XH174	EE Canberra PR9 <ff>	RAF, stored Shawbury
	XH175	EE Canberra PR9 <ff>	Privately owned, Stock, Essex
	XH177	EE Canberra PR9 <ff>	Newark Air Museum, Winthorpe
	XH278	DH115 Vampire T11 (8595M/ 7866M) [42]	Privately owned, Felton, Northumberland
	XH312	DH115 Vampire T11 [18]	Privately owned, Dodleston, Cheshire
	XH313	DH115 Vampire T11 (G-BZRD) [E]	Privately owned, Sandtoft
	XH318	DH115 Vampire T11 (7761M) [64]	Privately owned, Cadnam
	XH328	DH115 Vampire T11 <ff>	Privately owned, Duxford
	XH330	DH115 Vampire T11 [73]	Privately owned, Camberley, Surrey
	XH537	Avro 698 Vulcan B2MRR (8749M) <ff>	Bournemouth Aviation Museum
	XH558	Avro 698 Vulcan B2 (G-VLCN)	British Aviation Heritage, Bruntingthorpe
	XH560	Avro 698 Vulcan K2 <ff>	Privately owned, Foulness
	XH563	Avro 698 Vulcan B2MRR <ff>	Privately owned, Banchory, Fife
	XH568	EE Canberra B6(mod) (G-BVIC)	Classic Aviation Projects, Bruntingthorpe
	XH584	EE Canberra T4 (G-27-374) <ff>	Aeroventure, Doncaster
	XH592	HP80 Victor K1A (8429M) <ff>	Phoenix Aviation, Bruntingthorpe
	XH648	HP80 Victor K1A	Imperial War Museum, Duxford
	XH669	HP80 Victor K2 (9092M) <ff>	Privately owned, Foulness
	XH670	HP80 Victor SR2 <ff>	Privately owned, Foulness
	XH672	HP80 Victor K2	RAF Museum, Cosford
	XH673	HP80 Victor K2 (8911M)	RAF Marham, on display
	XH767	Gloster Javelin FAW9 (7955M) [A]	Yorkshire Air Museum, Elvington
	XH783	Gloster Javelin FAW7 (7798M) <ff>	Privately owned, Catford
	XH837	Gloster Javelin FAW7 (8032M) <ff>	Caernarfon Air World
	XH892	Gloster Javelin FAW9R (7982M) [J]	Norfolk & Suffolk Avn Museum, Flixton
	XH897	Gloster Javelin FAW9	Imperial War Museum, Duxford

Serial	Type (other identity) [code]	Owner/operator, location or fate	Notes
XH903	Gloster Javelin FAW9 (7938M) <ff>	Gloucestershire Avn Coll, stored Gloucester	
XH992	Gloster Javelin FAW8 (7829M) [P]	Newark Air Museum, Winthorpe	
XJ314	RR Thrust Measuring Rig	Science Museum, South Kensington	
XJ380	Bristol 171 Sycamore HR14 (8628M)	Montrose Air Station Museum	
XJ389	Fairey Jet Gyrodyne (XD759/ G-AJJP)	Museum of Berkshire Aviation, Woodley	
XJ409	WS55 Whirlwind HAR10 (XD779)	Maes Artro Craft Village, Llanbedr	
XJ435 use	WS55 Whirlwind HAR10 (XB804/ 8671M) [V]	RAF Manston History Museum, spares	
XJ476	DH110 Sea Vixen FAW1 <ff>	No 424 Sqn ATC, Southampton Hall of Avn	
XJ481	DH110 Sea Vixen FAW1 [VL]	FAA Museum, stored RNAS Yeovilton	
XJ482	DH110 Sea Vixen FAW1 [713/VL]	Norfolk & Suffolk Avn Museum, Flixton	
XJ488	DH110 Sea Vixen FAW1 <ff>	Robertsbridge Aviation Society, Mayfield	
XJ494	DH110 Sea Vixen FAW2	Privately owned, Bruntingthorpe	
XJ560	DH110 Sea Vixen FAW2 (8142M) [242]	Newark Air Museum, Winthorpe	
XJ565	DH110 Sea Vixen FAW2 [127/E]	Mosquito Aircraft Museum, London Colney	
XJ571	DH110 Sea Vixen FAW2 (8140M) [242/R]	Privately owned, Brooklands Museum, Weybridge	
XJ575	DH110 Sea Vixen FAW2 <ff> [SAH-13]	Wellesbourne Wartime Museum	
XJ579	DH110 Sea Vixen FAW2 <ff>	Midland Air Museum, Coventry	
XJ580	DH110 Sea Vixen FAW2 [131/E]	Tangmere Military Aviation Museum	
XJ615	Hawker Hunter T8C(mod) (XF357/ G-BWGL)	The Old Flying Machine Co, Duxford	
XJ639	Hawker Hunter F6A (8687M) [H]	Classic Jets (UK), Exeter	
XJ676	Hawker Hunter F6A (8844M) <ff>	Destroyed	
XJ714	Hawker Hunter FR10 (comp XG226)	Jet Avn Preservation Grp, Long Marston	
XJ723	WS55 Whirlwind HAR10	Montrose Air Station Museum	
XJ726	WS55 Whirlwind HAR10 [F]	Caernarfon Air World	
XJ727	WS55 Whirlwind HAR10 (8661M) [L]	RAF Manston History Museum	
XJ758	WS55 Whirlwind HAR10 (8464M) <ff>	Privately owned, Welshpool	
XJ771	DH115 Vampire T55 (U-1215/ G-HELV)	Privately owned, Bournemouth	
XJ772	DH115 Vampire T11 [H]	Mosquito Aircraft Museum, London Colney	
XJ823	Avro 698 Vulcan B2A	Solway Aviation Society, Carlisle	
XJ824	Avro 698 Vulcan B2A	Imperial War Museum, Duxford	
XJ917	Bristol 171 Sycamore HR14 [H-S]	Bristol Sycamore Group, stored Kemble	
XJ918	Bristol 171 Sycamore HR14 (8190M)	RAF Museum, Cosford	
XK149	Hawker Hunter F6A (8714M) [L]	Privately owned, Bruntingthorpe	
XK378	Auster AOP9 (TAD200/XS238)	Scrapped by early 2001	
XK416	Auster AOP9 (7855M/G-AYUA)	De Havilland Aviation, Swansea	
XK417	Auster AOP9 (G-AVXY)	Auster 9 Group, Melton Mowbray	
XK418	Auster AOP9 (7976M)	SWWAPS, Lasham	
XK421	Auster AOP9 (8365M) (frame)	Aeroventure, stored Doncaster	
XK482	Saro Skeeter AOP12 (7840M/ G-BJWC) [C]	Privately owned, Ongar	
XK488	Blackburn NA39 Buccaneer S1	FAA Museum, stored RNAS Yeovilton	
XK526	Blackburn NA39 Buccaneer S2 (8648M)	RAF Honington, at main gate	
XK527	Blackburn NA39 Buccaneer S2D (8818M) <ff>	Privately owned, Aberdeen	
XK532	Blackburn NA39 Buccaneer S1 (8867M) [632/LM]	The Fresson Trust, Inverness Airport	
XK533	Blackburn NA39 Buccaneer S1 <ff>	Royal Scottish Mus'm of Flight, E Fortune	
XK590	DH115 Vampire T11 [V]	Wellesbourne Wartime Museum	
XK623	DH115 Vampire T11 (G-VAMP) [56]	Caernarfon Air World	
XK624	DH115 Vampire T11 [32]	Norfolk & Suffolk Avn Museum, Flixton	
XK625	DH115 Vampire T11 [12]	Brenzett Aeronautical Museum	
XK627	DH115 Vampire T11	Privately owned, Barton	
XK632	DH115 Vampire T11 [67]	No 2370 Sqn ATC, Denham	
XK637	DH115 Vampire T11 [56]	RAF Millom Museum, Haverigg	

Notes	Serial	Type (other identity) [code]	Owner/operator, location or fate
	XK655	DH106 Comet C2(RC) (G-AMXA) <ff>	Gatwick Airport, on display (BOAC colours)
	XK695	DH106 Comet C2(RC) (G-AMXH/ 9164M) <ff>	Mosquito Aircraft Museum, London Colney
	XK699	DH106 Comet C2 (7971M)	RAF Lyneham on display
	XK724	Folland Gnat F1 (7715M)	RAF Museum, Cosford
	XK740	Folland Gnat F1 (8396M)	Southampton Hall of Aviation
	XK741	Folland Gnat F1 (fuselage)	Midland Air Museum, Coventry
	XK776	ML Utility 1	Museum of Army Flying, Middle Wallop
	XK788	Slingsby T38 Grasshopper TX1	Privately owned, Sproughton
	XK789	Slingsby T38 Grasshopper TX1	Midland Air Museum, stored Coventry
	XK790	Slingsby T38 Grasshopper TX1	Privately owned, stored Husbands Bosworth
	XK819	Slingsby T38 Grasshopper TX1	Privately owned, Selby
	XK822	Slingsby T38 Grasshopper TX1	Privately owned, Kenley
	XK895	DH104 Sea Devon C20 (G-SDEV) [19/CU]	Privately owned, Shoreham
	XK896	DH104 Sea Devon C20 (G-RNAS) (fuselage)	Privately owned, Filton (spares use)
	XK907	WS55 Whirlwind HAS7 [U]	Midland Air Museum, Coventry
	XK911	WS55 Whirlwind HAS7 [519/PO]	Privately owned, Adlington, Lancs
	XK936	WS55 Whirlwind HAS7 [62]	Imperial War Museum, Duxford
	XK940	WS55 Whirlwind HAS7 (G-AYXT) [911]	The Helicopter Museum, Weston-super-Mare
	XK944	WS55 Whirlwind HAS7	No 617 Sqn ATC, Malpas, Cheshire
	XK970	WS55 Whirlwind HAR10 (8789M)	Privately owned, Dunkeswell
	XL149	Blackburn B101 Beverley C1 (7988M) <ff>	Newark Air Museum, Winthorpe
	XL160	HP80 Victor K2 (8910M) <ff>	HP Victor Association, Walpole
	XL164	HP80 Victor K2 (9215M) <ff>	Gatwick Aviation Museum, Charlwood, Surrey
	XL188	HP80 Victor K2 (9100M) (fuselage)	RAF Kinloss Fire Section
	XL190	HP80 Victor K2 (9216M) <ff>	RAF Manston History Museum
	XL231	HP80 Victor K2	Yorkshire Air Museum, Elvington
	XL318	Avro 698 Vulcan B2 (8733M)	RAF Museum, Hendon
	XL319	Avro 698 Vulcan B2	North-East Aircraft Museum, Usworth
	XL360	Avro 698 Vulcan B2A	Midland Air Museum, Coventry
	XL388	Avro 698 Vulcan B2 <ff>	Blyth Valley Aviation Collection, Walpole
	XL391	Avro 698 Vulcan B2	Privately owned, Blackpool
	XL426	Avro 698 Vulcan B2 (G-VJET)	Vulcan Restoration Trust, Southend
	XL445	Avro 698 Vulcan K2 (8811M) <ff>	Blyth Valley Aviation Collection, Walpole
	XL449	Fairey Gannet AEW3 <ff>	Privately owned, Camberley, Surrey
	XL472	Fairey Gannet AEW3 [044/R]	Gatwick Aviation Museum, Charlwood, Surrey
	XL497	Fairey Gannet AEW3 [041/R]	RN, Prestwick
	XL500	Fairey Gannet AEW3 [CU]	World Naval Base, Chatham
	XL502	Fairey Gannet AEW3 (8610M/ G-BMYP)	Privately owned, Sandtoft
	XL503	Fairey Gannet AEW3 [070/E]	FAA Museum, RNAS Yeovilton
	XL563	Hawker Hunter T7 (9218M)	Privately owned, Bosbury, Hereford
	XL564	Hawker Hunter T7 (fuselage)	Boscombe Down Museum
	XL565	Hawker Hunter T7 (parts of WT745)	Delta Jets, Kemble
	XL567	Hawker Hunter T7 (8723M) [84]	Privately owned, Exeter
	XL568	Hawker Hunter T7A (9224M) [C]	AMIF, RAFC Cranwell
	XL569	Hawker Hunter T7 (8833M) [SC]	East Midlands Airport Aeropark
	XL571	Hawker Hunter T7 (XL572/8834M/ G-HNTR) [V]	Yorkshire Air Museum, Elvington
	XL573	Hawker Hunter T7 (G-BVGH)	Privately owned, Exeter
	XL577	Hawker Hunter T7 (G-BXKF/ 8676M)	Delta Jets, Kemble
	XL578	Hawker Hunter T7 (fuselage) [77]	Privately owned, Kemble
	XL580	Hawker Hunter T8M [723]	FAA Museum, RNAS Yeovilton
	XL586	Hawker Hunter T7 <rf>	Delta Jets, Kemble
	XL587	Hawker Hunter T7 (8807M/ G-HPUX) [Z]	The Old Flying Machine Company, stored Scampton
	XL591	Hawker Hunter T7	Delta Jets, Kemble
	XL592	Hawker Hunter T7 (8836M) [Y]	Classic Jets (UK), Exeter
	XL601	Hawker Hunter T7 (G-BZSR) [874/VL]	Classic Fighters, Brustem, Belgium
	XL602	Hawker Hunter T8M (G-BWFT)	Classic Jets (UK), Exeter
	XL612	Hawker Hunter T7 [2]	QinetiQ Boscombe Down, wfu
	XL613	Hawker Hunter T7 (G-BVMB)	*Sold to South Africa, 17 June 2001*

Serial	Type (other identity) [code]	Owner/operator, location or fate	Notes
XL618	Hawker Hunter T7 (8892M) [05]	Caernarfon Air World	
XL621	Hawker Hunter T7 (G-BNCX)	Privately owned, Brooklands Museum	
XL623	Hawker Hunter T7 (8770M)	The Planets Leisure Centre, Woking	
XL629	EE Lightning T4	QinetiQ Boscombe Down, at main gate	
XL703	SAL Pioneer CC1 (8034M)	RAF Museum, Cosford	
XL714	DH82A Tiger Moth II (T6099/ G-AOGR)	Privately owned, Swanton Morley	
XL716	DH82A Tiger Moth II (T7363/ G-AOIL)	Privately owned, Chandlers Ford	
XL735	Saro Skeeter AOP12	Privately owned, Tattershall Thorpe	
XL738	Saro Skeeter AOP12 (7860M)	Privately owned, Ivybridge, Devon	
XL739	Saro Skeeter AOP12	AAC Wattisham, on display	
XL762	Saro Skeeter AOP12 (8017M)	Royal Scottish Mus'm of Flight, E Fortune	
XL763	Saro Skeeter AOP12	Privately owned, Ivybridge, Devon	
XL764	Saro Skeeter AOP12 (7940M) [J]	Newark Air Museum, Winthorpe	
XL765	Saro Skeeter AOP12	Privately owned, Melksham, Wilts	
XL770	Saro Skeeter AOP12 (8046M)	Southampton Hall of Aviation	
XL809	Saro Skeeter AOP12 (G-BLIX)	Privately owned, Wilden, Beds	
XL811	Saro Skeeter AOP12	The Helicopter Museum, Weston-super-Mare	
XL812	Saro Skeeter AOP12 (G-SARO)	Privately owned, Old Buckenham	
XL813	Saro Skeeter AOP12	Museum of Army Flying, Middle Wallop	
XL814	Saro Skeeter AOP12	AAC Historic Aircraft Flight, Middle Wallop	
XL824	Bristol 171 Sycamore HR14 (8021M)	Gr Manchester Mus of Science & Industry	
XL829	Bristol 171 Sycamore HR14	Bristol Industrial Museum	
XL840	WS55 Whirlwind HAS7	Privately owned, Long Marston	
XL847	WS55 Whirlwind HAS7 [83]	AAC Middle Wallop Fire Section	
XL853	WS55 Whirlwind HAS7 [PO]	FAA Museum, stored RNAS Yeovilton	
XL875	WS55 Whirlwind HAR9	Perth Technical College	
XL929	Percival P66 Pembroke C1 (G-BNPU)	D-Day Museum, Shoreham Airport	
XL954	Percival P66 Pembroke C1 (9042M/N4234C/G-BXES)	Air Atlantique Historic Flight, Coventry	
XL993	SAL Twin Pioneer CC1 (8388M)	RAF Museum, Cosford	
XM135	BAC Lightning F1 [B]	Imperial War Museum, Duxford	
XM144	BAC Lightning F1 (8417M) <ff>	Privately owned, Booker	
XM169	BAC Lightning F1A (8422M) <ff>	N Yorks Aircraft Recovery Centre, Chop Gate	
XM172	BAC Lightning F1A (8427M)	Privately owned, Booker	
XM173	BAC Lightning F1A (8414M) [A]	RAF Bentley Priory, at main gate	
XM191	BAC Lightning F1A (7854M/ 8590M) <ff>	RAF EPTT, St Athan	
XM192	BAC Lightning F1A (8413M) [K]	Bomber County Aviation Museum, Hemswell	
XM223	DH104 Devon C2 (G-BWWC) [J]	Air Atlantique, Coventry	
XM279	EE Canberra B(I)8 <ff>	Privately owned, Flixton	
XM300	WS58 Wessex HAS1	Welsh Industrial & Maritime Mus'm, stored Cardiff	
XM328	WS58 Wessex HAS3 [653/PO]	SFDO, RNAS Culdrose	
XM330	WS58 Wessex HAS1	The Helicopter Museum, Weston-super-Mare	
XM349	Hunting Jet Provost T3A (9046M) [T]	Global Aviation, Binbrook	
XM350	Hunting Jet Provost T3A (9036M)	Aeroventure, Doncaster	
XM351	Hunting Jet Provost T3 (8078M) [Y]	RAF Museum, Cosford	
XM355	Hunting Jet Provost T3 (8229M) [D]	Privately owned, Shobdon	
XM358	Hunting Jet Provost T3A (8987M) [53]	Privately owned, Llanwrtyd Wells, Powys	
XM362	Hunting Jet Provost T3 (8230M)	RAF No 1 SoTT, Cosford	
XM363	Hunting Jet Provost T3 <ff>	RAF Cranwell	
XM365	Hunting Jet Provost T3A (G-BXBH) [37]	Privately owned, Little Snoring	
XM369	Hunting Jet Provost T3 (8084M) [C]	Privately owned, Portsmouth	
XM370	Hunting Jet Provost T3A (G-BVSP) [10]	Privately owned, Long Marston	
XM372	Hunting Jet Provost T3 (8917M) [55]	RAF Linton-on-Ouse Fire Section	
XM375	Hunting Jet Provost T3 (8231M) [B]	RAF Cottesmore Fire Section	
XM383	Hunting Jet Provost T3A [90]	Newark Air Museum, Winthorpe	
XM402	Hunting Jet Provost T3 (8055AM) [J]	Fenland & W Norfolk Aviation Museum, Wisbech	

Notes	Serial	Type (other identity) [code]	Owner/operator, location or fate
	XM404	Hunting Jet Provost T3 (8055BM)	FETC, Moreton-in-Marsh, Glos
	XM409	Hunting Jet Provost T3 (8082M) <rf>	Air Scouts, Guernsey Airport
	XM410	Hunting Jet Provost T3 (8054AM) [B]	RAF North Luffenham Training Area
	XM411	Hunting Jet Provost T3 (8434M) <ff>	Aeroventure, Doncaster
	XM412	Hunting Jet Provost T3A (9011M) [41]	Privately owned, Sproughton
	XM414	Hunting Jet Provost T3A (8996M)	Flight Experience Workshop, Belfast
	XM417	Hunting Jet Provost T3 (8054BM) [D] <ff>	Privately owned, Hednesford, Staffs
	XM419	Hunting Jet Provost T3A (8990M) [102]	DARA Training School, RAF St Athan
	XM424	Hunting Jet Provost T3A (G-BWDS)	Privately owned, North Weald
	XM425	Hunting Jet Provost T3A (8995M) [88]	Privately owned, Longton, Staffs
	XM426	Hunting Jet Provost T3 [64] <ff>	Really XN511
	XM459	Hunting Jet Provost T3A [F]	Sold abroad
	XM463	Hunting Jet Provost T3A [38] (fuselage)	RAF Museum, Hendon
	XM468	Hunting Jet Provost T3 (8081M)	Privately owned, Terrington St Clement
	XM470	Hunting Jet Provost T3A (G-BWZZ) [12]	Privately owned, Lincs
	XM473	Hunting Jet Provost T3A (8974M/ G-TINY)	Bedford College, instructional use
	XM474	Hunting Jet Provost T3 (8121M) <ff>	No 1804 Sqn ATC, Heaton Chapel, Greater Manchester
	XM478	Hunting Jet Provost T3A (8983M/ G-BXDL)	Transair(UK) Ltd, North Weald
	XM479	Hunting Jet Provost T3A (G-BVEZ) [54]	Privately owned, Newcastle
	XM480	Hunting Jet Provost T3 (8080M)	4x4 Car Centre, Chesterfield
	XM496	Bristol 253 Britannia C1 (EL-WXA)	Britannia Preservation Society, Kemble
	XM529	Saro Skeeter AOP12 (7979M/ G-BDNS)	Privately owned, Handforth
	XM553	Saro Skeeter AOP12 (G-AWSV)	Privately owned, Middle Wallop
	XM555	Saro Skeeter AOP12 (8027M)	RAF Museum, Cosford
	XM561	Saro Skeeter AOP12 (7980M)	Aeroventure, Doncaster
	XM564	Saro Skeeter AOP12	National Tank Museum, Bovington
	XM569	Avro 698 Vulcan B2 <ff>	Gloucestershire Avn Coll, stored Gloucester
	XM575	Avro 698 Vulcan B2A (G-BLMC)	East Midlands Airport Aeropark
	XM594	Avro 698 Vulcan B2	Newark Air Museum, Winthorpe
	XM597	Avro 698 Vulcan B2	Royal Scottish Mus'm of Flight, E Fortune
	XM598	Avro 698 Vulcan B2 (8778M)	RAF Museum, Cosford
	XM602	Avro 698 Vulcan B2 (8771M) <ff>	Avro Aircraft Heritage Society, Woodford
	XM603	Avro 698 Vulcan B2	Avro Aircraft Heritage Society, Woodford
	XM607	Avro 698 Vulcan B2 (8779M)	RAF Waddington, on display
	XM612	Avro 698 Vulcan B2	City of Norwich Aviation Museum
	XM652	Avro 698 Vulcan B2 <ff>	Privately owned, Welshpool
	XM655	Avro 698 Vulcan B2 (G-VULC)	Privately owned, Wellesbourne Mountford
	XM660	WS55 Whirlwind HAS7 [78]	RAF Millom Museum, Haverigg
	XM685	WS55 Whirlwind HAS7 (G-AYZJ) [513/PO]	Newark Air Museum, Winthorpe
	XM692	HS Gnat T1 <ff>	Boscombe Down Museum
	XM693	HS Gnat T1 (7891M)	BAE Systems Hamble, on display
	XM693	HS Gnat T1 (8618M/XP504/ G-TIMM) [04]	Kennet Aviation, Cranfield
	XM697	HS Gnat T1 (G-NAAT)	Bournemouth Aviation Museum
	XM708	HS Gnat T1 (8573M)	Privately owned, Kings Langley, Herts
	XM709	HS Gnat T1 (8617M) [67]	Sold to the USA
	XM715	HP80 Victor K2	British Aviation Heritage, Bruntingthorpe
	XM717	HP80 Victor K2 <ff>	RAF Museum, Hendon
	XM819	Lancashire EP9 Prospector (G-APXW)	Museum of Army Flying, Middle Wallop
	XM833	WS58 Wessex HAS3	SWWAPS, Lasham
	XM868	WS58 Wessex HAS1 [517]	RN, Predannack Fire School
	XM870	WS58 Wessex HAS3 [PO]	RN, Predannack Fire School
	XM874	WS58 Wessex HAS1 [521/CU]	RN, Predannack Fire School
	XM927	WS58 Wessex HAS3 (8814M) [660/PO]	RAF Shawbury Fire Section

Serial	Type (other identity) [code]	Owner/operator, location or fate	Notes
XN126	WS55 Whirlwind HAR10 (8655M) [S]	Pinewood Studios, Elstree	
XN157	Slingsby T21B Sedbergh TX1	Privately owned, stored Long Mynd	
XN185	Slingsby T21B Sedbergh TX1 (8942M/BGA 4077)	RAFGSA, Syerston	
XN187	Slingsby T21B Sedbergh TX1 (BGA 3903)	Privately owned, Seighford	
XN198	Slingsby T31B Cadet TX3	Privately owned, Challock Lees	
XN238	Slingsby T31B Cadet TX3 <ff>	Aeroventure, stored Doncaster	
XN239	Slingsby T31B Cadet TX3 (8889M) [G]	Welsh National Museum, Cardiff	
XN243	Slingsby T31B Cadet TX3 (BGA 3145)	Privately owned, Bicester	
XN246	Slingsby T31B Cadet TX3	Southampton Hall of Aviation	
XN258	WS55 Whirlwind HAR9 [589/CU]	North-East Aircraft Museum, Usworth	
XN263	WS55 Whirlwind HAS7	Privately owned, Bosham, W Sussex	
XN297	WS55 Whirlwind HAR9 (XN311) [12]	Privately owned, Hull	
XN298	WS55 Whirlwind HAR9 (810/LS]	International Fire Training Centre, Chorley	
XN299	WS55 Whirlwind HAS7 [ZZ]	Tangmere Military Aviation Museum	
XN304	WS55 Whirlwind HAS7 [64]	Norfolk & Suffolk Avn Museum, Flixton	
XN332	Saro P531 (G-APNV) [759]	FAA Museum, RNAS Yeovilton	
XN334	Saro P531	FAA Museum, stored RNAS Yeovilton	
XN341	Saro Skeeter AOP12 (8022M)	Stondon Transport Mus & Garden Centre, Beds	
XN344	Saro Skeeter AOP12 (8018M)	Science Museum, South Kensington	
XN351	Saro Skeeter AOP12 (G-BKSC)	Privately owned, Ipswich	
XN380	WS55 Whirlwind HAS7	RAF Manston History Museum	
XN385	WS55 Whirlwind HAS7	Botany Bay Villages, Chorley, Lancs	
XN386	WS55 Whirlwind HAR9 [435/ED]	Aeroventure, Doncaster	
XN412	Auster AOP9	Auster 9 Group, Melton Mowbray	
XN435	Auster AOP9 (G-BGBU)	Privately owned, Egham	
XN437	Auster AOP9 (G-AXWA)	Privately owned, North Weald	
XN441	Auster AOP9 (G-BGKT)	Auster 9 Group, Melton Mowbray	
XN459	Hunting Jet Provost T3A (G-BWOT)	Transair(UK) Ltd, North Weald	
XN462	Hunting Jet Provost T3A [17]	FAA Museum, stored RNAS Yeovilton	
XN466	Hunting Jet Provost T3A [29] <ff>	No 1005 Sqn ATC, Radcliffe, Gtr Manchester	
XN492	Hunting Jet Provost T3 (8079M) <ff>	Privately owned, Ellesmere Port, Cheshire	
XN493	Hunting Jet Provost T3 (XN137) <ff>	Privately owned, Camberley	
XN494	Hunting Jet Provost T3A (9012M) [43]	Crawley Technical College	
XN497	Hunting Jet Provost T3A [52]	DARA, RAF St Athan	
XN500	Hunting Jet Provost T3A [48]	Oxford Avn Services Ltd, Oxford, ground instruction	
XN501	Hunting Jet Provost T3A (8958M) [G]	Privately owned, Billockby, Norfolk	
XN503	Hunting Jet Provost T3 <ff>	No 1284 Sqn ATC, Milford Haven	
XN505	Hunting Jet Provost T3A [25]	Sold abroad	
XN508	Hunting Jet Provost T3A <ff>	DARA, RAF St Athan	
XN510	Hunting Jet Provost T3 (G-BXBI) [40]	Privately owned, Sproughton	
XN511	Hunting Jet Provost T3 [64] <ff>	Aeroventure, Doncaster	
XN549	Hunting Jet Provost T3 (8235M) [32,P]	RAF Shawbury Fire Section	
XN550	Hunting Jet Provost T3 <ff>	Privately owned, Stone, Staffs	
XN551	Hunting Jet Provost T3A (8984M)	DARA Training School, RAF St Athan	
XN554	Hunting Jet Provost T3 (8436M) [K]	RAF North Luffenham Training Area	
XN573	Hunting Jet Provost T3 [E] <ff>	Newark Air Museum, Winthorpe	
XN577	Hunting Jet Provost T3A (8956M) [89,F]	Privately owned, Billockby, Norfolk	
XN579	Hunting Jet Provost T3A (9137M) [14]	RAF North Luffenham Training Area	
XN582	Hunting Jet Provost T3A (8957M) [95,H]	Arbury College, Cambridge	
XN584	Hunting Jet Provost T3A (9014M) [E]	Phoenix Aviation, Bruntingthorpe	
XN586	Hunting Jet Provost T3A (9039M) [91,S]	Brooklands Technical College	

Notes	Serial	Type (other identity) [code]	Owner/operator, location or fate
	XN589	Hunting Jet Provost T3A (9143M) [46]	RAF Linton-on-Ouse, on display
	XN592	Hunting Jet Provost T3 <ff>	No 1105 Sqn ATC, Winchester
	XN593	Hunting Jet Provost T3A (8988M) [97,Q]	Privately owned, Billockby, Norfolk
XN594		Hunting Jet Provost T3 (8234M/ XN458)	Privately owned, Ashington, W Sussex
	XN597	Hunting Jet Provost T3 (7984M) <ff>	RAF Millom Museum, Haverigg
	XN607	Hunting Jet Provost T3 <ff>	N Yorks Aircraft Recovery Centre, Chop Gate
	XN629	Hunting Jet Provost T3A (G-BVEG/ G-KNOT) [49]	Transair (UK) Ltd, North Weald
	XN632	Hunting Jet Provost T3 (8352M)	Privately owned, Birlingham, Worcs
	XN634	Hunting Jet Provost T3A <ff>	Privately owned, Sproughton
	XN634	Hunting Jet Provost T3A [53] <rf>	BAE Systems Warton Fire Section
	XN636	Hunting Jet Provost T3A (9045M) [15]	Privately owned
	XN637	Hunting Jet Provost T3 (G-BKOU) [03]	Privately owned, Cranfield
	XN647	DH110 Sea Vixen FAW2 <ff>	Privately owned, stored Bruntingthorpe
	XN650	DH110 Sea Vixen FAW2 <ff>	Privately owned, Welshpool
	XN651	DH110 Sea Vixen FAW2 <ff>	Privately owned, Lavendon, Bucks
	XN657	DH110 Sea Vixen D3 [TR-1]	Privately owned, Yateley, Hants
	XN685	DH110 Sea Vixen FAW2 (8173M) [03/VL]	Midland Air Museum, Coventry
	XN691	DH110 Sea Vixen FAW2 (8143M) [247/H]	*Scrapped at North Weald, 26 July 2001*
	XN696	DH110 Sea Vixen FAW2 <ff>	Blyth Valley Aviation Collection, stored Walpole
	XN714	Hunting H126	RAF Museum, Cosford
	XN724	EE Lightning F2A (8513M) [F]	*Scrapped*
	XN726	EE Lightning F2A (8545M) <ff>	Boscombe Down Museum
	XN728	EE Lightning F2A (8546M) [V]	Privately owned, Balderton, Notts
	XN734	EE Lightning F3A (8346M/ G-BNCA) <ff>	Privately owned, Cranfield
	XN769	EE Lightning F2 (8402M) <ff>	*To Malta, Spring 2001*
	XN774	EE Lightning F2A (8551M) <ff>	Privately owned, Boston, Lincs
	XN776	EE Lightning F2A (8535M) [C]	Royal Scottish Mus'm of Flight, E Fortune
	XN795	EE Lightning F2A <ff>	Privately owned, Foulness
	XN817	AW660 Argosy C1	QinetiQ West Freugh Fire Section
	XN819	AW660 Argosy C1 (8205M) <ff>	Newark Air Museum, Winthorpe
	XN923	HS Buccaneer S1 [13]	Gatwick Aviation Museum, Charlwood, Surrey
	XN928	HS Buccaneer S1 (8179M) <ff>	Privately owned, Kent
	XN957	HS Buccaneer S1	FAA Museum, RNAS Yeovilton
	XN964	HS Buccaneer S1 [613/LM]	Newark Air Museum, Winthorpe
	XN967	HS Buccaneer S1 <ff>	Muckleburgh Collection, Weybourne, Norfolk
XN972		HS Buccaneer S1 (8183M/XN962) <ff>	RAF Museum, Hendon
	XN974	HS Buccaneer S2A	Yorkshire Air Museum, Elvington
	XN983	HS Buccaneer S2B <ff>	Fenland & W Norfolk Aviation Museum, Wisbech
	XP110	WS58 Wessex HAS3 [55/FL]	RN AESS, *HMS Sultan*, Gosport, BDRT
	XP137	WS58 Wessex HAS3 [711/DD]	SFDO, RNAS Culdrose
	XP142	WS58 Wessex HAS3	FAA Museum, stored Yeovilton
	XP150	WS58 Wessex HAS3 [LS]	FETC, Moreton-in-Marsh, Glos
	XP159	WS58 Wessex HAS1 (8877M) [047/R]	*Currently not known*
	XP160	WS58 Wessex HAS1	RN, Predannack Fire School
	XP165	WS Scout AH1	The Helicopter Museum, Weston-super-Mare
	XP166	WS Scout AH1 (G-APVL)	Privately owned, East Dereham, Norfolk
	XP190	WS Scout AH1	Aeroventure, Doncaster
	XP191	WS Scout AH1	Privately owned, Dunkeswell
	XP226	Fairey Gannet AEW3 [073/E]	Newark Air Museum, Winthorpe
	XP241	Auster AOP9	Privately owned, Eaglescott
	XP242	Auster AOP9 (G-BUCI)	AAC Historic Aircraft Flight, Middle Wallop
	XP244	Auster AOP9 (7864M/*M7922*)	Army SEAE, Arborfield
XP248		Auster AOP9 (7863M/WZ679)	Privately owned, Sandy, Beds
	XP254	Auster AOP11 (G-ASCC)	Privately owned, Tollerton

Serial	Type (other identity) [code]	Owner/operator, location or fate	Notes
XP279	Auster AOP9 (G-BWKK)	Privately owned, Popham	
XP280	Auster AOP9	Snibston Discovery Park, Coalville	
XP281	Auster AOP9	Imperial War Museum, Duxford	
XP283	Auster AOP9 (7859M) (frame)	Privately owned,	
XP299	WS55 Whirlwind HAR10 (8726M)	RAF Museum, Cosford	
XP329	WS55 Whirlwind HAR10 (8791M) [V]	Scrapped at Tattershall Thorpe	
XP330	WS55 Whirlwind HAR10	CAA Fire School, Tees-side Airport	
XP344	WS55 Whirlwind HAR10 (8764M) [H723]	RAF North Luffenham Training Area	
XP345	WS55 Whirlwind HAR10 (8792M) Elvington	York Helicopter Preservation Group,	
XP346	WS55 Whirlwind HAR10 (8793M)	Privately owned, Long Marston	
XP350	WS55 Whirlwind HAR10	Flambards Village Theme Park, Helston	
XP351	WS55 Whirlwind HAR10 (8672M) [Z]	RAF Shawbury, on display	
XP353	WS55 Whirlwind HAR10 (8720M)	Currently not known	
XP355	WS55 Whirlwind HAR10 (8463M/ G-BEBC)	City of Norwich Aviation Museum	
XP359	WS55 Whirlwind HAR10 (8447M)	Dundonald Aviation Centre, Strathclyde	
XP360	WS55 Whirlwind HAR10 [V]	Privately owned, Upper Hill, nr Leominster	
XP395	WS55 Whirlwind HAR10 (8674M) [A]	Scrapped at Tattershall Thorpe	
XP398	WS55 Whirlwind HAR10 (8794M)	Gatwick Aviation Museum, Charlwood, Surrey	
XP399	WS55 Whirlwind HAR10	Privately owned, Rettendon, Essex	
XP404	WS55 Whirlwind HAR10 (8682M)	The Helicopter Museum, Weston-super-Mare	
XP411	AW660 Argosy C1 (8442M) [C]	RAF Museum, Cosford	
XP454	Slingsby T38 Grasshopper TX1	Wellingborough School, Wellingborough	
XP458	Slingsby T38 Grasshopper TX1	Scrapped at Norwich	
XP488	Slingsby T38 Grasshopper TX1	Fenland & W Norfolk Aviation Museum, stored Wisbech	
XP493	Slingsby T38 Grasshopper TX1	Privately owned, stored Aston Down	
XP494	Slingsby T38 Grasshopper TX1	Privately owned, Rattlesden, Suffolk	
XP502	HS Gnat T1 (8576M)	Privately owned, Kemble	
XP505	HS Gnat T1	Science Museum, Wroughton	
XP516	HS Gnat T1 (8580M) [16]	QinetiQ Structures Dept, Farnborough	
XP540	HS Gnat T1 (8608M) [62]	Arbury College, Cambridge	
XP542	HS Gnat T1 (8575M) [42]	R. Military College of Science, Shrivenham	
XP556	Hunting Jet Provost T4 (9027M) [B]	RAF Cranwell Aviation Heritage Centre	
XP557	Hunting Jet Provost T4 (8494M) [72]	Bomber County Aviation Museum, Hemswell	
XP558	Hunting Jet Provost T4 (8627M)[20]	Privately owned, Sproughton	
XP563	Hunting Jet Provost T4 (9028M) [C]	Privately owned, Sproughton	
XP568	Hunting Jet Provost T4	Jet Avn Preservation Grp, Long Marston	
XP573	Hunting Jet Provost T4 (8236M) [19]	Jersey Airport Fire Section	
XP585	Hunting Jet Provost T4 (8407M) [24]	NE Wales Institute, Wrexham	
XP627	Hunting Jet Provost T4	North-East Aircraft Museum, Usworth	
XP629	Hunting Jet Provost T4 (9026M) [P]	RAF North Luffenham Training Area	
XP638	Hunting Jet Provost T4 (9034M) [A]	RAF Waddington, BDRT	
XP640	Hunting Jet Provost T4 (8501M) [27]	Yorkshire Air Museum, Elvington	
XP642	Hunting Jet Provost T4 <ff>	Privately owned, Lavendon, Bucks	
XP672	Hunting Jet Provost T4 (8458M/ G-RAFI) [03]	Privately owned, North Weald	
XP677	Hunting Jet Provost T4 (8587M) <ff>	No 1343 Sqn ATC, East Grinstead	
XP680	Hunting Jet Provost T4 (8460M)	FETC, Moreton-in-Marsh, Glos	
XP686	Hunting Jet Provost T4 (8401M/ 8502M) [G]	RAF North Luffenham Training Area	
XP688	Hunting Jet Provost T4 (9031M)	Botany Bay Villages, Chorley, Lancs	
XP701	BAC Lightning F3 (8924M) <ff>	Robertsbridge Aviation Society, Mayfield	
XP703	BAC Lightning F3 <ff>	The Cockpit Collection, RAF Coltishall	
XP706	BAC Lightning F3 (8925M)	Lincs Lightning Pres'n Society, Hemswell	
XP743	BAC Lightning F3 <ff>	No 351 Sqn ATC, Burton-upon-Trent	
XP745	BAC Lightning F3 (8453M) <ff>	Greenford Haulage, West London	
XP772	DHC2 Beaver AL1 (G-BUCJ)	AAC Historic Aircraft Flight, stored Duxford	
XP775	DHC2 Beaver AL1	Privately owned	
XP806	DHC2 Beaver AL1	To Canada, November 2000	
XP820	DHC2 Beaver AL1	AAC Historic Aircraft Flight, Middle Wallop	

Notes	Serial	Type (other identity) [code]	Owner/operator, location or fate
	XP821	DHC2 Beaver AL1 [MCO]	Museum of Army Flying, Middle Wallop
	XP822	DHC2 Beaver AL1	Museum of Army Flying, Middle Wallop
	XP831	Hawker P.1127 (8406M)	Science Museum, South Kensington
	XP841	Handley-Page HP115	FAA Museum, RNAS Yeovilton
	XP846	WS Scout AH1 [B,H] (fuselage)	RE 39 Regt, Waterbeach, instructional use
	XP847	WS Scout AH1	Museum of Army Flying, Middle Wallop
	XP848	WS Scout AH1	AAC Arborfield, on display
	XP849	WS Scout AH1	Privately owned, East Dereham, Norfolk
	XP853	WS Scout AH1	Privately owned, Dunkeswell
	XP854	WS Scout AH1 (7898M/TAD043)	Privately owned, Sproughton
	XP855	WS Scout AH1	Army SEAE, Arborfield
	XP856	WS Scout AH1	Privately owned, Dunkeswell
	XP883	WS Scout AH1	Privately owned, Oaksey Park, Wilts
	XP884	WS Scout AH1	AAC Middle Wallop, instructional use
	XP885	WS Scout AH1	AAC Wattisham, instructional use
	XP886	WS Scout AH1	Yeovil College
	XP888	WS Scout AH1	Privately owned, Sproughton
	XP890	WS Scout AH1 [G] (fuselage)	Privately owned, Ipswich
	XP893	WS Scout AH1	AAC Middle Wallop, BDRT
	XP899	WS Scout AH1 [D]	Army SEAE, Arborfield
	XP900	WS Scout AH1	AAC Wattisham, instructional use
	XP902	WS Scout AH1 <ff>	Aeroventure, stored Doncaster
	XP905	WS Scout AH1	Privately owned, Sproughton
	XP907	WS Scout AH1 (G-SROE)	Privately owned, Wattisham
	XP910	WS Scout AH1	Museum of Army Flying, Middle Wallop
	XP919	DH110 Sea Vixen FAW2 (8163M) [706/VL]	Blyth Valley Aviation Collection, Walpole
	XP924	DH110 Sea Vixen D3 (G-CVIX)	De Havilland Aviation, Bournemouth
	XP925	DH110 Sea Vixen FAW2 [752] <ff>	No 1268 Sqn ATC, Haslemere, Surrey
	XP956	DH110 Sea Vixen FAW2	Privately owned
	XP980	Hawker P.1127	FAA Museum, RNAS Yeovilton
	XP984	Hawker P.1127	Brooklands Museum, Weybridge
	XR220	BAC TSR2 (7933M)	RAF Museum, Cosford
	XR222	BAC TSR2	Imperial War Museum, Duxford
	XR232	Sud Alouette AH2 (F-WEIP)	Museum of Army Flying, Middle Wallop
	XR240	Auster AOP9 (G-BDFH)	Privately owned, Booker
	XR241	Auster AOP9 (G-AXRR)	The Aircraft Restoration Co, Duxford
	XR244	Auster AOP9	AAC Historic Aircraft Flight, Middle Wallop
	XR246	Auster AOP9 (7862M/G-AZBU)	Auster 9 Group, Melton Mowbray
	XR267	Auster AOP9 (G-BJXR)	Privately owned, Newark
	XR271	Auster AOP9	Museum of Artillery, Woolwich
	XR371	SC5 Belfast C1	RAF Museum, Cosford
	XR379	Sud Alouette AH2	AAC Historic Aircraft Flight, Middle Wallop
	XR453	WS55 Whirlwind HAR10 (8873M) [A]	RAF Odiham, on gate
	XR458	WS55 Whirlwind HAR10 (8662M) [H]	Museum of Army Flying, Middle Wallop
	XR485	WS55 Whirlwind HAR10 [Q]	Norfolk & Suffolk Avn Museum, Flixton
	XR486	WS55 Whirlwind HCC12 (8727M/ G-RWWW)	The Helicopter Museum, Weston-super-Mare
	XR497	WS58 Wessex HC2 [F]	RAF No 72 Sqn, Aldergrove
	XR498	WS58 Wessex HC2 [X]	RAF No 72 Sqn, Aldergrove
	XR499	WS58 Wessex HC2 [W]	RN AESS, *HMS Sultan*, Gosport
	XR501	WS58 Wessex HC2	Army, Keogh Barracks, Aldershot, instructional use
	XR502	WS58 Wessex HC2 [Z]	Privately owned, Colsterworth
	XR503	WS58 Wessex HC2	MoD FSCTE, Manston
	XR506	WS58 Wessex HC2 [V]	RAF No 72 Sqn, Aldergrove
	XR507	WS58 Wessex HC2	Privately owned, Hixon, Staffs
	XR508	WS58 Wessex HC2 [B]	RN AESS, *HMS Sultan*, Gosport
	XR511	WS58 Wessex HC2 [L]	RAF No 72 Sqn, Aldergrove
	XR516	WS58 Wessex HC2 [WB]	RN AESS, *HMS Sultan*, Gosport
	XR517	WS58 Wessex HC2 [N]	Shoreham Airport, on display
	XR518	WS58 Wessex HC2 [O]	
	XR520	WS58 Wessex HC2	RN AESS, *HMS Sultan*, Gosport
	XR523	WS58 Wessex HC2 [M]	RN AESS, *HMS Sultan*, Gosport
	XR525	WS58 Wessex HC2 [G]	RAF No 72 Sqn, Aldergrove
	XR526	WS58 Wessex HC2 (8147M)	The Helicopter Museum, Weston-super-Mare
	XR528	WS58 Wessex HC2	SFDO, RNAS Culdrose
	XR529	WS58 Wessex HC2 [E]	RAF No 72 Sqn, Aldergrove
	XR534	HS Gnat T1 (8578M) [65]	Newark Air Museum, Winthorpe

Serial	Type (other identity) [code]	Owner/operator, location or fate	Notes
XR537	HS Gnat T1 (8642M/G-NATY) [T]	Bournemouth Aviation Museum	
XR569	HS Gnat T1 (8560M) [08]	Sold to the USA, 2001	
XR571	HS Gnat T1 (8493M)	RAF Red Arrows, Scampton, on display	
XR574	HS Gnat T1 (8631M) [72]	RAF No 1 SoTT, Cosford	
XR588	WS58 Wessex HC2 [Hearts]	RAF No 84 Sqn, Akrotiri	
XR595	WS Scout AH1 (G-BWHU) [M]	Privately owned, Glenrothes	
XR597	WS Scout AH1 (fuselage)	Privately owned, Sproughton	
XR601	WS Scout AH1	Army SEAE, Arborfield	
XR625	WS Scout AH1 (XR633/XR777)	To Germany, Spring 2001	
XR627	WS Scout AH1 [X]	Privately owned, Sproughton	
XR628	WS Scout AH1	Privately owned, Ipswich	
XR629	WS Scout AH1 (fuselage)	Privately owned, Ipswich	
XR635	WS Scout AH1	Privately owned, Sproughton	
XR650	Hunting Jet Provost T4 (8459M) [28]	Boscombe Down Museum	
XR654	Hunting Jet Provost T4 <ff>	Privately owned, Sealand	
XR658	Hunting Jet Provost T4 (8192M)	Deeside College, Connah's Quay, Clwyd	
XR662	Hunting Jet Provost T4 (8410M) [25]	Boulton Paul Association, Wolverhampton	
XR672	Hunting Jet Provost T4 (8495M) [50]	RAF Halton, Fire Section	
XR673	Hunting Jet Provost T4 (G-BXLO/ 9032M) [L]	Privately owned, North Weald	
XR681	Hunting Jet Provost T4 (8588M) <ff>	No 1216 Sqn ATC, Newhaven, E Sussex	
XR700	Hunting Jet Provost T4 (8589M) <ff>	RAF EPTT, Aldergrove	
XR713	BAC Lightning F3 (8935M) [C]	RAF Leuchars, on display	
XR718	BAC Lightning F6 (8932M) [DA]	Blyth Valley Aviation Collection, Walpole	
XR724	BAC Lightning F6 (G-BTSY)	The Lightning Association, Binbrook	
XR725	BAC Lightning F6	Privately owned, Binbrook	
XR726	BAC Lightning F6 <ff>	Privately owned, Harrogate	
XR728	BAC Lightning F6 [JS]	Lightning Preservation Grp, Bruntingthorpe	
XR747	BAC Lightning F6 <ff>	Privately owned, Booker	
XR749	BAC Lightning F3 (8934M) [DA]	Tees-side Airport, on display	
XR751	BAC Lightning F3	Privately owned, Tremar, Cornwall	
XR753	BAC Lightning F6 (8969M) [BP]	RAF Leeming on display	
XR753	BAC Lightning F53 (ZF578) [A]	Privately owned, Quedgeley, Glos	
XR754	BAC Lightning F6 (8972M) <ff>	Aeroventure, Doncaster	
XR755	BAC Lightning F6	Privately owned, Callington, Cornwall	
XR757	BAC Lightning F6 <ff>	Privately owned, Grainthorpe, Lincs	
XR759	BAC Lightning F6 <ff>	Privately owned, Haxey, Lincs	
XR770	BAC Lightning F6 [AA]	Privately owned, Grainthorpe, Lincs	
XR771	BAC Lightning F6 [BM]	Midland Air Museum, Coventry	
XR806	BAC VC10 C1K <ff>	RAF Brize Norton, BDRT	
XR807	BAC VC10 C1K	DARA, stored RAF St Athan	
XR808	BAC VC10 C1K	RAF No 10 Sqn, Brize Norton	
XR810	BAC VC10 C1K	RAF No 10 Sqn, Brize Norton	
XR944	Wallis WA116 (G-ATTB)	RAF Museum, Hendon	
XR954	HS Gnat T1 (8570M) [30]	Privately owned, Bournemouth	
XR955	HS Gnat T1 (SAH-2)	Privately owned, Leavesden	
XR977	HS Gnat T1 (8640M) [3]	RAF Museum, Cosford	
XR985	HS Gnat T1 (7886M)	Scrapped	
XR991	HS Gnat T1 (8624M/XS102/ G-MOUR)	Privately owned, Kemble	
XR993	HS Gnat T1 (8620M/XP534/ G-BVPP)	Kennet Aviation, Cranfield	
XS100	HS Gnat T1 (8561M) [57]	Privately owned, Ongar	
XS101	HS Gnat T1 (8638M) (G-GNAT)	Privately owned, Cranfield	
XS122	WS58 Wessex HAS3 [655/PO]	RN AESS, HMS Sultan, Gosport	
XS128	WS58 Wessex HAS1 [37]	Scrapped at Yeovilton	
XS149	WS58 Wessex HAS3 [661/GL]	The Helicopter Museum, Weston-super-Mare	
XS165	Hiller UH12E (G-ASAZ) [37]	Privately owned, North Weald	
XS176	Hunting Jet Provost T4 (8514M)	Privately owned, Solihull	
XS177	Hunting Jet Provost T4 (9044M) [N]	RAF Valley Fire Section	
XS179	Hunting Jet Provost T4 (8237M) [20]	University of Salford, Manchester	
XS180	Hunting Jet Provost T4 (8238M) [21]	RAF St Athan, Fire Section	
XS181	Hunting Jet Provost T4 (9033M) <ff>	Communications & Electronics Museum, Bletchley Park	

Notes	Serial	Type (other identity) [code]	Owner/operator, location or fate
	XS183	Hunting Jet Provost T4 <ff>	Privately owned, Plymouth
	XS186	Hunting Jet Provost T4 (8408M) [M]	RAF North Luffenham Training Area
	XS209	Hunting Jet Provost T4 (8409M)	Privately owned, Kemble
	XS215	Hunting Jet Provost T4 (8507M) [17]	RAF Halton
	XS216	Hunting Jet Provost T4 <ff>	No 2357 Sqn ATC, Goole
	XS217	Hunting Jet Provost T4 (9029M) [O]	Privately owned, Bruntingthorpe
	XS218	Hunting Jet Provost T4 (8508M) <ff>	No 447 Sqn ATC, Henley-on-Thames, Berks
	XS231	BAC Jet Provost T5 (G-ATAJ)	Privately owned, Barnstaple
	XS235	DH106 Comet 4C (G-CPDA)	British Aviation Heritage, Bruntingthorpe
	XS416	BAC Lightning T5	Privately owned, Grainthorpe, Lincs
	XS417	BAC Lightning T5 [DZ]	Newark Air Museum, Winthorpe
	XS420	BAC Lightning T5	Privately owned, Norfolk
	XS421	BAC Lightning T5 <ff>	Privately owned, Foulness
	XS456	BAC Lightning T5 [DX]	Privately owned, Wainfleet
	XS457	BAC Lightning T5 <ff>	Privately owned, North Coates
	XS458	BAC Lightning T5 [T]	T5 Projects, Cranfield
	XS459	BAC Lightning T5 [AW]	Fenland & W Norfolk Aviation Museum, Wisbech
	XS463	WS Wasp HAS1 (comp XT431)	Privately owned, Sproughton
	XS479	WS58 Wessex HU5 (8819M) [XF]	*Scrapped at Stock, Essex*
	XS481	WS58 Wessex HU5	Aeroventure, Doncaster
	XS482	WS58 Wessex HU5 [A/D]	RAF Manston History Museum
	XS485	WS58 Wessex HC5C (comp XR503) [Hearts]	RN AESS, *HMS Sultan*, Gosport
	XS486	WS58 Wessex HU5 (9272M) [524/CU,F]	No 93 Sqn ATC, Bath
	XS488	WS58 Wessex HU5 (9056M) [XK]	RN AESS, *HMS Sultan*, Gosport
	XS489	WS58 Wessex HU5 [R]	RN AESS, *HMS Sultan*, Gosport
	XS492	WS58 Wessex HU5 [623]	RN, stored DARA Fleetlands
	XS493	WS58 Wessex HU5	RN, stored DARA Fleetlands
	XS496	WS58 Wessex HU5 [625/PO]	RN AESS, *HMS Sultan*, Gosport
	XS498	WS58 Wessex HC5C (comp XS677) [WK]	Privately owned, Hixon, Staffs
	XS507	WS58 Wessex HU5	RN AESS, *HMS Sultan*, Gosport
	XS508	WS58 Wessex HU5	FAA Museum, stored RNAS Yeovilton
	XS510	WS58 Wessex HU5 [626/PO]	RN AESS, *HMS Sultan*, Gosport
	XS511	WS58 Wessex HU5 [M]	RN AESS, *HMS Sultan*, Gosport
	XS513	WS58 Wessex HU5 [419/CU]	RN AESS, *HMS Sultan*, Gosport
	XS514	WS58 Wessex HU5 [L]	RN AESS, *HMS Sultan*, Gosport
	XS515	WS58 Wessex HU5 [N]	Army, Keogh Barracks, Aldershot, instructional use
	XS516	WS58 Wessex HU5 [Q]	RN, Predannack Fire School
	XS517	WS58 Wessex HC5C (comp XS679) [Diamonds]	RN AESS, *HMS Sultan*, Gosport, BDRT
	XS520	WS58 Wessex HU5 [F]	RN AESS, *HMS Sultan*, Gosport
	XS522	WS58 Wessex HU5 [ZL]	RN, Predannack Fire School
	XS527	WS Wasp HAS1	FAA Museum, stored RNAS Yeovilton
	XS529	WS Wasp HAS1	RN, Predannack Fire School
	XS539	WS Wasp HAS1 [435]	DARA Fleetlands Apprentice School
	XS567	WS Wasp HAS1 [434/E]	Imperial War Museum, Duxford
	XS568	WS Wasp HAS1 [441]	RN AESS, *HMS Sultan*, Gosport
	XS569	WS Wasp HAS1	DARA Fleetlands Apprentice School
	XS570	WS Wasp HAS1 [445/P]	Warship Preservation Trust, Birkenhead
	XS576	DH110 Sea Vixen FAW2 [125/E]	Imperial War Museum, Duxford
	XS587	DH110 Sea Vixen FAW(TT)2 (8828M/G-VIXN)	Gatwick Aviation Museum, Charlwood, Surrey
	XS590	DH110 Sea Vixen FAW2 [131/E]	FAA Museum, RNAS Yeovilton
	XS596	HS Andover C1(PR)	DPA/AFD/*Open Skies*, QinetiQ Boscombe Down
	XS598	HS Andover C1 (fuselage)	FETC, Moreton-in-Marsh, Glos
	XS606	HS Andover C1	DPA/AFD/ETPS, QinetiQ Boscombe Down
	XS639	HS Andover E3A	RAF Museum, Cosford
	XS641	HS Andover C1(PR) (9198M) [Z]	RAF No 1 SoTT, Cosford
	XS643	HS Andover E3A (9278M)	MoD FSCTE, Manston
	XS646	HS Andover C1(mod)	DPA/AFD, QinetiQ Boscombe Down
	XS652	Slingsby T45 Swallow TX1 (BGA 1107)	Privately owned, Rufforth
	XS674	WS58 Wessex HC2 [R]	Privately owned, Sproughton
	XS675	WS58 Wessex HC2 [Spades]	RAF No 84 Sqn, Akrotiri
	XS677	WS58 Wessex HC2 [WK]	*Sold as ZK-HBE August 2001*

Serial	Type (other identity) [code]	Owner/operator, location or fate	Notes
XS695	HS Kestrel FGA1	RAF Museum Restoration Centre, Cosford	
XS709	HS125 Dominie T1 [M]	RAF No 3 FTS/55(R) Sqn, Cranwell	
XS710	HS125 Dominie T1 (9259M) [O]	RAF No 1 SoTT, Cosford	
XS711	HS125 Dominie T1 [L]	RAF No 3 FTS/55(R) Sqn, Cranwell	
XS712	HS125 Dominie T1 [A]	RAF No 3 FTS/55(R) Sqn, Cranwell	
XS713	HS125 Dominie T1 [C]	RAF No 3 FTS/55(R) Sqn, Cranwell	
XS714	HS125 Dominie T1 (9246M) [P]	MoD FSCTE, Manston	
XS726	HS125 Dominie T1 (9273M) [T]	RAF No 1 SoTT, Cosford	
XS727	HS125 Dominie T1 [D]	RAF No 3 FTS/55(R) Sqn, Cranwell	
XS728	HS125 Dominie T1 [E]	RAF No 3 FTS/55(R) Sqn, Cranwell	
XS729	HS125 Dominie T1 (9275M) [G]	RAF No 1 SoTT, Cosford	
XS730	HS125 Dominie T1 [H]	RAF No 3 FTS/55(R) Sqn, Cranwell	
XS731	HS125 Dominie T1 [J]	RAF No 3 FTS/55(R) Sqn, Cranwell	
XS733	HS125 Dominie T1 (9276M) [Q]	RAF No 1 SoTT, Cosford	
XS734	HS125 Dominie T1 (9260M) [N]	RAF No 1 SoTT, Cosford	
XS735	HS125 Dominie T1 [R]	RAF Sealand, instructional use	
XS736	HS125 Dominie T1 [S]	RAF No 3 FTS/55(R) Sqn, Cranwell	
XS737	HS125 Dominie T1 [K]	RAF No 3 FTS/55(R) Sqn, Cranwell	
XS738	HS125 Dominie T1 (9274M) [U]	RAF No 1 SoTT, Cosford	
XS739	HS125 Dominie T1 [F]	RAF No 3 FTS/55(R) Sqn, Cranwell	
XS743	Beagle B206Z Basset CC1	DPA/AFD/ETPS, QinetiQ Boscombe Down	
XS765	Beagle B206Z Basset CC1 (G-BSET)	Privately owned, Cranfield	
XS770	Beagle B206Z Basset CC1 (G-HRHI)	Privately owned, Cranfield	
XS790	HS748 Andover CC2 <ff>	Boscombe Down Museum	
XS791	HS748 Andover CC2	Privately owned, Stock, Essex	
XS862	WS58 Wessex HAS3	Privately owned, Hixon, Staffs	
XS863	WS58 Wessex HAS1	Imperial War Museum, Duxford	
XS866	WS58 Wessex HAS1 [520/CU]	RN, Predannack Fire School	
XS868	WS58 Wessex HAS1	RN, Predannack Fire School	
XS870	WS58 Wessex HAS1 [PO]		
XS871	WS58 Wessex HAS1 (8457M) [265]	Privately owned, Chippenham, Wilts	
XS876	WS58 Wessex HAS1 [523/PO]	SFDO, RNAS Culdrose	
XS881	WS58 Wessex HAS1	RN, Predannack Fire School	
XS885	WS58 Wessex HAS1 [512/DD]	SFDO, RNAS Culdrose	
XS886	WS58 Wessex HAS1 [527/CU]	Sea Scouts, Evesham, Worcs	
XS887	WS58 Wessex HAS1 [403/FI]	Flambards Village Theme Park, Helston	
XS888	WS58 Wessex HAS1 [521]	Guernsey Airport Fire Section	
XS897	BAC Lightning F6	Aeroventure, Doncaster	
XS898	BAC Lightning F6 <ff>	Privately owned, Lavendon, Bucks	
XS899	BAC Lightning F6 <ff>	The Cockpit Collection, RAF Coltishall	
XS903	BAC Lightning F6 [BA]	Yorkshire Air Museum, Elvington	
XS904	BAC Lightning F6 [BQ]	Lightning Preservation Grp, Bruntingthorpe	
XS919	BAC Lightning F6	Wonderland Pleasure Park, Farnsfield, Notts	
XS922	BAC Lightning F6 (8973M) <ff>	The Air Defence Collection, Salisbury	
XS923	BAC Lightning F6 <ff>	Privately owned, Welshpool	
XS925	BAC Lightning F6 (8961M) [BA]	RAF Museum, Hendon	
XS928	BAC Lightning F6 [D]	BAE Systems Warton, on display	
XS932	BAC Lightning F6 <ff>	D-Day Museum, Shoreham	
XS933	BAC Lightning F6 <ff>	Privately owned, Terrington St Clement	
XS936	BAC Lightning F6	Castle Motors, Liskeard, Cornwall	
XT108	Agusta-Bell 47G-3 Sioux AH1 [U]	Museum of Army Flying, Middle Wallop	
XT123	WS Sioux AH1 (XT827) [D]	AAC Middle Wallop, at main gate	
XT131	Agusta-Bell 47G-3 Sioux AH1 [B]	AAC Historic Aircraft Flight, Middle Wallop	
XT133	Agusta-Bell 47G-3 Sioux AH1	Royal Engineers' Museum, stored Chattenden	
XT140	Agusta-Bell 47G-3 Sioux AH1	Perth Technical College	
XT141	Agusta-Bell 47G-3 Sioux AH1 (8509M)	Privately owned, Dunkeswell	
XT148	Agusta-Bell 47G-3 Sioux AH1	The Helicopter Museum, stored Weston-super-Mare	
XT150	Agusta-Bell 47G-3 Sioux AH1 (7883M) [R]	AAC Netheravon, at main gate	
XT151	WS Sioux AH1 [W]	Museum of Army Flying, stored Middle Wallop	
XT175	WS Sioux AH1 (TAD175)	Privately owned, Cambs	
XT176	WS Sioux AH1 [U]	FAA Museum, stored Yeovilton	
XT190	WS Sioux AH1	The Helicopter Museum, Weston-super-Mare	

Notes	Serial	Type (other identity) [code]	Owner/operator, location or fate
	XT200	WS Sioux AH1 [F]	Newark Air Museum, Winthorpe
	XT223	WS Sioux AH1 (G-BGZK/G-XTUN)	Privately owned, Sherburn-in-Elmet
	XT236	WS Sioux AH1 (frame only)	North-East Aircraft Museum, stored Usworth
	XT242	WS Sioux AH1 (composite) [12]	Aeroventure, Doncaster
	XT257	WS58 Wessex HAS3 (8719M)	Privately owned, East Grinstead
	XT277	HS Buccaneer S2A (8853M) <ff>	Privately owned, Welshpool
	XT280	HS Buccaneer S2A <ff>	Dundonald Aviation Centre, Strathclyde
	XT284	HS Buccaneer S2A (8855M) <ff>	Privately owned, Felixstowe
	XT288	HS Buccaneer S2B (9134M)	Royal Scottish Museum of Flight, stored E Fortune
	XT420	WS Wasp HAS1 [606]	Privately owned, East Dereham, Norfolk
	XT422	WS Wasp HAS1 [324]	Privately owned, Burgess Hill
	XT427	WS Wasp HAS1 [606]	FAA Museum, stored RNAS Yeovilton
	XT434	WS Wasp HAS1 [455]	DARA Fleetlands Apprentice School
	XT437	WS Wasp HAS1 [423]	Boscombe Down Museum
	XT439	WS Wasp HAS1 [605]	Privately owned, King's Lynn
	XT443	WS Wasp HAS1 [422/AU]	The Helicopter Museum, Weston-super-Mare
	XT453	WS58 Wessex HU5 [A/B]	RN AESS, *HMS Sultan*, Gosport
	XT455	WS58 Wessex HU5 [U]	RN AESS, *HMS Sultan*, Gosport
	XT456	WS58 Wessex HU5 (8941M) [XZ]	RAF Aldergrove, BDRT
	XT458	WS58 Wessex HU5 [622]	RN AESS, *HMS Sultan*, Gosport
	XT460	WS58 Wessex HU5	RN AESS, *HMS Sultan*, Gosport, BDRT
	XT463	WS58 Wessex HC5C (comp XR508) [*Clubs*]	Privately owned, Hixon, Staffs
	XT466	WS58 Wessex HU5 (8921M) [XV]	DARA, Fleetlands
	XT467	WS58 Wessex HU5 (8922M) [BF]	Privately owned, Dunkeswell
	XT468	WS58 Wessex HU5 (comp XT460) [628]	RN, Predannack Fire School
	XT469	WS58 Wessex HU5 (8920M)	RAF No 16 MU, Stafford, ground instruction
	XT472	WS58 Wessex HU5 [XC]	The Helicopter Museum, Weston-super-Mare
	XT474	WS58 Wessex HU5 [820]	RN AESS, *HMS Sultan*, Gosport
	XT480	WS58 Wessex HU5 [468/RG]	DARA, Fleetlands, on display
	XT482	WS58 Wessex HU5 [ZM/VL]	FAA Museum, RNAS Yeovilton
	XT484	WS58 Wessex HU5 [H]	RN AESS, *HMS Sultan*, Gosport
	XT485	WS58 Wessex HU5	RN AESS, *HMS Sultan*, Gosport
	XT575	Vickers Viscount 837 <ff>	Brooklands Museum, Weybridge
	XT595	McD F-4K Phantom FG1 (8851M) <ff>	
	XT596	McD F-4K Phantom FG1	FAA Museum, RNAS Yeovilton
	XT597	McD F-4K Phantom FG1	Boscombe Down Museum
	XT601	WS58 Wessex HC2 (9277M) (composite)	RAF Odiham, BDRT
	XT602	WS58 Wessex HC2	RN AESS, *HMS Sultan*, Gosport, BDRT
	XT604	WS58 Wessex HC2	Privately owned, Colsterworth
	XT606	WS58 Wessex HC2 [WL]	*Sold to New Zealand, August 2001*
	XT607	WS58 Wessex HC2 [P]	RAF, stored Shawbury
	XT617	WS Scout AH1	AAC Wattisham, on display
	XT621	WS Scout AH1	R. Military College of Science, Shrivenham
	XT623	WS Scout AH1	Army SEAE, Arborfield
	XT626	WS Scout AH1 [Q]	AAC Historic Aircraft Flt, Middle Wallop
	XT630	WS Scout AH1 (G-BXRL) [X]	Privately owned, Hinckley, Leics
	XT631	WS Scout AH1 [D]	Privately owned, Ipswich
	XT632	WS Scout AH1 (G-BZBD)	Privately owned, Thruxton (spares use)
	XT633	WS Scout AH1	Army SEAE, Arborfield
	XT634	WS Scout AH1 (G-BYRX) [T]	Privately owned, Humberside
	XT638	WS Scout AH1 [N]	AAC Middle Wallop, at gate
	XT640	WS Scout AH1	Privately owned, Sproughton
	XT643	WS Scout AH1 [Z]	Army, Thorpe Camp, East Wretham
	XT645	WS Scout AH1 (fuselage)	Privately owned, Ipswich
	XT668	WS58 Wessex HC2 [S]	RAF No 72 Sqn, Aldergrove
	XT670	WS58 Wessex HC2	RN AESS, *HMS Sultan*, Gosport, BDRT
	XT671	WS58 Wessex HC2 (G-BYRC) [D]	Privately owned, Redhill
	XT672	WS58 Wessex HC2 [WE]	Privately owned, Hixon, Staffs
	XT676	WS58 Wessex HC2 [I]	RAF No 72 Sqn, Aldergrove
	XT677	WS58 Wessex HC2 (8016M)	*Scrapped at Stock, Essex*
	XT680	WS58 Wessex HC2 [*Diamonds*]	RAF No 84 Sqn, Akrotiri
	XT681	WS58 Wessex HC2 (9279M) [U]	RAF Benson, BDRT
	XT761	WS58 Wessex HU5	RN AESS, *HMS Sultan*, Gosport
	XT762	WS58 Wessex HU5	RN, Predannack Fire School

Serial	Type (other identity) [code]	Owner/operator, location or fate	Notes
XT764	WS58 Wessex HU5 [G]	RN AESS, *HMS Sultan*, Gosport	
XT765	WS58 Wessex HU5 [J]	RN AESS, *HMS Sultan*, Gosport	
XT766	WS58 Wessex HU5 (9054M) [822/CU]	*Scrapped at Gosport, December 2000*	
XT769	WS58 Wessex HU5 [823]	FAA Museum, RNAS Yeovilton	
XT770	WS58 Wessex HU5 (9055M) [P]	Privately owned, Shawell, Leics	
XT771	WS58 Wessex HU5 [620/PO]	RN AESS, *HMS Sultan*, Gosport	
XT772	WS58 Wessex HU5 (8805M)	SARTU RAF Valley, ground instruction	
XT773	WS58 Wessex HU5 (9123M) [822/CU]	DARA, RAF St Athan, BDRT	
XT778	WS Wasp HAS1 [430]	FAA Museum, stored Yeovilton	
XT780	WS Wasp HAS1 [636]	DARA Fleetlands Apprentice School	
XT781	WS Wasp HAS1 (NZ3908/ G-KAWW) [426]	Kennet Aviation, Cranfield	
XT788	WS Wasp HAS1 (G-BMIR) [316] (painted as XT78?)	Privately owned, Dunkeswell	
XT793	WS Wasp HAS1 (G-BZPP) [456]	Privately owned, Thruxton	
XT803	WS Sioux AH1 [Y]	Privately owned, Panshanger	
XT852	McD YF-4M Phantom FGR2	QinetiQ West Freugh Fire Section	
XT863	McD F-4K Phantom FG1 <ff>	Privately owned, Cowes, IOW	
XT864	McD F-4K Phantom FG1 (8998M/ *XT684*) [BJ]	RAF Leuchars on display	
XT867	McD F-4K Phantom FG1 (9064M) [BH]	*Scrapped at Leuchars, April 2001*	
XT891	McD F-4M Phantom FGR2 (9136M) [Z]	RAF Coningsby, at main gate	
XT903	McD F-4M Phantom FGR2 <ff>	RAF Museum Restoration Centre, Cosford	
XT905	McD F-4M Phantom FGR2 [P]	RAF North Luffenham Training Area	
XT907	McD F-4M Phantom FGR2 (9151M) [W]	DEODS, Chattenden, Kent	
XT914	McD F-4M Phantom FGR2	RAF Brampton, Cambs, on display	
XV101	BAC VC10 C1K	RAF No 10 Sqn, Brize Norton	
XV102	BAC VC10 C1K	RAF No 10 Sqn, Brize Norton	
XV103	BAC VC10 C1K	*Scrapped at St Athan, December 2001*	
XV104	BAC VC10 C1K	RAF No 10 Sqn, Brize Norton	
XV105	BAC VC10 C1K	RAF No 10 Sqn, Brize Norton	
XV106	BAC VC10 C1K	DARA, RAF St Athan	
XV107	BAC VC10 C1K	RAF No 10 Sqn, Brize Norton	
XV108	BAC VC10 C1K	RAF No 10 Sqn, Brize Norton	
XV109	BAC VC10 C1K	RAF No 10 Sqn, Brize Norton	
XV118	WS Scout AH1 (9141M)	RAF Air Movements School, Brize Norton	
XV121	WS Scout AH1 (G-BYKJ)	Privately owned, Oaksey Park, Wilts	
XV122	WS Scout AH1 [D]	R. Military College of Science, Shrivenham	
XV123	WS Scout AH1	Privately owned, Ipswich	
XV124	WS Scout AH1 [W]	Army SEAE, Arborfield	
XV126	WS Scout AH1 (G-SCTA) [X]	Privately owned, Thruxton	
XV127	WS Scout AH1	Museum of Army Flying, Middle Wallop	
XV130	WS Scout AH1 (G-BWJW) [R]	Privately owned, Redhill	
XV131	WS Scout AH1 [Y]	AAC 70 Aircraft Workshops, Middle Wallop, BDRT	
XV134	WS Scout AH1 (G-BWLX) [P]	Privately owned, East Dereham, Norfolk	
XV136	WS Scout AH1 [X]	AAC Netheravon, on display	
XV137	WS Scout AH1 (G-CRUM)	Privately owned, Glenrothes	
XV137	WS Scout AH1 (XV139)	Yeovil College	
XV138	WS Scout AH1	Privately owned, East Dereham, Norfolk	
XV139	WS Scout AH1	*Repainted as XV137*	
XV140	WS Scout AH1 (G-KAXL) [K]	Kennet Aviation, Cranfield	
XV141	WS Scout AH1	REME Museum, Arborfield	
XV147	HS Nimrod MR1(mod) (fuselage)	BAE Systems, Warton	
XV148	HS Nimrod MR1(mod) <ff>	Privately owned, Guildford	
XV161	HS Buccaneer S2B (9117M) <ff>	Dundonald Aviation Centre, Strathclyde	
XV165	HS Buccaneer S2B <ff>	Gloucestershire Avn Coll, stored Gloucester	
XV168	HS Buccaneer S2B	BAE Systems Brough, on display	
XV176	Lockheed C-130K Hercules C3	*Returned to LMAC, 4 March 2001*	
XV177	Lockheed C-130K Hercules C3	RAF Lyneham Transport Wing	
XV179	Lockheed C-130K Hercules C1	RAF Lyneham Transport Wing	
XV181	Lockheed C-130K Hercules C1	RAF Lyneham, wfu	
XV183	Lockheed C-130K Hercules C3	RAF Lyneham Transport Wing	
XV184	Lockheed C-130K Hercules C3	RAF Lyneham Transport Wing	
XV185	Lockheed C-130K Hercules C1	*Returned to LMAC, 3 September 2001*	
XV186	Lockheed C-130K Hercules C1	*Returned to LMAC, 10 June 2001*	

Notes	Serial	Type (other identity) [code]	Owner/operator, location or fate
	XV187	Lockheed C-130K Hercules C1	*Returned to LMAC, 28 January 2001*
	XV188	Lockheed C-130K Hercules C3	RAF Lyneham Transport Wing
	XV190	Lockheed C-130K Hercules C3	RAF Lyneham Transport Wing
	XV191	Lockheed C-130K Hercules C1	*Returned to LMAC, 3 September 2001*
	XV192	Lockheed C-130K Hercules C1	*Returned to LMAC, 10 June 2001*
	XV195	Lockheed C-130K Hercules C1	*Returned to LMAC, 28 January 2001*
	XV196	Lockheed C-130K Hercules C1	RAF Lyneham Transport Wing
	XV197	Lockheed C-130K Hercules C3	RAF Lyneham Transport Wing
	XV199	Lockheed C-130K Hercules C3	RAF Lyneham Transport Wing
	XV200	Lockheed C-130K Hercules C1	RAF Lyneham Transport Wing
	XV201	Lockheed C-130K Hercules C1K	RAF, stored Cambridge
	XV202	Lockheed C-130K Hercules C3	RAF Lyneham Transport Wing
	XV205	Lockheed C-130K Hercules C1	RAF Lyneham Transport Wing
	XV206	Lockheed C-130K Hercules C1	RAF Lyneham Transport Wing
	XV208	Lockheed C-130K Hercules W2	DPA/AFD, QinetiQ Boscombe Down
	XV209	Lockheed C-130K Hercules C3	RAF Lyneham Transport Wing
	XV211	Lockheed C-130K Hercules C1	*Returned to LMAC, 10 June 2001*
	XV212	Lockheed C-130K Hercules C3	RAF Lyneham Transport Wing
	XV214	Lockheed C-130K Hercules C3	RAF Lyneham Transport Wing
	XV217	Lockheed C-130K Hercules C3	RAF Lyneham Transport Wing
	XV220	Lockheed C-130K Hercules C3	RAF Lyneham Transport Wing
	XV221	Lockheed C-130K Hercules C3	RAF Lyneham Transport Wing
	XV222	Lockheed C-130K Hercules C3	RAF Lyneham Transport Wing
	XV226	HS Nimrod MR2	RAF Kinloss MR Wing
	XV227	HS Nimrod MR2	RAF Kinloss MR Wing
	XV228	HS Nimrod MR2	RAF Kinloss MR Wing
	XV229	HS Nimrod MR2	RAF Kinloss MR Wing
	XV230	HS Nimrod MR2	RAF Kinloss MR Wing
	XV231	HS Nimrod MR2	RAF Kinloss MR Wing
	XV232	HS Nimrod MR2	RAF Kinloss MR Wing
	XV235	HS Nimrod MR2	RAF Kinloss MR Wing
	XV236	HS Nimrod MR2	RAF No 42(R) Sqn, Kinloss
	XV237	HS Nimrod MR2 <ff>	Privately owned, St Austell
	XV238	HS Nimrod <R> (parts of G-ALYW)	RAF EPTT, St Athan
	XV240	HS Nimrod MR2 [CXX]	RAF No 120 Sqn, Kinloss
	XV241	HS Nimrod MR2	RAF No 206 Sqn, Kinloss
	XV243	HS Nimrod MR2	RAF No 120 Sqn, Kinloss
	XV244	HS Nimrod MR2	RAF Kinloss MR Wing
	XV245	HS Nimrod MR2	RAF No 201 Sqn, Kinloss
	XV246	HS Nimrod MR2	RAF Kinloss MR Wing
	XV248	HS Nimrod MR2	RAF Kinloss MR Wing
	XV249	HS Nimrod R1	RAF No 51 Sqn, Waddington
	XV250	HS Nimrod MR2	RAF Kinloss MR Wing
	XV252	HS Nimrod MR2	RAF No 201 Sqn, Kinloss
	XV253	HS Nimrod MR2 (9118M)	DPA/BAE Systems, Woodford
	XV254	HS Nimrod MR2	RAF Kinloss MR Wing
	XV255	HS Nimrod MR2	RAF Kinloss MR Wing
	XV259	BAe Nimrod AEW3 <ff>	Privately owned, Carlisle
	XV260	HS Nimrod MR2	RAF Kinloss MR Wing
	XV263	BAe Nimrod AEW3P (8967M) <ff>	BAE Systems, Warton, instructional use
	XV263	BAe Nimrod AEW3P (8967M) <rf>	FR Aviation, Bournemouth
	XV268	DHC2 Beaver AL1 (G-BVER)	Privately owned, Lochearnhead
	XV277	HS P.1127(RAF)	Royal Scottish Mus'm of Flight, E Fortune
	XV279	HS P.1127(RAF) (8566M)	RAF Harrier Maintenance School, Wittering
	XV280	HS P.1127(RAF) <ff>	RNAS Yeovilton Fire Section
	XV290	Lockheed C-130K Hercules C3	RAF Lyneham Transport Wing
	XV291	Lockheed C-130K Hercules C1	RAF Lyneham, wfu
	XV292	Lockheed C-130K Hercules C1	RAF Lyneham, wfu
	XV293	Lockheed C-130K Hercules C1	*Returned to LMAC, 4 March 2001*
	XV294	Lockheed C-130K Hercules C3	RAF Lyneham Transport Wing
	XV295	Lockheed C-130K Hercules C1	RAF Lyneham Transport Wing
	XV296	Lockheed C-130K Hercules C1K	RAF, stored Cambridge
	XV297	Lockheed C-130K Hercules C1	*Returned to LMAC, 4 September 2001*
	XV299	Lockheed C-130K Hercules C3	RAF Lyneham Transport Wing
	XV300	Lockheed C-130K Hercules C1	*Returned to LMAC, 28 January 2001*
	XV301	Lockheed C-130K Hercules C3	RAF Lyneham Transport Wing
	XV302	Lockheed C-130K Hercules C3	RAF Lyneham Transport Wing
	XV303	Lockheed C-130K Hercules C3	RAF Lyneham Transport Wing
	XV304	Lockheed C-130K Hercules C3	RAF Lyneham Transport Wing
	XV305	Lockheed C-130K Hercules C3	RAF Lyneham Transport Wing
	XV306	Lockheed C-130K Hercules C1	*Returned to LMAC, 4 March 2001*
	XV307	Lockheed C-130K Hercules C3	RAF Lyneham Transport Wing

Serial	Type (other identity) [code]	Owner/operator, location or fate	Notes
XV328	BAC Lightning T5 <ff>	Phoenix Aviation, Bruntingthorpe	
XV332	HS Buccaneer S2B (9232M)	*Scrapped at Marham, July 2001*	
XV333	HS Buccaneer S2B [234/H]	FAA Museum, RNAS Yeovilton	
XV337	HS Buccaneer S2C (8852M) <ff>	Privately owned, Diseworth, Leics	
XV344	HS Buccaneer S2C	QinetiQ Farnborough, on display	
XV350	HS Buccaneer S2B	East Midlands Airport Aeropark	
XV352	HS Buccaneer S2B <ff>	RAF Manston History Museum	
XV353	HS Buccaneer S2B (9144M) <ff>	Privately owned, Dalkeith	
XV359	HS Buccaneer S2B [035/R]	RNAS Culdrose, on display	
XV361	HS Buccaneer S2B	Ulster Aviation Society, Langford Lodge	
XV370	Sikorsky SH-3D [260]	RN AESS, *HMS Sultan*, Gosport	
XV371	WS61 Sea King HAS1(DB) [261]	RN AESS, *HMS Sultan*, Gosport	
XV372	WS61 Sea King HAS1	RAF St Mawgan, instructional use	
XV399	McD F-4M Phantom FGR2 <ff>	Privately owned,	
XV401	McD F-4M Phantom FGR2 [I]	Boscombe Down Museum	
XV402	McD F-4M Phantom FGR2 <ff>	Robertsbridge Aviation Society, Mayfieldl	
XV406	McD F-4M Phantom FGR2 (9098M) [CK]	Solway Aviation Society, Carlisle Airport	
XV408	McD F-4M Phantom FGR2 (9165M) [Z]	RAF Halton	
XV411	McD F-4M Phantom FGR2 (9103M) [L]	MoD FSCTE, Manston	
XV415	McD F-4M Phantom FGR2 (9163M) [E]	RAF Boulmer, on display	
XV420	McD F-4M Phantom FGR2 (9247M) [BT]	RAF Neatishead, at main gate	
XV423	McD F-4M Phantom FGR2 [Y]	*Scrapped at Leeming, 19 July 2001*	
XV424	McD F-4M Phantom FGR2 (9152M) [I]	RAF Museum, Hendon	
XV426	McD F-4M Phantom FGR2 <ff>	The Cockpit Collection, RAF Coltishall	
XV426	McD F-4M Phantom FGR2 [P] <rf>	RAF Coningsby, BDRT	
XV435	McD F-4M Phantom FGR2 [R]	QinetiQ Llanbedr Fire Section	
XV460	McD F-4M Phantom FGR2 <ff>	No 2214 Sqn ATC, Usworth	
XV465	McD F-4M Phantom FGR2 [S]	*Scrapped at Leeming, 19 July 2001*	
XV468	McD F-4M Phantom FGR2 (9159M) [H]	*Scrapped at Woodvale, July 2001*	
XV474	McD F-4M Phantom FGR2 [T]	The Old Flying Machine Company, Duxford	
XV490	McD F-4M Phantom FGR2 <ff>	Privately owned, Nantwich	
XV497	McD F-4M Phantom FGR2 [W]	RAF Coningsby, decoy	
XV498	McD F-4M Phantom FGR2 (XV500/9113M) [U]	RAF St Athan, on display	
XV499	McD F-4M Phantom FGR2	RAF Leeming, WLT	
XV577	McD F-4K Phantom FG1 (9065M) [AM]	*Scrapped at Leuchars, April 2001*	
XV581	McD F-4K Phantom FG1 (9070M) <ff>	No 2481 Sqn ATC, Bridge of Don	
XV582	McD F-4K Phantom FG1 (9066M) [M]	RAF Leuchars, on display	
XV586	McD F-4K Phantom FG1 (9067M) [AJ]	RAF Leuchars, on display	
XV591	McD F-4K Phantom FG1 <ff>	RAF Museum, Cosford	
XV625	WS Wasp HAS1 [471]	RN, stored *HMS Sultan*, Gosport	
XV629	WS Wasp HAS1	AAC Middle Wallop, BDRT	
XV631	WS Wasp HAS1 (fuselage)	QinetiQ Acoustics Dept, Farnborough	
XV642	WS61 Sea King HAS2A [259]	RN AESS, *HMS Sultan*, Gosport	
XV643	WS61 Sea King HAS6 [262]	RN AESS, *HMS Sultan*, Gosport	
XV647	WS61 Sea King HU5 [707]	RN No 771 Sqn, Prestwick	
XV648	WS61 Sea King HU5 [708/PW]	DARA, RNAY Fleetlands	
XV649	WS61 Sea King AEW7 [182/CU]	RN AMG, Culdrose (conversion)	
XV650	WS61 Sea King AEW2 [181/CU]	RN AMG, Culdrose	
XV651	WS61 Sea King HU5 [599/CU]	RN, stored DARA Fleetlands	
XV653	WS61 Sea King HAS6 [513/CU]	RN, stored *HMS Sultan*, Gosport	
XV654	WS61 Sea King HAS6 [705] (wreck)	RN AESS, *HMS Sultan*, Gosport	
XV655	WS61 Sea King HAS6 [270/N]	RN, stored *HMS Sultan*, Gosport	
XV656	WS61 Sea King AEW2 [187/N]	RN No 849 Sqn, A Flt, Culdrose	
XV657	WS61 Sea King HAS5 (*ZA135*) [32/DD]	SFDO, RNAS Culdrose	
XV659	WS61 Sea King HAS6 [510/CU]	RN, stored *HMS Sultan*, Gosport	
XV660	WS61 Sea King HAS6 [69]	RN, stored *HMS Sultan*, Gosport	
XV661	WS61 Sea King HU5 [821]	RN No 771 Sqn, Culdrose	
XV663	WS61 Sea King HAS6	RN, stored *HMS Sultan*, Gosport	

Notes	Serial	Type (other identity) [code]	Owner/operator, location or fate
	XV664	WS61 Sea King AEW2 [186/N]	RN No 849 Sqn, A Flt, Culdrose
	XV665	WS61 Sea King HAS6 [507/CU]	RN, stored *HMS Sultan*, Gosport
	XV666	WS61 Sea King HU5 [823]	RN No 771 Sqn, Culdrose
	XV669	WS61 Sea King HAS1 [10]	Privately owned, Gosport
	XV670	WS61 Sea King HU5 [588]	RN, stored DARA Fleetlands
	XV671	WS61 Sea King AEW2 [181/N]	RN No 849 Sqn, HQ Flt, Culdrose
	XV672	WS61 Sea King AEW2 [182/L]	DPA/AFD Qinetiq, Boscombe Down
	XV673	WS61 Sea King HU5 [597]	RN, stored DARA, Fleetlands
	XV674	WS61 Sea King HAS6 [015/L]	RN No 820 Sqn, Culdrose
	XV675	WS61 Sea King HAS6 [701/PW]	RN, stored *HMS Sultan*, Gosport
	XV676	WS61 Sea King HAS6 [506]	RN No 771 Sqn, Culdrose
	XV677	WS61 Sea King HAS6 [269]	RN, stored *HMS Sultan*, Gosport
	XV696	WS61 Sea King HAS6 [267/N]	RN, stored *HMS Sultan*, Gosport
	XV697	WS61 Sea King AEW2 [185]	RN No 849 Sqn, B Flt, Culdrose
	XV699	WS61 Sea King HU5 [708]	RN
	XV700	WS61 Sea King HAS6 [005/CU]	RN/DARA, Fleetlands for HC4 conversion
	XV701	WS61 Sea King HAS6 [268/N]	RN, stored *HMS Sultan*, Gosport
	XV703	WS61 Sea King HAS6 [PW]	RN
	XV704	WS61 Sea King AEW7 [181/CU]	RN AMG, Culdrose (conversion)
	XV705	WS61 Sea King HU5 [821/CU]	RN, stored *HMS Sultan*, Gosport
	XV706	WS61 Sea King HAS6 [011/L]	RN No 820 Sqn, Culdrose
	XV707	WS61 Sea King AEW7	DPA/AFD/Qinetiq, Boscombe Down)
	XV708	WS61 Sea King HAS6 [501/CU]	RN, stored *HMS Sultan*, Gosport
	XV709	WS61 Sea King HAS6 [263]	RAF St Mawgan for ground instruction
	XV710	WS61 Sea King HAS6 [264]	RN AESS, *HMS Sultan*, Gosport
	XV711	WS61 Sea King HAS6 [515/CT]	RN No 810 Sqn, B Flt, Culdrose
	XV712	WS61 Sea King HAS6 [269]	RN AESS, *HMS Sultan*, Gosport
	XV713	WS61 Sea King HAS6 [018]	RN, stored *HMS Sultan*, Gosport
	XV714	WS61 Sea King AEW2 [180]	RN No 849 Sqn, HQ Flt, Culdrose
	XV720	WS58 Wessex HC2	RN AESS, *HMS Sultan*, Gosport
	XV721	WS58 Wessex HC2 [H]	RAF No 72 Sqn, Aldergrove
	XV722	WS58 Wessex HC2 [WH]	Privately owned, Hixon, Staffs
	XV723	WS58 Wessex HC2 [Q]	RAF Shawbury, instructional use
	XV724	WS58 Wessex HC2	RN AESS, *HMS Sultan*, Gosport
	XV725	WS58 Wessex HC2 [C]	RN AESS, *HMS Sultan*, Gosport
	XV726	WS58 Wessex HC2 [J]	RAF No 72 Sqn, Aldergrove
	XV728	WS58 Wessex HC2 [A]	Newark Air Museum, Winthorpe
	XV729	WS58 Wessex HC2 (G-HANA)	Privately owned, Redhill
	XV730	WS58 Wessex HC2 [*Clubs*]	RAF No 84 Sqn, Akrotiri
	XV731	WS58 Wessex HC2 [Y]	Privately owned, Redhill
	XV732	WS58 Wessex HCC4	RAF, stored Shawbury
	XV733	WS58 Wessex HCC4	The Helicopter Museum, Weston-super-Mare
	XV741	HS Harrier GR3 [41]	SFDO, RNAS Culdrose
	XV744	HS Harrier GR3 (9167M) [3K]	R. Military College of Science, Shrivenham
	XV748	HS Harrier GR3 [3D]	Yorkshire Air Museum, Elvington
	XV751	HS Harrier GR3	Privately owned, Bruntingthorpe
	XV752	HS Harrier GR3 (9078M) [B,HF]	RAF No 1 SoTT, Cosford
	XV753	HS Harrier GR3 (9075M) [53]	SFDO, RNAS Culdrose
	XV755	HS Harrier GR3 [M]	RNAS Yeovilton Fire Section
	XV759	HS Harrier GR3 [O] <ff>	Privately owned, Luton, Beds
	XV779	HS Harrier GR3 (8931M)	RAF Wittering on display
	XV783	HS Harrier GR3 [83]	SFDO, RNAS Culdrose
	XV784	HS Harrier GR3 (8909M) <ff>	Boscombe Down Museum
	XV786	HS Harrier GR3 <ff>	RNAS Culdrose
	XV786	HS Harrier GR3 [S] <rf>	RN, Predannack Fire School
	XV798	HS Harrier GR1(mod)	Bristol Aero Collection, stored Kemble
	XV804	HS Harrier GR3 (9280M) [O]	RAF North Luffenham Training Area
	XV808	HS Harrier GR3 (9076M) [08]	SFDO, RNAS Culdrose
	XV810	HS Harrier GR3 (9038M) [K]	Privately owned, Bruntingthorpe
	XV814	DH106 Comet 4 (G-APDF) <ff>	Privately owned, Chipping Campden
	XV863	HS Buccaneer S2B (9115M/ 9139M/9145M) [S]	RAF Lossiemouth
	XV864	HS Buccaneer S2B (9234M)	MoD FSCTE, Manston
	XV865	HS Buccaneer S2B (9226M)	Privately owned, Duxford
	XV867	HS Buccaneer S2B <ff>	N Yorks Aircraft Recovery Centre, Chop Gate
	XW175	HS Harrier T4(VAAC)	DPA/AFD, QinetiQ Boscombe Down
	XW198	WS Puma HC1	RAF No 230 Sqn, Aldergrove
	XW199	WS Puma HC1	RAF No 33 Sqn, Benson
	XW200	WS Puma HC1 (wreck)	RAF, stored Shawbury
	XW201	WS Puma HC1	RAF No 230 Sqn, Aldergrove

Serial	Type (other identity) [code]	Owner/operator, location or fate	Notes
XW202	WS Puma HC1	RAF No 33 Sqn, Benson	
XW204	WS Puma HC1	RAF No 72 Sqn, Aldergrove	
XW206	WS Puma HC1	RAF No 230 Sqn, Aldergrove	
XW207	WS Puma HC1	RAF Benson (spares use)	
XW208	WS Puma HC1	RAF No 33 Sqn, Benson	
XW209	WS Puma HC1	RAF No 72 Sqn, Aldergrove	
XW210	WS Puma HC1 (comp XW215)	RAF No 230 Sqn, Aldergrove	
XW211	WS Puma HC1	RAF No 33 Sqn, Benson	
XW212	WS Puma HC1	RAF No 230 Sqn, Aldergrove	
XW213	WS Puma HC1	RAF No 230 Sqn, Aldergrove	
XW214	WS Puma HC1	RAF No 230 Sqn, Aldergrove	
XW216	WS Puma HC1	DPA/Westland Helicopters, Weston-super-Mare	
XW217	WS Puma HC1	RAF No 33 Sqn, Benson	
XW218	WS Puma HC1	RAF No 33 Sqn, Benson	
XW219	WS Puma HC1	RAF No 33 Sqn, Benson	
XW220	WS Puma HC1	RAF No 230 Sqn, Aldergrove	
XW221	WS Puma HC1	RAF No 33 Sqn, Benson	
XW222	WS Puma HC1	RAF No 33 Sqn, Benson	
XW223	WS Puma HC1	RAF No 33 Sqn, Benson	
XW224	WS Puma HC1	RAF No 230 Sqn, Aldergrove	
XW225	WS Puma HC1	RAF Benson, spares use	
XW226	WS Puma HC1	RAF No 33 Sqn, Benson	
XW227	WS Puma HC1	RAF No 72 Sqn, Aldergrove	
XW229	WS Puma HC1	RAF No 33 Sqn, Benson	
XW231	WS Puma HC1	RAF No 230 Sqn, Aldergrove	
XW232	WS Puma HC1	RAF No 33 Sqn, Benson	
XW234	WS Puma HC1	RAF No 230 Sqn, Aldergrove	
XW235	WS Puma HC1	RAF No 33 Sqn, Benson	
XW236	WS Puma HC1	RAF No 230 Sqn, Aldergrove	
XW237	WS Puma HC1	RAF No 72 Sqn, Aldergrove	
XW241	Sud SA330E Puma	QinetiQ Avionics & Sensors Dept, Farnborough	
XW264	HS Harrier T2 <ff>	Jet Age Museum, Staverton	
XW265	HS Harrier T4A [W]	RAF No 1 SoTT, Cosford	
XW267	HS Harrier T4 [SA]	Territorial Army, Beeston, Notts	
XW269	HS Harrier T4	QinetiQ Boscombe Down, BDRT	
XW270	HS Harrier T4 (fuselage)	Phoenix Aviation, Bruntingthorpe	
XW271	HS Harrier T4 [71]	SFDO, RNAS Culdrose	
XW272	HS Harrier T4 (8783M) (fuselage) (comp XV281)	Marsh Lane Technical School, Preston	
XW276	Aérospatiale SA341 Gazelle (F-ZWRI)	Newark Air Museum, Winthorpe	
XW281	WS Scout AH1 (G-BYNZ) [U]	Privately owned, Thruxton (wreck)	
XW283	WS Scout AH1 [U]	RM, stored Yeovilton	
XW284	WS Scout AH1 [A] (fuselage)	Privately owned, Ipswich	
XW289	BAC Jet Provost T5A (G-BVXT/ G-JPVA) [73]	Kennet Aviation, Cranfield	
XW290	BAC Jet Provost T5A (9199M) [41,MA]	RAF No 1 SoTT, Cosford	
XW292	BAC Jet Provost T5A (9128M) [32]	RAF No 1 SoTT, Cosford	
XW293	BAC Jet Provost T5 (G-BWCS) [Z]	Privately owned, Sandtoft	
XW294	BAC Jet Provost T5A (9129M) [45]	RAF No 1 SoTT, Cosford	
XW299	BAC Jet Provost T5A (9146M) [60,MB]	RAF No 1 SoTT, Cosford	
XW301	BAC Jet Provost T5A (9147M) [63,MC]	RAF No 1 SoTT, Cosford	
XW303	BAC Jet Provost T5A (9119M) [127]	RAF No 1 SoTT, Cosford	
XW304	BAC Jet Provost T5 (9172M) [MD]	RAF No 1 SoTT, Cosford	
XW309	BAC Jet Provost T5 (9179M) [V,ME]	RAF No 1 SoTT, Cosford	
XW311	BAC Jet Provost T5 (9180M) [W,MF]	RAF No 1 SoTT, Cosford	
XW312	BAC Jet Provost T5A (9109M) [64]	RAF No 1 SoTT, Cosford	
XW315	BAC Jet Provost T5A <ff>	Privately owned, Wolverhampton	
XW318	BAC Jet Provost T5A (9190M) [78,MG]	RAF No 1 SoTT, Cosford	
XW320	BAC Jet Provost T5A (9015M) [71]	RAF No 1 SoTT, Cosford	
XW321	BAC Jet Provost T5A (9154M) [62,MH]	RAF No 1 SoTT, Cosford	
XW323	BAC Jet Provost T5A (9166M) [86]	RAF Museum, Hendon	
XW324	BAC Jet Provost T5 (G-BWSG)	Privately owned, North Weald	

Notes	Serial	Type (other identity) [code]	Owner/operator, location or fate
	XW325	BAC Jet Provost T5B (G-BWGF) [E]	Privately owned, Woodford
	XW327	BAC Jet Provost T5A (9130M) [62]	RAF No 1 SoTT, Cosford
	XW328	BAC Jet Provost T5A (9177M) [75,MI]	RAF No 1 SoTT, Cosford
	XW330	BAC Jet Provost T5A (9195M) [82,MJ]	RAF No 1 SoTT, Cosford
	XW333	BAC Jet Provost T5A (G-BVTC)	Global Aviation, Humberside
	XW335	BAC Jet Provost T5A (9061M) [74]	RAF No 1 SoTT, Cosford
	XW351	BAC Jet Provost T5A (9062M) [31]	RAF No 1 SoTT, Cosford
	XW353	BAC Jet Provost T5A (9090M) [3]	RAF Cranwell, on display
	XW358	BAC Jet Provost T5A (9181M) [59,MK]	RAF No 1 SoTT, Cosford
	XW360	BAC Jet Provost T5A (9153M) [61,ML]	RAF No 1 SoTT, Cosford
	XW361	BAC Jet Provost T5A (9192M) [81,MM]	RAF No 1 SoTT, Cosford
	XW363	BAC Jet Provost T5A [36]	BAE Systems North West Heritage Group, Warton
	XW364	BAC Jet Provost T5A (9188M) [35,MN]	RAF No 1 SoTT, Cosford
	XW365	BAC Jet Provost T5A (9018M) [73]	RAF No 1 SoTT, Cosford
	XW366	BAC Jet Provost T5A (9097M) [75]	RAF No 1 SoTT, Cosford
	XW367	BAC Jet Provost T5A (9193M) [64,MO]	RAF No 1 SoTT, Cosford
	XW370	BAC Jet Provost T5A (9196M) [72,MP]	RAF No 1 SoTT, Cosford
	XW375	BAC Jet Provost T5A (9149M) [52]	RAF No 1 SoTT, Cosford
	XW404	BAC Jet Provost T5A (9049M)	DARA Training School, RAF St Athan
	XW405	BAC Jet Provost T5A (9187M) [J,MQ]	RAF No 1 SoTT, Cosford
	XW409	BAC Jet Provost T5A (9047M)	DARA Training School, RAF St Athan
	XW410	BAC Jet Provost T5A (9125M) [80,MR]	RAF No 1 SoTT, Cosford
	XW413	BAC Jet Provost T5A (9126M) [69]	RAF No 1 SoTT, Cosford
	XW416	BAC Jet Provost T5A (9191M) [84,MS]	RAF No 1 SoTT, Cosford
	XW418	BAC Jet Provost T5A (9173M) [MT]	RAF No 1 SoTT, Cosford
	XW419	BAC Jet Provost T5A (9120M) [125]	RAF No 1 SoTT, Cosford
	XW420	BAC Jet Provost T5A (9194M) [83,MU]	RAF No 1 SoTT, Cosford
	XW421	BAC Jet Provost T5A (9111M) [60]	RAF No 1 SoTT, Cosford
	XW423	BAC Jet Provost T5A (G-BWUW) [14]	Privately owned, Little Snoring
	XW425	BAC Jet Provost T5A (9200M) [H,MV]	RAF No 1 SoTT, Cosford
	XW427	BAC Jet Provost T5A (9124M) [67]	RAF No 1 SoTT, Cosford
	XW430	BAC Jet Provost T5A (9176M) [77,MW]	RAF No 1 SoTT, Cosford
	XW432	BAC Jet Provost T5A (9127M) [76,MX]	RAF No 1 SoTT, Cosford
	XW433	BAC Jet Provost T5A (G-JPRO)	Global Aviation, Humberside
	XW434	BAC Jet Provost T5A (9091M) [78,MY]	RAF No 1 SoTT, Cosford
	XW436	BAC Jet Provost T5A (9148M) [68]	RAF No 1 SoTT, Cosford
	XW527	HS Buccaneer S2B <ff>	Privately owned, Wittering
	XW528	HS Buccaneer S2B (8861M) [C]	RAF Coningsby Fire Section
	XW530	HS Buccaneer S2B	Buccaneer Service Station, Elgin
	XW544	HS Buccaneer S2B (8857M) [Y]	Privately owned, Kemble
	XW547	HS Buccaneer S2B (9095M/ 9169M) [R]	RAF Museum, Cosford
	XW549	HS Buccaneer S2B (8860M) (fuselage)	Scrapped at Kinloss
	XW550	HS Buccaneer S2B <ff>	Privately owned, West Horndon, Essex
	XW563	SEPECAT Jaguar S (XX822/ 8563M)	RAF Coltishall, on display
	XW566	SEPECAT Jaguar B	QinetiQ Avionics & Sensors Dept, Farnborough
	XW613	WS Scout AH1 (G-BXRS) [W]	Privately owned, Thruxton
	XW616	WS Scout AH1	AAC Dishforth, instructional use
	XW630	HS Harrier GR3	RNAS Yeovilton, Fire Section
	XW635	Beagle D5/180 (G-AWSW)	Privately owned, Spanhoe Lodge

Serial	Type (other identity) [code]	Owner/operator, location or fate	Notes
XW664	HS Nimrod R1	RAF No 51 Sqn, Waddington	
XW665	HS Nimrod R1	RAF No 51 Sqn, Waddington	
XW666	HS Nimrod R1 <ff>	Aeroventure, Doncaster	
XW750	HS748 Series 107	DPA/AFD, QinetiQ Boscombe Down	
XW763	HS Harrier GR3 (9002M/9041M) <ff>	Privately owned, Bruntingthorpe	
XW768	HS Harrier GR3 (9072M) [N]	RAF No 1 SoTT, Cosford	
XW784	Mitchell-Procter Kittiwake I (G-BBRN) [VL]	Privately owned, Compton Abbas	
XW795	WS Scout AH1	Blessingbourne Museum, Fivemiletown, Co Tyrone, NI	
XW796	WS Scout AH1	Privately owned, Sproughton	
XW835	WS Lynx	AAC Wattisham, instructional use	
XW837	WS Lynx (fuselage)	*Scrapped at Yeovilton, 2000*	
XW838	WS Lynx (TAD 009)	Army SEAE, Arborfield	
XW839	WS Lynx	The Helicopter Museum, Weston-super-Mare	
XW844	WS Gazelle AH1	DARA Fleetlands Apprentice School	
XW845	WS Gazelle HT2 (47/CU)	RN, stored Shawbury	
XW846	WS Gazelle AH1 [M]	AAC No 671 Sqn/2 Regt, Middle Wallop	
XW847	WS Gazelle AH1 [H]	RM No 847 Sqn, Yeovilton	
XW848	WS Gazelle AH1 [D]	AAC No 671 Sqn/2 Regt, Middle Wallop	
XW849	WS Gazelle AH1 [G]	RM No 847 Sqn, Yeovilton	
XW851	WS Gazelle AH1	RM No 847 Sqn, Yeovilton	
XW852	WS Gazelle HCC4	RAF, stored Shawbury	
XW853	WS Gazelle HT2 (53/CU)	Privately owned, Somerset	
XW854	WS Gazelle HT2 (46/CU)	RN, stored Shawbury	
XW855	WS Gazelle HCC4	RAF, stored Shawbury	
XW856	WS Gazelle HT2 (G-CBBY) [49/CU]	Privately owned, Truro	
XW857	WS Gazelle HT2 (55/CU)	RN, stored Shawbury	
XW858	WS Gazelle HT3 (G-DMSS) [C]	Privately owned, Kirkham, Lincs	
XW860	WS Gazelle HT2 (TAD021)	Army SEAE, Arborfield	
XW861	WS Gazelle HT2 (G-BZFJ) [52/CU]	Privately owned, Ford, W Sussex	
XW862	WS Gazelle HT3 [D]	Privately owned, Stapleford Tawney	
XW863	WS Gazelle HT2 (TAD022) [42/CU]	Army SEAE, Arborfield	
XW864	WS Gazelle HT2 (54/CU)	RN, stored Shawbury	
XW865	WS Gazelle AH1 [5C]	AAC No 29 Flt, BATUS, Suffield, Canada	
XW866	WS Gazelle HT3 (G-BXTH) [E]	Flightline Ltd, Southend	
XW868	WS Gazelle HT2 (50/CU)	Privately owned, Stapleford Tawney	
XW870	WS Gazelle HT3 [F]	MoD FSCTE, Manston	
XW871	WS Gazelle HT2 (44/CU)	RN, stored Shawbury	
XW884	WS Gazelle HT2 (G-BZDV) [41/CU]	*Sold as 3D-HXL, June 2001*	
XW885	WS Gazelle AH1	Privately owned, Thruxton	
XW887	WS Gazelle HT2 (G-CBFD) [FL]	Privately owned, Hungerford	
XW888	WS Gazelle AH1 (TAD017)	Army SEAE, Arborfield	
XW889	WS Gazelle AH1 (TAD018)	Army SEAE, Arborfield	
XW890	WS Gazelle HT2	RNAS Yeovilton, on display	
XW892	WS Gazelle AH1 [C]	AAC, stored Shawbury	
XW893	WS Gazelle AH1 <ff>	Privately owned, Wellington, Somerset	
XW894	WS Gazelle HT2 (G-BZOS) [37/CU]	*Repainted as G-BZOS by October 2001*	
XW895	WS Gazelle HT2 (G-BXZD) [51/CU]	Privately owned, Barnard Castle	
XW897	WS Gazelle AH1 [Y]	AAC No 658 Sqn/7 Regt, Netheravon	
XW898	WS Gazelle HT3 [G]	Privately owned, Goodwood	
XW899	WS Gazelle AH1 [Z]	AAC No 658 Sqn/7 Regt, Netheravon	
XW900	WS Gazelle AH1 (TAD900)	Army SEAE, Arborfield	
XW902	WS Gazelle HT3 [H]	Qinetiq spares use, Boscombe Down	
XW903	WS Gazelle AH1 (G-BZYC)	Privately owned, Hungerford	
XW904	WS Gazelle AH1 [H]	AAC No 666(V) Sqn/7 Regt, Netheravon	
XW906	WS Gazelle HT3 [J]	QinetiQ Boscombe Down, Apprentice School	
XW907	WS Gazelle HT2 (G-BZOT) [48/CU]	Privately owned, Truro	
XW908	WS Gazelle AH1 [A]	AAC No 666(V) Sqn/7 Regt, Netheravon	
XW909	WS Gazelle AH1	AAC No 656 Sqn/9 Regt, Dishforth	
XW910	WS Gazelle HT3 (G-BXZE) [K]	Privately owned, Selsey, W Sussex	
XW911	WS Gazelle AH1 [H]	*Sold as N911XW, May 2001*	
XW912	WS Gazelle AH1 (TAD019)	Army SEAE, Arborfield	

Notes	Serial	Type (other identity) [code]	Owner/operator, location or fate
	XW913	WS Gazelle AH1	AAC No 662 Sqn/3 Regt, Wattisham
	XW917	HS Harrier GR3 (8975M)	RAF Cottesmore, at main gate
	XW919	HS Harrier GR3 [W]	R. Military College of Science, Shrivenham
	XW922	HS Harrier GR3 (8885M)	MoD FSCTE, Manston
	XW923	HS Harrier GR3 (8724M) <ff>	RAF Wittering, Fire Section
	XW924	HS Harrier GR3 (9073M) [G]	RAF Cottesmore, preserved
	XW934	HS Harrier T4 [Y]	DPA, QinetiQ Farnborough (wfu)
	XW986	HS Buccaneer S2B	*Sold to South Africa, 2001*
	XX105	BAC 1-11/201AC (G-ASJD)	DPA/AFD, QinetiQ Boscombe Down
	XX108	SEPECAT Jaguar GR3	DPA/BAE Systems, Warton
	XX109	SEPECAT Jaguar GR1 (8918M) [US]	RAF Coltishall, ground instruction
	XX110	SEPECAT Jaguar GR1 (8955M) [EP]	RAF No 1 SoTT, Cosford
	XX110	SEPECAT Jaguar GR1 <R> (BAPC 169)	RAF No 1 SoTT, Cosford
	XX112	SEPECAT Jaguar GR3A [EA]	RAF No 6 Sqn, Coltishall
	XX115	SEPECAT Jaguar GR1 (8821M) (fuselage)	RAF No 1 SoTT, Cosford
	XX116	SEPECAT Jaguar GR3A [EO]	DPA/AFD, QinetiQ Boscombe Down
	XX117	SEPECAT Jaguar GR3 [PA]	RAF No 16(R) Sqn, Coltishall
	XX119	SEPECAT Jaguar GR3A (8898M) [GD]	RAF No 54 Sqn, Coltishall
	XX121	SEPECAT Jaguar GR1 [EQ]	Privately owned, Charlwood, Surrey
	XX139	SEPECAT Jaguar T4	RAF No 16(R) Sqn, Coltishall
	XX140	SEPECAT Jaguar T2 (9008M) [D,JJ]	Privately owned, Charlwood, Surrey
	XX141	SEPECAT Jaguar T2A [T]	AMIF, RAFC Cranwell
	XX143	SEPECAT Jaguar T2B [X] (wreck)	*Scrapped at Charlwood*
	XX144	SEPECAT Jaguar T2A [U]	RAF, stored Shawbury
	XX145	SEPECAT Jaguar T2A	DPA/AFD/ETPS, QinetiQ Boscombe Down
	XX146	SEPECAT Jaguar T4 [GT]	RAF No 54 Sqn, Coltishall
	XX150	SEPECAT Jaguar T4 [PW]	RAF No 16(R) Sqn, Coltishall
	XX153	WS Lynx AH1	AAC Wattisham, instructional use
	XX154	HS Hawk T1	DPA/AFD/ETPS, QinetiQ Boscombe Down
	XX156	HS Hawk T1	RAF No 4 FTS/*208(R) Sqn*, Valley
	XX157	HS Hawk T1A	RN FRADU, Culdrose
	XX158	HS Hawk T1A	RAF No 4 FTS/*19(R) Sqn*, Valley
	XX159	HS Hawk T1A	DARA, RAF St Athan
	XX160	HS Hawk T1 [CP]	RAF No 100 Sqn, Leeming
	XX161	HS Hawk T1W	RAF No 4 FTS/*208(R) Sqn*, Valley
	XX162	HS Hawk T1	RAF Aviation Medicine Flt, Boscombe Down
	XX163	HS Hawk T1 (9243M) [PH] (wreck)	*Scrapped at Faygate*
	XX165	HS Hawk T1	RAF No 4 FTS/*208(R) Sqn*, Valley
	XX167	HS Hawk T1W	RN FRADU, Culdrose
	XX168	HS Hawk T1	RAF No 4 FTS/*208(R) Sqn*, Valley
	XX169	HS Hawk T1	RAF No 4 FTS/*208(R) Sqn*, Valley
	XX170	HS Hawk T1	RN FRADU, Culdrose
	XX171	HS Hawk T1	RN FRADU, Culdrose
	XX172	HS Hawk T1	RAF No 4 FTS/*208(R) Sqn*, Valley
	XX173	HS Hawk T1	RAF No 4 FTS/*208(R) Sqn*, Valley
	XX174	HS Hawk T1	RAF No 4 FTS/*208(R) Sqn*, Valley
	XX175	HS Hawk T1	RAF No 4 FTS/*208(R) Sqn*, Valley
	XX176	HS Hawk T1W	RAF No 4 FTS/*19(R) Sqn*, Valley
	XX177	HS Hawk T1	RAF No 4 FTS/*208(R) Sqn*, Valley
	XX178	HS Hawk T1W	RAF No 4 FTS/*19(R) Sqn*, Valley
	XX179	HS Hawk T1W	RAF No 4 FTS, Valley
	XX181	HS Hawk T1W	RAF No 4 FTS/*208(R) Sqn*, Valley
	XX183	HS Hawk T1	RAF No 4 FTS/*208(R) Sqn*, Valley
	XX184	HS Hawk T1	RAF No 4 FTS/*19(R) Sqn*, Valley
	XX185	HS Hawk T1	RAF No 4 FTS/*208(R) Sqn*, Valley
	XX187	HS Hawk T1A	RN FRADU, Culdrose
	XX188	HS Hawk T1A	RAF No 4 FTS, Valley
	XX189	HS Hawk T1A	RAF No 4 FTS/*19(R) Sqn*, Valley
	XX190	HS Hawk T1A	DPA/BAE Systems, Warton
	XX191	HS Hawk T1A	RAF No 4 FTS/*19(R) Sqn*, Valley
	XX194	HS Hawk T1A [CO]	RAF No 100 Sqn/JFACSTU, Leeming
	XX195	HS Hawk T1W	RAF No 4 FTS/*208(R) Sqn*, Valley
	XX196	HS Hawk T1A	DARA, RAF St Athan
	XX198	HS Hawk T1A	RAF No 4 FTS/*208(R) Sqn*, Valley
	XX199	HS Hawk T1A	RAF No 4 FTS/*19(R) Sqn*, Valley
	XX200	HS Hawk T1A [CF]	RAF No 100 Sqn, Leeming

Serial	Type (other identity) [code]	Owner/operator, location or fate	Notes
XX201	HS Hawk T1A	RN FRADU, Culdrose	
XX202	HS Hawk T1A	RAF No 4 FTS/*19(R) Sqn*, Valley	
XX203	HS Hawk T1A	RAF No 4 FTS, Valley	
XX204	HS Hawk T1A	RAF No 4 FTS/*208(R) Sqn*, Valley	
XX205	HS Hawk T1A	DPA/BAE Systems, Warton	
XX217	HS Hawk T1A [CC]	RAF No 100 Sqn, Leeming	
XX218	HS Hawk T1A	RAF No 4 FTS/*19(R) Sqn*, Valley	
XX219	HS Hawk T1A	RAF No 4 FTS/*208(R) Sqn*, Valley	
XX220	HS Hawk T1A	DARA, RAF St Athan	
XX221	HS Hawk T1A	RAF No 4 FTS, Valley	
XX222	HS Hawk T1A [CA]	RAF No 100 Sqn, Leeming	
XX223	HS Hawk T1 <ff>	Privately owned, Charlwood, Surrey	
XX224	HS Hawk T1W	RN FRADU, Culdrose	
XX225	HS Hawk T1	RAF No 4 FTS/*208(R) Sqn*, Valley	
XX226	HS Hawk T1 [CR]	RAF No 100 Sqn, Leeming	
XX226	HS Hawk T1 <R> (*XX263*/ BAPC 152)	RAF EPTT, St Athan	
XX227	HS Hawk T1A	RAF *Red Arrows*, Scampton	
XX228	HS Hawk T1A [CG]	DARA, RAF St Athan	
XX230	HS Hawk T1A	RN FRADU, Culdrose	
XX231	HS Hawk T1W	RN FRADU, Culdrose	
XX232	HS Hawk T1	RAF No 4 FTS/*208(R) Sqn*, Valley	
XX233	HS Hawk T1	RAF *Red Arrows*, Scampton	
XX234	HS Hawk T1	RN FRADU, Culdrose	
XX235	HS Hawk T1W	RAF No 4 FTS/*208(R) Sqn*, Valley	
XX236	HS Hawk T1W	RAF No 4 FTS, Valley	
XX237	HS Hawk T1	RAF *Red Arrows*, Scampton	
XX238	HS Hawk T1	RAF No 4 FTS/*19(R) Sqn*, Valley	
XX239	HS Hawk T1W	RAF No 4 FTS/*19(R) Sqn*, Valley	
XX240	HS Hawk T1	RN FRADU, Culdrose	
XX242	HS Hawk T1	RAF No 4 FTS, Valley	
XX244	HS Hawk T1	RAF No 4 FTS/*208(R) Sqn*, Valley	
XX245	HS Hawk T1	RAF No 4 FTS/*208(R) Sqn*, Valley	
XX246	HS Hawk T1A	RAF No 4 FTS, Valley	
XX246	HS Hawk T1A <rf>	RAF CTTS, St Athan	
XX247	HS Hawk T1A [CM]	RAF No 100 Sqn, Leeming	
XX248	HS Hawk T1A [CJ]	RAF No 100 Sqn, Leeming	
XX249	HS Hawk T1W	*Crashed 28 September 2001, Mona*	
XX250	HS Hawk T1	RAF No 4 FTS/*19(R) Sqn*, Valley	
XX252	HS Hawk T1A (fuselage)	Privately owned, Charlwood	
XX253	HS Hawk T1A	RAF *Red Arrows*, Scampton	
XX253	HS Hawk T1 <R> (*XX297*/ BAPC 171)	RAF EPTT, St Athan	
XX254	HS Hawk T1A <ff>	DARA, RAF St Athan	
XX254	HS Hawk T1A	DPA/BAE Systems, stored Scampton	
•*XX254*	HS Hawk T1A <R>	Privately owned, Marlow, Bucks	
XX255	HS Hawk T1A	RN FRADU, Culdrose	
XX256	HS Hawk T1A	RAF No 4 FTS/*19(R) Sqn*, Valley	
XX258	HS Hawk T1A	RAF No 4 FTS, Valley	
XX260	HS Hawk T1A	RAF *Red Arrows*, Scampton	
XX261	HS Hawk T1A	RAF No 4 FTS/*208(R) Sqn*, Valley	
XX263	HS Hawk T1A	RAF No 4 FTS/*208(R) Sqn*, Valley	
XX264	HS Hawk T1A	RAF *Red Arrows*, Scampton	
XX265	HS Hawk T1A	RAF No 4 FTS, Valley	
XX266	HS Hawk T1A	RAF *Red Arrows*, Scampton	
XX278	HS Hawk T1A [CD]	RAF No 100 Sqn, Leeming	
XX280	HS Hawk T1A	RAF No 4 FTS, Valley	
XX281	HS Hawk T1A	RAF No 4 FTS/*19(R) Sqn*, Valley	
XX283	HS Hawk T1W	DARA, RAF St Athan	
XX284	HS Hawk T1A	RAF No 4 FTS/*208(R) Sqn*, Valley	
XX285	HS Hawk T1A [CB]	RAF No 100 Sqn, Leeming	
XX286	HS Hawk T1A	DARA, RAF St Athan	
XX287	HS Hawk T1A	RAF No 4 FTS/*208(R) Sqn*, Valley	
XX289	HS Hawk T1A [CI]	RAF No 100 Sqn, Leeming	
XX290	HS Hawk T1W	RAF No 4 FTS/*19(R) Sqn*, Valley	
XX292	HS Hawk T1W	RAF *Red Arrows*, Scampton	
XX294	HS Hawk T1	RAF *Red Arrows*, Scampton	
XX295	HS Hawk T1W	RAF No 4 FTS/*19(R) Sqn*, Valley	
XX296	HS Hawk T1	RAF No 4 FTS/*19(R) Sqn*, Valley	
XX299	HS Hawk T1W [CS]	RAF No 100 Sqn, Leeming	
XX301	HS Hawk T1A	DARA, RAF St Athan	
XX303	HS Hawk T1A	RAF No 4 FTS, Valley	
XX304	HS Hawk T1A <ff>	RAF, stored Shawbury	

Notes	Serial	Type (other identity) [code]	Owner/operator, location or fate
	XX304	HS Hawk T1A <rf>	Cardiff International Airport Fire Section
	XX306	HS Hawk T1A	RAF *Red Arrows*, Scampton
	XX307	HS Hawk T1	RAF *Red Arrows*, Scampton
	XX308	HS Hawk T1	RAF *Red Arrows*, Scampton
	XX309	HS Hawk T1	RAF No 4 FTS, Valley
	XX310	HS Hawk T1W	RAF No 4 FTS/*208(R) Sqn*, Valley
	XX311	HS Hawk T1	RAF No 4 FTS/*19(R) Sqn*, Valley
	XX312	HS Hawk T1W [CW]	RAF No 100 Sqn, Leeming
	XX313	HS Hawk T1W	RAF No 4 FTS, Valley
	XX314	HS Hawk T1W [CN]	RAF No 100 Sqn, Leeming
	XX315	HS Hawk T1A	RAF No 4 FTS, Valley
	XX316	HS Hawk T1A	DARA, RAF St Athan
	XX317	HS Hawk T1A [CH]	DARA, RAF St Athan
	XX318	HS Hawk T1A	RAF No 4 FTS/*208(R) Sqn*, Valley
	XX319	HS Hawk T1A	DARA, RAF St Athan
	XX320	HS Hawk T1A	RAF No 4 FTS, Valley
	XX321	HS Hawk T1A [CG]	DARA, RAF St Athan
	XX322	HS Hawk T1A	RN FRADU, Culdrose
	XX323	HS Hawk T1A [CT]	RAF No 100 Sqn, Leeming
	XX324	HS Hawk T1A	RAF No 4 FTS/*19(R) Sqn*, Valley
	XX325	HS Hawk T1A	RAF No 4 FTS/*208(R) Sqn*, Valley
	XX326	HS Hawk T1A <ff>	DARA, RAF St Athan
	XX326	HS Hawk T1A	DPA/BAE Systems, Brough (on rebuild)
	XX327	HS Hawk T1	RAF Aviation Medicine Flt, Boscombe Down
	XX329	HS Hawk T1A	RAF No 4 FTS, Valley
	XX330	HS Hawk T1A [CL]	RAF No 100 Sqn, Leeming
	XX331	HS Hawk T1A]	RAF No 4 FTS/*208(R) Sqn*, Valley
	XX332	HS Hawk T1A	RAF No 4 FTS/*19(R) Sqn*, Valley
	XX335	HS Hawk T1A [CD]	RAF No 100 Sqn, Leeming
	XX337	HS Hawk T1A	RAF No 4 FTS, Valley
	XX338	HS Hawk T1W	RAF No 4 FTS/*19(R) Sqn*, Valley
	XX339	HS Hawk T1A	RAF No 4 FTS/*208(R) Sqn*, Valley
	XX341	HS Hawk T1 ASTRA [1]	DPA/AFD/ETPS, QinetiQ Boscombe Down
	XX342	HS Hawk T1 [2]	DPA/AFD/ETPS, QinetiQ Boscombe Down
	XX343	HS Hawk T1 [3] (wreck)	Boscombe Down Museum
	XX344	HS Hawk T1 (8847M) (fuselage)	QinetiQ Farnborough Fire Section
	XX345	HS Hawk T1A	RAF No 4 FTS, Valley
	XX346	HS Hawk T1A	RAF No 4 FTS, Valley
	XX348	HS Hawk T1A	RAF No 4 FTS, Valley
	XX349	HS Hawk T1W [CE]	RAF No 100 Sqn/JFACSTU, Leeming
	XX350	HS Hawk T1A	RAF No 4 FTS/*19(R) Sqn*, Valley
	XX351	HS Hawk T1A	DPA/BAE Systems, Warton
	XX352	HS Hawk T1A [CP]	RAF No 4 FTS, Valley
	XX370	WS Gazelle AH1	AAC No 665 Sqn/5 Regt, Aldergrove
	XX371	WS Gazelle AH1	AAC No 12 Flt, Brüggen
	XX372	WS Gazelle AH1	AAC No 9 Regt, Dishforth
	XX375	WS Gazelle AH1	AAC No 8 Flt, Middle Wallop
	XX378	WS Gazelle AH1 [Q]	AAC No 671 Sqn/2 Regt, Middle Wallop
	XX379	WS Gazelle AH1	AAC No 669 Sqn/4 Regt, Wattisham
	XX380	WS Gazelle AH1	RM No 847 Sqn, Yeovilton
	XX381	WS Gazelle AH1	AAC No 662 Sqn/3 Regt, Wattisham
	XX382	WS Gazelle HT3 (G-BZYB) [M]	Privately owned, Hungerford
	XX383	WS Gazelle AH1 [D]	AAC No 666(V) Sqn/7 Regt, Netheravon
	XX384	WS Gazelle AH1	AAC No 7 Air Assault Battalion, Wattisham
	XX385	WS Gazelle AH1	AAC No 663 Sqn/3 Regt, Wattisham
	XX386	WS Gazelle AH1	AAC No 12 Flt, Brüggen
	XX387	WS Gazelle AH1 (TAD 014)	Army SEAE, Arborfield
	XX388	WS Gazelle AH1	Privately owned, Hungerford
	XX389	WS Gazelle AH1	AAC No 656 Sqn/9 Regt, Dishforth
	XX391	WS Gazelle HT2 [56/CU]	*Sold as ZK-HTB, July 2001*
	XX392	WS Gazelle AH1	AAC No 3(V) Flt/7 Regt, Leuchars
	XX393	WS Gazelle AH1 (fuselage)	Privately owned, Wellington, Somerset
	XX394	WS Gazelle AH1 [X]	AAC No 669 Sqn/4 Regt, Wattisham
	XX396	WS Gazelle HT3 (8718M) [N]	ATF, RAFC Cranwell
	XX398	WS Gazelle AH1	AAC No 7 Air Assault Battalion, Wattisham
	XX399	WS Gazelle AH1	RM No 847 Sqn, Yeovilton
	XX403	WS Gazelle AH1	DARA, Fleetlands
	XX405	WS Gazelle AH1	AAC No 665 Sqn/5 Regt, Aldergrove
	XX406	WS Gazelle HT3 [P]	RAF stored, Shawbury
	XX409	WS Gazelle AH1	AAC No 7 Air Assault Battalion, Wattisham
	XX411	WS Gazelle AH1 <rf>	FAA Museum, RNAS Yeovilton
	XX412	WS Gazelle AH1 [B]	RM No 847 Sqn, Yeovilton

Serial	Type (other identity) [code]	Owner/operator, location or fate	Notes
XX413	WS Gazelle AH1 [C]	Privately owned, Wellington, Somerset	
XX414	WS Gazelle AH1	AAC, stored DARA Fleetlands	
XX416	WS Gazelle AH1	AAC No 9 Regt, Dishforth	
XX417	WS Gazelle AH1	AAC No 667 Sqn, Middle Wallop	
XX418	WS Gazelle AH1	Privately owned, Wellington, Somerset	
XX419	WS Gazelle AH1	AAC No 662 Sqn/3 Regt, Wattisham	
XX431	WS Gazelle HT2 (9300M) [43/CU]	RAF Shawbury, for display	
XX432	WS Gazelle AH1	AAC No 665 Sqn/5 Regt, Aldergrove	
XX433	WS Gazelle AH1 [F]	Privately owned, Hungerford	
XX435	WS Gazelle AH1 [V]	AAC No 658 Sqn/7 Regt, Netheravon	
XX436	WS Gazelle HT2 [39/CU]	RN, stored Shawbury	
XX437	WS Gazelle AH1	AAC No 669 Sqn/4 Regt, Wattisham	
XX438	WS Gazelle AH1	AAC No 9 Regt, Dishforth	
XX439	WS Gazelle AH1	AAC No 9 Regt, Dishforth	
XX440	WS Gazelle AH1 (G-BCHN)	DARA Fleetlands Apprentice School	
XX441	WS Gazelle HT2 [38/CU]	*Sold as ZK-HBH, July 2001*	
XX442	WS Gazelle AH1 [E]	AAC No 666(V) Sqn/7 Regt, Netheravon	
XX443	WS Gazelle AH1 [Y]	AAC Stockwell Hall, Middle Wallop, instructional use	
XX444	WS Gazelle AH1	AAC No 25 Flt, Belize	
XX445	WS Gazelle AH1 [T]	AAC, stored DARA Fleetlands	
XX446	WS Gazelle HT2 [57/CU]	*Sold as ZK-HTF, July 2001*	
XX447	WS Gazelle AH1 [D1]	AAC No 671 Sqn/2 Regt, Middle Wallop	
XX448	WS Gazelle AH1	AAC No 664 Sqn/9 Regt, Dishforth	
XX449	WS Gazelle AH1	AAC No 664 Sqn/9 Regt, Dishforth	
XX450	WS Gazelle AH1 [D]	Privately owned, Wellington, Somerset	
XX453	WS Gazelle AH1	AAC No 669 Sqn/4 Regt, Wattisham	
XX454	WS Gazelle AH1 (TAD 023) (fuselage)	Army SEAE, Arborfield	
XX455	WS Gazelle AH1	DARA, Fleetlands	
XX456	WS Gazelle AH1	AAC No 3(V) Flt/7 Regt, Leuchars	
XX457	WS Gazelle AH1 <ff>	Jet Avn Preservation Grp, Long Marston	
XX460	WS Gazelle AH1	AAC No 662 Sqn/3 Regt, Wattisham	
XX462	WS Gazelle AH1 [W]	AAC No 658 Sqn/7 Regt, Netheravon	
XX467	HS Hunter T66B/T7 (XL605/ G-TVII) [86]	Privately owned, Kemble	
XX475	HP137 Jetstream T2 (N1036S)	DPA, QinetiQ West Freugh	
XX476	HP137 Jetstream T2 (N1037S) [561/CU]	RN No 750 Sqn, Culdrose	
XX477	HP137 Jetstream T1 (G-AXXS/ 8462M) <ff>	RAF Cranwell, instructional use	
XX478	HP137 Jetstream T2 (G-AXXT) [564/CU]	RN No 750 Sqn, Culdrose	
XX479	HP137 Jetstream T2 (G-AXUR)	RN, Predannack Fire School	
XX481	HP137 Jetstream T2 (G-AXUP) [560/CU]	RN No 750 Sqn, Culdrose	
XX482	SA Jetstream T1 [J]	RAF No 3 FTS/45(R) Sqn, Cranwell	
XX483	SA Jetstream T2 <ff>	Privately owned, Welshpool	
XX484	SA Jetstream T2 [566/CU]	RN No 750 Sqn, Culdrose	
XX486	SA Jetstream T2 [569/CU]	RN No 750 Sqn, Culdrose	
XX487	SA Jetstream T2 [568/CU]	RN No 750 Sqn, Culdrose	
XX488	SA Jetstream T2 [562/CU]	RN No 750 Sqn, Culdrose	
XX491	SA Jetstream T1 [K]	RAF No 3 FTS/45(R) Sqn, Cranwell	
XX492	SA Jetstream T1 [A]	RAF No 3 FTS/45(R) Sqn, Cranwell	
XX493	SA Jetstream T1 [L]	RAF No 3 FTS/45(R) Sqn, Cranwell	
XX494	SA Jetstream T1 [B]	RAF No 3 FTS/45(R) Sqn, Cranwell	
XX495	SA Jetstream T1 [C]	RAF No 3 FTS/45(R) Sqn, Cranwell	
XX496	SA Jetstream T1 [D]	RAF No 3 FTS/45(R) Sqn, Cranwell	
XX497	SA Jetstream T1 [E]	RAF No 3 FTS/45(R) Sqn, Cranwell	
XX498	SA Jetstream T1 [F]	RAF No 3 FTS/45(R) Sqn, Cranwell	
XX499	SA Jetstream T1 [G]	RAF No 3 FTS/45(R) Sqn, Cranwell	
XX500	SA Jetstream T1 [H]	RAF No 3 FTS/45(R) Sqn, Cranwell	
XX510	WS Lynx HAS2 [69/DD]	SFDO, RNAS Culdrose	
XX513	SA Bulldog T1 (G-KKKK) [10]	Privately owned,	
XX514	SA122 Bulldog (G-BWIB)	Privately owned, Leicester	
XX515	SA Bulldog T1 (G-CBBC) [4]	Privately owned, Wellesbourne Mountford	
XX516	SA Bulldog T1 [A]	*Sold as N516BG, November 2001*	
XX518	SA Bulldog T1 [S]	RAF, stored Shawbury	
XX520	SA Bulldog T1 [A]	No .... Sqn ATC, Haywards Heath	
XX521	SA Bulldog T1 (G-CBEH) [H]	Privately owned, East Dereham, Norfolk	
XX522	SA Bulldog T1 [06]	Privately owned, Manchester	
XX523	SA Bulldog T1 (G-BZFM) [X]	*Sold as N523BD, March 2001*	
XX524	SA Bulldog T1 (G-DDOG) [04]	Privately owned, North Weald	

Notes	Serial	Type (other identity) [code]	Owner/operator, location or fate
	XX525	SA Bulldog T1 (G-CBJJ) [8]	Privately owned
	XX526	SA Bulldog T1 [C]	RAF, stored Shawbury
	XX528	SA Bulldog T1 (G-BZON) [D]	Privately owned, Carlisle
	XX529	SA Bulldog T1 (G-BZOJ) [08]	*Sold as N178BD, January 2001*
	XX530	SA Bulldog T1 (XX637/9197M) [F]	Rolls-Royce, Renfrew
	XX531	SA Bulldog T1 [G]	*Sold as F-AZLZ, August 2001*
	XX532	SA Bulldog T1 [1]	*Sold as F-AZOB, August 2001*
	XX533	SA Bulldog T1 [U]	*Sold as HA-TUI, October 2001*
	XX534	SA Bulldog T1 (G-EDAV) [B]	Privately owned,
	XX535	SA Bulldog T1 [$]	*Sold as F-AZOZ, August 2001*
	XX536	SA Bulldog T1 [6]	*Sold as N433UB, October 2001*
	XX537	SA Bulldog T1 (G-CBCB) [C]	Privately owned, Sleap
	XX538	SA Bulldog T1 (G-TDOG) [O]	Privately owned, Bewdley, Worcs
	XX539	SA Bulldog T1 [L]	Privately owned, Wellesbourne Mountford
	XX541	SA Bulldog T1 [F]	*Sold as N9179C, January 2001*
	XX543	SA Bulldog T1 (G-CBAB) [F]	Privately owned, Duxford
	XX546	SA Bulldog T1 (G-CBCO) [03]	Privately owned, Clacton
	XX547	SA Bulldog T1 [Q]	*To Armed Forces of Malta as AS0124, 30 July 2001*
	XX548	SA Bulldog T1 [06]	RAF, stored Shawbury
	XX549	SA Bulldog T1 (G-CBJD) [6]	Privately owned
	XX550	SA Bulldog T1 (G-CBBL) [Z]	Privately owned, Fenland
	XX551	SA Bulldog T1 (G-BZDP) [E]	Privately owned, Wellesbourne Mountford
	XX552	SA Bulldog T1 [08]	*Sold as N415BD, November 2001*
	XX553	SA Bulldog T1 [07]	Privately owned, Sproughton
	XX554	SA Bulldog T1 (G-BZMD) [09]	Privately owned, Grantham
	XX555	SA Bulldog T1 [U]	*Sold as F-AZKJ, June 2001*
	XX556	SA Bulldog T1 [M]	*Sold as N556WH, August 2001*
	XX558	SA Bulldog T1 [A]	*Sold as F-AZOG, September 2001*
	XX559	SA Bulldog T1 [F]	*Sold as F-AZOD, August 2001*
	XX560	SA Bulldog T1 [F]	*Sold as N560XX, June 2001*
	XX561	SA Bulldog T1 (G-BZEP) [7]	Privately owned, Biggin Hill
	XX562	SA Bulldog T1 [18]	RAF, stored Shawbury
	XX611	SA Bulldog T1 (G-CBDK) [7]	Privately owned, Wellesbourne Mountford
	XX612	SA Bulldog T1 (G-BZXC) [A,03]	Privately owned, West Sussex
	XX614	SA Bulldog T1 (G-GGRR) [V]	Privately owned, White Waltham
	XX615	SA Bulldog T1 [2]	*Sold as F-AZKI, June 2001*
	XX617	SA Bulldog T1 [2]	*Sold as N25AG, May 2001*
	XX619	SA Bulldog T1 (G-CBBW) [T]	Privately owned, Coventry
	XX620	SA Bulldog T1 [02]	*Sold as N620BD, January 2001*
	XX621	SA Bulldog T1 (G-CBEF) [H]	Privately owned, Sywell
	XX622	SA Bulldog T1 [B]	*Sold as G-CBGX, November 2001*
	XX623	SA Bulldog T1 [M]	Privately owned, Hurstbourne Tarrant
	XX624	SA Bulldog T1 (G-KDOG) [E]	Privately owned, North Weald
	XX625	SA Bulldog T1 (G-CBBR) [01,N]	Privately owned, Lincs
	XX626	SA Bulldog T1 (9290M) [W,02]	DARA Training School, RAF St Athan
	XX627	SA Bulldog T1 [7]	*Sold N321BD, 2001*
	XX628	SA Bulldog T1 (G-CBFU) [9]	Privately owned, Faversham
	XX629	SA Bulldog T1 (G-BZXZ) [V]	Privately owned, Sleap
	XX630	SA Bulldog T1 (G-SIJW) [5]	Privately owned, Sleap
	XX631	SA Bulldog T1 (G-BZXS) [W]	Privately owned, Newport, Ireland
	XX633	SA Bulldog T1 [X]	Privately owned, Mansfield
	XX634	SA Bulldog T1 [T]	Privately owned, Wellesbourne Mountford
	XX635	SA Bulldog T1 (8767M)	DARA Training School, RAF St Athan
	XX636	SA Bulldog T1 (G-CBFP) [Y]	Privately owned, Biggin Hill
	XX638	SA Bulldog T1 (G-DOGG)	Privately owned,
	XX639	SA Bulldog T1 [D]	Privately owned, Sleap
	XX640	SA Bulldog T1 [K]	*Sold as N640RH, August 2001*
	XX653	SA Bulldog T1 [E]	QinetiQ, stored Boscombe Down
	XX654	SA Bulldog T1 [3]	RAF, stored Shawbury
	XX655	SA Bulldog T1 [V]	MoD FSCTE, Manston
	XX656	SA Bulldog T1 [C]	Privately owned, Wellesbourne Mountford
	XX657	SA Bulldog T1 [U]	Privately owned, Hurstbourne Tarrant
	XX658	SA Bulldog T1 (G-BZPS) [07]	Privately owned, Wellesbourne Mountford
	XX659	SA Bulldog T1 [E]	Privately owned, Hixon, Staffs
	XX661	SA Bulldog T1 [6]	*Sold as N661BD, December 2001*
	XX663	SA Bulldog T1 [01]	*Sold as F-AZLK, January 2001*
	XX664	SA Bulldog T1 (G-CBCT) [04]	Privately owned, Sleap
	XX665	SA Bulldog T1	No 2409 Sqn ATC, Halton
	XX667	SA Bulldog T1 (G-BZFN) [16]	Privately owned, Sleap
	XX668	SA Bulldog T1 (G-CBAN) [1]	Privately owned, Calne, Wilts
	XX669	SA Bulldog T1 (8997M) [B]	Privately owned, Hurstbourne Tarrant, Hants

Serial	Type (other identity) [code]	Owner/operator, location or fate	Notes
XX670	SA Bulldog T1 [C]	RAF, stored Shawbury	
XX671	SA Bulldog T1 [D]	Privately owned, Wellesbourne Mountford	
XX672	SA Bulldog T1 [E]	Barry Technical College, Cardiff Airport	
XX685	SA Bulldog T1 (G-BZLB) [11]	Privately owned, Hurstbourne Tarrant	
XX686	SA Bulldog T1 (9291M) [5]	DARA Training School, RAF St Athan	
XX687	SA Bulldog T1 [F]	Barry Technical College, Cardiff Airport	
XX688	SA Bulldog T1 [8]	*Sold as F-AZOA, 2001*	
XX689	SA Bulldog T1 [D]	*Sold to the USA, 2001*	
XX690	SA Bulldog T1 [A]	RAF, stored Shawbury	
XX692	SA Bulldog T1 (G-BZMH) [A]	Privately owned, Wellesbourne Mountford	
XX693	SA Bulldog T1 (G-BZML) [07]	Privately owned, Elmsett	
XX694	SA Bulldog T1 (G-CBBS) [E]	Privately owned, Lincs	
XX695	SA Bulldog T1 (G-CBBT) [3]	Privately owned, Lincs	
XX697	SA Bulldog T1 [H]	*Sold as N697BD, June 2001*	
XX698	SA Bulldog T1 (G-BZME) [9]	Privately owned, Grantham	
XX699	SA Bulldog T1 (G-CBCV) [F]	Privately owned, Cheshire	
XX700	SA Bulldog T1 (G-CBEK) [17]	Privately owned, Sleap	
XX701	SA Bulldog T1 [2]	*Sold as N701AB, May 2001*	
XX702	SA Bulldog T1 (G-CBCR) [π]	Privately owned, Lincs	
XX705	SA Bulldog T1 [5]	QinetiQ Boscombe Down, Apprentice School	
XX706	SA Bulldog T1 [1]	RAF, stored Shawbury	
XX707	SA Bulldog T1 (G-CBDS) [4]	Privately owned, Wellesbourne Mountford	
XX708	SA Bulldog T1 [3]	RAF, stored Shawbury	
XX711	SA Bulldog T1 (G-CBBU) [X]	Privately owned, Lincs	
XX713	SA Bulldog T1 (G-CBJK) [2]	Privately owned	
XX720	SEPECAT Jaguar GR3A [GB]	RAF No 54 Sqn, Coltishall	
XX721	SEPECAT Jaguar GR1 [EF]	RAF, stored St Athan	
XX723	SEPECAT Jaguar GR3A [GQ]	RAF No 54 Sqn, Coltishall	
XX724	SEPECAT Jaguar GR3A [GC]	RAF No 54 Sqn, Coltishall	
XX725	SEPECAT Jaguar GR3A	RAF AWC/SAOEU, Boscombe Down	
XX725	SEPECAT Jaguar GR1 <R> (BAPC 150/*XX718*) [GU]	RAF EPTT, St Athan	
XX726	SEPECAT Jaguar GR1 (8947M) [EB]	RAF No 1 SoTT, Cosford	
XX727	SEPECAT Jaguar GR1 (8951M) [ER]	RAF No 1 SoTT, Cosford	
XX729	SEPECAT Jaguar GR3A [EL]	RAF No 6 Sqn, Coltishall	
XX730	SEPECAT Jaguar GR1 (8952M) [EC]	RAF No 1 SoTT, Cosford	
XX733	SEPECAT Jaguar GR1B [ER]	*Scrapped at Coltishall*	
XX734	SEPECAT Jaguar GR1 (8816M) (fuselage)	Gatwick Aviation Museum, Charlwood	
XX736	SEPECAT Jaguar GR1 (9110M) <ff>	BAE Systems Brough	
XX737	SEPECAT Jaguar GR3A [EE]	RAF No 6 Sqn, Coltishall	
XX738	SEPECAT Jaguar GR3A [GG]	RAF No 54 Sqn, Coltishall	
XX739	SEPECAT Jaguar GR1 (8902M) [I]	RAF No 1 SoTT, Cosford	
XX741	SEPECAT Jaguar GR1A [04]	RAF, stored Shawbury	
XX743	SEPECAT Jaguar GR1 (8949M) [EG]	RAF No 1 SoTT, Cosford	
XX744	SEPECAT Jaguar GR1	RAF Coltishall, instructional use	
XX745	SEPECAT Jaguar GR1A [GV]	RAF, stored Shawbury	
XX746	SEPECAT Jaguar GR1 (8895M) [09]	RAF No 1 SoTT, Cosford	
XX747	SEPECAT Jaguar GR1 (8903M)	ATF, RAFC Cranwell	
XX748	SEPECAT Jaguar GR3A [GK]	RAF No 54 Sqn, Coltishall	
XX751	SEPECAT Jaguar GR1 (8937M) [10]	RAF No 1 SoTT, Cosford	
XX752	SEPECAT Jaguar GR3A [PD]	RAF No 16(R) Sqn, Coltishall	
XX753	SEPECAT Jaguar GR1 (9087M) <ff>	RAF EPTT, St Athan	
XX756	SEPECAT Jaguar GR1 (8899M) [AM]	RAF No 1 SoTT, Cosford	
XX757	SEPECAT Jaguar GR1 (8948M) [CU]	RAF No 1 SoTT, Cosford	
XX761	SEPECAT Jaguar GR1 (8600M) <ff>	Boscombe Down Museum	
XX763	SEPECAT Jaguar GR1 (9009M)	DARA Training School, RAF St Athan	
XX764	SEPECAT Jaguar GR1 (9010M)	DARA Training School, RAF St Athan	
XX765	SEPECAT Jaguar ACT	RAF Museum, Cosford	
XX766	SEPECAT Jaguar GR3A [PE]	RAF No 16(R) Sqn, Coltishall	
XX767	SEPECAT Jaguar GR3A [GE]	RAF No 54 Sqn, Coltishall	

Notes	Serial	Type (other identity) [code]	Owner/operator, location or fate
	XX818	SEPECAT Jaguar GR1 (8945M) [DE]	RAF No 1 SoTT, Cosford
	XX819	SEPECAT Jaguar GR1 (8923M) [CE]	RAF No 1 SoTT, Cosford
	XX821	SEPECAT Jaguar GR1 (8896M) [P]	AMIF, RAFC Cranwell
XX822	*SEPECAT Jaguar S (XW563/ 8563M)*	*Repainted as XW563*
	XX824	SEPECAT Jaguar GR1 (9019M) [AD]	RAF No 1 SoTT, Cosford
	XX825	SEPECAT Jaguar GR1 (9020M) [BN]	RAF No 1 SoTT, Cosford
	XX826	SEPECAT Jaguar GR1 (9021M) [34,JH]	RAF No 1 SoTT, Cosford
	XX829	SEPECAT Jaguar T2A [GZ]	RAF, stored Shawbury
	XX830	SEPECAT Jaguar T2 <ff>	The Cockpit Collection, RAF Coltishall
	XX832	SEPECAT Jaguar T2A [EZ]	RAF, stored Shawbury
	XX833	SEPECAT Jaguar T2B	RAF AWC/SAOEU, Boscombe Down
	XX835	SEPECAT Jaguar T4 [FY]	RAF No 41 Sqn, Coltishall
	XX836	SEPECAT Jaguar T2A [X]	RAF, stored Shawbury
	XX837	SEPECAT Jaguar T2 (8978M) [Z]	RAF No 1 SoTT, Cosford
	XX838	SEPECAT Jaguar T4 [PR]	RAF No 16(R) Sqn, Coltishall
	XX839	SEPECAT Jaguar T2B (9256M)	RAF, stored St Athan
	XX840	SEPECAT Jaguar T4 [PS]	RAF No 16(R) Sqn, Coltishall
	XX841	SEPECAT Jaguar T4 [ES]	RAF No 6 Sqn, Coltishall
	XX842	SEPECAT Jaguar T2A [X]	DPA/BAE Systems, Warton
	XX845	SEPECAT Jaguar T4 [ET]	RAF No 6 Sqn, Coltishall
	XX846	SEPECAT Jaguar T4 [PV]	RAF No 16(R) Sqn, Coltishall
	XX847	SEPECAT Jaguar T2	RAF, St Athan (rebuild)
	XX885	HS Buccaneer S2B (9225M)	The Old Flying Machine Company, Scampton
	XX888	HS Buccaneer S2B <ff>	Dundonald Aviation Centre, Strathclyde
	XX889	HS Buccaneer S2B	Gloucestershire Avn Coll, stored Gloucester
	XX892	HS Buccaneer S2B <ff>	Dundonald Aviation Centre, Strathclyde
	XX893	HS Buccaneer S2B <ff>	Privately owned, Birtley, Tyne & Wear
	XX894	HS Buccaneer S2B [020/R]	Buccaneer Supporters Club, Kemble
	XX895	HS Buccaneer S2B <ff>	Privately owned, Oxford
	XX897	HS Buccaneer S2B(mod)	Bournemouth Aviation Museum
	XX899	HS Buccaneer S2B <ff>	Midland Air Museum, Coventry
	XX900	HS Buccaneer S2B	British Aviation Heritage, Bruntingthorpe
	XX901	HS Buccaneer S2B	Yorkshire Air Museum, Elvington
	XX907	WS Lynx AH1	QinetiQ Structures Dept, Farnborough
	XX910	WS Lynx HAS2	The Helicopter Museum, Weston-super-Mare
	XX914	BAC VC10/1103 (8777M) <rf>	RAF Air Movements School, Brize Norton
	XX919	BAC 1-11/402AP (PI-C1121) <ff>	Boscombe Down Museum
	XX946	Panavia Tornado (P02) (8883M)	RAF Museum, Hendon
	XX947	Panavia Tornado (P03) (8797M)	DARA, RAF St Athan, BDRT
	XX948	Panavia Tornado (P06) (8879M) [P]	RAF No 1 SoTT, Cosford
	XX955	SEPECAT Jaguar GR1A [GK]	RAF, stored Shawbury
	XX956	SEPECAT Jaguar GR1 (8950M) [BE]	RAF No 1 SoTT, Cosford
	XX958	SEPECAT Jaguar GR1 (9022M) [BK,JG]	RAF No 1 SoTT, Cosford
	XX959	SEPECAT Jaguar GR1 (8953M) [CJ]	RAF No 1 SoTT, Cosford
	XX962	SEPECAT Jaguar GR1B [E]	AMIF, RAFC Cranwell
	XX965	SEPECAT Jaguar GR1A [C]	AMIF, RAFC Cranwell
	XX966	SEPECAT Jaguar GR1 (8904M) [EL]	RAF No 1 SoTT, Cosford
	XX967	SEPECAT Jaguar GR1 (9006M) [AC,JD]	RAF No 1 SoTT, Cosford
	XX968	SEPECAT Jaguar GR1 (9007M) [AJ,JE]	RAF No 1 SoTT, Cosford
	XX969	SEPECAT Jaguar GR1 (8897M) [01]	RAF No 1 SoTT, Cosford
	XX970	SEPECAT Jaguar GR3A [EH]	DARA, RAF St Athan (conversion)
	XX974	SEPECAT Jaguar GR3 [PB]	RAF No 16(R) Sqn, Coltishall
	XX975	SEPECAT Jaguar GR1 (8905M) [07]	RAF No 1 SoTT, Cosford
	XX976	SEPECAT Jaguar GR1 (8906M) [BD]	RAF No 1 SoTT, Cosford

Serial	Type (other identity) [code]	Owner/operator, location or fate	Notes
XX977	SEPECAT Jaguar GR1 (9132M) [DL,05]	DARA, RAF St Athan, BDRT	
XX979	SEPECAT Jaguar GR1A	RAF, stored St Athan	
XZ101	SEPECAT Jaguar GR1A (9282M) [D]	QinetiQ Boscombe Down, GI use	
XZ103	SEPECAT Jaguar GR3A [FP]	RAF No 41 Sqn, Coltishall	
XZ104	SEPECAT Jaguar GR3A [FM]	RAF No 41 Sqn, Coltishall	
XZ106	SEPECAT Jaguar GR3 [FR]	RAF No 41 Sqn, Coltishall	
XZ107	SEPECAT Jaguar GR3 [FH]	RAF No 41 Sqn, Coltishall	
XZ109	SEPECAT Jaguar GR3	RAF No 6 Sqn, Coltishall	
XZ112	SEPECAT Jaguar GR3A [GA]	RAF No 54 Sqn, Coltishall	
XZ113	SEPECAT Jaguar GR3 [FD]	RAF No 41 Sqn, Coltishall	
XZ114	SEPECAT Jaguar GR1A [FB]	RAF, stored Shawbury	
XZ115	SEPECAT Jaguar GR3 [PD]	RAF No 16(R) Sqn, Coltishall	
XZ117	SEPECAT Jaguar GR3 [EP]	RAF No 6 Sqn, Coltishall	
XZ118	SEPECAT Jaguar GR3 [FF]	RAF No 41 Sqn, Coltishall	
XZ119	SEPECAT Jaguar GR1A [F]	AMIF, RAFC Cranwell	
XZ129	HS Harrier GR3 [ETS]	RN ETS, Yeovilton	
XZ130	HS Harrier GR3 (9079M) [A,HE]	RAF No 1 SoTT, Cosford	
XZ131	HS Harrier GR3 (9174M) <ff>	No 2156 Sqn ATC, Brierley Hill, W Midlands	
XZ132	HS Harrier GR3 (9168M) [C]	ATF, RAFC Cranwell	
XZ133	HS Harrier GR3 [10]	Imperial War Museum, Duxford	
XZ135	HS Harrier GR3 (8848M) <ff>	RAF EPTT, St Athan	
XZ138	HS Harrier GR3 (9040M) <ff>	RAFC Cranwell, Trenchard Hall	
XZ145	HS Harrier T4 [45]	SFDO, RNAS Culdrose	
XZ146	HS Harrier T4 (9281M) [S]	RAF Wittering, for display	
XZ170	WS Lynx AH9	DPA/Westland Helicopters, Yeovil	
XZ171	WS Lynx AH7	AAC No 654 Sqn/4 Regt, Wattisham	
XZ172	WS Lynx AH7	AAC No 655 Sqn/5 Regt, Aldergrove	
XZ173	WS Lynx AH7	AAC No 661 Sqn/1 Regt, Brüggen	
XZ174	WS Lynx AH7	AAC No 3 Regt, Wattisham	
XZ175	WS Lynx AH7	AAC No 25 Flt, Belize	
XZ176	WS Lynx AH7	DARA, Fleetlands	
XZ177	WS Lynx AH7	DARA, Fleetlands	
XZ178	WS Lynx AH7	AAC No 661 Sqn/1 Regt, Brüggen	
XZ179	WS Lynx AH7	AAC No 652 Sqn/1 Regt, Brüggen	
XZ180	WS Lynx AH7 [R]	RM No 847 Sqn, Yeovilton	
XZ181	WS Lynx AH1	Westland Helicopters, Yeovil, wfu	
XZ182	WS Lynx AH7 [M]	RM No 847 Sqn, Yeovilton	
XZ183	WS Lynx AH7	AAC No 656 Sqn/9 Regt, Dishforth	
XZ184	WS Lynx AH7 [Z]	AAC, stored DARA Fleetlands	
XZ185	WS Lynx AH7	AAC, stored DARA Fleetlands	
XZ186	WS Lynx AH7 (wreckage)	*Scrapped at Fleetlands*	
XZ187	WS Lynx AH7	DARA, Fleetlands	
XZ188	WS Lynx AH7	Army SEAE, Arborfield	
XZ190	WS Lynx AH7	AAC No 9 Regt, Dishforth	
XZ191	WS Lynx AH7 [A]	AAC No 671 Sqn/2 Regt, Middle Wallop	
XZ192	WS Lynx AH7	DPA/Westland Helicopters, Weston-super-Mare (on rebuild)	
XZ193	WS Lynx AH7 [I]	AAC No 671 Sqn/2 Regt, Middle Wallop	
XZ194	WS Lynx AH7	AAC No 664 Sqn/9 Regt, Dishforth	
XZ195	WS Lynx AH7	AAC, stored DARA Fleetlands	
XZ196	WS Lynx AH7	AAC No 7 Air Assault Battalion, Wattisham	
XZ197	WS Lynx AH7	AAC, stored DARA Fleetlands	
XZ198	WS Lynx AH7	DARA, Fleetlands	
XZ203	WS Lynx AH7 [L]	AAC No 671 Sqn/2 Regt, Middle Wallop	
XZ205	WS Lynx AH7	AAC No 655 Sqn/5 Regt, Aldergrove	
XZ206	WS Lynx AH7	AAC No 655 Sqn/5 Regt, Aldergrove	
XZ207	WS Lynx AH7	DARA, Fleetlands (damaged)	
XZ208	WS Lynx AH7	AAC No 669 Sqn/4 Regt, Wattisham	
XZ209	WS Lynx AH7	AAC No 655 Sqn/5 Regt, Aldergrove	
XZ210	WS Lynx AH7	AAC No 7 Air Assault Battalion, Wattisham	
XZ211	WS Lynx AH7	AAC, stored DARA Fleetlands	
XZ212	WS Lynx AH7	AAC No 656 Sqn/9 Regt, Dishforth	
XZ213	WS Lynx AH1 (TAD 213)	DARA Fleetlands Apprentice School	
XZ214	WS Lynx AH7	AAC No 657 Sqn, Odiham	
XZ215	WS Lynx AH7 [4]	AAC No 655 Sqn/5 Regt, Aldergrove	
XZ216	WS Lynx AH7	AAC No 661 Sqn/1 Regt, Brüggen	
XZ217	WS Lynx AH7	AAC No 654 Sqn/4 Regt, Wattisham	
XZ218	WS Lynx AH7	DARA, Fleetlands	
XZ219	WS Lynx AH7	AAC No 7 Air Assault Battalion, Wattisham	

Notes	Serial	Type (other identity) [code]	Owner/operator, location or fate
	XZ220	WS Lynx AH7	AAC No 7 Air Assault Battalion, Wattisham
	XZ221	WS Lynx AH7	AAC No 654 Sqn/4 Regt, Wattisham
	XZ222	WS Lynx AH7	AAC No 657 Sqn, Odiham
	XZ228	WS Lynx HAS3S [425/KT]	RN No 815 Sqn, *Kent* Flt, Yeovilton
	XZ229	WS Lynx HAS3S [457/LA]	RN No 815 Sqn, *Lancaster* Flt, Yeovilton
	XZ230	WS Lynx HAS3S [302]	DARA, Fleetlands
	XZ232	WS Lynx HAS3S [350/CL]	RN No 815 Sqn, *Cumberland* Flt, Yeovilton
	XZ233	WS Lynx HAS3(ICE) [644]	RN No 702 Sqn, Yeovilton
	XZ234	WS Lynx HAS3S [633]	RN No 702 Sqn, Yeovilton
	XZ235	WS Lynx HAS3S [635]	RN No 702 Sqn, Yeovilton
	XZ236	WS Lynx HMA8	DPA/AFD, QinetiQ Boscombe Down
	XZ237	WS Lynx HAS3S [630]	RN No 702 Sqn, Yeovilton
	XZ238	WS Lynx HAS3S(ICE) [435/EE]	RN No 815 Sqn, *Endurance* Flt, Yeovilton
	XZ239	WS Lynx HAS3S [417/NM]	RN No 815 Sqn, *Nottingham* Flt, Yeovilton
	XZ241	WS Lynx HAS3S(ICE) [435/EE]	RN AMG, Yeovilton
	XZ243	WS Lynx HAS3 <ff>	RNAS Culdrose, Fire Section
	XZ245	WS Lynx HAS3S [410/GC]	RN No 815 Sqn, *Gloucester* Flt, Yeovilton
	XZ246	WS Lynx HAS3S(ICE) [434/EE]	RN No 815 Sqn, *Endurance* Flt, Yeovilton
	XZ248	WS Lynx HAS3S [638]	RN No 702 Sqn, Yeovilton
	XZ250	WS Lynx HAS3S [631]	RN No 702 Sqn, Yeovilton
	XZ252	WS Lynx HAS3S	RN MASU, DARA Fleetlands
	XZ254	WS Lynx HAS3S [634]	RN No 702 Sqn, Yeovilton
	XZ255	WS Lynx HMA8 [462/WM]	RN No 815 Sqn, *Westminster* Flt, Yeovilton
	XZ256	WS Lynx HMA8 [474/RM]	RN No 815 Sqn, *Richmond* Flt, Yeovilton
	XZ257	WS Lynx HMA8	RN No 702 Sqn, Yeovilton
	XZ286	BAe Nimrod AEW3 <rf>	RAF Kinloss Fire Section
	XZ287	BAe Nimrod AEW3 (9140M) (fuselage)	RAF TSW, Stafford
	XZ290	WS Gazelle AH1	AAC No 665 Sqn/5 Regt, Aldergrove
	XZ291	WS Gazelle AH1	AAC No 12 Flt, Brüggen
	XZ292	WS Gazelle AH1	AAC No 9 Regt, Dishforth
	XZ294	WS Gazelle AH1 [X]	AAC No 658 Sqn/7 Regt, Netheravon
	XZ295	WS Gazelle AH1	AAC No 12 Flt, Brüggen
	XZ296	WS Gazelle AH1	AAC, No 657 Sqn, Odiham
	XZ298	WS Gazelle AH1	AAC No 656 Sqn/9 Regt, Dishforth
	XZ299	WS Gazelle AH1	AAC No 665 Sqn/5 Regt, Aldergrove
	XZ300	WS Gazelle AH1 [L] (wreck)	Army, Bramley, Hants
	XZ301	WS Gazelle AH1 [U]	AAC No 3 Regt, Wattisham
	XZ303	WS Gazelle AH1	AAC No 663 Sqn/3 Regt, Wattisham
	XZ304	WS Gazelle AH1	AAC No 6(V) Flt/7 Regt, Shawbury
	XZ305	WS Gazelle AH1 (TAD020)	Army SEAE, Arborfield
	XZ307	WS Gazelle AH1	DARA Fleetlands Apprentice School
	XZ308	WS Gazelle AH1	AAC No 9 Regt, Dishforth
	XZ309	WS Gazelle AH1	AAC No 6(V) Flt/7 Regt, Shawbury
	XZ311	WS Gazelle AH1	AAC No 6(V) Flt/7 Regt, Shawbury
	XZ312	WS Gazelle AH1	AAC No 9 Regt, Dishforth
	XZ313	WS Gazelle AH1	AAC No 667 Sqn, Middle Wallop
	XZ314	WS Gazelle AH1	AAC No 8 Flt, Middle Wallop
	XZ315	WS Gazelle AH1	AAC, stored DARA Fleetlands
	XZ316	WS Gazelle AH1 [B]	AAC No 666(V) Sqn/7 Regt, Netheravon
	XZ317	WS Gazelle AH1 [R]	*Sold as 3D-HGZ, Oct 01*
	XZ318	WS Gazelle AH1 (fuselage)	AAC, stored DARA Fleetlands
	XZ320	WS Gazelle AH1	AAC No 669 Sqn/4 Regt, Wattisham
	XZ321	WS Gazelle AH1	AAC No 665 Sqn/5 Regt, Aldergrove
	XZ322	WS Gazelle AH1 (9283M) [N]	DARA, RAF St Athan, BDRT
	XZ323	WS Gazelle AH1	AAC No 16 Flt, Dhekelia, Cyprus
	XZ324	WS Gazelle AH1	AAC No 3(V) Flt/7 Regt, Leuchars
	XZ325	WS Gazelle AH1 [T]	Army SEAE, Arborfield
	XZ326	WS Gazelle AH1	AAC No 665 Sqn/5 Regt, Aldergrove
	XZ327	WS Gazelle AH1	AAC, No 3(V) Flt/7 Regt, Leuchars
	XZ328	WS Gazelle AH1	AAC No 662 Sqn/3 Regt, Wattisham
	XZ329	WS Gazelle AH1 (G-BZYD) [J]	Privately owned, Hungerford
	XZ330	WS Gazelle AH1 [Y]	AAC, Middle Wallop (damaged)
	XZ331	WS Gazelle AH1	AAC No 654 Sqn/4 Regt, Wattisham
	XZ332	WS Gazelle AH1 [O]	Army SEAE, Arborfield
	XZ333	WS Gazelle AH1 [A]	Army SEAE, Arborfield
	XZ334	WS Gazelle AH1	AAC No 665 Sqn/5 Regt, Aldergrove
	XZ335	WS Gazelle AH1	AAC No 6(V) Flt/7 Regt, Shawbury
	XZ337	WS Gazelle AH1	AAC No 667 Sqn, Middle Wallop
	XZ338	WS Gazelle AH1	AAC, stored DARA Fleetlands
	XZ339	WS Gazelle AH1	AAC No 665 Sqn/5 Regt, Aldergrove

Serial	Type (other identity) [code]	Owner/operator, location or fate	Notes
XZ340	WS Gazelle AH1 [5B]	AAC No 29 Flt, BATUS, Suffield, Canada	
XZ341	WS Gazelle AH1	AAC DARA, Fleetlands	
XZ342	WS Gazelle AH1	AAC No 8 Flt, Credenhill	
XZ343	WS Gazelle AH1	DARA, Fleetlands, hack	
XZ344	WS Gazelle AH1	AAC No 9 Regt, Dishforth	
XZ345	WS Gazelle AH1	AAC No 656 Sqn/9 Regt, Dishforth	
XZ346	WS Gazelle AH1	AAC No 665 Sqn/5 Regt, Aldergrove	
XZ347	WS Gazelle AH1	AAC No 3 Regt, Wattisham	
XZ348	WS Gazelle AH1 (wreck)	AAC, stored DARA Fleetlands	
XZ349	WS Gazelle AH1 [G1]	AAC No 671 Sqn/2 Regt, Middle Wallop	
XZ355	SEPECAT Jaguar GR3A [FJ]	RAF No 41 Sqn, Coltishall	
XZ356	SEPECAT Jaguar GR1A [EP]	DARA, RAF St Athan	
XZ357	SEPECAT Jaguar GR3A [FK]	RAF No 41 Sqn, Coltishall	
XZ358	SEPECAT Jaguar GR1A [L]	AMIF, RAFC Cranwell	
XZ360	SEPECAT Jaguar GR3 [FN]	DARA, RAF St Athan	
XZ361	SEPECAT Jaguar GR3 [FT]	RAF No 41 Sqn, Coltishall	
XZ363	SEPECAT Jaguar GR3 [FO]	*Crashed Alaska, 23 July 2001*	
XZ363	SEPECAT Jaguar GR1A <R> (*XX824*/BAPC 151) [A]	RAF EPTT, St Athan	
XZ364	SEPECAT Jaguar GR3A [GJ]	RAF No 41 Sqn, Coltishall	
XZ366	SEPECAT Jaguar GR3A [FS]	RAF No 41 Sqn, Coltishall	
XZ367	SEPECAT Jaguar GR3 [GP]	RAF, stored Shawbury	
XZ368	SEPECAT Jaguar GR1 [8900M] [AG]	RAF No 1 SoTT, Cosford	
XZ369	SEPECAT Jaguar GR3A [EF]	RAF No 6 Sqn, Coltishall	
XZ370	SEPECAT Jaguar GR1 (9004M) [JB]	RAF No 1 SoTT, Cosford	
XZ371	SEPECAT Jaguar GR1 (8907M) [AP]	RAF No 1 SoTT, Cosford	
XZ372	SEPECAT Jaguar GR3 [ED]	RAF No 41 Sqn, Coltishall	
XZ374	SEPECAT Jaguar GR1 (9005M) [JC]	RAF No 1 SoTT, Cosford	
XZ375	SEPECAT Jaguar GR1A (9255M) [GR]	RAF, stored St Athan	
XZ377	SEPECAT Jaguar GR3A [EG]	RAF No 6 Sqn, Coltishall	
XZ378	SEPECAT Jaguar GR1A [EP]	RAF, stored Shawbury	
XZ382	SEPECAT Jaguar GR1 (8908M)	Privately owned, Bruntingthorpe	
XZ383	SEPECAT Jaguar GR1 (8901M) [AF]	RAF No 1 SoTT, Cosford	
XZ384	SEPECAT Jaguar GR1 (8954M) [BC]	RAF No 1 SoTT, Cosford	
XZ385	SEPECAT Jaguar GR3 [PC]	RAF No 16(R) Sqn, Coltishall	
XZ389	SEPECAT Jaguar GR1 (8946M) [BL]	RAF No 1 SoTT, Cosford	
XZ390	SEPECAT Jaguar GR1 (9003M) [35,JA]	RAF No 1 SoTT, Cosford	
XZ391	SEPECAT Jaguar GR3A [EB]	RAF AWC/SAOEU, Boscombe Down	
XZ392	SEPECAT Jaguar GR1A [GQ]	RAF, stored St Athan	
XZ394	SEPECAT Jaguar GR3 [GN]	RAF No 54 Sqn, Coltishall	
XZ396	SEPECAT Jaguar GR1A [EM]	RAF No 6 Sqn, Coltishall	
XZ398	SEPECAT Jaguar GR3 [FA]	RAF No 41 Sqn, Coltishall	
XZ399	SEPECAT Jaguar GR3A [EJ]	RAF No 6 Sqn, Coltishall	
XZ400	SEPECAT Jaguar GR3A [GR]	DPA/BAE Systems, Warton	
XZ431	HS Buccaneer S2B (9233M)	*Scrapped at Marham, July 2001*	
XZ439	BAe Sea Harrier FA2	DPA/BAE Systems, Warton	
XZ440	BAe Sea Harrier FA2 [127/R]	RN No 800 Sqn, Yeovilton	
XZ455	BAe Sea Harrier FA2 [001] (wreck)	RN FSAIU, Yeovilton	
XZ459	BAe Sea Harrier FA2 [126/R]	DPA/BAE Systems, Warton	
XZ493	BAe Sea Harrier FRS1 (comp XV760) [001/N]	FAA Museum, RNAS Yeovilton	
XZ493	BAe Sea Harrier FRS1 <ff>	RN Yeovilton, Fire Section	
XZ494	BAe Sea Harrier FA2 [128]	RN, St Athan	
XZ497	BAe Sea Harrier FA2 [001]	RN No 801 Sqn, Yeovilton	
XZ499	BAe Sea Harrier FA2 [003]	RN No 801 Sqn, Yeovilton	
XZ559	Slingsby T61F Venture T2 (G-BUEK)	Privately owned, Tibenham	
XZ570	WS61 Sea King HAS5(mod)	RN, stored *HMS Sultan*, Gosport	
XZ571	WS61 Sea King HAS6 [016/L]	RN No 820 Sqn, Culdrose	
XZ574	WS61 Sea King HAS6 [829/CU]	RN No 771 Sqn, Culdrose	
XZ575	WS61 Sea King HU5	DPA/AFD, QinetiQ Boscombe Down	
XZ576	WS61 Sea King HAS6	DPA/AFD, QinetiQ Boscombe Down	
XZ578	WS61 Sea King HU5 [709/PW]	RN	
XZ579	WS61 Sea King HAS6 [707/PW]	RN, stored *HMS Sultan*, Gosport	

Notes	Serial	Type (other identity) [code]	Owner/operator, location or fate
	XZ580	WS61 Sea King HAS6 [704/PW]	RN, stored HMS Sultan, Gosport
	XZ581	WS61 Sea King HAS6 [69/CU]	RN, stored HMS Sultan, Gosport
	XZ585	WS61 Sea King HAR3	RAF No 202 Sqn, A Flt, Boulmer
	XZ586	WS61 Sea King HAR3	RAF No 202 Sqn, A Flt, Boulmer
	XZ587	WS61 Sea King HAR3	DARA, Fleetlands
	XZ588	WS61 Sea King HAR3	RAF No 203(R) Sqn, St Mawgan
	XZ589	WS61 Sea King HAR3	RAF HMF, St Mawgan
	XZ590	WS61 Sea King HAR3	RAF No 78 Sqn, Mount Pleasant, FI
	XZ591	WS61 Sea King HAR3	RAF No 202 Sqn, D Flt, Lossiemouth
	XZ592	WS61 Sea King HAR3	RAF No 203(R) Sqn, St Mawgan
	XZ593	WS61 Sea King HAR3	RAF HMF St Mawgan
	XZ594	WS61 Sea King HAR3	RAF No 202 Sqn, D Flt, Lossiemouth
	XZ595	WS61 Sea King HAR3	RAF No 202 Sqn, E Flt, Leconfield
	XZ596	WS61 Sea King HAR3	RAF No 202 Sqn, E Flt, Leconfield
	XZ597	WS61 Sea King HAR3	RAF No 203(R) Sqn, St Mawgan
	XZ598	WS61 Sea King HAR3	RAF HMF St Mawgan
	XZ599	WS61 Sea King HAR3	RAF/DARA, Fleetlands (damaged)
	XZ605	WS Lynx AH7 [Y]	RM No 847 Sqn, Yeovilton
	XZ606	WS Lynx AH7	AAC No 667 Sqn, Middle Wallop
	XZ607	WS Lynx AH7	AAC No 9 Regt, Dishforth
	XZ608	WS Lynx AH7	AAC No 657 Sqn, Odiham
	XZ609	WS Lynx AH7	AAC No 9 Regt, Dishforth
	XZ611	WS Lynx AH7	AAC No 3 Regt, Wattisham
	XZ612	WS Lynx AH7	RM No 847 Sqn, Yeovilton
	XZ613	WS Lynx AH7 [F]	Army SEAE, Arborfield
	XZ614	WS Lynx AH7 [X]	RM No 847 Sqn, Yeovilton
	XZ615	WS Lynx AH7	AAC No 655 Sqn/5 Regt, Aldergrove
	XZ616	WS Lynx AH7	AAC No 657 Sqn, Odiham
	XZ617	WS Lynx AH7	AAC No 7 Air Assault Battalion, Wattisham
	XZ630	Panavia Tornado GR1 (8976M)	DARA, RAF St Athan, BDRT
	XZ631	Panavia Tornado GR1	DPA/BAE Systems, Warton
	XZ641	WS Lynx AH7	AAC No 7 Air Assault Battalion, Wattisham
	XZ642	WS Lynx AH7	AAC No 663 Sqn/3 Regt, Wattisham
	XZ643	WS Lynx AH7	AAC No 654 Sqn/4 Regt, Wattisham
	XZ645	WS Lynx AH7	AAC No 4 Regt, Wattisham
	XZ646	WS Lynx AH7	AAC No 657 Sqn, Odiham
	XZ647	WS Lynx AH7	AAC No 667 Sqn, Middle Wallop
	XZ648	WS Lynx AH7	AAC No 664 Sqn/9 Regt, Dishforth
	XZ649	WS Lynx AH7	DPA/AFD, QinetiQ Boscombe Down
	XZ651	WS Lynx AH7	AAC No 9 Regt, Dishforth
	XZ652	WS Lynx AH7 [T]	AAC No 671 Sqn/2 Regt, Middle Wallop
	XZ653	WS Lynx AH7	AAC No 663 Sqn/3 Regt, Wattisham
	XZ654	WS Lynx AH7	AAC No 655 Sqn/5 Regt, Aldergrove
	XZ655	WS Lynx AH7	AAC No 655 Sqn/5 Regt, Aldergrove
	XZ661	WS Lynx AH1	AAC No 655 Sqn/5 Regt, Aldergrove
	XZ663	WS Lynx AH7	AAC No 655 Sqn/5 Regt, Aldergrove
	XZ664	WS Lynx AH7	Crashed 23 February 2001, Leeming
	XZ665	WS Lynx AH7	AAC, stored DARA Fleetlands
	XZ666	WS Lynx AH7	Army SEAE, Arborfield
	XZ668	WS Lynx AH7 [UN] (wreckage)	AAC Middle Wallop
	XZ669	WS Lynx AH7	AAC No 4 Regt, Wattisham
	XZ670	WS Lynx AH7	AAC, stored DARA Fleetlands
	XZ671	WS Lynx AH7 <ff>	Westland Helicopters, Yeovil, instructional use
	XZ672	WS Lynx AH7	AAC No 655 Sqn/5 Regt, Aldergrove
	XZ673	WS Lynx AH7	AAC No 655 Sqn/5 Regt, Aldergrove
	XZ674	WS Lynx AH7	AAC No 25 Flt, Belize
	XZ675	WS Lynx AH7 [E]	AAC No 671 Sqn/2 Regt, Middle Wallop
	XZ676	WS Lynx AH7 [N]	AAC No 671 Sqn/2 Regt, Middle Wallop
	XZ677	WS Lynx AH7	AAC No 657 Sqn, Odiham
	XZ678	WS Lynx AH7	AAC No 3 Regt, Wattisham
	XZ679	WS Lynx AH7	AAC No 1 Regt, Bruggen
	XZ680	WS Lynx AH7	AAC No 1 Regt, Bruggen
	XZ689	WS Lynx HMA8 [674]	RN No 702 Sqn, Yeovilton
	XZ690	WS Lynx HMA8 [355/SM]	RN No 815 Sqn, HQ Flt, Yeovilton
	XZ691	WS Lynx HMA8 [670]	DARA, Fleetlands
	XZ692	WS Lynx HMA8 [365/AY]	DARA, Fleetlands
	XZ693	WS Lynx HAS3S [639]	RN No 702 Sqn, Yeovilton
	XZ694	WS Lynx HAS3S [411/EB]	RN No 815 Sqn, Edinburgh Flt, Yeovilton
	XZ695	WS Lynx HMA8	RN No 815 Sqn, Yeovilton
	XZ696	WS Lynx HAS3S [335/CF]	RN No 815 Sqn, Cardiff Flt, Yeovilton
	XZ697	WS Lynx HMA8 [437/GT]	RN No 815 Sqn, Grafton Flt, Yeovilton
	XZ698	WS Lynx HMA8 [672]	RN No 702 Sqn, Yeovilton

Serial	Type (other identity) [code]	Owner/operator, location or fate	Notes
XZ699	WS Lynx HAS8 [303]	DARA, Fleetlands	
XZ719	WS Lynx HMA8 [317]	RN No 815 Sqn OEU, Yeovilton	
XZ720	WS Lynx HAS3S [302]	RN No 815 Sqn, HQ Flt, Yeovilton	
XZ721	WS Lynx HMA8 [350/CL]	RN No 815 Sqn, *Cumberland* Flt, Yeovilton	
XZ722	WS Lynx HMA8	RN AMG, Yeovilton	
XZ723	WS Lynx HMA8 [426/PD]	RN No 815 Sqn, *Portland* Flt, Yeovilton	
XZ724	WS Lynx HAS3S [426/PD]	RN No 815 Sqn, *Portland* Flt, Yeovilton	
XZ725	WS Lynx HMA8 [633]	DARA, Fleetlands (conversion)	
XZ726	WS Lynx HMA8 [345/NC]	RN No 815 Sqn, *Newcastle* Flt, Yeovilton	
XZ727	WS Lynx HAS3S [303]	RN No 815 Sqn, HQ Flt, Yeovilton	
XZ728	WS Lynx HMA8 [415/MM]	RN, stored DARA Fleetlands	
XZ729	WS Lynx HMA8 [632]	DARA, Fleetlands (conversion)	
XZ730	WS Lynx HAS3CTS [632]	RN No 702 Sqn, Yeovilton	
XZ731	WS Lynx HMA8 [307]	DARA, Fleetlands	
XZ732	WS Lynx HMA8	RN AMG, Yeovilton	
XZ733	WS Lynx HAS3S	RN No 815 Sqn, HQ Flt, Yeovilton	
XZ735	WS Lynx HAS3S [304]	RN No 815 Sqn, HQ Flt, Yeovilton	
XZ736	WS Lynx HMA8 [352/SD]	RN No 815 Sqn, *Sheffield* Flt, Yeovilton	
XZ920	WS61 Sea King HU5 [828]	RN No 771 Sqn, Culdrose	
XZ921	WS61 Sea King HAS6 [269/N]	RN ETS, Culdrose	
XZ922	WS61 Sea King HAS6 [701]	RN, stored *HMS Sultan*, Gosport	
XZ930	WS Gazelle HT3 [Q]	RN AESS, *HMS Sultan*, Gosport	
XZ931	WS Gazelle HT3 [R]	*Sold as N931XZ, September 2001*	
XZ932	WS Gazelle HT3 [S]	Privately owned, Stapleford Tawney	
XZ933	WS Gazelle HT3 [T]	QinetiQ Boscombe Down, spares use	
XZ934	WS Gazelle HT3 [U]	RAF, stored Shawbury	
XZ935	WS Gazelle HCC4	RAF, stored Shawbury	
XZ936	WS Gazelle HT2 [6]	DPA/AFD/ETPS, QinetiQ Boscombe Down	
XZ937	WS Gazelle HT2 [Y]	Privately owned, Stapleford Tawney	
XZ938	WS Gazelle HT2 [45/CU]	RN, stored Shawbury	
XZ939	WS Gazelle HT2 [9]	DPA/AFD/ETPS, QinetiQ Boscombe Down	
XZ940	WS Gazelle HT2 (G-CBBV) [O]	Privately owned, Redhill	
XZ941	WS Gazelle HT2 [B]	DARA Trg School, RAF St Athan, BDRT	
XZ942	WS Gazelle HT2 [42/CU]	RN, stored Shawbury	
XZ964	BAe Harrier GR3 [D]	Royal Engineers Museum, Chatham	
XZ966	BAe Harrier GR3 (9221M) [G]	MoD FSCTE, Manston	
XZ968	BAe Harrier GR3 (9222M) [3G]	Muckleborough Collection, Weybourne	
XZ969	BAe Harrier GR3 [69]	SFDO, RNAS Culdrose	
XZ971	BAe Harrier GR3 (9219M) [G]	RAF, stored Shawbury	
XZ987	BAe Harrier GR3 (9185M) [C]	RAF Stafford, at main gate	
XZ990	BAe Harrier GR3 <ff>	No 1220 Sqn ATC, March, Cambs	
XZ990	BAe Harrier GR3 <rf>	RAF Wittering, derelict	
XZ991	BAe Harrier GR3 (9162M) [3A]	DARA, RAF St Athan, BDRT	
XZ993	BAe Harrier GR3 (9240M) (fuselage)	DARA, RAF St Athan, fire training	
XZ994	BAe Harrier GR3 (9170M) [U]	RAF Air Movements School, Brize Norton	
XZ995	BAe Harrier GR3 (G-CBGK) [3G]	Privately owned, Lowestoft	
XZ996	BAe Harrier GR3 [96]	SFDO, RNAS Culdrose	
XZ997	BAe Harrier GR3 (9122M) [V]	RAF Museum, Hendon	
ZA101	BAe Hawk 100 (G-HAWK)	DPA/BAE Systems, Warton	
ZA105	WS61 Sea King HAR3 [S]	RAF No 78 Sqn, Mount Pleasant, FI	
ZA110	BAe Jetstream T2 (F-BTMI) [563/CU]	RN No 750 Sqn, Culdrose	
ZA111	BAe Jetstream T2 (9Q-CTC) [565/CU]	RN No 750 Sqn, Culdrose	
ZA126	WS61 Sea King HAS6 [504/CU]	RN, stored *HMS Sultan*, Gosport	
ZA127	WS61 Sea King HAS6 [509/CU]	RN, stored *HMS Sultan*, Gosport	
ZA128	WS61 Sea King HAS6 [010/L]	RN No 810 Sqn, Culdrose	
ZA129	WS61 Sea King HAS6 [502/CU]	RN, stored *HMS Sultan*, Gosport	
ZA130	WS61 Sea King HU5 [824]	RN No 771 Sqn, Culdrose	
ZA131	WS61 Sea King HAS6 [271/N]	RN, stored *HMS Sultan*, Gosport	
ZA133	WS61 Sea King HAS6 [013]	RN No 820 Sqn, Culdrose	
ZA134	WS61 Sea King HU5 [825]	RN No 771 Sqn, Culdrose	
ZA135	WS61 Sea King HAS6 [705/PW]	RN No 771 Sqn, Prestwick	
ZA136	WS61 Sea King HAS6 [018/L]	RN, AESS, *HMS Sultan*, Gosport (wreck)	
ZA137	WS61 Sea King HU5 [820]	RN No 771 Sqn, Culdrose	
ZA140	BAe VC10 K2 (G-ARVL) [A]	*Scrapped at St Athan, January 2001*	
ZA142	BAe VC10 K2 (G-ARVI) [C]	RAF No 101 Squadron, Brize Norton	
ZA144	BAe VC10 K2 (G-ARVC) [E]	*Scrapped at St Athan, April 2001*	
ZA147	BAe VC10 K3 (5H-MMT) [F]	RAF No 101 Sqn, Brize Norton	
ZA148	BAe VC10 K3 (5Y-ADA) [G]	RAF No 101 Sqn, Brize Norton	

Notes	Serial	Type (other identity) [code]	Owner/operator, location or fate
	ZA149	BAe VC10 K3 (5X-UVJ) [H]	RAF No 101 Sqn, Brize Norton
	ZA150	BAe VC10 K3 (5H-MOG)	RAF No 101 Sqn, Brize Norton
	ZA166	WS61 Sea King HU5 [189/CU]	RN, stored DARA Fleetlands
	ZA167	WS61 Sea King HU5 [822/CU]	RN No 771 Sqn, Culdrose
	ZA168	WS61 Sea King HAS6	RN No 849 Sqn, HQ Flt, Culdrose
	ZA169	WS61 Sea King HAS6 [500/CU]	RN AMG, Culdrose
	ZA170	WS61 Sea King HU5	RN MASU, DARA Fleetlands
	ZA175	BAe Sea Harrier FA2	RN, St Athan
	ZA176	BAe Sea Harrier FA2	RN AMG, Yeovilton
	ZA195	BAe Sea Harrier FA2	DPA/BAE Systems, Warton
	ZA250	BAe Harrier T52 (G-VTOL)	Brooklands Museum, Weybridge
	ZA254	Panavia Tornado F2 (9253M) (fuselage)	RAF Coningsby, instructional use
	ZA267	Panavia Tornado F2 (9284M)	RAF Marham, instructional use
	ZA283	Panavia Tornado F2	*Scrapped at St Athan, January 2001*
	ZA291	WS61 Sea King HC4 [ZX]	RN No 848 Sqn, Yeovilton
	ZA292	WS61 Sea King HC4 [ZR]	DPA/Westland Helicopters, Weston-super-Mare
	ZA293	WS61 Sea King HC4 [ZO]	RN No 848 Sqn, Yeovilton
	ZA295	WS61 Sea King HC4 [ZR]	RN No 848 Sqn, Yeovilton
	ZA296	WS61 Sea King HC4 [VO]	RN No 846 Sqn, Yeovilton
	ZA297	WS61 Sea King HC4 [C]	RN No 845 Sqn, Yeovilton
	ZA298	WS61 Sea King HC4 [G]	RN No 845 Sqn, Yeovilton
	ZA299	WS61 Sea King HC4 [VV]	RN No 846 Sqn, Yeovilton
	ZA310	WS61 Sea King HC4 [ZY]	RN No 848 Sqn, Yeovilton
	ZA312	WS61 Sea King HC4 [ZS]	RN AMG, Yeovilton
	ZA313	WS61 Sea King HC4 [M]	RN No 845 Sqn, Yeovilton
	ZA314	WS61 Sea King HC4 [F]	RN No 845 Sqn, Yeovilton
	ZA319	Panavia Tornado GR1 [TAV]	RAF, stored St Athan
	ZA320	Panavia Tornado GR1 [TAW]	RAF, stored St Athan
	ZA321	Panavia Tornado GR1 [TAB]	RAF, stored St Athan
	ZA322	Panavia Tornado GR1 [TAC]	RAF Marham, WLT
	ZA323	Panavia Tornado GR1 [TAZ]	RAF No 15(R) Sqn, Lossiemouth
	ZA324	Panavia Tornado GR1 [TAY]	RAF Lossiemouth, BDRT
	ZA325	Panavia Tornado GR1	RAF, stored St Athan
	ZA326	Panavia Tornado GR1P	DPA/AFD, QinetiQ Boscombe Down
	ZA327	Panavia Tornado GR1	DPA/BAE Systems, Warton
	ZA328	Panavia Tornado GR1	DPA/BAE Systems, Warton
	ZA352	Panavia Tornado GR1 [TAU]	RAF, stored St Athan
	ZA353	Panavia Tornado GR1 [B-53]	DPA/AFD, QinetiQ Boscombe Down
	ZA354	Panavia Tornado GR1	DPA/BAE Systems, Warton
	ZA355	Panavia Tornado GR1 [TAA]	RAF Lossiemouth, WLT
	ZA356	Panavia Tornado GR1 [TP]	RAF No 15(R) Sqn, Lossiemouth
	ZA357	Panavia Tornado GR1 [TS]	RAF No 15(R) Sqn, Lossiemouth
	ZA358	Panavia Tornado GR1	RAF, stored St Athan
	ZA359	Panavia Tornado GR1	BAE Systems Warton, Overseas Customer Training Centre
	ZA360	Panavia Tornado GR1 [TC]	DPA/BAE Systems, Warton
	ZA361	Panavia Tornado GR1 [TD]	RAF, stored St Athan
	ZA362	Panavia Tornado GR1 [TR]	RAF No 15(R) Sqn, Lossiemouth
	ZA365	Panavia Tornado GR4 [AJ-Y]	RAF No 617 Sqn, Lossiemouth
	ZA367	Panavia Tornado GR4 [FW]	RAF No 12 Sqn, Lossiemouth
	ZA369	Panavia Tornado GR4A [U]	RAF No 13 Sqn, Marham
	ZA370	Panavia Tornado GR4A [A]	RAF, stored St Athan
	ZA371	Panavia Tornado GR4A [C]	RAF No 2 Sqn, Marham
	ZA372	Panavia Tornado GR4A [E]	RAF No 2 Sqn, Marham
	ZA373	Panavia Tornado GR4A [H]	RAF No 2 Sqn, Marham
	ZA374	Panavia Tornado GR1 [TTA]	RAF No 15(R) Sqn, Lossiemouth
	ZA375	Panavia Tornado GR1 [AJ-W]	RAF Marham, BDRT
	ZA393	Panavia Tornado GR4 [BE]	RAF, St Athan
	ZA395	Panavia Tornado GR4A [N]	RAF, St Athan
	ZA398	Panavia Tornado GR4A [S]	RAF No 2 Sqn, Marham
	ZA399	Panavia Tornado GR1 [AJ-C]	RAF, stored St Athan
	ZA400	Panavia Tornado GR4A [T]	RAF No 2 Sqn, Marham
	ZA401	Panavia Tornado GR4A [R]	DPA/BAE Systems, Warton (conversion)
	ZA402	Panavia Tornado GR4A	DPA/BAE Systems, Warton (conversion)
	ZA404	Panavia Tornado GR4A [W]	RAF No 2 Sqn, Marham
	ZA405	Panavia Tornado GR4A [Y]	RAF No 2 Sqn, Marham
	ZA406	Panavia Tornado GR4	DPA/BAE Systems, Warton (conversion)
	ZA407	Panavia Tornado GR1 [AJ-N]	RAF Marham, for display
	ZA409	Panavia Tornado GR1 [TV]	RAF No 15(R) Sqn, Lossiemouth
	ZA410	Panavia Tornado GR4 [DX]	RAF No 31 Sqn, Marham
	ZA411	Panavia Tornado GR1 [[TT]	RAF No 15(R) Sqn, Lossiemouth

Serial	Type (other identity) [code]	Owner/operator, location or fate	Notes
ZA412	Panavia Tornado GR1 [IV]	RAF/DARA, St Athan	
ZA446	Panavia Tornado GR1 [U]	RAF AWC/SAOEU, Boscombe Down	
ZA447	Panavia Tornado GR1 [TA]	RAF, stored St Athan	
ZA449	Panavia Tornado GR4 [AJ-N]	RAF No 617 Sqn, Lossiemouth	
ZA450	Panavia Tornado GR1 [TH]	RAF, stored St Athan	
ZA452	Panavia Tornado GR1 [TJ]	RAF No 15(R) Sqn, Lossiemouth	
ZA453	Panavia Tornado GR1 [TB]	RAF No 15(R) Sqn, Lossiemouth	
ZA455	Panavia Tornado GR1 [F]	RAF, stored St Athan	
ZA456	Panavia Tornado GR1 [AJ-Q]	RAF No 617 Sqn, Lossiemouth	
ZA457	Panavia Tornado GR1 [AJ-J]	RAF No 9 Sqn, Marham	
ZA458	Panavia Tornado GR4 [DG]	RAF No 31 Sqn, Marham	
ZA459	Panavia Tornado GR1 [TQ]	RAF No 15(R) Sqn, Lossiemouth	
ZA460	Panavia Tornado GR1 [AJ-A]	RAF, stored St Athan	
ZA461	Panavia Tornado GR1	RAF No 15(R) Sqn, Lossiemouth	
ZA462	Panavia Tornado GR4	DPA/BAE Systems, Warton (conversion)	
ZA463	Panavia Tornado GR4	DPA/BAE Systems, Warton (conversion)	
ZA465	Panavia Tornado GR1 [FF]	Imperial War Museum, Duxford	
ZA466	Panavia Tornado GR1 <ff>	DARA, RAF St Athan, BDRT	
ZA469	Panavia Tornado GR1 [TM]	DARA, RAF St Athan	
ZA470	Panavia Tornado GR1	DARA, RAF St Athan	
ZA471	Panavia Tornado GR1 [AJ-K]	RAF St Athan Fire Section	
ZA472	Panavia Tornado GR4	DPA/BAE Systems, Warton (conversion)	
ZA473	Panavia Tornado GR1 [TK]	RAF No 15(R) Sqn, Lossiemouth	
ZA474	Panavia Tornado GR1 [AJ-F]	RAF No 617 Sqn, Lossiemouth	
ZA475	Panavia Tornado GR1 [FH]	RAF Lossiemouth, on display	
ZA490	Panavia Tornado GR1 [FJ]	RAF No 12 Sqn, Lossiemouth	
ZA491	Panavia Tornado GR1 [TI]	RAF No 15(R) Sqn, Lossiemouth	
ZA492	Panavia Tornado GR1 [TE]	RAF No 14 Sqn, Lossiemouth	
ZA541	Panavia Tornado GR4 [DZ]	RAF No 31 Sqn, Marham	
ZA542	Panavia Tornado GR4 [DM]	RAF No 31 Sqn, Marham	
ZA543	Panavia Tornado GR4	DPA/AFD, QinetiQ Boscombe Down	
ZA544	Panavia Tornado GR4 [FZ]	RAF No 12 Sqn, Lossiemouth	
ZA546	Panavia Tornado GR4 [TB]	RAF Lossiemouth	
ZA547	Panavia Tornado GR4 [DC]	RAF No 31 Sqn, Marham	
ZA548	Panavia Tornado GR4 [III]	RAF No13 Sqn, Marham	
ZA549	Panavia Tornado GR4 [AJ-Z]	RAF No 617 Sqn, Lossiemouth	
ZA550	Panavia Tornado GR4 [DD]	RAF No 31 Sqn, Marham	
ZA551	Panavia Tornado GR4 [AX]	RAF No 9 Sqn, Marham	
ZA552	Panavia Tornado GR4 [TX]	RAF No 15(R) Sqn, Lossiemouth	
ZA553	Panavia Tornado GR4 [DI]	RAF No 31 Sqn, Marham	
ZA554	Panavia Tornado GR4 [DF]	RAF No 31 Sqn, Marham	
ZA556	Panavia Tornado GR2 [Z]	RAF No 13 Sqn, Marham	
ZA556	Panavia Tornado GR1 <R> (ZA368/BAPC 155) [Z]	RAF EPTT, St Athan	
ZA557	Panavia Tornado GR4 [AC]	RAF No 9 Sqn, Marham	
ZA559	Panavia Tornado GR4 [AD]	RAF No 9 Sqn, Marham	
ZA560	Panavia Tornado GR4 [BC]	RAF No 14 Sqn, Lossiemouth	
ZA562	Panavia Tornado GR1 [TO]	RAF No 15(R) Sqn, Lossiemouth	
ZA563	Panavia Tornado GR4 [AG]	RAF No 9 Sqn, Marham	
ZA564	Panavia Tornado GR4 [TTB]	RAF No 15(R) Sqn, Lossiemouth	
ZA585	Panavia Tornado GR4 [AH]	RAF No 9 Sqn, Marham	
ZA587	Panavia Tornado GR4	RAF Lossiemouth	
ZA588	Panavia Tornado GR4 [BB]	RAF No 14 Sqn, Lossiemouth	
ZA589	Panavia Tornado GR4	DPA/AFD, QinetiQ Boscombe Down	
ZA590	Panavia Tornado GR1	RAF St Athan Fire Section	
ZA591	Panavia Tornado GR4 [DJ]	RAF No 31 Sqn, Marham	
ZA592	Panavia Tornado GR4 [BJ]	RAF No 14 Sqn, Lossiemouth	
ZA594	Panavia Tornado GR4 [TTV]	RAF No 15(R) Sqn, Lossiemouth	
ZA595	Panavia Tornado GR4 [VIII]	RAF No 13 Sqn, Marham	
ZA596	Panavia Tornado GR4	RAF No 14 Sqn, Lossiemouth	
ZA597	Panavia Tornado GR4 [TA]	DPA/BAE Systems, Warton (conversion)	
ZA598	Panavia Tornado GR4 [TW]	RAF No 15(R) Sqn, Lossiemouth	
ZA599	Panavia Tornado GR4 [VI]	RAF No 2 Sqn, Marham	
ZA600	Panavia Tornado GR4	RAF No 12 Sqn, Lossiemouth	
ZA601	Panavia Tornado GR4 [TTE]	RAF No 15(R) Sqn, Lossiemouth	
ZA602	Panavia Tornado GR4 [BY]	RAF No 14 Sqn, Lossiemouth	
ZA604	Panavia Tornado GR4 [TY]	RAF No 15(R) Sqn, Lossiemouth	
ZA606	Panavia Tornado GR4	RAF No 14 Sqn, Lossiemouth	
ZA607	Panavia Tornado GR4 [AB]	RAF No 9 Sqn, Marham	
ZA608	Panavia Tornado GR4 [TN]	RAF No 15(R) Sqn, Lossiemouth	
ZA609	Panavia Tornado GR4	RAF AWC/SAOEU, Boscombe Down	
ZA611	Panavia Tornado GR4 [TK]	RAF No 15(R) Sqn, Lossiemouth	
ZA612	Panavia Tornado GR4	DPA/BAE Systems, Warton (conversion)	

Notes	Serial	Type (other identity) [code]	Owner/operator, location or fate
	ZA613	Panavia Tornado GR1 [TL]	RAF No 15(R) Sqn, Lossiemouth
	ZA614	Panavia Tornado GR4 [AJ-J]	RAF No 617 Sqn, Lossiemouth
	ZA634	Slingsby T61F Venture T2 (G-BUHA) [C]	Privately owned, Rufforth
	ZA670	B-V Chinook HC2 (N37010) [EY]	RAF No 7 Sqn, Odiham
	ZA671	B-V Chinook HC2 (N37011) [BB]	RAF No 18 Sqn, Odiham
	ZA673	B-V Chinook HC2 (N37016) [NX]	RAF No 27 Sqn, Odiham
	ZA674	B-V Chinook HC2 (N37019)	RAF No 27 Sqn, Odiham
	ZA675	B-V Chinook HC2 (N37020)	RAF No 7 Sqn, Odiham
	ZA676	B-V Chinook HC1 (N37021/9230M) [FG] (wreck)	AAC, Wattisham
	ZA677	B-V Chinook HC2 (N37022) [EG]	RAF No 7 Sqn, Odiham
	ZA678	B-V Chinook HC1 (N37023/9229M) [EZ] (wreck)	RAF Odiham, BDRT
	ZA679	B-V Chinook HC2 (N37025)	RAF No 18 Sqn, Odiham
	ZA680	B-V Chinook HC2 (N37026)	RAF No 27 Sqn, Odiham
	ZA681	B-V Chinook HC2 (N37027) [ED]	DARA, Fleetlands
	ZA682	B-V Chinook HC2 (N37029) [EW]	RAF No 27 Sqn, Odiham
	ZA683	B-V Chinook HC2 (N37030) [BD]	RAF No 18 Sqn, Odiham
	ZA684	B-V Chinook HC2 (N37031) [EL]	RAF No 7 Sqn, Odiham
	ZA704	B-V Chinook HC2 (N37033) [EJ]	DARA, Fleetlands (wreck)
	ZA705	B-V Chinook HC2 (N37035) [BE]	RAF No 27 Sqn, Odiham
	ZA707	B-V Chinook HC2 (N37040) [EV]	DARA, Fleetlands
	ZA708	B-V Chinook HC2 (N37042)	RAF No 18 Sqn, Odiham
	ZA709	B-V Chinook HC2 (N37043)	RAF No 27 Sqn, Odiham
	ZA710	B-V Chinook HC2 (N37044) [NC]	RAF No 27 Sqn, Odiham
	ZA711	B-V Chinook HC2 (N37046) [BA]	RAF No 27 Sqn, Odiham
	ZA712	B-V Chinook HC2 (N37047) [ER]	DARA, Fleetlands
	ZA713	B-V Chinook HC2 (N37048)	RAF No 27 Sqn, Odiham
	ZA714	B-V Chinook HC2 (N37051) [NT]	RAF No 27 Sqn, Odiham
	ZA717	B-V Chinook HC1 (N37056/9238M) (wreck)	Trenchard Hall, RAF Cranwell, instructional use
	ZA718	B-V Chinook HC2 (N37058) [BN]	RAF No 78 Sqn, Mount Pleasant, FI
	ZA720	B-V Chinook HC2 (N37060) [BR]	RAF No 18 Sqn, Odiham
	ZA726	WS Gazelle AH1 [F1]	AAC No 671 Sqn/2 Regt, Middle Wallop
	ZA728	WS Gazelle AH1	RM No 847 Sqn, Yeovilton
	ZA729	WS Gazelle AH1	AAC
	ZA730	WS Gazelle AH1	AAC, stored Shawbury
	ZA731	WS Gazelle AH1	AAC No 29 Flt, BATUS, Suffield, Canada
	ZA733	WS Gazelle AH1	DARA Fleetlands Apprentice School
	ZA734	WS Gazelle AH1	AAC No 25 Flt, Belize
	ZA735	WS Gazelle AH1	AAC No 25 Flt, Belize
	ZA736	WS Gazelle AH1	AAC No 29 Flt, BATUS, Suffield, Canada
	ZA737	WS Gazelle AH1	Museum of Army Flying, Middle Wallop
	ZA766	WS Gazelle AH1	AAC, stored DARA Fleetlands
	ZA768	WS Gazelle AH1 [F] (wreck)	AAC, stored DARA Fleetlands
	ZA769	WS Gazelle AH1 [K]	Army SEAE, Arborfield
	ZA771	WS Gazelle AH1	AAC No 663 Sqn/3 Regt, Wattisham
	ZA772	WS Gazelle AH1	AAC No 665 Sqn/5 Regt, Aldergrove
	ZA773	WS Gazelle AH1 [F]	AAC No 666(V) Sqn/7 Regt, Netheravon
	ZA774	WS Gazelle AH1	AAC No 665 Sqn/5 Regt, Aldergrove
	ZA775	WS Gazelle AH1	AAC No 665 Sqn/5 Regt, Aldergrove
	ZA776	WS Gazelle AH1 [F]	RM No 847 Sqn, Yeovilton
	ZA777	WS Gazelle AH1 [B]	Crashed 16 Nov 2001, Bruton, Somerset
	ZA802	WS Gazelle HT3 [W]	RAF, stored Shawbury
	ZA803	WS Gazelle HT3 [X]	Privately owned, Goodwood
	ZA804	WS Gazelle HT3 [I]	Qinetiq, for spares, Boscombe Down
	ZA934	WS Puma HC1 [BZ]	RAF No 72 Sqn, Aldergrove
	ZA935	WS Puma HC1	RAF No 33 Sqn, Benson
	ZA936	WS Puma HC1	RAF No 33 Sqn, Benson
	ZA937	WS Puma HC1	RAF No 33 Sqn, Benson
	ZA938	WS Puma HC1	RAF No 230 Sqn, Aldergrove
	ZA939	WS Puma HC1	RAF No 230 Sqn, Aldergrove
	ZA940	WS Puma HC1	RAF No 230 Sqn, Algergrove
	ZA947	Douglas Dakota C3 [YS-H]	RAF BBMF, Coningsby
	ZB500	WS Lynx 800 (G-LYNX/ZA500)	The Helicopter Museum, Weston-super-Mare
	ZB506	WS61 Sea King Mk 4X	DPA/AFD, QinetiQ Boscombe Down
	ZB507	WS61 Sea King HC4 [ZN]	RN No 848 Sqn, Yeovilton
	ZB600	BAe Harrier T4	BAE Systems RNAS Yeovilton, for Indian Navy
	ZB601	BAe Harrier T4 (fuselage)	RNAS Yeovilton, Fire Section

Serial	Type (other identity) [code]	Owner/operator, location or fate	Notes
ZB602	BAe Harrier T4	BAE Systems RNAS Yeovilton, for Indian Navy	
ZB603	BAe Harrier T8 [724]	RN No 899 Sqn, Yeovilton	
ZB604	BAe Harrier T8 [722]	RN No 899 Sqn, Yeovilton	
ZB605	BAe Harrier T8 [720/VL]	RN, St Athan	
ZB615	SEPECAT Jaguar T2A	DPA/AFD, QinetiQ Boscombe Down	
ZB625	WS Gazelle HT3 [N]	DPA/AFD, QinetiQ Boscombe Down	
ZB626	WS Gazelle HT3 (G-BZDW) [L]	Repainted as G-BZDW by July 2001	
ZB627	WS Gazelle HT3 [A]	RAF, stored Shawbury	
ZB629	WS Gazelle HCC4 [N]	RAF, stored Shawbury	
ZB646	WS Gazelle HT2 (G-CBGZ) [59/CU]	Privately owned, Knebworth	
ZB647	WS Gazelle HT2 [40/CU]	RN, stored Shawbury	
ZB649	WS Gazelle HT2 [VL]	RN, stored Shawbury	
ZB665	WS Gazelle AH1	AAC No 665 Sqn/5 Regt, Aldergrove	
ZB667	WS Gazelle AH1	AAC No 16 Flt, Dhekelia, Cyprus	
ZB668	WS Gazelle AH1 (TAD 015)	Army SEAE, Arborfield	
ZB669	WS Gazelle AH1	AAC No 654 Sqn/4 Regt, Wattisham	
ZB670	WS Gazelle AH1	AAC No 665 Sqn/5 Regt, Aldergrove	
ZB671	WS Gazelle AH1 [2]	AAC No 29 Flt, BATUS, Suffield, Canada	
ZB672	WS Gazelle AH1	Army Training Regiment, Winchester	
ZB673	WS Gazelle AH1 [P]	AAC No 671 Sqn/2 Regt, Middle Wallop	
ZB674	WS Gazelle AH1	AAC No 665 Sqn/5 Regt, Aldergrove	
ZB676	WS Gazelle AH1	RM No 847 Sqn, Yeovilton	
ZB677	WS Gazelle AH1	AAC No 29 Flt, BATUS, Suffield, Canada	
ZB678	WS Gazelle AH1	Army SEAE, Arborfield	
ZB679	WS Gazelle AH1	AAC No 16 Flt, Dhekelia, Cyprus	
ZB682	WS Gazelle AH1	AAC No 665 Sqn/5 Regt, Aldergrove	
ZB683	WS Gazelle AH1	AAC No 665 Sqn/5 Regt, Aldergrove	
ZB684	WS Gazelle AH1	AAC No 667 Sqn, Middle Wallop	
ZB685	WS Gazelle AH1	DARA, Fleetlands	
ZB686	WS Gazelle AH1	AAC No 665 Sqn/5 Regt, Aldergrove	
ZB688	WS Gazelle AH1 [H]	AAC No 671 Sqn/2 Regt, Middle Wallop	
ZB689	WS Gazelle AH1	AAC No 665 Sqn/5 Regt, Aldergrove	
ZB690	WS Gazelle AH1	AAC No 16 Flt, Dhekelia, Cyprus	
ZB691	WS Gazelle AH1	AAC No 9 Regt, Dishforth	
ZB692	WS Gazelle AH1	AAC No 9 Regt, Dishforth	
ZB693	WS Gazelle AH1	AAC No 29 Flt, BATUS, Suffield, Canada	
ZD230	BAC Super VC10 K4 (G-ASGA) [K]	RAF No 101 Sqn, Brize Norton	
ZD234	BAC Super VC10 (G-ASGF/8700M)	RAF Brize Norton, tanker simulator	
ZD235	BAC Super VC10 K4 (G-ASGG) [L]	RAF No 101 Sqn, Brize Norton	
ZD240	BAC Super VC10 K4 (G-ASGL) [M]	RAF No 101 Sqn, Brize Norton	
ZD241	BAC Super VC10 K4 (G-ASGM) [N]	RAF No 101 Sqn, Brize Norton	
ZD242	BAC Super VC10 K4 (G-ASGP)	RAF No 101 Sqn, Brize Norton	
ZD249	WS Lynx HAS3S [637]	RN No 702 Sqn, Yeovilton	
ZD250	WS Lynx HAS3S [302]	RN No 815 Sqn, HQ Flt, Yeovilton	
ZD251	WS Lynx HAS3S [636]	RN No 702 Sqn, Yeovilton	
ZD252	WS Lynx HMA8 [671]	RN No 702 Sqn, Yeovilton	
ZD253	WS Lynx HAS3S [407/YK]	Crashed into Arabian sea off Oman, 27 October 2001	
ZD254	WS Lynx HAS3S [457/LA]	RN/AMG, Yeovilton	
ZD255	WS Lynx HAS3S [372/NL]	RN No 815 Sqn, Northumberland Flt, Yeovilton	
ZD257	WS Lynx HMA8 [474/RM]	RN No 815 Sqn, Richmond Flt, Yeovilton	
ZD258	WS Lynx HMA8 (XZ258) [319]	RN No 815 Sqn OEU, Yeovilton	
ZD259	WS Lynx HMA8 [407/YK]	RN No 815 Sqn, York Flt, Yeovilton	
ZD260	WS Lynx HMA8 [334/SN]	RN No 815 Sqn, Southampton Flt, Yeovilton	
ZD261	WS Lynx HMA8	RN No 815 Sqn OEU, Yeovilton	
ZD262	WS Lynx HMA8 [444/MR]	RN No 815 Sqn, Montrose Flt, Yeovilton	
ZD263	WS Lynx HAS3S [305]	RN No 815 Sqn, HQ Flt, Yeovilton	
ZD264	WS Lynx HAS3S [334/SN]	RN No 815 Sqn, Southampton Flt, Yeovilton	
ZD265	WS Lynx HMA8	RN No 815 Sqn, HQ Flt, Yeovilton	
ZD266	WS Lynx HMA8	DPA/Westland Helicopters, Weston-super-Mare	
ZD267	WS Lynx HMA8	DPA/Westland Helicopters, Yeovil	
ZD268	WS Lynx HMA8	DARA, Fleetlands	

Notes	Serial	Type (other identity) [code]	Owner/operator, location or fate
	ZD272	WS Lynx AH7 [H]	AAC No 671 Sqn/2 Regt, Middle Wallop
	ZD273	WS Lynx AH7	AAC No 655 Sqn/5 Regt, Aldergrove
	ZD274	WS Lynx AH7	AAC No 664 Sqn/9 Regt, Dishforth
	ZD276	WS Lynx AH7 [X]	AAC No 671 Sqn/2 Regt, Middle Wallop
	ZD277	WS Lynx AH7	AAC No 3 Regt, Wattisham
	ZD278	WS Lynx AH7 [A]	AAC No 655 Sqn/5 Regt, Aldergrove
	ZD279	WS Lynx AH7	AAC No 655 Sqn/5 Regt, Aldergrove
	ZD280	WS Lynx AH7	AAC No 661 Sqn/1 Regt, Brüggen
	ZD281	WS Lynx AH7 [K]	AAC No 671 Sqn/2 Regt, Middle Wallop
	ZD282	WS Lynx AH7 [L]	RM No 847 Sqn, Yeovilton
	ZD283	WS Lynx AH7	AAC No 655 Sqn/5 Regt, Aldergrove
	ZD284	WS Lynx AH7 [H]	AAC No 1 Regt, Brüggen
	ZD285	WS Lynx AH7	DPA/AFD/QinetiQ, Boscombe Down
	ZD318	BAe Harrier GR7	DPA/AFD/QinetiQ, Boscombe Down
	ZD319	BAe Harrier GR7	DPA/BAE Systems, Warton
	ZD320	BAe Harrier GR7	DPA/BAE Systems, Warton
	ZD321	BAe Harrier GR7 [02]	RAF No 1 Sqn, Cottesmore
	ZD322	BAe Harrier GR7 [03]	RAF HOCU/No 20(R) Sqn, Wittering
	ZD323	BAe Harrier GR7 [04]	RAF ASF, Cottesmore
	ZD327	BAe Harrier GR7 [08]	RAF No 4 Sqn, Cottesmore
	ZD328	BAe Harrier GR7 [09]	RAF No 3 Sqn, Cottesmore
	ZD329	BAe Harrier GR7 [10]	RAF No 3 Sqn, Cottesmore
	ZD330	BAe Harrier GR7 [11]	RAF No 4 Sqn, Cottesmore
	ZD346	BAe Harrier GR7 [13]	RAF No 4 Sqn, Cottesmore
	ZD347	BAe Harrier GR7 [14]	DARA, RAF St Athan
	ZD348	BAe Harrier GR7	RAF, stored St Athan
	ZD350	BAe Harrier GR5 (9189M) <ff>	DARA, RAF St Athan, BDRT
	ZD351	BAe Harrier GR7 (fuselage)	RAF, stored St Athan
	ZD352	BAe Harrier GR7 [19]	DARA, RAF St Athan
	ZD353	BAe Harrier GR5 (fuselage)	BAE Systems, Brough
	ZD354	BAe Harrier GR7 [21]	RAF No 1 Sqn, Cottesmore
	ZD375	BAe Harrier GR7 [23]	RAF HOCU/No 20(R) Sqn, Wittering
	ZD376	BAe Harrier GR7 [24]	RAF No 1 Sqn, Cottesmore
	ZD378	BAe Harrier GR7 [26]	RAF HOCU/No 20(R) Sqn, Wittering
	ZD379	BAe Harrier GR7 [27]	RAF No 4 Sqn, Cottesmore
	ZD380	BAe Harrier GR7 [28]	RAF No 4 Sqn, Cottesmore
	ZD401	BAe Harrier GR7 [30]	RAF No 3 Sqn, Cottesmore
	ZD402	BAe Harrier GR7 [31]	RAF HOCU/No 20(R) Sqn, Wittering
	ZD403	BAe Harrier GR7 [32]	RAF, stored St Athan
	ZD404	BAe Harrier GR7 [33]	RAF HOCU/No 20(R) Sqn, Wittering
	ZD405	BAe Harrier GR7 [34]	RAF AWC/SAOEU, Boscombe Down
	ZD406	BAe Harrier GR7 [35]	RAF No 4 Sqn, Cottesmore
	ZD407	BAe Harrier GR7 [36]	RAF HOCU/No 20(R) Sqn, Wittering
	ZD408	BAe Harrier GR7 [37]	DPA/BAE Systems, Warton
	ZD409	BAe Harrier GR7 [38]	RAF No 4 Sqn, Cottesmore
	ZD410	BAe Harrier GR7 [39]	RAF No 3 Sqn, Cottesmore
	ZD411	BAe Harrier GR7	RAF AWC/SAOEU, Boscombe Down
	ZD412	BAe Harrier GR5 (fuselage)	BAE Systems Brough, fatigue testing
	ZD431	BAe Harrier GR7 [43]	RAF HOCU/No 20(R) Sqn, Wittering
	ZD433	BAe Harrier GR7 [45]	RAF HOCU/No 20(R) Sqn, Wittering
	ZD435	BAe Harrier GR7 [47]	RAF No 1 Sqn, Cottesmore
	ZD436	BAe Harrier GR7 [48]	RAF ASF, Cottesmore
	ZD437	BAe Harrier GR7 [49]	RAF HOCU/No 20(R) Sqn, Wittering
	ZD438	BAe Harrier GR7 [50]	RAF No 1 Sqn, Cottesmore
	ZD461	BAe Harrier GR7 [51]	RAF No 1 Sqn, Cottesmore
	ZD462	BAe Harrier GR7 (9302M) [52]	RAF No 1 SoTT, Cosford
	ZD463	BAe Harrier GR7 [53]	DPA/AFD/Qinetiq, Boscombe Down
	ZD464	BAe Harrier GR7 [54]	DARA, RAF St Athan
	ZD465	BAe Harrier GR7 [55]	RAF, stored St Athan
	ZD466	BAe Harrier GR7 [56]	DARA, RAF St Athan
	ZD467	BAe Harrier GR7 [57]	RAF No 1 Sqn, Cottesmore
	ZD468	BAe Harrier GR7 [58]	RAF, stored St Athan
	ZD469	BAe Harrier GR7 [59]	RAF No 1 Sqn, Cottesmore
	ZD470	BAe Harrier GR7 [60]	RAF No 4 Sqn, Cottesmore
	ZD476	WS61 Sea King HC4 [ZU]	RN No 848 Sqn, Yeovilton
	ZD477	WS61 Sea King HC4 [H]	RN No 845 Sqn, Yeovilton
	ZD478	WS61 Sea King HC4 [VX]	RN No 846 Sqn, Yeovilton
	ZD479	WS61 Sea King HC4 [ZV]	RN No 848 Sqn, Yeovilton
	ZD480	WS61 Sea King HC4 [E]	RN No 845 Sqn, Yeovilton
	ZD559	WS Lynx AH5X	DPA/AFD, QinetiQ Boscombe Down
	ZD560	WS Lynx AH7	DPA/AFD/ETPS, QinetiQ Boscombe Down
	ZD565	WS Lynx HMA8 [361/NF]	RN No 815 Sqn, *Norfolk* Flt, Yeovilton
	ZD566	WS Lynx HMA8 [422/SU]	RN AMG, Yeovilton

Serial	Type (other identity) [code]	Owner/operator, location or fate	Notes
ZD574	B-V Chinook HC2 (N37077)	RAF No 27 Sqn, Odiham	
ZD575	B-V Chinook HC2 (N37078) [BW]	RAF No 18 Sqn, Odiham	
ZD578	BAe Sea Harrier FA2 [714]	RN No 899 Sqn, Yeovilton	
ZD579	BAe Sea Harrier FA2	RN, St Athan	
ZD580	BAe Sea Harrier FA2	DPA/BAE Systems, Warton	
ZD581	BAe Sea Harrier FA2	DPA/BAE Systems, Warton	
ZD582	BAe Sea Harrier FA2 [124/R]	RN No 800 Sqn, Yeovilton	
ZD607	BAe Sea Harrier FA2	RN, St Athan	
ZD608	BAe Sea Harrier FA2 [710]	RN No 899 Sqn, Yeovilton	
ZD610	BAe Sea Harrier FA2 [711]	RN/AMG. Yeovilton	
ZD611	BAe Sea Harrier FA2 [122]	RN No 899 Sqn, Yeovilton	
ZD612	BAe Sea Harrier FA2 [122]	RN No 800 Sqn, Yeovilton	
ZD613	BAe Sea Harrier FA2 [007/L]	RN No 801 Sqn, Yeovilton	
ZD614	BAe Sea Harrier FA2 [122/R]	Crashed 8 October 2001, Yeovilton	
ZD615	BAe Sea Harrier FA2	DPA/BAE Systems, Warton	
ZD620	BAe 125 CC3	RAF No 32(The Royal) Sqn, Northolt	
ZD621	BAe 125 CC3	RAF No 32(The Royal) Sqn, Northolt	
ZD625	WS61 Sea King HC4 [VZ]	RN No 846 Sqn, Yeovilton	
ZD626	WS61 Sea King HC4 [ZZ]	RN No 848 Sqn, Yeovilton	
ZD627	WS61 Sea King HC4 [VR]	RN No 846 Sqn, Yeovilton	
ZD630	WS61 Sea King HAS6 [012/L]	RN No 820 Sqn, Culdrose	
ZD631	WS61 Sea King HAS6 [66] (fuselage)	RN, Predannack Fire School	
ZD633	WS61 Sea King HAS6 [014/L]	RN, stored HMS Sultan, Gosport	
ZD634	WS61 Sea King HAS6 [503]	RN No 771 Sqn, Culdrose	
ZD636	WS61 Sea King AEW2 [183/L]	RN No 849 Sqn, B Flt, Culdrose	
ZD637	WS61 Sea King HAS6 [700/PW]	RN, stored HMS Sultan, Gosport	
ZD657	Schleicher ASW-19B Valiant TX1	Sold as BGA 2893, 2000]	
ZD658	Schleicher ASW-19B Valiant TX1 (BGA 4989) [YX]	Privately owned,	
ZD659	Schleicher ASW-19B Valiant TX1	Sold as BGA2895, 2000	
ZD660	Schleicher ASW-19B Valiant TX1	Sold as BGA 2896, 2000	
ZD667	BAe Harrier GR3 (9201M) [67]	SFDO, RNAS Culdrose	
ZD668	BAe Harrier GR3 (G-CBCU) [3E]	Privately owned, Lowestoft	
ZD670	BAe Harrier GR3 [3A]	The Trocadero, Leicester Square, London	
ZD703	BAe 125 CC3	RAF No 32(The Royal) Sqn, Northolt	
ZD704	BAe 125 CC3	RAF No 32(The Royal) Sqn, Northolt	
ZD707	Panavia Tornado GR1 [BU]	RAF No 14 Sqn, Lossiemouth	
ZD708	Panavia Tornado GR4	DPA/BAE Systems, Warton	
ZD709	Panavia Tornado GR4 [DH]	RAF No 31 Sqn, Marham	
ZD710	Panavia Tornado GR1 <ff>	Privately owned, Welshpool	
ZD711	Panavia Tornado GR4 [II]	RAF No 2 Sqn, Marham	
ZD712	Panavia Tornado GR4 [TTR]	RAF No 14 Sqn, Lossiemouth	
ZD713	Panavia Tornado GR4 [TW]	RAF, St Athan	
ZD714	Panavia Tornado GR4 [AJ-W]	RAF No 617 Sqn, Lossiemouth	
ZD715	Panavia Tornado GR4 [AM]	RAF No 9 Sqn, Marham	
ZD716	Panavia Tornado GR4	DPA/BAE Systems, Warton (conversion)	
ZD719	Panavia Tornado GR4 [BS]	RAF No 15(R) Sqn, Lossiemouth	
ZD720	Panavia Tornado GR4	RAF, stored St Athan	
ZD739	Panavia Tornado GR4	DPA/BAE Systems, Warton (conversion)	
ZD740	Panavia Tornado GR4 [AF]	RAF No 9 Sqn, Marham	
ZD741	Panavia Tornado GR4 [BZ]	RAF No 14 Sqn, Lossiemouth	
ZD742	Panavia Tornado GR4 [FY]	RAF No 12 Sqn, Lossiemouth	
ZD743	Panavia Tornado GR4	RAF No 15(R) Sqn, Lossiemouth	
ZD744	Panavia Tornado GR4	RAF, St Athan	
ZD745	Panavia Tornado GR4 [DA]	RAF No 31 Sqn, Marham	
ZD746	Panavia Tornado GR4	RAF AWC/SAOEU, Boscombe Down	
ZD747	Panavia Tornado GR4 [AJ-P]	DPA/BAE Systems, Warton (conversion)	
ZD748	Panavia Tornado GR4 [FC]	RAF No 12 Sqn, Lossiemouth	
ZD749	Panavia Tornado GR4 [BG]	DPA/BAE Systems, Warton (conversion)	
ZD788	Panavia Tornado GR1 [BT]	DPA/BAE Systems, Warton (conversion)	
ZD789	Panavia Tornado GR1 <ff>	RAF, stored Shawbury	
ZD790	Panavia Tornado GR4 [FM]	RAF No 12 Sqn, Lossiemouth	
ZD792	Panavia Tornado GR4 [BE]	RAF No 14 Sqn, Lossiemouth	
ZD793	Panavia Tornado GR4	DPA/BAE Systems, Warton (conversion)	
ZD810	Panavia Tornado GR4 [TTD]	RAF No 12 Sqn, Lossiemouth	
ZD811	Panavia Tornado GR4 [BK]	RAF No 14 Sqn, Lossiemouth	
ZD812	Panavia Tornado GR4 [TU]	RAF No 15(R) Sqn, Lossiemouth	
ZD842	Panavia Tornado GR4 [VII]	RAF No 13 Sqn, Marham	
ZD843	Panavia Tornado GR4 [CJ]	DPA/BAE Systems, Warton (conversion)	
ZD844	Panavia Tornado GR4 [AJ-A]	RAF No 617 Sqn, Lossiemouth	
ZD847	Panavia Tornado GR4 [AA]	RAF No 9 Sqn, Marham	
ZD848	Panavia Tornado GR4	DPA/BAE Systems, Warton (conversion)	

Notes	Serial	Type (other identity) [code]	Owner/operator, location or fate
	ZD849	Panavia Tornado GR4 [FE]	RAF, St Athan
	ZD850	Panavia Tornado GR4 [AJ-T]	RAF No 617 Sqn, Lossiemouth
	ZD851	Panavia Tornado GR4 [FP]	RAF No 12 Sqn, Lossiemouth
	ZD890	Panavia Tornado GR4 [FR]	RAF No 12 Sqn, Lossiemouth
	ZD892	Panavia Tornado GR4 [TG]	RAF 15(R) Sqn, Lossiemouth
	ZD895	Panavia Tornado GR4 [S]	DPA/BAE Systems, Warton (conversion)
	ZD899	Panavia Tornado F2	DPA/BAE Systems, Warton
	ZD900	Panavia Tornado F2 (comp ZE343) (fuselage)	RAF Lossiemouth, GI use
	ZD901	Panavia Tornado F2 (comp ZE154)	RAF Brize Norton, GI use
	ZD902	Panavia Tornado F2A(TIARA)	DPA/AFD/QinetiQ, Boscombe Down
	ZD903	Panavia Tornado F2 (comp ZE728) (fuselage)	RAF St Athan, GI use
	ZD904	Panavia Tornado F2 (comp ZE759)	*Scrapped at St Athan, January 2001*
	ZD905	Panavia Tornado F2 (comp ZE258) (fuselage)	RAF, BDRT St Athan
	ZD906	Panavia Tornado F2 (comp ZE294) <ff>	*Scrapped at St Athan, January 2001*
	ZD932	Panavia Tornado F2 (comp ZE255) (fuselage)	RAF, stored St Athan
	ZD933	Panavia Tornado F2 (comp ZE729) (fuselage)	RAF, stored St Athan
	ZD934	Panavia Tornado F2 (comp ZE786) <ff>	RAF Leeming, GI use
	ZD935	Panavia Tornado F2 (comp ZE793) <ff>	RAF, stored Shawbury
	ZD936	Panavia Tornado F2 (comp ZE251)	*To EADS, Germany, 2001*
	ZD937	Panavia Tornado F2 (comp ZE736)	*Scrapped at St Athan, January 2001*
	ZD938	Panavia Tornado F2 (comp ZE295) <ff>	RAF, stored Shawbury
	ZD939	Panavia Tornado F2 (comp ZE292)	RAF, stored St Athan
	ZD940	Panavia Tornado F2 (comp ZE288) (fuselage)	RAF, stored St Athan
	ZD941	Panavia Tornado F2 (comp ZE254)	*Scrapped at St Athan, January 2001*
	ZD948	Lockheed TriStar KC1 (G-BFCA)	RAF No 216 Sqn, Brize Norton
	ZD949	Lockheed TriStar K1 (G-BFCB)	RAF No 216 Sqn, Brize Norton
	ZD950	Lockheed TriStar KC1 (G-BFCC)	RAF No 216 Sqn, Brize Norton
	ZD951	Lockheed TriStar K1 (G-BFCD)	RAF No 216 Sqn, Brize Norton
	ZD952	Lockheed TriStar KC1 (G-BFCE)	RAF No 216 Sqn, Brize Norton
	ZD953	Lockheed TriStar KC1 (G-BFCF)	RAF No 216 Sqn, Brize Norton
	ZD974	Schempp-Hirth Kestrel TX1 [SY]	Privately owned,
	ZD975	Schempp-Hirth Kestrel TX1 [SZ]	RAF, stored Barkston Heath
	ZD980	B-V Chinook HC2 (N37082)	RAF No 27 Sqn, Odiham
	ZD981	B-V Chinook HC2 (N37083) [BH]	RAF No 18 Sqn, Odiham
	ZD982	B-V Chinook HC2 (N37085) [BI]	DARA, Fleetlands
	ZD983	B-V Chinook HC2 (N37086)	RAF No 7 Sqn, Odiham
	ZD984	B-V Chinook HC2 (N37088) [BJ]	RAF No 18 Sqn, Odiham
	ZD990	BAe Harrier T8 [721]	RN No 899 Sqn, Yeovilton
	ZD991	BAe Harrier T8 (9228M) [722/VL]	DPA/BAE Systems, Chadderton (damaged)
	ZD992	BAe Harrier T8 [724/VL]	RN FSAIU, Yeovilton (wreck)
	ZD993	BAe Harrier T8 [723/VL]	RN No 899 Sqn, Yeovilton
	ZD996	Panavia Tornado GR4A [I]	RAF No 13 Sqn, Marham
	ZE116	Panavia Tornado GR4A [X]	RAF No 13 Sqn, Marham
	ZE154	Panavia Tornado F3 [LT] (comp ZD901)	RAF F3 OCU/No 56(R) Sqn, Coningsby
	ZE155	Panavia Tornado F3	DPA/BAE Systems, Warton
	ZE156	Panavia Tornado F3 [UX]	RAF F3 OCU/No 56(R) Sqn, Coningsby
	ZE157	Panavia Tornado F3	RAF F3 OCU/No 56(R) Sqn, Coningsby
	ZE158	Panavia Tornado F3 [UW]	RAF No 11 Sqn, Leeming
	ZE159	Panavia Tornado F3 [UV]	RAF No 111 Sqn, Leuchars
	ZE160	Panavia Tornado F3 [TX]	RAF No 25 Sqn, Leeming
	ZE161	Panavia Tornado F3 [GR]	RAF No 43 Sqn, Leuchars
	ZE162	Panavia Tornado F3 [FK]	RAF No 111 Sqn, Leuchars
	ZE163	Panavia Tornado F3 (comp ZG753)	RAF, stored St Athan
	ZE164	Panavia Tornado F3 [UQ]	RAF No 5 Sqn, Coningsby
	ZE165	Panavia Tornado F3 [Q]	RAF No 111 Sqn, Leuchars
	ZE168	Panavia Tornado F3]	RAF AWC/F3OEU, Coningsby
	ZE199	Panavia Tornado F3 [[TV]	RAF F3 OCU/No 56(R) Sqn, Coningsby
	ZE200	Panavia Tornado F3 [UM]	RAF No111 Sqn, Leuchars
	ZE201	Panavia Tornado F3 [GA]	RAF No 43 Sqn, Leuchars

Serial	Type (other identity) [code]	Owner/operator, location or fate	Notes
ZE203	Panavia Tornado F3 [UK]	RAF No 25 Sqn, Leeming	
ZE204	Panavia Tornado F3 [UJ]	RAF No 43 Sqn, Leuchars	
ZE206	Panavia Tornado F3 [UI]	RAF No 25 Sqn, Leeming	
ZE207	Panavia Tornado F3 [GC]	RAF No 43 Sqn, Leuchars	
ZE209	Panavia Tornado F3 [AX]	RAF No 111 Sqn, Leuchars	
ZE210	Panavia Tornado F3 (fuselage)	*Scrapped at St Athan, January 2001*	
ZE250	Panavia Tornado F3 [AM]	RAF ASF Lossiemouth	
ZE251	Panavia Tornado F3 (comp ZD936) [C]	RAF No 43 Sqn, Leuchars	
ZE253	Panavia Tornado F3 [AC]	RAF, stored St Athan	
ZE254	Panavia Tornado F3 (comp ZD941) [CW]	RAF No 25 Sqn, Leeming	
ZE255	Panavia Tornado F3 (comp ZD932) [CK]	RAF No 43 Sqn, Leuchars	
ZE256	Panavia Tornado F3 [TP]	RAF F3 OCU/No 56(R) Sqn, Coningsby	
ZE257	Panavia Tornado F3 [UB]	RAF No 25 Sqn, Leeming	
ZE258	Panavia Tornado F3 (comp ZD905) [AQ]	RAF No 5 Sqn, Coningsby	
ZE287	Panavia Tornado F3 [AF]	RAF F3 OCU/No 56(R) Sqn, Coningsby	
ZE288	Panavia Tornado F3 (comp ZD940) [AT]	RAF No 111 Sqn, Leuchars	
ZE289	Panavia Tornado F3 [VX]	RAF No 11 Sqn, Leeming	
ZE290	Panavia Tornado F3 [AG]	RAF, stored St Athan	
ZE291	Panavia Tornado F3 [GQ]	RAF, stored St Athan	
ZE292	Panavia Tornado F3 (comp ZD939) [YY]	RAF No 25 Sqn, Leeming	
ZE293	Panavia Tornado F3 [HT]	RAF, stored St Athan	
ZE294	Panavia Tornado F3 (comp ZD906) [YX]	RAF No 5 Sqn, Coningsby	
ZE295	Panavia Tornado F3 (comp ZD938) [AY]	RAF No 56(R) Sqn, Coningsby	
ZE296	Panavia Tornado F3	RAF, stored St Athan	
ZE338	Panavia Tornado F3 [YV]	RAF No 111 Sqn, Leuchars	
ZE339	Panavia Tornado F3	RAF, stored St Athan	
ZE340	Panavia Tornado F3 [AE]	*Marked as ZE758 by September 2001*	
ZE341	Panavia Tornado F3 [CL]	RAF No 11 Sqn, Leeming	
ZE342	Panavia Tornado F3 [W]	RAF No 111 Sqn, Leuchars	
ZE343	Panavia Tornado F3 (comp ZD900) [TI]	RAF F3 OCU/No 56(R) Sqn, Coningsby	
ZE350	McD F-4J(UK) Phantom (9080M) <ff>	Privately owned, Ingatestone, Essex	
ZE352	McD F-4J(UK) Phantom (9086M) <ff>	Privately owned, Hooton Park, Cheshire	
ZE353	McD F-4J(UK) Phantom (9083M) [E]	*Scrapped at Manston, July 2001*	
ZE354	McD F-4J(UK) Phantom (9084M) [R]	*Scrapped at Coningsby, 20 July 2001*	
ZE356	McD F-4J(UK) Phantom (9060M) [Q]	RAF Waddington, BDRT	
ZE360	McD F-4J(UK) Phantom (9059M) [O]	MoD FSCTE, Manston	
ZE361	McD F-4J(UK) Phantom (9057M) [P]	*Scrapped at Honington, December 2000*	
ZE368	WS61 Sea King HAR3	RAF No 22 Sqn, C Flt, Valley	
ZE369	WS61 Sea King HAR3	RAF/DARA, Fleetlands	
ZE370	WS61 Sea King HAR3	RAF No 22 Sqn, C Flt, Valley	
ZE375	WS Lynx AH9 [2,9]	AAC No 653 Sqn/3 Regt, Wattisham	
ZE376	WS Lynx AH9	AAC No 659 Sqn/4 Regt, Wattisham	
ZE378	WS Lynx AH7	AAC No 654 Sqn/4 Regt, Wattisham	
ZE379	WS Lynx AH7	AAC No 655 Sqn/5 Regt, Aldergrove	
ZE380	WS Lynx AH9 [3]	AAC No 659 Sqn/4 Regt, Wattisham	
ZE381	WS Lynx AH7	AAC No 655 Sqn/5 Regt, Aldergrove	
ZE382	WS Lynx AH9	AAC No 659 Sqn/4 Regt, Wattisham	
ZE395	BAe 125 CC3	RAF No 32(The Royal) Sqn, Northolt	
ZE396	BAe 125 CC3	RAF No 32(The Royal) Sqn, Northolt	
ZE410	Agusta A109A (AE-334)	AAC No 8 Flt, Credenhill	
ZE411	Agusta A109A (AE-331)	AAC No 8 Flt, Credenhill	
ZE412	Agusta A109A	AAC No 8 Flt, Credenhill	
ZE413	Agusta A109A	AAC No 8 Flt, Credenhill	
ZE418	WS61 Sea King AEW2 [182]	RN No 849 Sqn, HQ Flt, Culdrose	
ZE420	WS61 Sea King AEW2 [184/L]	RN No 849 Sqn, B Flt, Culdrose	
ZE422	WS61 Sea King HAS6 [508/CT]	RN No 771 Sqn, Culdrose	
ZE425	WS61 Sea King HC4 [ZJ]	RN No 848 Sqn, Yeovilton	

Notes	Serial	Type (other identity) [code]	Owner/operator, location or fate
	ZE426	WS61 Sea King HC4 [ZW]	RN No 848 Sqn, Yeovilton
	ZE427	WS61 Sea King HC4 [B]	RN No 845 Sqn, Yeovilton
	ZE428	WS61 Sea King HC4 [VS]	RN No 846 Sqn, Yeovilton
	ZE432	BAC 1-11/479FU (DQ-FBV)	DPA/AFD/ETPS, QinetiQ Boscombe Down
	ZE433	BAC 1-11/479FU (DQ-FBQ)	DPA/GEC-Ferranti, Edinburgh
	ZE438	BAe Jetstream T3 [76]	RN FONA/Heron Flight, Yeovilton
	ZE439	BAe Jetstream T3 [77]	RN, stored Shawbury
	ZE440	BAe Jetstream T3 [78]	RN FONA/Heron Flight, Yeovilton
	ZE441	BAe Jetstream T3 [79]	RN FONA/Heron Flight, Yeovilton
	ZE449	SA330L Puma HC1 (9017M/PA-12)	RAF No 33 Sqn, Benson
	ZE477	WS Lynx 3	The Helicopter Museum, Weston-super-Mare
	ZE495	Grob G103 Viking T1 (BGA3000) [VA]	RAF No 622 VGS, Upavon
	ZE496	Grob G103 Viking T1 (BGA3001) [VB]	RAF No 634 VGS, St Athan
	ZE498	Grob G103 Viking T1 (BGA3003) [VC]	RAF No 614 VGS, Wethersfield
	ZE499	Grob G103 Viking T1 (BGA3004) [VD]	RAF No 615 VGS, Kenley
	ZE501	Grob G103 Viking T1 (BGA3006) [VE]	RAF No 636 VGS, Swansea
	ZE502	Grob G103 Viking T1 (BGA3007) [VF]	RAF No 614 VGS, Wethersfield
	ZE503	Grob G103 Viking T1 (BGA3008) [VG]	RAF No 645 VGS, Catterick
	ZE504	Grob G103 Viking T1 (BGA3009) [VH]	RAF No 634 VGS, St Athan
	ZE520	Grob G103 Viking T1 (BGA3010) [VJ]	RAF No 636 VGS, Swansea
	ZE521	Grob G103 Viking T1 (BGA3011) [VK]	RAF No 626 VGS, Predannack
	ZE522	Grob G103 Viking T1 (BGA3012) [VL]	RAF No 634 VGS, St Athan
	ZE524	Grob G103 Viking T1 (BGA3014) [VM]	RAF No 645 VGS, Catterick
	ZE526	Grob G103 Viking T1 (BGA3016) [VN]	RAF No 636 VGS, Swansea
	ZE527	Grob G103 Viking T1 (BGA3017) [VP]	RAF ACCGS, Syerston
	ZE528	Grob G103 Viking T1 (BGA3018) [VQ]	RAF No 614 VGS, Wethersfield
	ZE529	Grob G103 Viking T1 (BGA3019) (comp ZE655) [VR]	RAF No 614 VGS, Wethersfield
	ZE530	Grob G103 Viking T1 (BGA3020) [VS]	RAF No 611 VGS, Watton
	ZE531	Grob G103 Viking T1 (BGA3021) [VT]	RAF No 615 VGS, Kenley
	ZE532	Grob G103 Viking T1 (BGA3022) [VU]	RAF No 614 VGS, Wethersfield
	ZE533	Grob G103 Viking T1 (BGA3023) [VV]	RAF No 622 VGS, Upavon
	ZE534	Grob G103 Viking T1 (BGA3024) [VW]	RAF No 614 VGS, Wethersfield
	ZE550	Grob G103 Viking T1 (BGA3025) [VX]	RAF ACCGS, Syerston
	ZE551	Grob G103 Viking T1 (BGA3026) [VY]	RAF No 614 VGS, Wethersfield
	ZE552	Grob G103 Viking T1 (BGA3027) [VZ]	RAF No 661 VGS, Kirknewton
	ZE553	Grob G103 Viking T1 (BGA3028) [WA]	RAF No 611 VGS, Watton
	ZE554	Grob G103 Viking T1 (BGA3029) [WB]	RAF No 611 VGS, Watton
	ZE555	Grob G103 Viking T1 (BGA3030) [WC]	RAF No 645 VGS, Catterick
	ZE556	Grob G103 Viking T1 (BGA3031) [WD]	RAF No 662 VGS, Arbroath
	ZE557	Grob G103 Viking T1 (BGA3032) [WE]	RAF No 622 VGS, Upavon
	ZE558	Grob G103 Viking T1 (BGA3033) [WF]	RAF No 615 VGS, Kenley

Serial	Type (other identity) [code]	Owner/operator, location or fate	Notes
ZE559	Grob G103 Viking T1 (BGA3034) [WG]	RAF No 631 VGS, Sealand	
ZE560	Grob G103 Viking T1 (BGA3035) [WH]	RAF No 661 VGS, Kirknewton	
ZE561	Grob G103 Viking T1 (BGA3036) [WJ]	RAF No 621 VGS, Hullavington	
ZE562	Grob G103 Viking T1 (BGA3037) [WK]	RAF No 626 VGS, Predannack	
ZE563	Grob G103 Viking T1 (BGA3038) [WL]	RAF No 631 VGS, Sealand	
ZE564	Grob G103 Viking T1 (BGA3039) [WN]	RAF No 625 VGS, Hullavington	
ZE584	Grob G103 Viking T1 (BGA3040) [WP]	RAF No 631 VGS, Sealand	
ZE585	Grob G103 Viking T1 (BGA3041) [WQ]	RAF ACCGS, Syerston	
ZE586	Grob G103 Viking T1 (BGA3042) [WR]	RAF No 631 VGS, Sealand	
ZE587	Grob G103 Viking T1 (BGA3043) [WS]	RAF No 611 VGS, Watton	
ZE589	Grob G103 Viking T1 (BGA3045) (wreck)	RAFGSA, stored Bicester	
ZE590	Grob G103 Viking T1 (BGA3046) [WT]	RAF No 661 VGS, Kirknewton	
ZE591	Grob G103 Viking T1 (BGA3047) [WU]	RAF No 631 VGS, Sealand	
ZE592	Grob G103 Viking T1 (BGA3048) [WV]	RAF No 615 VGS, Kenley	
ZE593	Grob G103 Viking T1 (BGA3049) [WW]	RAF No 621 VGS, Hullavington	
ZE594	Grob G103 Viking T1 (BGA3050) [WX]	RAF No 615 VGS, Kenley	
ZE595	Grob G103 Viking T1 (BGA3051) [WY]	RAF No 622 VGS, Upavon	
ZE600	Grob G103 Viking T1 (BGA3052) [WZ]	RAF No 622 VGS, Upavon	
ZE601	Grob G103 Viking T1 (BGA3053) [XA]	RAF No 611 VGS, Watton	
ZE602	Grob G103 Viking T1 (BGA3054) [XB]	RAF No 645 VGS, Catterick	
ZE603	Grob G103 Viking T1 (BGA3055) [XC]	RAF No 636 VGS, Swansea	
ZE604	Grob G103 Viking T1 (BGA3056) [XD]	RAF No 615 VGS, Kenley	
ZE605	Grob G103 Viking T1 (BGA3057) [XE]	RAF No 662 VGS, Arbroath	
ZE606	Grob G103 Viking T1 (BGA3058) [XF]	RAF No 625 VGS, Hullavington	
ZE607	Grob G103 Viking T1 (BGA3059) [XG]	RAF No 625 VGS, Hullavington	
ZE608	Grob G103 Viking T1 (BGA3060) [XH]	RAF No 621 VGS, Hullavington	
ZE609	Grob G103 Viking T1 (BGA3061) [XJ]	RAF No 661 VGS, Kirknewton	
ZE610	Grob G103 Viking T1 (BGA3062) [XK]	RAF No 626 VGS, Predannack	
ZE611	Grob G103 Viking T1 (BGA3063) [XL]	RAF No 611 VGS, Watton	
ZE613	Grob G103 Viking T1 (BGA3065) [XM]	RAF No 625 VGS, Hullavington	
ZE614	Grob G103 Viking T1 (BGA3066) [XN]	RAF No 631 VGS, Sealand	
ZE625	Grob G103 Viking T1 (BGA3067) [XP]	RAF No 625 VGS, Hullavington	
ZE626	Grob G103 Viking T1 (BGA3068) [XQ]	RAF No 626 VGS, Predannack	
ZE627	Grob G103 Viking T1 (BGA3069) [XR]	RAF No 634 VGS, St Athan	
ZE628	Grob G103 Viking T1 (BGA3070) [XS]	RAF ACCGS, Syerston	
ZE629	Grob G103 Viking T1 (BGA3071) [XT]	RAF No 662 VGS, Arbroath	

Notes	Serial	Type (other identity) [code]	Owner/operator, location or fate
	ZE630	Grob G103 Viking T1 (BGA3072) [XU]	RAF No 662 VGS, Arbroath
	ZE631	Grob G103 Viking T1 (BGA3073) [XV]	RAF No 662 VGS, Arbroath
	ZE632	Grob G103 Viking T1 (BGA3074) [XW]	RAF No 645 VGS, Catterick
	ZE633	Grob G103 Viking T1 (BGA3075) [XX]	RAF No 614 VGS, Wethersfield
	ZE635	Grob G103 Viking T1 (BGA3077) [XY]	RAF No 625 VGS, Hullavington
	ZE636	Grob G103 Viking T1 (BGA3078) [XZ]	RAF No 636 VGS, Swansea
	ZE637	Grob G103 Viking T1 (BGA3079) [YA]	RAF No 622 VGS, Upavon
	ZE650	Grob G103 Viking T1 (BGA3080) [YB]	RAF ACCGS, Syerston
	ZE651	Grob G103 Viking T1 (BGA3081) [YC]	RAF No 661 VGS, Kirknewton
	ZE652	Grob G103 Viking T1 (BGA3082) [YD]	RAF ACCGS, Syerston
	ZE653	Grob G103 Viking T1 (BGA3083) [YE]	RAF No 661 VGS, Kirknewton
	ZE656	Grob G103 Viking T1 (BGA3086) [YH]	RAF No 622 VGS, Upavon
	ZE657	Grob G103 Viking T1 (BGA3087) [YJ]	RAF No 615 VGS, Kenley
	ZE658	Grob G103 Viking T1 (BGA3088) [YK]	RAF No 621 VGS, Hullavington
	ZE659	Grob G103 Viking T1 (BGA3089) [YL]	AIB, Farnborough (damaged)
	ZE677	Grob G103 Viking T1 (BGA3090) [YM]	RAF No 645 VGS, Catterick
	ZE678	Grob G103 Viking T1 (BGA3091) [YN]	RAF No 621 VGS, Hullavington
	ZE679	Grob G103 Viking T1 (BGA3092) [YP]	RAF No 622 VGS, Upavon
	ZE680	Grob G103 Viking T1 (BGA3093) [YQ]	RAF No 662 VGS, Arbroath
	ZE681	Grob G103 Viking T1 (BGA3094) [YR]	RAF No 615 VGS, Kenley
	ZE682	Grob G103 Viking T1 (BGA3095) [YS]	RAF No 662 VGS, Arbroath
	ZE683	Grob G103 Viking T1 (BGA3096) [YT]	RAF CGMF, Syerston
	ZE684	Grob G103 Viking T1 (BGA3097) [YU]	RAF No 621 VGS, Hullavington
	ZE685	Grob G103 Viking T1 (BGA3098) [YV]	RAF No 631 VGS, Sealand
	ZE686	Grob G103 Viking T1 (BGA3099)	DPA/Slingsby Kirkbymoorside
	ZE690	BAe Sea Harrier FA2 [005]	RN No 801 Sqn, Yeovilton
	ZE691	BAe Sea Harrier FA2 [710/VL]	RN/DARA, St Athan
	ZE692	BAe Sea Harrier FA2 [715]	RN No 899 Sqn, Yeovilton
	ZE693	BAe Sea Harrier FA2 [731]	DPA/BAE Systems, Warton
	ZE694	BAe Sea Harrier FA2 [004]	RN No 801 Sqn, Yeovilton
	ZE695	BAe Sea Harrier FA2 [718]	RN/DARA, St Athan
	ZE696	BAe Sea Harrier FA2 [007]	RN No 801 Sqn, Yeovilton
	ZE697	BAe Sea Harrier FA2 [711]	RN No 899 Sqn, Yeovilton
	ZE698	BAe Sea Harrier FA2 [123/R]	RN No 800 Sqn, Yeovilton
	ZE700	BAe 146 CC2 (G-6-021)	RAF No 32(The Royal) Sqn, Northolt
	ZE701	BAe 146 CC2 (G-6-029)	RAF No 32(The Royal) Sqn, Northolt
	ZE702	BAe 146 CC2 (G-6-124)	RAF, stored Northolt
	ZE704	Lockheed TriStar C2 (N508PA)	RAF No 216 Sqn, Brize Norton
	ZE705	Lockheed TriStar C2 (N509PA)	RAF No 216 Sqn, Brize Norton
	ZE706	Lockheed TriStar C2A (N503PA)	RAF No 216 Sqn, Brize Norton
	ZE728	Panavia Tornado F3 (comp ZD903) [TH]	RAF No 111 Sqn, Leuchars
	ZE729	Panavia Tornado F3 (comp ZD933) [D]	RAF/DARA St Athan
	ZE731	Panavia Tornado F3 [GF]	RAF F3 OCU/No 56(R) Sqn, Coningsby
	ZE734	Panavia Tornado F3 [GB]	RAF/DARA stored St Athan
	ZE735	Panavia Tornado F3 [AL]	RAF F3 OCU/No 56(R) Sqn, Coningsby
	ZE736	Panavia Tornado F3 (comp ZD937)	RAF No 1435 Flt, Mount Pleasant, FI
	ZE737	Panavia Tornado F3 [FF]	RAF No 111 Sqn, Leuchars

Serial	Type (other identity) [code]	Owner/operator, location or fate	Notes
ZE755	Panavia Tornado F3 [YL]	RAF No 11 Sqn, Leuchars	
ZE756	Panavia Tornado F3	RAF, stored St Athan	
ZE757	Panavia Tornado F3 [YJ]	RAF No 25 Sqn, Leeming	
ZE758	Panavia Tornado F3 [YI]	RAF F3 OCU/No 56(R) Sqn, Coningsby	
ZE758	Panavia Tornado F3 (ZE340/ 9298M) [GO]	RAF No 1 SoTT, Cosford	
ZE763	Panavia Tornado F3 [DG]	RAF No 5 Sqn, Leeming	
ZE764	Panavia Tornado F3 [DH]	RAF No 25 Sqn, Leeming	
ZE785	Panavia Tornado F3 [YC]	RAF AWC/F3 OEU, Coningsby	
ZE786	Panavia Tornado F3 (comp ZD934) [AN]	RAF F3 OCU/No 56(R) Sqn, Coningsby	
ZE788	Panavia Tornado F3 [YA]	RAF No 25 Sqn, Leeming	
ZE790	Panavia Tornado F3 [VU]	RAF No 43 Sqn, Leuchars	
ZE791	Panavia Tornado F3 [XY]	RAF No 111 Sqn, Leuchars	
ZE793	Panavia Tornado F3 (comp ZD935)	RAF No 111 Sqn, Leuchars	
ZE794	Panavia Tornado F3	RAF No 5 Sqn, Coningsby	
ZE808	Panavia Tornado F3 [XV]	RAF No 25 Sqn, Leeming	
ZE810	Panavia Tornado F3 [HP]	RAF No 111 Sqn, Leuchars	
ZE812	Panavia Tornado F3 [XR]	RAF No 111 Sqn, Leuchars	
ZE831	Panavia Tornado F3 [GG]	RAF No 43 Sqn, Leuchars	
ZE834	Panavia Tornado F3 [XO]	RAF No 1435 Flt, Mount Pleasant, FI	
ZE838	Panavia Tornado F3 [GH]	RAF No 43 Sqn, Coningsby	
ZE839	Panavia Tornado F3	RAF No 5 Sqn, Coningsby	
ZE887	Panavia Tornado F3 [DJ]	RAF No 5 Sqn, Coningsby	
ZE888	Panavia Tornado F3 [TC]	RAF F3 OCU/No 56(R) Sqn, Coningsby	
ZE889	Panavia Tornado F3 [XI]	RAF No 111 Sqn, Leuchars	
ZE907	Panavia Tornado F3 [FM]	RAF No 5 Sqn, Coningsby	
ZE908	Panavia Tornado F3 [HV]	RAF No 25 Sqn, Leeming	
ZE934	Panavia Tornado F3 [TA]	RAF F3 OCU/No 56(R) Sqn, Coningsby	
ZE936	Panavia Tornado F3 [XF]	RAF No11 Sqn, Leeming	
ZE941	Panavia Tornado F3 [FE]	RAF F3 OCU/No 56(R) Sqn, Coningsby	
ZE942	Panavia Tornado F3	RAF No 5 Sqn, Coningsby	
ZE961	Panavia Tornado F3 [AW]	RAF F3 OCU/No 56(R) Sqn, Coningsby	
ZE962	Panavia Tornado F3 [FJ]	RAF No 11 Sqn, Leeming	
ZE963	Panavia Tornado F3 [GE]	RAF No 43 Sqn, Leuchars	
ZE964	Panavia Tornado F3 [GN]	RAF No 5 Sqn, Coningsby	
ZE965	Panavia Tornado F3 [WT]	RAF F3 OCU/No 56(R) Sqn, Coningsby	
ZE966	Panavia Tornado F3 [DX]	RAF No 11 Sqn, Leeming	
ZE967	Panavia Tornado F3 [UT]	RAF No 111 Sqn, Leuchars	
ZE968	Panavia Tornado F3 [DM]	RAF No 111 Sqn, Leuchars	
ZE969	Panavia Tornado F3 [XA]	RAF F3 OCU/No 56(R) Sqn, Coningsby	
ZE982	Panavia Tornado F3 [VV]	RAF No 5 Sqn, Coningsby	
ZE983	Panavia Tornado F3 [DN]	RAF No 11 Sqn, Leeming	
ZF115	WS61 Sea King HC4	Crashed 30 Nov 2001, Boscombe Down	
ZF116	WS61 Sea King HC4 [ZP]	RN No 848 Sqn, Yeovilton	
ZF117	WS61 Sea King HC4 [VQ]	RN No 846 Sqn, Yeovilton	
ZF118	WS61 Sea King HC4 [VP]	RN No 846 Sqn, Yeovilton	
ZF119	WS61 Sea King HC4 [VW]	RN No 846 Sqn, Yeovilton	
ZF120	WS61 Sea King HC4 [K]	RN No 845 Sqn, Yeovilton	
ZF121	WS61 Sea King HC4 [VT]	RN No 846 Sqn, Yeovilton	
ZF122	WS61 Sea King HC4 [VU]	RN No 846 Sqn, Yeovilton	
ZF123	WS61 Sea King HC4 [ZQ]	RN No 848 Sqn, Yeovilton	
ZF124	WS61 Sea King HC4 [L]	RN No 845 Sqn, Yeovilton	
ZF130	BAe 125-600B (G-BLUW)	Cranfield University	
ZF135	Shorts Tucano T1	RAF No 1 FTS, Linton-on-Ouse	
ZF136	Shorts Tucano T1	RAF No 1 FTS, Linton-on-Ouse	
ZF137	Shorts Tucano T1	RAF No 1 FTS, Linton-on-Ouse	
ZF138	Shorts Tucano T1	RAF No 1 FTS, Linton-on-Ouse	
ZF139	Shorts Tucano T1	RAF No 1 FTS, Linton-on-Ouse	
ZF140	Shorts Tucano T1	RAF No 1 FTS, Linton-on-Ouse	
ZF141	Shorts Tucano T1	RAF, stored Shawbury	
ZF142	Shorts Tucano T1	RAF No 1 FTS, Linton-on-Ouse	
ZF143	Shorts Tucano T1	RAF No 1 FTS, Linton-on-Ouse	
ZF144	Shorts Tucano T1	RAF No 1 FTS, Linton-on-Ouse	
ZF145	Shorts Tucano T1	RAF No 1 FTS, Linton-on-Ouse	
ZF160	Shorts Tucano T1	RAF No 1 FTS, Linton-on-Ouse	
ZF161	Shorts Tucano T1	RAF No 1 FTS, Linton-on-Ouse	
ZF162	Shorts Tucano T1	RAF No 1 FTS, Linton-on-Ouse	
ZF163	Shorts Tucano T1	RAF, stored Shawbury	
ZF164	Shorts Tucano T1	RAF, stored Shawbury	
ZF165	Shorts Tucano T1	RAF, stored Shawbury	
ZF166	Shorts Tucano T1	RAF No 1 FTS, Linton-on-Ouse	

Notes	Serial	Type (other identity) [code]	Owner/operator, location or fate
	ZF167	Shorts Tucano T1	RAF, stored Shawbury
	ZF168	Shorts Tucano T1	RAF No 1 FTS, Linton-on-Ouse
	ZF169	Shorts Tucano T1	RAF No 1 FTS, Linton-on-Ouse
	ZF170	Shorts Tucano T1	RAF No 1 FTS, Linton-on-Ouse
	ZF171	Shorts Tucano T1	RAF, stored Shawbury
	ZF172	Shorts Tucano T1	RAF, stored Shawbury
	ZF200	Shorts Tucano T1	RAF, stored Shawbury
	ZF201	Shorts Tucano T1	RAF, stored Shawbury
	ZF202	Shorts Tucano T1	RAF, stored Shawbury
	ZF203	Shorts Tucano T1	RAF No 1 FTS, Linton-on-Ouse
	ZF204	Shorts Tucano T1	RAF, stored Shawbury
	ZF205	Shorts Tucano T1	RAF, stored Shawbury
	ZF206	Shorts Tucano T1	RAF No 1 FTS, Linton-on-Ouse
	ZF207	Shorts Tucano T1	RAF No 1 FTS, Linton-on-Ouse
	ZF208	Shorts Tucano T1	RAF No 1 FTS, Linton-on-Ouse
	ZF209	Shorts Tucano T1	RAF, stored Shawbury
	ZF210	Shorts Tucano T1	RAF No 1 FTS, Linton-on-Ouse
	ZF211	Shorts Tucano T1	RAF, stored Shawbury
	ZF212	Shorts Tucano T1	RAF No 1 FTS, Linton-on-Ouse
	ZF238	Shorts Tucano T1	RAF No 1 FTS, Linton-on-Ouse
	ZF239	Shorts Tucano T1	RAF, stored Shawbury
	ZF240	Shorts Tucano T1	RAF No 1 FTS, Linton-on-Ouse
	ZF241	Shorts Tucano T1	RAF No 1 FTS, Linton-on-Ouse
	ZF242	Shorts Tucano T1	RAF No 1 FTS, Linton-on-Ouse
	ZF243	Shorts Tucano T1	RAF No 1 FTS, Linton-on-Ouse
	ZF244	Shorts Tucano T1	RAF No 1 FTS, Linton-on-Ouse
	ZF245	Shorts Tucano T1	RAF, stored Shawbury
	ZF263	Shorts Tucano T1	RAF No 1 FTS, Linton-on-Ouse
	ZF264	Shorts Tucano T1	RAF, stored Shawbury
	ZF265	Shorts Tucano T1	RAF, stored Shawbury
	ZF266	Shorts Tucano T1	RAF No 1 FTS, Linton-on-Ouse
	ZF267	Shorts Tucano T1	RAF, stored Shawbury
	ZF268	Shorts Tucano T1	RAF No 1 FTS, Linton-on-Ouse
	ZF269	Shorts Tucano T1	RAF, stored Shawbury
	ZF284	Shorts Tucano T1	RAF, stored Shawbury
	ZF285	Shorts Tucano T1	RAF, stored Shawbury
	ZF286	Shorts Tucano T1	RAF No 1 FTS, Linton-on-Ouse
	ZF287	Shorts Tucano T1	RAF, stored Shawbury
	ZF288	Shorts Tucano T1	RAF No 1 FTS, Linton-on-Ouse
	ZF289	Shorts Tucano T1	RAF No 1 FTS, Linton-on-Ouse
	ZF290	Shorts Tucano T1	RAF No 1 FTS, Linton-on-Ouse
	ZF291	Shorts Tucano T1	RAF No 1 FTS, Linton-on-Ouse
	ZF292	Shorts Tucano T1	RAF No 1 FTS, Linton-on-Ouse
	ZF293	Shorts Tucano T1	RAF No 1 FTS, Linton-on-Ouse
	ZF294	Shorts Tucano T1	RAF No 1 FTS, Linton-on-Ouse
	ZF295	Shorts Tucano T1	RAF No 1 FTS, Linton-on-Ouse
	ZF315	Shorts Tucano T1	RAF No 1 FTS, Linton-on-Ouse
	ZF317	Shorts Tucano T1	RAF No 1 FTS, Linton-on-Ouse
	ZF318	Shorts Tucano T1	RAF, stored Shawbury
	ZF319	Shorts Tucano T1	RAF No 1 FTS, Linton-on-Ouse
	ZF320	Shorts Tucano T1	RAF No 1 FTS, Linton-on-Ouse
	ZF338	Shorts Tucano T1	RAF No 1 FTS, Linton-on-Ouse
	ZF339	Shorts Tucano T1	RAF No 1 FTS, Linton-on-Ouse
	ZF340	Shorts Tucano T1	RAF, stored Shawbury
	ZF341	Shorts Tucano T1	RAF No 1 FTS, Linton-on-Ouse
	ZF342	Shorts Tucano T1	RAF No 1 FTS, Linton-on-Ouse
	ZF343	Shorts Tucano T1	RAF No 1 FTS, Linton-on-Ouse
	ZF344	Shorts Tucano T1	RAF, stored Shawbury
	ZF345	Shorts Tucano T1	RAF No 1 FTS, Linton-on-Ouse
	ZF346	Shorts Tucano T1	RAF No 1 FTS, Linton-on-Ouse
	ZF347	Shorts Tucano T1	RAF No 1 FTS, Linton-on-Ouse
	ZF348	Shorts Tucano T1	RAF No 1 FTS, Linton-on-Ouse
	ZF349	Shorts Tucano T1	RAF No 1 FTS, Linton-on-Ouse
	ZF350	Shorts Tucano T1	RAF No 1 FTS, Linton-on-Ouse
	ZF372	Shorts Tucano T1	RAF, stored Shawbury
	ZF373	Shorts Tucano T1	RAF, stored Shawbury
	ZF374	Shorts Tucano T1	RAF, stored Shawbury
	ZF375	Shorts Tucano T1	RAF No 1 FTS, Linton-on-Ouse
	ZF376	Shorts Tucano T1	RAF, stored Shawbury
	ZF377	Shorts Tucano T1	RAF St Athan
	ZF378	Shorts Tucano T1	RAF, stored Shawbury
	ZF379	Shorts Tucano T1	RAF No 1 FTS, Linton-on-Ouse
	ZF380	Shorts Tucano T1	RAF, stored Shawbury

Serial	Type (other identity) [code]	Owner/operator, location or fate	Notes
ZF405	Shorts Tucano T1	RAF No 1 FTS, Linton-on-Ouse	
ZF406	Shorts Tucano T1	RAF No 1 FTS, Linton-on-Ouse	
ZF407	Shorts Tucano T1	RAF No 1 FTS, Linton-on-Ouse	
ZF408	Shorts Tucano T1	RAF, stored Shawbury	
ZF409	Shorts Tucano T1	RAF, stored Shawbury	
ZF410	Shorts Tucano T1	RAF No 1 FTS, Linton-on-Ouse	
ZF411	Shorts Tucano T1	RAF, stored Shawbury	
ZF412	Shorts Tucano T1	RAF, stored Shawbury	
ZF413	Shorts Tucano T1	RAF No 1 FTS, Linton-on-Ouse	
ZF414	Shorts Tucano T1	RAF, stored Shawbury	
ZF415	Shorts Tucano T1	RAF, stored Shawbury	
ZF416	Shorts Tucano T1	RAF No 1 FTS, Linton-on-Ouse	
ZF417	Shorts Tucano T1	RAF No 1 FTS, Linton-on-Ouse	
ZF418	Shorts Tucano T1	RAF No 1 FTS, Linton-on-Ouse	
ZF445	Shorts Tucano T1	RAF No 1 FTS, Linton-on-Ouse	
ZF446	Shorts Tucano T1	RAF No 1 FTS, Linton-on-Ouse	
ZF447	Shorts Tucano T1	RAF No 1 FTS, Linton-on-Ouse	
ZF448	Shorts Tucano T1	RAF No 1 FTS, Linton-on-Ouse	
ZF449	Shorts Tucano T1	RAF No 1 FTS, Linton-on-Ouse	
ZF450	Shorts Tucano T1	RAF, stored Shawbury	
ZF483	Shorts Tucano T1	RAF No 1 FTS, Linton-on-Ouse	
ZF484	Shorts Tucano T1	RAF No 1 FTS, Linton-on-Ouse	
ZF485	Shorts Tucano T1 (G-BULU)	RAF No 1 FTS, Linton-on-Ouse	
ZF486	Shorts Tucano T1	RAF No 1 FTS, Linton-on-Ouse	
ZF487	Shorts Tucano T1	RAF No 1 FTS, Linton-on-Ouse	
ZF488	Shorts Tucano T1	RAF, stored Shawbury	
ZF489	Shorts Tucano T1	RAF No 1 FTS, Linton-on-Ouse	
ZF490	Shorts Tucano T1	RAF No 1 FTS, Linton-on-Ouse	
ZF491	Shorts Tucano T1	RAF No 1 FTS, Linton-on-Ouse	
ZF492	Shorts Tucano T1	RAF No 1 FTS, Linton-on-Ouse	
ZF510	Shorts Tucano T1	DPA/AFD, QinetiQ Boscombe Down	
ZF511	Shorts Tucano T1	DPA/AFD, QinetiQ Boscombe Down	
ZF512	Shorts Tucano T1	RAF No 1 FTS, Linton-on-Ouse	
ZF513	Shorts Tucano T1	RAF No 1 FTS, Linton-on-Ouse	
ZF514	Shorts Tucano T1	RAF No 1 FTS, Linton-on-Ouse	
ZF515	Shorts Tucano T1	RAF No 1 FTS, Linton-on-Ouse	
ZF516	Shorts Tucano T1	RAF, stored Shawbury	
ZF534	BAe EAP	Loughborough University	
ZF537	WS Lynx AH9	AAC No 653 Sqn/3 Regt, Wattisham	
ZF538	WS Lynx AH9	AAC No 659 Sqn/4 Regt, Wattisham	
ZF539	WS Lynx AH9	AAC No 7 Air Assault Battalion, Wattisham	
ZF540	WS Lynx AH9	AAC, stored DARA Fleetlands	
ZF557	WS Lynx HMA8 [420/EX]	RN No 815 Sqn, *Exeter* Flt, Yeovilton	
ZF558	WS Lynx HMA8 [307]	RN No 815 Sqn, HQ Flt, Yeovilton	
ZF560	WS Lynx HMA8 [365/AY]	RN No 815 Sqn, *Argyll* Flt, Yeovilton	
ZF562	WS Lynx HMA8 [336/CV]	RN No 815 Sqn, *Coventry* Flt, Yeovilton	
ZF563	WS Lynx HMA8 [306]	RN No 815 Sqn, Yeovilton	
ZF573	PBN 2T Islander CC2A (G-SRAY)	RAF Northolt Station Flight	
ZF578	BAC Lightning F53	*Repainted as XR753*	
ZF579	BAC Lightning F53	Gatwick Aviation Museum, Charlwood	
ZF580	BAC Lightning F53	BAE Systems Samlesbury, at main gate	
ZF581	BAC Lightning F53	Privately owned, Rochester	
ZF582	BAC Lightning F53 <ff>	Privately owned, Reading	
ZF583	BAC Lightning F53	Solway Aviation Society, Carlisle	
ZF584	BAC Lightning F53	Ferranti Ltd, South Gyle, Edinburgh	
ZF587	BAC Lightning F53 <ff>	Lashenden Air Warfare Museum, Headcorn	
ZF588	BAC Lightning F53 [L]	East Midlands Airport Aeropark	
ZF592	BAC Lightning F53	Privately owned, Portsmouth	
ZF593	BAC Lightning F53 (fuselage)	Pontypridd Technical College	
ZF594	BAC Lightning F53	North-East Aircraft Museum, Usworth	
ZF595	BAC Lightning T55 <ff>	*To the USA, Spring 2001*	
ZF596	BAC Lightning T55 <ff>	BAe North-West Heritage Group Warton	
ZF622	Piper PA-31 Navajo Chieftain 350 (N3548Y)	DPA/AFD, QinetiQ Boscombe Down	
ZF641	EHI-101 [PP1]	SFDO, RNAS Culdrose	
ZF649	EHI-101 Merlin [PP5]	RN AESS, *HMS Sultan*, Gosport	
ZG101	EHI-101 (mock-up) [GB]	Westland Helicopters/Agusta, Yeovil	
ZG471	BAe Harrier GR7 [61]	RAF No 1 Sqn, Cottesmore	
ZG474	BAe Harrier GR7 [64]	RAF No 1 Sqn, Cottesmore	
ZG474	BAe Harrier GR7 [64]	RAF No 1 Sqn, Cottesmore	
ZG477	BAe Harrier GR7 [67]	RAF No 3 Sqn, Cottesmore	

Notes	Serial	Type (other identity) [code]	Owner/operator, location or fate
	ZG478	BAe Harrier GR7 [68]	RAF No 1 Sqn, Cottesmore
	ZG479	BAe Harrier GR7 [69]	RAF No 1 Sqn, Cottesmore
	ZG480	BAe Harrier GR7 [70]	RAF AWC/SAOEU, Boscombe Down
	ZG500	BAe Harrier GR7 [71]	RAF No 4 Sqn, Cottesmore
	ZG501	BAe Harrier GR7 [72]	RAF No 3 Sqn, Cottesmore
	ZG502	BAe Harrier GR7 [73]	RAF No 4 Sqn, Cottesmore
	ZG503	BAe Harrier GR7 [74]	RAF No 1 Sqn, Cottesmore
	ZG504	BAe Harrier GR7 [75]	RAF No 4 Sqn, Cottesmore
	ZG505	BAe Harrier GR7 [76]	RAF No 4 Sqn, Cottesmore
	ZG506	BAe Harrier GR7 [77]	RAF HOCU/No 20(R) Sqn, Wittering
	ZG507	BAe Harrier GR7 [78]	RAF No 3 Sqn, Cottesmore
	ZG508	BAe Harrier GR7 [79]	RAF No 4 Sqn, Cottesmore
	ZG509	BAe Harrier GR7 [80]	RAF No 1 Sqn, Cottesmore
	ZG510	BAe Harrier GR7 [81]	RAF No 1 Sqn, Cottesmore
	ZG511	BAe Harrier GR7 [82]	DPA/AFD, QinetiQ Boscombe Down
	ZG512	BAe Harrier GR7 [83]	RAF No 3 Sqn, Cottesmore
	ZG530	BAe Harrier GR7 [84]	RAF No 1 Sqn, Cottesmore
	ZG531	BAe Harrier GR7 [85]	RAF No 4 Sqn, Cottesmore
	ZG705	Panavia Tornado GR4A [J]	RAF No 13 Sqn, Marham
	ZG706	Panavia Tornado GR1A [E]	RAF, stored St Athan
	ZG707	Panavia Tornado GR4A [B]	RAF No 13 Sqn, Marham
	ZG709	Panavia Tornado GR4A [V]	RAF No 13 Sqn, Marham
	ZG710	Panavia Tornado GR4A [D]	RAF No 13 Sqn, Marham
	ZG711	Panavia Tornado GR4A [O]	RAF No 2 Sqn, Marham
	ZG712	Panavia Tornado GR4A [F]	RAF No 13 Sqn, Marham
	ZG713	Panavia Tornado GR4A [G]	RAF No 13 Sqn, Marham
	ZG714	Panavia Tornado GR4A [Q]	RAF No 2 Sqn, Marham
	ZG726	Panavia Tornado GR4A [K]	RAF No 13 Sqn, Marham
	ZG727	Panavia Tornado GR4A [L]	DPA/BAE Systems, Warton (conversion)
	ZG729	Panavia Tornado GR4A [M]	RAF No 13 Sqn, Marham
	ZG731	Panavia Tornado F3	RAF AWC/F3 OEU, Coningsby
	ZG750	Panavia Tornado GR4 [DY]	RAF No 31 Sqn, Marham
	ZG751	Panavia Tornado F3 [WP]	RAF No 111 Sqn, Leuchars
	ZG752	Panavia Tornado GR4 [TO]	DPA/BAE Systems, Warton (conversion)
	ZG753	Panavia Tornado F3 [WO]	RAF No 1435 Flt, Mount Pleasant, FI
	ZG754	Panavia Tornado GR4 [TTP]	RAF No 15(R) Sqn, Lossiemouth)
	ZG755	Panavia Tornado F3	RAF No 25 Sqn, Leeming
	ZG756	Panavia Tornado GR4 [TTS]	RAF No 15(R) Sqn, Lossiemouth
	ZG757	Panavia Tornado F3 [WM]	RAF No 25 Sqn, Leeming
	ZG769	Panavia Tornado GR4 [TN]	RAF/DARA stored St Athan
	ZG770	Panavia Tornado F3 [CC]	RAF No 5 Sqn, Coningsby
	ZG771	Panavia Tornado GR4 [AZ]	RAF No 9 Sqn, Marham
	ZG772	Panavia Tornado F3 [WJ]	RAF No 25 Sqn, Leeming
	ZG773	Panavia Tornado GR4	DPA/BAE Systems, Warton
	ZG774	Panavia Tornado F3	RAF, stored St Athan
	ZG775	Panavia Tornado GR4 [FB]	RAF No 12 Sqn, Lossiemouth
	ZG776	Panavia Tornado F3	RAF No 1435 Flt, Mount Pleasant, FI
	ZG777	Panavia Tornado GR4 [TTC]	RAF No 15(R) Sqn, Lossiemouth
	ZG778	Panavia Tornado F3 [BG]	RAF F3 OCU/No 56(R) Sqn, Coningsby
	ZG779	Panavia Tornado GR4 [FA]	RAF No 12 Sqn, Lossiemouth
	ZG780	Panavia Tornado F3 [WF]	RAF No 11 Sqn, Leeming
	ZG791	Panavia Tornado GR4 [BI]	RAF No 14 Sqn, Lossiemouth
	ZG792	Panavia Tornado GR4 [AJ-G]	RAF No 617 Sqn, Lossiemouth
	ZG793	Panavia Tornado F3 [WE]	RAF No 11 Sqn, Leeming
	ZG794	Panavia Tornado GR4 [F]	RAF No 15(R) Sqn, Lossiemouth
	ZG795	Panavia Tornado F3 [H]	RAF Coningsby
	ZG796	Panavia Tornado F3 [WC]	RAF F3 OCU/No 56(R) Sqn, Coningsby
	ZG797	Panavia Tornado F3 [WB]	RAF F3 OCU/No 56(R) Sqn, Coningsby
	ZG798	Panavia Tornado F3 [WA]	RAF No 25 Sqn, Leeming
	ZG799	Panavia Tornado F3 [GP]	RAF No 43 Sqn, Leuchars
	ZG816	WS61 Sea King HAS6 [014/L]	RN No 820 Sqn, Culdrose
	ZG817	WS61 Sea King HAS6 [702/PW]	RN, stored HMS Sultan, Gosport
	ZG818	WS61 Sea King HAS6	RN, stored HMS Sultan, Gosport
	ZG819	WS61 Sea King HAS6 [265/N]	RN, stored HMS Sultan, Gosport
	ZG820	WS61 Sea King HC4 [A]	RN No 845 Sqn, Yeovilton
	ZG821	WS61 Sea King HC4 [D]	DARA, Fleetlands
	ZG822	WS61 Sea King HC4 [VN]	RN No 846 Sqn, Yeovilton
	ZG844	PBN 2T Islander AL1 (G-BLNE)	AAC AFWF, Middle Wallop
	ZG845	PBN 2T Islander AL1 (G-BLNT)	AAC No 1 Flt Aldergrove
	ZG846	PBN 2T Islander AL1 (G-BLNU)	AAC AFWF, Middle Wallop
	ZG847	PBN 2T Islander AL1 (G-BLNV)	AAC No 1 Flt, Aldergrove
	ZG848	PBN 2T Islander AL1 (G-BLNY)	AAC No 1 Flt, Aldergrove
	ZG857	BAe Harrier GR7 [89]	RAF No 4 Sqn, Cottesmore

Serial	Type (other identity) [code]	Owner/operator, location or fate	Notes
ZG858	BAe Harrier GR7	RAF AWC/SAOEU, Boscombe Down	
ZG859	BAe Harrier GR7 [91]	RAF HOCU/No 20(R) Sqn, Wittering	
ZG860	BAe Harrier GR7	DPA/BAE Systems, Warton (conversion)	
ZG862	BAe Harrier GR7 [94]	RAF No 1 Sqn, Cottesmore	
ZG875	WS61 Sea King HAS6 [013/L]	RN, stored *HMS Sultan*, Gosport (damaged)	
ZG879	Powerchute Raider Mk 1	DPA/Powerchute, Hereford	
ZG884	WS Lynx AH9	DPA/Westland Helicopters, Yeovil	
ZG885	WS Lynx AH9 [7]	AAC No 659 Sqn/4 Regt, Wattisham	
ZG886	WS Lynx AH9	AAC No 653 Sqn/3 Regt, Wattisham	
ZG887	WS Lynx AH9	AAC No 653 Sqn/3 Regt, Wattisham	
ZG888	WS Lynx AH9	AAC No 653 Sqn/3 Regt, Wattisham	
ZG889	WS Lynx AH9	AAC No 653 Sqn/3 Regt, Wattisham	
ZG914	WS Lynx AH9	AAC, stored DARA Fleetlands	
ZG915	WS Lynx AH9 [7]	DARA, Fleetlands	
ZG916	WS Lynx AH9 [8]	AAC No 653 Sqn/3 Regt, Wattisham	
ZG917	WS Lynx AH9 [2,9]	AAC No 7 Air Assault Battalion, Wattisham	
ZG918	WS Lynx AH9	AAC No 659 Sqn/4 Regt, Wattisham	
ZG919	WS Lynx AH9	AAC, stored DARA Fleetlands	
ZG920	WS Lynx AH9	AAC No 659 Sqn/4 Regt, Wattisham	
ZG921	WS Lynx AH9 [11]	AAC No 653 Sqn/3 Regt, Wattisham	
ZG922	WS Lynx AH9	DPA/Westland Helicopters, Weston-super-Mare (rebuild)	
ZG923	WS Lynx AH9	AAC No 653 Sqn/3 Regt, Wattisham	
ZG969	Pilatus PC-9 (HB-HQE)	BAE Systems Warton	
ZG989	PBN 2T Islander ASTOR (G-DLRA)	DPA/PBN, Bembridge	
ZG993	PBN 2T Islander AL1 (G-BOMD)	AAC No 1 Flight, Aldergrove	
ZG994	PBN 2T Islander AL1 (G-BPLN) (fuselage)	AAC, stored St Athan	
ZH101	Boeing E-3D Sentry AEW1	RAF No 8 Sqn/No 23 Sqn, Waddington	
ZH102	Boeing E-3D Sentry AEW1	RAF No 8 Sqn/No 23 Sqn, Waddington	
ZH103	Boeing E-3D Sentry AEW1	RAF No 8 Sqn/No 23 Sqn, Waddington	
ZH104	Boeing E-3D Sentry AEW1	RAF No 8 Sqn/No 23 Sqn, Waddington	
ZH105	Boeing E-3D Sentry AEW1	RAF No 8 Sqn/No 23 Sqn, Waddington	
ZH106	Boeing E-3D Sentry AEW1	RAF No 8 Sqn/No 23 Sqn, Waddington	
ZH107	Boeing E-3D Sentry AEW1	RAF No 8 Sqn/No 23 Sqn, Waddington	
ZH115	Grob G109B Vigilant T1 [TA]	RAF No 616 VGS, Henlow	
ZH116	Grob G109B Vigilant T1 [TB]	RAF No 664 VGS, Newtownards	
ZH117	Grob G109B Vigilant T1 [TC]	RAF No 642 VGS, Linton-on-Ouse	
ZH118	Grob G109B Vigilant T1 [TD]	RAF No 612 VGS, Abingdon	
ZH119	Grob G109B Vigilant T1 [TE]	RAF No 632 VGS, Ternhill	
ZH120	Grob G109B Vigilant T1 [TF]	RAF No 613 VGS, Halton	
ZH121	Grob G109B Vigilant T1 [TG]	RAF No 633 VGS, Cosford	
ZH122	Grob G109B Vigilant T1 [TH]	RAF No 635 VGS, Samlesbury	
ZH123	Grob G109B Vigilant T1 [TJ]	RAF No 637 VGS, Little Rissington	
ZH124	Grob G109B Vigilant T1 [TK]	RAF No 642 VGS, Linton-on-Ouse	
ZH125	Grob G109B Vigilant T1 [TL]	RAF No 633 VGS, Cosford	
ZH126	Grob G109B Vigilant T1 [TM]	RAF No 637 VGS, Little Rissington	
ZH127	Grob G109B Vigilant T1 [TN]	RAF No 642 VGS, Linton-on-Ouse	
ZH128	Grob G109B Vigilant T1 [TP]	RAF No 624 VGS, Chivenor RMB	
ZH129	Grob G109B Vigilant T1 [TQ]	RAF No 635 VGS, Samlesbury	
ZH139	BAe Harrier GR7 <R> (BAPC 191/ ZD472)	RAF EPTT, St Athan	
ZH141	AS355F-1 Twin Squirrel HCC1 (G-OILX)	RAF No 32(The Royal) Sqn, Northolt	
ZH144	Grob G109B Vigilant T1 [TR]	RAF No 616 VGS, Henlow	
ZH145	Grob G109B Vigilant T1 [TS]	RAF No 618 VGS, Odiham	
ZH146	Grob G109B Vigilant T1 [TT]	RAF No 624 VGS, Chivenor RMB	
ZH147	Grob G109B Vigilant T1 [TU]	RAF No 632 VGS, Ternhill	
ZH148	Grob G109B Vigilant T1 [TV]	RAF No 613 VGS, Halton	
ZH184	Grob G109B Vigilant T1 [TW]	RAF No 618 VGS, Odiham	
ZH185	Grob G109B Vigilant T1 [TX]	RAF No 663 VGS, Kinloss	
ZH186	Grob G109B Vigilant T1 [TY]	RAF No 613 VGS, Halton	
ZH187	Grob G109B Vigilant T1 [TZ]	RAF No 633 VGS, Cosford	
ZH188	Grob G109B Vigilant T1 [UA]	RAF No 612 VGS, Abingdon	
ZH189	Grob G109B Vigilant T1 [UB]	RAF No 635 VGS, Samlesbury	
ZH190	Grob G109B Vigilant T1 [UC]	RAF No 663 VGS, Kinloss	
ZH191	Grob G109B Vigilant T1 [UD]	RAF No 616 VGS, Henlow	
ZH192	Grob G109B Vigilant T1 [UE]	RAF No 635 VGS, Samlesbury	
ZH193	Grob G109B Vigilant T1 [UF]	RAF No 612 VGS, Abingdon	
ZH194	Grob G109B Vigilant T1 [UG]	RAF No 624 VGS, Chivenor RMB	
ZH195	Grob G109B Vigilant T1 [UH]	RAF ACCGS/No 644 VGS, Syerston	

Notes	Serial	Type (other identity) [code]	Owner/operator, location or fate
	ZH196	Grob G109B Vigilant T1 [UJ]	RAF No 612 VGS, Abingdon
	ZH197	Grob G109B Vigilant T1 [UK]	RAF No 633 VGS, Cosford
	ZH200	BAe Hawk 200	Overseas Customer Trade Centre, BAE Systems Warton
	ZH205	Grob G109B Vigilant T1 [UL]	RAF No 613 VGS, Halton
	ZH206	Grob G109B Vigilant T1 [UM]	RAF No 633 VGS, Cosford
	ZH207	Grob G109B Vigilant T1 [UN]	RAF ACCGS/No 644 VGS, Syerston
	ZH208	Grob G109B Vigilant T1 [UP]	RAF CGMF, Syerston
	ZH209	Grob G109B Vigilant T1 [UQ]	RAF No 664 VGS, Newtownards
	ZH211	Grob G109B Vigilant T1 [UR]	RAF No 618 VGS, Odiham
	ZH247	Grob G109B Vigilant T1 [US]	RAF ACCGS/No 644 VGS, Syerston
	ZH248	Grob G109B Vigilant T1 [UT]	RAF No 637 VGS, Little Rissington
	ZH249	Grob G109B Vigilant T1	RAF ACCGS/No 644 VGS, Syerston
	ZH257	B-V CH-47C Chinook (AE-520/9217M)	DARA, Fleetlands
	ZH263	Grob G109B Vigilant T1 [UV]	RAF No 632 VGS, Ternhill
	ZH264	Grob G109B Vigilant T1 [UW]	RAF No 616 VGS, Henlow
	ZH265	Grob G109B Vigilant T1 [UX]	RAF No 663 VGS, Kinloss
	ZH266	Grob G109B Vigilant T1 [UY]	RAF No 635 VGS, Samlesbury
	ZH267	Grob G109B Vigilant T1 [UZ]	RAF No 632 VGS, Ternhill
	ZH268	Grob G109B Vigilant T1 [SA]	RAF No 613 VGS, Halton
	ZH269	Grob G109B Vigilant T1 [SB]	RAF No 642 VGS, Linton-on-Ouse
	ZH270	Grob G109B Vigilant T1 [SC]	RAF No 616 VGS, Henlow
	ZH271	Grob G109B Vigilant T1 [SD]	RAF ACCGS/No 644 VGS, Syerston
	ZH278	Grob G109B Vigilant T1 [SFJ]	RAF CGMF, Syerston
	ZH279	Grob G109B Vigilant T1 [SG]	RAF CGMF, Syerston
	ZH536	PBN 2T Islander CC2 (G-BSAH)	RAF Northolt Station Flight
	ZH540	WS61 Sea King HAR3A	RAF No 203 Sqn, St Mawgan
	ZH541	WS61 Sea King HAR3A	RAF HMF, St Mawgan
	ZH542	WS61 Sea King HAR3A	RAF No 22 Sqn, B Flt, Wattisham
	ZH543	WS61 Sea King HAR3A	RAF No 22 Sqn, A Flt, Chivenor RMB
	ZH544	WS61 Sea King HAR3A	RAF HMF, St Mawgan
	ZH545	WS61 Sea King HAR3A	RAF No 22 Sqn, B Flt, Wattisham
	ZH552	Panavia Tornado F3 [AB]	RAF F3 OCU/No 56(R) Sqn, Coningsby
	ZH553	Panavia Tornado F3 [AB]	RAF No 11 Sqn, Leeming
	ZH554	Panavia Tornado F3	RAF AWC/F3 OEU, Coningsby
	ZH555	Panavia Tornado F3 [CV]	RAF F3 OCU/No 56(R) Sqn, Coningsby
	ZH556	Panavia Tornado F3 [AK]	RAF F3 OCU/No 56(R) Sqn, Coningsby
	ZH557	Panavia Tornado F3 [NT]	RAF No 5 Sqn, Coningsby
	ZH559	Panavia Tornado F3 [AJ]	RAF F3 OCU/No 56(R) Sqn, Coningsby
	ZH588	Eurofighter Typhoon (DA2)	DPA/BAE Systems, Warton
	ZH590	Eurofighter Typhoon (DA4)	DPA/BAE Systems, Warton
	ZH653	BAe Harrier T10	DPA/BAE Systems, Warton
	ZH654	BAe Harrier T10	QinetiQ, stored Boscombe Down (wreck)
	ZH655	BAe Harrier T10 [Q]	RAF, stored St Athan (damaged)
	ZH656	BAe Harrier T10 [104]	RAF No 1 Sqn, Cottesmore
	ZH657	BAe Harrier T10 [105]	RAF HOCU/No 20(R) Sqn, Wittering
	ZH658	BAe Harrier T10 [106]	RAF HOCU/No 20(R) Sqn, Wittering
	ZH659	BAe Harrier T10 [107]	RAF HOCU/No 20(R) Sqn, Wittering
	ZH660	BAe Harrier T10 [108]	RAF HOCU/No 20(R) Sqn, Wittering
	ZH661	BAe Harrier T10 [109]	DPA/BAE Systems, Warton
	ZH662	BAe Harrier T10 [110]	RAF HOCU/No 20(R) Sqn, Wittering
	ZH663	BAe Harrier T10 [111]	RAF HOCU/No 20(R) Sqn, Wittering
	ZH664	BAe Harrier T10 [112]	RAF No 1 Sqn, Cottesmore
	ZH665	BAe Harrier T10 [113]	RAF HOCU/No 20(R) Sqn, Wittering
	ZH762	Westinghouse Skyship 500 (G-SKSC)	Westinghouse, stored Cardington
	ZH763	BAC 1-11/539GL (G-BGKE)	DPA/AFD, QinetiQ Boscombe Down
	ZH775	B-V Chinook HC2 (N7424J) [NS]	RAF No 7 Sqn, Odiham
	ZH776	B-V Chinook HC2 (N7424L) [ES]	RAF No 7 Sqn, Odiham
	ZH777	B-V Chinook HC2 (N7424M) [BS]	RAF No 18 Sqn, Odiham
	ZH796	BAe Sea Harrier FA2 [716/VL]	RN, St Athan
	ZH797	BAe Sea Harrier FA2 [002]	RN No 801 Sqn, Yeovilton
	ZH798	BAe Sea Harrier FA2 [718]	RN No 899 Sqn, Yeovilton
	ZH799	BAe Sea Harrier FA2 [730]	DPA/BAE Systems, Warton
	ZH800	BAe Sea Harrier FA2 [005]	RN/DARA, St Athan
	ZH801	BAe Sea Harrier FA2 [006/L]	RN No 801 Sqn, Yeovilton
	ZH802	BAe Sea Harrier FA2 [717]	RN/DARA, St Athan
	ZH803	BAe Sea Harrier FA2 [128/R]	RN No 800 Sqn, Yeovilton
	ZH804	BAe Sea Harrier FA2 [125]	RN No 800 Sqn, Yeovilton
	ZH805	BAe Sea Harrier FA2 [730]	RN No 899 Sqn, Yeovilton
	ZH806	BAe Sea Harrier FA2 [717]	RN AMG Yeovilton
	ZH807	BAe Sea Harrier FA2 [719]	DPA/BAE Systems, Warton

Serial	Type (other identity) [code]	Owner/operator, location or fate	Notes
ZH808	BAe Sea Harrier FA2 [712]	RN No 899 Sqn, Yeovilton	
ZH809	BAe Sea Harrier FA2	RN AMG, Yeovilton	
ZH810	BAe Sea Harrier FA2 [716]	RN No 899 Sqn, Yeovilton	
ZH811	BAe Sea Harrier FA2	DPA/BAE Systems, Warton	
ZH812	BAe Sea Harrier FA2 [006]	DPA/BAE Systems, Warton	
ZH813	BAe Sea Harrier FA2 [000]	RN No 801 Sqn, Yeovilton	
ZH814	Bell 212 (G-BGMH)	AAC No 7 Flt, Brunei	
ZH815	Bell 212 (G-BGCZ)	AAC No 7 Flt, Brunei	
ZH816	Bell 212 (G-BGMG)	AAC No 7 Flt, Brunei	
ZH821	EHI-101 Merlin HM1	DPA/Westland Helicopters, Yeovil	
ZH822	EHI-101 Merlin HM1	DPA/Westland Helicopters, Yeovil	
ZH823	EHI-101 Merlin HM1	DPA/Westland Helicopters, Yeovil	
ZH824	EHI-101 Merlin HM1	DPA/AFD, QinetiQ Boscombe Down	
ZH825	EHI-101 Merlin HM1 [583/CU]	RN AMG, Culdrose	
ZH826	EHI-101 Merlin HM1	RN AMG, Culdrose	
ZH827	EHI-101 Merlin HM1	RN/DARA, Fleetlands	
ZH828	EHI-101 Merlin HM1 [583/CU]	DPA/Westland Helicopters, Weston-super-Mare	
ZH829	EHI-101 Merlin HM1	DPA/Westland Helicopters, Yeovil	
ZH830	EHI-101 Merlin HM1	DPA/AFD/QinetiQ, Boscombe Down	
ZH831	EHI-101 Merlin HM1	DPA/Westland Helicopters, Yeovil	
ZH832	EHI-101 Merlin HM1	DPA/AFD/QinetiQ, Boscombe Down	
ZH833	EHI-101 Merlin HM1	DPA/Westland Helicopters, Yeovil	
ZH834	EHI-101 Merlin HM1	DPA/Westland Helicopters, Yeovil	
ZH835	EHI-101 Merlin HM1 [581/CU]	RN No 824 Sqn, Culdrose	
ZH836	EHI-101 Merlin HM1 [582/CU]	RN No 824 Sqn, Culdrose	
ZH837	EHI-101 Merlin HM1	RN AMG, Culdrose	
ZH838	EHI-101 Merlin HM1	RN No 824 Sqn, Culdrose	
ZH839	EHI-101 Merlin HM1 [539/CU]	RN No 700M OEU, Culdrose	
ZH840	EHI-101 Merlin HM1	DPA/Westland Helicopters, Yeovil	
ZH841	EHI-101 Merlin HM1	DPA/AFD/QinetiQ, Boscombe Down	
ZH842	EHI-101 Merlin HM1 [585/CU]	RN No 824 Sqn, Culdrose	
ZH843	EHI-101 Merlin HM1 [533/CU]	RN No 700M OEU, Culdrose	
ZH844	EHI-101 Merlin HM1	DPA/Westland Helicopters, Yeovil	
ZH845	EHI-101 Merlin HM1 [535]	RN No 700M OEU, Culdrose	
ZH846	EHI-101 Merlin HM1 [586]	RN No 824 Sqn, Culdrose	
ZH847	EHI-101 Merlin HM1	DPA/Westland Helicopters, Yeovil	
ZH848	EHI-101 Merlin HM1	RN No 814 Sqn, Culdrose	
ZH849	EHI-101 Merlin HM1 [265/R]	RN No 814 Sqn, Culdrose	
ZH850	EHI-101 Merlin HM1 [266/R]	RN No 814 Sqn, Culdrose	
ZH851	EHI-101 Merlin HM1 [267/R]	RN No 814 Sqn, Culdrose	
ZH852	EHI-101 Merlin HM1 [583/CU]	RN No 824 Sqn, Culdrose	
ZH853	EHI-101 Merlin HM1	RN AMG, Culdrose	
ZH854	EHI-101 Merlin HM1 [580/CU]	RN No 824 Sqn, Culdrose	
ZH855	EHI-101 Merlin HM1 [587/CU]	RN No 824 Sqn, Culdrose	
ZH856	EHI-101 Merlin HM1	DPA/Westland Helicopters, Yeovil	
ZH857	EHI-101 Merlin HM1	DPA/Westland Helicopters, Yeovil	
ZH858	EHI-101 Merlin HM1	DPA/Westland Helicopters, Yeovil	
ZH859	EHI-101 Merlin HM1	DPA/Westland Helicopters, Yeovil	
ZH860	EHI-101 Merlin HM1	Westland Helicopters, Yeovil, for RN	
ZH861	EHI-101 Merlin HM1	Westland Helicopters, Yeovil, for RN	
ZH862	EHI-101 Merlin HM1	Westland Helicopters, Yeovil, for RN	
ZH863	EHI-101 Merlin HM1	Westland Helicopters, Yeovil, for RN	
ZH864	EHI-101 Merlin HM1	Westland Helicopters, Yeovil, for RN	
ZH865	Lockheed C-130J-30 Hercules C4 (N130JA)	DPA/Lockheed-Martin, Marietta	
ZH866	Lockheed C-130J-30 Hercules C4 (N130JE)	RAF Lyneham Transport Wing	
ZH867	Lockheed C-130J-30 Hercules C4 (N130JJ)	RAF Lyneham Transport Wing	
ZH868	Lockheed C-130J-30 Hercules C4 (N130JN)	RAF Lyneham Transport Wing	
ZH869	Lockheed C-130J-30 Hercules C4 (N130JV)	RAF Lyneham Transport Wing	
ZH870	Lockheed C-130J-30 Hercules C4 (N73235/N78235)	RAF Lyneham Transport Wing	
ZH871	Lockheed C-130J-30 Hercules C4 (N73238)	DPA/AFD, QinetiQ Boscombe Down	
ZH872	Lockheed C-130J-30 Hercules C4 (N4249Y)	RAF Lyneham Transport Wing	
ZH873	Lockheed C-130J-30 Hercules C4 (N4242N)	RAF Lyneham Transport Wing	

Notes	Serial	Type (other identity) [code]	Owner/operator, location or fate
	ZH874	Lockheed C-130J-30 Hercules C4 (N41030)	RAF Lyneham Transport Wing
	ZH875	Lockheed C-130J-30 Hercules C4 (N4099R)	RAF Lyneham Transport Wing
	ZH876	Lockheed C-130J-30 Hercules C4 (N4080M)	RAF Lyneham Transport Wing
	ZH877	Lockheed C-130J-30 Hercules C4 (N4081M)	RAF Lyneham Transport Wing
	ZH878	Lockheed C-130J-30 Hercules C4 (N73232)	RAF Lyneham Transport Wing
	ZH879	Lockheed C-130J-30 Hercules C4 (N4080M)	RAF Lyneham Transport Wing
	ZH880	Lockheed C-130J Hercules C5 (N73238)	DPA/AFD, QinetiQ Boscombe Down
	ZH881	Lockheed C-130J Hercules C5 (N4081M)	RAF Lyneham Transport Wing
	ZH882	Lockheed C-130J Hercules C5 (N4099R)	RAF Lyneham Transport Wing
	ZH883	Lockheed C-130J Hercules C5 (N4242N)	RAF Lyneham Transport Wing
	ZH884	Lockheed C-130J Hercules C5 (N4249Y)	RAF Lyneham Transport Wing
	ZH885	Lockheed C-130J Hercules C5 (N41030)	RAF Lyneham Transport Wing
	ZH886	Lockheed C-130J Hercules C5 (N73235)	RAF Lyneham Transport Wing
	ZH887	Lockheed C-130J Hercules C5 (N4187W)	RAF Lyneham Transport Wing
	ZH888	Lockheed C-130J Hercules C5 (N4187)	RAF Lyneham Transport Wing
	ZH889	Lockheed C-130J Hercules C5 (N4099R)	RAF Lyneham Transport Wing
	ZH890	Grob G109B Vigilant T1 [SE]	RAF ACCGS/No 644 VGS, Syerston
	ZH891	B-V Chinook HC2A (N20075)	RAF No 18 Sqn, Odiham
	ZH892	B-V Chinook HC2A (N2019V) [BL]	RAF No 18 Sqn, Odiham
	ZH893	B-V Chinook HC2A (N2025L) [BM]	RAF No 18 Sqn, Odiham
	ZH894	B-V Chinook HC2A (N2026E) [BO]	RAF No 18 Sqn, Odiham
	ZH895	B-V Chinook HC2A (N2034K) [BP]	RAF No 18 Sqn, Odiham
	ZH896	B-V Chinook HC2A (N2038G)	DPA/AFD, QinetiQ Boscombe Down
	ZH897	B-V Chinook HC3 (N2045G)	DPA/AFD, QinetiQ Boscombe Down
	ZH898	B-V Chinook HC3 (N2057Q)	DPA/AFD, QinetiQ Boscombe Down
	ZH899	B-V Chinook HC3 (N2057R)	DPA/AFD, QinetiQ Boscombe Down
	ZH900	B-V Chinook HC3 (N2060H)	DPA/AFD, QinetiQ Boscombe Down
	ZH901	B-V Chinook HC3 (N2060M)	Boeing, Philadelphia, for RAF
	ZH902	B-V Chinook HC3 (N2064W)	DPA/AFD, QinetiQ Boscombe Down
	ZH903	B-V Chinook HC3 (N20671)	Boeing, Philadelphia, for RAF
	ZH904	B-V Chinook HC3 (N2083K)	Boeing, Philadelphia, for RAF
	ZJ100	BAe Hawk 102D	BAE Systems Warton
	ZJ116	EHI-101 (G-OIOI) (PP8)	*Repainted as G-17-101 by August 2001*
	ZJ117	EHI-101 Merlin HC3	DPA/Westland Helicopters, Yeovil
	ZJ118	EHI-101 Merlin HC3 [B]	DPA/AFD, QinetiQ Boscombe Down
	ZJ119	EHI-101 Merlin HC3 [C]	DPA/Westland Helicopters, Yeovil
	ZJ120	EHI-101 Merlin HC3	DPA/Westland Helicopters, Yeovil
	ZJ121	EHI-101 Merlin HC3 [E]	RAF No 28 Sqn, Benson
	ZJ122	EHI-101 Merlin HC3 [F]	RAF No 28 Sqn, Benson
	ZJ123	EHI-101 Merlin HC3 [G]	RAF No 28 Sqn, Benson
	ZJ124	EHI-101 Merlin HC3 [H]	RAF No 28 Sqn, Benson
	ZJ125	EHI-101 Merlin HC3 [J]	RAF No 28 Sqn, Benson
	ZJ126	EHI-101 Merlin HC3 [K]	RAF No 28 Sqn, Benson
	ZJ127	EHI-101 Merlin HC3 [L]	RAF No 28 Sqn, Benson
	ZJ128	EHI-101 Merlin HC3 [M]	DPA/Westland Helicopters, Yeovil
	ZJ129	EHI-101 Merlin HC3 [N]	DPA/Westland Helicopters, Yeovil
	ZJ130	EHI-101 Merlin HC3	DPA/Westland Helicopters, Yeovil
	ZJ131	EHI-101 Merlin HC3	DPA/Westland Helicopters, Yeovil
	ZJ132	EHI-101 Merlin HC3	DPA/Westland Helicopters, Yeovil
	ZJ133	EHI-101 Merlin HC3	DPA/Westland Helicopters, Yeovil
	ZJ134	EHI-101 Merlin HC3	DPA/Westland Helicopters, Yeovil
	ZJ135	EHI-101 Merlin HC3	DPA/Westland Helicopters, Yeovil
	ZJ136	EHI-101 Merlin HC3	Westland Helicopters, Yeovil, for RAF
	ZJ137	EHI-101 Merlin HC3	Westland Helicopters, Yeovil, for RAF
	ZJ138	EHI-101 Merlin HC3	Westland Helicopters, Yeovil, for RAF

Serial	Type (other identity) [code]	Owner/operator, location or fate	Notes
ZJ139	AS355F-1 Twin Squirrel HCC1 (G-NUTZ)	RAF No 32(The Royal) Sqn, Northolt	
ZJ140	AS355F-1 Twin Squirrel HCC1 (G-FFHI)	RAF No 32(The Royal) Sqn, Northolt	
ZJ164	AS365N-2 Dauphin 2 (G-BTLC)	RN/Bond Helicopters, Plymouth	
ZJ165	AS365N-2 Dauphin 2 (G-NTOO)	RN/Bond Helicopters, Plymouth	
ZJ166	WAH-64 Apache AH1 (N9219G)	DPA/Westland Helicopters, Yeovil	
ZJ167	WAH-64 Apache AH1 (N3266B)	AAC No 651 Sqn, Middle Wallop	
ZJ168	WAH-64 Apache AH1 (N3123T)	AAC No 651 Sqn, Middle Wallop	
ZJ169	WAH-64 Apache AH1 (N3114H)	AAC No 651 Sqn, Middle Wallop	
ZJ170	WAH-64 Apache AH1 (N3065U)	Boeing Helicopters, Mesa, for AAC	
ZJ171	WAH-64 Apache AH1 (N3266T)	DPA/AFD, QinetiQ Boscombe Down	
ZJ172	WAH-64 Apache AH1	AAC No 651 Sqn, Middle Wallop	
ZJ173	WAH-64 Apache AH1 (N3266W)	DPA/Westland Helicopters, Yeovil	
ZJ174	WAH-64 Apache AH1	AAC No 651 Sqn, Middle Wallop	
ZJ175	WAH-64 Apache AH1 (N3218V)	AAC No 651 Sqn, Middle Wallop	
ZJ176	WAH-64 Apache AH1	AAC No 651 Sqn, Middle Wallop	
ZJ177	WAH-64 Apache AH1	DPA/Westland Helicopters, Yeovil	
ZJ178	WAH-64 Apache AH1	AAC No 651 Sqn, Middle Wallop	
ZJ179	WAH-64 Apache AH1	AAC No 651 Sqn, Middle Wallop	
ZJ180	WAH-64 Apache AH1	AAC No 651 Sqn, Middle Wallop	
ZJ181	WAH-64 Apache AH1	DPA/Westland Helicopters, Yeovil	
ZJ182	WAH-64 Apache AH1	AAC/ DARA, Fleetlands	
ZJ183	WAH-64 Apache AH1	AAC/ DARA, Fleetlands	
ZJ184	WAH-64 Apache AH1	DPA/Westland Helicopters, Yeovil	
ZJ185	WAH-64 Apache AH1	DPA/Westland Helicopters, Yeovil	
ZJ186	WAH-64 Apache AH1	DPA/Westland Helicopters, Yeovil	
ZJ187	WAH-64 Apache AH1	DPA/Westland Helicopters, Yeovil	
ZJ188	WAH-64 Apache AH1	DPA/Westland Helicopters, Yeovil	
ZJ189	WAH-64 Apache AH1	DPA/Westland Helicopters, Yeovil	
ZJ190	WAH-64 Apache AH1	Westland Helicopters, for AAC	
ZJ191	WAH-64 Apache AH1	Westland Helicopters, for AAC	
ZJ192	WAH-64 Apache AH1	Westland Helicopters, for AAC	
ZJ193	WAH-64 Apache AH1	Westland Helicopters, for AAC	
ZJ194	WAH-64 Apache AH1	Westland Helicopters, for AAC	
ZJ195	WAH-64 Apache AH1	Westland Helicopters, for AAC	
ZJ196	WAH-64 Apache AH1	Westland Helicopters, for AAC	
ZJ197	WAH-64 Apache AH1	Westland Helicopters, for AAC	
ZJ198	WAH-64 Apache AH1	Westland Helicopters, for AAC	
ZJ199	WAH-64 Apache AH1	Westland Helicopters, for AAC	
ZJ200	WAH-64 Apache AH1	Westland Helicopters, for AAC	
ZJ202	WAH-64 Apache AH1	Westland Helicopters, for AAC	
ZJ203	WAH-64 Apache AH1	Westland Helicopters, for AAC	
ZJ204	WAH-64 Apache AH1	Westland Helicopters, for AAC	
ZJ205	WAH-64 Apache AH1	Westland Helicopters, for AAC	
ZJ206	WAH-64 Apache AH1	Westland Helicopters, for AAC	
ZJ207	WAH-64 Apache AH1	Westland Helicopters, for AAC	
ZJ208	WAH-64 Apache AH1	Westland Helicopters, for AAC	
ZJ209	WAH-64 Apache AH1	Westland Helicopters, for AAC	
ZJ210	WAH-64 Apache AH1	Westland Helicopters, for AAC	
ZJ211	WAH-64 Apache AH1	Westland Helicopters, for AAC	
ZJ212	WAH-64 Apache AH1	Westland Helicopters, for AAC	
ZJ213	WAH-64 Apache AH1	Westland Helicopters, for AAC	
ZJ214	WAH-64 Apache AH1	Westland Helicopters, for AAC	
ZJ215	WAH-64 Apache AH1	Westland Helicopters, for AAC	
ZJ216	WAH-64 Apache AH1	Westland Helicopters, for AAC	
ZJ217	WAH-64 Apache AH1	Westland Helicopters, for AAC	
ZJ218	WAH-64 Apache AH1	Westland Helicopters, for AAC	
ZJ219	WAH-64 Apache AH1	Westland Helicopters, for AAC	
ZJ220	WAH-64 Apache AH1	Westland Helicopters, for AAC	
ZJ221	WAH-64 Apache AH1	Westland Helicopters, for AAC	
ZJ222	WAH-64 Apache AH1	Westland Helicopters, for AAC	
ZJ223	WAH-64 Apache AH1	Westland Helicopters, for AAC	
ZJ224	WAH-64 Apache AH1	Westland Helicopters, for AAC	
ZJ225	WAH-64 Apache AH1	Westland Helicopters, for AAC	
ZJ226	WAH-64 Apache AH1	Westland Helicopters, for AAC	
ZJ227	WAH-64 Apache AH1	Westland Helicopters, for AAC	
ZJ228	WAH-64 Apache AH1	Westland Helicopters, for AAC	
ZJ229	WAH-64 Apache AH1	Westland Helicopters, for AAC	
ZJ230	WAH-64 Apache AH1	Westland Helicopters, for AAC	
ZJ231	WAH-64 Apache AH1	Westland Helicopters, for AAC	
ZJ232	WAH-64 Apache AH1	Westland Helicopters, for AAC	
ZJ233	WAH-64 Apache AH1	Westland Helicopters, for AAC	

Notes	Serial	Type (other identity) [code]	Owner/operator, location or fate
	ZJ234	Bell 412EP Griffin HT1 (G-BWZR) [S]	DHFS No 60(R) Sqn, RAF Shawbury
	ZJ235	Bell 412EP Griffin HT1 (G-BXBF) [I]	DHFS No 60(R) Sqn, RAF Shawbury
	ZJ236	Bell 412EP Griffin HT1 (G-BXBE) [X]	DHFS No 60(R) Sqn, RAF Shawbury
	ZJ237	Bell 412EP Griffin HT1 (G-BXFF) [T]	DHFS No 60(R) Sqn, RAF Shawbury
	ZJ238	Bell 412EP Griffin HT1 (G-BXHC) [Y]	DHFS No 60(R) Sqn, RAF Shawbury
	ZJ239	Bell 412EP Griffin HT1 (G-BXFH) [R]	DHFS No 60(R) Sqn, RAF Shawbury
	ZJ240	Bell 412EP Griffin HT1 (G-BXIR) [U]	DHFS No 60(R) Sqn/SARTU, RAF Valley
	ZJ241	Bell 412EP Griffin HT1 (G-BXIS) [L]	DHFS No 60(R) Sqn/SARTU, RAF Valley
	ZJ242	Bell 412EP Griffin HT1 (G-BXDK) [E]	DHFS No 60(R) Sqn/SARTU, RAF Valley
	ZJ243	AS350BA Squirrel HT2 (G-BWZS)	DHFS, RAF Shawbury
	ZJ244	AS350BA Squirrel HT2 (G-BXMD)	School of Army Aviation/No 670 Sqn, Middle Wallop
	ZJ245	AS350BA Squirrel HT2 (G-BXME)	School of Army Aviation/No 670 Sqn, Middle Wallop
	ZJ246	AS350BA Squirrel HT2 (G-BXMJ)	School of Army Aviation/No 670 Sqn, Middle Wallop
	ZJ247	AS350BA Squirrel HT2 (G-BXNB)	School of Army Aviation/No 670 Sqn, Middle Wallop
	ZJ248	AS350BA Squirrel HT2 (G-BXNE)	School of Army Aviation/No 670 Sqn, Middle Wallop
	ZJ249	AS350BA Squirrel HT2 (G-BXNJ)	School of Army Aviation/No 670 Sqn, Middle Wallop
	ZJ250	AS350BA Squirrel HT2 (G-BXNY)	School of Army Aviation/No 670 Sqn, Middle Wallop
	ZJ251	AS350BA Squirrel HT2 (G-BXOG)	School of Army Aviation/No 670 Sqn, Middle Wallop
	ZJ252	AS350BA Squirrel HT2 (G-BXOK)	School of Army Aviation/No 670 Sqn, Middle Wallop
	ZJ253	AS350BA Squirrel HT2 (G-BXPG)	School of Army Aviation/No 670 Sqn, Middle Wallop
	ZJ254	AS350BA Squirrel HT2 (G-BXPJ)	DHFS, RAF Shawbury
	ZJ255	AS350BB Squirrel HT1 (G-BXAG)	DHFS, RAF Shawbury
	ZJ256	AS350BB Squirrel HT1 (G-BXCE)	DHFS, RAF Shawbury
	ZJ257	AS350BB Squirrel HT1 (G-BXDJ)	DHFS, RAF Shawbury
	ZJ258	AS350BB Squirrel HT1 (G-BXEO)	DHFS, RAF Shawbury
	ZJ259	AS350BB Squirrel HT1 (G-BXFJ)	DHFS, RAF Shawbury
	ZJ260	AS350BB Squirrel HT1 (G-BXGB)	DHFS, RAF Shawbury
	ZJ261	AS350BB Squirrel HT1 (G-BXGJ)	DHFS, RAF Shawbury
	ZJ262	AS350BB Squirrel HT1 (G-BXHB)	DHFS, RAF Shawbury
	ZJ263	AS350BB Squirrel HT1 (G-BXHK)	DHFS, RAF Shawbury
	ZJ264	AS350BB Squirrel HT1 (G-BXHW)	DHFS, RAF Shawbury
	ZJ265	AS350BB Squirrel HT1 (G-BXHX)	DHFS, RAF Shawbury
	ZJ266	AS350BB Squirrel HT1 (G-BXIL)	DHFS, RAF Shawbury
	ZJ267	AS350BB Squirrel HT1 (G-BXIP)	DHFS, RAF Shawbury
	ZJ268	AS350BB Squirrel HT1 (G-BXJE)	DHFS, RAF Shawbury
	ZJ269	AS350BB Squirrel HT1 (G-BXJN)	DHFS, RAF Shawbury
	ZJ270	AS350BB Squirrel HT1 (G-BXJR)	DHFS, RAF Shawbury
	ZJ271	AS350BB Squirrel HT1 (G-BXKE)	DHFS, RAF Shawbury
	ZJ272	AS350BB Squirrel HT1 (G-BXKN)	DHFS, RAF Shawbury
	ZJ273	AS350BB Squirrel HT1 (G-BXKP)	DHFS, RAF Shawbury
	ZJ274	AS350BB Squirrel HT1 (G-BXKR)	DHFS, RAF Shawbury
	ZJ275	AS350BB Squirrel HT1 (G-BXLB)	DHFS, RAF Shawbury
	ZJ276	AS350BB Squirrel HT1 (G-BXLE)	DHFS, RAF Shawbury
	ZJ277	AS350BB Squirrel HT1 (G-BXLH)	DHFS, RAF Shawbury
	ZJ278	AS350BB Squirrel HT1 (G-BXMB)	DHFS, RAF Shawbury
	ZJ279	AS350BB Squirrel HT1 (G-BXMC)	DHFS, RAF Shawbury
	ZJ280	AS350BB Squirrel HT1 (G-BXMI)	DHFS, RAF Shawbury
	ZJ281 to ZJ480	GEC Phoenix UAV	For Army
	ZJ514	BAE Systems Nimrod MRA4 (XV251) [PA-4]	DPA/BAE Systems, Woodford (conversion)
	ZJ515	BAE Systems Nimrod MRA4 (XV258) [PA-5]	DPA/BAE Systems, Woodford (conversion)

Serial	Type (other identity) [code]	Owner/operator, location or fate	Notes
ZJ516	BAE Systems Nimrod MRA4 (XV247) [PA-1]	DPA/BAE Systems, Woodford (conversion)	
ZJ517	BAE Systems Nimrod MRA4 (XV242) [PA-3]	DPA/BAE Systems, Woodford (conversion)	
ZJ518	BAE Systems Nimrod MRA4 (XV234) [PA-2]	DPA/BAE Systems, Woodford (conversion)	
ZJ519	BAE Systems Nimrod MRA4 (XZ284) [PA-6]	DPA/BAE Systems, Woodford (conversion)	
ZJ520	BAE Systems Nimrod MRA4 (XV233) [PA-7]	DPA/BAE Systems, Woodford (conversion)	
ZJ521	BAE Systems Nimrod MRA4	BAE Systems, for RAF	
ZJ522	BAE Systems Nimrod MRA4	BAE Systems, for RAF	
ZJ523	BAE Systems Nimrod MRA4	BAE Systems, for RAF	
ZJ524	BAE Systems Nimrod MRA4	BAE Systems, for RAF	
ZJ525	BAE Systems Nimrod MRA4	BAE Systems, for RAF	
ZJ526	BAE Systems Nimrod MRA4	BAE Systems, for RAF	
ZJ527	BAE Systems Nimrod MRA4	BAE Systems, for RAF	
ZJ528	BAE Systems Nimrod MRA4	BAE Systems, for RAF	
ZJ529	BAE Systems Nimrod MRA4	BAE Systems, for RAF	
ZJ530	BAE Systems Nimrod MRA4	BAE Systems, for RAF	
ZJ531	BAE Systems Nimrod MRA4	BAE Systems, for RAF	
ZJ532	BAE Systems Nimrod MRA4	BAE Systems, for RAF	
ZJ533	BAE Systems Nimrod MRA4	BAE Systems, for RAF	
ZJ534	BAE Systems Nimrod MRA4	BAE Systems, for RAF	
ZJ554	WS Super Lynx Mk 99	*To S Korean Navy as 00-0735, 2000*	
ZJ619	Eurofighter Typhoon <Sim>	RAF No 1 SoTT, Cosford	
ZJ632	BAE Systems Hawk 127	*To R.Australian AF as A27-01, 28 January 2001*	
ZJ635	AS355F-1 Twin Squirrel (G-NEXT)	DPA/AFD/ETP, QinetiQ, Boscombe Down	
ZJ642	BAE Systems Hawk 127	*To R.Australian AF as A27-11, 28 January 2001*	
ZJ643	BAE Systems Hawk 127	*To R.Australian AF as A27-15, 26 September 2001*	
ZJ644	BAE Systems Hawk 127	*To R.Australian AF as A27-27, 26 September 2001*	
ZJ645	D-BD Alpha Jet (98+62)	DPA/AFD/ETPS QinetiQ, Boscombe Down	
ZJ646	D-BD Alpha Jet (98+55)	DPA/AFD/QinetiQ, Llanbedr	
ZJ647	D-BD Alpha Jet (98+71)	DPA/AFD/ETPS, QinetiQ Boscombe Down	
ZJ648	D-BD Alpha Jet (98+09)	DPA/AFD/QinetiQ, Boscombe Down	
ZJ649	D-BD Alpha Jet (98+73)	DPA/AFD/QinetiQ, Llanbedr	
ZJ650	D-BD Alpha Jet (98+35)	DPA/AFD/QinetiQ, Boscombe Down	
ZJ651	D-BD Alpha Jet (41+42)	QinetiQ, Boscombe Down, spares use	
ZJ652	D-BD Alpha Jet (41+09)	QinetiQ, Boscombe Down, spares use	
ZJ653	D-BD Alpha Jet (40+22)	QinetiQ, Boscombe Down, spares use	
ZJ654	D-BD Alpha Jet (41+02)	QinetiQ, Boscombe Down, spares use	
ZJ655	D-BD Alpha Jet (41+19)	QinetiQ, Boscombe Down, spares use	
ZJ656	D-BD Alpha Jet (41+40)	QinetiQ, Boscombe Down, spares use	
ZJ675	BAE Systems Hawk 115	*To Canada as 155207, 7 December 2000*	
ZJ676	BAE Systems Hawk 115	*To Canada as 155208, 7 December 2000*	
ZJ677	BAE Systems Hawk 115	*To Canada as 155209, 1 February 2001*	
ZJ678	BAE Systems Hawk 115	*To Canada as 155210, 14 January 2001*	
ZJ679	BAE Systems Hawk 115	*To Canada as 155211, 7 January 2001*	
ZJ680	BAE Systems Hawk 115	*To Canada as 155212, 24 January 2001*	
ZJ681	BAE Systems Hawk 115	*To Canada as 155213, 27 February 2001*	
ZJ682	BAE Systems Hawk 115	*To Canada as 155214, 25 March 2001*	
ZJ683	BAE Systems Hawk 115	*To Canada as 155215, 21 May 2001*	
ZJ684	BAE Systems Hawk 115	*To Canada as 155216, 18 June 2001*	
ZJ685	BAE Systems Hawk 115	*To Canada as 155217, 18 June 2001*	
ZJ686	BAE Systems Hawk 115	*To Canada as 155218, 27 August 2001*	
ZJ695	Eurofighter Training Rig	RAF No 1 SoTT, Cosford	
ZJ696	Eurofighter Training Rig	RAF No 1 SoTT, Cosford	
ZJ699	Eurofighter Typhoon (PT001)	DPA/BAE Systems, Warton	
ZJ700	Eurofighter Typhoon (PS002)	DPA/BAE Systems, Warton	
ZJ701	WS Super Lynx Mk 88A	WHL, Yeovil, for German Navy as 83+03	
ZJ800	Eurofighter Typhoon (BT001)	DPA/BAE Systems, for RAF	
ZJ801	Eurofighter Typhoon (BT002)	DPA/BAE Systems, for RAF	
ZJ802	Eurofighter Typhoon (BT003)	DPA/BAE Systems, for RAF	
ZJ803	Eurofighter Typhoon (BT004)	DPA/BAE Systems, for RAF	
ZJ804	Eurofighter Typhoon (BT005)	DPA/BAE Systems, for RAF	
ZJ805	Eurofighter Typhoon (BT006)	DPA/BAE Systems, for RAF	
ZJ806	Eurofighter Typhoon (BT007)	DPA/BAE Systems, for RAF	
ZJ807	Eurofighter Typhoon (BT008)	DPA/BAE Systems, for RAF	
ZJ808	Eurofighter Typhoon (BT009)	DPA/BAE Systems, for RAF	

Notes	Serial	Type (other identity) [code]	Owner/operator, location or fate
	ZJ809	Eurofighter Typhoon (BT010)	DPA/BAE Systems, for RAF
	ZJ810	Eurofighter Typhoon (BT011)	DPA/BAE Systems, for RAF
	ZJ811	Eurofighter Typhoon (BT012)	DPA/BAE Systems, for RAF
	ZJ812	Eurofighter Typhoon (BT013)	DPA/BAE Systems, for RAF
	ZJ813	Eurofighter Typhoon (BT014)	DPA/BAE Systems, for RAF
	ZJ814	Eurofighter Typhoon (BT015)	DPA/BAE Systems, for RAF
	ZJ815	Eurofighter Typhoon (BT016)	DPA/BAE Systems, for RAF
	ZJ902	WS Lynx Mk 90B	*To Danish Navy as S-170 by July 2001*
	ZJ910	Eurofighter Typhoon (BS0001)	DPA/BAE Systems, for RAF
	ZJ911	Eurofighter Typhoon (BS0002)	DPA/BAE Systems, for RAF
	ZJ912	Eurofighter Typhoon (BS0003)	DPA/BAE Systems, for RAF
	ZJ913	Eurofighter Typhoon (BS0004)	DPA/BAE Systems, for RAF
	ZJ914	Eurofighter Typhoon (BS0005)	DPA/BAE Systems, for RAF
	ZJ915	Eurofighter Typhoon (BS0006)	DPA/BAE Systems, for RAF
	ZJ916	Eurofighter Typhoon (BS0007)	DPA/BAE Systems, for RAF
	ZJ917	Eurofighter Typhoon (BS0008)	DPA/BAE Systems, for RAF
	ZJ918	Eurofighter Typhoon (BS0009)	DPA/BAE Systems, for RAF
	ZJ919	Eurofighter Typhoon (BS0010)	DPA/BAE Systems, for RAF
	ZJ920	Eurofighter Typhoon (BS0011)	DPA/BAE Systems, for RAF
	ZJ921	Eurofighter Typhoon (BS0012)	DPA/BAE Systems, for RAF
	ZJ922	Eurofighter Typhoon (BS0013)	DPA/BAE Systems, for RAF
	ZJ923	Eurofighter Typhoon (BS0014)	DPA/BAE Systems, for RAF
	ZJ924	Eurofighter Typhoon (BS0015)	DPA/BAE Systems, for RAF
	ZJ925	Eurofighter Typhoon (BS0016)	DPA/BAE Systems, for RAF
	ZJ926	Eurofighter Typhoon (BS0017)	DPA/BAE Systems, for RAF
	ZJ927	Eurofighter Typhoon (BS0018)	DPA/BAE Systems, for RAF
	ZJ928	Eurofighter Typhoon (BS0019)	DPA/BAE Systems, for RAF
	ZJ929	Eurofighter Typhoon (BS0020)	DPA/BAE Systems, for RAF
	ZJ930	Eurofighter Typhoon (BS0021)	DPA/BAE Systems, for RAF
	ZJ931	Eurofighter Typhoon (BS0022)	DPA/BAE Systems, for RAF
	ZJ932	Eurofighter Typhoon (BS0023)	DPA/BAE Systems, for RAF
	ZJ933	Eurofighter Typhoon (BS0024)	DPA/BAE Systems, for RAF
	ZJ934	Eurofighter Typhoon (BS0025)	DPA/BAE Systems, for RAF
	ZJ935	Eurofighter Typhoon (BS0026)	DPA/BAE Systems, for RAF
	ZJ936	Eurofighter Typhoon (BS0027)	DPA/BAE Systems, for RAF
	ZJ937	Eurofighter Typhoon (BS0028)	DPA/BAE Systems, for RAF
	ZJ938	Eurofighter Typhoon (BS0029)	DPA/BAE Systems, for RAF
	ZJ939	Eurofighter Typhoon (BS0030)	DPA/BAE Systems, for RAF
	ZJ940	Eurofighter Typhoon (BS0031)	DPA/BAE Systems, for RAF
	ZJ941	Eurofighter Typhoon (BS0032)	DPA/BAE Systems, for RAF
	ZJ942	Eurofighter Typhoon (BS0033)	DPA/BAE Systems, for RAF
	ZJ943	Eurofighter Typhoon (BS0034)	DPA/BAE Systems, for RAF
	ZJ944	Eurofighter Typhoon (BS0035)	DPA/BAE Systems, for RAF
	ZJ945	Eurofighter Typhoon (BS0036)	DPA/BAE Systems, for RAF
	ZJ951	BAE Systems Hawk 100	BAE Systems, Warton
	ZK531	BAe Hawk T53 (LL-5306)	BAE Systems, Warton
	ZK532	BAe Hawk T53 (LL-5315)	BAE Systems, Warton
	ZK533	BAe Hawk T53 (LL-5317)	BAE Systems, Warton
	ZK534	BAe Hawk T53 (LL-5319)	BAE Systems, Warton
	ZK535	BAe Hawk T53 (LL-5320)	BAE Systems, Warton
	ZT800	WS Super Lynx Mk 300	DPA/Westland Helicopters, Yeovil
	ZZ171	Boeing C-17A Globemaster III (00-201/N171UK)	RAF No 99 Sqn, Brize Norton
	ZZ172	Boeing C-17A Globemaster III (00-202/N172UK)	RAF No 99 Sqn, Brize Norton
	ZZ173	Boeing C-17A Globemaster III (00-203/N173UK)	RAF No 99 Sqn, Brize Norton
	ZZ174	Boeing C-17A Globemaster III (00-204/N174UK)	RAF No 99 Sqn, Brize Norton

DHFS Squirrel HT1 ZJ276 is based at RAF Shawbury. *PRM*

This replica Avro 504 D8781 is based with the ARC at Duxford. *PRM*

The Shuttleworth Collection's Sopwith Pup N6181. *PRM*

Bristol Blenhiem IV (Bolingbroke IVT) G-BPIV carries the RAF serial 'R3821' and code 'UX-N. *PRM*

Replica Hurricane I R4115 is for ground display purposes only. *Daniel March*

Hawker Nimrod replica S1581 is based at Duxford with The Fighter Collection. *PRM*

This rare Spitfire XI PL965 has gone to the USA for an indefinite period. *PRM*

This all-black Hunter T7 WV318 is painted in the colours of No 111 Squadron 'The Black Arrows'. *PRM*

Meteor NF11 WM167 is the only example of its type currently airworthy in the UK. *PRM*

This Hunting Percival Pembroke C1 WV740 still carries No 60 Squadron, RAF markings. *PRM*

Civil Registered Aircraft in UK Military Service

Serial	Type (other identity) [code]	Owner/operator, location or fate	Notes
G-BLVI	Slingsby T.67M Firefly 2	HCS/CFS, Cranwell	
G-BNSO	Slingsby T.67M Firefly 2	HCS/JEFTS, Barkston Heath	
G-BNSP	Slingsby T.67M Firefly 2	HCS/CFS, Cranwell	
G-BNSR	Slingsby T.67M Firefly 2	HCS/CFS, Cranwell	
G-BONT	Slingsby T.67M Firefly 2	HCS/CFS, Cranwell	
G-BUUA	Slingsby T.67M Firefly 2	HCS/JEFTS, Middle Wallop	
G-BUUB	Slingsby T.67M Firefly 2	HCS/JEFTS, Middle Wallop	
G-BUUC	Slingsby T.67M Firefly 2	HCS/JEFTS, Middle Wallop	
G-BUUD	Slingsby T.67M Firefly 2	HCS/JEFTS, Middle Wallop	
G-BUUE	Slingsby T.67M Firefly 2	HCS/JEFTS, Middle Wallop	
G-BUUF	Slingsby T.67M Firefly 2	HCS/JEFTS, Middle Wallop	
G-BUUG	Slingsby T.67M Firefly 2	HCS/JEFTS, Middle Wallop	
G-BUUI	Slingsby T.67M Firefly 2	HCS/JEFTS, Middle Wallop	
G-BUUJ	Slingsby T.67M Firefly 2	HCS/JEFTS, Middle Wallop	
G-BUUK	Slingsby T.67M Firefly 2	HCS/JEFTS, Middle Wallop	
G-BUUL	Slingsby T.67M Firefly 2	HCS/JEFTS, Middle Wallop	
G-BVHC	Grob G.115D-2 Heron	Shorts Bros/NFGF, Plymouth	
G-BVHD	Grob G.115D-2 Heron	Shorts Bros/NFGF, Plymouth	
G-BVHE	Grob G.115D-2 Heron	Shorts Bros/NFGF, Plymouth	
G-BVHF	Grob G.115D-2 Heron	Shorts Bros/NFGF, Plymouth	
G-BVHG	Grob G.115D-2 Heron	Shorts Bros/NFGF, Plymouth	
G-BWXA	Slingsby T.67M Firefly 260	HCS/JEFTS, Barkston Heath	
G-BWXB	Slingsby T.67M Firefly 260	HCS/JEFTS, Barkston Heath	
G-BWXC	Slingsby T.67M Firefly 260	HCS/JEFTS, Barkston Heath	
G-BWXD	Slingsby T.67M Firefly 260	HCS/JEFTS, Barkston Heath	
G-BWXE	Slingsby T.67M Firefly 260	HCS/JEFTS, Barkston Heath	
G-BWXF	Slingsby T.67M Firefly 260	HCS/JEFTS, Barkston Heath	
G-BWXG	Slingsby T.67M Firefly 260	HCS/JEFTS, Church Fenton	
G-BWXH	Slingsby T.67M Firefly 260	HCS/JEFTS, Barkston Heath	
G-BWXI	Slingsby T.67M Firefly 260	HCS/JEFTS, Barkston Heath	
G-BWXJ	Slingsby T.67M Firefly 260	HCS/JEFTS, Barkston Heath	
G-BWXK	Slingsby T.67M Firefly 260	HCS/JEFTS, Barkston Heath	
G-BWXL	Slingsby T.67M Firefly 260	HCS/JEFTS, Barkston Heath	
G-BWXM	Slingsby T.67M Firefly 260	HCS/JEFTS, Barkston Heath	
G-BWXN	Slingsby T.67M Firefly 260	HCS/JEFTS, Barkston Heath	
G-BWXO	Slingsby T.67M Firefly 260	HCS/JEFTS, Barkston Heath	
G-BWXP	Slingsby T.67M Firefly 260	HCS/JEFTS, Barkston Heath	
G-BWXR	Slingsby T.67M Firefly 260	HCS/JEFTS, Barkston Heath	
G-BWXS	Slingsby T.67M Firefly 260 [6]	HCS/JEFTS, Barkston Heath	
G-BWXT	Slingsby T.67M Firefly 260	HCS/JEFTS, Barkston Heath	
G-BWXU	Slingsby T.67M Firefly 260	HCS/JEFTS, Barkston Heath	
G-BWXV	Slingsby T.67M Firefly 260	HCS/JEFTS, Barkston Heath	
G-BWXW	Slingsby T.67M Firefly 260	HCS/JEFTS, Barkston Heath	
G-BWXX	Slingsby T.67M Firefly 260	HCS/JEFTS, Barkston Heath	
G-BWXY	Slingsby T.67M Firefly 260	HCS/JEFTS, Barkston Heath	
G-BWXZ	Slingsby T.67M Firefly 260	HCS/JEFTS, Barkston Heath	
G-BYOA	Slingsby T.67M Firefly 260	HCS/JEFTS, Barkston Heath	
G-BYOB	Slingsby T.67M Firefly 260	HCS/JEFTS, Barkston Heath	
G-BYUA	Grob G.115E Tutor	Bombardier/Cambridge UAS, Wyton	
G-BYUB	Grob G.115E Tutor	Bombardier/University of Wales AS, St Athan	
G-BYUC	Grob G.115E Tutor	Bombardier/CFS/East Midlands Universities AS, Cranwell	
G-BYUD	Grob G.115E Tutor	Bombardier/Northumbrian Universities AS, Leeming	
G-BYUE	Grob G.115E Tutor	Bombardier/CFS/East Midlands Universities AS, Cranwell	
G-BYUF	Grob G.115E Tutor	Bombardier/Cambridge UAS/University of London AS, Wyton	
G-BYUG	Grob G.115E Tutor	Bombardier/Universities of Glasgow & Strathclyde AS, Glasgow	
G-BYUH	Grob G.115E Tutor	Bombardier/Bristol UAS, Colerne	
G-BYUI	Grob G.115E Tutor	Bombardier/Liverpool UAS/Manchester and Salford Universities AS, Woodvale	
G-BYUJ	Grob G.115E Tutor	Bombardier/Northumbrian Universities AS, Leeming	
G-BYUK	Grob G.115E Tutor	Bombardier/Cambridge UAS, Wyton	

Civil Registered Aircraft in UK Military Service

Notes	Serial	Type (other identity) [code]	Owner/operator, location or fate
	G-BYUL	Grob G.115E Tutor	Bombardier/University of London AS, Wyton
	G-BYUM	Grob G.115E Tutor	Bombardier/Southampton UAS, Boscombe Down
	G-BYUN	Grob G.115E Tutor	Bombardier/Cambridge UAS/University of London AS, Wyton
	G-BYUO	Grob G.115E Tutor	Bombardier/University of London AS, Wyton
	G-BYUP	Grob G.115E Tutor	Bombardier/East Lowlands UAS/Aberdeen, Dundee & St Andrews UAS, Leuchars
	G-BYUR	Grob G.115E Tutor	Bombardier/East Lowlands UAS/Aberdeen, Dundee & St Andrews UAS, Leuchars
	G-BYUS	Grob G.115E Tutor	Bombardier/Oxford UAS, Benson
	G-BYUT	Grob G.115E Tutor	Bombardier/Oxford UAS, Benson
	G-BYUU	Grob G.115E Tutor	Bombardier/Universities of Glasgow & Strathclyde AS, Glasgow
	G-BYUV	Grob G.115E Tutor	Bombardier/Oxford UAS, Benson
	G-BYUW	Grob G.115E Tutor	Bombardier/East Lowlands UAS/Aberdeen, Dundee & St Andrews UAS, Leuchars
	G-BYUX	Grob G.115E Tutor	Bombardier/Liverpool UAS/Manchester and Salford Universities AS, Woodvale
	G-BYUY	Grob G.115E Tutor	Bombardier/East Lowlands UAS/Aberdeen, Dundee & St Andrews UAS, Leuchars
	G-BYUZ	Grob G.115E Tutor	Bombardier/Liverpool UAS/Manchester and Salford Universities AS, Woodvale
	G-BYVA	Grob G.115E Tutor	Bombardier/CFS/East Midlands Universities AS, Cranwell
	G-BYVB	Grob G.115E Tutor	Bombardier/Universities of Glasgow & Strathclyde AS, Glasgow
	G-BYVC	Grob G.115E Tutor	Bombardier/Bristol UAS, Colerne
	G-BYVD	Grob G.115E Tutor	Bombardier/Cambridge UAS/University of London AS, Wyton
	G-BYVE	Grob G.115E Tutor	Bombardier/Southampton UAS, QinetiQ Boscombe Down
	G-BYVF	Grob G.115E Tutor	Bombardier/Universities of Glasgow & Strathclyde AS, Glasgow
	G-BYVG	Grob G.115E Tutor	Bombardier/Yorkshire Universities AS, Church Fenton
	G-BYVH	Grob G.115E Tutor	Bombardier/East Lowlands UAS/Aberdeen, Dundee & St Andrews UAS, Leuchars
	G-BYVI	Grob G.115E Tutor	Bombardier/Universities of Glasgow & Strathclyde AS, Glasgow
	G-BYVJ	Grob G.115E Tutor	Bombardier/Northumbrian Universities AS, Leeming
	G-BYVK	Grob G.115E Tutor	Bombardier/East Lowlands UAS/Aberdeen, Dundee & St Andrews UAS, Leuchars
	G-BYVL	Grob G.115E Tutor	Bombardier/University of Wales AS, St Athan
	G-BYVM	Grob G.115E Tutor	Bombardier/East Lowlands UAS/Aberdeen, Dundee & St Andrews UAS, Leuchars
	G-BYVN	Grob G.115E Tutor	Bombardier/Bristol UAS, Colerne
	G-BYVO	Grob G.115E Tutor	Bombardier/University of Birmingham AS, Cosford
	G-BYVP	Grob G.115E Tutor	Bombardier/Oxford UAS, Benson
	G-BYVR	Grob G.115E Tutor	Bombardier/CFS/East Midlands Universities AS, Cranwell
	G-BYVS	Grob G.115E Tutor	Bombardier/Cambridge UAS/University of London AS, Wyton
	G-BYVT	Grob G.115E Tutor	Bombardier/Cambridge UAS/University of London AS, Wyton
	G-BYVU	Grob G.115E Tutor	Bombardier/Oxford UAS, Benson
	G-BYVV	Grob G.115E Tutor	Bombardier/Yorkshire Universities AS, Church Fenton
	G-BYVW	Grob G.115E Tutor	Bombardier/Yorkshire Universities AS, Church Fenton
	G-BYVX	Grob G.115E Tutor	Bombardier/Yorkshire Universities AS, Church Fenton
	G-BYVY	Grob G.115E Tutor	Bombardier/Yorkshire Universities AS, Church Fenton
	G-BYVZ	Grob G.115E Tutor	Bombardier/Yorkshire Universities AS, Church Fenton
	G-BYWA	Grob G.115E Tutor	Bombardier/University of Wales AS, St Athan
	G-BYWB	Grob G.115E Tutor	Bombardier/Bristol UAS, Colerne
	G-BYWC	Grob G.115E Tutor	Bombardier/Bristol UAS, Colerne

Serial	Type (other identity) [code]	Owner/operator, location or fate	Notes
G-BYWD	Grob G.115E Tutor	Bombardier/Liverpool UAS/Manchester and Salford Universities AS, Woodvale	
G-BYWE	Grob G.115E Tutor	Bombardier/Bristol UAS, Colerne	
G-BYWF	Grob G.115E Tutor	Bombardier/CFS/East Midlands Universities AS, Cranwell	
G-BYWG	Grob G.115E Tutor	Bombardier/Bristol UAS, Colerne	
G-BYWH	Grob G.115E Tutor	Bombardier/Northumbrian Universities AS, Leeming	
G-BYWI	Grob G.115E Tutor	Bombardier/Bristol UAS, Colerne	
G-BYWJ	Grob G.115E Tutor	Bombardier/Liverpool UAS/Manchester and Salford Universities AS, Woodvale	
G-BYWK	Grob G.115E Tutor	Grob/Bombardier for RAF	
G-BYWL	Grob G.115E Tutor	Bombardier/Liverpool UAS/Manchester and Salford Universities AS, Woodvale	
G-BYWM	Grob G.115E Tutor	Bombardier/CFS/East Midlands Universities AS, Cranwell	
G-BYWN	Grob G.115E Tutor	Bombardier/Liverpool UAS/Manchester and Salford Universities AS, Woodvale	
G-BYWO	Grob G.115E Tutor	Bombardier/University of Birmingham AS, Cosford	
G-BYWP	Grob G.115E Tutor	Bombardier/Yorkshire Universities AS, Church Fenton	
G-BYWR	Grob G.115E Tutor	Bombardier/Cambridge UAS/University of London AS, Wyton	
G-BYWS	Grob G.115E Tutor	Bombardier/Northumbrian Universities AS, Leeming	
G-BYWT	Grob G.115E Tutor	Bombardier/Northumbrian Universities AS, Leeming	
G-BYWU	Grob G.115E Tutor	Bombardier/Cambridge UAS/University of London AS, Wyton	
G-BYWV	Grob G.115E Tutor	Bombardier/University of Birmingham AS, Cosford	
G-BYWW	Grob G.115E Tutor	Bombardier/CFS/East Midlands Universities AS, Cranwell	
G-BYWX	Grob G.115E Tutor	Bombardier/Cambridge UAS/University of London AS, Wyton	
G-BYWY	Grob G.115E Tutor	Bombardier/CFS/East Midlands Universities AS, Cranwell	
G-BYWZ	Grob G.115E Tutor	Bombardier/CFS/East Midlands Universities AS, Cranwell	
G-BYXA	Grob G.115E Tutor	Bombardier/Liverpool UAS/Manchester and Salford Universities AS, Woodvale	
G-BYXB	Grob G.115E Tutor	Bombardier/Southampton UAS, Boscombe Down	
G-BYXC	Grob G.115E Tutor	Bombardier/CFS/East Midlands Universities AS, Cranwell	
G-BYXD	Grob G.115E Tutor	Bombardier/CFS/East Midlands Universities AS, Cranwell	
G-BYXE	Grob G.115E Tutor	Bombardier/Yorkshire Universities AS, Church Fenton	
G-BYXF	Grob G.115E Tutor	Bombardier/University of Birmingham AS, Cosford	
G-BYXG	Grob G.115E Tutor	Bombardier/University of Birmingham AS, Cosford	
G-BYXH	Grob G.115E Tutor	Bombardier/Cambridge UAS/University of London AS, Wyton	
G-BYXI	Grob G.115E Tutor	Bombardier/Liverpool UAS/Manchester and Salford Universities AS, Woodvale	
G-BYXJ	Grob G.115E Tutor	Bombardier/Southampton UAS, Boscombe Down	
G-BYXK	Grob G.115E Tutor	Bombardier/University of Wales AS, St Athan	
G-BYXL	Grob G.115E Tutor	Bombardier/University of Birmingham AS, Cosford	
G-BYXM	Grob G.115E Tutor	Bombardier/Southampton UAS, Boscombe Down	
G-BYXN	Grob G.115E Tutor	Bombardier/Southampton UAS, Boscombe Down	
G-BYXO	Grob G.115E Tutor	Bombardier/University of Birmingham AS, Cosford	
G-BYXP	Grob G.115E Tutor	Bombardier/Cambridge UAS/University of London AS, Wyton	
G-BYXR	Grob G.115E Tutor	Bombardier/Oxford UAS, Benson	

Civil Registered Aircraft in UK Military Service

Notes	Serial	Type (other identity) [code]	Owner/operator, location or fate
	G-BYXS	Grob G.115E Tutor	Bombardier/Oxford UAS, Benson
	G-BYXT	Grob G.115E Tutor	Bombardier/CFS/East Universities AS, Cranwell
	G-BYXX	Grob G.115E Tutor	Bombardier/Liverpool UAS/Manchester and Salford Universities AS, Woodvale
	G-BYXY	Grob G.115E Tutor	Bombardier/Northumbrian Universities AS, Leeming
	G-BYXZ	Grob G.115E Tutor	Bombardier/CFS/East Midlands Universities AS, Cranwell
	G-BYYA	Grob G.115E Tutor	Bombardier/CFS/East Midlands Universities AS, Cranwell
	G-BYYB	Grob G.115E Tutor	Bombardier/CFS/East Midlands Universities AS, Cranwell
	G-FFRA	Dassault Falcon 20DC (N902FR)	FR Aviation, Tees-side
	G-FRAE	Dassault Falcon 20E (N910FR)	FR Aviation, Bournemouth
	G-FRAF	Dassault Falcon 20E (N911FR)	FR Aviation, Bournemouth
	G-FRAH	Dassault Falcon 20DC (N900FR)	FR Aviation, Tees-side
	G-FRAI	Dassault Falcon 20E (N901FR)	FR Aviation, Tees-side
	G-FRAJ	Dassault Falcon 20E (N903FR)	FR Aviation, Tees-side
	G-FRAK	Dassault Falcon 20DC (N905FR)	FR Aviation, Bournemouth
	G-FRAL	Dassault Falcon 20DC (N904FR)	FR Aviation, Tees-side
	G-FRAM	Dassault Falcon 20DC (N907FR)	FR Aviation, Bournemouth
	G-FRAO	Dassault Falcon 20DC (N906FR)	FR Aviation, Bournemouth
	G-FRAP	Dassault Falcon 20DC (N908FR)	FR Aviation, Bournemouth
	G-FRAR	Dassault Falcon 20DC (N909FR)	FR Aviation, Bournemouth
	G-FRAS	Dassault Falcon 20C (117501)	FR Aviation, Tees-side
	G-FRAT	Dassault Falcon 20C (117502)	FR Aviation, Tees-side
	G-FRAU	Dassault Falcon 20C (117504)	FR Aviation, Tees-side
	G-FRAW	Dassault Falcon 20ECM (117507)	FR Aviation, Tees-side
	G-FRBA	Dassault Falcon 20C	FR Aviation, Bournemouth
	G-HONG	Slingsby T.67M Firefly 2	HCS/JEFTS, Middle Wallop
	G-KONG	Slingsby T.67M Firefly 2	HCS/JEFTS, Middle Wallop
	G-XXEA	Sikorsky S-76C+	Air Hanson/The Royal Flight, Blackbushe

The stalky undercarriage identifies this Jet Provost T1. *PRM*

Hunter F6A XF515 taking off for a display. *PRM*

Specially marked No 20 (R) Squadron Harrier GR7 in 'the hover'. *PRM*

1764M/K4972	7530M/WT648	7851M/WZ706	8023M/XD463
2015M/K5600	7532M/WT651	7852M/XG506	8027M/XM555
2292M/K8203	7533M/WT680	7854M/XM191	8032M/XH837
2361M/K6035	7544M/WN904	7855M/XK416	8033M/XD382
3118M/H5199/(BK892)	7548M/PS915	7859M/XP283	8034M/XL703
3858M/X7688	7556M/WK584	7860M/XL738	8041M/XF690
4354M/BL614	7564M/XE982	7862M/XR246	8043M/XF836
4552M/T5298	7570M/XD674	7863M/*XP248*	8046M/XL770
5377M/EP120	7582M/WP190	7864M/XP244	8049M/WE168
5405M/LF738	7583M/WP185	7865M/TX226	8050M/XG329
5466M/*BN230*/(LF751)	7602M/WE600	7866M/XH278	8052M/WH166
5690M/MK356	7605M/WS692	7868M/WZ736	8054AM/XM410
5718M/BM597	7606M/WV562	7869M/WK935	8054BM/XM417
5758M/DG202	7607M/TJ138	7872M/*WZ826*/(XD826)	8055AM/XM402
6457M/ML427	7615M/WV679	7882M/XD525	8055BM/XM404
6490M/LA255	7616M/WW388	7883M/XT150	8056M/XG337
6640M/RM694	7618M/WW442	7891M/XM693	8057M/XR243
6850M/TE184	7622M/WV606	7894M/XD818	8063M/WT536
6946M/RW388	7631M/VX185	7895M/WF784	8070M/EP120
6948M/DE673	7641M/XA634	7898M/XP854	8072M/PK624
6960M/MT847	7645M/WD293	7900M/WA576	8073M/TB252
7008M/EE549	7646M/VX461	7906M/WH132	8078M/XM351
7014M/N6720	7648M/XF785	7917M/WA591	8079M/XN492
7015M/NL985	7659M/WH701	7920M/WL360	8080M/XM480
7035M/*K2567*/(DE306)	7673M/WV332	7923M/XT133	8081M/XM468
7060M/VF301	7688M/WW421	7928M/XE849	8082M/XM409
7090M/EE531	7693M/WV483	7930M/WH301	8086M/TB752
7118M/LA198	7696M/WV493	7931M/RD253	8092M/WK654
7119M/LA226	7698M/WV499	7932M/WZ744	8094M/WT520
7150M/PK683	7704M/TW536	7933M/XR220	8101M/WH984
7154M/WB188	7705M/WL505	7937M/WS843	8102M/WT486
7174M/VX272	7706M/WB584	7938M/XH903	8103M/WR985
7175M/VV106	7709M/WT933	7939M/XD596	8106M/WR982
7200M/VT812	7711M/PS915	7940M/XL764	8108M/WV703
7241M/*MK178*/(TE311)	7712M/WK281	7955M/XH767	8114M/WL798
7243M/TE462	7715M/XK724	7957M/XF545	8117M/WR974
7244M/*MK673*/(TB382)	7716M/WS776	7959M/WS774	8118M/WZ549
7246M/TD248	7718M/WA577	7960M/WS726	8119M/WR971
7256M/TB752	7719M/WK277	7961M/WS739	8121M/XM474
7257M/TB252	7729M/WB758	7964M/WS760	8128M/WH775
7279M/TB252	7734M/XD536	7965M/WS792	8131M/WT507
7281M/TB252	7737M/XD602	7967M/WS788	8140M/XJ571
7288M/PK724	7741M/VZ477	7970M/WP907	8142M/XJ560
7293M/RW393	7750M/*WK864*/(WL168)	7971M/XK699	8147M/XR526
7323M/VV217	7751M/WL131	7973M/WS807	8151M/WV795
7325M/R5868	7755M/WG760	7976M/XK418	8153M/WV903
7326M/VN485	7758M/PM651	7979M/XM529	8154M/WV908
7362M/475081/(VP546)	7759M/PK664	7980M/XM561	8155M/WV797
7416M/WN907	7761M/XH318	7982M/XH892	8156M/XE339
7421M/WT660	7762M/XE670	7983M/XD506	8158M/XE369
7422M/WT684	7764M/XH318	7984M/XN597	8159M/XD528
7428M/WK198	7770M/WT746	7986M/WG777	8160M/XD622
7432M/WZ724	7793M/XG523	7988M/XL149	8161M/XE993
7438M/*18671*/(WP905)	7796M/WJ676	7990M/XD452	8162M/WM913
7443M/WX853	7798M/XH783	7997M/XG452	8163M/XP919
7458M/WX905	7806M/TA639	7998M/*XM515*/(XD515)	8164M/*WN105*/(WF299)
7464M/XA564	7809M/XA699	8005M/WG768	8165M/WH791
7467M/WP978	7816M/WG763	8009M/XG518	8169M/WH364
7470M/XA553	7817M/TX214	8010M/XG547	8173M/XN685
7473M/XE946	7825M/WK991	8012M/VS562	8176M/WH791
7491M/WT569	7827M/XA917	8017M/XL762	8177M/*WM311*/(WM224)
7496M/WT612	7829M/XH992	8018M/XN344	8179M/XN928
7499M/WT555	7839M/WV781	8019M/WZ869	8183M/*XN972*/(XN962)
7510M/WT694	7840M/XK482	8021M/XL824	8184M/WT520
7525M/WT619	7841M/WV783	8022M/XN341	8185M/WH946

RAF Maintenance Cross-reference

8186M/WR977	8427M/XM172	8589M/XR700	8743M/WD790
8187M/WH791	8429M/XH592	8590M/XM191	8746M/XH171
8189M/*WD615* (WD646)	8434M/XM411	8591M/XA813	8749M/XH537
8190M/XJ918	8436M/XN554	8595M/XH278	8751M/XT255
8192M/XR658	8437M/WG362	8598M/WP270	8753M/WL795
8196M/XE920	8439M/WZ846	8600M/XX761	8762M/WH740
8198M/WT339	8440M/WD935	8602M/*PF179*/(XR541)	8763M/WH665
8203M/XD377	8442M/XP411	8606M/XP530	8764M/XP344
8205M/XN819	8447M/XP359	8608M/XP540	8767M/XX635
8206M/WG419	8453M/XP745	8610M/XL502	8768M/A-522
8207M/WD318	8457M/XS871	8611M/WF128	8769M/A-528
8208M/WG303	8458M/XP672	8618M/*XM693*/(XP504)	8770M/XL623
8209M/WG418	8459M/XR650	8620M/XP534	8771M/XM602
8210M/WG471	8460M/XP680	8624M/*XR991*/(XS102)	8772M/WR960
8211M/WK570	8462M/XX477	8627M/XP558	8777M/XX914
8213M/WK626	8463M/XP355	8628M/XJ380	8778M/XM598
8216M/WP927	8464M/XJ758	8630M/WG362	8779M/XM607
8218M/WB645	8465M/W1048	8631M/XR574	8780M/WK102
8229M/XM355	8466M/L-866	8633M/3W-17/MK732	8781M/WE982
8230M/XM362	8467M/WP912	8634M/WP314	8782M/XH136
8231M/XM375	8468M/MM5701/(BT474)	8638M/XS101	8783M/XW272
8234M/XN458	8470M/584219	8640M/XR977	8785M/XS642
8235M/XN549	8471M/701152	8642M/XR537	8791M/XP329
8236M/XP573	8472M/120227/(VN679)	8645M/XD163	8792M/XP345
8237M/XS179	8473M/WP190	8648M/XK526	8793M/XP346
8238M/XS180	8474M/494083	8653M/XS120	8794M/XP398
8344M/WH960	8475M/360043/(PJ876)	8655M/XN126	8796M/XK943
8350M/WH840	8476M/24	8656M/XP405	8797M/XX947
8352M/XN632	8477M/4101/(DG200)	8657M/VZ634	8799M/WV787
8355M/*KG374*/(KN645)	8478M/10639	8661M/XJ727	8800M/XG226
8357M/WK576	8479M/730301	8662M/XR458	8805M/XT772
8359M/WF825	8481M/191614	8664M/WJ603	8807M/XL587
8361M/WB670	8482M/112372/(VK893)	8666M/XE793	8810M/XJ825
8362M/WG477	8483M/420430	8668M/WJ821	8814M/XM927
8364M/WG464	8484M/5439	8671M/XJ435	8816M/XX734
8365M/XK421	8485M/997	8672M/XP351	8818M/XK527
8366M/XG454	8486M/BAPC 99	8673M/XD165	8820M/VP952
8367M/XG474	8487M/J-1172	8676M/XL577	8821M/XX115
8368M/XF926	8488M/WL627	8677M/*XF519*/(XJ695)	8822M/VP957
8369M/WE139	8491M/WJ880	8679M/XF526	8828M/XS587
8370M/N1671	8492M/WJ872	8680M/XF527	8830M/XF515
8371M/XA847	8493M/XR571	8681M/XG164	8831M/XG160
8372M/K8042	8494M/XP557	8682M/XP404	8832M/XG172
8373M/P2617	8495M/XR672	8685M/XF516	8833M/XL569
8375M/NX611	8501M/XP640	8687M/XJ639	8834M/*XL571*
8376M/RF398	8502M/XP686	8693M/WH863	8836M/XL592
8377M/R9125	8507M/XS215	8696M/WH773	8838M/*34037*/(429356)
8378M/*T9707*	8508M/XS218	8700M/ZD234	8839M/*69*/(XG194)
8379M/DG590	8509M/XT141	8702M/XG196	8840M/XG252
8380M/Z7197	8514M/XS176	8703M/VW453	8841M/XE606
8382M/VR930	8535M/XN776	8706M/XF383	8847M/XX344
8383M/K9942	8538M/XN781	8708M/XF509	8848M/XZ135
8384M/X4590	8545M/XN726	8709M/XG209	8851M/XT595
8385M/N5912	8546M/XN728	8710M/XG274	8852M/XV337
8386M/NV778	8548M/WT507	8711M/XG290	8853M/XT277
8387M/T6296	8549M/WT534	8713M/XG225	8855M/XT284
8388M/XL993	8551M/XN774	8714M/XK149	8857M/XW544
8389M/VX573	8554M/TG511	8718M/XX396	8861M/XW528
8392M/SL674	8561M/XS100	8719M/XT257	8863M/XG154
8394M/WG422	8563M/*XX822*/(XW563)	8720M/XP353	8867M/XK532
8395M/WF408	8565M/*WT720*/(E-408)	8722M/WJ640	8868M/WH775
8396M/XK740	8566M/XV279	8723M/XL567	8869M/WH967
8399M/WR539	8570M/XR954	8724M/XW923	8870M/WH964
8401M/XP686	8573M/XM708	8726M/XP299	8871M/WJ565
8406M/XP831	8575M/XP542	8727M/XR486	8873M/XR453
8407M/XP585	8576M/XP502	8728M/WT532	8874M/XE597
8408M/XS186	8578M/XR534	8729M/WJ815	8875M/XE624
8409M/XS209	8582M/XE874	8733M/XL318	8876M/*VM791*/(XA312)
8410M/XR662	8583M/BAPC 94	8736M/XF375	8877M/XP159
8413M/XM192	8585M/XE670	8738M/*XF519*/(XJ695)	8879M/XX948
8414M/XM173	8586M/XE643	8739M/XH170	8880M/XF435
8417M/XM144	8587M/XP677	8740M/WE173	8881M/XG254
8422M/XM169	8588M/XR681	8741M/XW329	8883M/XX946

8884M/VX275	8987M/XM358	9093M/WK124	9190M/XW318
8885M/XW922	8988M/XN593	9095M/XW547	9191M/XW416
8886M/XA243	8990M/XM419	9096M/WV322	9192M/XW361
8888M/XA231	8995M/XM425	9097M/XW366	9193M/XW367
8889M/XN239	8996M/XM414	9098M/XV406	9194M/XW420
8890M/WT532	8997M/XX669	9100M/XL188	9195M/XW330
8892M/XL618	8998M/XT864	9103M/XV411	9196M/XW370
8895M/XX746	9002M/XW763	9109M/XW312	9197M/*XX530*/(XX637)
8896M/XX821	9003M/XZ390	9110M/XX736	9198M/XS641
8897M/XX969	9004M/XZ370	9111M/XW421	9199M/XW290
8898M/XX119	9005M/XZ374	9113M/*XV498*	9200M/XW425
8899M/XX756	9006M/XX967	9115M/XV863	9201M/ZD667
8900M/XZ368	9007M/XX968	9117M/XV161	9203M/*3066*
8901M/XZ383	9008M/XX140	9118M/XV253	9205M/*E449*
8902M/XX739	9009M/XX763	9119M/XW303	9206M/F6314
8903M/XX747	9010M/XX764	9120M/XW419	9207M/8417/18
8904M/XX966	9011M/XM412	9122M/XZ997	9208M/F938
8905M/XX975	9012M/XN494	9123M/XT773	9210M/MF628
8906M/XX976	9014M/XN584	9124M/XW427	9211M/733682
8907M/XZ371	9015M/XW320	9125M/XW410	9212M/*KL216*/(45-49295)
8908M/XZ382	9017M/ZE449	9126M/XW413	9213M/N5182
8909M/XV784	9018M/XW365	9127M/XW432	9215M/XL164
8910M/XL160	9019M/XX824	9128M/XW292	9216M/XL190
8911M/XH673	9020M/XX825	9129M/XW394	9217M/ZH257
8917M/XM372	9021M/XX826	9130M/XW327	9218M/XL563
8918M/XX109	9022M/XX958	9131M/*DD931*	9219M/XZ971
8920M/XT469	9026M/XP629	9132M/XX977	9220M/XZ995
8921M/XT466	9027M/XP556	9133M/*413573*	9221M/XZ966
8922M/XT467	9028M/XP563	9134M/XT288	9222M/XZ968
8923M/XX819	9029M/XS217	9136M/XT891	9224M/XL568
8924M/XP701	9031M/XP688	9137M/XN579	9225M/XX885
8925M/XP706	9032M/XR673	9139M/XV863	9226M/XV865
8931M/XV779	9033M/XS181	9140M/XZ287	9227M/XB812
8932M/XR718	9034M/XP638	9141M/XV118	9228M/ZD991
8934M/XR749	9036M/XM350	9143M/XN589	9229M/ZA678
8935M/XR713	9038M/XV810	9144M/XV353	9230M/ZA676
8937M/XX751	9039M/XN586	9145M/XV863	9234M/XV864
8938M/WV746	9040M/XZ138	9146M/XW299	9237M/XF445
8941M/XT456	9041M/XW763	9147M/XW301	9238M/ZA717
8942M/XN185	9042M/XL954	9148M/XW436	9239M/7198/18
8943M/XE799	9044M/XS177	9149M/XW375	9243M/XX163
8944M/WZ791	9045M/XN636	9150M/*FX760*	9246M/XS714
8945M/XX818	9046M/XM349	9151M/XT907	9247M/XV420
8946M/XZ389	9047M/XW409	9152M/XV424	9248M/WB627
8947M/XX726	9048M/XM403	9153M/XW360	9249M/WV396
8948M/XX757	9049M/XW404	9154M/XW321	9250M/162068
8949M/XX743	9050M/XG577	9155M/WL679	9253M/ZA254
8950M/XX956	9052M/WJ717	9162M/XZ991	9255M/XZ375
8951M/XX727	9055M/XT770	9163M/XV415	9256M/XX839
8952M/XX730	9056M/XS488	9165M/XV408	9259M/XS710
8953M/XX959	9059M/ZE360	9166M/XW323	9260M/XS734
8954M/XZ384	9060M/ZE356	9167M/XV744	9272M/XS486
8955M/XX110	9061M/XW335	9168M/XZ132	9273M/XS726
8956M/XN577	9062M/XW351	9169M/XW547	9274M/XS738
8957M/XN582	9066M/XV582	9170M/XZ994	9275M/XS729
8958M/XN501	9067M/XV586	9172M/XW304	9276M/XS733
8961M/XS925	9070M/XV581	9173M/XW418	9277M/XT601
8967M/XV263	9072M/XW768	9174M/XZ131	9278M/XS643
8969M/XR753	9073M/XW924	9175M/P1344	9279M/XT681
8972M/XR754	9075M/XV753	9176M/XW430	9280M/XV804
8973M/XS922	9076M/XV808	9177M/XW328	9281M/XZ146
8974M/XM473	9078M/XV752	9179M/XW309	9282M/XZ101
8975M/XW917	9079M/XZ130	9180M/XW311	9283M/XZ322
8976M/XZ630	9080M/ZE350	9181M/XW358	9284M/ZA267
8978M/XX837	9086M/ZE352	9183M/*XF519*/(XJ695)	9290M/XX626
8983M/XM478	9087M/XX753	9185M/XZ987	9291M/XX686
8984M/XN551	9090M/XW353	9187M/XW405	9298M/*ZE758*/(ZE340)
8985M/WK127	9091M/XW434	9188M/XW364	9300M/XX431
8986M/XV261	9092M/XH669	9189M/ZD350	9302M/ZD462

DH Sea Vixen XP924 is operated from Bournemouth. *PRM*

RN Landing Platform and Shore Station Code-letters

Code	Deck Letters	Vessel Name & Pennant No	Vessel Type & Unit
—	AS	RFA *Argus* (A135)	Aviation Training ship
365/6	AY	HMS *Argyll* (F231)	Type 23 (815 Sqn)
—	BD	RFA *Sir Bedivere* (L3004)	Landing ship
—	BV	RFA *Black Rover* (A273)	Fleet tanker
335	CF	HMS *Cardiff* (D108)	Type 42 (815 Sqn)
350/1	CL	HMS *Cumberland* (F85)	Type 22 (815 Sqn)
-	CM	HMS *Chatham* (F87)	Type 22
508	CT	HMS *Campbeltown* (F86)	Type 22 (771 Sqn)
—	CU	RNAS Culdrose (HMS *Seahawk*)	
412/3	CW	HMS *Cornwall* (F99)	Type 22 (815 Sqn)
—	DC	HMS *Dumbarton Castle* (P265)	Fishery protection
—	DG	RFA *Diligence* (A132)	Maintenance
411	EB	HMS *Edinburgh* (D97)	Type 42 (815 Sqn)
434/5	EE	HMS *Endurance* (A171)	Ice Patrol (815 Sqn)
420	EX	HMS *Exeter* (D89)	Type 42 (815 Sqn)
—	FA	RFA *Fort Austin* (A386)	Support ship
—	FG	RFA *Fort Rosalie* (A385)	Support ship
—	FL	RNAY Fleetlands	
—	FS	HMS *Fearless* (L10)	Assault
410	GC	HMS *Gloucester* (D96)	Type 42 (815 Sqn)
—	GD	RFA *Sir Galahad* (L3005)	Landing ship
—	GR	RFA *Sir Geraint* (L3027)	Landing ship
437	GT	HMS *Grafton* (F80)	Type 23 (815 Sqn)
—	GV	RFA *Gold Rover* (A271)	Fleet tanker
344	GW	HMS *Glasgow* (D88)	Type 42 (815 Sqn)
—	GY	RFA *Grey Rover* (A269)	Fleet tanker
404	IR	HMS *Iron Duke* (F234)	Type 23 (815 Sqn)
425	KT	HMS *Kent* (F78)	Type 23 (815 Sqn)
—	L	HMS *Illustrious* (R06)	Carrier
457	LA	HMS *Lancaster* (F229)	Type 23 (815 Sqn)
—	LC	HMS *Leeds Castle* (P258)	Fishery protection
332	LP	HMS *Liverpool* (D92)	Type 42 (815 Sqn)
363/4	MA	HMS *Marlborough* (F233)	Type 23 (815 Sqn)
360	MC	HMS *Manchester* (D95)	Type 42 (815 Sqn)
415	MM	HMS *Monmouth* (F235)	Type 23 (815 Sqn)
444	MR	HMS *Montrose* (F236)	Type 23 (815 Sqn)
—	N	HMS *Invincible* (R05)	Carrier
345	NC	HMS *Newcastle* (D87)	Type 42 (815 Sqn)
361/2	NF	HMS *Norfolk* (F230)	Type 23 (815 Sqn)
372	NL	HMS *Northumberland* (F238)	Type 23 (815 Sqn)
417	NM	HMS *Nottingham* (D91)	Type 42 (815 Sqn)
—	O	HMS *Ocean* (L12)	Helicopter carrier
—	PV	RFA *Sir Percivale* (L3036)	Landing ship
—	R	HMS *Ark Royal* (R07)	Carrier
474	RM	HMS *Richmond* (F239)	Type 23 (815 Sqn)
352/3	SD	HMS *Sheffield* (F96)	Type 22 (815 Sqn)
355	SM	HMS *Somerset* (F82)	Type 23 (815 Sqn)
334	SN	HMS *Southampton* (D90)	Type 42 (815 Sqn)
422	SU	HMS *Sutherland* (F81)	Type 23 (815 Sqn)
—	TM	RFA *Sir Tristram* (L3055)	Landing ship
—	VL	RNAS Yeovilton (HMS *Heron*)	
462	WM	HMS *Westminster* (F237)	Type 23 (815 Sqn)
407	YK	HMS *York* (D98)	Type 42 (815 Sqn)
—	—	HMS *Albion* (L14)	Assault
—	—	HMS *Bulwark* (L15)	Assault
—	—	RFA *Fort Victoria* (A387)	Auxiliary Oiler
—	—	RFA *Fort George* (A388)	Auxiliary Oiler
—	—	HMS *St Albans* (F83)	Type 23
—	—	RFA *Wave Knight* (A389)	Fleet-tanker
—	—	RFA *Wave Ruler* (A390)	Fleet tanker

BAe Jetstream T3 ZE440 taking off from its home base at RNAS Yeovilton. *Daniel March*

Ships' Numeric Code – Deck Letters Analysis

	0	1	2	3	4	5	6	7	8	9
33			LP		**SN**	CF	CV	CV		
34					GW	NC				
35	CL	CL	SD	SD		SM				
36	MC	NF	NF	MA	MA	AY	AY			
37		NL								
40					IR			YK		
41	GC	EB	CW	CW		MM		NM		
42	EX		SU			KT	PD			
43					EE	EE		GT		
44					MR					
45								LA		
46			WM							
47					RM					

RN Code – Squadron – Base – Aircraft Cross-check

Deck/Base Code Numbers	Letters	Unit	Location	Aircraft Type(s)
000 — 006	L	801 Sqn	Yeovilton	Sea Harrier FA2
010 — 020	L	820 Sqn	Culdrose	Sea King HAS6
122 — 129	R	800 Sqn	Yeovilton	Sea Harrier FA2
180 — 182	CU	849 Sqn HQ Flt	Culdrose	Sea King AEW2
183 — 185	L	849 Sqn B Flt	Culdrose	Sea King AEW2
186 — 188	R	849 Sqn A Flt	Culdrose	Sea King AEW2
264 — 274	R	814 Sqn	Culdrose	Merlin HM1
300 — 308	PO	815 Sqn	Yeovilton	Lynx HAS3/HMA8
318 — 319	PO	815 Sqn OEU	Yeovilton	Lynx HMA8
332 — 479	*	815 Sqn	Yeovilton	Lynx HAS3/HMA8
535 — 541	CU	700M OEU	Culdrose	Merlin HM1
560 — 573	CU	750 Sqn	Culdrose	Jetstream T2
576 — 579	-	FONA	Yeovilton	Jetstream T3
580 — 585	CU	824 Sqn	Culdrose	Merlin HM1
630 — 648	PO	702 Sqn	Yeovilton	Lynx HAS3
670 — 676	PO	702 Sqn	Yeovilton	Lynx HMA8
700 — 707	PW	771 Sqn	Prestwick	Sea King HAS6
710 — 719	VL	899 Sqn	Yeovilton	Sea Harrier FA2
720 — 724	VL	899 Sqn	Yeovilton	Harrier T8
730 — 731	VL	899 Sqn	Yeovilton	Sea Harrier FA2
820 — 827	CU	771 Sqn	Culdrose	Sea King HU5

*See foregoing separate ships' Deck Letter Analysis.
Note that only the 'last two' digits of the Code are worn by some aircraft types, especially helicopters.

Royal Air Force Squadron Markings

This table gives brief details of the markings worn by aircraft of RAF squadrons. While this may help to identify the operator of a particular machine, it may not always give the true picture. For example, from time to time aircraft are loaned to other units while others (such as those with No 4 FTS at Valley) wear squadron marks but are actually operated on a pool basis. Squadron badges are usually located on the front fuselage.

Squadron	Type(s) operated	Base(s)	Distinguishing marks & other comments
No 1 Sqn	Harrier GR7/T10	RAF Cottesmore	Badge: A red & white winged number 1 on a white diamond. Tail fin has a red stripe with the badge repeated on it.
No 2 Sqn	Tornado GR1/GR1A/GR4A	RAF Marham	Badge: A wake knot on a white circular background flanked on either side by black and white triangles. Tail fin has a black stripe with white triangles and the badge repeated on it. Codes are single letters inside a white triangle on the tail.
No 3 Sqn	Harrier GR7/T10	RAF Cottesmore	Badge: A blue cockatrice on a white circular background flanked by two green bars edged with yellow. Tail fin has a green stripe edged with yellow.
No 4 Sqn	Harrier GR7/T10	RAF Cottesmore	Badge: A yellow lightning flash inside a red and black circle flanked by bars on either side repeating this design. Tail fin has a yellow lightning flash on a red and black stripe.
No 5 Sqn	Tornado F3	RAF Coningsby	Tail fin has a red stripe with a green maple leaf in the middle.
No 6 Sqn	Jaguar GR1A/GR3/T2A	RAF Coltishall	Badge: A red winged can opener inside a circle edged in red. Tail has a light blue bar with red diagonal lines. Aircraft are coded E*.
No 7 Sqn	Chinook HC2/ Gazelle HT3	RAF Odiham	Badge (on tail): A blue badge containing the seven stars of Ursa Major ('The Plough') in yellow. Aircraft are coded E*. Aircraft pooled with No 18 Sqn and No 27 Sqn.
No 8 Sqn	Sentry AEW1	RAF Waddington	Badge (on tail): A grey, sheathed, Arabian dagger. Aircraft pooled with No 23 Sqn.
No 9 Sqn	Tornado GR4	RAF Marham	Badge: A green bat on a black circular background, flanked by yellow and green horizontal stripes. The green bat also appears on the tail, edged in yellow. Aircraft are coded A*.
No 10 Sqn	VC10 C1K	RAF Brize Norton	Badge (on tail): A yellow arrow with red wings.
No 11 Sqn	Tornado F3	RAF Leeming	Roundel is superimposed over a yellow diamond on a black background. Badge (on tail): Two black eagles in flight. Aircraft are coded D*.
No 12 Sqn	Tornado GR1/GR4	RAF Lossiemouth	Roundel is superimposed on a green chevron. Tail fin has a black & white horizontal stripe with the squadron badge, a fox's head on a white circle, in the middle. Aircraft are coded F*.

Squadron	Type(s) operated	Base(s)	Distinguishing marks & other comments
No 13 Sqn	Tornado GR4/GR4A	RAF Marham	A yellow lightning flash on a green and blue background on the nose. Badge (on tail): A lynx's head over a dagger on a white shield.
No 14 Sqn	Tornado GR1/GR4	RAF Lossiemouth	Badge: A red cross on a white circle, with wings either side, flanked by blue diamonds on a white background. The blue diamonds are repeated horizontally across the tail. Aircraft are coded B*.
No 15(R) Sqn	Tornado GR1/GR1B/GR4	RAF Lossiemouth	Roman numerals XV appear in white on the tail. Aircraft are either coded T*, TA*, or TT*.
No 16(R) Sqn	Jaguar GR3/T2A/T4	RAF Coltishall	Badge: Two keys crossed on a black circle. On the tail is a black circle containing the 'Saint' emblem from the 60's TV series.
No 18 Sqn	Chinook HC2	RAF Odiham	Badge (on tail): A red winged horse on a black circle. Aircraft are coded B*. Aircraft pooled with No 7 Sqn and No 27 Sqn.
No 19(R) Sqn	Hawk T1/T1A/T1W	RAF Valley	Badge (on tail): A fish flanked by two wings on a yellow circle. Aircraft also carry black and white checks either side of the roundel on the fuselage. Aircraft pooled with No 208(R) Sqn; part of No 4 FTS.
No 20(R) Sqn [HOCU]	Harrier GR7/T10	RAF Wittering	Badge: An eagle in a white circle flanked by a white stripe on a blue background. On the tail is a stripe made up of black, yellow, green and red triangles.
No 22 Sqn	Sea King HAR3/HAR3A	A Flt: RMB Chivenor B Flt: Wattisham C Flt: RAF Valley	Badge: A black in front of a white Maltese cross on a red circle.
No 23 Sqn	Sentry AEW1	RAF Waddington	Badge (on tail): A red eagle preying on a yellow falcon. Aircraft pooled with No 8 Sqn.
No 24 Sqn	Hercules C1/C3/C4/C5	RAF Lyneham	No squadron markings carried. Aircraft pooled with No 30 Sqn, No 47 Sqn, No 57(R) Sqn and No 70 Sqn.
No 25 Sqn	Tornado F3	RAF Leeming	Badge (on tail): A hawk on a gauntlet.
No 27 Sqn	Chinook HC2	RAF Odiham	Badge (on tail): An dark green elephant on a green circle, flanked by green and dark green stripes. Aircraft pooled with No 7 Sqn and No 18 Sqn.
No 28 Sqn	Merlin HC3	RAF Benson	Badge: A winged horse above white two crosses on a red shield.
No 30 Sqn	Hercules C1/C3	RAF Lyneham	No squadron markings carried. Aircraft pooled with No 24 Sqn, No 47 Sqn, No 57(R) Sqn and No 70 Sqn.
No 31 Sqn	Tornado GR4	RAF Marham	Badge: A gold, five-pointed star on a yellow circle flanked by yellow and green checks. The star is repeated on the tail. Aircraft are coded D*.

RAF Squadron Markings

Squadron	Type(s) operated	Base(s)	Distinguishing marks & other comments
No 32 (The Royal) Sqn	125 CC3/146 CC2/ Twin Squirrel HCC1	RAF Northolt	No squadron markings carried but aircraft carry a distinctive livery with a blue flash along the middle of the fuselage and a red tail.
No 33 Sqn	Puma HC1	RAF Benson	Badge: A stag's head.
No 39 (1 PRU) Sqn	Canberra PR9/T4	RAF Marham	Badge (on tail): A winged bomb on a light blue circle. Aircraft are coded A*.
No 41 Sqn	Jaguar GR3/T4	RAF Coltishall	Badge: A red, double armed cross, flanked by red and white horizontal stipes. Stripes repeated on tail. Aircraft are coded F*.
No 42(R) Sqn	Nimrod MR2	RAF Kinloss	No squadron markings usually carried. Aircraft pooled with No 120 Sqn, No 201 Sqn and No 206 Sqn.
No 43 Sqn	Tornado F3	RAF Leuchars	Badge (on tail): A black and red gamecock..
No 45(R) Sqn	Jetstream T1	RAF Cranwell	No squadron markings usually carried. Part of No 3 FTS.
No 47 Sqn	Hercules C1/C3	RAF Lyneham	No squadron markings usually carried. Aircraft pooled with No 24 Sqn, 30 Sqn, No 57(R) Sqn and No 70 Sqn.
No 51 Sqn	Nimrod R1	RAF Waddington	Badge (on tail): A red goose in flight.
No 54 Sqn	Jaguar GR3/GR3A/T2/T4	RAF Coltishall	Badge: A blue lion on a yellow shield, flanked by blue and yellow checks. A stripe of blue and yellow checks also appears on the tail. Aircraft are coded G*.
No 55(R) Sqn	Dominie T1	RAF Cranwell	Badge (on tail): A blue fist holding an arrow on a white circle.
No 56(R) Sqn [F3OCU]	Tornado F3	RAF Coningsby	Badge (on tail): A gold phoenix rising from red flames. The tail fin has a stripe made up of red and white checks.
No 57(R) Sqn	Hercules C1/C3/C4/C5	RAF Lyneham	No squadron markings usually carried. Aircraft pooled with No 24 Sqn, No 30 Sqn, No 47 Sqn and No 70 Sqn.
No 60(R) Sqn	Griffin HT1	RAF Shawbury [DHFS] & RAF Valley [SARTU]	No squadron markings usually carried.
No 70 Sqn	Hercules C1/C3/C4/C5	RAF Lyneham	No squadron markings usually carried. Aircraft pooled with No 24 Sqn, No 30 Sqn, No 47 Sqn and No 57(R) Sqn.
No 72 Sqn	Wessex HC2/Puma HC1	RAF Aldergrove	Badge: A blue swift in flight on a red circle, flanked by red bars. The badge appears on the tail of the Wessex and by the cockpit on the Puma. Aircraft are sometimes coded A*.
No 78 Sqn	Chinook HC2/ Sea King HAR3	RAF Mount Pleasant	Badge: A yellow, heraldic tiger with two tails, on a black circle. The badge appears on the tail of the Chinook and by the cockpit on the Sea King.
No 84 Sqn	Wessex HC2	RAF Akrotiri	Badge (on tail): A scorpion on a playing card symbol (diamonds, clubs etc.). Aircraft carry a vertical blue stripe through the roundel on the fuselage.

Squadron	Type(s) operated	Base(s)	Distinguishing marks & other comments
No 99 Sqn	Globemaster III	RAF Brize Norton	Badge (on tail): A black puma leaping.
No 100 Sqn	Hawk T1/T1A	RAF Leeming	Badge (on tail): A skull in front of two bones crossed. Aircraft are usually coded C*.
No 101 Sqn	VC10 K3/K4	RAF Brize Norton	Badge (on tail): A lion behind a castle turret.
No 111 Sqn	Tornado F3	RAF Leuchars	Badge (on tail): A cross in front of crossed swords on a light grey circle, flanked by a stripe of darker grey.
No 120 Sqn	Nimrod MR2	RAF Kinloss	No squadron markings usually carried. Aircraft pooled with No 42(R) Sqn, No 201 Sqn and No 206 Sqn.
No 201 Sqn	Nimrod MR2	RAF Kinloss	No squadron markings usually carried. Aircraft pooled with No 42(R) Sqn, No 120 Sqn and No 206 Sqn.
No 202 Sqn	Sea King HAR3	A Flt: RAF Boulmer D Flt: RAF Lossiemouth E Flt: RAF Leconfield	Badge: A mallard alighting on a white circle.
No 203(R) Sqn	Sea King HAR3	RAF St Mawgan	Badge: A green sea horse on a white circle.
No 206 Sqn	Nimrod MR2	RAF Kinloss	No squadron markings usually carried. Aircraft pooled with No 42(R) Sqn, No 120 Sqn and No 201 Sqn.
No 208(R) Sqn	Hawk T1/T1A/T1W	RAF Valley	Badge (on tail): A Sphinx inside a white circle, flanked by flashes of yellow. Aircraft also carry blue and yellow bars either side of the roundel on the fuselage and a blue and yellow chevron on the nose. Aircraft pooled with No 19(R) Sqn; part of No 4 FTS.
No 216 Sqn	TriStar K1/KC1/C2/C2A	RAF Brize Norton	Badge (on tail): An eagle in flight with a bomb in its claws.
No 230 Sqn	Puma HC1	RAF Aldergrove	Badge: A tiger in front of a palm tree on a black pentagon.
No 617 Sqn	Tornado GR1/GR4	RAF Lossiemouth	Badge: Dam breached, flanked on either side by red lightning flashes on a black background. Tail fin is black with a red lightning flash. Aircraft are coded AJ-*.
No 1435 Flt	Tornado F3	RAF Mount Pleasant	Badge (on tail): A red Maltese cross on a white circle, flanked by red and white horizontal bars.

University Air Squadrons/ Air Experience Flights

Now that the conversion to the Tutor has taken place, UAS aircraft have begun to carry squadron badges and markings, usually on the tail. Squadron crests all consist of a white circle surrounded by a blue circle, topped with a red crown and having a yellow scroll beneath. Each differs by the motto on the scroll, the UAS name running around the blue circle and by the contents at the centre and it is the latter which are described below. From April 1996 all AEFs have come under the administration of local UASs and these are listed here.

UAS	Base(s)	Marks
Aberdeen, Dundee & St Andrews UAS	RAF Leuchars	A red lion holding a stone turret between its paws above a crown.
University of Birmingham AS/No 8 AEF	RAF Cosford	A blue griffon with two heads.
Bristol UAS/No 3 AEF	RAF Colerne	A sailing ship on water.
Cambridge UAS/No 5 AEF	RAF Wyton	A heraldic lion in front of a red badge.
East Lowlands UASs/No 12 AEF	RAF Leuchars	An open book in front of a white diagonal cross, edged in blue.
East Midlands Universities AS/ No 7 AEF	RAF Cranwell	A yellow quiver, full of arrows.
Universities of Glasgow and Strathclyde AS/ No 4 AEF	Glasgow	A bird of prey in flight, holding a branch in its beak, in front of an upright sword.
Liverpool UAS	RAF Woodvale	A bird atop an open book, holding a branch in its beak.
University of London AS/No 6 AEF	RAF Wyton	A globe superimposed over an open book.
Manchester and Salford Universities AS/ No 10 AEF	RAF Woodvale	A bird of prey with a green snake in its beak
Northumbrian Universities AS/No 11 AEF	RAF Leeming	A white cross on a blue background.
Oxford UAS	RAF Benson	An open book in front of crossed swords.
Southampton UAS/No 2 AEF	QinetiQ Boscombe Down	A red stag in front of a stone pillar.
University of Wales AS/No 1 AEF	DARA St Athan	A red Welsh dragon in front of an open book, clasping a sword. Some aircraft have the dragon in front of white and green squares.
Yorkshire Universities AS/No 9 AEF	RAF Church Fenton	An open book in front of a Yorkshire rose with leaves.

Historic Aircraft in Overseas Markings

Some *historic, classic and warbird* aircraft carry the markings of overseas air arms and can be seen in the UK, mainly preserved in museums and collections or taking part in air shows.

Notes	Serial	Type (other identity)	Owner/operator, location

ARGENTINA

	0729	Beech T-34C Turbo Mentor	FAA Museum, stored RNAS Yeovilton
	0767	Aermacchi MB339AA	Rolls-Royce Heritage Trust, Filton
	A-515	FMA IA58 Pucara (ZD485)	RAF Museum, Cosford
	A-517	FMA IA58 Pucara (G-BLRP)	Privately owned, Channel Islands
	A-522	FMA IA58 Pucara (8768M)	FAA Museum, at NE Aircraft Museum, Usworth
	A-528	FMA IA58 Pucara (8769M)	Norfolk & Suffolk Avn Museum, Flixton
	A-533	FMA IA58 Pucara (ZD486) <ff>	Boscombe Down Museum
	A-549	FMA IA58 Pucara (ZD487)	Imperial War Museum, Duxford
	AE-409	Bell UH-1H Iroquois [656]	Museum of Army Flying, Middle Wallop
	AE-422	Bell UH-1H Iroquois	FAA Museum, stored RNAS Yeovilton

AUSTRALIA

	A2-4	Supermarine Seagull V (VH-ALB)	RAF Museum, Hendon
	A16-199	Lockheed Hudson IIIA (G-BEOX) [SF-R]	RAF Museum, Hendon
	A17-48	DH82A Tiger Moth (G-BPHR)	Privately owned, Swindon
	A19-144	Bristol 156 Beaufighter XIc (JM135/A8-324)	The Fighter Collection, Duxford
	A79-808	DH115 Vampire T33	De Havilland Aviation, Swansea
	A92-480	GAF Jindivik 4A (A92-LLAN-1)	QinetiQ Llanbedr, on display
	A92-664	GAF Jindivik 4A	Privately owned, Llanbedr
	A92-708	GAF Jindivik 4A	Bristol Aero Collection, stored Kemble
	N6-766	DH115 Sea Vampire T22 (XG766/ G-SPDR)	De Havilland Aviation, Swansea

BELGIUM

	FT-36	Lockheed T-33A	Dumfries & Galloway Avn Mus, Dumfries
	H-50	Noorduyn AT-16 Harvard IIB (OO-DAF)	Privately owned, Brasschaat, Belgium
	HD-75	Hanriot HD1 (G-AFDX)	RAF Museum, Hendon
	IF-68	Hawker Hunter F6 <ff>	Privately owned, Welshpool
	K-16	Douglas C-53D Skytrooper (OT-CWG/N49G)	Air Dakota, Brussels, Belgium
	L-44	Piper L-18C Super Cub (OO-SPQ)	BSD Aeroclub FBA, Bierset, Belgium
	L-47	Piper L-18C Super Cub (OO-SPG)	BSD Aeroclub FBA, Bierset, Belgium
	L-57	Piper L-18C Super Cub (OO-GDH)	BSD Aeroclub FBA, Bierset, Belgium
	L-156	Piper L-18C Super Cub (OO-LGB)	BSD Aeroclub FBA, Bierset, Belgium
	V-18	Stampe SV-4B (OO-GWD)	Antwerp Stampe Centre, Antwerp-Deurne, Belgium
	V-29	Stampe SV-4B (OO-GWB)	Antwerp Stampe Centre, Antwerp-Deurne, Belgium

BOLIVIA

	FAB184	SIAI-Marchetti SF.260W (G-SIAI)	Privately owned, Booker

BOTSWANA

	OJ1	BAC Strikemaster 83 (ZG805/ G-BXFU)	Global Aviation, Humberside
	OJ4	BAC Strikemaster 87 (G-AYHR/ G-UNNY) [Z2]	Privately owned, Duxford
	OJ10	BAC Strikemaster 87 (G-UVNR)	Privately owned, North Weald

BRAZIL

	1317	Embraer T-27 Tucano	Shorts, Belfast (engine test bed)

BURKINA FASO

	BF-8431	SIAI-Marchetti SF.260 (G-NRRA) [31]	Privately owned, Elstree

Historic Aircraft

Notes	Serial	Type (other identity)	Owner/operator, location
	CANADA		
	622	Piasecki HUP-3 Retriever (51-16622/N6699D)	The Helicopter Museum, Weston-super-Mare
	920	VS Stranraer (CF-BXO) [Q-N]	RAF Museum, Hendon
	3349	NA64 Yale (G-BYNF)	Privately owned, Duxford
	5450	Hawker Hurricane XII (G-TDTW)	Hawker Restorations Ltd, Milden
	9754	Consolidated PBY-5A Catalina (VP-BPS) [P]	Privately owned, Lee-on-Solent
	9893	Bristol 149 Bolingbroke IVT	Imperial War Museum store, Duxford
	9940	Bristol 149 Bolingbroke IVT	Royal Scottish Mus'm of Flight, E Fortune
	15195	Fairchild PT-19A Cornell	RAF MuseumRestoration Centre. Cosford
	16693	Auster J/1N Alpha (G-BLPG) [693]	Privately owned, Headcorn
	18013	DHC1 Chipmunk 22 (G-TRIC) [013]	The Shuttleworth Collection, Old Warden
	18393	Avro Canada CF-100 Canuck 4B (G-BCYK)	Imperial War Museum, Duxford
	18671	DHC1 Chipmunk 22 (WP905/ 7438M/G-BNZC) [671]	Privately owned, Wombleton
	20310	CCF T-6J Harvard IV (G-BSBG) [310]	Privately owned, Liverpool
	21261	Lockheed T-33A-N Silver Star (G-TBRD)	Golden Apple Operations/OFMC, Duxford
	21417	Canadair CT-133 Silver Star	Yorkshire Air Museum, Elvington
	23140	Canadair CL-13 Sabre [AX] <rf>	Midland Air Museum, Coventry
	23380	Canadair CL-13 Sabre <rf>	RAF Millom Museum, Haverigg
	FJ777	Boeing-Stearman PT-13D Kaydet (42-17786/G-BRTK)	Privately owned, Swanton Morley
	CHINA		
	2632016	Nanchang CJ-6A Chujiao (G-BXZB) (also wears *2632019*)	Privately owned, Hibaldstow
	2751219	Nanchang CJ-6A Chujiao (G-BVVG)	Privately owned, Breighton
	CZECH REPUBLIC		
	3677	Letov S-102 (MiG-15) (613677)	Royal Scottish Mus'm of Flight, E Fortune
	3794	Letov S-102 (MiG-15) (623794)	Imperial War Museum, stored Duxford
	9147	Mil Mi-4	The Helicopter Museum, Weston-super-Mare
	DENMARK		
	A-011	SAAB A-35XD Draken	Privately owned, Grainthorpe, Lincs
	AR-107	SAAB S-35XD Draken	Newark Air Museum, Winthorpe
	E-402	Hawker Hunter F51	Bournemouth Aviation Museum
	E-419	Hawker Hunter F51	North-East Aircraft Museum, Usworth
	E-420	Hawker Hunter F51 (G-9-442)	Privately owned, Walton-on-Thames
	E-421	Hawker Hunter F51	Brooklands Museum, Weybridge
	E-423	Hawker Hunter F51 (G-9-444)	SWWAPS, Lasham
	E-424	Hawker Hunter F51 (G-9-445)	Aeroventure, Doncaster
	ET-272	Hawker Hunter T7 <ff>	Boulton Paul Association, Wolverhampton
	ET-273	Hawker Hunter T7 <ff>	Aeroventure, Doncaster
	K-682	Douglas C-47A Skytrain (OY-BPB)	Foreningen For Flyvende Mus, Vaerløse, Denmark
	L-866	Consolidated PBY-6A Catalina (8466M)	RAF Museum, Cosford
	R-756	Lockheed F-104G Starfighter	Midland Air Museum, Coventry
	S-881	Sikorsky S-55C	The Helicopter Museum, Weston-super-Mare
	S-882	Sikorsky S-55C	The Helicopter Museum, Weston-super-Mare
	S-886	Sikorsky S-55C	
	S-887	Sikorsky S-55C	The Helicopter Museum, Weston-super-Mare
	EGYPT		
	0446	Mikoyan MiG-21UM <ff>	Thameside Aviation Museum, Tilbury
	7907	Sukhoi Su-7 <ff>	Robertsbridge Aviation Society, Mayfield
	FINLAND		
	VI-3	Valtion Viima 2 (OO-EBL)	Privately owned, Brasschaat, Belgium

Serial	Type (other identity)	Owner/operator, location	Notes
	FRANCE		
3	Mudry/CAARP CAP-10B (G-BXRA)	Privately owned, Sedlescombe, Sussex	
06	Dewoitine D27 (290/F-AZJD)	The Old Flying Machine Company, Duxford	
20	MH1521C1 Broussard (G-BWGG) [315-SQ]	Privately owned, Rednal	
37	Nord 3400 (G-ZARA) [MAB]	Privately owned, Boston	
57	Dassault Mystère IVA [8-MT]	Imperial War Museum, Duxford	
67	SNCAN 1101 Noralpha (F-GMCY) [CY]	Privately owned, la Ferté-Alais, France	
46	Yakovlev Yak-52 (9111413/ RA-44413)	Privately owned, White Waltham	
68	Nord 3400 [MHA]	Privately owned,	
70	Dassault Mystère IVA	Midland Air Museum, Coventry	
78	Nord 3202 (G-BIZK)	Privately owned, Swanton Morley	
79	Dassault Mystère IVA [2-EG]	Norfolk & Suffolk Avn Museum, Flixton	
83	Dassault Mystère IVA [8-MS]	Newark Air Museum, Winthorpe	
84	Dassault Mystère IVA [8-NF]	Lashenden Air Warfare Museum, Headcorn	
85	Dassault Mystère IVA [8-MV]	British Aviation Heritage, Bruntingthorpe	
100	Mudry/CAARP CAP-10B (G-BXRB)	Privately owned, Sedlescombe, Sussex	
101	Dassault Mystère IVA [8-MN]	Bomber County Aviation Museum, Hemswell	
104	MH1521M Broussard (F-GHFG) [307-FG]	Privately owned, France	
105	Nord N2501F Noratlas (F-AZVM) [62-SI]	Le Noratlas de Provence, Bretigny, France	
FR108	SO1221 Djinn [CDL]	The Helicopter Museum, Weston-super-Mare	
120	SNCAN Stampe SV4C (G-AZGC)	Privately owned, Reading	
121	Dassault Mystère IVA	City of Norwich Aviation Museum	
134	Mudry/CAARP CAP-10B (G-BXRC)	Privately owned, Sedlescombe, Sussex	
135	Mudry/CAARP CAP-10B (G-BXFE)	Privately owned, Sedlescombe, Sussex	
143	Morane-Saulnier MS733 Alcyon (G-MSAL)	The Squadron, North Weald	
FR145	SO1221 Djinn [CDL]	Privately owned, Luton	
146	Dassault Mystère IVA [8-MC]	North-East Aircraft Museum, Usworth	
185	MH1521M Broussard (G-BWLR)	Privately owned, Longhope	
282	Dassault MD311 Flamant (F-AZFX) [316-KY]	Memorial Flt Association, la Ferté-Alais, France	
316	MH1521M Broussard (F-GGKR) [315-SN]	The Old Flying Machine Company, Duxford	
318	Dassault Mystère IVA [8-NY]	Dumfries & Galloway Avn Mus, Dumfries	
319	Dassault Mystère IVA [8-ND]	Rebel Air Museum, Andrewsfield	
396	Stampe SV4A (G-BWRE)	Privately owned, stored Sandown	
538	Dassault Mirage IIIE [3-QH]	Yorkshire Air Museum, Elvington	
1417	SA.341G Gazelle I (G-BXJK)	Privately owned, Stapleford Tawney	
17473	Lockheed T-33A	Midland Air Museum, Coventry	
42157	NA F-100D Super Sabre [11-ML]	North-East Aviation Museum, Usworth	
63938	NA F-100F Super Sabre [11-MU]	Lashenden Air Warfare Museum, Headcorn	
121748	Grumman F8F-2P Bearcat (F-AZRJ) [5834/P]	Privately owned, Anemasse, France	
125716	Douglas AD-4N Skyraider (F-AZFN) [22-DG]	Privately owned, Etampes, France	
126965	Douglas AD-4NA Skyraider (OO-FOR)	Privately owned, Braaschaat, Belgium	
133704	CV F4U-7 Corsair (125541/ F-AZYS)	Privately owned, Cuers, France	
517545	NA T-28S Fennec (N14113) [CD-113]	Privately owned, Duxford	
517692	NA T-28S Fennec (F-AZFV/ G-TROY) [142]	Privately owned, Duxford	
56-5395	Piper L-18C Super Cub (52-2436/ G-CUBJ) [CDG]	Privately owned, Oaksey Park	
C850	Salmson 2A2 <R>	Barton Aviation Heritage Society, Barton	
MS824	Morane-Saulnier Type N <R> (G-AWBU)	Privately owned, Booker	
TE184	VS361 Spitfire LF XVIE (6850M/ G-MXVI) [D]	De Cadenet Motor Racing, Halton	

Historic Aircraft

Notes	Serial	Type (other identity)	Owner/operator, location
		GERMANY	
	-	Fieseler Fi103R-IV (V-1) (BAPC 91)	Lashenden Air Warfare Museum, Headcorn
	-	Focke-Achgelis Fa330A-1 (8469M)	RAF Museum, Cosford
	-	Fokker Dr1 Dreidekker <R> (G-BVGZ)	Museum of Army Flying, Middle Wallop
	-	Fokker Dr1 Dreidekker <R> (BAPC 88)	FAA Museum, RNAS Yeovilton
	3	SNCAN 1101 Noralpha (G-BAYV)	Barton Aviation Heritage Society, Barton
	6	Messerschmitt Bf109G-2/Trop (10639/8478M/G-USTV)	RAF/Imperial War Museum, Duxford
	8	Focke Wulf Fw190 <R> (G-WULF)	The Real Aeroplane Company, Breighton
	14	Messerschmitt Bf109 <R> (BAPC 67)	Kent Battle of Britain Museum, Hawkinge
	14	SNCAN 1101 Noralpha (G-BSMD)	Privately owned, North Weald
	152/17	Fokker Dr1 Dreidekker <R> (G-ATJM)	Privately owned, North Weald
	210/16	Fokker EIII (BAPC 56)	Science Museum, South Kensington
	214	SPP Yak C-11 (G-DYAK)	Classic Aviation Company, Hannover, Germany
	422/15	Fokker EIII <R> (G-AVJO)	Privately owned, Booker
	425/17	Fokker Dr1 Dreidekker <R> (BAPC 133)	Kent Battle of Britain Museum, Hawkinge
	626/8	Fokker DVII <R> (N6268)	Blue Max Movie Aircraft Museum, Booker
	959	Mikoyan MiG-21SPS	Midland Air Museum, Coventry
	1190	Messerschmitt Bf109E-3 [4]	Imperial War Museum, Duxford
	1480	Messerschmitt Bf109 <R> (BAPC 66) [6]	Kent Battle of Britain Museum, Hawkinge
	2100	Focke-Wulf Fw189A-1 (G-BZKY) [V7+1H]	Privately owned, W Sussex
	4101	Messerschmitt Bf109E-3 (DG200/ 8477M) [12]	RAF Museum, Hendon
	6357	Messerschmitt Bf109 <R> (BAPC 74) [6]	Kent Battle of Britain Museum, Hawkinge
	7198/18	LVG CVI (G-AANJ/9239M)	The Shuttleworth Collection, Old Warden
	8147	Messerschmitt Bf109F-4	Charleston Aviation Services, Colchester
	8417/18	Fokker DVII (9207M)	RAF Museum, Hendon
	12802	Antonov An-2T (D-FOFM)	Privately owned, Lahr, Germany
	100143	Focke-Achgelis Fa330A-1	Imperial War Museum, Duxford
	100502	Focke-Achgelis Fa330A-1	The Real Aeroplane Company, Breighton
	100509	Focke-Achgelis Fa330A-1	Science Museum, stored Wroughton
	100545	Focke-Achgelis Fa330A-1	Fleet Air Arm Museum, stored RNAS Yeovilton
	100549	Focke-Achgelis Fa330A-1	Lashenden Air Warfare Museum, Headcorn
	112372	Messerschmitt Me262A-2a (AM.51/VK893/8482M) [9K+XK]	RAF Museum, Cosford
	120227	Heinkel He162A-2 Salamander (VN679/AM.65/8472M) [2]	RAF Museum, Hendon
	120235	Heinkel He162A-1 Salamander (AM.68)	Imperial War Museum, Lambeth
	191316	Messerschmitt Me163B Komet	Science Museum, South Kensington
	191614	Messerschmitt Me163B Komet (8481M)	RAF Museum, Cosford
	191659	Messerschmitt Me163B Komet (8480M) [15]	Royal Scottish Mus'm of Flight, E Fortune
	191660	Messerschmitt Me163B Komet (AM.214) [3]	Imperial War Museum, Duxford
	280020	Flettner Fl282/B-V20 Kolibri (frame only)	Midland Air Museum, Coventry
	360043	Junkers Ju88R-1 (PJ876/8475M) [D5+EV]	RAF Museum, Hendon
	420430	Messerschmitt Me410A-1/U2 (AM.72/8483M) [3U+CC]	RAF Museum, Cosford
	475081	Fieseler Fi156C-7 Storch (VP546/ AM.101/7362M)[GM+AK]	RAF Museum, Cosford
	494083	Junkers Ju87D-3 (8474M) [RI+JK]	RAF Museum, Hendon
	584219	Focke Wulf Fw190F-8/U1 (AM.29/8470M) [38]	RAF Museum, Hendon
	701152	Heinkel He111H-23 (8471M) [NT+SL]	RAF Museum, Hendon

Serial	Type (other identity)	Owner/operator, location	Notes
730301	Messerschmitt Bf110G-4 (AM.34/8479M) [D5+RL]	RAF Museum, Hendon	
733682	Focke Wulf Fw190A-8/R7 (AM.75/9211M)	Imperial War Museum, Lambeth	
2+1	Focke Wulf Fw190 <R> (G-SYFW) [7334]	Privately owned, Guernsey, CI	
2E+RA	Fieseler Fi-156C-2 Storch (NX436FS)	Privately owned, North Weald	
4+1	Focke Wulf Fw190 <R> (G-BSLX)	Privately owned, Riseley	
4V+GH	Amiot AAC1/Ju52 (Port.AF 6316) [9]	Imperial War Museum, Duxford	
22+35	Lockheed F-104G Starfighter	SWWAPS, Lasham	
22+57	Lockheed F-104G Starfighter	Privately owned, Grainthorpe, Lincs	
58+89	Dornier Do28D-2 Skyservant (D-ICDY)	Moosreiner Consulting, Hamburg, Germany	
96+21	Mil Mi-24D (406)	Imperial War Museum, Duxford	
96+26	Mil Mi-24D (429)	The Helicopter Museum, Weston-super-Mare	
97+04	Putzer Elster B (G-APVF)	Privately owned, Breighton	
98+14	Sukhoi Su-22M-4	The Old Flying Machine Company, stored Scampton	
99+24	NA OV-10B Bronco (F-AZKM)	Privately owned, Montelimar, France	
99+26	NA OV-10B Bronco (G-BZGL)	Privately owned, Duxford	
99+32	NA OV-10B Bronco (G-BZGK)	Privately owned, Duxford	
BU+CC	CASA 1.131E Jungmann (G-BUCC)	Privately owned, Goodwood	
BU+CK	CASA 1.131E Jungmann (G-BUCK)	Privately owned, White Waltham	
CC+43	Pilatus P-2 (G-CJCI)	Privately owned, Norwich	
CF+HF	Morane-Saulnier MS502 (EI-AUY)	Imperial War Museum, Duxford	
CW+BG	CASA 1.131E Jungmann [483] (G-BXBD)	Privately owned, Kemble	
D5397/17	Albatros DVA <R> (G-BFXL)	FAA Museum, RNAS Yeovilton	
ES+BH	Messerschmitt Bf108B-2 (D-ESBH)	Messerschmitt Stiftung, Germany	
FI+S	Morane-Saulnier MS505 (G-BIRW)	Royal Scottish Mus'm of Flight, E Fortune	
FM+BB	Messerschmitt Bf109G-6 (D-FMBB)	Messerschmitt Stiftung, Germany	
JA+120	Canadair CL-13 Sabre 4 (MM19607)	Privately owned	
KG+EM	Nord 1002 (G-ETME)	Privately owned, Booker	
LG+01	Bücker Bü133C Jungmeister (G-AYSJ)	The Fighter Collection, Duxford	
LG+03	Bücker Bü133C Jungmeister (G-AEZX)	Privately owned, Milden	
NJ+C11	Nord 1002 (G-ATBG)	Privately owned, Sutton Bridge	
S4+A07	CASA 1.131E Jungmann (G-BWHP)	Privately owned, Yarcombe, Devon	
S5+B06	CASA 1.131E Jungmann 2000 (G-BSFB)	Privately owned, Stretton, Cheshire	
TA+RC	Morane-Saulnier MS505 (G-BPHZ)	The Aircraft Restoration Co, Duxford	

GHANA

G-102	SA122 Bulldog	Privately owned, Bourne Park, Hants	
G-108	SA122 Bulldog (G-BCUP)	Privately owned, Bourne Park, Hants	

GREECE

51-6171	NA F-86D Sabre	North-East Aircraft Museum, Usworth	
52-6541	Republic F-84F Thunderflash [541]	North-East Aircraft Museum, Usworth	

HONG KONG

HKG-5	SA128 Bulldog (G-BULL)	Privately owned, Slinfold	
HKG-6	SA128 Bulldog (G-BPCL)	Privately owned, Elstree	
HKG-11	Slingsby T.67M Firefly 200 (VR-HZQ)	Slingsby, stored Kirkbymoorside	
HKG-13	Slingsby T.67M Firefly 200 (G-BXKW)	Slingsby, stored Kirkbymoorside	

HUNGARY

501	Mikoyan MiG-21PF	Imperial War Museum, Duxford	

Historic Aircraft

Notes	Serial	Type (other identity)	Owner/operator, location
	INDIA		
	Q497	EE Canberra T4 (WE191) (fuselage)	Dumfries & Galloway Avn Mus, Dumfries
	INDONESIA		
	LL-5313	BAe Hawk T53	FR Aviation, stored Bournemouth
	IRAQ		
	333	DH115 Vampire T55 <ff>	Military Aircraft Pres'n Grp, Barton
	ITALY		
	MM5701	Fiat CR42 (BT474/8468M) [13-95]	RAF Museum, Hendon
	MM52801	Fiat G46-3B (G-BBII) [4-97]	Privately owned, Duxford
	MM53692	CCF T-6G Texan	RAeS Medway Branch, Rochester
	MM53774	Fiat G59-4B (I-MRSV) [181]	Privately owned, Parma, Italy
	MM54099	NA T-6G Texan (G-BRBC) [RR-56]	Privately owned, Chigwell
	MM54-2372	Piper L-21B Super Cub	Privately owned, Kesgrave, Suffolk
	W7	Avia FL3 (G-AGFT)	Privately owned, Leicester
	JAPAN		
	-	Yokosuka MXY 7 Ohka II (BAPC 159)	Defence School, Chattenden
	24	Kawasaki Ki100-1B (8476M/ BAPC 83)	RAF Museum, Cosford
	3685	Mitsubishi A6M3-2 Zero	Imperial War Museum, Duxford
	5439	Mitsubishi Ki46-III (8484M/ BAPC 84)	RAF Museum, Cosford
	15-1585	Yokosuka MXY 7 Ohka II (BAPC 58)	Science Museum, at FAA Museum, RNAS Yeovilton
	997	Yokosuka MXY 7 Ohka II (8485M/ BAPC 98)	Gr Manchester Mus of Science & Industry
	I-13	Yokosuka MXY 7 Ohka II (8486M/ BAPC 99)	RAF Museum, Cosford
	MYANMAR		
	UB441	VS361 Spitfire IX (ML119)	Privately owned, Rochester
	NETHERLANDS		
	204	Lockheed SP-2H Neptune [V]	RAF Museum, Cosford
	A-12	DH82A Tiger Moth (PH-TYG)	Privately owned, Gilze-Rijen, The Netherlands
	B-64	Noorduyn AT-16 Harvard IIB (PH-LSK)	Privately owned, Gilze-Rijen, The Netherlands
	B-71	Noorduyn AT-16 Harvard IIB (PH-MLM)	Privately owned, Gilze-Rijen, The Netherlands
	B-118	Noorduyn AT-16 Harvard IIB (PH-IIB)	Privately owned, Gilze-Rijen, The Netherlands
	E-14	Fokker S-11 Instructor (PH-AFS) The Netherlands	Privately owned, Lelystad,
	E-15	Fokker S-11 Instructor (G-BIYU)	Privately owned, White Waltham
	E-18	Fokker S-11 Instructor (PH-HTC)	Dukes of Brabant AF, Eindhoven, The Netherlands
	E-20	Fokker S-11 Instructor (PH-GRB)	Privately owned, Gilze-Rijen, The Netherlands
	E-27	Fokker S-11 Instructor (PH-HOL)	Privately owned, Lelystad, The Netherlands
	E-31	Fokker S-11 Instructor (G-BEPV)	Privately owned, Elstree
	E-32	Fokker S-11 Instructor (PH-HOI)	Privately owned, Gilze-Rijen, The Netherlands
	E-36	Fokker S-11 Instructor (PH-ACG)	Privately owned, Lelystad, The Netherlands
	E-39	Fokker S-11 Instructor (PH-HOG)	Privately owned, Lelystad, The Netherlands
	G-29	Beech D18S (N5369X)	KLu Historic Flt, Gilze-Rijen, The Netherlands
	MK732	VS 361 Spitfire LF IXC (8633M/ PH-OUQ) [3W-17]	KLu Historic Flight, Lelystad, The Netherlands
	N-202	Hawker Hunter F6 [10] <ff>	Privately owned, Eaglescott
	N-250	Hawker Hunter F6 (G-9-185) <ff>	Imperial War Museum, Duxford
	N-268	Hawker Hunter FGA78 (Qatar QA-10)	Yorkshire Air Museum, Elvington

126

Serial	Type (other identity)	Owner/operator, location	Notes
N-315	Hawker Hunter T7 (XM121)	Jet Avn Preservation Grp, Long Marston	
N5-149	NA B-25J Mitchell (44-29507/ HD346/N320SQ) [232511]	Duke of Brabant AF, Eindhoven, The Netherlands	
R-559	Piper L-21B Super Cub (54-2466/ G-BLMI)	Privately owned, White Waltham	
R-109	Piper L-21B Super Cub (54-2337/ PH-GAZ)	Privately owned, Gilze-Rijen, The Netherlands	
R-122	Piper L-21B Super Cub (54-2412/ PH-PPW)	Privately owned, Gilze-Rijen, The Netherlands	
R-137	Piper L-21B Super Cub (54-2427/ PH-PSC)	Privately owned, Gilze-Rijen, The Netherlands	
R-151	Piper L-21B Super Cub (54-2441/ G-BIYR)	Privately owned, Dunkeswell	
R-156	Piper L-21B Super Cub (54-2446/ G-ROVE)	Privately owned, Headcorn	
R-163	Piper L-21B Super Cub (54-2453/ G-BIRH)	Privately owned, Lee-on-Solent	
R-167	Piper L-21B Super Cub (54-2457/ G-LION)	Privately owned, Turweston, Bucks	
R-177	Piper L-21B Super Cub (54-2467/ PH-KNR)	Privately owned, Gilze-Rijen, The Netherlands	
R-181	Piper L-21B Super Cub (54-2471/ PH-GAU)	Privately owned, Gilze-Rijen, The Netherlands	
R-345	Piper J-3C Cub (PH-UCS)	Privately owned, The Netherlands	
S-9	DHC2 L-20A Beaver (PH-DHC) The Netherlands	KLu Historic Flt, Gilze-Rijen,	
Y-74	Consolidated PBY-5A Catalina (2459/PH-PBY)	Neptune Association, Valkenburg, The Netherlands	

NEW ZEALAND

Serial	Type (other identity)	Owner/operator, location	Notes
NZ3009	Curtiss P-40E Kittyhawk (ZK-RMH)	The Old Flying Machine Company, Duxford	
NZ3905	WS Wasp HAS1 (XT787)	Kennet Aviation, Cranfield	
NZ3907	WS Wasp HAS1 (XT435/G-RIMM)	Privately owned, Cranfield	
NZ3909	WS Wasp HAS1 (XT782)	Kennet Aviation, Cranfield, spares use	
NZ5648	Goodyear FG-1D Corsair (G-BXUL) [648]	The Old Flying Machine Company, Duxford	
NZ6361	BAC Strikemaster 87 (OJ5/ G-BXFP)	Privately owned, Chalgrove	

NORTH KOREA

Serial	Type (other identity)	Owner/operator, location	Notes
-	WSK Lim-2 (MiG-15) (01420/ G-BMZF)	FAA Museum, RNAS Yeovilton	
1211	WSK Lim-5 (MiG-17F) (G-BWUF)	Privately owned, Sussex	

NORWAY

Serial	Type (other identity)	Owner/operator, location	Notes
423/427	Gloster Gladiator I (L8032/ G-AMRK/N2308)	The Shuttleworth Collection, Old Warden	
848	Piper L-18C Super Cub (LN-ACL) [FA-N]	Privately owned, Norway	
56321	SAAB S91B Safir (G-BKPY) [U-AB]	Newark Air Museum, Winthorpe	

POLAND

Serial	Type (other identity)	Owner/operator, location	Notes
05	WSK SM-2 (Mi-2) (1005)	The Helicopter Museum, Weston-super-Mare	
309	WSK SBLim-2A (MiG-15UTI) <ff>	Royal Scottish Mus'm of Flight, E Fortune	
408	WSK-PZL Mielec TS-11 Iskra (1H-0408)	Privately owned,	
1018	WSK-PZL Mielec TS-11 Iskra (1H-1018/G-ISKA)	Privately owned, Bruntingthorpe	
1120	WSK Lim-2 (MiG-15bis)	RAF Museum, Cosford	

PORTUGAL

Serial	Type (other identity)	Owner/operator, location	Notes
85	Isaacs Fury II (G-BTPZ)	Privately owned, Ormskirk	
1372	OGMA/DHC1 Chipmunk T20 (HB-TUM)	Privately owned, Switzerland	
1377	DHC1 Chipmunk 22 (G-BARS)	Privately owned, Yeovilton	
1741	CCF Harvard IV (G-HRVD)	Air Atlantique Historic Flight, Coventry	
1747	CCF T-6J Harvard IV (20385/ G-BGPB)	The Aircraft Restoration Co, Duxford	

Historic Aircraft

Notes	Serial	Type (other identity)	Owner/operator, location
	QATAR		
	QA12	Hawker Hunter FGA78 <ff>	The Planets Leisure Centre, Woking
	QP30	WS Lynx Mk 28 (G-BFDV/TD 013)	Army SEAE, Arborfield
	QP31	WS Lynx Mk 28	DARA Fleetlands Apprentice School
	QP32	WS Lynx Mk 28 (TD 016)	AAC Stockwell Hall, Middle Wallop
	RUSSIA (& FORMER SOVIET UNION)		
	-	Mil Mi-24V (3532424810853)	Privately owned, Hawarden
	01	Yakovlev Yak-52 (9311709/ G-YKSZ)	Privately owned, Old Buckenham
	2	Yakovlev Yak-52 (9311708/ G-YAKS)	Privately owned, North Weald
	03	Mil Mi-24D (3532461715415)	Privately owned, Hawarden
	03	Yakovlev Yak-9UM (0470403/ F-AZYJ)	Privately owned, Dijon, France
	04	Mikoyan MiG-23ML (024003607)	Privately owned, Hawarden
	04	Yakovlev Yak-52 (9211612/ RA-22521)	Privately owned, Wellesbourne Mountford
	05	Yakovlev Yak-50 (832507/YL-CBH)	Privately owned, Strathallan
	06	Mil Mi-24D (3532464505029)	Privately owned, Hawarden
	07	WSK SM-1 (Mi-1) (Czech. 2007)	The Helicopter Museum, Weston-super-Mare
	07	Yakovlev Yak-18M (G-BMJY)	Privately owned, North Weald
	09	Yakovlev Yak-52 (9411809/ G-BVMU)	Privately owned, Sandy, Beds
	10	Yakovlev Yak-52 (9110580)	Privately owned, White Waltham
	11	SPP Yak C-11 (G-YCII)	Privately owned, North Weald
	11	SPP Yak C-11 (G-BZMY)	Privately owned, North Weald
	12	LET L-29 Delfin (194555/ES-YLM/ G-DELF)	Privately owned, Manston
	14	Yakovlev Yak-52 (899404/ G-CCCP)	Privately owned, North Weald
	15	Yakovlev Yak-52 (866915/LY-ABQ)	Privately owned, Leicester
	18	LET L-29S Delfin (591771/YL-PAF)	Privately owned, Hawarden
	19	Yakovlev Yak-52 (811202/YL-CBI)	Privately owned, Cumbernauld
	20	Lavochkin La-11	The Fighter Collection, Duxford
	20	Yakovlev Yak-52 (790404/YL-CBJ)	Privately owned, Strathallan
	23	Mikoyan MiG-27D (83712515040)	Privately owned, Hawarden
	26	Yakovlev Yak-52 (9111306/ G-BVXK)	Privately owned, White Waltham
	27	SPP Yak C-11 (G-OYAK)	Privately owned, North Weald
	27	Yakovlev Yak-52 (9111307/ G-YAKX)	Privately owned, Old Sarum
	31	Yakovlev Yak-52 (9111311/ RA-02209)	Privately owned, Rendcomb
	35	Sukhoi Su-17M-3 (25102)	Privately owned, Hawarden
	35	Yakovlev Yak-52 (9010508/ RA-02080)	Privately owned, White Waltham
	36	LET/Yak C-11 (G-KYAK)	Privately owned, North Weald
	36	SPP Yak C-11 (G-IYAK)	Privately owned, Earls Colne
	40	Yakovlev Yak-55M (920506/ RA-01333/G-YAKM)	Privately owned, White Waltham
	42	Yakovlev Yak-52 (833901/ LY-AMU)	Privately owned, North Weald
	48	Yakovlev Yak-52 (RA-44514)	Privately owned, White Waltham
	49	Yakovlev Yak-55M (880606/ RA-44526)	Privately owned, White Waltham
	50	Mikoyan MiG-23MF (023003508)	Privately owned, Hawarden
	50	Yakovlev Yak-50 (812003/ G-BWJT)	Privately owned, Little Gransden
	50	Yakovlev Yak-50 (812101/ LY-ASG)	Privately owned,
	50	Yakovlev Yak-50 (822305/ G-BXNO)	Privately owned, Denham
	50	Yakovlev Yak-52 (9111415/ RA-44464)	Privately owned, White Waltham
	51	Curtiss P-40E Warhawk (41-13570)	Privately owned, stored Sandown
	51	LET L-29S Delfin (491273/ YL-PAG)	Privately owned, Hawarden

Serial	Type (other identity)	Owner/operator, location	Notes
52	Yakovlev Yak-52 (878202/ G-BWVR)	Privately owned, Barton	
52	Yakovlev Yak-52 (800708/LY-AMP)	Privately owned, Breighton	
54	Sukhoi Su-17M (69004)	Privately owned, Hawarden	
55	Yakovlev Yak-52 (9111505/ G-BVOK)	Intrepid Aviation, North Weald	
56	Yakovlev Yak-52 (811504/ LY-AKW)	Privately owned, Hawarden	
56	Yakovlev Yak-52 (9111506/ RA-44516)	Privately owned, White Waltham	
69	Hawker Hunter FGA9 (8839M/ XG194)	RAF North Luffenham Training Area	
69	Yakovlev Yak-50 (801810/G-BTZB)	Privately owned, Audley End	
69	Yakovlev Yak-52 (855509/LY-ALS)	Privately owned, North Weald	
71	Mikoyan MiG-27M (61912507006)	Privately owned, Hawarden	
72	Yakovlev Yak-52 (9111608/ G-BXAV)	Privately owned, North Weald	
74	Yakovlev Yak-52 (877404/LY-AOK)	Privately owned, Tollerton	
74	Yakovlev Yak-52 (888802/G-BXID)	Privately owned, Wellesbourne Mountford	
96	Yakovlev Yak-55 (901103/ RA-44525)	Privately owned, White Waltham	
98	Yakovlev Yak-52 (888911/ RA-02042)	Privately owned, White Waltham	
100	Yakovlev Yak-52 (866904/G-YAKI)	Privately owned, Popham	
101	Yakovlev Yak-52 (888914/ RA-02075)	Privately owned, White Waltham	
107	Yakovlev Yak-50 (822210/ LY-AGG)	Privately owned, Old Sarum	
111	Aero L-39ZO Albatros (28+02/ G-OTAF)	The Old Flying Machine Company, Duxford	
112	Yakovlev Yak-52 (822610/LY-AFB)	Privately owned, Little Gransden	
114	Yakovlev Yak-52 (8890012/ LY-ALM)	Privately owned, Compton Abbas	
139	Yakovlev Yak-52 (833810/ G-BWOD)	Privately owned, Sywell	
503	Mikoyan MiG-21SMT (G-BRAM)	Bournemouth Aviation Museum	
1342	Yakovlev Yak-1 (G-BTZD)	Privately owned, Milden	
1-12	Yakovlev Yak-52 (9011013/ RA-02293)	Privately owned, Halfpenny Green	
1870710	Ilyushin Il-2 (G-BZVW)	Privately owned, Sandtoft	
1878576	Ilyushin Il-2 (G-BZVX)	Privately owned, Sandtoft	
BH328	Hawker Hurricane IIb	Privately owned, Isle of Wight	
PT879	VS361 Spitfire LF IX (G-BYDE)	Privately owned, Isle of Wight	
(RK858)	VS361 Spitfire LF IX	The Fighter Collection, Duxford	
(SM639)	VS361 Spitfire LF IX	Privately owned, Catfield	

SAUDI ARABIA

405	Agusta-Bell AB.212	Privately owned, Margate	
420	Agusta-Bell AB.212	Privately owned, Margate	
1104	BAC Strikemaster 80	Global Aviation, Humberside	
1105	BAC Strikemaster 80 (G-BZYF)	Privately owned, Sproughton	
1107	BAC Strikemaster 80	Global Aviation, Humberside	
1108	BAC Strikemaster 80	Privately owned, Duxford	
1112	BAC Strikemaster 80 (G-FLYY)	Privately owned, Hawarden	
1114	BAC Strikemaster 80A (G-BZYH)	Privately owned, Sproughton	
1115	BAC Strikemaster 80A	Global Aviation, Humberside	
1120	BAC Strikemaster 80A	Global Aviation, Humberside	
1121	BAC Strikemaster 80A	Privately owned, North Weald	
1125	BAC Strikemaster 80A	Privately owned, Sproughton	
1129	BAC Strikemaster 80A	Global Aviation, Humberside	
1130	BAC Strikemaster 80A	Global Aviation, Humberside	
1133	BAC Strikemaster 80A (G-BESY)	Imperial War Museum, Duxford	
55-713	BAC Lightning T55 (ZF598)	Midland Air Museum, Coventry	

SLOVAKIA

7708	Mikoyan MiG-21MF	Boscombe Down Museum	

SOUTH AFRICA

92	Westland Wasp HAS1 (G-BYCX)	Privately owned, Thruxton	
6130	Lockheed Ventura II (AJ469)	RAF Museum, Cosford	
7429	NA AT-6D Harvard III (D-FASS)	Privately owned, Germany	

Historic Aircraft

Serial	Type (other identity)	Owner/operator, location
SOUTH VIETNAM		
24550	Cessna L-19E Bird Dog (G-PDOG)	Privately owned, Lincs
SPAIN		
B.2l-27	CASA 2.111B (He111H-16) (B.2l-103)	Imperial War Museum, stored Duxford
C.4E-88	Messerschmitt Bf109E	Privately owned, Hungerford
C.4K-102	Hispano HA 1.112M1L Buchon (G-BWUE)	Privately owned, Breighton
E.3B-114	CASA 1.131E Jungmann (G-BJAL)	Privately owned, Breighton
E.3B-143	CASA 1.131E Jungmann (G-JUNG)	Privately owned, White Waltham
E.3B-153	CASA 1.131E Jungmann (G-BPTS) [781-75]	Privately owned, Duxford
E.3B-336	CASA 1.131E Jungmann (G-BUTA)	Privately owned, Breighton
E.3B-350	CASA 1.131E Jungmann (G-BHPL) [05-97]	Privately owned, Kemble
(E.3B-369)	CASA 1.131E Jungmann (G-BPDM) [781-32]	Privately owned, Chilbolton
E.3B-521	CASA 1.131E Jungmann [781-3]	RAF Museum, Hendon
EM-01	DH60G Moth (G-AAOR)	Privately owned, Rendcomb
ES-9	CASA 1.133L Jungmeister (E.1-9/G-BVXJ)	The Real Aeroplane Company, Newby Wiske
ES.1-16	CASA 1.133L Jungmeister	Privately owned, Stretton, Cheshire
SWEDEN		
081	CFM 01 Tummelisa <R> (SE-XIL)	Privately owned, Karlstad, Sweden
05108	DH60 Moth	Privately owned, Langham
17239	SAAB B-17A (SE-BYH) [7-J]	Flygvapenmuseum, Linköping, Sweden
26158	NA P-51D Mustang (SE-BKG) [16-K]	Privately owned, Hässlo, Sweden
28693	DH100 Vampire FB6 (J-1184/ SE-DXY) [9-G]	Scandinavian Historic Flight, North Weald
29640	SAAB J-29F [20-08]	Midland Air Museum, Coventry
29670	SAAB J-29F (SE-DXB) [10-R]	Flygvapenmuseum/F10 Wing, Angelholm, Sweden
32028	SAAB 32A Lansen (G-BMSG)	Privately owned, Cranfield
34066	Hawker Hunter F58 (J-4089/ SE-DXA) [9-G]	Scandinavian Historic Flight, North Weald
35075	SAAB J-35J Draken [40]	Imperial War Museum, Duxford
A14	Thulin A/Bleriot XI (SE-XMC)	Privately owned, Karlstad, Sweden
SWITZERLAND		
A-10	CASA 1.131E Jungmann (G-BECW)	Privately owned, Denham
A-57	CASA 1.131E Jungmann (G-BECT)	Privately owned, Goodwood
A-701	Junkers Ju52/3m (HB-HOS)	Ju-Air, Dubendorf, Switzerland
A-702	Junkers Ju52/3m (HB-HOT)	Ju-Air, Dubendorf, Switzerland
A-703	Junkers Ju52/3m (HB-HOP)	Ju-Air, Dubendorf, Switzerland
A-806	Pilatus P3-03 (G-BTLL)	Privately owned, stored Headcorn
C-552	EKW C-3605 (G-DORN)	Privately owned, North Weald
C-558	EKW C-3605	Privately owned, Catfield
J-1008	DH100 Vampire FB6	Mosquito Aircraft Museum, London Colney
J-1149	DH100 Vampire FB6 (G-SWIS)	Privately owned, Bournemouth
J-1172	DH100 Vampire FB6 (8487M)	RAF Museum Restoration Centre, Cosfird
J-1573	DH112 Venom FB50 (G-VICI)	Source Classic Jet Flight, Bournemouth
J-1605	DH112 Venom FB50 (G-BLID)	Gatwick Aviation Museum, Charlwood, Surrey
J-1629	DH112 Venom FB50	Source Classic Jet Flight, Bournemouth
J-1632	DH112 Venom FB50 (G-VNOM)	Mosquito Museum, London Colney
J-1649	DH112 Venom FB50	Source Classic Jet Flight, Bournemouth
J-1704	DH112 Venom FB54	RAF Museum, Cosford
J-1712	DH112 Venom FB54 <ff>	Botany Bay Village, Chroley, Lancs
J-1758	DH112 Venom FB54 (N203DM)	Privately owned, stored North Weald
J-2001	Hawker Hunter F58 (J-4095/ F-AZHS)	Privately owned, Cuers, France
J-4015	Hawker Hunter F58 (J-4040/ HB-RVS)	Privately owned, Altenrhein, Switzerland
J-4021	Hawker Hunter F58 (G-BWIU)	Historic Flying Ltd/OFMC, Scampton

Serial	Type (other identity)	Owner/operator, location	Notes
J-4031	Hawker Hunter F58 (G-BWFR)	The Old Flying Machine Company, Scampton	
J-4058	Hawker Hunter F58 (G-BWFS)	The Old Flying Machine Company, Scampton	
J-4066	Hawker Hunter F58 (G-BXNZ)	The Old Flying Machine Company, Scampton	
J-4072	Hawker Hunter F58	Privately owned, Scampton	
J-4081	Hawker Hunter F58 (G-BWKB)	The Old Flying Machine Company, Scampton	
J-4083	Hawker Hunter F58 (G-EGHH)	Privately owned, Bournemouth	
J-4086	Hawker Hunter F58 (HB-RVU)	Privately owned, Altenrhein, Switzerland	
J-4090	Hawker Hunter F58 (G-SIAL)	The Old Flying Machine Company, Scampton	
J-4091	Hawker Hunter F58	British Aviation Heritage, Bruntingthorpe	
J-4201	Hawker Hunter T68 (HB-RVR)	Privately owned, Altenrhein, Switzerland	
J-4205	Hawker Hunter T68 (HB-RVP)	Privately owned, Altenrhein, Switzerland	
U-80	Bücker Bü133D Jungmeister (G-BUKK)	Privately owned, White Waltham	
U-99	Bücker Bü133C Jungmeister (G-AXMT)	Privately owned, Breighton	
U-110	Pilatus P-2 (G-PTWO)	Privately owned, Earls Colne	
U-125	Pilatus P-2 (G-BLKZ)	Privately owned, North Weald	
U-142	Pilatus P-2 (G-BONE)	Privately owned, Hibaldstow	
V-54	SE3130 Alouette II (G-BVSD)	Privately owned, Staverton	

USA

Serial	Type (other identity)	Owner/operator, location	Notes
-	Noorduyn AT-16 Harvard IIB (KLu B-168)	American Air Museum, Duxford	
1	Spad XIII <R> (G-BFYO/*S3398*)	American Air Museum, Duxford	
2	Boeing-Stearman N2S-5 Kaydet (G-AZLE)	Privately owned, Tongham	
5	Boeing P-26A Peashooter <R> (G-BEEW)	Privately owned, Barton	
14	Boeing-Stearman A75N-1 Kaydet (G-ISDN)	Privately owned, Rendcomb	
23	Fairchild PT-23 (N49272)	Privately owned, Halfpenny Green	
26	Boeing-Stearman A75N-1 Kaydet (G-BAVO)	Privately owned, Old Buckenham	
27	NA SNJ-7 Texan (90678/G-BRVG)	Privately owned, Goodwood	
33-K	PA-18 Super Cub 95 (51-15541/ G-BJLH)	Privately owned, Felthorpe	
43	Noorduyn AT-16 Harvard IIB (43-13064/G-AZSC) [SC]	Privately owned, Duxford	
44	Boeing-Stearman D75N-1 Kaydet (42-15852/G-RJAH)	Privately owned, Rendcomb	
44	Piper L-21B Super Cub (54-2405/ G-BWHH)	Privately owned, Felthorpe	
49	Curtiss P-40M Kittyhawk (43-5802/ G-KITT/*P8196*)	The Fighter Collection, Duxford	
57	WS55 Whirlwind HAS7 (XG592)	*Task Force* Adventure Park, Cowbridge, S Glam	
85	WAR P-47 Thunderbolt <R> (G-BTBI)	Privately owned, Carlisle	
112	Boeing-Stearman PT-13D Kaydet (42-17397/G-BSWC)	Privately owned, Old Sarum	
118	Boeing-Stearman PT-13A Kaydet (38-470/G-BSDS)	Privately owned, Swanton Morley	
379	Boeing-Stearman PT-13D Kaydet (42-14865/G-ILLE)	Privately owned, Compton Abbas	
441	Boeing-Stearman N2S-4 Kaydet (30010/G-BTFG)	Privately owned, Perth	
540	Piper L-4H Grasshopper (43-29877/G-BCNX)	Privately owned, Monewden	
578	Boeing-Stearman N2S-5 Kaydet (N1364V)	Privately owned, North Weald	
628	Beech D17S (44-67761/N18V)	Privately owned, stored North Weald	
718	Boeing-Stearman PT-13D Kaydet (42-17555/N5345N)	Privately owned, Tibenham	
744	Boeing-Stearman A75N-1 Kaydet (42-16532/OO-USN)	Privately owned, Wevelghem, Belgium	
817	Boeing-Stearman PT-17 Kaydet (N59269)	Privately owned, North Weald	

Historic Aircraft

Notes	Serial	Type (other identity)	Owner/operator, location
	854	Ryan PT-22 Recruit (42-17378/ G-BTBH)	Privately owned, Wellesbourne Mountford
	855	Ryan PT-22 Recruit (41-15510/ N56421)	Privately owned, Halfpenny Green
	897	Aeronca 11AC Chief (G-BJEV) [E]	Privately owned, English Bicknor, Glos
	1164	Beech D18S (G-BKGL)	The Aircraft Restoration Co, Duxford
,	1180	Boeing-Stearman N2S-3 Kaydet (3403/G-BRSK)	Privately owned, Tibenham
	2807	NA T-6G Texan (49-3072/G-BHTH) [V-103]	Northbrook College, Shoreham
	6136	Boeing-Stearman A75N-1 Kaydet (42-16136/G-BRUJ) [205]	Privately owned, Liverpool
	6771	Republic F-84F Thunderstreak (BAF FU-6)	RAF Museum, stored Cosford
	7797	Aeronca L-16A (47-0797/G-BFAF)	Privately owned, Finmere
	8178	NA F-86A Sabre (48-0178/ G-SABR) [FU-178]	Golden Apple Operations/ARC, Duxford
	8242	NA F-86A Sabre (48-0242) [FU-242]	American Air Museum, Duxford
	01532	Northrop F-5E Tiger II <R>	RAF Alconbury on display
	02538	Fairchild PT-19B (N33870)	Privately owned, North Weald
	07539	Boeing-Stearman N2S-3 Kaydet (N63590) [143]	Privately owned, Tibenham
	14286	Lockheed T-33A (51-4286)	American Air Museum, Duxford
	O-14419	Lockheed T-33A (51-4419)	Midland Air Museum, Coventry
	14863	NA AT-6D Harvard III (41-33908/ G-BGOR)	Privately owned, Goudhurst, Kent
	15154	Bell OH-58A Kiowa (70-15154)	R. Military College of Science, Shrivenham
	16445	Bell AH-1F Hueycobra (69-16445)	R. Military College of Science, Shrivenham
	16506	Hughes OH-6A Cayuse (67-16506)	The Helicopter Museum, Weston-super-Mare
	16579	Bell UH-1H Iroquois (66-16579)	The Helicopter Museum, Weston-super-Mare
	16718	Lockheed T-33A (51-6718)	City of Norwich Aviation Museum
	17962	Lockheed SR-71A (64-17962)	American Air Museum, Duxford
	18263	Boeing-Stearman PT-17 Kaydet (41-8263/N38940) [822]	Privately owned, Tibenham
	19252	Lockheed T-33A (51-9252)	Tangmere Military Aviation Museum
	20249	Noorduyn AT-16 Harvard IIB (PH-KLU) [XS-249]	Privately owned, Lelystad, The Netherlands
	21605	Bell UH-1H Iroquois (72-21605)	American Air Museum, Duxford
	21714	Grumman F8F-2P Bearcat (121714/G-RUMM) [201-B]	The Fighter Collection, Duxford
	24538	Kaman HH-43F Huskie (62-4535)	Midland Air Museum, Coventry
	24541	Cessna L-19E Bird Dog (F-GFVE)	Privately owned, Redhill
	24568	Cessna L-19E Bird Dog (LN-WNO)	Army Aviation Norway, Kjeller, Norway
	28521	CCF Harvard IV (G-TVIJ) [TA-521]	Privately owned, Woodchurch, Kent
	30861	NA TB-25J Mitchell (44-30861/ N9089Z)	Privately owned, North Weald
	31145	Piper L-4B Grasshopper (43-1145/ G-BBLH) [26-G]	Privately owned, Biggin Hill
	31171	NA B-25J Mitchell (44-31171/ N7614C)	American Air Museum, Duxford
	31952	Aeronca O-58B Defender (G-BRPR)	Privately owned, Earls Colne
	34037	NA TB-25N Mitchell (44-29366/ N9115Z/8838M)	RAF Museum, Hendon
	37414	McD F-4C Phantom (63-7414)	Midland Air Museum, Coventry
	38674	Thomas-Morse S4 Scout <R> (G-MTKM)	Privately owned, Rugby
	39624	Wag Aero Sport Trainer (G-BVMH) [39-D]	Privately owned, Lincoln
	40467	Grumman F6F-5K Hellcat (80141/ G-BTCC) [19]	The Fighter Collection, Duxford
	41386	Thomas-Morse S4 Scout <R> (G-MJTD)	Privately owned, Hitchin
	42163	NA F-100D Super Sabre (54-2163) [HE]	Dumfries & Galloway Avn Mus, Dumfries
	42165	NA F-100D Super Sabre (54-2165) [VM]	American Air Museum, Duxford

Serial	Type (other identity)	Owner/operator, location	Notes
42174	NA F-100D Super Sabre (54-2174) [UH]	Midland Air Museum, Coventry	
42196	NA F-100D Super Sabre (54-2196) [LT]	Norfolk & Suffolk Avn Museum, Flixton	
46214	Grumman TBM-3E Avenger (69327/CF-KCG) [X-3]	American Air Museum, Duxford	
46867	Grumman FM-2 Wildcat (N909WJ)	Flying A Services, North Weald	
48846	Boeing B-17G Fortress (44-8846/F-AZDX) [DS-M]	Assoc Fortresse Toujours Volant, Paris, France	
53319	Grumman TBM-3R Avenger (G-BTDP) [319-RB]	Privately owned, North Weald	
54137	CCF Harvard IV (MM54137/G-CTKL) [69]	Privately owned, North Weald	
54433	Lockheed T-33A (55-4433)	Norfolk & Suffolk Avn Museum, Flixton	
54439	Lockheed T-33A (55-4439)	North-East Aircraft Museum, Usworth	
58811	NA B-25J Mitchell (45-8811/F-AZID) [HD]	Privately owned, Athens, Greece	
60312	McD F-101F Voodoo (56-0312)	Midland Air Museum, Coventry	
60689	Boeing B-52D Stratofortress (56-0689)	American Air Museum, Duxford	
63000	NA F-100D Super Sabre (54-2212) [FW-000]	USAF Croughton, Oxon, at gate	
63319	NA F-100D Super Sabre (54-2269) [FW-319]	RAF Lakenheath, on display	
63428	Republic F-105G Thunderchief (62-4428)	USAF Croughton, Oxon, at gate	
66692	Lockheed U-2CT (56-6692)	American Air Museum, Duxford	
70270	McD F-101B Voodoo (57-270) (fuselage)	Midland Air Museum, Coventry	
80425	Grumman F7F-3P Tigercat (N7235C/G-RUMT) [WT-14]	The Fighter Collection, Duxford	
82062	DHC U-6A Beaver (58-2062)	Midland Air Museum, Coventry	
91007	Lockheed T-33A (51-8566/G-NASA) [TR-007]	De Havilland Aviation, Swansea	
91822	Republic F-105D Thunderchief (59-1822)	American Air Museum, Duxford	
92399	Goodyear FG-1D Corsair (G-CCMV) [17]	Privately owned, Duxford	
93542	CCF Harvard IV (G-BRLV) [LTA-542]	Privately owned, North Weald	
96995	CV F4U-4 Corsair (OE-EAS) [BR-37]	Tyrolean Jet Services, Innsbruck, Austria	
97264	CV F4U-4 Corsair (F-AZVJ) [403]	Flying Legend, Dijon, France	
111836	NA AT-6C Harvard IIA (41-33262/G-TSIX) [JZ-6]	The Real Aeroplane Company, Breighton	
111989	Cessna L-19A Bird Dog (51-11989/N33600)	Museum of Army Flying, Middle Wallop	
115042	NA T-6G Texan (51-15042/G-BGHU) [TA-042]	Privately owned, Headcorn	
115227	NA T-6G Texan (51-15227/G-BKRA)	Privately owned, Sandown	
115302	Piper L-18C Super Cub (51-15302/G-BJTP) [TP]	Privately owned, Bidford	
115684	Piper L-21A Super Cub (51-15684/G-BKVM) [DC]	Privately owned, North Coates	
122351	Beech C-45G (51-11665/G-BKRG)	Privately owned, Bruntingthorpe	
124143	Douglas AD-4NA Skyraider (F-AZDP) [205-RM]	Amicale J-B Salis, la Ferté-Alais, France	
124485	Boeing B-17G Fortress (44-85784/G-BEDF) [DF-A]	B-17 Preservation Ltd, Duxford	
124724	CV F4U-5NL Corsair (F-AZEG) [22]	Amicale J-B Salis, la Ferté-Alais, France	
126922	Douglas AD-4NA Skyraider (G-RAID) [402-AK]	The Fighter Collection, Duxford	
126956	Douglas AD-4NA Skyraider (F-AZDQ) [3-RM]	Aéro Retro, St Rambert d'Albon, France	
127002	Douglas AD-4NA Skyraider (F-AZHK) [618-G]	Privately owned, Cuers, France	
138179	NA T-28A Trojan (OE-ESA) [BA]	Tyrolean Jet Services, Innsbruck, Austria	
140547	NA T-28C Trojan (N2800Q)	Privately owned	
146289	NA T-28C Trojan (N99153) [2W]	Norfolk & Suffolk Aviation Museum, Flixton	
150225	WS58 Wessex 60 (G-AWOX) [123]	Privately owned, Lulsgate	

Historic Aircraft

Notes	Serial	Type (other identity)	Owner/operator, location
	151632	NA TB-25N Mitchell (44-30925/ G-BWGR)	Privately owned, Sandtoft
	155529	McD F-4S Phantom (ZE359) [AJ-114]	American Air Museum, Duxford
	155848	McD F-4S Phantom [WT-11]	Royal Scottish Mus'm of Flight, E Fortune
	159233	HS AV-8A Harrier [CG-33]	IWM North, Salford Quay
	162068	McD AV-8B Harrier II (9250M) (fuselage)	RAF Cottesmore BDRT
	162071	McD AV-8B Harrier II (fuselage)	Rolls-Royce, Filton
	162730	McD AV-8B Harrier II (fuselage)	DARA, stored St Athan
	162958	McD AV-8B Harrier II	Qinetiq, Boscombe Down
	211072	Boeing-Stearman PT-17 Kaydet (N50755)	Privately owned, Swanton Morley
	217786	Boeing-Stearman PT-17 Kaydet (41-8169/CF-EQS) [25]	American Air Museum, Duxford
	219993	Bell P-39Q Airacobra (42-19993/ N139DP)	The Fighter Collection
	226413	Republic P-47D Thunderbolt (45-49192/N47DD) [ZU-N]	American Air Museum, Duxford
	226671	Republic P-47M Thunderbolt (G-THUN) [MX-X]	The Fighter Collection, Duxford
	231983	Boeing B-17G Fortress (44-83735/ F-BDRS) [IY-G]	American Air Museum, Duxford
	234539	Fairchild PT-19B Cornell (42-34539/N50429) [63]	Privately owned, Dunkeswell
	237123	Waco CG-4A Hadrian (BAPC 157) (fuselage)	Yorkshire Air Museum, Elvington
	238410	Piper L-4A Grasshopper (42-38410/G-BHPK) [44-A]	Privately owned, Tibenham
	243809	Waco CG-4A Hadrian (BAPC 185)	Museum of Army Flying, Middle Wallop
	252983	Schweizer TG-3A (42-52983/ N66630)	American Air Museum, Duxford
	314887	Fairchild Argus III (43-14887/ G-AJPI)	Privately owned, Felthorpe
	315211	Douglas C-47A (43-15211/ N1944A) [J8-Z]	Privately owned, Booker
	315509	Douglas C-47A (43-15509/ G-BHUB) [W7-S]	American Air Museum, Duxford
	329405	Piper L-4H Grasshopper (43-29405/G-BCOB) [23-A]	Privately owned, South Walsham
	329417	Piper L-4A Grasshopper (42-38400/G-BDHK)	Privately owned, Coleford
	329471	Piper L-4H Grasshopper (43-29471/G-BGXA) [44-F]	Privately owned, Martley, Worcs
	329601	Piper L-4H Grasshopper (43-29601/G-AXHR) [44-D]	Privately owned, Nayland
	329854	Piper L-4H Grasshopper (43-29854/G-BMKC) [44-R]	Privately owned, St Just
	329934	Piper L-4H Grasshopper (43-29934/G-BCPH) [72-B]	Privately owned, White Waltham
	330238	Piper L-4H Grasshopper (43-30238/G-LIVH) [24-A]	Privately owned, Barton
	330485	Piper L-4H Grasshopper (43-30485/G-AJES) [44-C]	Privately owned, Shifnal
	343251	Boeing-Stearman N2S-5 Kaydet (43517/G-NZSS) [27]	Privately owned, Swanton Morley
	413573	NA P-51D Mustang (44-73415/ 9133M/N6526D) [B6-V]	RAF Museum, Hendon
	414151	NA P-51D Mustang (44-73140/ NL314BG) [HO-M]	Flying A Services, North Weald
	414419	NA P-51D Mustang (45-15118/ G-MSTG) [LH-F]	Privately owned, Norwich
	414450	NA P-51D Mustang (44-73877/ N167F) [B6-S]	Scandinavian Historic Flight, North Weald
	434602	Douglas A-26B Invader (44-34602/N167B) [S]	Scandinavian Historic Flight, North Weald
	435710	Douglas A-26C Invader (44-35710/ OO-INV)	Historic Invader Avn, Schiphol, The Netherlands
	442268	Noorduyn AT-16 Harvard IIB (KF568/LN-TEX) [TA-268]	Scandinavian Historic Flight, Oslo, Norway

Serial	Type (other identity)	Owner/operator, location	Notes
454467	Piper L-4J Grasshopper (45-4467/ G-BILI) [44-J]	Privately owned, White Waltham	
454537	Piper L-4J Grasshopper (45-4537/ G-BFDL) [04-J]	Privately owned, Pontefract	
461748	Boeing B-29A Superfortress (44-61748/G-BHDK) [Y]	American Air Museum, Duxford	
463209	NA P-51D Mustang <R> (BAPC 255) [WZ-S]	American Air Museum, Duxford	
463221	NA P-51D Mustang (44-73149/ G-BTCD) [E2-Z]	The Old Flying Machine Company, Duxford	
472035	NA P-51D Mustang (44-72035/ F-AZMU)	Aéro Retro, St Rambert d'Albon, France	
472216	NA P-51D Mustang (44-72216/ G-BIXL) [HO-M]	Privately owned, North Weald	
472218	CAC-18 Mustang 22 (A68-192/ G-HAEC) [WZ-I]	Privately owned, Woodchurch, Kent	
472218	NA P-51D Mustang (44-73979) [WZ-I]	Imperial War Museum, Lambeth	
472773	NA P-51D Mustang (44-72773/ G-SUSY) [QP-M]	Privately owned, Sywell	
474008	NA P-51D Mustang (44-73339/ G-SIRR) [VF-R]	Intrepid Aviation, North Weald	
474425	NA P-51D Mustang (44-74425/ NL11T) [OC-G]	Dutch Mustang Flt, Lelystad, The Netherlands	
474832	NA P-51D Mustang (44-74506/ F-AZJJ) [GA-N]	Air B Aviation, Annemasse, France	
474923	NA P-51D Mustang (44-74923/ N6395)	Privately owned, Lelystad, The Netherlands	
479744	Piper L-4H Grasshopper (44-79744/G-BGPD) [49-M]	Privately owned, Marsh, Bucks	
479766	Piper L-4H Grasshopper (44-79766/G-BKHG) [63-D]	Privately owned, Goldcliff, Gwent	
480015	Piper L-4H Grasshopper (44-80015/G-AKIB) [44-M]	Privately owned, Bodmin	
480133	Piper L-4J Grasshopper (44-80133/G-BDCD) [44-B]	Privately owned, Slinfold	
480321	Piper L-4J Grasshopper (44-80321/G-FRAN) [44-H]	Privately owned, Rayne, Essex	
480480	Piper L-4J Grasshopper (44-80480/G-BECN) [44-E]	Privately owned, Kersey, Suffolk	
480551	Piper L-4J Grasshopper (44-80551/LN-KLT) [43-S]	Scandinavian Historic Flight, Oslo, Norway	
480636	Piper L-4J Grasshopper (44-80636/G-AXHP) [58-A]	Privately owned, Southend	
480723	Piper L-4J Grasshopper (44-80723/G-BFZB)	Privately owned, Egginton	
480752	Piper L-4J Grasshopper (44-80752/G-BCXJ) [39-E]	Privately owned, Old Sarum	
483868	Boeing B-17G Fortress (44-83868/N5237V) [A-N]	RAF Museum, Hendon	
486893	NA B-25J Mitchell (N6123C)	Tyrolean Jet Services, Innsbruck, Austria	
493209	NA T-6G Texan (49-3209/ G-DDMV/41)	Privately owned, Duxford	
511701A	Beech C-45H (51-11701/G-BSZC) [AF258]	Privately owned, Bryngwyn Bach	
607327	PA-18 Super Cub 95 (G-ARAO) [09-L]	Privately owned, Denham	
2106449	NA P-51C Mustang (43-25147/ N51PR/G-PSIC) [HO-W]	The Fighter Collection, Duxford	
2-134	NA T-6G Texan (114700)	Privately owned, North Weald	
3-1923	Aeronca O-58B Defender (43-1923/G-BRHP)	Privately owned, Chiseldon	
18-2001	Piper L-18C Super Cub (52-2401/G-BIZV)	Privately owned, Oxenhope	
39-139	Beech YC-43 Traveler (N295BS)	Dukes of Brabant AF, Eindhoven, The Netherlands	
40-1766	Boeing-Stearman PT-17 Kaydet	Privately owned, Swanton Morley	
41-33275	NA AT-6C Texan (G-BICE) [CE]	Privately owned, Ipswich	
42-12417	Noorduyn AT-16 Harvard IIB (Klu. B-163)	Northants Aviation Mus'm, Harrington, Northants	
42-40557	Consolidated B-24D Liberator <ff>	American Air Museum, Duxford	

Historic Aircraft

Notes	Serial	Type (other identity)	Owner/operator, location
	42-58678	Taylorcraft DF-65 (G-BRIY) [IY]	Privately owned, North Weald
	42-78044	Aeronca 11AC Chief (G-BRXL)	Privately owned, High Cross, Herts
	42-84555	NA AT-6D Harvard III (FAP.1662/ G-ELMH) [EP-H]	Privately owned, Hardwick, Norfolk
	42-93510	Douglas C-47A Skytrain [CM] <ff>	Privately owned, Kew
	43-9628	Douglas A-20G Havoc <ff>	Privately owned, Hinckley, Leics
	44-13954	NA P-51D Mustang	Privately owned, Coventry
	44-14574	NA P-51D Mustang (fuselage)	East Essex Aviation Museum, Clacton
	44-51228	Consolidated B-24M Liberator [RE-N]	American Air Museum, Duxford
	44-79609	Piper L-4H Grasshopper (G-BHXY) [PR]	Privately owned, Bodmin
	44-80594	Piper L-4J Grasshopper (G-BEDJ)	Privately owned, White Waltham
	44-80647	Piper L-4J Grasshopper (D-EGAF)	The Vintage Aircraft Co, Fürstenwalde, Germany
	44-83184	Fairchild UC-61K Argus III (G-RGUS)	Privately owned, Sturgate, Lincs
	51-9036	Lockheed T-33A	Newark Air Museum, Winthorpe
	54-223	NA F-100D Super Sabre (54-2223)	Newark Air Museum, Winthorpe
	54-2447	Piper L-21B Super Cub (G-SCUB)	Privately owned, Anwick
	63-699	McD F-4C Phantom (63-7699) [CG]	Midland Air Museum, Coventry
	64-17657	Douglas A-26A Invader (N99218) <ff>	Tower Museum, Ludham, Norfolk
	65-777	McD F-4C Phantom (63-7419) [LN]	RAF Lakenheath, on display
	67-120	GD F-111E Aardvark (67-0120) [UH]	American Air Museum, Duxford
	68-0060	GD F-111E Aardvark <ff>	Dumfries & Galloway Avn Mus, Dumfries
	72-1447	GD F-111F Aardvark <ff>	American Air Museum, Duxford
	72-448	GD F-111E Aardvark (68-0011) [LN]	RAF Lakenheath, on display
	76-020	McD F-15A Eagle (76-0020) [BT]	American Air Museum, Duxford
	76-124	McD F-15B Eagle (76-0124) [LN]	RAF Lakenheath, instructional use
	77-259	Fairchild A-10A Thunderbolt (77-0259) [AR]	American Air Museum, Duxford
	80-219	Fairchild GA-10A Thunderbolt (80-0219) [AR]	RAF Alconbury, on display
	92-048	McD F-15A Eagle (74-0131) [LN]	RAF Lakenheath, on display
	146-11042	Wolf WII <R> (G-BMZX) [7]	Privately owned, Haverfordwest
	146-11083	Wolf WII <R> (G-BNAI) [5]	Privately owned, Haverfordwest
	998-8888	Bell UH-1H Iroquois (Arg. AE-406)	Museum of Army Flying, Middle Wallop
	H-57	Piper L-4A Grasshopper (42-36375/G-AKAZ)	Privately owned, Duxford

YUGOSLAVIA

Notes	Serial	Type (other identity)	Owner/operator, location
	23170	Soko G-2A Galeb (YU-YAB)	Privately owned, Biggin Hill
	23187	Soko G-2A Galeb (YU-YAD)	Privately owned, Biggin Hill
	23194	Soko G-2A Galeb (YU-YAG)	Privately owned, Biggin Hill
	23196	Soko G-2A Galeb (YU-YAC)	Privately owned, Biggin Hill
	30139	Soko P-2 Kraguj [139]	Privately owned, Biggin Hill
	30140	Soko P-2 Kraguj (G-RADA) [140]	Privately owned, Biggin Hill
	30146	Soko P-2 Kraguj (G-BSXD) [146]	Privately owned, Elstree
	30149	Soko P-2 Kraguj (G-SOKO) [149]	Privately owned, Liverpool
	30151	Soko P-2 Kraguj [151]	Privately owned, North Gorley, Hants
	51182	UTVA-66 (YU-DMN)	Privately owned, Biggin Hill
	51183	UTVA-66 (YU-DMT)	Privately owned, Biggin Hill

Former Botswana Defence Force Strikemaster OJ4 is now flown from Duxford. *PRM*

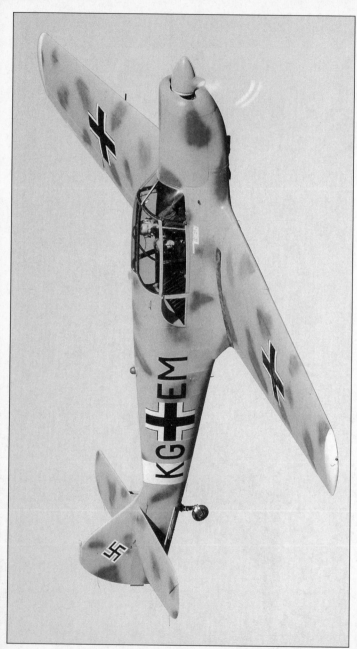

Painted to represent a Messerschmitt Bf108 this Nord 1002 G-ETME is based at White Waltham. *PRM*

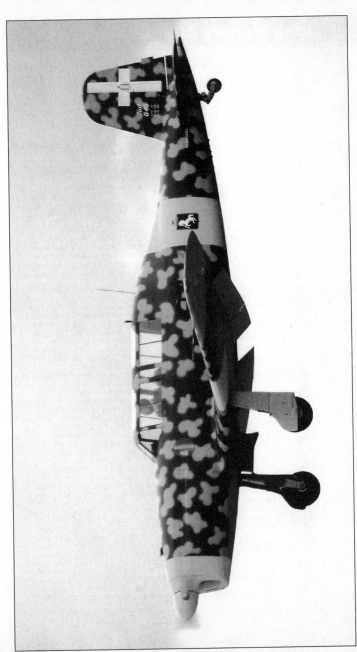

Rare Italian Fiat G46-3B G-BBII retains its original markings and serial MM52801. *PRM*

Notes	Serial	Type (other identity)	Owner/operator, location
	34	Miles M14A Magister (N5392)	IAC Engineering Wing stored, Baldonnel
	141	Avro 652A Anson C19	IAC Engineering Wing stored, Baldonnel
	164	DHC1 Chipmunk T20	IAC Engineering Wing stored, Baldonnel
	168	DHC1 Chipmunk T20	IAC No 2 Support Wing, Gormanston
	172	DHC1 Chipmunk T20	IAC Training Wing stored, Gormanston
	173	DHC1 Chipmunk T20	South East Aviation Enthusiasts, Waterford
	176	DH104 Dove 4 (VP-YKF)	Privately owned, Baldonnel
	177	Percival P56 Provost T51 (G-BLIW)	Privately owned, Shoreham
	183	Percival P56 Provost T51	IAC Engineering Wing stored, Baldonnel
	184	Percival P56 Provost T51	South East Aviation Enthusiasts, Waterford
	187	DH115 Vampire T55	South East Aviation Enthusiasts, Waterford
	189	Percival P56 Provost T51 (comp XF846)	IAC Baldonnel Fire Section
	191	DH115 Vampire T55	IAC Museum, Baldonnel
	192	DH115 Vampire T55	South East Aviation Enthusiasts, Waterford
	193	DH115 Vampire T55	IAC Baldonnel Fire Section
	195	Sud SA316 Alouette III	IAC No 3 Support Wing, Baldonnel
	196	Sud SA316 Alouette III	IAC No 3 Support Wing, Baldonnel
	197	Sud SA316 Alouette III	IAC No 3 Support Wing, Baldonnel
	198	DH115 Vampire T11 (XE977)	IAC Engineering Wing stored, Baldonnel
	199	DHC1 Chipmunk T22	IAC Engineering Wing stored, Baldonnel
	203	Reims-Cessna FR172H	IAC No 2 Support Wing, Gormanston
	205	Reims-Cessna FR172H	IAC No 2 Support Wing, Gormanston
	206	Reims-Cessna FR172H	IAC No 2 Support Wing, Gormanston
	207	Reims-Cessna FR172H	IAC Engineering Wing stored, Waterford
	208	Reims-Cessna FR172H	IAC No 2 Support Wing, Gormanston
	210	Reims-Cessna FR172H	IAC No 2 Support Wing, Gormanston
	211	Sud SA316 Alouette III	IAC No 3 Support Wing, Baldonnel
	212	Sud SA316 Alouette III	IAC No 3 Support Wing, Baldonnel
	213	Sud SA316 Alouette III	IAC No 3 Support Wing, Baldonnel
	214	Sud SA316 Alouette III	IAC No 3 Support Wing, Baldonnel
	215	Fouga CM170 Super Magister	IAC, stored Baldonnel
	216	Fouga CM170 Super Magister	IAC Engineering Wing, Baldonnel
	217	Fouga CM170 Super Magister	IAC, stored Baldonnel
	218	Fouga CM170 Super Magister	IAC, stored Baldonnel
	219	Fouga CM170 Super Magister	IAC, stored Baldonnel
	220	Fouga CM170 Super Magister	Carlow Institute of Technology, instructional use
	222	SIAI SF-260WE Warrior	IAC Training Wing, Baldonnel
	225	SIAI SF-260WE Warrior	IAC Training Wing, Baldonnel
	226	SIAI SF-260WE Warrior	IAC Training Wing, Baldonnel
	227	SIAI SF-260WE Warrior	IAC Training Wing, Baldonnel
	229	SIAI SF-260WE Warrior	IAC Training Wing, Baldonnel
	230	SIAI SF-260WE Warrior	IAC Training Wing, Baldonnel
	231	SIAI SF-260WE Warrior	IAC Training Wing, Baldonnel
	237	Aérospatiale SA342L Gazelle	IAC No 3 Support Wing, Baldonnel
	240	Beech Super King Air 200MR	IAC No 1 Support Wing, Baldonnel
	241	Aérospatiale SA342L Gazelle	IAC No 3 Support Wing, Baldonnel
	243	Reims-Cessna FR172K	IAC No 2 Support Wing, Gormanston
	244	Aérospatiale SA365F Dauphin II	IAC No 3 Support Wing, Baldonnel
	245	Aérospatiale SA365F Dauphin II	IAC No 3 Support Wing, Baldonnel
	246	Aérospatiale SA365F Dauphin II	IAC No 3 Support Wing, Baldonnel
	247	Aérospatiale SA365F Dauphin II	IAC No 3 Support Wing, Baldonnel
	251	Grumman G1159C Gulfstream IV	IAC No 1 Support Wing, Baldonnel
	252	Airtech CN.235 MPA Persuader	IAC No 1 Support Wing, Baldonnel
	253	Airtech CN.235 MPA Persuader	IAC No 1 Support Wing, Baldonnel
	254	PBN-2T Defender 4000 (G-BWPN)	Garda Air Support Unit, Baldonnel
	255	AS355N Twin Squirrel (G-BXEV)	Garda Air Support Unit, Baldonnel
	256	Eurocopter EC135T-1	Garda Air Support Unit, Baldonnel

Overseas Military Aircraft Markings

Aircraft included in this section are a selection of those likely to be seen visiting UK civil and military airfields on transport flights, exchange visits, exercises and for air shows. It is not a comprehensive list of *all* aircraft operated by the air arms concerned.

ALGERIA
Force Aérienne Algérienne/
Al Quwwat al Jawwiya al
Jaza'eriya
Lockheed C-130H
Hercules

7T-WHE	(4935)
7T-WHF	(4934)
7T-WHI	(4930)
7T-WHJ	(4928)
7T-WHQ	(4926)
7T-WHR	(4924)
7T-WHS	(4912)
7T-WHT	(4911)
7T-WHY	(4913)
7T-WHZ	(4914)

Lockheed C-130H-30
Hercules

7T-WHA	(4997)
7T-WHB	(5224)
7T-WHD	(4987)
7T-WHL	(4989)
7T-WHM	(4919)
7T-WHN	(4894)
7T-WHO	(4897)
7T-WHP	(4921)

Grumman
G.1159A Gulfstream III/
G.1159C Gulfstream IV/
G.1159C Gulfstream IVSP
Ministry of Defence, Boufarik

7T-VPC	(1418)
	Gulfstream IV
7T-VPM	(1421)
	Gulfstream IV
7T-VPR	(1288)
	Gulfstream IVSP
7T-VPS	(1291)
	Gulfstream IVSP
7T-VRD	(399)
	Gulfstream III

Gulfstream Aerospace
Gulfstream V
Ministry of Defence, Boufarik
7T-VPG (617)

AUSTRALIA
Royal Australian Air Force
Boeing 707-338C/368C*
33 Sqn, Amberley
A20-261*
A20-623
A20-624
A20-629

Canadair CL.604
Challenger
34 Sqn, Canberra
A37-001
A37-002
A37-003

Dassault Falcon 900
34 Sqn, Canberra
A26-070
A26-073
A26-074
A26-076
A26-077

Lockheed C-130H Hercules
36 Sqn, Richmond, NSW
A97-001
A97-002
A97-003
A97-004
A97-005
A97-006
A97-007
A97-008
A97-009
A97-010
A97-011
A97-012

Lockheed C-130J-30
Hercules
37 Sqn, Richmond, NSW
A97-440
A97-441
A97-442
A97-447
A97-448
A97-449
A97-450
A97-464
A97-465
A97-466
A97-467
A97-468

Lockheed P-3C Orion
10/11 Sqns, Maritime Patrol
Group, Edinburgh, NSW

A9-656	10 Sqn
A9-657	11 Sqn
A9-658	10 Sqn
A9-659	11 Sqn
A9-660	11 Sqn
A9-661	10 Sqn
A9-662	11 Sqn
A9-663	11 Sqn
A9-664	11 Sqn
A9-665	10 Sqn
A9-751	11 Sqn
A9-752	10 Sqn
A9-753	10 Sqn
A9-755	11 Sqn
A9-756	11 Sqn
A9-757	10 Sqn
A9-758	10 Sqn
A9-759	10 Sqn
A9-760	10 Sqn

AUSTRIA
Oesterreichische
Luftstreitkräfte
Airtech CN.235-300
Fliegerregiment I
Flachenstaffel, Tulln
6T-AA

SAAB 35ÖE Draken
Fliegerregiment II
1 Staffel/Uberwg, Zeltweg;
2 Staffel/Uberwg, Graz

01	(351401)	1 Staffel
02	(351402)	1 Staffel
03	(351403)	1 Staffel
04	(351404)	1 Staffel
05	(351405)	1 Staffel
06	(351406)	1 Staffel
07	(351407)	1 Staffel
08	(351408)	1 Staffel
09	(351409)	1 Staffel
10	(351410)	1 Staffel
11	(351411)	1 Staffel
12	(351412)	1 Staffel
13	(351413)	2 Staffel
14	(351414)	2 Staffel
15	(351415)	2 Staffel
16	(351416)	2 Staffel
18	(351418)	2 Staffel
19	(351419)	2 Staffel
20	(351420)	2 Staffel
21	(351421)	2 Staffel
22	(351422)	2 Staffel
23	(351423)	2 Staffel
24	(351424)	2 Staffel

SAAB 105ÖE
Dusenstastaffel, Linz
(yellow)

B	(105402)
D	(105404)
E	(105405)
F	(105406)
G	(105407)
I	(105409)
J	(105410)

(green)

A	(105411)
B	(105412)
D	(105414)
GF-16	(105416)
GG-17	(105417)

(red)

B	(105422)
C	(105423)
D	(105424)

E	(105425)
F	(105426)
G	(105427)
H	(105428)
I	(105429)
J	(105430)
(blue)	
A	(105431)
B	(105432)
C	(105433)
D	(105434)
E	(105435)
F	(105436)
G	(105437)
I	(105439)
J	(105440)

Short SC7 Skyvan 3M
Fliegerregiment I
  Flachenstaffel, Tulln
5S-TA
5S-TB

BAHRAIN
BAE RJ.100
Bahrain Defence Force
A9C-BDF1

Boeing 747SP-21
Bahrain Amiri Flt
A9C-HHH

Grumman
G.1159 Gulfstream IITT/
G.1159C Gulfstream IV
Govt of Bahrain
A9C-BAH Gulfstream IV
A9C-BG   Gulfstream IITT

BELGIUM
Force Aérienne Belge/
  Belgische Luchtmacht
  D-BD Alpha Jet E
  7/11 Smaldeel (1 Wg),
    Bevekom
AT-01
AT-02
AT-03
AT-05
AT-06
AT-08
AT-10
AT-11
AT-12
AT-13
AT-14
AT-15
AT-17
AT-18
AT-19
AT-20
AT-21
AT-22
AT-23
AT-24
AT-25
AT-26
AT-27
AT-28
AT-29
AT-30
AT-31
AT-32
AT-33

Airbus A.310-322
21 Smaldeel (15 Wg),
  Melsbroek
CA-01
CA-02

Dassault Falcon 900B
21 Smaldeel (15 Wg),
  Melsbroek
CD-01 VERJ 145LR

Embraer ERJ.135/
ERJ.145LR*
21 Smaldeel (15 Wg),
  Melsbroek
CE-01
CE-02
CE-03*
CE-04*

Swearingen Merlin IIIA
21 Smaldeel (15 Wg),
  Melsbroek
CF-04

Lockheed C-130H Hercules
20 Smaldeel (15 Wg),
  Melsbroek
CH-01
CH-02
CH-03
CH-04
CH-05
CH-07
CH-08
CH-09
CH-10
CH-11
CH-12

Dassault Falcon 20E
21 Smaldeel (15 Wg),
  Melsbroek
CM-01
CM-02

Hawker-Siddeley
HS748 Srs 2A
21 Smaldeel (15 Wg),
  Melsbroek
CS-01
CS-02

General Dynamics F-16
(MLU aircraft are marked
with a *)
1,2,350 Smaldeel (2 Wg),
  Florennes [FS];
23,31,349 Smaldeel, OCU
  (10 Wg), Kleine-Brogel
  [BL]

FA-27	F-16A*	2 Wg
FA-46	F-16A	2 Wg
FA-47	F-16A	2 Wg
FA-48	F-16A*	2 Wg
FA-49	F-16A(R)	2 Wg
FA-50	F-16A*	2 Wg
FA-53	F-16A(R)	2 Wg
FA-55	F-16A*	2 Wg
FA-56	F-16A*	10 Wg
FA-57	F-16A*	10 Wg
FA-58	F-16A*	2 Wg
FA-60	F-16A*	10 Wg
FA-61	F-16A*	10 Wg

FA-65	F-16A*	10 Wg
FA-66	F-16A*	2 Wg
FA-67	F-16A*	2 Wg
FA-68	F-16A	2 Sm
FA-69	F-16A	31 Sm
FA-70	F-16A*	10 Wg
FA-71	F-16A*	2 Wg
FA-72	F-16A*	2 Wg
FA-73	F-16A*	10 Wg
FA-74	F-16A*	10 Wg
FA-75	F-16A*	2 Wg
FA-76	F-16A*	10 Wg
FA-77	F-16A*	10 Wg
FA-78	F-16A*	10 Wg
FA-81	F-16A*	10 Wg
FA-82	F-16A*	10 Wg
FA-83	F-16A*	2 Wg
FA-84	F-16A*	2 Wg
FA-86	F-16A*	10 Wg
FA-87	F-16A*	2 Wg
FA-88	F-16A*	2 Wg
FA-89	F-16A*	2 Wg
FA-90	F-16A*	10 Wg
FA-91	F-16A*	10 Wg
FA-92	F-16A*	2 Wg
FA-93	F-16A*	10 Wg
FA-94	F-16A*	10 Wg
FA-95	F-16A*	10 Wg
FA-97	F-16A*	2 Wg
FA-98	F-16A*	10 Wg
FA-99	F-16A*	10 Wg
FA-100	F-16A*	10 Wg
FA-101	F-16A*	10 Wg
FA-102	F-16A*	2 Wg
FA-103	F-16A	349 Sm
FA-104	F-16A*	2 Wg
FA-106	F-16A*	10 Wg
FA-107	F-16A	2 Wg
FA-108	F-16A*	2 Wg
FA-109	F-16A	2 Wg
FA-110	F-16A*	2 Wg
FA-111	F-16A	10 Wg
FA-112	F-16A*	10 Wg
FA-114	F-16A	10 Wg
FA-115	F-16A*	2 Wg
FA-116	F-16A*	10 Wg
FA-117	F-16A*	10 Wg
FA-118	F-16A	2 Sm
FA-119	F-16A*	2 Wg
FA-120	F-16A*	10 Wg
FA-121	F-16A	2 Wg
FA-122	F-16A*	10 Wg
FA-123	F-16A*	10 Wg
FA-124	F-16A*	10 Wg
FA-125	F-16A	2 Wg
FA-126	F-16A*	10 Wg
FA-127	F-16A	2 Wg
FA-128	F-16A	2 Wg
FA-129	F-16A	2 Wg
FA-130	F-16A	2 Wg
FA-131	F-16A(R)	2 Wg
FA-132	F-16A	2 Wg
FA-133	F-16A	2 Wg
FA-134	F-16A	2 Wg
FA-135	F-16A	10 Wg
FA-136	F-16A*	10 Wg
FB-01	F-16B	2 Wg
FB-02	F-16B	OCU
FB-04	F-16B*	2 Wg
FB-05	F-16B	2 Wg
FB-07	F-16B*	10 Wg
FB-08	F-16B*	10 Wg
FB-09	F-16B	2 Wg
FB-10	F-16B	10 Wg

FB-12	F-16B	2 Wg
FB-14	F-16B*	10 Wg
FB-15	F-16B*	OCU
FB-17	F-16B*	OCU
FB-18	F-16B*	10 Wg
FB-19	F-16B*	10 Wg
FB-20	F-16B*	2 Wg
FB-21	F-16B*	2 Wg
FB-22	F-16B*	OCU
FB-23	F-16B	10 Wg
FB-24	F-16B*	OCU

Fouga CM170 Magister
Fouga Flight/7 Smaldeel
(1 Wg), Bevekom
MT-04
MT-13
MT-14
MT-26
MT-34
MT-35
MT-40
MT-44
MT-48

**Westland Sea King
Mk48/48A***
40 Smaldeel, Koksijde
RS-01
RS-02
RS-03*
RS-04
RS-05

**SIAI Marchetti
SF260MB/SF260D***
Ecole de Pilotage
Elementaire (5 Sm/1 Wg),
Bevekom
ST-02
ST-03
ST-04
ST-06
ST-12
ST-15
ST-16
ST-17
ST-18
ST-19
ST-20
ST-22
ST-23
ST-24
ST-25
ST-26
ST-27
ST-30
ST-31
ST-32
ST-34
ST-35
ST-36
ST-40*
ST-41*
ST-42*
ST-43*
ST-44*
ST-45*
ST-46*
ST-47*
ST-48*

**Aviation Légère de la
Force Terrestre/**

**Belgische Landmacht
Sud SA318C/SE3130***
Alouette II
16 BnHLn, Bierset;
SLV, Brasschaat

A-22*	16 BnHLn
A-37*	16 BnHLn
A-40	SLV
A-41	SLV
A-43	SLV
A-44	SLV
A-46	SLV
A-47	16 BnHLn
A-49	16 BnHLn
A-50	16 BnHLn
A-53	16 BnHLn
A-54	SLV
A-55	SLV
A-57	SLV
A-59	16 BnHLn
A-61	SLV
A-62	16 BnHLn
A-64	SLV
A-65	SLV
A-66	SLV
A-68	16 BnHLn
A-69	16 BnHLn
A-70	SLV
A-72	SLV
A-73	16 BnHLn
A-74	SLV
A-75	16 BnHLn
A-77	16 BnHLn
A-78	16 BnHLn
A-79	SLV
A-80	16 BnHLn

**Britten-Norman
BN-2A/BN-2B-21* Islander**
16 BnHLn, Bierset;
SLV, Brasschaat

B-01	LA	16 BnHLn
B-02*	LB	SLV
B-03*	LC	16 BnHLn
B-04*	LD	SLV
B-07*	LG	16 BnHLn
B-08*	LH	16 BnHLn
B-09*	LI	16 BnHLn
B-10*	LJ	16 BnHLn
B-11*	LK	SLV
B-12	LL	SLV

Agusta A109HA/HO*
17 BnHATk, Bierset;
18 BnHATk, Bierset;
SLV, Brasschaat

H-01*	SLV
H-02*	SLV
H-03*	SLV
H-04*	SLV
H-05*	17 BnHATk
H-06*	17 BnHATk
H-07*	17 BnHATk
H-08*	18 BnHATk
H-09*	18 BnHATk
H-10*	18 BnHATk
H-11*	SLV
H-12*	SLV
H-13*	SLV
H-14*	SLV
H-15*	SLV
H-16*	18 BnHATk
H-17*	17 BnHATk
H-18*	18 BnHATk

H-20	18 BnHATk
H-21	18 BnHATk
H-22	17 BnHATk
H-23	18 BnHATk
H-24	17 BnHATk
H-25	18 BnHATk
H-26	18 BnHATk
H-27	18 BnHATk
H-28	18 BnHATk
H-29	18 BnHATk
H-30	17 BnHATk
H-31	18 BnHATk
H-32	18 BnHATk
H-33	18 BnHATk
H-34	17 BnHATk
H-35	18 BnHATk
H-36	17 BnHATk
H-37	17 BnHATk
H-38	17 BnHATk
H-39	18 BnHATk
H-40	SLV
H-41	17 BnHATk
H-42	17 BnHATk
H-43	17 BnHATk
H-44	17 BnHATk
H-45	17 BnHATk
H-46	17 BnHATk

**Force Navale Belge/Belgische
Zeemacht
Sud SA316B Alouette III**
Koksijde Heli Flight

M-1	(OT-ZPA)
M-2	(OT-ZPB)
M-3	(OT-ZPC)

**Gendarmerie/Rijkswacht
Cessna 182 Skylane**
Luchsteundetachment,
Melsbroek

G-01	C.182Q
G-03	C.182R
G-04	C.182R

MDH MD.520N
Luchsteundetachment,
Melsbroek
G-14
G-15

MDH MD.900 Explorer
Luchsteundetachment,
Melsbroek
G-10
G-11
G-12

**BOTSWANA
Botswana Defence Force
Grumman G.1159C
Gulfstream IV**
OK-1

Lockheed C-130B Hercules
OM-1
OM-2
OM-3

**BRAZIL
Força Aérea Brasileira
Boeing KC-137**
2º GT 2º Esq, Galeão
2401
2402

2403
2404

Lockheed C-130E Hercules
1° GT, 1° Esq, Galeão;
1° GTT, 1° Esq, Afonsos

2451	C-130E	1° GTT
2453	C-130E	1° GTT
2454	C-130E	1° GTT
2456	C-130E	1° GTT
2458	SC-130E	1° GT
2459	SC-130E	1° GT
2461	KC-130H	1° GT
2462	KC-130H	1° GT
2463	C-130H	1° GT
2464	C-130H	1° GT
2465	C-130H	1° GT
2467	C-130H	1° GT

BRUNEI
Airbus A.340
Brunei Govt, Bandar Seri
Bergawan
V8-BKH   A.340-212

Boeing 747-430
Brunei Govt, Bandar Seri
Bergawan
V8-ALI

Boeing 767-27GER
Brunei Govt, Bandar Seri
Bergawan
V8-MHB

**Gulfstream Aerospace
Gulfstream V**
Brunei Govt, Bandar Seri
Bergawan
V8-007

BULGARIA
**Bulgarsky Voenno-
Vazdushni Sily**
Antonov An-30
16 TAP, Sofia/Dobroslavtzi
055

Bulgarian Govt
Dassault Falcon 2000
Bulgarian Govt, Sofia
LZ-OOI

Tupolev Tu-134A-3
Bulgarian Govt, Sofia
LZ-TUG

Tupolev Tu-154M
Bulgarian Govt, Sofia
LZ-BTQ
LZ-BTZ

BURKINA FASO
Boeing 727-14
Govt of Burkina Faso,
Ouagadougou
XT-BBE

CAMEROON
**Grumman
G.1159A Gulfstream III**
Govt of Cameroon, Yaounde
TJ-AAW

CANADA
Canadian Forces
**Lockheed CC-130
Hercules CC-130E/
CC-130E(SAR)***
413 Sqn, Greenwood (SAR)
(14 Wing);
424 Sqn, Trenton (SAR)
(8 Wing);
426 Sqn, Trenton (8 Wing);
429 Sqn, Trenton (8 Wing);
435 Sqn, Winnipeg (17 Wing);
436 Sqn, Trenton (8 Wing)

130305*	8 Wing
130306*	14 Wing
130307	8 Wing
130308*	8 Wing
130310*	8 Wing
130311*	14 Wing
130313	8 Wing
130314*	14 Wing
130315*	14 Wing
130316	8 Wing
130317	8 Wing
130319	8 Wing
130320	8 Wing
130323	8 Wing
130324*	8 Wing
130325	8 Wing
130326	8 Wing
130327	8 Wing
130328	8 Wing

CC-130H/CC-130H(T)*
130332	17 Wing
130333	17 Wing
130334	8 Wing
130335	8 Wing
130336	17 Wing
130337	8 Wing
130338*	17 Wing
130339*	17 Wing
130340*	17 Wing
130341*	17 Wing
130342*	17 Wing

CC-130H-30
| 130343 | 8 Wing |
| 130344 | 8 Wing |

**Lockheed CP-140 Aurora/
CP-140A Arcturus***
404/405/415 Sqns,
Greenwood (14 Wing);
407 Sqn, Comox (19 Wing)

140101	14 Wing
140102	14 Wing
140103	14 Wing
140104	14 Wing
140105	14 Wing
140106	14 Wing
140107	14 Wing
140108	14 Wing
140109	407 Sqn
140110	14 Wing
140111	14 Wing
140112	14 Wing
140113	14 Wing
140114	14 Wing
140115	14 Wing
140116	407 Sqn
140117	14 Wing
140118	407 Sqn
140119*	14 Wing
140120*	14 Wing
140121*	14 Wing

**De Havilland Canada
CT-142**
402 Sqn, Winnipeg
(17 Wing)
142803	CT-142
142804	CT-142
142805	CT-142
142806	CT-142

**Canadair CC-144
Challenger**
412 Sqn, Ottawa (8 Wing)
144601	CC-144A
144602	CC-144A
144604	CC-144A
144614	CC-144B
144615	CC-144B
144616	CC-144B

**Airbus CC-150 Polaris
(A310-304/A310-304F*)**
437 Sqn, Trenton (8 Wing)
15001	216
15002*	212
15003*	202
15004*	205
15005*	204

CHILE
Fuerza Aérea de Chile
Boeing 707
Grupo 10, Santiago
902	707-351C
903	707-330B
904	707-358C

Boeing 737
Grupo 10, Santiago
| 921 | 737-58N |
| 922 | 737-330 |

Extra EA-300
Los Halcones
021	[6]
022	[7]
024	[2]
025	[3]
027	[4]
028	[5]
029	[1]

**Lockheed C-130B/H
Hercules**
Grupo 10, Santiago
994	C-130B
995	C-130H
996	C-130H
997	C-130B
998	C-130B

CROATIA
Canadair CL.601 Challenger
Croatian Govt, Zagreb
9A-CRO
9A-CRT

CZECH REPUBLIC
Ceske Vojenske Letectvo
Aero L-39/L-59 Albatros
42 slt/4 zTL, Cáslav;
321 tpzlt & 322 tlt/32 zTL,
Náměšt;
341 vlt/34 zSL, Pardubice;
LZO, Praha/Kbely

0001	L-39MS	LZO
0004	L-39MS	LZO
0005	L-39MS	LZO
0103	L-39C	341 vlt/34 zSL
0105	L-39C	341 vlt/34 zSL
0106	L-39C	341 vlt/34 zSL
0107	L-39C	341 vlt/34 zSL
0108	L-39C	341 vlt/34 zSL
0113	L-39C	341 vlt/34 zSL
0115	L-39C	341 vlt/34 zSL
0440	L-39C	341 vlt/34 zSL
0441	L-39C	341 vlt/34 zSL
0444	L-39C	341 vlt/34 zSL
0445	L-39C	341 vlt/34 zSL
0448	L-39C	341 vlt/34 zSL
2341	L-39ZA	42 slt/4 zTL
2344	L-39ZA	42 slt/4 zTL
2347	L-39ZA	42 slt/4 zTL
2350	L-39ZA	42 slt/4 zTL
2415	L-39ZA	42 slt/4 zTL
2418	L-39ZA	42 slt/4 zTL
2421	L-39ZA	42 slt/4 zTL
2424	L-39ZA	32 zTL
2427	L-39ZA	42 slt/4 zTL
2430	L-39ZA	42 slt/4 zTL
2433	L-39ZA	42 slt/4 zTL
2436	L-39ZA	42 slt/4 zTL
3903	L-39ZA	32 zTL
4605	L-39C	341 vlt/34 zSL
4606	L-39C	341 vlt/34 zSL
5013	L-39ZA	32 zTL
5015	L-39ZA	32 zTL
5017	L-39ZA	32 zTL
5019	L-39ZA	32 zTL

Aero L-159 ALCA/L-159T*
4 zTL, Cáslav;
LZO, Praha/Kbely

5831*	LZO
5832	LZO
6001	4 zTL
6002	4 zTL
6003	4 zTL
6004	4 zTL
6005	4 zTL
6006	4 zTL
6007	4 zTL
6008	4 zTL
6009	4 zTL
6010	4 zTL
6011	4 zTL
6012	4 zTL
6013	
6014	
6015	
6016	
6017	
6018	
6019	
6020	
6021	
6022	
6023	
6024	
6025	
6026	
6027	
6028	

Antonov An-24V
1 dlt/6 zDL, Praha/Kbely
7109
7110

**Antonov An-26/
An-26Z-1M***
1 dlt/6 zDL, Praha/Kbely
2408
2409
2507
3209*
4201

Antonov An-30FG
344 pzdlt/34 zSL, Pardubice
1107

**Canadair CL.601-3A
Challenger**
1 dlt/6 zDL, Praha/Kbely
5105

Let 410 Turbolet
1 dlt/6 zDL, Praha/Kbely;
344 pzdlt/34 zSL, Pardubice

0503	L-410MA	344 pzdlt/34 zSL
0712	L-410UVP-S	344 pzdlt/34 zSL
0731	L-410UVP	1 dlt/6 zDL
0926	L-410UVP-T	1 dlt/6 zDL [4]
0928	L-410UVP-T	1 dlt/6 zDL
0929	L-410UVP-T	1 dlt/6 zDL [2]
1132	L-410UVP-T	1 dlt/6 zDL [3]
1134	L-410UVP	1 dlt/6 zDL
1504	L-410UVP	1 dlt/6 zDL
1523	L-410FG	344 pzdlt/34 zSL
1525	L-410FG	344 pzdlt/34 zSL
1526	L-410FG	344 pzdlt/34 zSL
2312	L-410UVP-E	1 dlt/6 zDL
2601	L-410UVP-E	1 dlt/6 zDL
2602	L-410UVP-E	1 dlt/6 zDL
2710	L-410UVP-E	1 dlt/6 zDL

Let 610M
1 dlt/6 zDL, Praha/Kbely;
LZO, Praha/Kbely

0003	1 dlt/6 zDL	
0005	LZO	

**Mikoyan MiG-21MF/
MiG-21UM***
42 slt/4 zTL, Cáslav;
LZO, Ceske Budejovice

2205	42 slt/4 zTL
2500	42 slt/4 zTL
2614	42 slt/4 zTL
3186*	42 slt/4 zTL
3746*	42 slt/4 zTL
4017	42 slt/4 zTL
4175	42 slt/4 zTL
4307	LZO
5031*	42 slt/4 zTL
5201	42 slt/4 zTL

5203	LZO
5210	42 slt/4 zTL
5212	42 slt/4 zTL
5213	42 slt/4 zTL
5214	42 slt/4 zTL
5301	42 slt/4 zTL
5302	42 slt/4 zTL
5303	42 slt/4 zTL
5304	42 slt/4 zTL
5305	42 slt/4 zTL
5508	42 slt/4 zTL
5512	42 slt/4 zTL
5581	42 slt/4 zTL
5603	42 slt/4 zTL
7701	42 slt/4 zTL
7802	42 slt/4 zTL
9011*	42 slt/4 zTL
9332*	42 slt/4 zTL
9333*	42 slt/4 zTL
9341*	42 slt/4 zTL
9399*	42 slt/4 zTL
9410	42 slt/4 zTL
9414	42 slt/4 zTL
9707	42 slt/4 zTL
9711	42 slt/4 zTL
9801	42 slt/4 zTL
9802	LZO
9804	42 slt/4 zTL
9805	42 slt/4 zTL

**Mikoyan MiG-23ML/
MiG-23UB***
41 slt/4 zTL, Cáslav

2402
2406
2409
2410
2422
2423
2425
3303
3304
3307
4641
4645
4850
4855
4860
8107*
8109*
8327*

Mil Mi-24
331 ltBVr/33 zVrL, Přerov

0103	Mi-24D
0140	Mi-24D
0142	Mi-24D
0146	Mi-24D
0151	Mi-24D
0214	Mi-24D
0216	Mi-24D
0217	Mi-24D
0218	Mi-24D
0219	Mi-24D
0220	Mi-24D
0701	Mi-24V1
0702	Mi-24V1
0703	Mi-24V1
0705	Mi-24V1
0709	Mi-24V1
0710	Mi-24V1
0788	Mi-24V1
0789	Mi-24V1
0790	Mi-24V1

Czech Republic - Denmark

0812	Mi-24V1
0815	Mi-24V1
0816	Mi-24V1
0834	Mi-24V2
0835	Mi-24V2
0836	Mi-24V2
0837	Mi-24V2
0838	Mi-24V2
0839	Mi-24V2
4010	Mi-24D
4011	Mi-24D
6050	Mi-24DU

Sukhoi Su-22M-4K/ Su-22UM-3K*
321 tpzlt/32 zTL, Náměšt

2217	01	
2218	18	
2619	34	NA-2D
2620	35	NA-2D
2701	36	
3402	05	
3701	02	NA-1A
3703	43	NA-1D
3704	44	NA-1D
3705	51	
3706	52	NA-1E
3802	26	NA-2B
3803	27	NA-2B
4005	30	NA-2C
4008	29	NA-2B
4010	28	NA-2B
4011	22	NA-2A
4208	53	NA-1E
4209	54	NA-1E
6602	55	*
7103	03	NA-1A*
7104	40	NA-2C*
7309	41	NA-2D*
7310	25	NA-2A*

Tupolev Tu-154
1 dlt/6 zDL, Praha/Kbely
0601	Tu-154B-2
1003	Tu-154M
1016	Tu-154M

Yakovlev Yak-40
1 dlt/6 zDL, Praha/Kbely
| 0260 | Yak-40 |
| 1257 | Yak-40K |

Sukhoi Su-25K/ Su-25UBK*
322 tlt/32 zTL, Náměšt
1002	
1004	
1005	
3348*	
5007	
5039	
5040	
8076	
8077	
8078	
8079	
8080	
8081	
9013	
9014	
9093	
9094	
9098	
9099	

Tupolev Tu-154
1 dlt/6 zDL, Praha/Kbely
0601	Tu-154B-2
1003	Tu-154M
1016	Tu-154M

Yakovlev Yak-40
1 dlt/6 zDL, Praha/Kbely
| 0260 | Yak-40 |
| 1257 | Yak-40K |

DENMARK
Flyvevåbnet

Lockheed C-130H Hercules
Eskadrille 721, Vaerløse
| B-678 |
| B-679 |
| B-680 |

Canadair CL.604 Challenger
Eskadrille 721, Vaerløse
| C-080 |
| C-168 |
| C-172 |

General Dynamics F-16
(MLU aircraft are marked with a *)
Eskadrille 726, Aalborg;
Eskadrille 727, Skrydstrup;
Eskadrille 730, Skrydstrup

E-004	F-16A*	Esk 726
E-005	F-16A*	Esk 726
E-006	F-16A*	Esk 726
E-007	F-16A*	Esk 726
E-008	F-16A*	Esk 726
E-011	F-16A	Esk 726
E-016	F-16A*	Esk 726
E-017	F-16A*	Esk 726
E-018	F-16A*	Esk 726
E-024	F-16A	Esk 730
E-074	F-16A	Esk 730
E-075	F-16A	Esk 730
E-107	F-16A*	Esk 730
E-174	F-16A	Esk 727
E-176	F-16A	Esk 726
E-177	F-16A*	Esk 727
E-180	F-16A	Esk 730
E-181	F-16A	Esk 726
E-182	F-16A	Esk 730
E-183	F-16A	Esk 730
E-184	F-16A	Esk 727
E-187	F-16A	Esk 727
E-188	F-16A	
E-190	F-16A*	Esk 730
E-191	F-16A	Esk 730
E-192	F-16A*	Esk 727
E-193	F-16A	Esk 727
E-194	F-16A*	Esk 726
E-195	F-16A	Esk 730
E-196	F-16A	Esk 727
E-197	F-16A	Esk 727
E-198	F-16A	Esk 726
E-199	F-16A	Esk 727
E-200	F-16A	Esk 727
E-202	F-16A*	Esk 730
E-203	F-16A	Esk 730
E-596	F-16A*	Esk 727
E-597	F-16A*	Esk 727
E-598	F-16A*	Esk 726
E-599	F-16A*	Esk 727
E-600	F-16A*	Esk 726
E-601	F-16A	Esk 726
E-602	F-16A	Esk 730
E-603	F-16A*	Esk 730
E-604	F-16A*	Esk 726
E-605	F-16A*	Esk 730
E-606	F-16A*	Esk 730
E-607	F-16A*	Esk 730
E-608	F-16A*	Esk 726
E-609	F-16A*	Esk 726
E-610	F-16A*	Esk 726
E-611	F-16A	Esk 726
ET-022	F-16B	Esk 730
ET-197	F-16B	Esk 727
ET-198	F-16B*	Esk 730
ET-199	F-16B*	Esk 730
ET-204	F-16B*	Esk 726
ET-206	F-16B	Esk 730
ET-207	F-16B*	Esk 726
ET-208	F-16B	Esk 730
ET-210	F-16B	Esk 727
ET-612	F-16B*	Esk 730
ET-613	F-16B*	Esk 726
ET-614	F-16B*	Esk 727
ET-615	F-16B*	Esk 726
ET-626	F-16B	Esk 730

Grumman G.1159A Gulfstream III
Eskadrille 721, Vaerløse
| F-249 |
| F-313 |

SAAB T-17 Supporter
Eskadrille 721, Vaerløse;
Flyveskolen, Karup (FLSK)
T-401	FLSK
T-402	FLSK
T-403	FLSK
T-404	FLSK
T-405	FLSK
T-407	Esk 721
T-408	FLSK
T-409	FLSK
T-410	FLSK
T-411	FLSK
T-412	FLSK
T-413	FLSK
T-414	FLSK
T-415	FLSK
T-417	FLSK
T-418	Esk 721
T-419	FLSK
T-420	Esk 721
T-421	FLSK
T-423	FLSK
T-425	FLSK
T-426	FLSK
T-427	FLSK
T-428	FLSK
T-429	FLSK
T-430	FLSK
T-431	Esk 721
T-432	FLSK

Sikorsky S-61A Sea King
Eskadrille 722, Vaerløse
Detachments at:
Aalborg, Ronne, Skrydstrup
| U-240 |
| U-275 |
| U-276 |
| U-277 |
| U-278 |
| U-279 |
| U-280 |
| U-481 |

Søvaernets Flyvetjaeneste (Navy)
Westland Lynx
Mk 80/90/90B
Eskadrille 722, Vaerløse
S-134 Mk 80
S-142 Mk 80
S-170 Mk 90B
S-175 Mk 80
S-181 Mk 80
S-191 Mk 90B
S-249 Mk 90
S-256 Mk 90

Haerens Flyvetjaeneste (Army)
Hughes 500M
OVH Kmp, Vandel;
PVH Kmp, Vandel
H-201
H-202
H-203
H-205
H-206
H-207
H-209
H-211
H-213
H-244
H-245
H-246

Aérospatiale AS.550C-2 Fennec
PVH Kmp, Vandel
P-090
P-234
P-254
P-275
P-276
P-287
P-288
P-319
P-320
P-339
P-352
P-369

EGYPT
Al Quwwat al-Jawwiya ilMisriya
Lockheed C-130H/ C-130H-30* Hercules
16 Sqn, Cairo West
1271/SU-BAB
1272/SU-BAC
1273/SU-BAD
1274/SU-BAE
1275/SU-BAF
1277/SU-BAI
1278/SU-BAJ
1279/SU-BAK
1280/SU-BAL
1281/SU-BAM
1282/SU-BAN
1283/SU-BAP
1284/SU-BAQ
1285/SU-BAR
1286/SU-BAS
1287/SU-BAT
1288/SU-BAU
1289/SU-BAV
1290/SU-BAW
1291/SU-BAX

1292/SU-BAY
1293/SU-BKS*
1294/SU-BKT*
1295/SU-BKU*

Egyptian Govt
Airbus A.340-211
Egyptian Govt, Cairo
SU-GGG

Boeing 707-366C
Egyptian Govt, Cairo
SU-AXJ

Grumman G.1159A
Gulfstream III/G.1159C
Gulfstream IV
Egyptian Air Force/Govt, Cairo
SU-BGM Gulfstream IV
SU-BGU Gulfstream III
SU-BGV Gulfstream III
SU-BNC Gulfstream IV
SU-BND Gulfstream IV

FINLAND
Suomen Ilmavoimat
Fokker F.27 Friendship
Tukilentolaivue,
Jyväskylä/Tikkakoski
FF-1   F.27-100
FF-2   F.27-100
FF-3   F.27-400M

FRANCE
Armée de l'Air Aérospatiale
SN601 Corvette
CEV, Bretigny
1   MV
2   MW
10   MX

Aérospatiale TB-30 Epsilon
Cartouche Dorée,
(EPAA 00.315) Cognac;
EPAA 00.315, Cognac;
SOCATA, Tarbes
1   315-UA
2   315-UB
3   FZ SOCATA
4   315-UC
5   315-UD
6   315-UE
7   315-UF
8   315-UG
9   315-UH
10   315-UI
12   315-UK
13   315-UL
14   315-UM
15   315-UN
16   315-UO
17   315-UP
19   315-UR
20   315-US
21   315-UT
23   315-UV
24   315-UW
24   315-UW
25   315-UX
26   315-UY
27   315-UZ
28   315-VA

29   315-VB
30   315-VC
31   315-VD
32   315-VE
33   315-VF
34   315-VG
35   315-VH
36   315-VI
37   315-VJ
38   315-VK
39   315-VL
40   315-VM
41   315-VN
42   315-VO
43   315-VP
44   315-VQ
45   315-VR
46   315-VS
47   315-VT
48   315-VU
49   315-VV
50   315-VW
52   315-VX
53   315-VY
54   315-VZ
56   315-WA
57   F-ZVLB
61   315-WD
62   315-WE
63   315-WF
64   315-WG
65   315-WH
66   315-WI
67   315-WJ
68   315-WK
69   315-WL
70   315-WM
72   315-WO
73   315-WP
74   315-WQ
75   315-WR
76   315-WS
77   315-WT
78   315-WU
79   315-WV
80   315-WW
81   315-WX
82   315-WY
83   315-WZ
84   315-XA
85   315-XB
86   315-XC
87   315-XD
88   315-XE
89   315-XF
90   315-XG
91   315-XH
92   F-SEXI [1]*
93   315-XJ
94   315-XK
95   315-XL
96   315-XM
97   315-XN
98   315-XO
99   315-XP
100   F-SEXQ [2]*
101   315-XR
102   315-XS
103   315-XT
104   315-XU
105   F-SEXV [4]*
106   315-XW
107   315-XX
108   315-XY

109	315-XZ	
110	315-YA	
111	315-YB	
112	315-YC	
113	315-YD	
114	315-YE	
115	315-YF	
116	315-YG	
117	F-SEYH [3]*	
118	315-YI	
119	315-YJ	
120	315-YK	
121	315-YL	
122	315-YM	
123	315-YN	
124	315-YO	
125	315-YP	
126	315-YQ	
127	315-YR	
128	315-YS	
129	315-YT	
130	315-YU	
131	315-YV	
132	315-YW	
133	315-YX	
134	315-YY	
135	315-YZ	
136	315-ZA	
137	315-ZB	
138	315-ZC	
139	315-ZD	
140	315-ZE	
141	315-ZF	
142	315-ZG	
143	315-ZH	
144	315-ZI	
145	315-ZJ	
146	315-ZK	
149	315-ZM	
150	315-ZN	
152	315-ZO	
153	315-ZP	
154	315-ZQ	
155	315-ZR	
158	315-ZS	
159	315-ZT	

Airbus A.310-304
ET 03.060 *Esterel*,
  Paris/Charles de Gaulle

418	F-RADC
421	F-RADA
422	F-RADB

Airbus A.319CJ-115
ETEC 00.065, Villacoublay

1485	65-VU
1556	65-VV

Airtech CN-235M-200
ETL 01.062 *Vercours*, Creil;
ETOM 00.052 *La Tontouta*,
  Noumea;
ETOM 00.082 *Maine*,
  Faaa-Tahiti

043	62-IA	01.062
045	62-IB	01.062
065	82-IC	00.082
066	52-ID	00.052
071	62-IE	01.062
072	82-IF	00.082
105	62-IG	01.062
107	52-IH	00.052
111	62-II	01.062

114	62-IJ	01.062
123	62-IM	01.062
128	62-IK	01.062
129	62-IL	01.062
137	62-IN	01.062
141	62-IO	01.062

Boeing C-135 Stratotanker
ERV 00.093 *Bretagne*, Istres

470	C-135FR	93-CA
471	C-135FR	93-CB
472	C-135FR	93-CC
474	C-135FR	93-CE
475	C-135FR	93-CF
497	KC-135R	93-CM
525	KC-135R	93-CN
574	KC-135R	93-CP
735	C-135FR	93-CG
736	C-135FR	93-CH
737	C-135FR	93-CI
738	C-135FR	93-CJ
739	C-135FR	93-CK
740	C-135FR	93-CL

Boeing E-3F Sentry
EDCA 00.036, Avord

201	36-CA
202	36-CB
203	36-CC
204	36-CD

CASA 212-300 Aviocar
CEV, Cazaux & Istres

377	MO
378	MP
386	MQ
387	MR
388	MS

Cessna 310
CEV, Cazaux & Istres

046	310L	AV
185	310N	AU
187	310N	BJ
188	310N	BK
190	310N	BL
192	310N	BM
193	310N	BG
194	310N	BH
242	310K	AW
244	310K	AX
513	310N	BE
693	310N	BI
820	310Q	CL
981	310Q	BF

D-BD Alpha Jet
AMD-BA, Istres;
CEAM (EC 05.330),
  Mont-de-Marsan;
CEV, Cazaux & Istres;
CITac 00.339 *Aquitaine*,
  Luxeuil;
EAC 00.314, Tours;
EC 01.002 *Cicogne*, Dijon;
EC 01.007 *Provence* &
  EC 02.007 *Argonne*,
  St Dizier;
EPNER, Istres;
ERS 01.091 *Gascogne*,
  Mont-de-Marsan;
ETO 01.008 *Saintonge* &
  ETO 02.008 *Nice*, Cazaux;

GI 00.312, Salon de Provence;
Patrouille de France (PDF)
  (EPAA 20.300),
  Salon de Provence

01	F-ZJTS	CEV
E1		CEV
E3	314-LV	00.314
E4		CEV
E5	339-WH	00.339
E7	314-LJ	00.314
E8		CEV
E9	8-MJ	01.008
E10	314-LK	00.314
E11	8-MW	01.008
E12		CEV
E13	8-NM	02.008
E14	2-EI	01.002
E15	8-NO	02.008
E17	314-TE	00.314
E18	8-NN	02.008
E19	330-AH	CEAM
E20	339-DI	00.339
E21	330-AL	CEAM
E22	314-UB	00.314
E23	8-MQ	01.008
E24	314-TJ	00.314
E25	314-UK	00.314
E26	F-TERO	PDF
E28	8-NK	02.008
E29	314-TM	00.314
E30	339-WN	00.339
E31		
E32	8-NQ	02.008
E33	8-MZ	01.008
E34	8-MF	01.008
E35	7-HY	01.007
E36	2-EF	01.002
E37	8-NI	02.008
E38	339-DG	00.339
E41	F-TERA	PDF [4]
E42	7-PX	02.007
E43	314-LI	00.314
E44	314-LP	00.314
E45	330-AK	CEAM
E46		CEV
E47	7-PJ	02.007
E48	314-TD	00.314
E49	314-TA	00.314
E51	314-TH	00.314
E52		
E53		
E55	314-UC	00.314
E58	314-LF	00.314
E59	314-LY	00.314
E60		EPNER
E61		
E63	314-LN	00.314
E64	314-TL	00.314
E65	8-ND	02.008
E66	8-ME	01.008
E67	314-TB	00.314
E68	2-EL	01.002
E69	314-TO	00.314
E72	314-LA	00.314
E73	314-TV	00.314
E74	8-MS	01.008
E75	F-TERW	PDF [2]
E76	8-MR	01.008
E79	8-MI	01.008
E80		CEV
E81	F-TERI	PDF
E82	8-NB	02.008
E83	2-EI	01.002
E84	8-MH	01.008

E85	314-LF	00.314
E86	8-NS	02.008
E87	314-LU	00.314
E88	314-TF	00.314
E89	314-TQ	00.314
E90		
E91	8-NL	02.008
E92	314-UE	00.314
E93	314-LD	00.314
E94	314-TE	00.314
E95		
E96	8-MT	01.008
E97	314-UN	00.314
E98	314-TT	00.314
E99	314-LW	00.314
E100		EPNER
E101	314-LX	00.314
E102		
E103	314-UA	00.314
E104	314-TG	00.314
E105	314-LE	00.314
E106	8-NA	02.008
E107	312-RT	00.312
E108	8-NF	02.008
E109	8-NJ	02.008
E110	8-NG	02.008
E112	DA	01.091
E113	312-RU	00.312
E114	314-TU	00.314
E115	8-NW	02.008
E116	8-MG	01.008
E117		
E118	314-LM	00.314
E119	7-PZ	02.007
E120	F-TERG	PDF [1]
E121	F-TERK	PDF [9]
E122		
E123	8-ML	01.008
E124	312-RS	00.312
E125		
E126	314-LI	00.314
E127	8-MB	01.008
E128	F-TERN	PDF [3]
E129	314-TO	00.314
E130	314-LQ	00.314
E131	312-RV	00.312
E132	314-TR	00.314
E133	8-NE	02.008
E134	7-PX	02.007
E135	F-TERX	PDF [7]
E136	314-TN	00.314
E137	339-DE	00.339
E138		
E139	330-AH	CEAM
E140	314-UH	00.314
E141	314-LC	00.314
E142	314-LB	00.314
E143	8-MM	01.008
E144	314-LO	00.314
E145	314-LZ	00.314
E146		
E147	8-NH	02.008
E148	8-NP	02.008
E149	8-MO	01.008
E150	8-NC	02.008
E151	8-MC	01.008
E152	339-DH	00.339
E153	F-TERH	PDF [5]
E154	339-DF	00.339
E155	314-TP	00.314
E156	314-TI	00.314
E157	314-LG	00.314
E158	F-TERG	PDF [2]
E159	7-PP	02.007

E160	F-TERC	PDF [8]
E161	8-MK	01.008
E162	314-TZ	00.314
E163	F-TERB	PDF
E164	8-MB	01.008
E165	F-TER.	PDF
E166	314-TX	00.314
E167	314-LL	00.314
E168	314-TS	00.314
E169	F-TERQ	PDF [0]
E170	7-PQ	02.007
E171		
E173	314-LH	00.314
E175	F-TERL	PDF [6]
E176	8-MA	01.008

Dassault Falcon 20
CEV, Cazaux & Istres;
CITac 00.339 Aquitaine,
  Luxeuil;
EAM 09.120, Cazaux;
ETEC 00.065, Villacoublay

22	CS	CEV
49	120-FA	09.120
79	CT	CEV
86	CG	CEV
93	F-RAED	00.065
96	CB	CEV
104	CW	CEV
115	339-JG	00.339
124	CC	CEV
131	CD	CEV
138	CR	CEV
145	CU	CEV
167	(F-RAEB)	00.065
182	339-JA	00.339
188	CX	CEV
238	F-RAEE	00.065
252	CA	CEV
260	F-RAEA	00.065
263	CY	CEV
268	F-RAEF	00.065
288	CV	CEV
291	65-EG	00.065
342	F-RAEC	00.065
375	CZ	CEV
422	65-EH	00.065
451	339-JC	00.339
483	339-JI	00.339

Dassault Falcon 50
ETEC 00.065, Villacoublay

5	F-RAFI
27	(F-RAFK)
34	(F-RAFL)
78	F-RAFJ

Dassault Falcon 900
ETEC 00.065, Villacoublay

2	(F-RAFP)
4	(F-RAFQ)

Dassault Mirage IVP
ERS 01.091 Gascogne,
  Mont-de-Marsan

25	AX
36	BI
53	BZ
59	CF
61	CH

Dassault Mirage F.1
CEAM (EC 05.330),
  Mont-de-Marsan;

CEV, Cazaux & Istres;
EC 01.030 Alsace &
  EC 02.030 Normandie
  Niemen, Colmar;
ER 01.033 Belfort,
  ER 02.033 Savoie
  & EC 03.033 Lorraine,
  Reims;
EC 04.033 Vexin, Djibouti
Mirage F.1C/F.1CT*

5		
24		
31	33-FC	03.033
32	33-FV	03.033
33		
52	33-FB	03.033
62		
64	33-FK	03.033
74		
76	33-FI	03.033
77	33-FF	03.033
80	33-FP	03.033
81	33-LJ	04.033
82		
83	33-FO	03.033
84		
85		
87	33-FS	03.033
90	33-FE	03.033
100	33-LA	04.033
103	33-FU	03.033
201	33-FJ	03.033
202	33-FN	03.033
203	33-LB	04.033
205	33-FR	03.033
206	33-FN	03.033
207*	330-AO	CEAM
210	33-LC	04.033
211	33-FQ	03.033
213	33-FW	03.033
214		
218	33-LC	04.033
219*	30-SN	01.030
220*	330-AJ	CEAM
221*		
223*	30-QX	02.030
224	33-LG	04.033
225*	30-QE	02.030
226*	30-QU	02.030
227*	330-AP	CEAM
228*	30-QT	02.030
229*	30-QC	02.030
230*		
231*	30-SA	01.030
232*	30-QW	02.030
233*	30-QG	02.030
234*	30-SI	01.030
235*	30-SK	01.030
236*	30-SB	01.030
237*	30-SM	01.030
238*		
239*	30-QD	02.030
241*	30-QA	02.030
242*		
243*	30-QJ	02.030
244*	30-QH	02.030
245*	30-SX	01.030
246*	30-ST	01.030
247*	30-QP	02.030
248*	30-SQ	01.030
251*		
252*	30-QO	02.030
253*	30-SJ	01.030
254*	330-AI	CEAM

255*			643	33-NR	02.033	EC 04.033 *Vexin*, Djibouti
256*	30-QK	02.030	645	33-CC	01.033	1		
257*	30-SF	01.030	646	33-NW	02.033	2		CEV
258*	30-SZ	01.030	647			3	5-NP	01.005
259*	30-QZ	02.030	648	33-NT	02.033	4	5-NK	01.005
260*			649	33-CZ	01.033	5	5-OO	02.005
261*			650	33-CJ	01.033	8	5-OA	01.005
262*	30-SE	01.030	651	33-NB	02.033	9	5-OJ	02.005
264*	30-SW	01.030	653	33-NV	02.033	11	5-NJ	01.005
265*	30-SH	01.030	654	33-CL	01.033	12	5-NN	01.005
267*	30-QB	02.030	655	330-AT	CEAM	13	5-NM	01.005
268*	30-SR	01.030	656	33-CS	01.033	14	5-NW	01.005
271*	30-QQ		657			15	5-NA	01.005
272*	30-QL	02.030	658	33-CW	01.033	16	5-NE	01.005
273*			659			17	5-NR	01.005
274*			660	33-ND	02.033	18	5-OF	02.005
275*	30-QM	02.030	661	33-CX	01.033	19	5-OB	02.005
278*	30-QY	02.030	662	33-NA	02.033	20	5-NB	02.005
279*	30-SC	01.030				21	5-NG	01.005
280*	30-SD	01.030	**Dassault Mirage 2000B/**			22	5-ND	01.005
281*			**2000-5***			25	5-NU	01.005
283*	30-SV	01.030	AMD-BA, Istres;			27	5-NT	01.005
Mirage F.1B			CEAM (EC 05.330),			28	5-NN	01.005
501			Mont-de-Marsan;			29	5-NO	01.005
502	33-FX	03.033	CEV, Cazaux & Istres;			30	5-OZ	02.005
503	33-FG	03.033	EC 02.002 *Côte d'Or*, Dijon;			32	5-NQ	02.005
504			EC 01.005 *Vendée* &			34	5-NH	01.005
505			EC 02.005 *Ile de France*,			35	5-NL	01.005
507	33-FA	03.033	Orange;			36	5-OC	02.005
509			EC 01.012 *Cambrésis* &			37	5-NF	01.005
510	33-FI	03.033	EC 02.012 *Picardie*,			38*	2-FK	02.002
511	33-FT	03.033	Cambrai			40*	2-FG	02.002
512	33-FL	03.033	501*	(BX1)	CEV	41*	2-EJ	01.002
513	330-AD	CEAM	502	5-OH	02.005	42*	2-FH	02.002
514	33-FZ	03.033	504*		CEV	43*	2-FB	02.002
516	33-FH	03.033	505	5-OY	02.005	44*	2-EQ	01.002
517	33-FB	03.033	506	5-OD	02.005	45*		
518	33-FF	03.033	507	5-OX	02.005	46*	2-EN	01.002
519	33-FM	03.033	508	5-OT	02.005	47*	2-EP	01.002
520	33-FJ	03.033	509	5-OP	02.005	48*	2-ER	01.002
Mirage F.1CR			510	5-OQ	02.005	49*	2-FF	02.002
602		CEV	511	5-OR	02.005	51*	330-AS	CEAM
603	33-CB	01.033	512	5-OU	02.005	52*	2-FC	02.002
604	33-NU	02.033	513	5-OI	02.005	53*		CEAM
605	33-CO	01.033	514	5-OE	02.005	54*	2-EA	01.002
606	33-NP	02.033	515	5-OG	02.005	55*	330-AM	CEAM
607	33-CE	01.033	516	5-OL	02.005	56*	2-EG	01.002
608	33-NG	02.033	518	5-OM	02.005	57*	2-ET	01.002
610	33-NQ	02.033	519	5-OW	02.005	58*	2-FO	02.002
611	33-NN	02.033	520	5-OS	02.005	59*	2-EV	01.002
612	33-NJ	02.033	521	5-ON	02.005	61*	2-EM	01.002
613	33-CU	01.033	522	5-OV	02.005	62*	2-ED	01.002
614	33-CN	01.033	523			63*	2-FQ	02.002
615	33-NZ	02.033	524	330-AZ	CEAM	64	330-AQ	CEAM
616	33-NM	02.033	525	12-KP	02.012	65*		
617	33-NO	02.033	526	12-KM	02.012	66*	2-FD	02.002
620	33-CT	01.033	527	12-KJ	02.012	67*	2-FL	02.002
622	33-NH	02.033	528	330-AN	CEAM	68*	2-FP	02.002
623	33-CA	01.033	529			69*	2-FE	02.002
624	330-AB	CEAM	530	12-YA	01.012	70*	2-EC	01.002
627	33-CF	01.033				71*	2-EH	01.002
628	33-NB	02.033	**Dassault Mirage 2000C/**			72*	2-FR	02.002
629	33-NN	02.033	**2000-5***			73*	2-ES	01.002
630	330-AF	CEAM	CEAM (EC 05.330),			74*	2-EU	01.002
631	33-NS	02.033	Mont-de-Marsan;			76*	2-EB	01.002
632	33-NE	02.033	CEV, Istres;			77*	330-AX	CEAM
634	33-CK	01.033	EC 01.002 *Cicogne* &			78*	2-FS	2.002
635	33-NX	02.033	EC 02.002 *Côte d'Or*, Dijon;			79	12-KL	02.012
636	33-CG	01.033	EC 01.005 *Vendée* &			80		04.033
637	33-CP	01.033	EC 02.005 *Ile de France*,			81	12-YI	01.012
638	33-CI	01.033	Orange;			82		04.033
640	33-CH	01.033	EC 01.012 *Cambrésis* &			83	12-YL	01.012
641	33-CD	01.033	EC 02.012 *Picardie*,			85	12-YE	01.012
642	33-NC	02.033	Cambrai			86	12-KH	02.012

87	12-YQ	01.012
88	12-YR	01.012
89	12-KU	02.012
90	12-YS	01.012
91	12-YO	01.012
92	330-AW	CEAM
93		
94	12-KA	02.012
95	12-YF	01.012
96	12-KK	02.012
97	12-YT	01.012
98	12-YB	01.012
99		
100	12-KG	02.012
101	2-FB	02.002
102	12-KO	02.012
103	12-YN	01.012
104	12-YK	01.012
105		04.033
106	2-FP	02.002
107	12-KQ	02.012
108	12-KE	02.012
109	12-KR	02.012
111		04.033
112	12-YC	01.012
113	12-KN	02.012
114	12-KS	02.012
115	12-YE	01.012
116	12-KF	02.012
117	12-YH	01.012
118		04.033
119	12-KD	02.012
120	12-KU	02.012
121	12-YD	01.012
122	12-YU	01.012
123		
124	12-KB	02.012
X7		CEV

Dassault Mirage 2000D
AMD-BA, Istres;
CEAM (EC 05.330),
  Mont-de-Marsan;
CEV, Istres;
EC 01.003 *Navarre*,
  EC 02.003 *Champagne* &
  EC 03.003 *Ardennes*,
Nancy

601	3-IA	01.003
602		
603	330-AA	CEAM
604	3-IN	01.003
605	3-IE	01.003
606	3-IH	01.003
607		CEV
609		
610	3-II	01.003
611	3-XS	03.003
612	3-IL	01.003
613		
614	330-A	CEAM
615	3-JA	02.003
616	3-IJ	01.003
617	3-XA	03.003
618	3-JF	02.003
619	3-JE	02.003
620	3-IM	01.003
621	3-XC	03.003
622	3-IW	01.003
623	3-IB	01.003
624	3-XF	03.003
625	3-JC	02.003
626	3-XH	03.003
627	3-JG	02.003

628	330-AE	CEAM
629	3-XJ	03.003
630	3-XD	03.003
631	3-XI	03.003
632	3-XJ	03.003
634	3-JD	02.003
635	3-XP	03.003
636	3-JJ	02.003
637	3-JH	02.003
638	3-IQ	01.003
639	3-XQ	03.003
640	3-IR	01.003
641	3-XG	03.003
642	3-JB	02.003
643	330-AG	CEAM
644		
645	3-JO	02.003
646	3-JP	02.003
647	3-IU	01.003
648	3-XT	03.003
649	3-JW	02.003
650		
651		
652	3-XN	03.003
653	3-JK	02.003
654	3-IT	01.003
655	3-XE	03.003
656	3-JL	02.003
657	3-JM	02.003
658	3-JN	02.003
659	3-XR	03.003
660		
661	3-IH	01.003
662	3-XU	03.003
663	330-AU	CEAM
664	3-JU	02.003
665	3-XV	03.003
666	3-IK	01.003
667	3-JX	02.003
668	3-XX	03.003
669	3-JZ	02.003
670	3-IQ	01.003
671	3-IO	01.003
672	3-JQ	02.003
673	3-XA	03.003
674	3-XL	03.003
675	3-JI	02.003
676		CEV
677	3-XY	03.003
678	3-IC	01.003
679	3-IP	01.003
680	3-IG	01.003
681		
682	3-JR	02.003
683	3-JT	02.003
684	3-IF	01.003
685		
686		

Dassault Mirage 2000N
CEAM (EC 05.330),
  Mont-de-Marsan;
CEV, Istres;
EC 01.004 *Dauphiné* &
  EC 02.004 *Lafayette*,
  Luxeuil;
EC 03.004 *Limousin*, Istres

301		CEV
303	4-CL	03.004
304	4-CK	03.004
305	4-CS	03.004
306	4-BL	02.004
307	4-CH	03.004

309	4-AO	01.004
310	4-CE	03.004
311	4-BT	02.004
312	4-CN	03.004
313	4-CV	03.004
314	4-AX	01.004
315	4-BF	02.004
316	4-BH	02.004
317	4-CR	03.004
318	4-BP	02.004
319	4-AC	01.004
320	4-CD	03.004
322		
323	4-CV	03.004
325	4-CC	03.004
326	4-CM	03.004
327	4-CJ	03.004
329	4-AU	01.004
330	4-AT	01.004
331	4-CQ	03.004
332	4-BN	02.004
333	4-AB	01.004
334	330-AV	CEAM
335	4-CI	03.004
336	4-BI	02.004
337	4-AK	01.004
338		
339	4-AD	01.004
340	4-AA	01.004
341	4-AF	01.004
342	4-BA	02.004
343	4-AH	01.004
344	4-AJ	01.004
345	4-BU	02.004
348	4-AL	01.004
349	4-BM	02.004
350		
351	4-AQ	01.004
353	4-BD	02.004
354	4-BJ	02.004
355	4-AE	01.004
356	4-AN	01.004
357	4-CO	03.004
358	4-AM	01.004
359	4-BG	02.004
360	4-AI	01.004
361	4-CL	03.004
362		
363	4-BK	02.004
364	4-BB	02.004
365	4-BE	02.004
366	4-BO	02.004
367	4-AS	01.004
368	4-AR	01.004
369	4-BQ	02.004
370	4-CA	03.004
371	4-AV	01.004
372	4-BR	02.004
373	4-CF	03.004
374	4-BS	02.004
375	4-BC	02.004

Dassault Rafale-B
AMD-BA, Istres;
CEV, Istres

B01		CEV
B1	AMD-BA	
301	AMD-BA	
302	AMD-BA	

Dassault Rafale-C
AMD-BA, Istres

C01	AMD-BA

France

DHC-6 Twin Otter 200/300*
ET 00.042 *Ventoux*,
  Mont-de-Marsan;
GAM 00.056 *Vaucluse*,
  Evreux

292	CC	00.056
298	CD	00.056
300	CE	00.056
730*	CA	00.042
742*	CB	00.042
745*	CV	00.042
786*	CT	00.042
790*	CW	00.042

Douglas DC-8-72CF
EE 00.051 *Aubrac*, Evreux;
ET 03.060 *Esterel*,
  Paris/Charles de Gaulle

46013	F-RAFG	03.060
46043		00.051
46130	F-RAFF	03.060

Embraer EMB.121AA/AN* Xingu
EAT 00.319, Avord

054	YX
055*	YZ
064	YY
066*	
069*	
070*	
072	YA
073	YB
075	YC
076	YD
077*	
078	YE
080	YF
082	YG
083*	ZE
084	YH
086	YI
089	YJ
090*	ZF
091	YK
092	YL
095	YM
096	YN
098	YO
099	YP
101	YR
102	YS
103	YT
105	YU
107	YV
108	YW
111	YQ

Embraer EMB.312F Tucano
GI 00.312, Salon de Provence

438	312-UW
439	312-UY
456	312-JA
457	312-JB
458	312-JC
459	312-JD
460	312-JE
461	312-JF
462	312-JG
463	312-JH
464	312-JI
466	312-JK
467	312-JL
468	312-JM
469	312-JN
470	312-JO
471	312-JP
472	312-JQ
473	312-JR
474	312-JS
475	312-JT
477	312-JU
478	312-JV
479	312-JX
480	312-JY
481	312-JZ
483	312-UB
484	312-UC
485	312-UD
486	312-UE
487	312-UF
488	312-UG
489	312-UH
490	312-UI
491	312-UJ
492	312-UK
493	312-UL
494	312-UM
495	312-UN
496	312-UO
497	312-UP
498	312-UQ
499	312-UR
500	312-US
501	312-UT
502	312-UU
503	312-UV
504	312-UX

Eurocopter AS.332 Super Puma/AS.532 Cougar
EH 03.067 *Parisis*,
  Villacoublay;
EH 05.067 *Alpilles*,
  Aix-en-Provence;
ETOM 00.082 *Maine*,
  Faaa-Tahiti;
GAM 00.056 *Vaucluse*,
  Evreux

2014	AS.332C	PN	05.067
2057	AS.332C	PO	00.082
2093	AS.332L	F-ZKCM	
2233	AS.332L-1	67-FY	03.067
2235	AS.332L-1	67-FZ	03.067
2244	AS.332C	PM	00.082
2342	AS.532UL	FX	00.056
2369	AS.532UL	FW	00.056
2375	AS.532UL	FV	00.056
2377	AS.332L-1	67-FU	03.067

Lockheed C-130H/ C-130H-30* Hercules
ET 02.061 *Franche-Comté*,
  Orléans

4588	61-PM
4589	61-PN
5114	61-PA
5116	61-PB
5119	61-PC
5140	61-PD
5142*	61-PE
5144*	61-PF
5150*	61-PG
5151*	61-PH
5152*	61-PI
5153*	61-PJ
5226*	61-PK
5227*	61-PL

Morane Saulnier MS.760 Paris
CEV, Cazaux & Istres

68	NB	
115	OV	CEV
116	ON	CEV
118	NQ	CEV
119	NL	CEV

Nord 262A/262D* Frégate
CEV, Istres;
EPNER, Istres;
ETE 00.041 *Verdun*, Metz;
ET 00.042 *Ventoux*,
  Mont-de-Marsan;
ETE 00.043 *Médoc*,
  Bordeaux;
ETE 00.044 *Mistral*,
  Villacoublay;
ETEC 00.065, Villacoublay

58	MJ	EPNER
64*	AA	00.065
67	MI	CEV
77*	AK	00.044
80*	AW	00.065
81*	AH	00.041
88*	AL	00.042
89*	AZ	00.041
91*	AT	00.042
93*	AP	00.065
95*	AR	00.065
105*	AE	00.065
106*	AY	00.041
107*	AX	00.065
108*	AG	00.041
109*	AM	00.043
110*	AS	00.065

SEPECAT Jaguar
CEV, Cazaux & Istres;
CEAM (EC 05.330),
  Mont-de-Marsan;
CITac 00.339 *Aquitaine*,
  Luxeuil;
EC 01.007 *Provence*,
  St Dizier

Jaguar A

A99	7-HC	01.007
A101	7-HB	01.007
A104	7-HM	01.007
A113	7-HT	01.007
A120	7-HL	01.007
A122	7-HA	01.007
A124	7-HD	01.007
A126	7-HJ	01.007
A128	7-HP	01.007
A131	7-HF	01.007
A135	7-HK	01.007
A137	7-HQ	01.007
A138	7-HV	01.007
A139	7-HU	01.007
A140	7-HI	01.007
A145	7-HG	01.007

Serial	Code	Unit
A148	7-HN	01.007
A151	7-HE	01.007
A154	7-HO	01.007
A157	7-HH	01.007
A160	7-HS	01.007

Jaguar E

Serial	Code	Unit
E3	339-WF	00.339
E6	7-HR	01.007
E10	339-WL	00.339
E12	339-WI	00.339
E19	339-WG	00.339
E21	339-WM	00.339
E29	339-WJ	00.339
E35	7-HY	01.007
E37	7-HZ	01.007
E40	7-HX	01.007

SOCATA TBM 700
CEV, Cazaux & Istres;
ETE 00.041 *Verdun*, Metz;
ETE 00.043 *Médoc*, Bordeaux;
ETE 00.044 *Mistral*, Villacoublay;
ETEC 00.065, Villacoublay;
EdC 00.070, Chateaudun

Serial	Code	Unit
33	XA	00.043
35	XB	00.043
70	XC	00.043
77	XD	00.065
78	65-XE	00.044
80	41-XF	00.041
93	XL	00.043
94	65-XG	00.070
95	65-XH	00.065
103	41-XI	00.041
104	XJ	00.070
105	XK	00.065
106	MN	CEV
110	XP	00.041
111	XM	00.065
117	XN	00.044
125	65-XO	00.065
131	XQ	00.065
146	XR	00.065
147	XS	00.065

Transall C-160F/C-160NG GABRIEL*/C-160R
CEAM (EET 06.330), Mont-de-Marsan;
CEV, Cazaux & Istres;
EET 01.054 *Dunkerque*, Metz;
ET 01.061 *Touraine* & ET 03.061 *Poitou*, Orléans;
ET 01.064 *Bearn* & ET 02.064 *Anjou*, Evreux;
ETOM 00.050 *Réunion*, St Denis;
ETOM 00.055 *Ouessant*, Dakar;
ETOM 00.058 *Guadeloupe*, Pointe-à-Pitre;
ETOM 00.088 *Larzac*, Djibouti

Serial	Type	Code/Unit
RA02	C-160R	61-MI / 01.061
RA04	C-160R	61-MS / 01.061
RA06	C-160R	61-ZB / 03.061
R1	C-160R	61-MA / 01.061
R2	C-160R	61-MB / 01.061
R3	C-160R	61-MC / 00.058
R4	C-160R	61-MD / 01.061
R5	C-160R	61-ME / 01.061
R11	C-160R	61-MF / 01.061
R12	C-160R	61-MG / 01.061
R13	C-160R	61-MH / 00.050
R15	C-160R	61-MJ / 01.061
R17	C-160R	61-ML / 01.061
R18	C-160R	61-MM / 01.061
R42	C-160R	61-MN / 01.061
R43	C-160R	61-MO / 01.061
R44	C-160R	61-MP / 01.061
R45	C-160R	61-MQ / 01.061
R46	C-160R	61-MR / 01.061
R48	C-160R	61-MT / 01.061
F49	C-160F	59-MU / CEV
R51	C-160R	61-MW / 01.061
R52	C-160R	61-MX / 01.061
R53	C-160R	61-MY / 01.061
R54	C-160R	61-MZ / 01.061
R55	C-160R	61-ZC / 03.061
R86	C-160R	61-ZD / 03.061
R87	C-160R	61-ZE / 00.050
R88	C-160R	61-ZF / 03.061
R89	C-160R	61-ZG / 03.061
R90	C-160R	61-ZH / 03.061
R91	C-160R	61-ZI / 03.061
R92	C-160R	61-ZJ / 03.061
R93	C-160R	61-ZK / 03.061
R94	C-160R	61-ZL / 03.061
R95	C-160R	61-ZM / 03.061
R96	C-160R	61-ZN / 03.061
R97	C-160R	61-ZO / 03.061
R98	C-160R	61-ZP / 03.061
R99	C-160R	61-ZQ / 03.061
R100	C-160R	61-ZR / 03.061
R153	C-160R	61-ZS / 03.061
R154	C-160R	61-ZT / 03.061
R157	C-160R	61-ZW / 03.061
R158	C-160R	61-ZX / 03.061
R159	C-160R	61-ZY / 03.061
R160	C-160R	61-ZZ / 03.061
R201	C-160R	64-GA / 01.064
R202	C-160R	64-GB / 02.064
R203	C-160R	64-GC / 01.064
R204	C-160R	64-GD / 02.064
R205	C-160R	64-GE / 02.064
R206	C-160R	64-GF / 02.064
R207	C-160R	64-GG / 01.064
R208	C-160R	64-GH / 02.064
R210	C-160R	64-GJ / 02.064
R211	C-160R	64-GK / 01.064
R212	C-160R	64-GL / 02.064
R213	C-160R	64-GM / 01.064
R214	C-160R	64-GN / 02.064
R215	C-160R	64-GO / 01.064
F216	C-160NG*	54-GT / 01.054
R217	C-160R	64-GQ / 01.064
R218	C-160R	64-GR / 02.064
F221	C-160NG*	61-GS / 01.061
R223	C-160R	64-GW / 01.064
R224	C-160R	64-GX / 02.064
R225	C-160R	64-GY / 01.064
R226	C-160R	64-GZ / 02.064

Aéronavale/Marine
Aérospatiale SA.321G Super Frelon
32 Flottille, Lanvéoc/Poulmic;
35 Flottille, St Mandrier

Serial	Unit
101	32F
102	32F
106	32F
118	32F
120	32F
134	32F
137	32F
144	32F
148	32F
150	32F

160	32F		M02	AMD-BA	67	2S
162	32F		1	CEV	68	2S
163	35F		2	CEPA	71	28F
164	32F		3	CEPA	74	2S
165			4	CEPA	79	2S
			5	CEPA	81	2S
Dassault-Breguet			6	CEPA	85	28F
Atlantique 2					87	2S

Dassault-Breguet Atlantique 2
21 Flottille, Nimes/Garons;
23 Flottille, Lorient/Lann Bihoué

			Dassault Super Etendard		**Eurocopter SA.365/AS.565**	
1	21F		11 Flottille, Landivisiau;		**Panther**	
2	21F		17 Flottille, Landivisiau;		35 Flottille, St Mandrier	
3	23F		CEV, Cazaux & Istres		(with detachments at	
4	21F		1	11F	Cherbourg, Hyères,	
5	23F		2	11F	La Rochelle & Le	
6	21F		3	11F	Touquet)	
7	21F		4	11F	36 Flottille, St Mandrier	
8	23F		6	11F	17	SA.365N	35F
9	21F		8	17F	19	SA.365N	35F
10	23F		10	11F	24	SA.365N	35F
11	23F		11	17F	81	SA.365N	35F
12	23F		12	17F	91	SA.365N	35F
13	21F		13	17F	313	SA.365F1	35F
14	21F		14	17F	318	SA.365F1	35F
15	21F		15	17F	322	SA.365F1	35F
16	21F		16	11F	355	AS.565MA	35F
17	23F		17	11F	362	AS.565MA	35F
18	23F		18	11F	436	AS.565MA	36F
19	23F		19	11F	452	AS.565MA	36F
20	23F		23	11F	453	AS.565MA	35F
21	21F		24	11F	466	AS.565MA	36F
22	21F		25	17F	482	AS.565MA	35F
23	21F		26	17F	486	AS.565MA	36F
24	21F		28	17F	503	AS.565MA	36F
25	21F		30	11F	505	AS.565MA	35F
26	23F		31	11F	506	AS.565MA	36F
27	23F		32	11F	507	AS.565MA	36F
28	21F		33	11F	511	AS.565MA	
29			35	CEV	519	AS.565MA	36F
30			37	11F	522	AS.565MA	36F
			38	11F			
			39	11F			
Dassault Falcon 10(MER)			41	11F	**Nord 262E Frégate**	
ES 57, Landivisiau			43	11F	28 Flottille, Hyères;	
32			44	17F	ERCE, Hyères;	
101			45	11F	ES 2, Lorient/Lann Bihoué;	
129			46	17F	ES 55, Aspretto;	
133			47	17F	ES 56, Nimes/Garons	
143			48	11F	45	56S
185			49	11F	46	56S
			50	11F	51	2S
			51	11F	53	2S
Dassault Falcon 20G			52	11F	60	2S
Guardian			55	11F	63	56S
25 Flottille, Papeete &			57	11F	69	56S
Tontouta			59	11F	70	56S
48			60	11F	71	56S
65			61	17F	72	56S
72			62	11F	73	56S
77			64	11F	75	56S
80			65	11F	79	28F
			66	17F	100	2S
Dassault Falcon 50			68	CEV		
SURMAR			69	11F	**Northrop Grumman**	
24 Flottille,			71	17F	**E-2C Hawkeye**	
Lorient/Lann Bihoué					4 Flottille, Lorient/Lann	
7					Bihoué	
30			**Embraer EMB.121AN**		1	(165455)
36			**Xingu**		2	(165456)
			24 Flottille, Lorient/Lann			
Dassault Rafale-M			Bihoué		**Westland**	
AMD-BA, Istres;			28 Flottille, Hyères;		**Lynx HAS2(FN)/HAS4(FN)***	
CEPA, Landivisiau;			ES 2, Lorient/Lann Bihoué		31 Flottille, St Mandrier;	
CEV, Istres			30	24F	34 Flottille, Lanvéoc/Poulmic	
M01	AMD-BA		47	2S	260	
			65	2S		

262	34F
263	31F
264	34F
265	34F
266	34F
267	31F
268	
269	34F
270	31F
271	34F
272	31F
273	
274	34F
275	34F
276	34F
620	34F
621	34F
622	34F
623	34F
624	31F
625	34F
627	34F
801*	34F
802*	34F
804*	34F
806*	34F
807*	34F
808*	34F
810*	34F
811*	34F
812*	31F
813*	34F
814*	31F

Aviation Legére de l'Armée de Terre (ALAT)
Cessna F.406 Caravan II
EAAT, Rennes
0008	ABM
0010	ABN

SOCATA TBM 700
EAAT, Rennes
99	ABO
100	ABP
115	ABQ
136	ABR
139	ABS
156	ABT
159	ABU
160	ABV

French Govt
Aérospatiale AS.355F-1 Twin Ecureuil
Douanes Francaises
F-ZBAC	(5026)
F-ZBEF	(5236)
F-ZBEJ	(5003)
F-ZBEK	(5298)
F-ZBEL	(5299)

Beech Super King Air B200
Sécurité Civile
F-ZBFJ	98
F-ZBFK	96

Cessna F.406 Caravan II
Douanes Francaises
F-ZBAB	(0025)
F-ZBBB	(0039)
F-ZBCE	(0042)
F-ZBCF	(0077)
F-ZBCG	(0066)

F-ZBCH	(0075)
F-ZBCI	(0070)
F-ZBCJ	(0074)
F-ZBEP	(0006)
F-ZBES	(0017)
F-ZBFA	(0001)
F-ZBGA	(0086)

Dassault Falcon 20
AVDEF, Nimes/Garons
F-GPAA	Falcon 20ECM
F-GPAB	Falcon 20E

Fokker F-27-600
Sécurité Civile
F-ZBFF	71	(10432)
F-ZBFG	72	(10440)

GERMANY
Luftwaffe, Marineflieger
Airbus A.310-304/MRTT*
1/FBS, Köln-Bonn
10+21
10+22
10+23
10+24*
10+25*
10+26*
10+27*

Canadair CL601-1A Challenger
1/FBS, Köln-Bonn
12+02
12+03
12+04
12+05
12+06
12+07

Mikoyan MiG-29A/ MiG-29UB*
JG-73 Steinhoff, Laage
29+01
29+02
29+03
29+04
29+05
29+06
29+07
29+08
29+10
29+11
29+12
29+14
29+15
29+16
29+17
29+18
29+19
29+20
29+21
29+22*
29+23*
29+24*
29+25*

McD F-4F Phantom
JG-71 Richthoven, Wittmundhaven;
JG-72 Westfalen, Hopsten;
JG-73 Steinhoff, Laage;
JG-74 Molders, Neuburg/Donau;

TsLw-1, Kaufbeuren;
WTD-61, Ingolstadt
37+01	JG-74
37+03	JG-71
37+04	TsLw-1
37+06	JG-72
37+07	JG-72
37+08	JG-74
37+09	JG-72
37+10	JG-72
37+11	JG-73
37+12	JG-72
37+13	JG-74
37+14	TsLw-1
37+15	WTD-61
37+16	WTD-61
37+17	JG-74
37+22	JG-71
37+26	JG-73
37+28	JG-71
37+29	JG-72
37+31	JG-72
37+32	JG-71
37+33	JG-72
37+34	JG-72
37+35	JG-72
37+36	JG-72
37+37	JG-72
37+38	JG-72
37+39	JG-71
37+42	JG-72
37+43	JG-72
37+44	JG-72
37+45	JG-72
37+48	JG-74
37+49	JG-71
37+50	JG-72
37+52	JG-72
37+54	JG-74
37+55	JG-71
37+58	JG-72
37+61	JG-74
37+63	JG-71
37+64	JG-72
37+65	JG-71
37+66	JG-71
37+67	JG-74
37+71	JG-74
37+75	JG-73
37+76	JG-71
37+77	JG-74
37+78	JG-71
37+79	JG-71
37+81	JG-74
37+82	JG-71
37+83	JG-71
37+84	JG-74
37+85	JG-71
37+86	JG-71
37+88	JG-74
37+89	JG-73
37+92	JG-74
37+93	JG-72
37+94	JG-74
37+96	JG-72
37+97	JG-74
37+98	JG-71
38+00	JG-74
38+01	JG-73
38+02	JG-73
38+03	JG-72
38+04	JG-72
38+05	JG-73
38+06	JG-74

Reg	Unit	Reg	Unit	Reg	Unit
38+07	JG-71	43+06[1]	JbG-38	44+14	JbG-31
38+09	JG-74	43+07[1]	JbG-38	44+15	AkG-51
38+10	JG-74	43+08[1]	JbG-32	44+16[1]	JbG-31
38+12	JG-71	43+09[1]	JbG-38	44+17	AkG-51
38+13	WTD-61	43+10[1]	JbG-38	44+19	JbG-31
38+14	JG-71	43+11[1]	JbG-38	44+21	JbG-31
38+16	JG-74	43+13	EADS	44+23	JbG-33
38+17	JG-74	43+15[1]	JbG-38	44+24	AkG-51
38+18	JG-74	43+16[1]	JbG-38	44+25[1]	JbG-38
38+20	JG-72	43+17[1]	JbG-38	44+26	JbG-31
38+24	JG-74	43+20	JbG-31	44+27	JbG-33
38+25	JG-74	43+22[1]	JbG-34	44+29	JbG-31
38+26	JG-74	43+23[1]	JbG-38	44+30	JbG-31
38+27	JG-72	43+25	JbG-31	44+31	JbG-31
38+28	JG-74	43+27	JbG-34	44+32	JbG-38
38+29	JG-74	43+29[1]	JbG-31	44+33	JbG-33
38+30	JG-71	43+31[1]	JbG-31	44+34	JbG-33
38+31	JG-72	43+32	JbG-31	44+35	JbG-31
38+32	JG-71	43+33[1]	JbG-33	44+37[1]	JbG-34
38+33	JG-73	43+34	TsLw-1	44+40	JbG-33
38+34	JG-72	43+35[1]	AkG-51	44+41	JbG-31
38+36	JG-71	43+37[1]	JbG-32	44+42	AkG-51
38+37	JG-72	43+38	JbG-33	44+43	JbG-34
38+39	JG-74	43+40	JbG-33	44+44	JbG-31
38+40	JG-71	43+41	JbG-31	44+46	JbG-34
38+42	JG-73	43+43[1]	AkG-51	44+48	JbG-33
38+43	JG-72	43+46	AkG-51	44+49	JbG-33
38+44	JG-71	43+47	AkG-51	44+50	AkG-51
38+45	JG-71	43+48	AkG-51	44+52	JbG-34
38+46	JG-71	43+50	AkG-51	44+54	JbG-33
38+48	JG-74	43+52	JbG-38	44+55	JbG-38
38+49	JG-71	43+53	JbG-34	44+56	JbG-34
38+50	JG-72	43+54	JbG-34	44+57	JbG-31
38+53	JG-74	43+55	MFG-2	44+58	JbG-31
38+54	JG-73	43+58	JbG-34	44+61	AkG-51
38+55	JG-71	43+59	TsLw-1	44+62	JbG-33
38+56	JG-73	43+60	JbG-34	44+63	JbG-33
38+57	JG-74	43+61	TsLw-1	44+64	AkG-51
38+58	JG-73	43+62	JbG-34	44+65	AkG-51
38+60	JG-74	43+63	JbG-34	44+66	JbG-31
38+61	JG-72	43+64	JbG-33	44+68	AkG-51
38+62	JG-72	43+65	JbG-38	44+69	AkG-51
38+64	JG-72	43+67	JbG-34	44+70	JbG-31
38+66	JG-73	43+68	JbG-34	44+71	JbG-31
38+67	JG-73	43+69	JbG-31	44+72[1]	JbG-33
38+68	JG-74	43+70	JbG-33	44+75[1]	JbG-33
38+69	JG-74	43+71	JbG-38	44+76	JbG-34
38+70	JG-74	43+72	JbG-38	44+78	JbG-31
38+73	JG-72	43+73	AkG-51	44+79	JbG-33
38+74	JG-74	43+76	JbG-38	44+80	JbG-31
38+75	JG-71	43+77	JbG-34	44+83	JbG-33
99+91	WTD-61	43+78	JbG-34	44+84	JbG-33
		43+79	AkG-51	44+85	JbG-33
		43+80	AkG-51	44+86	AkG-51
		43+81	AkG-51	44+87	AkG-51
		43+82	AkG-51	44+88	AkG-51
		43+85	JbG-38	44+89	JbG-33
		43+86	JbG-34	44+90	JbG-33
		43+87	MFG-2	44+91	JbG-33
		43+90[1]	JbG-31	44+92	JbG-38
		43+94[1]	JbG-34	44+94	JbG-33
		43+96	AkG-51	44+95	JbG-38
		43+98	AkG-51	44+96	JbG-31
		44+00	JbG-31	44+97	JbG-38
		44+04	AkG-51	45+00	JbG-33
		44+06	JbG-34	45+02	JbG-34
		44+07	JbG-31	45+04	JbG-33
		44+08	JbG-31	45+06	AkG-51
		44+09	JbG-33	45+07	JbG-33
		44+10[1]	JbG-32	45+08	JbG-33
		44+11	JbG-34	45+12[1]	MFG-2
		44+13	TsLw-1	45+13[1]	MFG-2
				45+14[1]	JbG-38
				45+15[1]	MFG-2

Panavia Tornado Strike/Trainer[1]/ECR[2]
AkG-51 *Immelmann*, Schleswig/Jagel;
EADS, Manching;
JbG-31 *Boelcke*, Nörvenich;
JbG-32, Lechfeld;
JbG-33, Büchel;
JbG-34 *Algäu*, Memmingen;
JbG-38 *Ostfriesland*, Jever;
MFG-2, Eggebek;
TsLw-1, Kaufbeuren;
WTD-61, Ingolstadt

43+01[1] JbG-38
43+02[1] JbG-38
43+03[1] JbG-38
43+04[1] JbG-38
43+05[1] JbG-38

45+16[1]	MFG-2	46+07[1]	JbG-34	50+44	LTG-62
45+17	JbG-33	46+08[1]	AkG-51	50+45	LTG-63
45+18	JbG-33	46+10	WTD-61	50+46	LTG-62
45+19	JbG-33	46+11	MFG-2	50+47	LTG-61
45+20	AkG-51	46+12	MFG-2	50+48	LTG-61
45+21	JbG-33	46+13	JbG-34	50+49	LTG-63
45+22	JbG-33	46+14	JbG-34	50+50	LTG-63
45+23	JbG-31	46+15	MFG-2	50+51	LTG-61
45+24	JbG-33	46+18	MFG-2	50+52	LTG-62
45+25	AkG-51	46+19	MFG-2	50+53	LTG-61
45+27	MFG-2	46+20	MFG-2	50+54	LTG-63
45+28	MFG-2	46+21	MFG-2	50+55	LTG-62
45+29	WTD-61	46+22	MFG-2	50+56	LTG-63
45+30	MFG-2	46+23[2]	JbG-32	50+57	WTD-61
45+31	MFG-2	46+24[2]	JbG-32	50+58	LTG-62
45+33	MFG-2	46+25[2]	JbG-32	50+59	LTG-63
45+34	MFG-2	46+26[2]	JbG-32	50+60	LTG-62
45+35	MFG-2	46+27[2]	JbG-32	50+61	LTG-63
45+36	MFG-2	46+28[2]	JbG-32	50+62	LTG-62
45+37	MFG-2	46+29[2]	JbG-32	50+64	LTG-61
45+38	MFG-2	46+30[2]	JbG-32	50+65	LTG-62
45+39	MFG-2	46+31[2]	JbG-32	50+66	LTG-61
45+40	MFG-2	46+32[2]	JbG-32	50+67	LTG-63
45+41	MFG-2	46+33[2]	JbG-32	50+68	LTG-61
45+42	MFG-2	46+34[2]	JbG-32	50+69	LTG-63
45+43	MFG-2	46+35[2]	JbG-32	50+70	LTG-63
45+44	MFG-2	46+36[2]	JbG-32	50+71	LTG-63
45+45	MFG-2	46+37[2]	JbG-32	50+72	LTG-63
45+46	MFG-2	46+38[2]	JbG-32	50+73	LTG-63
45+47	MFG-2	46+39[2]	JbG-32	50+74	LTG-61
45+49	MFG-2	46+40[2]	JbG-32	50+75	LTG-63
45+50	MFG-2	46+41[2]	JbG-32	50+76	LTG-63
45+51	AkG-51	46+42[2]	JbG-32	50+77	LTG-63
45+52	MFG-2	46+43[2]	JbG-32	50+78	LTG-62
45+53	MFG-2	46+44[2]	JbG-32	50+79	LTG-63
45+54	MFG-2	46+45[2]	JbG-32	50+81	LTG-62
45+55	MFG-2	46+46[2]	JbG-32	50+82	LTG-63
45+56	MFG-2	46+47[2]	JbG-32	50+83	LTG-62
45+57	JbG-34	46+48[2]	JbG-32	50+84	LTG-61
45+59	MFG-2	46+49[2]	JbG-32	50+85	LTG-63
45+64	TsLw-1	46+50[2]	JbG-32	50+86	LTG-61
45+66	MFG-2	46+51[2]	JbG-32	50+87	LTG-63
45+67	AkG-51	46+52[2]	JbG-32	50+88	LTG-61
45+68	MFG-2	46+53[2]	JbG-32	50+89	LTG-62
45+69	MFG-2	46+54[2]	JbG-32	50+90	LTG-62
45+70[1]	JbG-33	46+55[2]	JbG-32	50+91	LTG-62
45+71	MFG-2	46+56[2]	JbG-32	50+92	LTG-61
45+72	MFG-2	46+57[2]	JbG-32	50+93	LTG-61
45+73[1]	JbG-31	98+59	WTD-61	50+94	LTG-63
45+74	MFG-2	98+60	WTD-61	50+95	LTG-63
45+76	JbG-38	98+79[2]	WTD-61	50+96	LTG-61
45+77[1]	JbG-33			50+97	LTG-62
45+78	JbG-33	**Transall C-160D**		50+98	LTG-61
45+79	JbG-31	LTG-61, Landsberg;		50+99	LTG-61
45+81	JbG-34	LTG-62, Wunstorf;		51+00	LTG-62
45+82	JbG-31	LTG-63, Hohn;		51+01	LTG-62
45+84	AkG-51	WTD-61, Ingolstadt		51+02	LTG-63
45+85	AkG-51	50+06	LTG-63	51+03	LTG-62
45+86	JbG-33	50+07	LTG-61	51+04	LTG-61
45+87	JbG-34	50+08	LTG-63	51+05	LTG-62
45+88	JbG-33	50+09	LTG-62	51+06	LTG-63
45+89	JbG-34	50+10	LTG-62	51+07	LTG-62
45+90	JbG-31	50+17	LTG-62	51+08	WTD-61
45+91	AkG-51	50+29	LTG-62	51+09	LTG-63
45+92	JbG-31	50+33	LTG-62	51+10	LTG-61
45+93	AkG-51	50+34	LTG-63	51+11	LTG-62
45+94	JbG-33	50+35	LTG-62	51+12	LTG-63
45+95	JbG-34	50+36	LTG-62	51+13	LTG-61
45+99[1]	AkG-51	50+37	LTG-62	51+14	LTG-63
46+01	JbG-34	50+38	LTG-62	51+15	LTG-61
46+02	JbG-33	50+40	LTG-61		
46+04[1]	JbG-32	50+41	LTG-62	**Dornier Do.228/Do.228LM***	
46+05[1]	MFG-2	50+42	LTG-63	MFG-3, Nordholz;	
				WTD-61, Ingolstadt	

Germany

57+01*	MFG-3
57+02*	MFG-3
57+03	MFG-3
57+04*	MFG-3
98+78	WTD-61

Breguet Br.1150 Atlantic
*Elint
MFG-3, Nordholz
61+03*
61+04
61+05
61+06*
61+08
61+09
61+10
61+11
61+12
61+13
61+14
61+15
61+16
61+17
61+18*
61+19*
61+20

Eurocopter AS.532U-2
Cougar
3/FBS, Berlin-Tegel
82+01
82+02
82+03

Westland Lynx Mk88/
Super Lynx Mk88A*
MFG-3, Nordholz
83+02
83+03
83+04
83+05
83+06
83+07
83+09
83+10
83+11
83+12
83+13
83+15
83+17
83+18
83+19
83+20*
83+21*
83+22*
83+23*
83+24*
83+25*
83+26*

Westland Sea King HAS41
MFG-5, Kiel-Holtenau
89+50
89+51
89+52
89+53
89+54
89+55
89+56
89+57
89+58
89+60
89+61
89+62

89+63
89+64
89+65
89+66
89+67
89+68
89+69
89+70
89+71

Eurofighter
Typhoon
WTD-61, Ingolstadt
98+29 WTD-61
98+30 WTD-61

NH Industries
NH.90
98+90

Heeresfliegertruppe
Eurocopter EC.135P-1
HFWS, Bückeburg
82+51
82+52
82+53
82+54
82+55
82+56
82+57
82+58
82+59
82+60
82+61
82+62
82+63
82+64
82+65

MBB Bo.105
HFlgRgt-15,
 Rheine-Bentlage;
HFlgRgt-16, Celle;
HFlgRgt-25, Laupheim;
HFlgRgt-26, Roth;
HFlgRgt-35, Mendig;
HFlgRgt-36, Fritzlar;
HFS-400, Cottbus;
HFVS-910, Bückeburg;
HFWS, Bückeburg;
TsLw-3, Fassberg;
WTD-61, Ingolstadt

80+01	Bo.105M	HFR-35
80+02	Bo.105M	HFWS
80+03	Bo.105M	HFWS
80+04	Bo.105M	HFWS
80+05	Bo.105M	HFR-35
80+06	Bo.105M	HFWS
80+07	Bo.105M	HFWS
80+08	Bo.105M	HFR-25
80+09	Bo.105M	HFR-35
80+10	Bo.105M	HFR-25
80+11	Bo.105M	HFWS
80+12	Bo.105M	HFWS
80+13	Bo.105M	HFR-15
80+14	Bo.105M	HFWS
80+15	Bo.105M	HFR-15
80+16	Bo.105M	HFR-15
80+18	Bo.105M	HFR-15
80+19	Bo.105M	HFR-15
80+20	Bo.105M	HFS-400
80+21	Bo.105M	HFR-15
80+22	Bo.105M	HFS-400
80+23	Bo.105M	HFR-15

80+24	Bo.105M	HFR-15
80+25	Bo.105M	HFR-35
80+26	Bo.105M	HFR-35
80+27	Bo.105M	HFR-35
80+28	Bo.105M	TsLw-3
80+29	Bo.105M	HFR-35
80+30	Bo.105M	HFR-35
80+31	Bo.105M	HFR-35
80+32	Bo.105M	HFR-35
80+33	Bo.105M	HFR-35
80+34	Bo.105M	HFR-25
80+35	Bo.105M	HFS-400
80+36	Bo.105M	HFR-25
80+37	Bo.105M	HFS-400
80+38	Bo.105M	HFR-25
80+39	Bo.105M	HFR-25
80+40	Bo.105M	HFR-25
80+41	Bo.105M	HFR-25
80+42	Bo.105M	HFR-25
80+43	Bo.105M	HFR-25
80+44	Bo.105M	HFR-25
80+46	Bo.105M	TsLw-3
80+47	Bo.105M	HFR-26
80+48	Bo.105M	HFR-25
80+49	Bo.105M	HFS-400
80+50	Bo.105M	HFS-400
80+51	Bo.105M	HFR-15
80+53	Bo.105M	HFS-400
80+54	Bo.105M	HFR-15
80+55	Bo.105M	HFS-400
80+56	Bo.105M	HFS-400
80+57	Bo.105M	HFR-35
80+58	Bo.105M	HFR-35
80+59	Bo.105M	HFR-35
80+60	Bo.105M	HFR-35
80+61	Bo.105M	HFS-400
80+62	Bo.105M	HFR-35
80+64	Bo.105M	HFR-35
80+65	Bo.105M	HFR-15
80+66	Bo.105M	HFR-15
80+67	Bo.105M	HFR-15
80+68	Bo.105M	HFR-15
80+69	Bo.105M	HFR-15
80+70	Bo.105M	HFR-15
80+71	Bo.105M	HFR-15
80+72	Bo.105M	HFR-15
80+73	Bo.105M	HFR-15
80+74	Bo.105M	HFR-15
80+76	Bo.105M	HFR-15
80+77	Bo.105M	HFR-35
80+78	Bo.105M	HFR-35
80+79	Bo.105M	HFR-35
80+80	Bo.105M	HFS-400
80+81	Bo.105M	HFR-26
80+82	Bo.105M	HFR-25
80+83	Bo.105M	HFR-25
80+84	Bo.105M	HFR-25
80+85	Bo.105M	HFR-25
80+86	Bo.105M	HFWS
80+87	Bo.105M	HFR-25
80+88	Bo.105M	HFS-400
80+89	Bo.105M	HFS-400
80+90	Bo.105M	HFS-400
80+91	Bo.105M	HFR-35
80+92	Bo.105M	HFR-35
80+93	Bo.105M	HFS-400
80+94	Bo.105M	HFR-25
80+95	Bo.105M	HFS-400
80+96	Bo.105M	HFR-25
80+97	Bo.105M	HFR-35
80+98	Bo.105M	HFR-25
80+99	Bo.105M	HFR-25
81+00	Bo.105M	HFR-25
86+01	Bo.105P	HFR-16

86+02	Bo.105P	HFWS	86+77	Bo.105P	HFR-16	87+55	Bo.105P	HFVS-910
86+03	Bo.105P	HFWS	86+78	Bo.105P	HFR-26	87+56	Bo.105P	HFR-26
86+04	Bo.105P	HFR-36	86+80	Bo.105P	HFR-16	87+57	Bo.105P	HFR-26
86+05	Bo.105P	HFWS	86+81	Bo.105P	HFR-16	87+58	Bo.105P	HFR-26
86+06	Bo.105P	HFWS	86+83	Bo.105P	HFR-16	87+59	Bo.105P	HFR-36
86+07	Bo.105P	HFWS	86+84	Bo.105P	HFR-16	87+60	Bo.105P	HFR-36
86+08	Bo.105P	HFWS	86+85	Bo.105P	HFR-16	87+61	Bo.105P	HFR-35
86+09	Bo.105P	HFWS	86+86	Bo.105P	HFR-16	87+62	Bo.105P	HFR-36
86+10	Bo.105P	HFR-16	86+87	Bo.105P	HFR-16	87+63	Bo.105P	HFWS
86+11	Bo.105P	HFWS	86+88	Bo.105P	HFR-16	87+64	Bo.105P	HFR-36
86+12	Bo.105P	HFWS	86+89	Bo.105P	HFR-16	87+65	Bo.105P	HFR-36
86+13	Bo.105P	HFWS	86+90	Bo.105P	HFR-26	87+66	Bo.105P	TsLw-3
86+14	Bo.105P	HFR-16	86+91	Bo.105P	HFR-26	87+67	Bo.105P	HFWS
86+15	Bo.105P	HFR-16	86+92	Bo.105P	HFR-36	87+68	Bo.105P	HFR-16
86+16	Bo.105P	HFWS	86+93	Bo.105P	HFVS-910	87+69	Bo.105P	HFR-26
86+17	Bo.105P	HFVS-910	86+94	Bo.105P	HFWS	87+70	Bo.105P	HFR-16
86+18	Bo.105P	HFR-26	86+95	Bo.105P	HFR-16	87+71	Bo.105P	HFR-26
86+19	Bo.105P	HFR-26	86+96	Bo.105P	HFR-26	87+72	Bo.105P	HFR-16
86+20	Bo.105P	HFWS	86+97	Bo.105P	HFR-36	87+73	Bo.105P	HFWS
86+21	Bo.105P	HFR-36	86+98	Bo.105P	HFR-16	87+74	Bo.105P	HFVS-910
86+22	Bo.105P	HFWS	86+99	Bo.105P	HFR-26	87+75	Bo.105P	HFR-16
86+23	Bo.105P	HFWS	87+00	Bo.105P	HFR-26	87+76	Bo.105P	HFR-16
86+24	Bo.105P	HFVS-910	87+01	Bo.105P	HFR-26	87+77	Bo.105P	HFR-16
86+25	Bo.105P	HFR-16	87+02	Bo.105P	HFR-26	87+78	Bo.105P	HFR-16
86+26	Bo.105P	HFS-400	87+03	Bo.105P	HFR-26	87+79	Bo.105P	HFR-16
86+27	Bo.105P	HFR-26	87+04	Bo.105P	HFR-26	87+80	Bo.105P	HFR-16
86+28	Bo.105P	HFR-16	87+05	Bo.105P	HFR-26	87+81	Bo.105P	HFR-16
86+29	Bo.105P	HFR-16	87+06	Bo.105P	HFR-36	87+82	Bo.105P	HFR-16
86+30	Bo.105P	HFR-26	87+07	Bo.105P	HFR-26	87+83	Bo.105P	HFR-16
86+31	Bo.105P	HFR-16	87+08	Bo.105P	HFR-16	87+84	Bo.105P	HFVS-910
86+32	Bo.105P	HFR-26	87+09	Bo.105P	HFR-36	87+85	Bo.105P	HFR-26
86+33	Bo.105P	HFR-26	87+10	Bo.105P	HFR-36	87+86	Bo.105P	HFR-26
86+34	Bo.105P	HFR-26	87+11	Bo.105P	HFR-36	87+87	Bo.105P	HFR-16
86+35	Bo.105P	HFR-26	87+12	Bo.105P	HFR-36	87+88	Bo.105P	HFR-26
86+36	Bo.105P	HFR-36	87+13	Bo.105P	HFR-36	87+89	Bo.105P	HFR-26
86+37	Bo.105P	HFR-16	87+14	Bo.105P	HFR-36	87+90	Bo.105P	HFWS
86+38	Bo.105P	HFR-36	87+15	Bo.105P	HFR-36	87+91	Bo.105P	HFR-26
86+39	Bo.105P	HFR-16	87+16	Bo.105P	HFR-36	87+92	Bo.105P	HFR-26
86+41	Bo.105P	HFR-16	87+17	Bo.105P	HFR-26	87+93	Bo.105P	HFR-26
86+42	Bo.105P	HFR-26	87+18	Bo.105P	HFWS	87+94	Bo.105P	HFR-26
86+43	Bo.105P	HFR-16	87+19	Bo.105P	HFR-36	87+95	Bo.105P	HFR-26
86+44	Bo.105P	HFR-26	87+20	Bo.105P	HFR-26	87+96	Bo.105P	HFR-26
86+45	Bo.105P	HFVS-910	87+21	Bo.105P	HFWS	87+97	Bo.105P	HFR-36
86+46	Bo.105P	HFR-26	87+22	Bo.105P	HFR-16	87+98	Bo.105P	HFR-26
86+47	Bo.105P	HFR-16	87+23	Bo.105P	HFR-36	87+99	Bo.105P	HFR-36
86+48	Bo.105P	HFR-16	87+24	Bo.105P	HFR-16	88+01	Bo.105P	HFR-26
86+49	Bo.105P	HFR-26	87+25	Bo.105P	HFR-26	88+02	Bo.105P	HFR-36
86+50	Bo.105P	HFR-16	87+26	Bo.105P	HFR-16	88+03	Bo.105P	HFR-36
86+51	Bo.105P	HFR-36	87+27	Bo.105P	HFR-16	88+04	Bo.105P	HFR-16
86+52	Bo.105P	HFR-16	87+28	Bo.105P	HFR-16	88+05	Bo.105P	HFVS-910
86+53	Bo.105P	HFR-26	87+29	Bo.105P	HFVS-910	88+06	Bo.105P	HFR-36
86+54	Bo.105P	HFR-16	87+30	Bo.105P	HFR-16	88+07	Bo.105P	HFR-36
86+55	Bo.105P	HFR-16	87+31	Bo.105P	HFR-16	88+08	Bo.105P	HFR-36
86+56	Bo.105P	HFR-36	87+32	Bo.105P	HFR-16	88+09	Bo.105P	HFR-36
86+57	Bo.105P	HFR-16	87+33	Bo.105P	HFR-26	88+10	Bo.105P	HFWS
86+58	Bo.105P	HFR-36	87+34	Bo.105P	HFR-26	88+11	Bo.105P	HFR-58
86+59	Bo.105P	HFR-16	87+35	Bo.105P	HFR-26	88+12	Bo.105P	HFR-36
86+60	Bo.105P	HFR-16	87+36	Bo.105P	HFR-26	98+28	Bo.105C	WTD-61
86+61	Bo.105P	HFR-26	87+37	Bo.105P	HFR-26			
86+62	Bo.105P	HFVS-910	87+38	Bo.105P	HFR-36			
86+63	Bo.105P	HFR-26	87+39	Bo.105P	HFR-36			
86+64	Bo.105P	HFR-26	87+41	Bo.105P	HFR-16			
86+65	Bo.105P	HFR-26	87+42	Bo.105P	HFR-36			
86+66	Bo.105P	HFVS-910	87+43	Bo.105P	HFR-36			
86+67	Bo.105P	HFR-26	87+44	Bo.105P	HFR-36			
86+68	Bo.105P	HFR-36	87+45	Bo.105P	TsLw-3			
86+69	Bo.105P	HFR-26	87+46	Bo.105P	HFR-16			
86+70	Bo.105P	HFR-16	87+47	Bo.105P	HFR-16			
86+71	Bo.105P	HFR-36	87+48	Bo.105P	HFR-16			
86+72	Bo.105P	HFR-36	87+49	Bo.105P	HFR-16			
86+73	Bo.105P	HFWS	87+50	Bo.105P	HFR-26			
86+74	Bo.105P	HFR-36	87+51	Bo.105P	HFR-16			
86+75	Bo.105P	HFR-36	87+52	Bo.105P	HFR-16			
86+76	Bo.105P	HFR-26	87+53	Bo.105P	HFR-26			

**Sikorsky/VFW CH-53G/
CH-53GS***

HFlgRgt-15, Rheine-
Bentlage;
HFlgRgt-25, Laupheim;
HFlgRgt-35, Mendig;
HFWS, Bückeburg;
TsLw-3, Fassberg;
WTD-61, Ingolstadt

84+01*	WTD-61	
84+02	WTD-61	
84+03	HFR-15	
84+04	HFWS	
84+05	HFR-35	
84+06	HFR-15	

84+07	HFWS
84+09	HFR-25
84+10	HFWS
84+11	HFWS
84+12	HFR-15
84+13	HFWS
84+14	HFWS
84+15*	HFR-25
84+16	HFWS
84+17	HFR-25
84+18	HFWS
84+19	HFWS
84+20	HFR-35
84+21	HFWS
84+22	HFR-15
84+23	HFR-35
84+24	HFR-35
84+25*	HFR-35
84+26	HFR-35
84+27	HFR-25
84+28	HFR-25
84+29	HFR-35
84+30	HFR-35
84+31	HFR-35
84+32	HFR-35
84+33	HFR-35
84+34	HFR-35
84+35	HFR-35
84+36	HFR-35
84+37	HFWS
84+38	HFR-35
84+39	HFR-35
84+40	HFR-25
84+41	HFWS
84+42	HFR-25
84+43	HFR-25
84+44	HFR-25
84+45*	HFR-25
84+46	HFR-35
84+47	HFR-25
84+48	HFR-25
84+49	HFWS
84+50	HFR-25
84+51	HFR-25
84+52*	HFR-25
84+53	HFR-25
84+54	HFR-25
84+55	HFR-25
84+56	HFR-35
84+57	HFR-25
84+58	HFR-25
84+59	HFR-25
84+60	HFR-25
84+62	HFR-25
84+63	HFR-25
84+64	HFR-35
84+65	HFR-35
84+66	HFR-35
84+67	HFR-35
84+68	HFWS
84+69	HFR-15
84+70	HFR-15
84+71	HFR-15
84+72	HFR-15
84+73	HFR-15
84+74	HFR-15
84+75	HFR-15
84+76	HFR-15
84+77	HFR-15
84+78	HFR-15
84+79*	HFR-15
84+80	HFR-15
84+82	HFR-35
84+83	HFR-15

84+84	HFR-15
84+85	HFR-15
84+86	HFR-15
84+87	HFR-15
84+88	HFR-15
84+89	HFR-15
84+90	HFR-15
84+91	HFR-15
84+93	HFR-35
84+94	HFR-35
84+95	HFR-25
84+96	HFR-25
84+97	HFR-25
84+98	HFWS
84+99	HFR-15
85+00*	HFWS
85+01	HFR-35
85+02	HFR-35
85+03	HFR-35
85+04	HFR-25
85+05	HFR-25
85+06	HFR-25
85+07	HFR-15
85+08	HFR-15
85+09*	HFR-15
85+10	HFR-35
85+11	HFR-25
85+12*	HFR-15

Eurocopter AS.665 Tiger
WTD-61, Ingolstadt
98+23
98+25

GHANA
Ghana Air Force
   Fokker F-28
   Fellowship 3000
   VIP Flight, Accra
   G-530

   Grumman G.1159A
   Gulfstream III
   VIP Flight, Accra
   G-540

GREECE
Ellinikí Polemikí Aeroporía
   Embraer ERJ.135LR
   356 MTM/112 PM, Elefsís
   145-209

   Lockheed C-130H Hercules
   356 MTM/112 PM, Elefsís
   *ECM
   741*
   742
   743
   744
   745
   746
   747*
   749
   751
   752

   Lockheed F-16C/F-16D*
   Fighting Falcon
   330 Mira/111 PM,
      Nea Ankhialos;
   341 Mira/111 PM,
      Nea Ankhialos;
   346 MAPK/110 PM, Larissa;

347 Mira/111 PM,	
Nea Ankhialos	
045	347 Mira
046	341 Mira
047	347 Mira
048	341 Mira
049	347 Mira
050	341 Mira
051	347 Mira
052	341 Mira
053	347 Mira
054	341 Mira
055	347 Mira
056	347 Mira
057	347 Mira
058	341 Mira
059	347 Mira
060	347 Mira
061	347 Mira
062	341 Mira
063	347 Mira
064	341 Mira
065	347 Mira
066	341 Mira
067	347 Mira
068	341 Mira
069	347 Mira
070	341 Mira
071	347 Mira
072	341 Mira
073	347 Mira
074	341 Mira
075	341 Mira
076	341 Mira
077*	341 Mira
078*	341 Mira
079*	347 Mira
080*	341 Mira
081*	341 Mira
082*	341 Mira
083*	341 Mira
084*	341 Mira
110	330 Mira
111	330 Mira
112	346 MAPK
113	330 Mira
114	346 MAPK
115	330 Mira
116	330 Mira
117	346 MAPK
118	346 MAPK
119	330 Mira
120	330 Mira
121	330 Mira
122	346 MAPK
124	330 Mira
125	330 Mira
126	346 MAPK
127	330 Mira
128	346 MAPK
129	330 Mira
130	346 MAPK
132	346 MAPK
133	330 Mira
134	346 MAPK
136	346 MAPK
138	346 MAPK
139	330 Mira
140	346 MAPK
141	330 Mira
143	346 MAPK
144*	330 Mira
145*	330 Mira
146*	346 MAPK

147* 330 Mira
148* 346 MAPK
149* 330 Mira

SAAB SF.340AEW&C
380 Mira, Elefsis
004

Greek Govt
Dassault Falcon 900
Greek Govt/Olympic Airways, Athens
SX-ECH

HUNGARY
Magyar Honvédseg Repülö Csapatai
Antonov An-26
89 VSD, Szolnok

405	(03405)
406	(03406)
407	(03407)
603	(03603)

Mikoyan MiG-29/29UB*
59 HRO, Kecskemét
01
02
03
04
05
06
07
08
09
10
11
12
14
15
16
18
19
20
21
23
24*
25*
26*
27*
28*
29*

ISRAEL
Heyl ha'Avir
Boeing 707
120 Sqn, Tel Aviv

120	RC-707
128	RC-707
137	RC-707
140	KC-707
242	VC-707
248	KC-707
250	KC-707
255	EC-707
258	EC-707
260	KC-707
264	RC-707
272	VC-707
275	KC-707
290	VC-707

Lockheed C-130 Hercules
103 Sqn & 131 Sqn, Tel Aviv

102	C-130H
106	C-130H
208	C-130H
305	C-130E
309	C-130E
310	C-130E
313	C-130E
314	C-130E
316	C-130E
420	C-130H
427	C-130H
428	C-130H
435	C-130H
436	KC-130H
522	KC-130H
545	KC-130H

Israeli Govt
Hawker 800XP
Israeli Govt, Tel Aviv
4X-COV

ITALY
Aeronautica Militare Italiana
Aeritalia G222/C-27J
9ª Brigata Aerea, Pratica di Mare: 8° Gruppo & 71° Gruppo;
46ª Brigata Aerea, Pisa: 2° Gruppo & 98° Gruppo;
RSV, Pratica di Mare

G222AAA

CSX62144	46-98	RSV

G222RM

MM62139	14-20	8
MM62140	14-21	8
MM62141	14-22	8
MM62142	14-23	8

G222TCM

MM62104	46-91	98
MM62109	46-96	98
MM62111	46-83	98
MM62117	46-25	2
MM62119	46-21	2
MM62124	46-88	98
MM62125	14-24	8
MM62135	46-94	98
MM62136	46-97	98
MM62137	46-95	98
MM62145	46-50	8
MM62146	46-51	8
MM62147	46-52	8
MM62152	RS-45	RSV
MM62153X	RS-46	RSV
MM62154	46-54	8
MM62155	46-53	8

G222VS

MM62107		71

C-27J

CSX62127		Alenia

Aeritalia-EMB AMX/AMX-T*
2° Stormo, Rivolto: 14° Gruppo;
32° Stormo, Amendola: 13° Gruppo & 101° Gruppo;
51° Stormo, Istrana: 103° Gruppo & 132° Gruppo;
RSV, Pratica di Mare

MMX595		Alenia
MMX596		Alenia
MMX597		Alenia
MMX599		Alenia
MM7089		
MM7090		
MM7091	32-64	101
MM7092	RS-14	RSV
MM7093		
MM7094	3-37	
MM7095		103
MM7096		
MM7097	3-36	
MM7098	3-35	
MM7099		
MM7100	32-66	101
MM7101	51-25	103
MM7102	2-03	14
MM7103		
MM7104	51-26	103
MM7106	3-25	
MM7107		
MM7110		
MM7111	51-50	132
MM7112		
MM7115	2-12	14
MM7116	32-11	13
MM7117	3-34	
MM7118	2-11	14
MM7119		
MM7120	51-52	132
MM7122	3-32	
MM7123		
MM7124	51-15	103
MM7125	RS-11	RSV
MM7126		
MM7127	3-24	
MM7128		
MM7129	2-03	14
MM7130		
MM7131	2-19	14
MM7132	51-14	103
MM7133	2-18	14
MM7134		
MM7135		
MM7138		
MM7139	51-16	103
MM7140	51-26	132
MM7141		
MM7142	51-37	132
MM7143	51-20	103
MM7144	51-41	132
MM7145	51-44	132
MM7146	51-42	132
MM7147	32-04	13
MM7148	51-22	103
MM7149		
MM7150	32-65	101
MM7151	2-14	14
MM7152		
MM7153	2-20	14
MM7154	51-54	132
MM7155	32-05	13
MM7156	32-10	13
MM7157	32-06	13
CSX7158	RS-12	RSV
MM7159		
MM7160	32-14	13
MM7161	2-21	14
MM7162	51-01	103
MM7163	2-25	14
MM7164	51-30	132
MM7165	51-31	132
MM7166	32-14	13
MM7167	2-01	14
MM7168	2-04	14
MM7169	2-06	14

Italy

MM7170	2-23	14
MM7171	2-15	14
MM7172	2-07	14
MM7173	2-16	14
MM7174		
MM7175	51-43	132
MM7176	2-20	14
MM7177	2-22	14
MM7178	2-24	14
MM7179	51-11	103
MM7180		
MM7181	51-32	132
MM7182	51-04	103
MM7183	32-01	13
MM7184	51-33	132
MM7185	51-35	132
MM7186	51-05	103
MM7187	32-16	13
MM7189	51-03	103
MM7190	32-17	13
MM7191		
MM7192	51-06	103
MM7193	51-07	103
MM7194	32-07	13
MM7195	51-37	132
MM7196	32-13	13
MM7197	32-21	13
MM7198	32-03	13
MM55024*	15	RSV
MM55025*	RS-16	RSV
MM55026*	32-43	101
MM55027*		
MM55029*	3-55	
MM55030*	32-41	101
MM55031*	32-40	101
MM55034*	18	RSV
MM55035*	32-50	101
MM55036*	32-51	101
MM55037*	32-64	101
MM55038*	32-53	101
MM55039*	32-54	101
MM55040*	32-52	101
MM55041*	32-55	101
MM55042*	32-56	101
MM55043*	51-10	103
MM55044*	32-57	101
MM55045*	2-10	14
MM55046*	32-47	101
MM55047*	32-45	101
MM55048*	32-44	101
MM55049*	32-46	101
MM55050*	32-43	101
MM55051*	32-42	101

Aermacchi MB339A/MB339CD*

61° Stormo, Lecce:
212° Gruppo & 213° Gruppo;
Aermacchi, Venegono;
Frecce Tricolori [FT] (313° Gruppo), Rivolto (MB339A/PAN);
RSV, Pratica di Mare

MMX606*		RSV
MM54438	61-93	
MM54440	61-00	
MM54441	61-71	
MM54442	61-95	
MM54443	61-50	
MM54445	61-25	
MM54446	61-01	
MM54447	61-02	
MM54449	61-04	
MM54450	61-94	
MM54451	61-86	
MM54452		
MM54453	61-05	
MM54454	61-06	
MM54455	61-07	
MM54456	61-10	
MM54457	61-11	
MM54458	61-12	
MM54459	61-13	
MM54460	61-14	
MM54461		
MM54462	61-16	
MM54463	61-17	
MM54467	61-23	
MM54468	61-24	
MM54471	61-27	
MM54472	61-30	
MM54473	8	[FT]
MM54475	1	[FT]
MM54477	9	[FT]
MM54478		[FT]
MM54479	12	[FT]
MM54480	7	[FT]
MM54482	13	[FT]
MM54483	61-102	
MM54484	61-101	
MM54485		[FT]
MM54486	10	[FT]
MM54487	61-31	
MM54488	61-32	
MM54489	61-33	
MM54490	61-34	
MM54491	61-35	
MM54492	61-36	
MM54493	61-37	
MM54494	61-40	
MM54496	61-42	
MM54497	61-43	
MM54498	61-44	
MM54499	61-45	
MM54500	4	[FT]
MM54503	61-51	
MM54504	61-52	
MM54505	61-53	
MM54506	61-54	
MM54507	61-55	
MM54508	61-56	
MM54509	61-57	
MM54510	61-60	
MM54511	61-61	
MM54512	61-62	
MM54513	61-63	
MM54514	61-64	
MM54515	61-65	
MM54516	61-66	
MM54517	3	[FT]
MM54518	61-70	
MM54532		
MM54533	61-72	
MM54534	61-73	
MM54535	61-74	
MM54536		[FT]
MM54537		
MM54538	61-75	
MM54539	61-76	
MM54541	61-100	
MM54542		[FT]
MM54543	6	[FT]
MM54544*	(Aermacchi)	
MM54545	61-84	
MM54546	5	[FT]
MM54547	0	[FT]
MM54548	61-90	
MM54549	61-107	
MM54550	61-110	
MM54551	2	[FT]
MM55052	61-96	
MM55053	61-97	
MM55054	61-15	
MM55055	61-20	
MM55058	61-41	
MM55059	61-26	
MM55062*	RS-26	RSV
MM55063*	RS-27	RSV
MM55064*	61-130	
MM55065*	61-131	
MM55066*	61-132	
MM55067*	61-133	
MM55068*	61-134	
MM55069*	61-135	
MM55070*	61-136	
MM55072*	61-140	
MM55073*	61-141	
MM55074*	61-142	
MM55075*	61-143	
MM55076*	61-144	

Airbus A.319CJ-115

31° Stormo,
Roma-Ciampino:
93° Gruppo

MM62173
MM62174

Boeing 707-328B/-3F5C*

9ª Brigata Aerea,
Pratica di Mare:
8° Gruppo;

MM62148	14-01
MM62149	14-02
MM62150*	14-03
MM62151*	14-04

Breguet Br.1150 Atlantic

30° Stormo, Cagliari:
86° Gruppo;
41° Stormo, Catania:
88° Gruppo

MM40108	41-70
MM40109	30-71
MM40110	41-72
MM40111	41-73
MM40112	30-74
MM40113	30-75
MM40114	41-76
MM40115	41-77
MM40116	30-01
MM40117	41-02
MM40118	30-03
MM40119	30-04
MM40120	41-05
MM40121	41-06
MM40122	30-07
MM40123	30-10
MM40124	41-11
MM40125	41-12

Dassault Falcon 50

31° Stormo,
Roma-Ciampino:
93° Gruppo

MM62020
MM62021
MM62026
MM62029

Dassault Falcon 900EX
31° Stormo,
Roma-Ciampino:
93° Gruppo

| MM62171 | | |
| MM62172 | | |

Eurofighter Typhoon
Aeritalia, Torino/Caselle;
RSV, Pratica di Mare

| MMX602 | RS-01 | RSV |
| MMX603 | (Aeritalia) | |

Grumman G.1159A Gulfstream III
31° Stormo,
Roma-Ciampino:
306° Gruppo

| MM62022 | | |
| MM62025 | | |

Lockheed F-104 Starfighter
4° Stormo, Grosseto:
9° Gruppo & 20° Gruppo;
5° Stormo, Cervia:
23° Gruppo;
9° Stormo, Grazzanise:
10° Gruppo;
37° Stormo, Trapani:
18° Gruppo;
RSV, Pratica di Mare

F-104S-ASA/F104ASA-M*

CMX611*	RS-06	RSV
MM6704	4-7	9
MM6705	4-5	9
MM6710		
MM6713	4-2	9
MM6714		
MM6716*	4-50	20
MM6717*	5-41	23
MM6719*	9-52	10
MM6720*	9-51	10
MM6721*	4-1	9
MM6722*	5-31	23
MM6726		
MM6731*	37-03	18
MM6732*	37-04	18
MM6733*	9-33	10
MM6734*	4-11	9
MM6735*	9-50	10
MM6736		
MM6737*	5-46	23
MM6739*	5-47	23
MM6740*	4-56	20
MM6748		
MM6756*	5-42	23
MM6759*	37-20	18
MM6762*	37-02	18
MM6763*	4-58	20
MM6764*	9-39	10
MM6767	37-05	18
MM6769	4-53	20
MM6770*	9-35	10
MM6771*	5-35	23
MM6772	37-11	18
MM6773		
MM6776*	9-46	10
MM6778*	9-40	10
MM6787*	9-32	10
MM6805	4-10	9
MM6812*	9-41	10
MM6816	4-6	9
MM6818		
MM6823		
MM6830	4-42	20
MM6838*	4-57	20
MM6839		
MM6841		
MM6848*	4-52	20
MM6849*	5-32	23
MM6850*	37-24	18
MM6870*	5-45	23
MM6872*	37-23	18
MM6873		
MM6875	4-14	9
MM6876*	37-21	18
MM6879	4-15	9
MM6880*		
MM6881*	5-41	23
MM6886	5-02	
MM6887*	5-33	23
MM6890*	37-25	18
MM6912*	9-42	10
MM6914*	37-01	18
MM6923*	9-32	10
MM6924		
MM6925*	37-15	18
MM6926*	37-12	18
MM6929*	9-43	10
MM6930*	9-53	10
MM6932*	5-40	23
MM6934	RS-07	RSV
MM6935*	5-30	23
MM6936*	9-41	10
MM6939*	37-22	18
MM6940	4-50	20
MM6941	4-4	9
MM6942		
MM6943	4-1	9
MM6944		

TF-104G/TF-104G-M*

MM54226*	4-23	20
MM54228	4-26	20
MM54232	4-29	20
MM54233	RS-09	RSV
MM54237*	4-32	20
MM54250*	4-33	20
MM54251*	4-34	20
MM54253	4-35	20
MM54254*	4-36	20
MM54255	4-37	20
MM54256	4-38	20
MM54258	4-40	20
MM54260	4-41	20
MM54261*	4-42	20
MM54553*	4-44	20
MM54554*	4-48	20
MM54555*	4-45	20
MM54556*	4-47	20

Lockheed C-130H Hercules
46ª Brigata Aerea, Pisa:
50° Gruppo

MM61988	46-02
MM61989	46-03
MM61990	46-04
MM61991	46-05
MM61992	46-06
MM61993	46-07
MM61994	46-08
MM61995	46-09
MM61997	46-11
MM61998	46-12

Lockheed C-130J Hercules II
46ª Brigata Aerea, Pisa:
2° Gruppo

MM62175	46-40
MM62176	46-41
MM62177	46-42
MM62178	46-43
MM62179	46-44
MM62180	46-45
MM62181	46-46
MM62182	46-47
MM62183	46-48
MM62184	46-49

Panavia Tornado ADV/Trainer[1]
36° Stormo, Gioia del Colle:
12° Gruppo

MM7202	36-33	(ZE832)
MM7203	36-02	(ZE761)
MM7204	36-05	(ZE730)
MM7205	36-06	(ZE787)
MM7206	36-26	(ZE760)
MM7207	36-27	(ZE762)
MM7208	36-32	(ZE811)
MM7209	36-25	(ZE835)
MM7210	36-14	(ZE836)
MM7211	36-16	(ZE792)
MM7225	36-04	(ZE252)
MM7226	36-21	(ZE911)
MM7227	36-22	(ZG732)
MM7228	36-34	(ZG733)
MM7229	36-07	(ZG728)
MM7230	36-11	(ZG730)
MM7231	36-12	(ZG734)
MM7232	36-10	(ZG735)
MM7233	36-23	(ZG768)
MM7234	36-24	(ZE167)
MM55056[1]	36-01	(ZE202)
MM55057[1]	36-03	(ZE837)
MM55060[1]	36-30	(ZE208)
MM55061[1]	36-20	(ZE205)

Panavia Tornado Strike/Trainer[1]/ECR[2]
6° Stormo, Ghedi:
102° Gruppo &
154° Gruppo;
50° Stormo, Piacenza:
155° Gruppo;
156° Gruppo Autonomo,
Gioia del Colle;
RSV, Pratica di Mare

MM7002	6-10	154
MM7003	6-23	154
MM7004	50-52	155
MM7005	6-05	154
MM7006	6-16	154
MM7007	36-37	156
MM7008		
MM7009		
MM7011	6-33	102
MM7013	36-40	156
MM7014		
MM7015	50-53	155
MM7016	6-26	154
MM7018	6-46	102
MM7019[2]	50-19	155
MM7020[2]	50-21	155
MM7021[2]	50-01	155
MM7022	6-02	154
MM7023	6-13	154
MM7025	6-43	102
MM7026		
MM7027	6-47	102
MM7028	6-18	154
MM7029	6-19	154

MM7030		
MM7031	6-21	154
MM7033	50-50	155
MM7034	6-30	154
MM7035	36-47	156
MM7036[2]	50-..	155
MM7037	6-07	154
MM7038	36-41	156
MM7039	50-03	155
CMX7040	RS-01	RSV
MM7041		
MM7042	6-31	102
MM7043		
MM7044	6-20	154
MM7046[2]	6-06	154
MM7047[2]	50-43	155
MM7048	36-54	Alenia
MM7049	6-34	102
MM7050	36-44	156
MM7051	50-45	155
MM7052		
MM7053[2]	50-07	155
MM7054[2]	50-40	155
MM7055	50-42	155
MM7056	50-47	155
MM7057	6-12	154
MM7058	6-36	102
MM7059	50-47	155
MM7060	6-32	102
MM7061	6-01	154
MM7062[2]	50-44	155
MM7063	36-42	156
MM7064	6-24	154
MM7065	6-25	154
MM7066	6-44	102
MM7067	67	156
MM7068[2]		Alenia
MM7070[2]	50-06	155
MM7071	6-35	102
MM7072	36-57	156
MM7073	36-43	156
MM7075	50-05	155
MM7078	50-02	155
CMX7079[2]		Alenia
MM7080	6-41	102
MM7081	6-02	154
MM7082[2]	6-14	154
MM7083	6-37	102
MM7084	6-36	102
CMX7085	36-50	Alenia
MM7086	6-04	154
MM7087	36-35	156
MM7088	6-18	154
MM55000[1]	6-51	102
MM55001[1]	6-42	102
MM55002[1]	6-..	102
MM55003[1]	6-..	154
MM55004[1]	6-53	102
MM55005[1]	6-40	102
MM55006[1]	6-44	102
MM55007[1]	36-55	156
MM55008[1]	6-45	102
MM55009[1]	36-56	156
MM55010[1]	6-42	102
MM55011[1]		

Piaggio P-180AM Avanti
14° Stormo, Guidonia:
  303° Gruppo;
36° Stormo, Gioia del Colle:
  636° SC;
RSV, Pratica di Mare

MM62159		636
MM62160	54	RSV

MM62161		303
MM62162		303
MM62163		303
CSX62164		RSV

**Piaggio-Douglas
PD-808-GE/PD-808-RM/
PD-808-TA**
9ª Brigata Aerea,
  Pratica di Mare:
  8° Gruppo &
  71° Gruppo;
RSV, Pratica di Mare

MM61952	GE	71
MM61954	TA	71
MM61955	GE	71
MM61960	GE	71
MM61961	GE	71
MM61962	GE	71
MM62014	RM	8

**Guardia di Finanza
Aérospatiale
ATR.42-400MP**
2° Gruppo EM,
  Pratica di Mare

MM62165	GF-13
MM62166	GF-14

**Marina Militare Italiana
McDonnell Douglas
AV-8B/TAV-8B Harrier II+**
Gruppo Aerei Imbarcarti,
  Taranto/Grottaglie
AV-8B

MM7199	1-03
MM7200	1-04
MM7201	1-05
MM7212	1-06
MM7213	1-07
MM7214	1-08
MM7215	1-09
MM7216	1-10
MM7217	1-11
MM7218	1-12
MM7219	1-13
MM7220	1-14
MM7221	1-15
MM7222	1-16
MM7223	1-18
MM7224	1-19

TAV-8B

MM55032	1-01
MM55033	1-02

**Italian Govt
Dassault Falcon 200**
Italian Govt/Soc. CAI,
  Roma/Ciampino
I-CNEF
I-SOBE

Dassault Falcon 900
Italian Govt/Soc. CAI,
  Roma/Ciampino
I-DIES
I-FICV
I-NUMI

**IVORY COAST
Fokker 100**
Ivory Coast Govt, Abidjan
TU-VAA

**Grumman G.1159C
Gulfstream IV**
Ivory Coast Govt, Abidjan
TU-VAD

**JAPAN
Japan Air Self Defence Force
Boeing 747-47C**
701st Flight Sqn, Chitose
20-1101
20-1102

**JORDAN
Al Quwwat al Jawwiya
al Malakiya al Urduniya
Extra EA-300S**
*Royal Jordanian Falcons,
  Amman*
JY-RNA
JY-RNC
JY-RND
JY-RNE
JY-RNG

Lockheed C-130H Hercules
3 Sqn, Al Matar AB/Amman
344
345
346
347

**Jordanian Govt
Airbus A.340-211**
Jordanian Govt, Amman
JY-ABH

Canadair CL.604 Challenger
Jordanian Govt, Amman
JY-ONE
JY-TWO

**Lockheed L.1011
TriStar 500**
Jordanian Govt, Amman
JY-HKJ

**KAZAKHSTAN
Boeing 757-2M6**
Govt of Kazakhstan, Almaty
P4-NSN

Tupolev Tu-134A-3
Govt of Kazakhstan, Almaty
UN-65799

**KENYA
Kenyan Air Force
Fokker 70ER**
308

**KUWAIT
Al Quwwat al Jawwiya
al Kuwaitiya
Lockheed L100-30
Hercules**
41 Sqn, Kuwait International
KAF 323
KAF 324
KAF 325

**Kuwaiti Govt
Airbus A.300C4-620**
Kuwaiti Govt, Safat
9K-AHI

Airbus A.310-308
Kuwaiti Govt, Safat
9K-ALD

Grumman G.1159C
Gulfstream IV
Kuwaiti Govt/Kuwait
Airways, Safat
9K-AJA
9K-AJB

Gulfstream Aerospace
Gulfstream V
Kuwaiti Govt/Kuwait
Airways, Safat
9K-AJD
9K-AJE
9K-AJF

KYRGYZSTAN
Tupolev Tu-134A-3
Govt of Kyrgyzstan, Bishkek
EX-65119

Tupolev Tu-134B/Tu-154M
Govt of Kyrgyzstan, Bishkek
EX-85294 Tu-154B
EX-85718 Tu-154M
EX-85762 Tu-154M

LITHUANIA
Karines Oro Pajegos
Let 410 Turbolet
I Transporto Eskadrile,
Zokniai
01
02

Lithuanian Govt
Lockheed L.1329
Jetstar 731
Lithuanian Govt, Vilnius
LY-AMB

LUXEMBOURG
NATO
Boeing 707-307C
NAEWF, Geilenkirchen
LX-N19997
LX-N19999
LX-N20000

Boeing E-3A
NAEWF, Geilenkirchen
LX-N90442
LX-N90443
LX-N90444
LX-N90445
LX-N90446
LX-N90447
LX-N90448
LX-N90449
LX-N90450
LX-N90451
LX-N90452
LX-N90453
LX-N90454
LX-N90455
LX-N90456
LX-N90458
LX-N90459

MALAYSIA
Royal Malaysian Air Force/
Tentera Udara Diraja
Malaysia
Bombardier BD.700-1A10
Global Express
2 Sqn, Simpang
M48-01

Lockheed C-130 Hercules
4 Sqn, Subang;
14 Sqn, Labuan;
20 Sqn, Subang

M30-01	C-130H(MP)	4 Sqn
M30-02	C-130H	14 Sqn
M30-03	C-130H	14 Sqn
M30-04	C-130H	14 Sqn
M30-05	C-130H	14 Sqn
M30-06	C-130H	14 Sqn
M30-07	C-130T	4 Sqn
M30-08	C-130H(MP)	20 Sqn
M30-09	C-130H(MP)	20 Sqn
M30-10	C-130H-30	20 Sqn
M30-11	C-130H-30	20 Sqn
M30-12	C-130H-30	20 Sqn
M30-14	C-130H-30	20 Sqn
M30-15	C-130H-30	20 Sqn
M30-16	C-130H-30	20 Sqn

MEXICO
Fuerza Aérea Mexicana
Boeing 757-225
8° Grupo Aéreo, Mexico City
TP-01 (XC-UJM)

MOROCCO
Force Aérienne Royaume
Marocaine/ Al Quwwat al
Jawwiya al Malakiya
Marakishiya
Airtech CN.235M-100
Escadrille de Transport,
Rabat
023 CNA-MA
024 CNA-MB
025 CNA-MC
026 CNA-MD
027 CNA-ME
028 CNA-MF
031 CNA-MG

CAP-231/CAP-232
Marche Verte
CAP-231
09 CN-ABL
22 CN-ABM
23 CN-ABN
24 CN-ABO
CAP-232
28 CNA-BP
29 CN-ABQ
31 CN-ABR

Lockheed C-130H Hercules
Escadrille de Transport,
Rabat
4535 CN-AOA
4551 CN-AOC
4575 CN-AOD
4581 CN-AOE
4583 CN-AOF
4713 CN-AOG
4717 CN-AOH
4733 CN-AOI

4738 CN-AOJ
4739 CN-AOK
4742 CN-AOL
4875 CN-AOM
4876 CN-AON
4877 CN-AOO
4888 CN-AOP
4892 CN-AOQ
4907 CN-AOR
4909 CN-AOS
4940 CN-AOT

Govt of Morocco
Boeing 707-138B
Govt of Morocco, Rabat
CNA-NS

Cessna 560 Citation V
Govt of Morocco, Rabat
CNA-NW

Dassault Falcon 50
Govt of Morocco, Rabat
CN-ANO

Grumman G.1159
Gulfstream IITT/G.1159A
Gulfstream III
Govt of Morocco, Rabat
CNA-NL Gulfstream IITT
CNA-NU Gulfstream III
CNA-NV Gulfstream III

NAMIBIA
Dassault Falcon 900B
Namibian Govt, Windhoek
V5-NAM

NETHERLANDS
Koninklijke Luchtmacht
Agusta-Bell AB.412SP
303 Sqn, Leeuwarden
R-01
R-02
R-03

Boeing-Vertol CH-47D
Chinook
298 Sqn, Soesterberg
D-101
D-102
D-103
D-104
D-105
D-106
D-661
D-662
D-663
D-664
D-665
D-666
D-667

Eurocopter AS.532U-2
Cougar
300 Sqn, Gilze-Rijen
S-400
S-419
S-433
S-438
S-440
S-441
S-442
S-444

Netherlands

S-445		
S-447		
S-450		
S-453		
S-454		
S-456		
S-457		
S-458		
S-459		

Fokker 50
334 Sqn, Eindhoven
U-05
U-06

Fokker 60UTA-N
334 Sqn, Eindhoven
U-01
U-02
U-03
U-04

General Dynamics F-16
(MLU aircraft are marked
with a *)
TGp/306/311/312 Sqns,
 Volkel;
313/315 Sqns, Twenthe;
322/323 Sqns, Leeuwarden

J-001	F-16A*	322 Sqn
J-002	F-16A*	322 Sqn
J-003	F-16A*	322 Sqn
J-004	F-16A*	322 Sqn
J-005	F-16A*	322 Sqn
J-006	F-16A*	322 Sqn
J-008	F-16A*	322 Sqn
J-009	F-16A*	322 Sqn
J-010	F-16A*	323 Sqn
J-011	F-16A*	322 Sqn
J-013	F-16A*	322 Sqn
J-014	F-16A*	322 Sqn
J-015	F-16A*	313 Sqn
J-016	F-16A*	312 Sqn
J-017	F-16A*	312 Sqn
J-018	F-16A*	323 Sqn
J-019	F-16A*	323 Sqn
J-020	F-16A*	313 Sqn
J-021	F-16A*	311 Sqn
J-055	F-16A*	322 Sqn
J-057	F-16A*	323 Sqn
J-058	F-16A*	315 Sqn
J-060	F-16A*	315 Sqn
J-061	F-16A*	322 Sqn
J-062	F-16A*	322 Sqn
J-063	F-16A*	322 Sqn
J-064	F-16B*	322 Sqn
J-065	F-16B*	313 Sqn
J-066	F-16B*	TGp
J-067	F-16B*	315 Sqn
J-068	F-16B*	322 Sqn
J-135	F-16A*	312 Sqn
J-136	F-16A*	315 Sqn
J-137	F-16A*	322 Sqn
J-138	F-16A*	315 Sqn
J-139	F-16A	312 Sqn
J-141	F-16A*	315 Sqn
J-142	F-16A*	323 Sqn
J-143	F-16A*	315 Sqn
J-144	F-16A*	315 Sqn
J-145	F-16A*	313 Sqn
J-146	F-16A*	313 Sqn
J-192	F-16A*	311 Sqn
J-193	F-16A*	312 Sqn
J-194	F-16A*	312 Sqn

J-196	F-16A	312 Sqn
J-197	F-16A	312 Sqn
J-198	F-16A	306 Sqn
J-199	F-16A*	312 Sqn
J-201	F-16A*	312 Sqn
J-202	F-16A*	312 Sqn
J-203	F-16A*	311 Sqn
J-204	F-16A*	323 Sqn
J-205	F-16A*	322 Sqn
J-207	F-16A*	312 Sqn
J-208	F-16B*	312 Sqn
J-209	F-16B*	313 Sqn
J-210	F-16B*	312 Sqn
J-211	F-16B*	322 Sqn
J-243	F-16A	306 Sqn
J-251	F-16A*	306 Sqn
J-253	F-16A	312 Sqn
J-254	F-16A*	306 Sqn
J-255	F-16A*	306 Sqn
J-257	F-16A	312 Sqn
J-267	F-16B*	306 Sqn
J-269	F-16B*	312 Sqn
J-270	F-16B*	306 Sqn
J-360	F-16A*	323 Sqn
J-362	F-16A*	315 Sqn
J-363	F-16A*	323 Sqn
J-364	F-16A	312 Sqn
J-365	F-16A*	313 Sqn
J-366	F-16A*	315 Sqn
J-367	F-16A*	322 Sqn
J-368	F-16B*	306 Sqn
J-369	F-16B*	313 Sqn
J-508	F-16A*	315 Sqn
J-509	F-16A*	315 Sqn
J-510	F-16A*	312 Sqn
J-511	F-16A*	315 Sqn
J-512	F-16A*	313 Sqn
J-513	F-16A*	323 Sqn
J-514	F-16A*	315 Sqn
J-515	F-16A*	322 Sqn
J-516	F-16A*	311 Sqn
J-616	F-16A	312 Sqn
J-617	F-16A*	313 Sqn
J-619	F-16A*	311 Sqn
J-620	F-16A*	315 Sqn
J-622	F-16A*	323 Sqn
J-623	F-16A	306 Sqn
J-624	F-16A*	313 Sqn
J-627	F-16A(R)	306 Sqn
J-628	F-16A*	315 Sqn
J-630	F-16A*	311 Sqn
J-631	F-16A*	311 Sqn
J-632	F-16A*	311 Sqn
J-633	F-16A*	312 Sqn
J-635	F-16A*	312 Sqn
J-636	F-16A*	311 Sqn
J-637	F-16A*	312 Sqn
J-638	F-16A*	312 Sqn
J-640	F-16A*	311 Sqn
J-641	F-16A*	311 Sqn
J-642	F-16A*	312 Sqn
J-643	F-16A(R)	322 Sqn
J-644	F-16A*	313 Sqn
J-646	F-16A*	306 Sqn
J-647	F-16A*	311 Sqn
J-648	F-16A*	312 Sqn
J-649	F-16B	306 Sqn
J-650	F-16B*	306 Sqn
J-652	F-16B*	313 Sqn
J-653	F-16B*	TGp
J-654	F-16B*	323 Sqn
J-655	F-16B*	313 Sqn
J-656	F-16B*	306 Sqn
J-657	F-16B*	313 Sqn

J-864	F-16A*	306 Sqn
J-866	F-16A*	312 Sqn
J-867	F-16A(R)	312 Sqn
J-868	F-16A*	311 Sqn
J-869	F-16A	312 Sqn
J-870	F-16A	312 Sqn
J-871	F-16A*	311 Sqn
J-872	F-16A*	312 Sqn
J-873	F-16A	306 Sqn
J-874	F-16A*	311 Sqn
J-875	F-16A*	313 Sqn
J-876	F-16A*	311 Sqn
J-877	F-16A*	312 Sqn
J-878	F-16A*	311 Sqn
J-879	F-16A*	312 Sqn
J-881	F-16A*	323 Sqn
J-882	F-16B*	306 Sqn
J-884	F-16B*	311 Sqn
J-885	F-16B*	323 Sqn

**Grumman G-1159C
Gulfstream IV**
334 Sqn, Eindhoven
V-11

**Lockheed C-130H-30
Hercules**
334 Sqn, Eindhoven
G-273
G-275

**MBB Bo.105CB/
Bo.105CB-4***
299 Sqn, Gilze-Rijen
B-39*
B-40*
B-41*
B-43
B-44
B-47
B-48
B-63
B-64
B-66
B-68
B-69
B-70
B-74
B-75
B-76
B-77
B-78*
B-79
B-80

**MDH AH-64DN Apache
Longbow**
301 Sqn, Gilze-Rijen;
302 Sqn, Gilze-Rijen

Q-01	302 Sqn
Q-02	302 Sqn
Q-03	302 Sqn
Q-04	301 Sqn
Q-05	302 Sqn
Q-06	302 Sqn
Q-07	302 Sqn
Q-08	302 Sqn
Q-09	301 Sqn
Q-10	301 Sqn
Q-11	
Q-12	
Q-13	302 Sqn
Q-14	302 Sqn
Q-15	301 Sqn

Q-16	301 Sqn
Q-17	302 Sqn
Q-18	301 Sqn
Q-19	
Q-20	301 Sqn
Q-21	302 Sqn
Q-22	
Q-23	
Q-24	
Q-25	
Q-26	
Q-27	
Q-28	
Q-29	
Q-30	

**McDonnell Douglas
KDC-10**
334 Sqn, Eindhoven
T-235
T-264

Pilatus PC-7
131 EMVO Sqn,
    Woensdrecht
L-01
L-02
L-03
L-04
L-05
L-06
L-07
L-08
L-09
L-10
L-11
L-12
L-13

Sud Alouette III
300 Sqn, Soesterberg
A-247
A-275
A-292
A-301

**Marine Luchtvaart Dienst
Beech Super King Air 200**
OVALK, Valkenburg
PH-SBK

Lockheed P-3C Orion
MARPAT (320 Sqn &
    321 Sqn), Valkenburg
    and Keflavik
300
301
302
303
304
305
306
307
308
309
311
312

Westland SH-14D Lynx
HELIGRP (7 Sqn &
    860 Sqn), De Kooij
    (7 Sqn operates
    860 Sqn aircraft on loan)
260

261
262
264
265
266
267
268
269
270
271
272
273
274
276
277
278
279
280
281
283

**Netherlands Govt
Fokker 70**
Dutch Royal Flight, Schiphol
PH-KBX

**NEW ZEALAND
Royal New Zealand Air Force
    Boeing 727-22C**
40 Sqn, Whenuapai
NZ7271
NZ7272

Lockheed C-130H Hercules
40 Sqn, Whenuapai
NZ7001
NZ7002
NZ7003
NZ7004
NZ7005

Lockheed P-3K Orion
5 Sqn, Whenuapai
NZ4201
NZ4202
NZ4203
NZ4204
NZ4205
NZ4206

**NIGERIA
Federal Nigerian Air Force
    Lockheed C-130H Hercules**
NAF-910
NAF-912
NAF-913
NAF-915
NAF-917
NAF-918

**Nigerian Govt
    Boeing 727-2N6**
Federal Govt of Nigeria,
    Lagos
5N-FGN   [001]

Dassault Falcon 900
Federal Govt of Nigeria,
    Lagos
5N-FGE
5N-FGO

**Grumman G.1159
Gulfstream II/G.1159A
Gulfstream III**
Federal Govt of Nigeria,
    Lagos

5N-AGV	Gulfstream II
5N-FGP	Gulfstream III

**Gulfstream Aerospace
Gulfstream V**
Federal Govt of Nigeria,
    Logos
5N-FGS

Hawker 1000
Federal Govt of Nigeria,
    Lagos
5N-FGR

**NORWAY
Kongelige Norske Luftforsvaret
    Bell 412SP**
339 Skv, Bardufoss;
720 Skv, Rygge

139	339 Skv
140	339 Skv
141	720 Skv
142	720 Skv
143	339 Skv
144	339 Skv
145	720 Skv
146	720 Skv
147	720 Skv
148	339 Skv
149	339 Skv
161	339 Skv
162	339 Skv
163	720 Skv
164	720 Skv
165	720 Skv
166	720 Skv
167	720 Skv
194	720 Skv

Dassault Falcon 20 ECM
717 Skv, Rygge
041
053
0125

General Dynamics F-16
(MLU aircraft are marked
    with a *)
331 Skv, Bodø (r/w/bl);
332 Skv, Rygge (y/bk);
334 Skv, Bodø (r/w);
338 Skv, Ørland

272	F-16A*	332 Skv
273	F-16A	332 Skv
275	F-16A*	332 Skv
276	F-16A	338 Skv
277	F-16A*	332 Skv
279	F-16A	338 Skv
281	F-16A	332 Skv
282	F-16A	338 Skv
284	F-16A*	332 Skv
285	F-16A	338 Skv
286	F-16A*	338 Skv
288	F-16A*	338 Skv
289	F-16A	338 Skv
291	F-16A*	338 Skv
292	F-16A*	338 Skv
293	F-16A*	332 Skv
295	F-16A*	338 Skv

297	F-16A*	332 Skv
298	F-16A	338 Skv
299	F-16A*	332 Skv
302	F-16B*	332 Skv
304	F-16B*	332 Skv
305	F-16B*	332 Skv
306	F-16B*	332 Skv
658	F-16A	334 Skv
659	F-16A*	334 Skv
660	F-16A*	331 Skv
661	F-16A*	338 Skv
662	F-16A*	334 Skv
663	F-16A	334 Skv
664	F-16A*	331 Skv
665	F-16A*	334 Skv
666	F-16A*	334 Skv
667	F-16A*	331 Skv
668	F-16A*	331 Skv
669	F-16A*	334 Skv
670	F-16A	332 Skv
671	F-16A*	338 Skv
672	F-16A	334 Skv
673	F-16A*	331 Skv
674	F-16A	332 Skv
675	F-16A*	331 Skv
677	F-16A	331 Skv
678	F-16A	331 Skv
680	F-16A*	338 Skv
681	F-16A*	338 Skv
682	F-16A*	331 Skv
683	F-16A	334 Skv
686	F-16A	331 Skv
687	F-16A*	331 Skv
688	F-16A*	331 Skv
689	F-16B*	332 Skv
690	F-16B	334 Skv
691	F-16B	334 Skv
692	F-16B*	332 Skv
693	F-16B*	338 Skv
711	F-16B*	332 Skv

Lockheed C-130H Hercules
335 Skv, Gardermoen
952
953
954
955
956
957

Lockheed P-3C Orion
333 Skv, Andøya
3296
3297
3298
3299

Lockheed P-3N Orion
333 Skv, Andøya
4576
6603

Northrop F-5A
Eye of the Tiger Project,
Rygge
128
130
131
133
134
896
902

Northrop F-5B
Eye of the Tiger Project,
Rygge
136
243
244
387
906
907
908
909

**Westland Sea King Mk 43/
Mk 43A/Mk 43B**
330 Skv:
  A Flt, Bodø;
  B Flt, Banak;
  C Flt, Ørland;
  D Flt, Sola

060	Mk 43
062	Mk 43
066	Mk 43
069	Mk 43
070	Mk 43
071	Mk 43B
072	Mk 43
073	Mk 43
074	Mk 43
189	Mk 43A
322	Mk 43B
329	Mk 43B
330	Mk 43B

**Kystvakt (Coast Guard)
Westland Lynx Mk86**
337 Skv, Bardufoss
207
216
228
232
237
350

OMAN
**Royal Air Force of Oman
BAC 1-11/485GD**
4 Sqn, Seeb
551
552
553

Lockheed C-130H Hercules
4 Sqn, Seeb
501
502
503

**Omani Govt
Boeing 747SP-27**
Govt of Oman, Seeb
A4O-SO
A4O-SP

**Grumman G.1159C
Gulfstream IV**
Govt of Oman, Seeb
A4O-AB
A4O-AC

PAKISTAN
**Pakistan Fiza'ya
Boeing 707-340C**

68-19866	12 Sqn
69-19635	12 Sqn

**Pakistani Govt
Boeing 737-33A**
Govt of Pakistan, Karachi
AP-BEH

PERU
**Fuerza Aérea Peruana
Douglas DC-8-62AF**

370	(OB-1372)
371	(OB-1373)

POLAND
**Polskie Wojska Lotnicze
Antonov An-26**
13 PLT, Krakow/Balice
1307
1310
1402
1403
1406
1407
1508
1509
1602
1603
1604

Mikoyan MiG-29A/UB*
1 ELT, Minsk/Mazowiecki
15*
28*
29
38
40
42*
54
56
59
64*
65
66
67
70
77
83
89
92
105
108
111
114
115

Tupolev Tu-154M
36 SPLT, Warszawa
101
102

Yakovlev Yak-40
36 SPLT, Warszawa
032
034
036
037
038
039
040
041
042
043
044
045
047
048

Lotnictwo Marynarki Wojennej
Antonov An-28B-1R Bryza
1 DLMW, Gydnia/Babie
  Doly;
3 DLMW, Cewice/
  Siemirowice

0404	3 DLMW
0405	1 DLMW
0810	1 DLMW
1006	1 DLMW
1007	1 DLMW
1008	3 DLMW
1017	3 DLMW
1022	3 DLMW
1114	3 DLMW
1115	3 DLMW
1116	3 DLMW

PORTUGAL
Força Aérea Portuguesa
  Aérospatiale
  SA.330C Puma
  Esq 711, Lajes;
  Esq 751, Montijo

19502	Esq 751
19503	Esq 751
19504	Esq 751
19505	Esq 751
19506	Esq 711
19508	Esq 711
19509	Esq 751
19511	Esq 711
19512	Esq 751
19513	Esq 711

  CASA 212A/212ECM*
  Aviocar
  Esq 401, Sintra;
  Esq 501, Sintra;
  Esq 502, Sintra;
  Esq 711, Lajes

16501*	Esq 501
16502*	Esq 501
16503	Esq 501
16504	Esq 501
16505	Esq 502
16506	Esq 502
16507	Esq 502
16508	Esq 502
16509	Esq 501
16510	Esq 401
16511	Esq 502
16512	Esq 401
16513	Esq 711
16514	Esq 711
16515	Esq 711
16517	Esq 711
16519	Esq 401
16520	Esq 711
16521*	Esq 401
16522*	Esq 401
16523*	Esq 401
16524*	Esq 401

  CASA 212-300 Aviocar
  Esq 401, Sintra
  17201
  17202

  D-BD Alpha Jet
  Esq 103, Beja;
  Esq 301, Beja
  15201
  15202

15204
15205
15206
15208
15209
15210
15211
15213
15214
15215
15216
15217
15218
15219
15220
15221
15222
15223
15224
15225
15226
15227
15228
15229
15230
15231
15232
15233
15234
15235
15236
15237
15238
15239
15240
15241
15242
15243
15244
15246
15247
15250

  Dassault Falcon 20DC
  Esq 504, Lisbon/Montijo
  17103

  Dassault Falcon 50
  Esq 504, Lisbon/Montijo
  17401
  17402
  17403

  Lockheed C-130H/
  C-130H-30* Hercules
  Esq 501, Lisbon/Montijo
  16801*
  16802*
  16803
  16804
  16805
  16806*

  Lockheed (GD)
  F-16A/F-16B*
  Esq 201, Monte Real
  15101
  15102
  15103
  15104
  15105
  15106
  15107
  15108

15109
15110
15111
15112
15113
15114
15115
15116
15117
15118*
15119*
15120*

  Lockheed P-3P Orion
  Esq 601, Lisbon/Montijo
  14801
  14802
  14803
  14804
  14805
  14806

Marinha
  Westland Super Lynx
  Mk 95
  Esq de Helicopteros,
    Lisbon/Montijo
  19201
  19202
  19203
  19204
  19205

QATAR
  Airbus A.310-304
  Qatari Govt, Doha
  A7-AAF

  Airbus A.320-232
  Qatari Govt, Doha
  A7-AAG

  Airbus A.340-211
  Qatari Govt, Doha
  A7-HHK

ROMANIA
Fortele Aeriene Romania
  Lockheed C-130B Hercules
  19 FMT, Bucharest/Otapeni
  5927
  5930
  6150
  6166

RUSSIA
Voenno-Vozdushniye Sily
  Rossioki Federatsii (Russian
  Air Force)
  Sukhoi Su-27
  TsAGI, Gromov Flight
    Institute, Zhukhovsky
  595 Su-27P
  597 Su-30
  598 Su-27P

Russian Govt
  Ilyushin Il-62M
  Russian Govt, Moscow
  RA-86466
  RA-86467
  RA-86468
  RA-86536
  RA-86537

RA-86540
RA-86553
RA-86554
RA-86559
RA-86561
RA-86710
RA-86711
RA-86712

Ilyushin Il-96-300
Russian Govt, Moscow
RA-96012

Tupolev Tu-134A
Russian Govt, Moscow
RA-65904

Tupolev Tu-154B-2
Russian Govt, Moscow
RA-85426
RA-85594

Tupolev Tu-154M
Russian Govt, Moscow;
Open Skies*
RA-85629
RA-85630
RA-85631
RA-85645
RA-85651
RA-85653
RA-85655*
RA-85658
RA-85659
RA-85666
RA-85675
RA-85676
RA-85843

SAUDI ARABIA
Al Quwwat al Jawwiya as Sa'udiya

BAe 125-800/-800B*
1 Sqn, Riyadh
HZ-105
HZ-109*
110*

Boeing E-3A/KE-3A* Sentry
18 Sqn, Riyadh;
19 Sqn, Riyadh
1801
1802
1803
1804
1805
1811*
1812*
1813*
1814*
1815*
1816*
1818*
1901*

Grumman G.1159A Gulfstream III/G.1159C Gulfstream IV
1 Sqn, Riyadh
HZ-103 Gulfstream IV
HZ-108 Gulfstream III

Lockheed C-130/L.100 Hercules
1 Sqn, Riyadh;
4 Sqn, Jeddah;
16 Sqn, Jeddah;
32 Sqn, Prince Sultan AB

111	VC-130H	1 Sqn
112	VC-130H	1 Sqn
451	C-130E	4 Sqn
452	C-130H	4 Sqn
455	C-130E	4 Sqn
461	C-130H	4 Sqn
462	C-130H	4 Sqn
463	C-130H	4 Sqn
464	C-130H	4 Sqn
465	C-130H	4 Sqn
466	C-130H	4 Sqn
467	C-130H	4 Sqn
468	C-130H	4 Sqn
471	C-130H-30	4 Sqn
472	C-130H	4 Sqn
473	C-130H	4 Sqn
474	C-130H	4 Sqn
475	C-130H	4 Sqn
476	C-130H	4 Sqn
477	C-130H	4 Sqn
478	C-130H	4 Sqn
479	C-130H	4 Sqn
1601	C-130H	16 Sqn
1602	C-130H	16 Sqn
1603	C-130H	16 Sqn
1604	C-130H	16 Sqn
1605	C-130H	16 Sqn
1606	C-130E	16 Sqn
1607	C-130E	16 Sqn
1608	C-130E	16 Sqn
1609	C-130E	16 Sqn
1610	C-130E	16 Sqn
1611	C-130E	16 Sqn
1612	C-130H	16 Sqn
1613	C-130H	16 Sqn
1614	C-130H	16 Sqn
1615	C-130H	16 Sqn
1618	C-130H	16 Sqn
1619	C-130H	16 Sqn
1622	C-130H-30	16 Sqn
1623	C-130H-30	16 Sqn
1624	C-130H	16 Sqn
1625	C-130H	16 Sqn
1626	C-130H	16 Sqn
3201	KC-130H	32 Sqn
3202	KC-130H	32 Sqn
3203	KC-130H	32 Sqn
3204	KC-130H	32 Sqn
3205	KC-130H	32 Sqn
3206	KC-130H	32 Sqn
3207	KC-130H	32 Sqn
3208	KC-130H	32 Sqn
HZ-114	VC-130H	1 Sqn
HZ-115	VC-130H	1 Sqn
HZ-116	VC-130H	1 Sqn
HZ-117	L.100-30	1 Sqn
HZ-128	L.100-30	1 Sqn
HZ-129	L.100-30	1 Sqn

Saudi Govt

Airbus A.340-211
Royal Embassy of Saudi Arabia, Riyadh
HZ-124

Boeing 737-268
Saudi Royal Flight, Jeddah
HZ-HM4

Boeing 747-3G1
Saudi Royal Flight, Jeddah
HZ-HM1A

Boeing 747SP-68
Saudi Govt, Jeddah;
Saudi Royal Flight, Jeddah
HZ-AIF Govt
HZ-AIJ Royal Flight
HZ-HM1B Royal Flight

Boeing MD-11
Saudi Royal Flight, Jeddah
HZ-AFA1
HZ-HM7

Canadair CL.604 Challenger
Saudi Royal Flight, Jeddah
HZ-AFA2

Dassault Falcon 900
Saudi Govt, Jeddah
HZ-AFT
HZ-AFZ

Grumman G.1159A Gulfstream III
Armed Forces Medical Services, Riyadh;
Saudi Govt, Jeddah
HZ-AFN Govt
HZ-AFR Govt
HZ-MS3 AFMS

Grumman G.1159C Gulfstream IV
Armed Forces Medical Services, Riyadh;
Saudi Govt, Jeddah
HZ-AFU Govt
HZ-AFV Govt
HZ-AFW Govt
HZ-AFX Govt
HZ-AFY Govt
HZ-MS4 AFMS

Gulfstream Aerospace Gulfstream V
Armed Forces Medical Services, Riyadh
HZ-MS5

Lockheed C-130H/L.100 Hercules
Armed Forces Medical Services, Riyadh
HZ-MS6 L.100-30
HZ-MS7 C-130H
HZ-MS8 C-130H-30
HZ-MS09 L.100-30
HZ-MS019 C-130H

Lockheed L.1011 TriStar 500
Saudi Royal Flight, Jeddah
HZ-HM5
HZ-HM6

SINGAPORE
Republic of Singapore Air Force

Boeing KC-135R Stratotanker
750

751		
752		
753		

Lockheed C-130 Hercules
122 Sqn, Paya Labar

720	KC-130B
721	KC-130B
724	KC-130B
725	KC-130B
730	C-130H
731	C-130H
732	C-130H
733	C-130H
734	KC-130H
735	C-130H

SLOVAKIA
Slovenské Vojenske Letectvo
Aero L-39/L-59 (L-39MS)
Albatros
31 SLK/3 Letka, Sliač [SL];
VSL, Košice;
White Albatroses,
Košice *(WA)*

0002	L-39MS	VSL
0003	L-39MS	VSL
0101	L-39C	WA [4]
0102	L-39C	WA [6]
0103	L-39C	VSL
0111	L-39C	WA [5]
0112	L-39C	WA [1]
0442	L-39C	WA [2]
0443	L-39C	WA [7]
0730	L-39V	VSL
0745	L-39V	VSL
1701	L-39ZA	31 SLK
1725	L-39ZA	31 SLK
1730	L-39ZA	31 SLK
4701	L-39ZA	31 SLK
4703	L-39ZA	31 SLK
4705	L-39ZA	31 SLK
4707	L-39ZA	31 SLK
4711	L-39ZA	31 SLK

Antonov An-24V
32 ZmDK/1 Letka, Pieštany
2903
5605

Antonov An-26
32 ZmDK/1 Letka, Pieštany
2506
3208

LET 410 Turbolet
31 SLK/4 Letka, Sliač [SL];
32 ZmDK/1 Letka, Pieštany;
VSL, Košice

0730	L-410UVP	32 ZmDK
0927	L-410T	31 SLK
0930	L-410T	32 ZmDK
1133	L-410T	VSL
1203	L-410FG	32 ZmDK
1521	L-410FG	32 ZmDK
2311	L-410UVP	32 ZmDK

Mikoyan MiG-29A/UB*
31 SLK/1 & 2 Letka,
Sliač [SL]
0619
0820
0921
1303*

2022	
2123	
3709	
3911	
4401*	
5113	
5304*	
5515	
5817	
6124	
6425	
6526	
6627	
6728	
6829	
6930	
7501	
8003	
8605	
9308	

Sukhoi Su-25K/UBK*
33 SBoLK/2 Letka, Malacky

| 1006 |
| 1007 |
| 1008 |
| 1027 |
| 3237* |
| 5033 |
| 5036 |
| 6017 |
| 6018 |
| 8072 |
| 8073 |
| 8074 |
| 8075 |

Slovak Govt
Tupolev Tu-154M
Slovak Govt,
Bratislava/Ivanka
OM-BYO
OM-BYR

Yakovlev Yak-40
Slovak Govt,
Bratislava/Ivanka
OM-BYE
OM-BYL

SLOVENIA
Slovene Army
Let 410UVP-E
15 Brigada, Ljubljana
L4-01

Pilatus PC-9
15 Brigada, Ljubljana

| L9-51 |
| L9-52 |
| L9-53 |
| L9-54 |
| L9-55 |
| L9-56 |
| L9-57 |
| L9-58 |
| L9-59 |
| L9-60 |
| L9-61 |
| L9-62 |
| L9-63 |
| L9-64 |
| L9-65 |
| L9-66 |

| L9-67 |
| L9-68 |
| L9-69 |

Slovenian Govt
Gates LearJet
Slovenian Govt, Ljubljana
S5-BAA LearJet 35A
S5-BAB LearJet 24D

SOUTH AFRICA
South African Air Force/
Suid Afrikaanse Lugmag
Boeing 707
60 Sqn, Waterkloof

1415	328C
1417	328C
1419	328C
1423	344C

Boeing 737-7ED
21 Sqn, Waterkloof
ZS-RSA

Dassault Falcon 900
21 Sqn, Waterkloof
ZS-NAN

Lockheed C-130B/
C-130BZ* Hercules
28 Sqn, Waterkloof

| 401 |
| 402 |
| 403 |
| 404 |
| 405 |
| 406 |
| 407* |
| 408* |
| 409* |

SPAIN
Ejército del Aire Airtech
CN.235M-10 (T.19A)/
CN.235M-100 (T.19B)
Ala 35, Getafe

T.19A-01	35-60
T.19A-02	35-61
T.19B-03	35-21
T.19B-04	35-22
T.19B-05	35-23
T.19B-06	35-24
T.19B-07	35-25
T.19B-08	35-26
T.19B-09	35-27
T.19B-10	35-28
T.19B-11	35-29
T.19B-12	35-30
T.19B-13	35-31
T.19B-14	35-32
T.19B-15	35-33
T.19B-16	35-34
T.19B-17	35-35
T.19B-18	35-36
T.19B-19	35-37
T.19B-20	35-38

Boeing 707
408 Esc, Torrejón;
Grupo 45, Torrejón

T.17-1	331B	45-10
T.17-2	331B	45-11
T.17-3	368C	45-12
TM.17-4	351C	408-21

Spain

CASA 101EB Aviojet

Grupo 54, Torrejón;
Grupo de Escuelas de Matacán (74);
AGA, San Javier (79);
Patrulla Aguila, San Javier*

E.25-01	79-01	
E.25-05	79-05	
E.25-06	79-06	
E.25-07	79-07	
E.25-08	79-08	[5]*
E.25-09	79-09	
E.25-10	79-10	
E.25-11	79-11	
E.25-12	79-12	
E.25-13	79-13	
E.25-14	79-14	[1]*
E.25-15	79-15	
E.25-16	79-16	
E.25-17	74-40	
E.25-18	74-42	
E.25-19	79-19	
E.25-20	79-20	
E.25-21	79-21	
E.25-22	79-22	[4]*
E.25-23	79-23	[3]*
E.25-24	79-24	
E.25-25	79-25	
E.25-26	79-26	[7]*
E.25-27	79-27	
E.25-28	79-28	[2]*
E.25-29		
E.25-31	79-31	
E.25-33	74-02	
E.25-34	79-34	
E.25-35	54-20	
E.25-37	79-37	
E.25-38	79-38	
E.25-40	79-40	
E.25-41	74-41	
E.25-43	74-43	
E.25-44	79-44	
E.25-45	79-45	
E.25-46	79-46	
E.25-47	79-47	
E.25-48	79-48	
E.25-49	79-49	
E.25-50	79-33	
E.25-51	74-07	
E.25-52	79-34	[6]*
E.25-53	74-09	
E.25-54	79-35	
E.25-55	44-05	
E.25-56	74-11	
E.25-57	74-12	
E.25-59	74-13	
E.25-61	54-22	
E.25-62	79-62	
E.25-63	74-17	
E.25-64	74-18	
E.25-65	79-95	
E.25-66	74-20	
E.25-67	74-21	
E.25-68	74-22	
E.25-69	79-97	
E.25-71	74-25	
E.25-72	74-26	
E.25-73	79-98	
E.25-74	74-28	
E.25-75	74-29	
E.25-76	74-30	
E.25-78	79-02	
E.25-79	74-32	
E.25-80	79-03	
E.25-81	74-34	
E.25-83	74-35	
E.25-84	79-04	
E.25-86	79-32	
E.25-87	79-29	
E.25-88	74-39	

CASA 212 Aviocar

212 (XT.12)/
212A (T.12B)/
212B (TR.12A)/
212D (TE.12B)/
212DE (TM.12D)/
212E (T.12C)/
212S (D.3A)/
212S1 (D.3B)/
212-200 (T.12D)/
212-200 (TR.12D)
Ala 22, Morón;
Ala 37, Villanubla;
Ala 46, Gando, Las Palmas;
CLAEX, Torrejón (54);
Grupo 72, Alcantarilla;
Grupo Esc, Matacán (74);
AGA (Ala 79), San Javier;
403 Esc, Getafe;
408 Esc, Torrejón;
801 Esc, Palma/
  Son San Juan;
803 Esc, Cuatro Vientos;
INTA, Torrejón

D.3A-1	(801 Esc)	
D.3A-2	(803 Esc)	
D.3B-3	(803 Esc)	
D.3B-4	(801 Esc)	
D.3B-5	(801 Esc)	
D.3B-6	(801 Esc)	
D.3B-7	(803 Esc)	
D.3B-8	(801 Esc)	
XT.12A-1	54-10	
TR.12A-4	403-02	
TR.12A-5	403-03	
TR.12A-6	403-04	
TR.12A-8	403-06	
T.12B-9	74-83	
TE.12B-10	79-92	
T.12B-12	74-82	
T.12B-13	74-70	
T.12B-14	37-01	
T.12B-15	37-02	
T.12B-16	74-71	
T.12B-17	37-03	
T.12B-18	46-31	
T.12B-19	46-32	
T.12B-20	37-04	
T.12B-21	37-05	
T.12B-22	37-06	
T.12B-23	72-01	
T.12B-24	37-07	
T.12B-25	74-72	
T.12B-26	72-02	
T.12B-27	46-33	
T.12B-28	72-03	
T.12B-29	37-08	
T.12B-30	74-73	
T.12B-31	46-34	
T.12B-33	72-04	
T.12B-34	74-74	
T.12B-35	37-09	
T.12B-36	37-10	
T.12B-37	72-05	
T.12B-39	74-75	
TE.12B-40	79-93	
TE.12B-41	79-94	
T.12C-43	46-50	
T.12C-44	37-50	
T.12B-46	74-76	
T.12B-47	72-06	
T.12B-48	37-11	
T.12B-49	72-07	
T.12B-51	74-78	
T.12B-52	46-35	
T.12B-53	46-36	
T.12B-54	46-37	
T.12B-55	46-38	
T.12B-56	74-79	
T.12B-57	72-08	
T.12B-58	46-39	
T.12C-59	37-51	
T.12C-60	37-52	
T.12C-61	37-53	
T.12B-63	37-14	
T.12B-64	46-40	
T.12B-65	74-80	
T.12B-66	72-09	
T.12B-67	74-81	
T.12B-68	37-15	
T.12B-69	37-16	
T.12B-70	37-17	
T.12B-71	37-18	
TM.12D-72	408-01	
TM.12D-74	54-11	
T.12D-75	403-07	
TR.12D-76	37-60	
TR.12D-77	37-61	
TR.12D-78	37-62	
TR.12D-79	37-63	
TR.12D-80	37-64	
TR.12D-81	37-65	

CASA 295

Ala 35, Getafe; CASA, Getafe

XT.21-01	
XT.21-02	
T.21-01	35.39
T.21-02	35.40

Cessna 560 Citation VI

403 Esc, Getafe

TR.20-01	403-11
TR.20-02	403-12

Dassault Falcon 20D/E/F

Grupo 45, Torrejón;
408 Esc, Torrejón

TM.11-1	20E	45-02
TM.11-2	20D	45-03
TM.11-3	20D	408-11
TM.11-4	20E	408-12
T.11-5	20F	45-05

Dassault Falcon 50

Grupo 45, Torrejón

T.16-1	45-20

Dassault Falcon 900

Grupo 45, Torrejón

T.18-1	45-40
T.18-2	45-41

Eurofighter Typhoon

CASA, Getafe

XCE.16-01

Fokker F.27M Friendship 400MPA

802 Esc, Gando, Las Palmas

D.2-01	802-10
D.2-02	802-11
D.2-03	802-12

**Lockheed C-130H/
C-130H-30/KC-130H
Hercules**
311 Esc/312 Esc (Ala 31),
Zaragoza

TL.10-01	C-130H-30	31-01
T.10-02	C-130H	31-02
T.10-03	C-130H	31-03
T.10-04	C-130H	31-04
TK.10-5	KC-130H	31-50
TK.10-6	KC-130H	31-51
TK.10-7	KC-130H	31-52
T.10-8	C-130H	31-05
T.10-9	C-130H	31-06
T.10-10	C-130H	31-07
TK.10-11	KC-130H	31-53
TK.10-12	KC-130H	31-54

**Lockheed P-3A/
P-3B* Orion**
Grupo 22, Morón

P.3-01	22-21
P.3-03	22-22
P.3-08	22-31*
P.3-09	22-32*
P.3-10	22-33*
P.3-11	22-34*
P.3-12	22-35*

**McDonnell Douglas
F-18 Hornet**
Ala 11, Morón;
Ala 12, Torrejón;
Ala 15, Zaragoza;
Escuadron 462, Gran
Canaria
EF-18A/EF-18B* Hornet

CE.15-1	15-70*
CE.15-2	15-71*
CE.15-3	15-72*
CE.15-4	15-73*
CE.15-5	15-74*
CE.15-6	15-75*
CE.15-7	15-76*
CE.15-8	12-71*
CE.15-9	15-77*
CE.15-10	12-73*
CE.15-11	12-74*
CE.15-12	12-75*
C.15-13	12-01
C.15-14	15-01
C.15-15	15-02
C.15-16	15-03
C.15-18	15-05
C.15-20	15-07
C.15-21	15-08
C.15-22	15-09
C.15-23	15-10
C.15-24	15-11
C.15-25	15-12
C.15-26	15-13
C.15-27	15-14
C.15-28	15-15
C.15-29	15-16
C.15-30	15-17
C.15-31	15-18
C.15-32	15-19
C.15-33	15-20
C.15-34	15-21
C.15-35	15-22

C.15-36	15-23
C.15-37	15-24
C.15-38	15-25
C.15-39	15-26
C.15-40	15-27
C.15-41	15-28
C.15-43	15-30
C.15-44	12-02
C.15-45	12-03
C.15-46	12-04
C.15-47	15-31
C.15-48	12-06
C.15-49	12-07
C.15-50	12-08
C.15-51	12-09
C.15-52	12-10
C.15-53	12-11
C.15-54	12-12
C.15-55	12-13
C.15-56	12-14
C.15-57	12-15
C.15-58	12-16
C.15-59	12-17
C.15-60	12-18
C.15-61	12-19
C.15-62	12-20
C.15-64	12-22
C.15-65	12-23
C.15-66	12-24
C.15-67	15-33
C.15-68	12-26
C.15-69	12-27
C.15-70	12-28
C.15-72	12-30

F/A-18A Hornet

C.15-73	11-01
C.15-74	21-02
C.15-75	11-03
C.15-76	21-04
C.15-77	21-05
C.15-78	11-06
C.15-79	11-07
C.15-80	21-08
C.15-81	11-09
C.15-82	46-10
C.15-83	21-11
C.15-84	46-12
C.15-85	21-13
C.15-86	11-14
C.15-87	11-15
C.15-88	11-16
C.15-89	21-17
C.15-90	11-18
C.15-91	21-19
C.15-92	21-20
C.15-93	21-21
C.15-94	21-22
C.15-95	46-01
C.15-96	21-24

**Arma Aérea de l'Armada
Española**
**BAe/McDonnell Douglas
EAV-8B/EAV-8B+/
TAV-8B Harrier II**
Esc 009, Rota
EAV-8B

VA.1A-15	01-903
VA.1A-16	01-904
VA.1A-17	01-905
VA.1A-18	01-906
VA.1A-19	01-907
VA.1A-21	01-909

VA.1A-22	01-910
VA.1A-23	01-911
VA.1A-24	01-912

EAV-8B+

VA.1B-25	01-914
VA.1B-26	01-915
VA.1B-27	01-916
VA.1B-28	01-917
VA.1B-29	01-918
VA.1B-30	01-919
VA.1B-31	01-920
VA.1B-32	01-921

TAV-8B

VAE.1A-33	01-922

Cessna 550 Citation 2
Esc 004, Rota

U.20-1	01-405
U.20-2	01-406
U.20-3	01-407

**SWEDEN
Svenska Flygvapnet
Beechcraft
Super King Air (Tp.101)**
Flottilji 7, Såtenäs;
Flottilji 17, Ronneby/
Kallinge;
Flottiljer 21, Luleå/
Kallax

101002	012	F21
101003	013	F17
101004	014	F7

**Grumman G.1159C
Gulfstream 4 (Tp.102A/
S.102B Korpen/
Tp.102C)**
Flottiljer 16, Uppsala;
Flottiljer 16M,
Stockholm/Bromma
Tp.102A

102001	021	F16M

S.102B Korpen

102002	022	F16
102003	023	F16

Tp.102C

102004	024	F16M

**Lockheed C-130 Hercules
(Tp.84)**
Flottiljer 7, Såtenäs

84001	841	C-130E
84002	842	C-130E
84003	843	C-130H
84004	844	C-130H
84005	845	C-130H
84006	846	C-130H
84007	847	C-130H
84008	848	C-130H

**Rockwell Sabreliner-40
(Tp.86)**
FMV, Malmslätt

86001	861
86002	862

SAAB 37 Viggen
Flottiljer 4, Östersund/
Frösön;
Flottiljer 16, Uppsala;
Flottiljer 17, Ronneby/
Kallinge;

Sweden

JA 37/JA 37D^D/JA 37DI^I

37304	01	F17
37305	05	F17
37311	03	F21
37316	16	F17
37317	06	F21
37318	58	F16
37319	59	F16
37320	60	F16
37322	62	F16
37325	25	F4
37326^i	26	FMV
37327	08	F4
37329	29	F4
37330	30	F16
37331	31	F4
37336	04	F21
37337	05	F21
37339	07	F17
37341	41	F4
37343	43	F4
37345	45	F17
37350	50	F21
37351	51	F17
37353	33	F21
37354	42	F17
37355	43	F17
37357	57	F4
37359	29	F17
37363	10	F21
37364	11	F21
37365	12	F21
37366	13	F16
37367	14	F21
37369	16	F21
37370	17	F21
37371	18	F21
37375	25	F17
37376	36	F4
37377	37	F4
37379	15	F21
37380	50	F4
37382	52	F4
37385	55	F4
37386^D	46	F17
37388	58	F4
37389^D	59	F17
37390	60	F4
37393	63	F4
37394	47	F17
37395	65	F4
37397^i	20	F17
37398^i	08	F17
37400	50	F16
37401^D	01	F17
37402^D	02	F17
37403	23	F21
37404^D	24	F17
37405	25	F21
37406	26	F21
37407	27	F21
37408	28	F21
37409	29	F21
37410	10	F16
37411	11	F16
37412^D	12	F17
37413^D	13	F17
37414^i	14	F17
37415^i	15	F16
37416^D	36	F17
37417	17	F17
37418^D	18	F17
37419	19	F16
37420	20	F16
37421^i	21	F17
37422^D	22	F17
37423	23	F16
37424^i	24	F21
37426^i	26	F17
37427^i	27	F16
37428^i	28	F16
37429^D	29	F17
37431^D	31	F17
37432	32	F16
37433	33	F16
37434	34	F16
37435^D	35	F17
37436^i	32	F16
37437^i	37	F17
37438^D	38	F17
37439	01	F4
37440^i	40	F17
37441^i	41	F17
37442^i	52	F17
37443^D	43	F17
37444^i	04	F17
37445^D	45	F17
37446^i	06	F17
37447	35	F21
37448	04	F4
37449^D	49	F17

Sk 37/Sk 37E*

37801	80	F4
37802	81	F4
37804	83	F4
37807*	70	F4
37808*	71	F4
37809*	72	F4
37811*	74	F4
37813*	75	F4
37814*	76	F4
37815*	77	F4
37816*	78	F4
37817*	79	F4

AJSH 37

37901	51	F21
37903	05	F21
37911	33	F21
37913		
37914	61	F21
37915	69	F21
37916	37	FMV
37918	71	F21
37922	61	F21
37925	75	F21

AJSF 37

37950	48	F21
37951	50	F21
37952	52	F21
37954	54	F21
37957	56	F21
37958	58	F21
37960	60	F21
37971	62	F21
37974	64	F21
37976	66	F21

SAAB JAS 39 Gripen

Flottiljer 7, Såtenäs [G];
Flottiljer 10, Angelholm;
FMV, Malmslätt

JAS 39

39-3	53	SAAB
39-5	55	FMV

JAS 39A

39101	51	FMV
39103	103	FMV
39104	04	F7
39105	105	F10
39106	106	F10
39107	07	F7
39108	108	F7
39109	09	F7
39110	10	F7
39111	11	F7
39112	112	F7
39113	13	F7
39114	14	F7
39115	15	F7
39116	16	SAAB
39117	17	F7
39118	18	SAAB
39119	19	F7
39120	120	F7
39121	21	F7
39122	122	F7
39123	23	F7
39124	24	F7
39125	125	F7
39126	26	F7
39127	27	F7
39128	28	F7
39129	29	F7
39131	31	F7
39132	132	F10
39133	33	F7
39134	134	F10
39135	35	F10
39136	36	F7
39137	137	F10
39138	38	F7
39139	139	F10
39140	40	F10
39141	41	F7
39142	42	F7
39143	43	F10
39144	44	F10
39145	45	F10
39146	46	F10
39147	47	F10
39148	48	F10
39149	49	F10
39150	50	F10
39151	51	F7
39152	52	F7
39153	53	F10
39154	54	F7
39155	55	F7
39157	57	F7
39158	58	F7
39159	59	F7
39160	60	F7
39161	61	F7
39162	62	F7
39163	63	F10
39164	64	F10
39165	65	F10
39166	66	F7
39167	67	F10
39168	168	F10
39169	169	F7
39170	170	F10
39171	171	F10
39172	172	F7
39173	173	F10
39174	174	F10
39175	175	F10
39176	176	F10

39177	177	FMV
39178	178	F10
39179	179	F10
39180		
39181	181	F7
39182	182	F7
39183	183	F10
39184	184	F10
39185	185	FMV
39186	186	F7
39187	187	F7
39188	188	F7
39189	189	FMV
39190	190	FMV
39191	191	F10
39192	192	F7
39193	193	
39194	194	FMV
39195		
39196	196	FMV
39197	197	FMV
39198	198	FMV
39199	199	SAAB
39200		
39200		
39200		
39201		
39202		
39203		
39204		
39205		
39206		
39208		
39209		
39210		
39211		
39212		
39213		
39214		
39215		
39216		
39217		
39218		
39219		
39220		
39221		
39222		
39223		
39224		
39225		

JAS 39B

39800	58	FMV
39801	70	F7
39802	802	FMV
39803	803	F7
39804	804	F7
39805	805	F7
39806	806	FMV
39807	807	F7
39808	808	FMW
39809	809	SAAB
39810		
39811		
39812		
39813		

JAS 39C

39-6		FMV
39227		
39228		
39229		
39230		
39231		
39232		
39233		

39234		
39235		
39236		
39237		
39238		
39239		
39240		

**SAAB SF.340AEW&C
(S.100B) Argus**

Flottiljer 16, Uppsala;

100002	002
100005	005
100006	006
100007	007

**Förvarsmaktens
Helikopterflottilj
Aerospatiale
AS.332M-1 Super Puma
(Hkp.10)**
1.HkpBat/
 Flygräddningsgrupp F4,
 Östersund/Frösön;
1.HkpBat/
 Flygräddningsgrupp F21,
 Luleå/Kallax;
2.HkpBat/
 Flygräddningsgrupp F16,
 Uppsala;
3.HkpBat/
 Flygräddningsgrupp F7,
 Såtenäs;
3.HkpBat/
 Flygräddningsgrupp F17,
 Ronneby/Kallinge;

10401	91	F7
10402	92	F7
10403	93	F21
10405	95	F17
10406	96	F17
10407	97	F17
10408	98	F17
10409	99	F17
10410	90	F17
10411	88	F21
10412	89	

**Agusta-Bell AB.412HP
(Hkp.11)**
1.HkpBat/1.Hkp Skv, Boden

11331	31
11332	32
11333	33
11334	34
11335	35
11336	36
11337	37
11338	38
11339	39
11340	40
11341	41
11342	42

MBB Bo.105CBS (Hkp.9A)
1.HkpBat/1.Hkp Skv, Boden;
4.HkpBat/Armeflyget 2
 (AF2), Malmslätt;
FMV (Flygvapnet),
 Malmslätt

09202	02	1.Hkp Skv
09203	03	AF2
09204	04	AF2
09205	05	1.Hkp Skv

09206	06	1.Hkp Skv
09207	07	1.Hkp Skv
09208	08	1.Hkp Skv
09209	09	AF2
09210	10	1.Hkp Skv
09211	11	1.Hkp Skv
09212	12	1.Hkp Skv
09213	13	AF2
09214	14	AF2
09215	15	AF2
09216	16	AF2
09217	17	AF2
09218	18	AF2
09219	19	AF1
09220	20	AF2
09221	90	FMV

Vertol/Kawasaki-Vertol 107
2.HkpBat/11
 Helikopterdivison,
 Berga;
3.HkpBat/
 12 Helikopterdivison,
 Goteborg/Säve;
3.HkpBat/
 13 Helikopterdivison,
 Ronneby/Kallinge;
FMV (Flygvapnet),
 Malmslätt
Vertol 107-II-15 (Hkp.4B)

04061	61	11 Hkp Div
04063	63	11 Hkp Div
04064	64	11 Hkp Div

**Kawasaki-Vertol
KV.107-II-16 (Hkp.4C)**

04065	65	12 Hkp Div
04067	67	12 Hkp Div
04068	68	12 Hkp Div
04069	69	12 Hkp Div
04070	70	11 Hkp Div
04071	71	12 Hkp Div
04072	72	FMV

Vertol 107-II-15 (Hkp.4D)

04073	73	11 Hkp Div
04074	74	13 Hkp Div
04075	75	13 Hkp Div
04076	76	13 Hkp Div

**SWITZERLAND
Schweizerische Flugwaffe**
(Most aircraft are pooled
 centrally. Some carry unit
 badges but these rarely
 indicate actual operators.)
**Aérospatiale
AS.332M-1/AS.532UL
Super Puma**
Leichte Flieger Staffel 5
 (LtSt 5), Interlaken;
Leichte Flieger Staffel 6
 (LtSt 6), Alpnach;
Leichte Flieger Staffel 8
 (LtSt 8), Ulrichen
Detachments at Alpnach,
 Emmen, Meiringen,
 Payerne & Sion
AS.332M-1
T-311
T-312
T-313
T-314
T-315
T-316

Switzerland

T-317
T-318
T-319
T-320
T-321
T-322
T-323
T-324
T-325

AS.532UL
T-331
T-332
T-333
T-334
T-335
T-336
T-337
T-338
T-339
T-340
T-341
T-342

Beechcraft
Super King Air 350C
Flugswaffenbrigade 31,
  Dübendorf
HB-GII

Dassault Falcon 50
VIP Flight, Dübendorf
T-783

Dassault Mirage III
Flieger Staffel 3 (FISt 3),
  Sion;
Flieger Staffel 4 (FISt 4),
  Payerne;
Flieger Staffel 10 (FISt 10),
  Buochs;
Gruppe fur Rustunggdienste
  (GRD), Emmen;
Instrumentation Flieger
  Staffel 14 (InstruFISt 14),
  Payerne
Mirage IIIBS
J-2001   InstruFISt 14
U-2004   InstruFISt 14
Mirage IIIUDS
J-2011   InstruFISt 14
J-2012   InstruFISt 14
Mirage IIIRS
R-2102
R-2103
R-2104
R-2105
R-2106
R-2107
R-2108
R-2109
R-2110
R-2111
R-2112
R-2113
R-2114
R-2115
R-2116
R-2117
R-2118

Gates Learjet 35A
VIP Flight, Dübendorf
T-781

McDonnell Douglas
F/A-18 Hornet
Flieger Staffel 11 (FISt 11),
  Meiringen;
Flieger Staffel 17 (FISt 17),
  Payerne;
Flieger Staffel 18 (FISt 18),
  Payerne
F/A-18C
J-5001
J-5002
J-5003
J-5004
J-5005
J-5006
J-5007
J-5008
J-5009
J-5010
J-5011
J-5012
J-5013
J-5014
J-5015
J-5016
J-5017
J-5018
J-5019
J-5020
J-5021
J-5022
J-5023
J-5024
J-5025
J-5026
F/A-18D
J-5232
J-5233
J-5234
J-5235
J-5236
J-5237
J-5238

Northrop F-5 Tiger II
Flieger Staffel 1 (FISt 1),
  Turtman;
Flieger Staffel 6 (FISt 6),
  Sion;
Flieger Staffel 8 (FISt 8),
  Meiringen;
Flieger Staffel 11 (FISt 11),
  Meiringen;
Flieger Staffel 13 (FISt 13),
  Meiringen;
Flieger Staffel 18 (FISt 18),
  Payerne;
Flieger Staffel 19 (FISt 19),
  Mollis;
Gruppe fur Rustunggdienste
  (GRD), Emmen;
Instrumentation Flieger
  Staffel 14 (InstruFISt 14),
  Dübendorf;
Patrouille Suisse, Emmen
  (*P. Suisse*)
F-5E
J-3001
J-3002
J-3004
J-3005
J-3006
J-3007
J-3008   InstruFISt 14

J-3009
J-3010
J-3011
J-3014
J-3015
J-3016
J-3024
J-3025
J-3027
J-3029
J-3030
J-3033
J-3034
J-3036
J-3037
J-3038
J-3041
J-3043
J-3044
J-3046
J-3047
J-3049
J-3051
J-3052
J-3053
J-3054
J-3055
J-3056
J-3057
J-3058
J-3060
J-3061
J-3062
J-3063
J-3065
J-3066
J-3067
J-3068
J-3069
J-3070
J-3072
J-3073
J-3074
J-3075
J-3076
J-3077
J-3079
J-3080   *P. Suisse*
J-3081   *P. Suisse*
J-3082
J-3083   *P. Suisse*
J-3084   *P. Suisse* [4]
J-3085   *P. Suisse* [3]
J-3086   *P. Suisse* [6]
J-3087   *P. Suisse*
J-3088   *P. Suisse* [5]
J-3089
J-3090   *P. Suisse* [2]
J-3091   *P. Suisse* [1]
J-3092
J-3093
J-3094
J-3095
J-3096
J-3097   GRD
J-3098
F-5F
J-3201
J-3202
J-3203
J-3204   GRD
J-3205
J-3206
J-3207

J-3208
J-3209
J-3210
J-3211
J-3212

SYRIA
Tupolev Tu-134A
Govt of Syria, Damascus
YK-AYA

TUNISIA
Boeing 737-7HJ
Govt of Tunisia, Tunis
TS-IOO

TURKEY
Türk Hava Kuvvetleri
Boeing KC-135R
Stratotanker
101 Filo, Incirlik
00325
00326
23539
23563
23567
72609
80110

Cessna 650 Citation VII
224 Filo, Ankara/Etimesğut
004
005

Grumman G.1159C
Gulfstream 4
224 Filo, Ankara/Etimesğut
001
002
003

Lockheed C-130B Hercules
222 Filo, Erkilet
3496 (23496)
10960
10963
70527
80736

Lockheed C-130E Hercules
222 Filo, Erkilet
01468   12-468
01947
13186   12-186
13187
13188
13189
73-991

Transall C-160D
221 Filo, Erkilet
019
68-020
021
022
023
024
025   12-025
69-026
027
69-028   12-028
029
69-031
032

69-033	
034	
035	
036	
037	12-037
038	
039	
69-040	

TUSAS-GD F-16C/F-16D*
Fighting Falcon
4 AJÜ, Mürted:
  141 Filo & Öncel Filo;
5 AJÜ, Merzifon:
  151 Filo & 152 Filo;
6 AJÜ, Bandirma:
  161 Filo & 162 Filo;
8 AJÜ, Diyarbakir:
  181 Filo & 182 Filo;
9 AJÜ, Balikesir:
  191 Filo & 192 Filo

86-0066	Öncel Filo
86-0068	Öncel Filo
86-0069	Öncel Filo
86-0070	Öncel Filo
86-0071	Öncel Filo
86-0072	Öncel Filo
86-0191*	Öncel Filo
86-0192*	Öncel Filo
86-0193*	Öncel Filo
86-0194*	Öncel Filo
86-0195*	Öncel Filo
86-0196*	Öncel Filo
87-0002*	Öncel Filo
87-0003*	Öncel Filo
87-0009	Öncel Filo
87-0010	Öncel Filo
87-0011	Öncel Filo
87-0013	Öncel Filo
87-0014	Öncel Filo
87-0015	Öncel Filo
87-0016	Öncel Filo
87-0017	Öncel Filo
87-0018	Öncel Filo
87-0019	Öncel Filo
87-0020	Öncel Filo
87-0021	Öncel Filo
88-0013*	Öncel Filo
88-0014*	141 Filo
88-0015*	141 Filo
88-0019	Öncel Filo
88-0020	Öncel Filo
88-0021	Öncel Filo
88-0024	Öncel Filo
88-0025	141 Filo
88-0026	Öncel Filo
88-0027	Öncel Filo
88-0028	191 Filo
88-0029	Öncel Filo
88-0030	191 Filo
88-0031	Öncel Filo
88-0032	Öncel Filo
88-0033	141 Filo
88-0034	141 Filo
88-0035	141 Filo
88-0036	141 Filo
88-0037	141 Filo
89-0022	141 Filo
89-0023	141 Filo
89-0024	141 Filo
89-0025	141 Filo
89-0026	141 Filo
89-0027	141 Filo
89-0028	141 Filo

89-0030	141 Filo
89-0031	141 Filo
89-0032	141 Filo
89-0034	162 Filo
89-0035	162 Filo
89-0036	162 Filo
89-0037	162 Filo
89-0038	162 Filo
89-0039	162 Filo
89-0040	162 Filo
89-0041	162 Filo
89-0042*	141 Filo
89-0043*	162 Filo
89-0044*	162 Filo
89-0045*	182 Filo
90-0001	162 Filo
90-0004	162 Filo
90-0005	162 Filo
90-0006	162 Filo
90-0007	162 Filo
90-0008	162 Filo
90-0009	162 Filo
90-0010	162 Filo
90-0011	162 Filo
90-0012	161 Filo
90-0013	161 Filo
90-0014	161 Filo
90-0015	161 Filo
90-0016	161 Filo
90-0017	161 Filo
90-0018	161 Filo
90-0019	161 Filo
90-0020	162 Filo
90-0021	161 Filo
90-0022*	161 Filo
90-0023*	161 Filo
90-0024*	161 Filo
91-0001	161 Filo
91-0002	161 Filo
91-0003	161 Filo
91-0004	161 Filo
91-0005	161 Filo
91-0006	161 Filo
91-0007	161 Filo
91-0008	141 Filo
91-0010	141 Filo
91-0011	141 Filo
91-0012	141 Filo
91-0013	192 Filo
91-0014	141 Filo
91-0015	182 Filo
91-0016	182 Filo
91-0017	182 Filo
91-0018	182 Filo
91-0019	192 Filo
91-0020	182 Filo
91-0022*	141 Filo
91-0024*	141 Filo
92-0001	182 Filo
92-0002	191 Filo
92-0003	162 Filo
92-0004	191 Filo
92-0005	191 Filo
92-0006	182 Filo
92-0007	182 Filo
92-0008	191 Filo
92-0009	191 Filo
92-0010	
92-0011	182 Filo
92-0012	191 Filo
92-0013	182 Filo
92-0014	182 Filo
92-0015	182 Filo
92-0016	182 Filo

92-0017	182 Filo
92-0018	182 Filo
92-0019	
92-0020	
92-0021	181 Filo
92-0022*	181 Filo
92-0023*	181 Filo
92-0024*	182 Filo
93-0001	181 Filo
93-0002	181 Filo
93-0003	181 Filo
93-0004	181 Filo
93-0005	181 Filo
93-0006	181 Filo
93-0007	181 Filo
93-0008	181 Filo
93-0009	182 Filo
93-0010	181 Filo
93-0011	181 Filo
93-0012	181 Filo
93-0013	181 Filo
93-0014	181 Filo
93-0657	141 Filo
93-0658	
93-0659	
93-0660	151 Filo
93-0661	
93-0662	151 Filo
93-0663	
93-0664	
93-0665	
93-0666	
93-0667	151 Filo
93-0668	
93-0669	152 Filo
93-0670	
93-0671	
93-0672	152 Filo
93-0673	Öncel Filo
93-0674	192 Filo
93-0675	192 Filo
93-0676	192 Filo
93-0677	192 Filo
93-0678	192 Filo
93-0679	192 Filo
93-0680	192 Filo
93-0681	192 Filo
93-0682	192 Filo
93-0683	192 Filo
93-0684	192 Filo
93-0685	192 Filo
93-0686	192 Filo
93-0687	192 Filo
93-0688	192 Filo
93-0689	Öncel Filo
93-0690	192 Filo
93-0691*	
93-0692*	152 Filo
93-0693*	Öncel Filo
93-0694*	
93-0695*	192 Filo
93-0696*	192 Filo
94-0071	192 Filo
94-0072	191 Filo
94-0073	191 Filo
94-0074	191 Filo
94-0075	191 Filo
94-0076	191 Filo
94-0077	
94-0078	191 Filo
94-0079	191 Filo
94-0080	191 Filo
94-0081	191 Filo
94-0082	191 Filo

94-0083	191 Filo
94-0084	191 Filo
94-0085	191 Filo
94-0086	191 Filo
94-0087	191 Filo
94-0088	
94-0089	
94-0090	
94-0091	152 Filo
94-0092	
94-0093	
94-0094	Öncel Filo
94-0095	
94-0096	
94-0105*	191 Filo
94-0106*	191 Filo
94-0107*	191 Filo
94-0108*	151 Filo
94-0109*	
94-0110*	
94-1557*	
94-1558*	Öncel Filo
94-1559*	152 Filo
94-1560*	151 Filo
94-1561*	191 Filo
94-1562*	192 Filo
94-1563*	192 Filo
94-1564*	191 Filo

TURKMENISTAN
BAe 1000B
Govt of Turkmenistan,
　Ashkhabad
EZ-B021

Boeing 757-23A
Govt of Turkmenistan,
　Ashkhabad
EZ-A010

UGANDA
Grumman G.1159C
Gulfstream IV
Govt of Uganda,
　Entebbe
5X-UEF

UKRAINE
Ukrainian Air Force
Ilyushin Il-76MD
321 TAP, Uzin
78820
UR-76413
UR-76537
UR-76624
UR-76677
UR-76687
UR-76697
UR-76699

Ilyushin Il-62M
Govt of Ukraine, Kiev
UR-86527
UR-86528

Tupolev Tu-134
Govt of Ukraine, Kiev
UR-63982

UNITED ARAB EMIRATES
United Arab Emirates Air Force
Abu Dhabi
Lockheed C-130H/
L.100-30* Hercules

1211	
1212	
1213	
1214	
1215*	

Dubai
311*
312*

UAE Govt
Airbus A.300B4-620
Govt of Abu Dhabi
A6-PFD
A6-SHZ

Airbus A.319CJ-113X
Dubai Air Wing
A6-ESH

Boeing 737-7F0/7Z5*
Govt of Abu Dhabi;
Govt Of Dubai

A6-AIN*	Abu Dhabi
A6-DAS*	Abu Dhabi
A6-HRS	Dubai
A6-LIW*	Dubai
A6-SIR*	Dubai

Boeing 747SP-31/747SP-Z5*
Govt of Dubai
A6-SMM
A6-SMR
A6-ZSN*

Boeing 747-2B4BF/
747-4F6*
Dubai Air Wing;
Govt of Abu Dhabi

A6-GDP	Dubai
A6-YAS*	Abu Dhabi

Boeing 767-341ER
Govt of Abu Dhabi
A6-SUL

Dassault Falcon 900
Govt of Abu Dhabi
A6-AUH

Grumman
G.1159C Gulfstream IV
Dubai Air Wing
A6-HHH

YEMEN
Boeing 747SP-27
Govt of Yemen, Sana'a
7O-YMN

YUGOSLAVIA
Dassault Falcon 50
Govt of Yugoslavia,
　Belgrade
YU-BNA
YU-BPZ

Gates LearJet 25B/
LearJet 25D*
Govt of Yugoslavia,
　Belgrade
YU-BJG
YU-BKR*

French AF Embraer Xingu 108 'YW' is based at Avord. *Daniel March*

This colourful Antonov An-26 '405' is operated by the Hungarian Air Force. *PRM*

One of four Boeing 707s in service with Italian AF from Pratica di Mare. *PRM*

The Italian Air Force *Freece Tricolori* display team flies 10 Aermacchi MB339s. *PRM*

Royal Netherlands Air Force F-16A 2001 season display aircraft. *PRM*

US Military Aircraft Markings

All USAF aircraft have been allocated a fiscal year (FY) number since 1921. Individual aircraft are given a serial according to the fiscal year in which they are ordered. The numbers commence at 0001 and are prefixed with the year of allocation. For example F-15C Eagle 84-001 (84-0001) was the first aircraft ordered in 1984. The fiscal year (FY) serial is carried on the technical data block which is usually stencilled on the left-hand side of the aircraft just below the cockpit. The number displayed on the fin is a corruption of the FY serial. Most tactical aircraft carry the fiscal year in small figures followed by the last three or four digits of the serial in large figures. For example Aviano-based F-16C Fighting Falcon 89-2009 carries 89-009/AV on its tail. Large transport and tanker aircraft such as C-130s and KC-135s sometimes display a five-figure number commencing with the last digit of the appropriate fiscal year and four figures of the production number. An example of this is KC-135R 58-0128 which displays 80128 on its fin.

USN serials follow a straightforward numerical sequence which commenced, for the present series, with the allocation of 00001 to an SB2C Helldiver by the Bureau of Aeronautics in 1940. Numbers in the 165000 series are presently being issued. They are usually carried in full on the rear fuselage of the aircraft.

UK-based USAF Aircraft

The following aircraft are normally based in the UK. They are listed in numerical order of type with individual aircraft in serial number order, as depicted on the aircraft. The number in brackets is either the alternative presentation of the five-figure number commencing with the last digit of the fiscal year, or the fiscal year where a five-figure serial is presented on the aircraft. Where it is possible to identify the allocation of aircraft to individual squadrons by means of colours carried on fin or cockpit edge, this is also provided.

Notes	Type				Notes	Type			
	McDonnell Douglas F-15C Eagle/					86-0176	(86-0176)	F-15C	y
	F-15D Eagle/F-15E Strike Eagle					86-0178	(86-0178)	F-15C	y
	LN: 48th FW, RAF Lakenheath:					86-0182	(86-0182)	F-15D	y
	492nd FS blue/white								[48th OSS]
	493rd FS black/yellow					91-0300	(91-0300)	F-15E	r
	494th FS red/white					91-0301	(91-0301)	F-15E	bl
	83-0018	(83-0018)	F-15C	y		91-0302	(91-0302)	F-15E	bl
	84-0001	(84-0001)	F-15C	y		91-0303	(91-0303)	F-15E	bl
	84-0004	(84-0004)	F-15C	y		91-0304	(91-0304)	F-15E	bl
	84-0009	(84-0009)	F-15C	y		91-0305	(91-0305)	F-15E	bl
	84-0010	(84-0010)	F-15C	y		91-0306	(91-0306)	F-15E	r
	84-0014	(84-0014)	F-15C	y		91-0307	(91-0307)	F-15E	bl
	84-0015	(84-0015)	F-15C	y		91-0308	(91-0308)	F-15E	bl
	84-0019	(84-0019)	F-15C	y		91-0309	(91-0309)	F-15E	bl
	84-0027	(84-0027)	F-15C	y		91-0310	(91-0310)	F-15E	r
	84-0044	(84-0044)	F-15D	y		91-0311	(91-0311)	F-15E	bl
	86-0147	(86-0147)	F-15C	y		91-0312	(91-0312)	F-15E	bl
	86-0154	(86-0154)	F-15C	y		91-0313	(91-0313)	F-15E	m
	86-0156	(86-0156)	F-15C	y					[48th OG]
	86-0159	(86-0159)	F-15C	y		91-0314	(91-0314)	F-15E	r
	86-0160	(86-0160)	F-15C	y					[494th FS]
	86-0163	(86-0163)	F-15C	y		91-0315	(91-0315)	F-15E	r
	86-0164	(86-0164)	F-15C	y		91-0316	(91-0316)	F-15E	r
				[493rd FS]		91-0317	(91-0317)	F-15E	r
	86-0165	(86-0165)	F-15C	y		91-0318	(91-0318)	F-15E	r
	86-0166	(86-0166)	F-15C	y		91-0319	(91-0319)	F-15E	r
	86-0167	(86-0167)	F-15C	y		91-0320	(91-0320)	F-15E	r
	86-0171	(86-0171)	F-15C	y		91-0321	(91-0321)	F-15E	r
	86-0172	(86-0172)	F-15C	y		91-0322	(91-0322)	F-15E	r
	86-0174	(86-0174)	F-15C	y		91-0323	(91-0323)	F-15E	r
	86-0175	(86-0175)	F-15C	y		91-0324	(91-0324)	F-15E	r

Type			Notes
91-0326	(91-0326)	F-15E *bl*	
91-0328	(91-0328)	F-15E *r*	
91-0329	(91-0329)	F-15E *bl*	
91-0330	(91-0330)	F-15E *r*	
91-0331	(91-0331)	F-15E *r*	
91-0332	(91-0332)	F-15E *bl*	
91-0333	(91-0333)	F-15E *r*	
91-0334	(91-0334)	F-15E *r*	
91-0601	(91-0601)	F-15E *r*	
91-0602	(91-0602)	F-15E *r*	
91-0603	(91-0603)	F-15E *r*	
91-0604	(91-0604)	F-15E *r*	
91-0605	(91-0605)	F-15E *r*	
92-0364	(92-0364)	F-15E *r*	
96-0201	(96-0201)	F-15E *bl*	
96-0202	(96-0202)	F-15E *bl*	
96-0204	(96-0204)	F-15E *bl*	
96-0205	(96-0205)	F-15E *bl*	
97-0217	(97-0217)	F-15E *bl*	
97-0218	(97-0218)	F-15E *m*	
		[48th FW]	
97-0219	(97-0219)	F-15E *bl*	
97-0220	(97-0220)	F-15E *bl*	
97-0221	(97-0221)	F-15E *bl*	
		[492nd FS]	
97-0222	(97-0222)	F-15E *bl*	
98-0131	(98-0131)	F-15E *bl*	
98-0132	(98-0132)	F-15E *bl*	
98-0133	(98-0133)	F-15E *bl*	
98-0134	(98-0134)	F-15E *bl*	
98-0135	(98-0135)	F-15E *bl*	

Sikorsky MH-53M
21st SOS/352nd SOG, RAF Mildenhall

01625	(FY70)
01630	(FY70)
14994	(FY67)
31649	(FY73)
31652	(FY73)
95784	(FY69)
95795	(FY69)
95796	(FY69)

Type			Notes

Lockheed C-130 Hercules
352nd SOG, RAF Mildenhall:
  7th SOS* & 67th SOS,

37814	(FY63)	C-130E
61699	(FY86)	MC-130H*
70023	(FY87)	MC-130H*
80193	(FY88)	MC-130H*
80194	(FY88)	MC-130H*
90280	(FY89)	MC-130H*
95823	(FY69)	MC-130P
95826	(FY69)	MC-130P
95828	(FY69)	MC-130P
95831	(FY69)	MC-130P
95832	(FY69)	MC-130P

Boeing KC-135R
Stratotanker
351st ARS/100th ARW,
  RAF Mildenhall [D] (*r/w/bl*)

00360	(FY60)
10302	(FY61)
14829	(FY64)
14835	(FY64)
14838	(FY64)
23538	(FY62)
23551	(FY62)
37978	(FY63)
37980	(FY63)
38008	(FY63)
38025	(FY63)
38879	(FY63)
38887	(FY63)
72605	(FY57)
91459	(FY59)

UK-based US Navy Aircraft

Beech UC-12M Super King Air
Naval Air Facility, Mildenhall
3836 (163836) [7C]
3843 (163843)

These aircraft are normally based in Western Europe with the USAFE. They are shown in numerical order of type designation, with individual aircraft in serial number order as carried on the aircraft. An alternative five-figure presentation of the serial is shown in brackets where appropriate. Fiscal year (FY) details are also provided if necessary. The unit allocation and operating bases are given for most aircraft.

Notes	Type				Notes	Type			
	Lockheed U-2S					**SP:** 52nd FW, Spangdahlem,			
	OL-FR/9th RW, Istres, France [BB]					Germany:			
	01081 (FY80)					22nd FS red/white			
	01082 (FY80)					23rd FS blue/white			
	01083 (FY80)					87-350 (87-0350) AV gn			
						87-351 (87-0351) AV m [31st OSS]			
	McDonnell Douglas					87-355 (87-0355) AV pr			
	C-9A Nightingale					87-359 (87-0359) AV pr			
	86th AW, Ramstein,					88-413 (88-0413) AV pr [510th FS]			
	Germany:					88-425 (88-0425) AV gn			
	75th AS & 76th AS[1]					88-435 (88-0435) AV gn			
	FY71					88-443 (88-0443) AV pr			
	10876[1] (VIP)					88-444 (88-0444) AV pr			
	10879					88-446 (88-0446) AV pr			
	10880					88-491 (88-0491) AV pr			
	10881					88-525 (88-0525) AV pr			
	10882					88-526 (88-0526) AV gn			
	FY67					88-529 (88-0529) AV gn			
	22585					88-532 (88-0532) AV gn			
						88-535 (88-0535) AV gn [555th FS]			
	Fairchild A-10A Thunderbolt II					88-541 (88-0541) AV pr			
	SP: 52nd FW, Spangdahlem,					89-001 (89-2001) AV m [31st FW]			
	Germany:					89-009 (89-2009) AV gn			
	81st FS black/yellow					89-011 (89-2011) AV pr			
	81-951 (81-0951) bk				89-016 (89-2016) AV gn [16th AF]			
	81-952 (81-0952) m [52nd FW]				89-018 (89-2018) AV gn			
	81-954 (81-0954) bk [81st FS]				89-023 (89-2023) AV gn			
	81-956 (81-0956) bk				89-024 (89-2024) AV pr			
	81-962 (81-0962) bk				89-026 (89-2026) AV pr			
	81-963 (81-0963) bk				89-029 (89-2029) AV pr			
	81-966 (81-0966) bk				89-030 (89-2030) AV pr			
	81-976 (81-0976) bk				89-035 (89-2035) AV gn			
	81-978 (81-0978) bk				89-038 (89-2038) AV gn			
	81-980 (81-0980) bk				89-039 (89-2039) AV gn			
	81-983 (81-0983) bk				89-044 (89-2044) AV gn			
	81-984 (81-0984) bk				89-046 (89-2046) AV pr			
	81-985 (81-0985) bk				89-047 (89-2047) AV pr			
	81-988 (81-0988) bk				89-049 (89-2049) AV gn			
	81-991 (81-0991) bk				89-057 (89-2057) AV gn			
	81-992 (81-0992) m [52nd OG]				89-068 (89-2068) AV gn			
	82-649 (82-0649) bk				89-102 (89-2102) AV gn			
	82-650 (82-0650) bk				89-137 (89-2137) AV pr [31st OG]			
	82-654 (82-0654) bk				89-178 (89-2178)* AV pr			
	82-655 (82-0655) bk [81st FS]				90-709 (90-0709) AV gn			
	82-656 (82-0656) bk				90-772 (90-0772) AV gn			
						90-773 (90-0773) AV gn			
	Beech C-12C/C-12D/C-12F					90-795 (90-0795)* AV gn			
	JUSMG, Ankara, Turkey;					90-796 (90-0796)* AV pr			
	US Embassy Flight, Budapest,					90-800 (90-0800)* AV gn			
	Hungary					90-813 (90-0813) SP r			
	FY83					90-818 (90-0818) SP r			
	30495 C-12D Budapest				90-827 (90-0827) SP r			
	FY73					90-828 (90-0828) SP r			
	31216 C-12C Ankara				90-829 (90-0829) SP r [22nd FS]			
						90-831 (90-0831) SP r			
	Lockheed (GD) F-16C/F-16D*					90-833 (90-0833) SP r			
	AV: 31st FW, Aviano, Italy:					90-843 (90-0843)* SP r			
	510th FS purple/white					90-846 (90-0846)* SP bl			
	555th FS green/yellow					91-336 (91-0336) SP r			

Type			Notes
91-337	(91-0337)	SP r	
91-338	(91-0338)	SP r	
91-339	(91-0339)	SP r	[22nd FS]
91-340	(91-0340)	SP r	
91-341	(91-0341)	SP r	
91-342	(91-0342)	SP r	
91-343	(91-0343)	SP r	
91-344	(91-0344)	SP r	
91-351	(91-0351)	SP r	
91-352	(91-0352)	SP m	[52nd FW]
91-391	(91-0391)	SP bl	
91-402	(91-0402)	SP bl	
91-403	(91-0403)	SP bl	
91-405	(91-0405)	SP bl	
91-406	(91-0406)	SP bl	[23rd FS]
91-407	(91-0407)	SP bl	
91-408	(91-0408)	SP bl	
91-409	(91-0409)	SP bl	
91-410	(91-0410)	SP bl	
91-412	(91-0412)	SP bl	
91-414	(91-0414)	SP bl	
91-415	(91-0415)	SP bl	
91-416	(91-0416)	SP bl	[52nd OG]
91-417	(91-0417)	SP bl	
91-418	(91-0418)	SP bl	
91-419	(91-0419)	SP bl	
91-420	(91-0420)	SP bl	
91-421	(91-0421)	SP bl	
91-464	(91-0464)*	SP r	
91-472	(91-0472)*	SP bl	
91-474	(91-0474)*	SP bl	
92-915	(92-3915)	SP bl	
92-918	(92-3918)	SP bl	
96-080	(96-0080)	SP bl	[23rd FS]
96-081	(96-0081)	SP bl	
96-082	(96-0082)	SP m	[52nd FW]
96-083	(96-0083)	SP bl	

Grumman C-20A Gulfstream III
76th AS/86th AW, Ramstein,
  Germany
FY83
30500
30501
30502

Gates C-21A Learjet
76th AS/86th AW, Ramstein,
  Germany;
*7005th ABS/HQ USEUCOM,
  Stuttgart, Germany
FY84
40068*
40081*
40082*

Type		Notes
40083*		
40084		
40085		
40086		
40087		
40108		
40109		
40110		
40111		
40112		

Gulfstream Aerospace
C-37A Gulfstream V
Det 1, 86th OG/SHAPE, Chievres,
  Belgium
FY99
90404

Sikorsky HH-60G Blackhawk
56th RQS/85th Wing, Keflavik,
  Iceland [IS]

26109	(FY88)	
26205	(FY89)	
26206	(FY89)	
26208	(FY89)	
26212	(FY89)	

Lockheed C-130E Hercules
37th AS/86th AW, Ramstein,
  Germany [RS] (*bl/w*)

01260	(FY70)	
01264	(FY70)	[86th AW]
01271	(FY70)	
01274	(FY70)	[86th AW]
10935	(FY68)	
10938	(FY68)	
10943	(FY68)	[86th OG]
10947	(FY68)	
17681	(FY64)	
18240	(FY64)	
37885	(FY63)	
37887	(FY63)	
40502	(FY64)	
40527	(FY64)	
40533	(FY64)	
40550	(FY64)	
96566	(FY69)	[37th AS]
96582	(FY69)	
96583	(FY69)	

European-based US Navy Aircraft

Notes	Type			Notes	Type		
	Lockheed P-3 Orion				**Fairchild C-26D**		
	CinCUSNFE				NAF Naples, Italy;		
	NAF Sigonella, Italy;				NAF Sigonella, Italy		
	NAF Keflavik, Iceland;				900528	Sigonella	
	VQ-2, NAF Rota, Spain				900530	Sigonella	
	150495		P-3A NAF Keflavik		900531	Sigonella	
	150496		VP-3A CinCUSNFE		910502	Naples	
	156519	[21]	EP-3E VQ-2				
	156525	[11]	P-3C VQ-2		**Sikorsky MH-53E Sea Stallion**		
	156529	[24]	EP-3E VQ-2		HC-4, NAF Sigonella, Italy		
	157316	[23]	EP-3E VQ-2		162505	[HC-47]	
	157325	[25]	EP-3E VQ-2		162509	[HC-49]	
	157326	[22]	EP-3E VQ-2		162516	[HC-46]	
	159886	[09]	P-3C VQ-2		163053	[HC-44]	
					163055	[HC-45]	
	Beech UC-12M Super King Air				163057	[HC-41]	
	NAF Rota, Spain				163065	[HC-43]	
	3839	(163839)	Rota		163068	[HC-42]	
	3842	(163842)	Rota		164864	[HC-48]	

European-based US Army Aircraft

Notes	Type			Notes	Type		
	Bell UH-1H Iroquois				**Beech**		
	LANDSOUTHEAST, Cigli, Turkey;				**C-12 Super King Air**		
	'B' Co, 2nd Btn, 502nd Avn Reg't,				214th Avn, Heidelberg;		
	Coleman Barracks;				'A' Co, 2nd Btn, 228th Avn Reg't,		
	7th Army Training Center, Grafenwöhr;				Heidelberg;		
	Combat Manoeuvre Training Centre,				'B' Co, 2nd Btn, 228th Avn Reg't,		
	Hohenfels;				Heidelberg;		
	HQ/USEUCOM, Stuttgart;				HQ/USEUCOM, Stuttgart;		
	6th Avn Co, Vicenza, Italy				6th Avn Co, Vicenza, Italy;		
	FY69				1st Military Intelligence Btn,		
	15605	HQ/USEUCOM			Wiesbaden		
	15606	HQ/USEUCOM			*FY84*		
	FY68				40144	C-12F	214th Avn
	16341	LANDSOUTHEAST			40152	C-12F	214th Avn
	16662	LANDSOUTHEAST			40153	C-12F	1st MIB
	FY72				40155	C-12F	214th Avn
	21569	CMTC			40156	C-12F	214th Avn
	21632	CMTC			40157	C-12F	214th Avn
	21636	CMTC			40158	C-12F	HQ/USEUCOM
	FY73				40160	C-12F	HQ/USEUCOM
	21668	CMTC			40161	C-12F	6th Avn Co
	21725	7th ATC			40162	C-12F	6th Avn Co
	21786	CMTC			40164	C-12F	214th Avn
	21806	LANDSOUTHEAST			40165	C-12F	214th Avn
	21824	7th ATC			*FY94*		
	22127	B/2-502nd Avn			40315	C-12R	A/2-228th Avn
	FY74				40316	C-12R	A/2-228th Avn
	22303	CMTC			40318	C-12R	A/2-228th Avn
	22318	6th Avn Co			40319	C-12R	A/2-228th Avn
	22330	CMTC			*FY85*		
	22347	CMTC			50147	RC-12K 1st MIB	
	22355	CMTC			50148	RC-12K 1st MIB	
	22368	HQ/USEUCOM			50149	RC-12K 1st MIB	
	22370	CMTC			50150	RC-12K 1st MIB	
	22410	CMTC			50152	RC-12K 1st MIB	
	22448	CMTC			50153	RC-12K 1st MIB	
	22465	CMTC			50155	RC-12K 1st MIB	
	22504	7th ATC					
	22513	HQ/USEUCOM			**Beech C-12J**		
	22514	HQ/USEUCOM			HQ/USEUCOM, Stuttgart		

Type	Notes
FY86	
60079	
Cessna UC-35A Citation V	
214th Avn Reg't, Heidelberg	
FY95	
50123	
50124	
FY97	
70101	
70102	
Boeing-Vertol CH-47D Chinook	
'F' Co, 159th Avn Reg't Giebelstadt	
FY87	
70072	
70073	
FY88	
80098	
80099	
80100	
80101	
80102	
80103	
80104	
80106	
FY89	
90138	
90139	
90140	
90141	
90142	
90143	
90144	
90145	
Bell OH-58D(I) Kiowa Warrior	
1st Btn, 1st Cavalry Reg't, Budingen;	
1st Btn, 4th Cavalry Reg't,	
Schweinfurt	
FY90	
00348	1-1st Cav
00371	1-1st Cav
00373	1-4th Cav
FY91	
10540	1-1st Cav
10544	1-1st Cav
10564	1-1st Cav
FY92	
20520	1-1st Cav
20529	1-1st Cav
20545	1-1st Cav
FY93	
30971	1-4th Cav
30996	1-4th Cav
30998	1-4th Cav
31002	1-4th Cav
31005	1-4th Cav
31006	1-4th Cav
31007	1-4th Cav
31008	1-4th Cav
FY94	
40149	1-4th Cav
40150	1-4th Cav
40151	1-4th Cav
40152	1-1st Cav
40153	1-4th Cav
40154	1-4th Cav
40174	1-4th Cav
40175	1-1st Cav
40176	1-4th Cav
40178	1-1st Cav
40179	1-1st Cav

Type		Notes
40180	1-1st Cav	
FY89		
90114	1-1st Cav	
90116	1-1st Cav	
90117	1-1st Cav	
Sikorsky H-60 Black Hawk		
2nd Btn, 1st Avn Reg't, Ansbach;		
45th Medical Co, Ansbach;		
'B' Co, 5th Btn, 158th Avn Reg't,		
Aviano;		
'A' Co, 127th Divisional Avn		
Support Btn, Bad Kreuznach;		
357th Avn Det/SHAPE, Chievres;		
'B' Co, 70th Transportation Reg't,		
Coleman Barracks;		
'A' Co, 5th Btn, 158th Avn Reg't,		
Giebelstadt;		
'C' Co, 5th Btn, 158th Avn Reg't,		
Giebelstadt;		
'C' Co, 158th Avn Reg't, Giebelstadt;		
'D' Co, 158th Avn Reg't, Giebelstadt;		
2nd Btn, 501st Avn Reg't, Hanau;		
214th Avn, Heidelberg;		
'B' Co, 7th Btn, 159th AVIM, Illesheim;		
236th Medical Co (HA), Landstuhl;		
6th Avn Co, Vicenza, Italy;		
159th Medical Co, Wiesbaden		
FY82		
23675	UH-60A	45th Med Co
23685	UH-60A	159th Med Co
23692	UH-60A	C/158th Avn
23693	UH-60A	45th Med Co
23727	UH-60A	159th Med Co
23729	UH-60A	45th Med Co
23735	UH-60A	236th Med Co
23736	UH-60A	236th Med Co
23737	UH-60A	236th Med Co
23738	UH-60A	159th Med Co
23745	UH-60A	236th Med Co
23749	UH-60A	236th Med Co
23750	UH-60A	159th Med Co
23751	UH-60A	45th Med Co
23752	UH-60A	236th Med Co
23753	UH-60A	159th Med Co
23754	UH-60A	45th Med Co
23755	UH-60A	236th Med Co
23756	UH-60A	236th Med Co
23757	UH-60A	214th Avn
23761	UH-60A	2-501st Avn
FY83		
23854	UH-60A	357th Avn Det
23855	UH-60A	214th Avn
23868	UH-60A	214th Avn
23869	UH-60A	214th Avn
FY84		
23951	UH-60A	45th Med Co
23970	UH-60A	C/5-158th Avn
23975	UH-60A	C/5-158th Avn
24019	EH-60A	2-1st Avn
FY85		
24391	UH-60A	45th Med Co
24467	EH-60A	2-1st Avn
24475	EH-60A	2-1st Avn
24478	EH-60A	2-1st Avn
FY86		
24498	UH-60A	2-501st Avn
24530	UH-60A	2-501st Avn
24531	UH-60A	45th Med Co
24532	UH-60A	45th Med Co
24538	UH-60A	214th Avn
24550	UH-60A	236th Med Co
24551	UH-60A	236th Med Co

US Army Europe

Type				Type		
24552	UH-60A	159th Med Co		**FY95**		
24554	UH-60A	C/5-158th Avn		26621	UH-60L	2-1st Avn
24555	UH-60A	159th Med Co		26628	UH-60L	2-1st Avn
24566	EH-60C	2-501st Avn		26629	UH-60L	2-1st Avn
FY87				26630	UH-60L	2-1st Avn
24579	UH-60A	A/5-158th Avn		26631	UH-60L	2-1st Avn
24581	UH-60A	159th Med Co		26632	UH-60L	2-1st Avn
24583	UH-60A	357th Avn Det		26633	UH-60L	2-1st Avn
24584	UH-60A	357th Avn Det		26635	UH-60L	2-1st Avn
24589	UH-60A	214th Avn		26636	UH-60L	2-1st Avn
24621	UH-60A	214th Avn		26637	UH-60L	2-1st Avn
24628	UH-60A	2-1st Avn		26638	UH-60L	2-1st Avn
24634	UH-60A	159th Med Co		26639	UH-60L	2-1st Avn
24642	UH-60A	214th Avn		26640	UH-60L	2-1st Avn
24643	UH-60A	2-1st Avn		26641	UH-60L	D/158th Avn
24644	UH-60A	45th Med Co		26642	UH-60L	D/158th Avn
24645	UH-60A	45th Med Co		26643	UH-60L	D/158th Avn
24646	UH-60A	2-1st Avn		26644	UH-60L	2-1st Avn
24647	UH-60A	214th Avn		26645	UH-60L	D/158th Avn
24650	UH-60A	159th Med Co		26646	UH-60L	2-1st Avn
24656	UH-60A	159th Med Co		26647	UH-60L	2-1st Avn
24660	EH-60C	2-501st Avn		26648	UH-60L	2-1st Avn
24664	EH-60A	2-501st Avn		26649	UH-60L	D/158th Avn
24667	EH-60A	2-501st Avn		26650	UH-60L	D/158th Avn
26001	UH-60A	45th Med Co		26651	UH-60L	C/158th Avn
26002	UH-60A	159th Med Co		26652	UH-60L	C/158th Avn
26003	UH-60A	B/5-158th Avn		26653	UH-60L	C/158th Avn
26004	UH-60A	2-1st Avn		26654	UH-60L	C/158th Avn
FY88				26655	UH-60L	C/158th Avn
26019	UH-60A	214th Avn		**FY96**		
26020	UH-60A	236th Med Co		26674	UH-60L	D/158th Avn
26023	UH-60A	236th Med Co		26675	UH-60L	D/158th Avn
26025	UH-60A	214th Avn		26676	UH-60L	D/158th Avn
26026	UH-60A	B/5-158th Avn		26677	UH-60L	D/158th Avn
26027	UH-60A	214th Avn		26678	UH-60L	D/158th Avn
26028	UH-60A	C/5-158th Avn		26679	UH-60L	D/158th Avn
26031	UH-60A	2-1st Avn		26680	UH-60L	D/158th Avn
26034	UH-60A	236th Med Co		26681	UH-60L	D/158th Avn
26037	UH-60A	B/7-159th AVIM		26682	UH-60L	D/158th Avn
26038	UH-60A	A/5-158th Avn		26683	UH-60L	C/158th Avn
26039	UH-60A	45th Med Co		26684	UH-60L	C/158th Avn
26040	UH-60A	2-1st Avn		26685	UH-60L	C/158th Avn
26041	UH-60A	A/5-158th Avn		26686	UH-60L	C/158th Avn
26042	UH-60A	A/5-158th Avn		26687	UH-60L	C/158th Avn
26045	UH-60A	45th Med Co		26688	UH-60L	C/158th Avn
26050	UH-60A	159th Med Co		26689	UH-60L	C/158th Avn
26051	UH-60A	A/5-158th Avn		26690	UH-60L	C/158th Avn
26052	UH-60A	B/5-158th Avn		26691	UH-60L	C/158th Avn
26053	UH-60A	A/5-158th Avn		26692	UH-60L	C/158th Avn
26054	UH-60A	236th Med Co		**FY97**		
26055	UH-60A	236th Med Co		26762	UH-60L	2-501st Avn
26056	UH-60A	A/5-158th Avn		26763	UH-60L	2-501st Avn
26058	UH-60A	159th Med Co		26764	UH-60L	2-501st Avn
26063	UH-60A	B/5-158th Avn		26765	UH-60L	2-501st Avn
26067	UH-60A	B/5-158th Avn		26766	UH-60L	2-501st Avn
26068	UH-60A	2-501st Avn		26767	UH-60L	2-501st Avn
26071	UH-60A	2-501st Avn		**FY98**		
26072	UH-60A	236th Med Co		26795	UH-60L	2-501st Avn
26075	UH-60A	2-501st Avn		26796	UH-60L	2-501st Avn
26077	UH-60A	C/5-158th Avn		26797	UH-60L	2-501st Avn
26080	UH-60A	236th Med Co		26798	UH-60L	2-501st Avn
26083	UH-60A	B/5-158th Avn		26799	UH-60L	2-501st Avn
26085	UH-60A	2-501st Avn		26800	UH-60L	2-501st Avn
26086	UH-60A	2-501st Avn		26801	UH-60L	2-501st Avn
FY89				26802	UH-60L	2-501st Avn
26138	UH-60A	2-1st Avn		26813	UH-60L	2-501st Avn
26142	UH-60A	B/7-159th AVIM		26814	UH-60L	2-501st Avn
26145	UH-60A	B/5-158th Avn				
26146	UH-60A	159th Med Co				
26153	UH-60A	B/5-158th Avn				
26155	UH-60A	2-1st Avn				
26164	UH-60A	C/5-158th Avn				
26165	UH-60A	214th Avn				

MDH AH-64A Apache
1st Btn, 1st Avn Reg't, Ansbach;
127th ASB, Hanau;
1st Btn, 501st Avn Reg't, Hanau;
2nd Btn, 6th Cavalry Reg't, Illesheim;

Type		Notes	Type		Notes
6th Btn, 6th Cavalry Reg't, Illesheim;			70442	1-1st Avn	
'A' Co, 7th Btn, 159th Avn Reg't,			70443	2-6th Cav	
Illesheim			70444	1-501st Avn	
FY86			70445	1-501st Avn	
68940	2-6th Cav		70446	1-501st Avn	
68941	6-6th Cav		70447	1-501st Avn	
68942	2-6th Cav		70449	1-501st Avn	
68943	2-6th Cav		70451	1-501st Avn	
68946	2-6th Cav		70453		
68947	6-6th Cav		70454		
68948	2-6th Cav		70455	1-501st Avn	
68949	2-6th Cav		70457	1-1st Avn	
68951	2-6th Cav		70465	2-6th Cav	
68952	2-6th Cav		70470	1-1st Avn	
68955	2-6th Cav		70471	1-1st Avn	
68956	2-6th Cav		70474	1-1st Avn	
68957	2-6th Cav		70475	1-1st Avn	
68959	2-6th Cav		70476	1-1st Avn	
68960	2-6th Cav		70477	1-1st Avn	
68961	2-6th Cav		70478	1-1st Avn	
68981	2-6th Cav		70481	1-1st Avn	
69011	2-6th Cav		70487	1-501st Avn	
69026	2-6th Cav		70496	1-501st Avn	
69030	2-6th Cav		70503	1-501st Avn	
69032	2-6th Cav		70504	1-501st Avn	
69037	2-6th Cav		70505	1-501st Avn	
69039	2-6th Cav		70506	1-501st Avn	
69041	1-501st Avn		*FY88*		
69048	2-6th Cav		80197	1-501st Avn	
FY87			80198	1-501st Avn	
70409	1-1st Avn		80203	6-6th Cav	
70410	1-501st Avn		80212	6-6th Cav	
70411	6-6th Cav		80213	6-6th Cav	
70412	1-1st Avn		80214	6-6th Cav	
70413	1-1st Avn		80215	6-6th Cav	
70415	1-501st Avn		80216	6-6th Cav	
70417	1-1st Avn		80217	6-6th Cav	
70418	1-501st Avn		80219	6-6th Cav	
70420	1-1st Avn		80222	6-6th Cav	
70428	1-1st Avn		80225	6-6th Cav	
70431	6-6th Cav		80228	6-6th Cav	
70432	1-1st Avn		80229	6-6th Cav	
70435	1-501st Avn		80232	6-6th Cav	
70436	1-1st Avn		80233	6-6th Cav	
70437	1-1st Avn		80234	6-6th Cav	
70438	1-501st Avn		80236	6-6th Cav	
70439	1-1st Avn		80243	6-6th Cav	
70440	1-501st Avn		80246	6-6th Cav	
70441	2-6th Cav				

US-based USAF Aircraft

The following aircraft are normally based in the USA but are likely to be seen visiting the UK from time to time. The presentation is in numerical order of the type, commencing with the B-**1B** and concluding with the C-**141**. The aircraft are listed in numerical progression by the serial actually carried externally. Fiscal year information is provided, together with details of mark variations and in some cases operating units. Where base-code letter information is carried on the aircrafts' tails, this is detailed with the squadron/base data; for example the 7th Wing's B-1B 30069 carries the letters DY on its tail, thus identifying the Wing's home base as Dyess AFB, Texas.

Rockwell B-1B Lancer

7th BW, Dyess AFB, Texas [DY]:
 9th BS (*bk*), 13th BS (*r*)
 & 28th BS (*bl/w*);
28th BW, Ellsworth AFB,
 South Dakota [EL]:
 13th BS (*bl/br*), 37th BS (*bl*)
 & 77th BS (*pr/y*);
127th BS/184th BW, Kansas ANG,
 McConnell AFB, Kansas (*r/w*);
128th BS/116th BW, Georgia ANG,
 Robins AFB, Georgia [GA];
419th FLTS/412th TW, Edwards AFB,
 California [ED]

Notes	Type			Notes	Type		
					50084	28th BW	pr/y
					50086	28th BW	pr/y
					50087	28th BW	pr/y
					50088	127th BS	r/w
					50089	128th BS	
					50090	28th BW	pr/y
					50091	28th BW	bl
					50092	128th BS	
	FY83				*FY86*		
	30065	7th BW	bk		60093	28th BW	pr/y
	30066	7th BW	bl/w		60094	28th BW	pr/y
	30067	7th BW	bk		60095	127th BS	r/w
	30068	7th BW	bl/w		60096	28th BW	bl
	30069	7th BW	bl/w		60097	28th BW	pr/y
	30070	7th BW	bl/w		60098	128th BS	
	30071	7th BW	bk		60099	28th BW	pr/y
	FY84				60100	7th BW	bl/w
	40049	412th TW			60101	7th BW	bl/w
	40050	7th BW	bl/w		60102	28th BW	pr/y
	40051	7th BW	bk		60103	7th BW	bk
	40053	7th BW			60104	28th BW	pr/y
	40054	7th BW	bl/w		60105	7th BW	bl/w
	40055	7th BW	bl/w		60107	128th BS	
	40056	7th BW	bl/w		60108	7th BW	bl/w
	40058	7th BW	bk		60109	7th BW	bl/w
	FY85				60110	7th BW	bl/w
	50059	128th BS			60111	28th BW	pr/y
	50060	127th BS	r/w		60112	7th BW	bk
	50061	128th BS			60113	28th BW	bl
	50062	7th BW	bk		60114	28th BW	pr/y
	50064	127th BS	r/w		60115	127th BS	r/w
	50065	7th BW	bk		60116			
	50066	28th BW	pr/y		60117	7th BW	bl/w
	50067	7th BW	bl/w		60118			
	50068	412th TW			60119	7th BW	bl/w
	50069	127th BS	r/w		60120	7th BW	bk
	50070	127th BS	r/w		60121			
	50071	128th BS			60122	7th BW	r
	50072	28th BW	bk		60123	7th BW	bk
	50073	7th BW	bk		60124	128th BS	
	50074	28th BW			60125			
	50075	28th BW	pr/y		60126	127th BS	r/w
	50077	28th BW	pr/y		60127	128th BS	
	50079	28th BW	pr/y		60128	28th BW	pr/y
	50080	127th BS	r/w		60129	28th BW	pr/y
	50081	127th BS	r/w		60130	7th BW	bl/w
	50082	412th TW			60131			
	50083	28th BW	bl		60132	7th BW	bl/w
					60133	128th BS	
					60134			
					60135	7th BW	bk
					60136	127th BS	r/w
					60137	7th BW	r
					60138	366th Wg	r/bk

Type			Notes
60139	366th Wg	r/bk	
60140	7th BW	bk	

Northrop B-2 Spirit
419th FLTS/412th TW, Edwards AFB,
California [ED];
509th BW, Whiteman AFB,
Missouri [WM]:
  325th BS, 393rd BS & 715th BS
(Names are given where known.
Each begins Spirit of ...)

FY90			
00040	509th BW	Alaska	
00041	509th BW	Hawaii	
FY92			
20700	509th BW	Florida	
FY82			
21066	509th BW	America	
21067	509th BW	Arizona	
21068	412th TW	New York	
21069	509th BW	Indiana	
21070	Northrop	Ohio	
21071	509th BW	Mississippi	
FY93			
31085	509th BW	Oklahoma	
31086	509th BW	Kitty Hawk	
31087	509th BW	Pennsylvania	
31088	509th BW	Louisiana	
FY88			
80328	509th BW	Texas	
80329	509th BW	Missouri	
80330	509th BW	California	
80331	509th BW	South Carolina	
80332	509th BW	Washington	
FY89			
90127	509th BW	Kansas	
90128	509th BW	Nebraska	
90129	509th BW	Georgia	

Boeing E-3 Sentry
552nd ACW, Tinker AFB,
Oklahoma [OK]:
  960th AACS (w), 963rd AACS (bk),
  964th AACS (r), 965th AACS (y)
  & 966th AACS (bl);
961st AACS/18th Wg, Kadena AB,
Japan [ZZ] (or);
962nd AACS/3rd Wg, Elmendorf AFB,
Alaska [AK] (gn);

FY80			
00137	E-3C	bk	
00138	E-3C	y	
00139	E-3C	bl	
FY81			
10004	E-3C	bk	
10005	E-3C	or	
FY71			
11407	E-3B	wh	
11408	E-3B	bk	
FY82			
20006	E-3C	y	
20007	E-3C	m	
FY83			
30008	E-3C	gn	
30009	E-3C	bk	
FY73			
31674	JE-3C	Boeing	
31675	E-3B	gn	
FY75			
50556	E-3B	or	
50557	E-3B	gn	
50558	E-3B	y	
50559	E-3B	bl	

Type			Notes
50560	E-3B	y	
FY76			
61604	E-3B	r	
61605	E-3B	gn	
61606	E-3B	gn	
61607	E-3B	bl	
FY77			
70351	E-3B	or	
70352	E-3B	r	
70353	E-3B	y	
70355	E-3B	r	
70356	E-3B	y	
FY78			
80576	E-3B	r	
80577	E-3B	r	
80578	E-3B	w	
FY79			
90001	E-3B	r	
90002	E-3B	y	
90003	E-3B	bl	

Boeing E-4B
1st ACCS/55th Wg, Offutt AFB,
Nebraska [OF]

31676	(FY73)		
31677	(FY73)		
40787	(FY74)		
50125	(FY75)		

Lockheed C-5 Galaxy
60th AMW, Travis AFB, California:
  21st AS (bk/gd) & 22nd AS (bk/bl);
56th AS/97th AMW, Altus AFB,
Oklahoma (r/y);
137th AS/105th AW, Stewart AFB,
New York (bl);
68th AS/433rd AW AFRC, Kelly AFB,
Texas;
436th AW, Dover AFB, Delaware:
  3rd AS & 9th AS (y/r & y/bl);
337th AS/439th AW AFRC, Westover
ARB, Massachusetts (bl/r)

FY70			
00445	C-5A	433rd AW	
00446	C-5A	433rd AW	
00447	C-5A	436th AW	y
00448	C-5A	439th AW	bl/r
00449	C-5A	60th AMW	bk/gd
00450	C-5A	60th AMW	bk/gd
00451	C-5A	60th AMW	
00452	C-5A	97th AMW	r/y
00453	C-5A	436th AW	y
00454	C-5A	97th AMW	r/y
00455	C-5A	97th AMW	r/y
00456	C-5A	60th AMW	bk/gd
00457	C-5A	60th AMW	bk/gd
00458	C-5A	433rd AW	
00459	C-5A	60th AMW	bk/gd
00460	C-5A	105th AW	bl
00461	C-5A	436th AW	y
00462	C-5A	97th AMW	r/y
00463	C-5A	436th AW	y
00464	C-5A	60th AMW	bk/bl
00465	C-5A	436th AW	
00466	C-5A	436th AW	
00467	C-5A	436th AW	y
FY83			
31285	C-5B	436th AW	y/r
FY84			
40059	C-5B	436th AW	
40060	C-5B	60th AMW	bk/bl
40061	C-5B	436th AW	y
40062	C-5B	60th AMW	bk/gd

Notes	Type			
	FY85			
	50001	C-5B	436th AW	*m*
	50002	C-5B	60th AMW	*bk/bl*
	50003	C-5B	436th AW	*y*
	50004	C-5B	60th AMW	*bk/bl*
	50005	C-5B	436th AW	*y*
	50006	C-5B	60th AMW	*bk/gd*
	50007	C-5B	436th AW	*y/bl*
	50008	C-5B	60th AMW	*bk/gd*
	50009	C-5B	436th AW	*y*
	50010	C-5B	60th AMW	*bk/gd*
	FY86			
	60011	C-5B	436th AW	*y/bl*
	60012	C-5B	60th AMW	*bk/bl*
	60013	C-5B	436th AW	*y*
	60014	C-5B	60th AMW	*bk/bl*
	60015	C-5B	436th AW	*y/r*
	60016	C-5B	60th AMW	*bk/bl*
	60017	C-5B	436th AW	*y*
	60018	C-5B	60th AMW	*bk/gd*
	60019	C-5B	436th AW	*y*
	60020	C-5B	436th AW	*y*
	60021	C-5B	60th AMW	*bk/gd*
	60022	C-5B	60th AMW	*bk/bl*
	60023	C-5B	436th AW	*y*
	60024	C-5B	60th AMW	*bk/bl*
	60025	C-5B	436th AW	*y*
	60026	C-5B	60th AMW	*bk/gd*
	FY66			
	68304	C-5A	439th AW	*bl/r*
	68305	C-5A	433rd AW	
	68306	C-5A	433rd AW	
	68307	C-5A	433rd AW	
	FY87			
	70027	C-5B	436th AW	*y/bl*
	70028	C-5B	60th AMW	*bk/bl*
	70029	C-5B	436th AW	*y*
	70030	C-5B	60th AMW	*bk/bl*
	70031	C-5B	436th AW	*y*
	70032	C-5B	60th AMW	*bk/bl*
	70033	C-5B	436th AW	*y*
	70034	C-5B	60th AMW	*bk/gd*
	70035	C-5B	436th AW	*y*
	70036	C-5B	60th AMW	*bk/gd*
	70037	C-5B	436th AW	*y*
	70038	C-5B	60th AMW	*bk/bl*
	70039	C-5B	436th AW	*y*
	70040	C-5B	60th AMW	*bk/gd*
	70041	C-5B	436th AW	*y*
	70042	C-5B	60th AMW	*bk/gd*
	70043	C-5B	436th AW	*y/bl*
	70044	C-5B	60th AMW	*bk/gd*
	70045	C-5B	436th AW	*y*
	FY67			
	70167	C-5A	439th AW	*bl/r*
	70168	C-5A	433rd AW	
	70169	C-5A	105th AW	*bl*
	70170	C-5A	105th AW	*bl*
	70171	C-5A	433rd AW	
	70173	C-5A	105th AW	*bl*
	70174	C-5A	105th AW	*bl*
	FY68			
	80211	C-5A	439th AW	*bl/r*
	80212	C-5A	105th AW	*bl*
	80213	C-5C	60th AMW	*bk/bl*
	80214	C-5B	436th AW	
	80215	C-5A	439th AW	*bl/r*
	80216	C-5C	60th AMW	*bk/gd*
	80217	C-5A	97th AMW	*r/y*
	80219	C-5A	439th AW	*bl/r*
	80220	C-5A	433rd AW	
	80221	C-5A	433rd AW	
	80222	C-5A	439th AW	*bl/r*

Notes	Type			
	80223	C-5A	433rd AW	
	80224	C-5A	105th AW	*bl*
	80225	C-5A	439th AW	*bl/r*
	80226	C-5A	105th AW	*bl*
	FY69			
	90001	C-5A	60th AMW	*bk/gd*
	90002	C-5A	433rd AW	
	90003	C-5A	439th AW	*bl/r*
	90004	C-5A	433rd AW	
	90005	C-5A	439th AW	*bl/r*
	90006	C-5A	433rd AW	
	90007	C-5A	433rd AW	
	90008	C-5A	105th AW	*bl*
	90009	C-5A	105th AW	*bl*
	90010	C-5A	60th AMW	*bk/gd*
	90011	C-5A	439th AW	*bl/r*
	90012	C-5A	105th AW	*bl*
	90013	C-5A	439th AW	*bl/r*
	90014	C-5A	97th AMW	*r/y*
	90015	C-5A	105th AW	*bl*
	90016	C-5A	433rd AW	
	90017	C-5A	439th AW	*bl/r*
	90018	C-5A	97th AMW	*r/y*
	90019	C-5A	439th AW	*bl/r*
	90020	C-5A	439th AW	*bl/r*
	90021	C-5A	105th AW	*bl*
	90022	C-5A	439th AW	*bl/r*
	90023	C-5A	60th AMW	*bk/bl*
	90024	C-5A	436th AW	*y*
	90025	C-5A	97th AMW	*r/y*
	90026	C-5A	60th AMW	*bk/bl*
	90027	C-5A	436th AW	*y*

Boeing E-8 J-STARS

Grumman, Melbourne, Florida;
12th ACCS/93rd ACW, Robins AFB,
  Georgia [WR] (*gn*)

Type			
FY00			
02000	E-8C		
FY90			
00175	E-8A	Grumman	
FY92			
23289	E-8C	93rd ACW	
23290	E-8C	93rd ACW	
FY93			
30597	E-8C	93rd ACW	
31097	E-8C	93rd ACW	
FY94			
40284	E-8C	93rd ACW	
40285	E-8C		
FY95			
50121	E-8C	93rd ACW	
50122	E-8C	93rd ACW	
50123	E-8C		
FY96			
60042	E-8C	93rd ACW	
60043	E-8C		
FY86			
60417	TE-8A	93rd ACW	
FY97			
70100	E-8C	93rd ACW	
70200	E-8C		
70201	E-8C		
FY99			
90006	E-8C		

McDonnell Douglas C-9 Nightingale

86th AW, Ramstein, Germany:
  75th AS & 76th AS;
99th AS/89th AW, Andrews AFB,
  Maryland;
30th AS/374th AW, Yokota AB,
  Japan;

Type			Notes
11th AS/375th AW, Scott AFB, Illinois			
FY71			
10874	C-9A	374th AW	
10875	C-9A	374th AW	
10876	C-9A	76th AS (VIP)	
10877	C-9A	374th AW	
10878	C-9A	375th AW	
10879	C-9A	75th AS	
10880	C-9A	75th AS	
10881	C-9A	75th AS	
10882	C-9A	75th AS	
FY68			
10958	C-9A	375th AW	
10959	C-9A	375th AW	
10960	C-9A	375th AW	
10961	C-9A	375th AW	
FY67			
22583	C-9A	374th AW	
22584	C-9A	375th AW	
22585	C-9A	75th AS	
FY73			
31681	C-9C	89th AW	
31682	C-9C	89th AW	
31683	C-9C	89th AW	
FY68			
88932	C-9A	375th AW	
88933	C-9A	375th AW	
88934	C-9A	374th AW	
88935	C-9A	375th AW	

McDonnell Douglas KC-10A Extender
60th AMW, Travis AFB, California: 6th ARS (*bk/r*) & 9th ARS (*bk/bl*); 305th AMW, McGuire AFB, New Jersey: 2nd ARS (*bl/r*) & 32nd ARS (*bl*)

FY82			
20191	60th AMW	*bk/bl*	
20192	60th AMW	*bk/r*	
20193	60th AMW	*bk/bl*	
FY83			
30075	60th AMW	*bk/r*	
30076	60th AMW	*bk/bl*	
30077	60th AMW	*bk/r*	
30078	60th AMW	*bk/bl*	
30079	305th AMW	*bl/r*	
30080	60th AMW	*bk/bl*	
30081	305th AMW	*bl*	
30082	305th AMW	*bl*	
FY84			
40185	60th AMW	*bk/bl*	
40186	305th AMW	*bl/r*	
40187	60th AMW	*bk/bl*	
40188	305th AMW	*bl/r*	
40189	305th AMW	*bl*	
40190	305th AMW	*bl/r*	
40191	60th AMW	*bk/bl*	
40192	305th AMW	*bl/r*	
FY85			
50027	305th AMW	*bl/r*	
50028	305th AMW	*bl/r*	
50029	60th AMW	*bk/r*	
50030	305th AMW	*bl/r*	
50031	305th AMW	*bl/r*	
50032	305th AMW	*bl/r*	
50033	305th AMW	*bl*	
50034	305th AMW	*bl/r*	
FY86			
60027	305th AMW	*bl*	
60028	305th AMW	*bl/r*	
60029	60th AMW	*bk/r*	

Type			Notes
60030	305th AMW	*bl/r*	
60031	60th AMW	*bk/r*	
60032	60th AMW	*bk/r*	
60033	60th AMW	*bk/r*	
60034	60th AMW	*bk/r*	
60035	305th AMW	*bl*	
60036	305th AMW	*bl*	
60037	60th AMW	*bk/r*	
60038	60th AMW	*bk/r*	
FY87			
70117	60th AMW	*bk/r*	
70118	60th AMW	*bk/bl*	
70119	60th AMW	*bk/r*	
70120	305th AMW	*bl*	
70121	305th AMW	*bl*	
70122	305th AMW	*bl/r*	
70123	305th AMW	*bl*	
70124	305th AMW	*bl/r*	
FY79			
90433	305th AMW	*bl*	
90434	305th AMW	*bl/r*	
91710	305th AMW	*bl/r*	
91711	305th AMW	*bl*	
91712	305th AMW	*bl/r*	
91713	305th AMW	*bl*	
91946	60th AMW	*bk/bl*	
91947	305th AMW	*bl*	
91948	60th AMW	*bk/bl*	
91949	305th AMW	*bl/r*	
91950	60th AMW	*bk/bl*	
91951	60th AMW	*bk/bl*	

McDonnell Douglas C-17 Globemaster III
62nd AW, McChord AFB, Washington: 4th AS, 7th AS & 8th AS; 58th AS/97th AMW, Altus AFB, Oklahoma (*r/y*); 417th FLTS/412th TW, Edwards AFB, California [ED]; 437th AW, Charleston AFB, South Carolina (*y/bl*): 14th AS, 15th AS & 17th AS

FFY00			
00171	C-17A	62nd AW	
00172	C-17A	62nd AW	
00173	C-17A	62nd AW	
00174	C-17A	62nd AW	
00175	C-17A	437th AW	*y/bl*
00176	C-17A	437th AW	*y/bl*
00177	C-17A	437th AW	*y/bl*
00178	C-17A	62nd AW	
00179	C-17A	62nd AW	
00180	C-17A	62nd AW	
00181	C-17A		
00182	C-17A		
00183	C-17A		
00184	C-17A		
00185	C-17A		
FY90			
00532	C-17A	437th AW	*y/bl*
00533	C-17A	97th AMW	*r/y*
00534	C-17A	437th AW	*y/bl*
00535	C-17A	97th AMW	*r/y*
FY92			
23291	C-17A	97th AMW	*r/y*
23292	C-17A	437th AW	*y/bl*
23293	C-17A	437th AW	*y/bl*
23294	C-17A	437th AW	*y/bl*
FY93			
30599	C-17A	97th AMW	*r/y*
30600	C-17A	97th AMW	*r/y*

Notes	Type				Notes	Type	
	30601	C-17A	437th AW	y/bl		Oklahoma [OK]:	
	30602	C-17A	97th AMW	r/y		966th AACS (bl)	
	30603	C-17A	437th AW	y/bl		FY81	
	30604	C-17A	437th AW	y/bl		10893	
	FY94					10898	
	40065	C-17A	437th AW	y/bl			
	40066	C-17A	437th AW	y/bl		**Grumman C-20 Gulfstream III/IV**	
	40067	'C-17A	437th AW	y/bl		99th AS/89th AW, Andrews AFB,	
	40068	C-17A	437th AW	y/bl		Maryland;	
	40069	C-17A	97th AMW	r/y		OSAC/PAT, US Army, Andrews AFB,	
	40070	C-17A	437th AW	y/bl		Maryland;	
	FY95					Pacific Flight Detachment,	
	50102	C-17A	437th AW	y/bl		Hickam AFB, Hawaii	
	50103	C-17A	437th AW	y/bl		**C-20B Gulfstream III**	
	50104	C-17A	437th AW	y/bl		FY86	
	50105	C-17A	97th AMW	r/y		60201	89th AW
	50106	C-17A	437th AW	y/bl		60202	89th AW
	50107	C-17A	437th AW	y/bl		60203	89th AW
	FY96					60204	89th AW
	60001	C-17A	437th AW	y/bl		60206	89th AW
	60002	C-17A	437th AW	y/bl		60403	89th AW
	60003	C-17A	437th AW	y/bl		**C-20C Gulfstream III**	
	60004	C-17A	437th AW	y/bl		FY85	
	60005	C-17A	437th AW	y/bl		50049	89th AW
	60006	C-17A	437th AW	y/bl		50050	89th AW
	60007	C-17A	437th AW	y/bl		**C-20E Gulfstream III**	
	60008	C-17A	437th AW	y/bl		FY87	
	FY87					70139	Pacific Flt Det
	70025	C-17A	412th TW			70140	OSAC/PAT
	FY97					**C-20F Gulfstream IV**	
	70041	C-17A	437th AW	y/bl		FY91	
	70042	C-17A	97th AMW	r/y		10108	OSAC/PAT
	70043	C-17A	437th AW	y/bl		**C-20H Gulfstream IV**	
	70044	C-17A	437th AW	y/bl		FY90	
	70045	C-17A	437th AW	y/bl		00300	89th AW
	70046	C-17A	437th AW	y/bl		FY92	
	70047	C-17A	437th AW	y/bl		20375	89th AW
	70048	C-17A	437th AW	y/bl			
	FY98					**Boeing C-22B**	
	80049	C-17A	62nd AW			201st AS/113th FW, DC ANG,	
	80050	C-17A	62nd AW			Andrews AFB, Maryland	
	80051	C-17A	62nd AW			FY83	
	80052	C-17A	62nd AW			34615	
	80053	C-17A	62nd AW			34616	
	80054	C-17A	62nd AW				
	80055	C-17A	62nd AW			**Boeing VC-25A**	
	80056	C-17A	62nd AW			89th AW, Andrews AFB, Maryland	
	80057	C-17A	62nd AW			FY82	
	FY88					28000	
	80265	C-17A	437th AW	y/bl		FY92	
	80266	C-17A	97th AMW	r/y		29000	
	FY99						
	90058	C-17A	62nd AW			**Boeing C-32A**	
	90059	C-17A	62nd AW			1st AS/89th AW, Andrews AFB,	
	90060	C-17A	62nd AW			Maryland	
	90061	C-17A	62nd AW			FY98	
	90062	C-17A	62nd AW			80001	
	90063	C-17A	62nd AW			80002	
	90064	C-17A	62nd AW			FY99	
	90165	C-17A	62nd AW			90003	
	90166	C-17A	62nd AW			90004	
	90167	C-17A	62nd AW				
	90168	C-17A	62nd AW			**Gulfstream Aerospace C-37A**	
	90169	C-17A	62nd AW			**Gulfstream V**	
	90170	C-17A	62nd AW			310th AS/6th AMW,	
	FY89					MacDill AFB, Florida;	
	91189	C-17A	437th AW	y/bl		99th AS/89th AW, Andrews AFB,	
	91190	C-17A	437th AW	y/bl		Maryland;	
	91191	C-17A	437th AW	y/bl		OSAC/PAT, US Army, Andrews AFB,	
	91192	C-17A	437th AW	y/bl		Maryland	
						FY01	
	Boeing TC-18E					10028	6th AMW
	552nd ACW, Tinker AFB,					10029	6th AMW

Type		Notes
10030	6th AMW	
FY97		
70049	OSAC/PAT	
70400	89th AW	
70401	89th AW	
FY99		
90402	89th AW	

IAI C-38A Astra
201st AS/113th FW, DC ANG,
  Andrews AFB, Maryland
FY94

41569		
41570		

Boeing T-43A/CT-43A*
310th AS/6th AMW,
  MacDill AFB, Florida;
562nd FTS/12th FTW, Randolph
  AFB, Texas [RA] (*bk/y*)

FY71		
11403	12th FTW	bk/y
11404	12th FTW	bk/y
11405	12th FTW	bk/y
FY72		
20283*	6th AMW	
20288	12th FTW	bk/y
FY73		
31150	12th FTW	bk/y
31151	12th FTW	bk/y
31152	12th FTW	bk/y
31153	12th FTW	bk/y
31154	12th FTW	bk/y
31156	12th FTW	bk/y

Boeing B-52H Stratofortress
2nd BW, Barksdale AFB,
  Louisiana [LA]:
  11th BS (*gd*), 20th BS (*bl*)
  & 96th BS (*r*);
23rd BS/5th BW, Minot AFB,
  North Dakota [MT] (*r/y*);
93rd BS/917th Wg AFRC,
  Barksdale AFB, Louisiana [BD] (*y/bl*);
419th FLTS/412th TW Edwards AFB,
  California [ED]

FY60		
00001	2nd BW	bl
00002	2nd BW	gd
00003	93rd BS	y/bl
00004	5th BW	r/y
00005	5th BW	r/y
00007	5th BW	r/y
00008	2nd BW	r
00009	5th BW	r/y
00010	2nd BW	r
00011	2nd BW	gd
00012	2nd BW	r
00013	2nd BW	r
00014	2nd BW	bl
00015	5th BW	r/y
00016	2nd BW	r
00017	2nd BW	gd
00018	5th BW	r/y
00019	2nd BW	r
00020	2nd BW	bl
00022	2nd BW	r
00023	5th BW	r/y
00024	5th BW	r/y
00025	2nd BW	bl
00026	5th BW	r/y
00028	2nd BW	r
00029	5th BW	r/y

00030	2nd BW	bl
00031	2nd BW	bl
00032	2nd BW	gd
00033	5th BW	r/y
00034	5th BW	r/y
00035	2nd BW	gd
00036	419th FLTS	
00037	2nd BW	r
00038	2nd BW	gd
00041	93rd BS	y/bl
00042	93rd BS	y/bl
00043	2nd BW	bl
00044	5th BW	r/y
00045	93rd BS	y/bl
00046	2nd BW	bl
00048	2nd BW	gd
00049	2nd BW	bl
00050	412th TW	
00051	5th BW	r/y
00052	2nd BW	r
00053	2nd BW	r
00054	2nd BW	r
00055	5th BW	r/y
00056	5th BW	r/y
00057	2nd BW	bl
00058	2nd BW	gd
00059	2nd BW	r
00060	5th BW	r/y
00061	2nd BW	gd
00062	2nd BW	bl
FY61		
10001	5th BW	r/y
10002	2nd BW	bl
10003	2nd BW	gd
10004	2nd BW	bl
10005	5th BW	r/y
10006	2nd BW	gd
10007	5th BW	r/y
10008	93rd BS	y/bl
10009	2nd BW	r
10010	2nd BW	bl
10011	2nd BW	gd
10012	2nd BW	gd
10013	2nd BW	r
10014	5th BW	r/y
10015	2nd BW	gd
10016	2nd BW	r
10017	93rd BS	y/bl
10018	5th BW	r/y
10019	2nd BW	r
10020	2nd BW	r
10021	93rd BS	y/bl
10022	93rd BS	y/bl
10023	2nd BW	bl
10024	2nd BW	r
10027	5th BW	r/y
10028	2nd BW	gd
10029	93rd BS	y/bl
10031	2nd BW	gd
10032	93rd BS	y/bl
10034	5th BW	r/y
10035	5th BW	r/y
10036	5th BW	r/y
10038	2nd BW	gd
10039	2nd BW	gd
10040	5th BW	r/y

Lockheed F-117A Nighthawk
49th FW, Holloman AFB, New Mexico
  [HO]:
  7th FS (*si*), 8th FS (*y*) & 9th FS (*r*)
53rd Wg, Nellis AFB, Nevada [OT]
  (*gy/w*);

Notes	Type	Notes	Type

445th FLTS/412th TW, Edwards AFB,
California [ED]
79-783 (79-10783) ED
79-784 (79-10784) ED
80-786 (80-0786) HO *r*
80-787 (80-0787) HO *y*
80-788 (80-0788) HO *si*
80-789 (80-0789) HO *r*
80-790 (80-0790) HO *r*
80-791 (80-0791) HO *y*
81-794 (81-10794) HO *r*
81-795 (81-10795) HO *y*
81-796 (81-10796) HO *si*
81-797 (81-10797) HO *r*
81-798 (81-10798) HO *r*
82-799 (82-0799) HO *y*
82-800 (82-0800) HO *y*
82-801 (82-0801) HO
82-802 (82-0802) HO *y*
82-803 (82-0803) HO *y*
82-804 (82-0804) HO *y*
82-805 (82-0805) HO *si*
83-807 (83-0807) HO *r*
83-808 (83-0808) HO *si*
84-809 (84-0809) HO *r* [9th FS]
84-810 (84-0810) HO *r*
84-811 (84-0811) HO *si*
84-812 (84-0812) HO *si* [49th OG]
84-824 (84-0824) HO *r*
84-825 (84-0825) HO *y*
84-826 (84-0826) HO *r*
84-827 (84-0827) HO *y*
84-828 (84-0828) HO *r*
85-813 (85-0813) HO *y*
85-814 (85-0814) HO *y*
85-816 (85-0816) HO *y* [49th FW]
85-817 (85-0817) HO *y*
85-818 (85-0818) HO *y*
85-819 (85-0819) HO *y* [8th FS]
85-820 (85-0820) HO *r*
85-829 (85-0829) HO *y*
85-830 (85-0830) HO *r*
85-831 (85-0831) ED
85-832 (85-0832) HO *y*
85-833 (85-0833) HO *si* [49th OG]
85-834 (85-0834) HO *y*
85-835 (85-0835) HO *r*
85-836 (85-0836) HO *y*
86-821 (86-0821) HO *r*
86-822 (86-0822) HO
86-823 (86-0823) HO *r*
86-837 (86-0837) HO *y*
86-838 (86-0838) HO *y* [8th FS]
86-839 (86-0839) HO *r*
86-840 (86-0840) HO *y*
88-841 (88-0841) HO *r* [9th FS]
88-842 (88-0842) HO *y*
88-843 (88-0843) HO *si* [49th FW]

Lockheed C-130 Hercules
1st SOS/353rd SOG, Kadena AB,
Japan;
3rd Wg, Elmendorf AFB, Alaska [AK]:
517th AS (*w*);
4th SOS/16th SOW, Hurlburt Field,
Florida;
7th SOS/352nd SOG,
RAF Mildenhall, UK;
8th SOS/16th SOW, Duke Field,
Florida;
9th SOS/16th OG, Eglin AFB, Florida;
15th SOS/16th SOW, Hurlburt Field,
Florida;

16th SOS/16th SOW, Hurlburt Field,
Florida;
17th SOS/353rd SOG, Kadena AB,
Japan;
37th AS/86th AW, Ramstein AB,
Germany [RS] (*bl/w*);
39th RQS/939th RQW AFRC,
Patrick AFB, Florida [FL];
41st ECS/355th Wg, Davis-Monthan
AFB, Arizona [DM] (*bl*);
42nd ACCS/355th Wg, Davis-Monthan
AFB, Arizona [DM] (*w*);
43rd AW, Pope AFB,
North Carolina [FT]:
2nd AS (*gn/bl*) & 41st AS (*gn/or*);
43rd ECS/355th Wg, Davis-Monthan
AFB, Arizona [DM] (*r*);
53rd WRS/403rd AW AFRC,
Keesler AFB, Missouri;
58th SOW, Kirtland AFB, New Mexico:
550th SOS;
67th SOS/352nd SOG,
RAF Mildenhall, UK;
71st RQS/347th Wg, Moody AFB,
Georgia [MY] (*bl*);
95th AS/440th AW AFRC,
General Mitchell ARS,
Wisconsin (*w/r*);
96th AS/934th AW AFRC,
Minneapolis/St Paul, Minnesota (*pr*);
102nd RQS/106th RQW, Suffolk
Field, New York ANG [LI];
105th AS/118th AW, Nashville,
Tennessee ANG (*r*);
109th AS/133rd AW,
Minneapolis/St Paul, Minnesota
ANG [MN] (*gn/bl*);
115th AS/146th AW, Channel Island
ANGS, California [CI] (*gn*);
122nd FS/159th FW, NAS New
Orleans, Louisiana ANG [JZ];
129th RQS/129th RQW, Moffet Field,
California ANG [CA] (*bl*);
130th AS/130th AW, Yeager Int'l
Airport, Charleston West Virginia
ANG [WV] (*pr/y*);
135th AS/135th AW, Martin State
Airport, Maryland ANG [MD] (*bk/y*);
139th AS/109th AW, Schenectady,
New York ANG [NY];
142nd AS/166th AW, New Castle
County Airport, Delaware
ANG [DE] (*bl*);
143rd AS/143rd AW, Quonset,
Rhode Island ANG [RI] (*r*);
144th AS/176th CW, Kulis ANGB,
Alaska [AK] (*bk/y*);
154th TS/189th AW, Little Rock,
Arkansas ANG (*r*);
156th AS/145th AW, Charlotte,
North Carolina ANG [NC] (*bl*);
157th FS/169th FW, McEntire ANGS,
South Carolina ANG [SC];
158th AS/165th AW, Savannah,
Georgia ANG (*r*);
159th FS/125th FW, Jacksonville,
Florida ANG;
164th AS/179th AW, Mansfield,
Ohio ANG [OH] (*bl*);
165th AS/123rd AW, Standiford Field,
Kentucky ANG [KY];
167th AS/167th AW, Martinsburg,
West Virginia ANG [WV] (*r*);

Type	Notes				Type			Notes
169th AS/182nd AW, Peoria, Illinois ANG [IL];					00322	C-130H	158th AS	r
171st AS/191st AW, Selfridge ANGB, Michigan ANG (y/bk);					00323	C-130H	158th AS	r
180th AS/139th AW, Rosencrans Memorial Airport, Missouri ANG [XP] (y);					00324	C-130H	158th AS	r
					00325	C-130H	158th AS	r
					00326	C-130H	158th AS	r
					00332	C-130H	158th AS	r
181st AS/136th AW, NAS Dallas, Texas ANG (bl/w);					**FY90**			
					01057	C-130H	204th AS	
					01058	C-130H	204th AS	
185th AS/137th AW, Will Rogers World Airport, Oklahoma ANG [OK] (bl);	•				**FY70**			
					01259	C-130E	43rd AW	gn/or
					01260	C-130E	37th AS	bl/w
187th AS/153rd AW, Cheyenne, Wyoming ANG [WY];					01261	C-130E	43rd AW	gn/bl
					01262	C-130E	43rd AW	gn/or
189th AS/124th Wg, Boise, Idaho ANG [ID];					01263	C-130E	43rd AW	gn/or
					01264	C-130E	37th AS	bl/w
192nd AS/152nd AW, Reno, Nevada ANG [NV] (w);					01265	C-130E	43rd AW	gn/bl
					01266	C-130E	43rd AW	gn/or
193rd SOS/193rd SOW, Harrisburg, Pennsylvania ANG [PA];					01267	C-130E	43rd AW	gn/bl
					01268	C-130E	43rd AW	gn/bl
198th AS/156th AW, San Juan, Puerto Rico ANG;					01270	C-130E	43rd AW	gn/bl
					01271	C-130E	37th AS	bl/w
204th AS/154th Wg, Hickam AFB, Hawaii ANG [HM];					01272	C-130E	43rd AW	gn/bl
					01273	C-130E	43rd AW	gn/bl
210th RQS/176th CW, Kulis ANGB, Alaska ANG [AK];					01274	C-130E	37th AS	bl/w
					01275	C-130E	43rd AW	gn/bl
303rd RQS/939th RQW AFRC, Portland, Oregon [PD] (y);					01276	C-130E	43rd AW	gn/bl
					FY90			
314th AW, Little Rock AFB, Arkansas: 53rd AS (bk) & 62nd AS (bl);					01791	C-130H	164th AS	bl
					01792	C-130H	164th AS	bl
317th AG, Dyess AFB, Texas: 39th AS (r) & 40th AS (bl);					01793	C-130H	164th AS	bl
					01794	C-130H	164th AS	bl
327th AS/913th AW AFRC, NAS Willow Grove, Pennsylvania (bk);					01795	C-130H	164th AS	bl
					01796	C-130H	164th AS	bl
328th AS/914th AW AFRC, Niagara Falls, New York [NF] (bl);					01797	C-130H	164th AS	bl
					01798	C-130H	164th AS	bl
357th AS/908th AW AFRC, Maxwell AFB, Alabama (bl);					**FY00**			
					01934	EC-130J	LMTAS	
36th AS/374th AW, Yokota AB, Japan [YJ] (r);					**FY90**			
					02103	HC-130N	210th RQS	
412th TW Edwards AFB, California: 452nd FLTS [ED];					09107	C-130H	757th AS	bl
					09108	C-130H	757th AS	bl
463rd AG Little Rock AFB, Arkansas [LK]:					**FY81**			
					10626	C-130H	700th AS	bl
50th AS (r) & 61st AS (gn);					10627	C-130H	700th AS	bl
645th Materiel Sqn, Palmdale, California [D4];					10628	C-130H	700th AS	bl
					10629	C-130H	700th AS	bl
700th AS/94th AW AFRC, Dobbins ARB, Georgia [DB] (bl);					10630	C-130H	700th AS	bl
					10631	C-130H	700th AS	bl
711th SOS/919th SOW AFRC, Duke Field, Florida;					**FY68**			
					10934	C-130E	43rd AW	gn/bl
731st AS/302nd AW AFRC, Peterson AFB, Colorado (pr/w);					10935	C-130E	37th AS	bl/w
					10937	C-130E	43rd AW	gn/or
757th AS/910th AW AFRC, Youngstown ARS, Ohio [YO] (bl);					10938	C-130E	37th AS	bl/w
					10939	C-130E	43rd AW	gn/bl
758th AS/911th AW AFRC, Pittsburgh ARS, Pennsylvania (bk/y);					10940	C-130E	43rd AW	gn/or
					10941	C-130E	43rd AW	gn/bl
773rd SOS/910th AW AFRC, Youngstown ARS, Ohio [YO] (r);					10942	C-130E	43rd AW	gn/bl
					10943	C-130E	37th AS	bl/w
815th AS/403rd AW AFRC, Keesler AFB, Missouri [KT] (r);					10947	C-130E	37th AS	bl/w
					10948	C-130E	463rd AG	gn
LMTAS, Marietta, Georgia					**FY91**			
FY90					11231	C-130H	165th AS	
00161	MC-130H	15th SOS			11232	C-130H	165th AS	
00162	MC-130H	15th SOS			11233	C-130H	165th AS	
00163	AC-130U	4th SOS			11234	C-130H	165th AS	
00164	AC-130U	4th SOS			11235	C-130H	165th AS	
00165	AC-130U	4th SOS			11236	C-130H	165th AS	
00166	AC-130U	4th SOS			11237	C-130H	165th AS	
00167	AC-130U	4th SOS			11238	C-130H	165th AS	
FY80					11239	C-130H	165th AS	
00320	C-130H	158th AS	r		11651	C-130H	165th AS	
00321	C-130H	158th AS	r		11652	C-130H	165th AS	

C-130

Notes	Type				Notes	Type			
	11653	C-130H	165th AS			21537	C-130H	187th AS	
	FY61					21538	C-130H	187th AS	
	12358	C-130E	171st AS	y/bk		*FY62*			
	12359	C-130E	115th AS	gn		21784	C-130E	154th TS	r
	12367	C-130E	115th AS	gn		21786	C-130E	189th AS	
	12369	C-130E	198th AS			21787	C-130E	154th TS	r
	12370	C-130E	171st AS	y/bk		21788	C-130E	154th TS	r
	12372	C-130E	115th AS	gn		21789	C-130E	314th AW	bk
	FY64					21791	EC-130E	42nd ACCS	w
	14852	HC-130P	71st RQS	bl		21792	C-130E	463rd AG	gn
	14853	HC-130P	71st RQS	bl		21793	C-130E	115th AS	gn
	14854	MC-130P	9th SOS			21795	C-130E	154th TS	r
	14855	HC-130P	303rd RQS	y		21798	C-130E	314th AW	bk
	14858	MC-130P	58th SOW			21799	C-130E	115th AS	gn
	14859	C-130E	16th SOW			21801	C-130E	115th AS	gn
	14860	HC-130P	303rd RQS	y		21804	C-130E	154th TS	r
	14861	WC-130H	53rd WRS			21806	C-130E	96th AS	pr
	14862	EC-130H	645th MS			21808	C-130E	314th AW	bk
	14863	HC-130P	71st RQS	bl		21810	C-130E	314th AW	bl
	14864	HC-130P	303rd RQS	y		21811	C-130E	115th AS	gn
	14865	HC-130P	71st RQS	bl		21812	C-130E	115th AS	gn
	14866	WC-130H	53rd WRS			21816	C-130E	314th AW	bl
	17680	C-130E	314th AW	bk		21817	C-130E	189th AS	
	17681	C-130E	37th AS	bl/w		21818	EC-130E	42nd ACCS	w
	18240	C-130E	37th AS	bl/w		21820	C-130E	171st AS	y/bk
	FY91					21823	C-130E	96th AS	pr
	19141	C-130H	773rd AS	r		21824	C-130E	154th TS	r
	19142	C-130H	773rd AS	r		21825	EC-130E	42nd ACCS	w
	19143	C-130H	773rd AS	r		21826	C-130E	115th AS	gn
	19144	C-130H	773rd AS	r		21829	C-130E	171st AS	y/bk
	FY82					21832	EC-130E	42nd ACCS	w
	20054	C-130H	144th AS	bk/y		21833	C-130E	115th AS	gn
	20055	C-130H	144th AS	bk/y		21834	C-130E	374th AW	r
	20056	C-130H	144th AS	bk/y		21835	C-130E	96th AS	pr
	20057	C-130H	144th AS	bk/y		21836	EC-130E	42nd ACCS	w
	20058	C-130H	144th AS	bk/y		21837	C-130E	189th AS	
	20059	C-130H	144th AS	bk/y		21839	C-130E	96th AS	pr
	20060	C-130H	144th AS	bk/y		21842	C-130E	171st AS	y/bk
	20061	C-130H	144th AS	bk/y		21843	MC-130E	711th SOS	
	FY92					21844	C-130E	96th AS	pr
	20253	AC-130U	4th SOS			21846	C-130E	189th AS	
	20547	C-130H	463rd AG	r		21847	C-130E	96th AS	pr
	20548	C-130H	463rd AG	r		21848	C-130E	96th AS	pr
	20549	C-130H	463rd AG	r		21849	C-130E	463rd AG	gn
	20550	C-130H	463rd AG	r		21850	C-130E	314th AW	bk
	20551	C-130H	463rd AG	r		21851	C-130E	115th AS	gn
	20552	C-130H	463rd AG	r		21852	C-130E	96th AS	pr
	20553	C-130H	463rd AG	r		21855	C-130E	374th AW	r
	20554	C-130H	463rd AG	r		21856	C-130E	143rd AS	r
	21094	LC-130H	139th AS			21857	EC-130E	42nd ACCS	w
	21095	LC-130H	139th AS			21858	C-130E	171st AS	y/bk
	FY72					21859	C-130E	122nd FS	
	21288	C-130E	374th AW	r		21862	C-130E	115th AS	gn
	21289	C-130E	374th AW	r		21863	EC-130E	42nd ACCS	w
	21290	C-130E	374th AW	r		21864	C-130E	189th AS	
	21291	C-130E	314th AW	bk		21866	C-130E	314th AW	bk
	21292	C-130E	463rd AG	gn		*FY92*			
	21293	C-130E	463rd AG	gn		23021	C-130H	773rd AS	r
	21294	C-130E	463rd AG	gn		23022	C-130H	773rd AS	r
	21295	C-130E	314th AW	bl		23023	C-130H	773rd AS	r
	21296	C-130E	314th AW	bk		23024	C-130H	773rd AS	r
	21299	C-130E	374th AW	r		23281	C-130H	328th AS	bl
	FY92					23282	C-130H	328th AS	bl
	21451	C-130H	156th AS	bl		23283	C-130H	328th AS	bl
	21452	C-130H	156th AS	bl		23284	C-130H	328th AS	bl
	21453	C-130H	156th AS	bl		23285	C-130H	328th AS	bl
	21454	C-130H	156th AS	bl		23286	C-130H	328th AS	bl
	21531	C-130H	187th AS			23287	C-130H	328th AS	bl
	21532	C-130H	187th AS			23288	C-130H	328th AS	bl
	21533	C-130H	187th AS			*FY83*			
	21534	C-130H	187th AS			30486	C-130H	139th AS	
	21535	C-130H	187th AS			30487	C-130H	139th AS	
	21536	C-130H	187th AS			30488	C-130H	139th AS	

Type			Notes	Type			Notes
30489	C-130H	139th AS		37800	C-130E	169th AS	
30490	LC-130H	139th AS		37804	C-130E	314th AW	bl
30491	LC-130H	139th AS		37805	C-130E	327th AS	bk
30492	LC-130H	139th AS		37808	C-130E	463rd AG	gn
30493	LC-130H	139th AS		37809	C-130E	463rd AG	gn
FY93				37811	C-130E	143rd AS	r
31036	C-130H	463rd AG	r	37812	C-130E	169th AS	
31037	C-130H	463rd AG	r	37814	C-130E	67th SOS	
31038	C-130H	463rd AG	r	37815	C-130E	193rd SOS	
31039	C-130H	463rd AG	r	37816	C-130E	193rd SOS	
31040	C-130H	463rd AG	r	37817	C-130E	314th AW	
31041	C-130H	463rd AG	r	37818	C-130E	169th AS	
31096	LC-130H	139th AS		37819	C-130E	374th AW	r
FY83				37821	C-130E	374th AW	r
31212	MC-130H	15th SOS		37822	C-130E	96th AS	pr
FY93				37823	C-130E	327th AS	bk
31455	C-130H	156th AS	bl	37824	C-130E	143rd AS	r
31456	C-130H	156th AS	bl	37825	C-130E	169th AS	
31457	C-130H	156th AS	bl	37826	C-130E	327th AS	bk
31458	C-130H	156th AS	bl	37828	EC-130E	193rd SOS	
31459	C-130H	156th AS	bl	37829	C-130E	463rd AG	gn
31561	C-130H	156th AS	bl	37830	C-130E	314th AW	bk
31562	C-130H	156th AS	bl	37831	C-130E	115th AS	gn
31563	C-130H	156th AS	bl	37832	C-130E	327th AS	bk
FY73				37833	C-130E	327th AS	bk
31580	EC-130H	43rd ECS	r	37834	C-130E	327th AS	bk
31581	EC-130H	43rd ECS	r	37835	C-130E	314th AW	bk
31582	C-130H	317th AG	r	37837	C-130E	374th AW	r
31583	EC-130H	43rd ECS	r	37838	C-130E	314th AW	bl
31584	EC-130H	43rd ECS	r	37839	C-130E	463rd AG	gn
31585	EC-130H	41st ECS	bl	37840	C-130E	143rd AS	r
31586	EC-130H	41st ECS	bl	37841	C-130E	198th AS	
31587	EC-130H	41st ECS	bl	37842	C-130E	303rd RQS	y
31588	EC-130H	41st ECS	bl	37845	C-130E	463rd AG	
31590	EC-130H	43rd ECS	r	37846	C-130E	314th AW	
31592	EC-130H	41st ECS	bl	37847	C-130E	154th TS	r
31594	EC-130H	41st ECS	bl	37848	C-130E	327th AS	bk
31595	EC-130H	43rd ECS	r	37849	C-130E	314th AW	bl
31597	C-130H	317th AG	r	37850	C-130E	374th AW	r
31598	C-130H	317th AG	r	37851	C-130E	198th AS	
FY93				37852	C-130E	463rd AG	
32041	C-130H	204th AS		37853	C-130E	327th AS	bk
32042	C-130H	204th AS		37856	C-130E	815th AS	r
32104	HC-130N	210th RQS		37857	C-130E	463rd AG	gn
32105	HC-130N	210th RQS		37858	C-130E	169th AS	
32106	HC-130N	210th RQS		37859	C-130E	143rd AS	r
37311	C-130H	731st AS	pr/w	37860	C-130E	314th AW	bl
37312	C-130H	731st AS	pr/w	37861	C-130E	129th RQS	bl
37313	C-130H	731st AS	pr/w	37864	C-130E	314th AW	bl
37314	C-130H	731st AS	pr/w	37865	C-130E	374th AW	r
FY63				37866	C-130E	314th AW	bk
37764	C-130E	463rd AG	gn	37867	C-130E	327th AS	bk
37765	C-130E	314th AW	bl	37868	C-130E	143rd AS	r
37767	C-130E	314th AW	bl	37869	EC-130E	193rd SOS	
37768	C-130E	314th AW	bl	37871	C-130E	374th AW	r
37769	C-130E	327th AS	bk	37872	C-130E	169th AS	
37770	C-130E	96th AS	pr	37874	C-130E	314th AW	bk
37773	EC-130E	193rd SOS		37876	C-130E	463rd AG	gn
37776	C-130E	327th AS	bk	37877	C-130E	169th AS	
37777	C-130E	198th AS		37879	C-130E	374th AW	r
37778	C-130E	314th AW	bk	37880	C-130E	314th AW	bl
37781	C-130E	463rd AG	gn	37882	C-130E	314th AW	bk
37782	C-130E	143rd AS	r	37883	C-130E	327th AS	bk
37783	EC-130E	193rd SOS		37884	C-130E	463rd AG	gn
37784	C-130E	314th AW	bl	37885	C-130E	37th AS	bl/w
37785	MC-130E	711th SOS		37887	C-130E	37th AS	bl/w
37786	C-130E	171st AS	y/bk	37888	C-130E	463rd AG	gn
37788	C-130E	143rd AS	r	37889	C-130E	143rd AS	r
37790	C-130E	374th AW	r	37890	C-130E	314th AW	bl
37791	C-130E	314th AW	bl	37892	C-130E	327th AS	bk
37792	C-130E	169th AS		37893	C-130E	314th AW	bk
37796	C-130E	314th AW	bk	37894	C-130E	463rd AG	gn
37799	C-130E	314th AW	bl	37895	C-130E	171st AS	y/bk

C-130

Notes	Type				Notes	Type			
	37896	C-130E	314th AW	bk		41663	C-130H	317th AG	bl
	37897	C-130E	169th AS	or		41664	C-130H	3rd Wg	w
	37898	C-130E	8th SOS			41665	C-130H	317th AG	bl
	37899	C-130E	314th AW	bl		41666	C-130H	317th AG	bl
	39810	C-130E	71st RQS	bl		41667	C-130H	317th AG	r
	39812	C-130E	314th AW	bk		41668	C-130H	3rd Wg	w
	39813	C-130E	171st AS	y/bk		41669	C-130H	317th AG	bl
	39814	C-130E	314th AW	bl		41670	C-130H	317th AG	r
	39815	C-130E	198th AS			41671	C-130H	317th AG	bl
	39816	EC-130E	193rd SOS			41673	C-130H	317th AG	bl
	39817	EC-130E	193rd SOS			41674	C-130H	317th AG	r
	FY84					41675	C-130H	317th AG	r
	40204	C-130H	700th AS	bl		41676	C-130H	3rd Wg	m
	40205	C-130H	700th AS	bl		41677	C-130H	317th AG	bl
	40206	C-130H	142nd AS	bl		41679	C-130H	317th AG	bl
	40207	C-130H	142nd AS	bl		41680	C-130H	317th AG	r
	40208	C-130H	142nd AS	bl		41682	C-130H	3rd Wg	w
	40209	C-130H	142nd AS	bl		41684	C-130H	3rd Wg	w
	40210	C-130H	142nd AS	bl		41685	C-130H	3rd Wg	w
	40211	C-130H	142nd AS	bl		41687	C-130H	317th AG	r
	40212	C-130H	142nd AS	bl		41688	C-130H	317th AG	bl
	40213	C-130H	142nd AS	bl		41689	C-130H	317th AG	bl
	40475	MC-130H	15th SOS			41690	C-130H	3rd Wg	w
	40476	MC-130H	15th SOS			41691	C-130H	317th AG	r
	FY64					41692	C-130H	3rd Wg	w
	40495	C-130E	43rd AW	gn/or		42061	C-130H	317th AG	r
	40496	C-130E	43rd AW	gn/bl		42062	C-130H	3rd Wg	w
	40498	C-130E	43rd AW	gn/bl		42063	C-130H	317th AG	bl
	40499	C-130E	43rd AW	gn/bl		42065	C-130H	317th AG	bl
	40502	C-130E	37th AS	bl/w		42066	C-130H	3rd Wg	w
	40504	C-130E	43rd AW	gn/bl		42067	C-130H	317th AG	r
	40510	C-130E	198th AS			42069	C-130H	317th AG	r
	40512	C-130E	154th TS	r		42070	C-130H	3rd Wg	w
	40514	C-130E	154th TS	r		42071	C-130H	3rd Wg	w
	40515	C-130E	198th AS			42072	C-130H	317th AG	bl
	40517	C-130E	43rd AW	gn/bl		42130	C-130H	317th AG	r
	40518	C-130E	463rd AG	gn		42131	C-130H	3rd Wg	w
	40519	C-130E	314th AW	bl		42132	C-130H	317th AG	r
	40520	C-130E	157th FS			42133	C-130H	3rd Wg	w
	40521	C-130E	159th FS			42134	C-130H	317th AG	r
	40523	MC-130E	8th SOS			*FY94*			
	40525	C-130E	43rd AW	gn/bl		46701	C-130H	167th AS	r
	40526	C-130E	154th TS	r		46702	C-130H	167th AS	r
	40527	C-130E	37th AS	bl/w		46703	C-130H	167th AS	r
	40529	C-130E	43rd AW	gn/or		46704	C-130H	167th AS	r
	40531	C-130E	43rd AW	gn/bl		46705	C-130H	167th AS	r
	40533	C-130E	37th AS	bl/w		46706	C-130H	167th AS	r
	40537	C-130E	43rd AW	gn/or		46707	C-130H	167th AS	r
	40538	C-130E	314th AW	bk		46708	C-130H	167th AS	r
	40539	C-130E	43rd AW	gn/or		47310	C-130H	731st AS	pr/w
	40540	C-130E	43rd AW	gn/bl		47315	C-130H	731st AS	pr/w
	40541	C-130E	314th AW	bk		47316	C-130H	731st AS	pr/w
	40542	C-130E	314th AW	bk		47317	C-130H	731st AS	pr/w
	40544	C-130E	198th AS			47318	C-130H	731st AS	pr/w
	40550	C-130E	37th AS	bl/w		47319	C-130H	731st AS	pr/w
	40551	MC-130E	711th SOS			47320	C-130H	731st AS	pr/w
	40555	MC-130E	711th SOS			47321	C-130H	731st AS	pr/w
	40559	MC-130E	8th SOS			48151	C-130J	815th AS	r
	40561	MC-130E	711th SOS			48152	C-130J	412th TW	
	40562	MC-130E	711th SOS			*FY85*			
	40565	MC-130E	711th SOS			50011	MC-130H	58th SOW	
	40566	MC-130E	8th SOS			50012	MC-130H	15th SOS	
	40567	MC-130E	8th SOS			50035	C-130H	357th AS	bl
	40568	MC-130E	8th SOS			50036	C-130H	357th AS	bl
	40569	C-130E	314th AW	bl		50037	C-130H	357th AS	bl
	40570	C-130E	43rd AW	gn/or		50038	C-130H	357th AS	bl
	40571	MC-130E	711th SOS			50039	C-130H	357th AS	bl
	40572	MC-130E	8th SOS			50040	C-130H	357th AS	bl
	FY74					50041	C-130H	357th AS	bl
	41658	C-130H	3rd Wg	w		50042	C-130H	357th AS	bl
	41659	C-130H	3rd Wg	w		*FY65*			
	41660	C-130H	3rd Wg	w		50962	EC-130H	42nd ACCS	w
	41661	C-130H	3rd Wg	w		50963	WC-130H	53rd WRS	

Type			Notes
50964	MC-130P		
50966	WC-130H	53rd WRS	
50967	WC-130H	53rd WRS	
50968	WC-130H	53rd WRS	
50970	HC-130P	303rd RQS	y
50971	MC-130P	58th SOW	
50973	HC-130P	71st RQS	bl
50974	HC-130P	102nd RQS	
50975	MC-130P	58th SOW	
50976	HC-130P		
50977	WC-130H	53rd WRS	
50978	HC-130P	102nd RQS	
50979	NC-130H	412th TW	
50980	WC-130H	53rd WRS	
50981	HC-130P	71st RQS	bl
50982	HC-130P	71st RQS	bl
50983	MC-130P	71st RQS	bl
50984	WC-130H	53rd WRS	
50985	WC-130H	53rd WRS	
50986	HC-130P	71st RQS	bl
50987	HC-130P	71st RQS	bl
50988	HC-130P	71st RQS	bl
50989	EC-130H	41st ECS	bl
50991	MC-130P	9th SOS	
50992	MC-130P	17th SOS	
50993	MC-130P	17th SOS	
50994	MC-130P	17th SOS	
FY95			
51001	C-130H	109th AS	gn/bl
51002	C-130H	109th AS	gn/bl
FY85			
51361	C-130H	181st AS	bl/w
51362	C-130H	181st AS	bl/w
51363	C-130H	181st AS	bl/w
51364	C-130H	181st AS	bl/w
51365	C-130H	181st AS	bl/w
51366	C-130H	181st AS	bl/w
51367	C-130H	181st AS	bl/w
51368	C-130H	181st AS	bl/w
FY95			
56709	C-130H	167th AS	r
56710	C-130H	167th AS	r
56711	C-130H	167th AS	r
56712	C-130H	167th AS	r
FY66			
60212	HC-130P	129th RQS	bl
60213	MC-130P	9th SOS	
60215	MC-130P	17th SOS	
60216	HC-130P	129th RQS	bl
60217	MC-130P	9th SOS	
60219	HC-130P	129th RQS	bl
60220	MC-130P	17th SOS	
60221	HC-130P	129th RQS	bl
60222	HC-130P	102nd RQS	
60223	MC-130P	9th SOS	
60224	HC-130P	39th RQS	
60225	MC-130P	9th SOS	
FY86			
60410	C-130H	758th AS	bk/y
60411	C-130H	758th AS	bk/y
60412	C-130H	758th AS	bk/y
60413	C-130H	758th AS	bk/y
60414	C-130H	758th AS	bk/y
60415	C-130H	758th AS	bk/y
60418	C-130H	758th AS	bk/y
60419	C-130H	758th AS	bk/y
FY96			
61003	C-130H	109th AS	gn/bl
61004	C-130H	109th AS	gn/bl
61005	C-130H	109th AS	gn/bl
61006	C-130H	109th AS	gn/bl
61007	C-130H	109th AS	gn/bl
61008	C-130H	109th AS	gn/bl

Type			Notes
FY86			
61391	C-130H	180th AS	y
61392	C-130H	180th AS	y
61393	C-130H	180th AS	y
61394	C-130H	180th AS	y
61395	C-130H	180th AS	y
61396	C-130H	180th AS	y
61397	C-130H	180th AS	y
61398	C-130H	180th AS	y
61699	MC-130H	7th SOS	
FY76			
63300	LC-130R	139th AS	
63301	LC-130R	139th AS	
63302	LC-130R	139th AS	
FY96			
65300	WC-130J	53rd WRS	
65301	WC-130J	53rd WRS	
65302	WC-130J	53rd WRS	
67322	C-130H	731st AS	pr/w
67323	C-130H	731st AS	pr/w
67324	C-130H	731st AS	pr/w
67325	C-130H	731st AS	pr/w
68153	C-130J	815th AS	r
68154	C-130J	815th AS	r
FY87			
70023	MC-130H	7th SOS	
70024	MC-130H	15th SOS	
70125	MC-130H	58th SOW	
70126	MC-130H	58th SOW	
70127	MC-130H	58th SOW	
70128	AC-130U	4th SOS	
FY97			
71351	C-130J	135th AS	bk/y
71352	C-130J	135th AS	bk/y
71353	C-130J	135th AS	bk/y
71354	C-130J	135th AS	bk/y
71931	EC-130J	LMTAS	
75303	WC-130J	53rd WRS	
75304	WC-130J	53rd WRS	
75305	WC-130J	53rd WRS	
75306	WC-130J	53rd WRS	
FY87			
79281	C-130H	95th AS	w/r
79282	C-130H	95th AS	w/r
79283	C-130H	95th AS	w/r
79284	C-130H	700th AS	bl
79285	C-130H	95th AS	w/r
79286	C-130H	357th AS	bl
79287	C-130H	95th AS	w/r
79288	C-130H	758th AS	bk/y
FY88			
80191	MC-130H	1st SOS	
80192	MC-130H	1st SOS	
80193	MC-130H	7th SOS	
80194	MC-130H	7th SOS	
80195	MC-130H	1st SOS	
80264	MC-130H	1st SOS	
FY78			
80806	C-130H	185th AS	bl
80807	C-130H	185th AS	bl
80808	C-130H	185th AS	bl
80809	C-130H	185th AS	bl
80810	C-130H	185th AS	bl
80811	C-130H	185th AS	bl
80812	C-130H	185th AS	bl
80813	C-130H	185th AS	bl
FY88			
81301	C-130H	130th AS	pr/y
81302	C-130H	130th AS	pr/y
81303	C-130H	130th AS	pr/y
81304	C-130H	130th AS	pr/y
81305	C-130H	130th AS	pr/y
81306	C-130H	130th AS	pr/y

Notes	Type			
	81307	C-130H	130th AS	pr/y
	81308	C-130H	130th AS	pr/y
	FY98			
	81355	C-130J	135th AS	bk/y
	81356	C-130J	135th AS	bk/y
	81357	C-130J	135th AS	bk/y
	81358	C-130J	135th AS	bk/y
	FY88			
	81803	MC-130H	1st SOS	
	FY98			
	81932	EC-130J	LMTAS	
	FY88			
	82101	HC-130N	102nd RQS	
	82102	HC-130N	102nd RQS	
	84401	C-130H	95th AS	w/r
	84402	C-130H	95th AS	w/r
	84403	C-130H	95th AS	w/r
	84404	C-130H	95th AS	w/r
	84405	C-130H	95th AS	w/r
	84406	C-130H	95th AS	w/r
	84407	C-130H	95th AS	w/r
	FY98			
	85307	WC-130J	53rd WRS	
	85308	WC-130J	53rd WRS	
	FY89			
	90280	MC-130H	7th SOS	
	90281	MC-130H	15th SOS	
	90282	MC-130H	15th SOS	
	90283	MC-130H	15th SOS	
	FY79			
	90473	C-130H	192nd AS	w
	90474	C-130H	192nd AS	w
	90475	C-130H	192nd AS	w
	90476	C-130H	192nd AS	w
	90477	C-130H	192nd AS	w
	90478	C-130H	192nd AS	w
	90479	C-130H	192nd AS	w
	90480	C-130H	192nd AS	w
	FY89			
	90509	AC-130U	4th SOS	
	90510	AC-130U	4th SOS	
	90511	AC-130U	4th SOS	
	90512	AC-130U	4th SOS	
	90513	AC-130U	4th SOS	
	90514	AC-130U	4th SOS	
	91051	C-130H	105th AS	r
	91052	C-130H	105th AS	r
	91053	C-130H	105th AS	r
	91054	C-130H	105th AS	r
	91055	C-130H	204th AS	
	91056	C-130H	180th AS	y
	91181	C-130H	105th AS	r
	91182	C-130H	105th AS	r
	91183	C-130H	105th AS	r
	91184	C-130H	105th AS	r
	91185	C-130H	105th AS	r
	91186	C-130H	105th AS	r
	91187	C-130H	105th AS	r
	91188	C-130H	105th AS	r
	FY99			
	91431	C-130J-30	143rd AS	r
	91432	C-130J-30	143rd AS	r
	91433	C-130J-30	143rd AS	r
	91933	EC-130J	LMTAS	
	95309	WC-130J	53rd WRS	
	FY69			
	95819	MC-130P	9th SOS	
	95820	MC-130P	9th SOS	
	95821	MC-130P	58th SOW	
	95822	MC-130P	9th SOS	
	95823	MC-130P	67th SOS	
	95825	MC-130P	9th SOS	
	95826	MC-130P	67th SOS	

Notes	Type			
	95827	MC-130P	9th SOS	
	95828	MC-130P	67th SOS	
	95829	HC-130N	39th RQS	
	95830	HC-130N	39th RQS	
	95831	MC-130P	67th SOS	
	95832	MC-130P	67th SOS	
	95833	HC-130N	39th RQS	
	96566	C-130E	37th AS	bl/w
	96568	AC-130H	16th SOS	
	96569	AC-130H	16th SOS	
	96570	AC-130H	16th SOS	
	96572	AC-130H	16th SOS	
	96573	AC-130H	16th SOS	
	96574	AC-130H	16th SOS	
	96575	AC-130H	16th SOS	
	96577	AC-130H	16th SOS	
	96580	C-130E	43rd AW	gn/or
	96582	C-130E	37th AS	bl/w
	96583	C-130E	37th AS	bl/w
	FY89			
	99101	C-130H	757th AS	bl
	99102	C-130H	757th AS	bl
	99103	C-130H	757th AS	bl
	99104	C-130H	757th AS	bl
	99105	C-130H	757th AS	bl
	99106	C-130H	757th AS	bl

Boeing C-135/C-137

6th AMW, MacDill AFB, Florida:
  91st ARS (*y/bl*);
15th ABW, Hickam AFB, Hawaii:
  65th AS;
18th Wg, Kadena AB, Japan [ZZ]:
  909th ARS (*w*);
19th ARG, Robins AFB, Georgia:
  99th ARS (*y/bl*);
22nd ARW, McConnell AFB, Kansas:
  344th ARS (*y/bk*), 349th ARS (*y/bl*)
  350th ARS (*y/r*) & 384th ARS (*y/pr*);
55th Wg, Offutt AFB, Nebraska [OF]:
  38th RS (*gn*) & 45th RS (*bk*);
88th ABW, Wright-Patterson AFB, Ohio;
89th AW, Andrews AFB, Maryland:
  1st AS;
92nd ARW, Fairchild AFB, Washington:
  92nd ARS (*bk*), 93rd ARS (*bl*)
  96th ARS (*gn*) & 97th ARS (*y*);
97th AMW, Altus AFB, Oklahoma:
  55th ARS (*y/r*);
100th ARW, RAF Mildenhall, UK [D]:
  351st ARS (*r/w/bl*);
106th ARS/117th ARW, Birmingham,
  Alabama ANG (*w/r*);
108th ARS/126th ARW,
  Scott AFB, Illinois ANG (*w/bl*);
108th ARW, McGuire AFB,
  New Jersey ANG:
  141st ARS (*bk/y*) & 150th ARS (*bl*);
116th ARS/141st ARW, Fairchild AFB,
  Washington ANG (*gn/w*);
117th ARS/190th ARW, Forbes Field,
  Kansas ANG (*bl/y*);
121st ARW, Rickenbacker ANGB,
  Ohio ANG:
  145th ARS & 166th ARS (*bl*);
126th ARS/128th ARW, Mitchell Field,
  Wisconsin ANG (*w/bl*);
132nd ARS/101st ARW, Bangor,
  Maine ANG (*w/gn*);
133rd ARS/157th ARW, Pease ANGB,
  New Hampshire ANG (*bl*);
136th ARS/107th ARW,
  Niagara Falls, New York ANG (*bl*);

Type	Notes
151st ARS/134th ARW, Knoxville, Tennessee ANG (w/or);	
153rd ARS/186th ARW, Meridian, Mississippi ANG (bk/gd);	
168th ARS/168th ARW, Eielson AFB, Alaska ANG (bl/y);	
171st ARW, Greater Pittsburgh, Pennsylvania ANG:	
146th ARS (y/bk) &	
147th ARS (bk/y);	
173rd ARS/155th ARW, Lincoln, Nebraska ANG (r/w);	
191st ARS/151st ARW, Salt Lake City, Utah ANG (bl/bk);	
196th ARS/163rd ARW, March ARB, California ANG (bl/w);	
197th ARS/161st ARW, Phoenix, Arizona ANG;	
203rd ARS/154th Wg, Hickam AFB, Hawaii ANG [HH] (y/bk);	
319th ARW, Grand Forks AFB, North Dakota:	
905th ARS (bl), 906th ARS (y), 911th ARS (r) & 912th ARS (w);	
366th Wg, Mountain Home AFB, Idaho [MO]:	
22nd ARS (y/gn);	
412th TW, Edwards AFB, California [ED]:	
452nd FLTS (bl);	
434th ARW AFRC, Grissom AFB, Indiana:	
72nd ARS (bl) & 74th ARS (r/w);	
452nd AMW AFRC, March ARB, California:	
336th ARS (y);	
507th ARW AFRC, Tinker AFB, Oklahoma:	
465th ARS (bl/y);	
645th Materiel Sqn, Greenville, Texas;	
916th ARW AFRC, Seymour Johnson AFB, North Carolina:	
77th ARS (gn);	
927th ARW AFRC, Selfridge ANGB, Michigan:	
63rd ARS (pr/w);	
940th ARW AFRC, McClellan AFB, California:	
314th ARS (or/bk);	
CinC CentCom (CinC CC)/6th AMW, MacDill AFB, Florida	

FY60

Type			Notes
00313	KC-135R	22nd ARW	
00314	KC-135R	434th ARW	r/w
00315	KC-135R	126th ARS	w/bl
00316	KC-135E	116th ARS	gn/w
00318	KC-135R	203rd ARS	y/bk
00319	KC-135R	319th ARW	
00320	KC-135R	319th ARW	w
00321	KC-135R	97th AMW	y/r
00322	KC-135R	434th ARW	bl
00323	KC-135R	203rd ARS	y/bk
00324	KC-135R	319th ARW	
00327	KC-135E	191st ARS	bl/bk
00328	KC-135R	22nd ARW	
00329	KC-135R	203rd ARS	y/bk
00331	KC-135R	92nd ARW	
00332	KC-135R	92nd ARW	y
00333	KC-135R	97th AMW	y/r
00334	KC-135R	168th ARS	bl/y
00335	KC-135T	22nd ARW	y/bk
00336	KC-135T	92nd ARW	gn

Type			Notes
00337	KC-135T	92nd ARW	m
00339	KC-135T	92nd ARW	bl
00341	KC-135R	121st ARW	bl
00342	KC-135R	319th ARW	y
00343	KC-135T	319th ARW	w
00344	KC-135T	319th ARW	r
00345	KC-135T	92nd ARW	y
00346	KC-135T	92nd ARW	bk
00347	KC-135R	121st ARW	bl
00348	KC-135R	319th ARW	r
00349	KC-135R	916th ARW	gn
00350	KC-135R	22nd ARW	y/bk
00351	KC-135R	22nd ARW	
00353	KC-135R	22nd ARW	
00355	KC-135R	22nd ARW	
00356	KC-135R	22nd ARW	y/bl
00357	KC-135R	22nd ARW	y/bk
00358	KC-135R	136th ARS	bl
00359	KC-135R	434th ARW	r/w
00360	KC-135R	100th ARW	r/w/bl
00362	KC-135R	22nd ARW	y/r
00363	KC-135R	434th ARW	bl
00364	KC-135R	434th ARW	r/w
00365	KC-135R	366th Wg	y/gn
00366	KC-135R	19th ARG	y/bl
00367	KC-135R	121st ARW	bl
00372	C-135E	412th TW	bl

FY61

Type			Notes
10264	KC-135R	121st ARW	bl
10266	KC-135R	173rd ARS	r/w
10267	KC-135R		
10268	KC-135R	940th ARW	or/bk
10270	KC-135E	927th ARW	pr/w
10271	KC-135E	927th ARW	pr/w
10272	KC-135R	434th ARW	r/w
10275	KC-135R	6th AMW	y/bl
10276	KC-135R	173rd ARS	r/w
10277	KC-135R	366th Wg	y/gn
10280	KC-135R	452nd AMW	y
10281	KC-135E	197th ARS	
10284	KC-135R		
10288	KC-135R	92nd ARW	bk
10290	KC-135R	203rd ARS	y/bk
10292	KC-135R	6th AMW	y/bl
10293	KC-135R	22nd ARW	y/r
10294	KC-135R	19th ARG	y/bl
10295	KC-135R	6th AMW	y/bl
10298	KC-135R	126th ARS	w/bl
10299	KC-135R	92nd ARW	y
10300	KC-135R	6th AMW	y/bl
10302	KC-135R	100th ARW	r/w/bl
10303	KC-135E	452nd AMW	y
10304	KC-135R	92nd ARW	y
10305	KC-135R	92nd ARW	bl
10306	KC-135R	18th Wg	w
10307	KC-135R	434th ARW	r/w
10308	KC-135R	97th AMW	y/r
10309	KC-135R	126th ARS	w/bl
10310	KC-135R	133rd ARS	bl
10311	KC-135R	22nd ARW	y/r
10312	KC-135R	319th ARW	r
10313	KC-135R	916th ARW	gn
10314	KC-135R	97th AMW	y/r
10315	KC-135R	97th AMW	y/r
10317	KC-135R	18th Wg	w
10318	KC-135R	6th AMW	y/bl
10320	KC-135R	412th TW	
10321	KC-135R	92nd ARW	bl
10323	KC-135R	3/9th ARW	
10324	KC-135R	452nd AMW	y
10330	EC-135E	412th TW	bl
12662	RC-135S	55th Wg	bk
12663	RC-135S	55th Wg	bk

Notes	Type				Notes	Type			
	12666	NC-135W	645th MS			23548	KC-135R	18th Wg	w
	12669	C-135C	412th TW	bl		23549	KC-135R	319th ARW	r
	12670	OC-135B	55th Wg			23550	KC-135R	22nd ARW	
	12672	OC-135B	55th Wg			23551	KC-135R	100th ARW	r/w/bl
	FY64					23552	KC-135R	319th ARW	r
	14828	KC-135R	22nd ARW	y/pr		23553	KC-135R	22nd ARW	y/r
	14829	KC-135R	100th ARW	r/w/bl		23554	KC-135R	19th ARG	y/bl
	14830	KC-135R	6th AMW	y/bl		23556	KC-135R	916th ARW	gn
	14831	KC-135R	22nd ARW			23557	KC-135R	18th Wg	w
	14832	KC-135R	203rd ARS	y/bk		23558	KC-135R	22nd ARW	y/bk
	14833	KC-135R	22nd ARW			23559	KC-135R	22nd ARW	y/pr
	14834	KC-135R	434th ARW	r/w		23561	KC-135R		
	14835	KC-135R	100th ARW	r/w/bl		23562	KC-135R	319th ARW	w
	14836	KC-135R	319th ARW	r		23564	KC-135R	22nd ARW	
	14837	KC-135R	6th AMW	y/bl		23565	KC-135R	22nd ARW	
	14838	KC-135R	100th ARW	r/w/bl		23566	KC-135E	153rd ARS	bk/gd
	14839	KC-135R	136th ARS	bl		23568	KC-135R	319th ARW	w
	14840	KC-135R	121st ARW	bl		23569	KC-135R	19th ARG	y/bl
	14841	RC-135V	55th Wg	gn		23571	KC-135R	168th ARS	bl/y
	14842	RC-135V	55th Wg	gn		23572	KC-135R	366th Wg	y/gn
	14843	RC-135V	55th Wg	gn		23573	KC-135R	92nd ARW	
	14844	RC-135V	55th Wg	gn		23575	KC-135R	22nd ARW	
	14845	RC-135V	55th Wg	gn		23576	KC-135R	133rd ARS	bl
	14846	RC-135V	55th Wg	gn		23577	KC-135R	916th ARW	gn
	14847	RC-135U	55th Wg	gn		23578	KC-135R		
	14848	RC-135V	55th Wg	gn		23580	KC-135R	97th AMW	y/r
	14849	RC-135U	55th Wg	gn		23582	WC-135C	55th Wg	bk
	FY67					24125	RC-135W	55th Wg	gn
	19417	EC-137D	6th AMW			24126	C-135B	108th ARW	bk/y
	FY62					24127	RC-135W	55th Wg	
	23498	KC-135R	366th Wg	y/gn		24128	RC-135S	55th Wg	
	23499	KC-135R	22nd ARW	y/pr		24129	TC-135W	55th Wg	gn
	23500	KC-135R	126th ARS	w/bl		24130	RC-135W	55th Wg	gn
	23502	KC-135R	18th Wg	w		24131	RC-135W	55th Wg	gn
	23503	KC-135R	18th Wg	w		24132	RC-135W	55th Wg	gn
	23504	KC-135R	6th AMW	y/bl		24133	TC-135S	55th Wg	bk
	23505	KC-135R	22nd ARW			24134	RC-135W	55th Wg	gn
	23506	KC-135R	133rd ARS	bl		24135	RC-135W	55th Wg	gn
	23507	KC-135R	18th Wg	w		24138	RC-135W	55th Wg	gn
	23508	KC-135R	19th ARG	y/bl		24139	RC-135W	55th Wg	gn
	23509	KC-135R	916th ARW	gn		*FY63*			
	23510	KC-135R	434th ARW	r/w		37976	KC-135R	6th AMW	y/bl
	23511	KC-135R	121st ARW	bl		37977	KC-135R	6th AMW	y/bl
	23512	KC-135R	126th ARS	w/bl		37978	KC-135R	100th ARW	r/w/bl
	23513	KC-135R	366th Wg	y/gn		37979	KC-135R	22nd ARW	
	23514	KC-135R	203rd ARS	y/bk		37980	KC-135R	100th ARW	r/w/bl
	23515	KC-135R	133rd ARS	bl		37981	KC-135R	136th ARS	bl
	23516	KC-135R	22nd ARW			37982	KC-135R	319th ARW	y
	23517	KC-135R	22nd ARW			37984	KC-135R	106th ARS	w/r
	23518	KC-135R	434th ARW	bl		37985	KC-135R	507th ARW	bl/y
	23519	KC-135R	319th ARW	r		37987	KC-135R	319th ARW	bl
	23520	KC-135R	6th AMW	y/bl		37988	KC-135R	173rd ARS	r/w
	23521	KC-135R	434th ARW	r/w		37991	KC-135R	173rd ARS	r/w
	23523	KC-135R	19th ARG	y/bl		37992	KC-135R	121st ARW	bl
	23524	KC-135R	106th ARS	w/r		37993	KC-135R	121st ARW	m
	23526	KC-135R	173rd ARS	r/w		37995	KC-135R	22nd ARW	y/bl
	23527	KC-135E	108th ARW	bl		37996	KC-135R	434th ARW	bl
	23528	KC-135R				37997	KC-135R	319th ARW	bl
	23529	KC-135R	319th ARW	w		37999	KC-135R	97th AMW	y/r
	23530	KC-135R	434th ARW	bl		38000	KC-135R	22nd ARW	
	23531	KC-135R	121st ARW	bl		38002	KC-135R	22nd ARW	
	23533	KC-135R	319th ARW	bl		38003	KC-135R	18th Wg	w
	23534	KC-135R	19th ARG	y/bl		38004	KC-135R	366th Wg	y/gn
	23537	KC-135R	22nd ARW			38006	KC-135R	319th ARW	w
	23538	KC-135R	100th ARW	r/w/bl		38007	KC-135R	106th ARS	w/r
	23540	KC-135R	22nd ARW			38008	KC-135R	100th ARW	r/w/bl
	23541	KC-135R	22nd ARW			38011	KC-135R	6th AMW	y/bl
	23542	KC-135R	916th ARW	gn		38012	KC-135R		
	23543	KC-135R	434th ARW	bl		38013	KC-135R	121st ARW	bl
	23544	KC-135R	19th ARG	y/bl		38014	KC-135R	319th ARW	bl
	23545	KC-135R	22nd ARW			38015	KC-135R	168th ARS	bl/y
	23546	KC-135R	97th AMW	y/r		38017	KC-135R	92nd ARW	bk
	23547	KC-135R	133rd ARS	bl		38018	KC-135R	173rd ARS	r/w

Type		Unit	Notes
38019	KC-135R	22nd ARW	y/pr
38020	KC-135R	97th AMW	y/r
38021	KC-135R	18th Wg	w
38022	KC-135R	22nd ARW	m
38023	KC-135R	97th AMW	y/r
38024	KC-135R	452nd AMW	y
38025	KC-135R	100th ARW	r/w/bl
38026	KC-135R	319th ARW	y
38027	KC-135R	92nd ARW	gn
38028	KC-135R	168th ARS	bl/y
38029	KC-135R	126th ARS	w/bl
38030	KC-135R	203rd ARS	y/bk
38031	KC-135R	92nd ARW	
38032	KC-135R	434th ARW	bl
38033	KC-135R	92nd ARW	bl
38034	KC-135R	97th AMW	y/r
38035	KC-135R	106th ARS	w/r
38036	KC-135R	136th ARS	bl
38037	KC-135R	97th AMW	y/r
38038	KC-135R	133rd ARS	bl
38039	KC-135R	507th ARW	bl/y
38040	KC-135R	22nd ARW	
38041	KC-135R	434th ARW	bl
38043	KC-135R	168th ARS	bl/y
38044	KC-135R	18th Wg	w
38045	KC-135R	97th AMW	y/r
38050	NKC-135B	412th TW	bl
38058	KC-135D	117th ARS	bl/y
38059	KC-135D	117th ARS	bl/y
38060	KC-135D	117th ARS	bl/y
38061	KC-135D	117th ARS	bl/y
38871	KC-135R	18th Wg	w
38872	KC-135R	136th ARS	bl
38873	KC-135R	6th AMW	y/bl
38874	KC-135R		
38875	KC-135R	366th Wg	y/gn
38876	KC-135R	168th ARS	bl/y
38877	KC-135R	97th AMW	y/r
38878	KC-135R	319th ARW	r
38879	KC-135R	100th ARW	r/w/bl
38880	KC-135R	507th ARW	bl/y
38881	KC-135R	97th AMW	y/r
38883	KC-135R	319th ARW	w
38884	KC-135R	22nd ARW	y/r
38885	KC-135R	18th Wg	w
38886	KC-135R	97th AMW	y/r
38887	KC-135R	100th ARW	r/w/bl
38888	KC-135R	97th AMW	y/r
39792	RC-135V	55th Wg	gn
FY55			
53132	NKC-135E	412th TW	bl
53135	NKC-135E	412th TW	bl
53141	KC-135E	116th ARS	gn/w
53143	KC-135E	197th ARS	
53145	KC-135E	940th ARW	or/bk
53146	KC-135E	108th ARW	bk/y
FY56			
63593	KC-135E	108th ARW	bk/y
63604	KC-135E	108th ARW	bk/y
63606	KC-135E	132nd ARS	w/gn
63607	KC-135E	151st ARS	w/or
63609	KC-135E	151st ARS	w/or
63611	KC-135E	171st ARW	y/bk
63612	KC-135E	171st ARW	y/bk
63622	KC-135E	132nd ARS	w/gn
63626	KC-135E	171st ARW	y/bk
63630	KC-135E	171st ARW	y/bk
63631	KC-135E	191st ARS	bl/bk
63638	KC-135E	197th ARS	
63640	KC-135E	132nd ARS	w/gn
63641	KC-135E	117th ARS	bl/y
63643	KC-135E	151st ARS	w/or
63648	KC-135E	171st ARW	y/bk
63650	KC-135E	116th ARS	gn/w
63654	KC-135E	132nd ARS	w/gn
63658	KC-135E	117th ARS	bl/y
FY57			
71418	KC-135R	153rd ARS	bk/gd
71419	KC-135R	19th ARG	y/bl
71421	KC-135E	116th ARS	gn/w
71422	KC-135E	927th ARW	pr/w
71423	KC-135E	171st ARW	bk/y
71425	KC-135E	151st ARS	w/or
71426	KC-135E	197th ARS	
71427	KC-135E	121st ARW	bl
71428	KC-135E	196th ARS	bl/w
71429	KC-135E	117th ARS	bl/y
71430	KC-135E	133rd ARS	bl
71431	KC-135E	108th ARW	bk/y
71432	KC-135E	106th ARS	w/r
71433	KC-135E	197th ARS	
71434	KC-135R	116th ARS	gn/w
71435	KC-135R	18th Wg	w
71436	KC-135E	196th ARS	bl/w
71437	KC-135E	916th ARW	gn
71438	KC-135E	927th ARW	pr/w
71439	KC-135R	6th AMW	y/bl
71440	KC-135R	319th ARW	r
71441	KC-135E	108th ARS	w/bl
71443	KC-135E	132nd ARS	w/gn
71445	KC-135E	108th ARS	bk/y
71447	KC-135E	171st ARW	y/bk
71448	KC-135E	132nd ARS	w/gn
71450	KC-135E	132nd ARS	w/gn
71451	KC-135R	196th ARS	bl/w
71452	KC-135R	197th ARS	
71453	KC-135E	106th ARS	w/r
71454	KC-135E	319th ARW	y
71455	KC-135E	151st ARS	w/or
71456	KC-135E	319th ARW	y
71458	KC-135E	108th ARS	w/bl
71459	KC-135E	196th ARS	bl/w
71460	KC-135E	117th ARS	bl/y
71461	KC-135E	173rd ARS	r/w
71462	KC-135E	121st ARW	bl
71463	KC-135E	117th ARS	bl/y
71464	KC-135E	108th ARW	bk/y
71465	KC-135E	151st ARS	w/or
71468	KC-135E	452nd AMW	y
71469	KC-135E	121st ARW	bl
71471	KC-135E	132nd ARS	w/gn
71472	KC-135R	434th ARW	bl
71473	KC-135R	19th ARG	y/bl
71474	KC-135R		
71475	KC-135R	197th ARS	
71479	KC-135R	452nd AMW	y
71480	KC-135E	108th ARS	w/bl
71482	KC-135E	108th ARS	w/bl
71483	KC-135R	92nd ARW	
71484	KC-135E	197th ARS	
71485	KC-135R	151st ARS	w/or
71486	KC-135R	92nd ARW	bk
71487	KC-135R	434th ARW	bl
71488	KC-135R	319th ARW	w
71491	KC-135E	132nd ARS	w/gn
71492	KC-135E	151st ARS	w/or
71493	KC-135R	22nd ARW	
71494	KC-135R	108th ARS	w/bl
71495	KC-135R	197th ARS	
71496	KC-135R	197th ARS	
71497	KC-135E	191st ARS	bl/bk
71499	KC-135R	92nd ARW	gn
71501	KC-135R	116th ARS	gn/w
71502	KC-135R	97th AMW	y/r
71503	KC-135E	151st ARS	w/or
71504	KC-135E	927th ARW	pr/w

Notes	Type			
	71505	KC-135E	132nd ARS	w/gn
	71506	KC-135R	319th ARW	w
	71507	KC-135R	108th ARW	bk/y
	71508	KC-135R	203rd ARS	y/bk
	71509	KC-135E	171st ARS	bk/y
	71510	KC-135E	191st ARS	bl/bk
	71511	KC-135R	940th ARW	or/bk
	71512	KC-135E	452nd AMW	y
	71514	KC-135R	126th ARS	w/bl
	72589	KC-135E	15th ABW	
	72593	KC-135R	121st ARW	bl
	72594	KC-135E	108th ARS	w/bl
	72595	KC-135R	171st ARW	bk/y
	72597	KC-135R	153rd ARS	bk/gd
	72598	KC-135R	452nd AMW	y
	72599	KC-135R	916th ARW	gn
	72600	KC-135R	116th ARS	gn/w
	72601	KC-135E	151st ARS	w/or
	72602	KC-135E	108th ARW	bl
	72603	KC-135R	452nd AMW	y
	72604	KC-135E	171st ARW	y/bk
	72605	KC-135E	100th ARW	r/w/bl
	72606	KC-135E	108th ARW	bl
	72607	KC-135R	171st ARW	bk/y
	72608	KC-135R	171st ARW	bk/y
	FY58			
	80001	KC-135R	6th AMW	y/bl
	80003	KC-135E	108th ARS	w/bl
	80004	KC-135R	153rd ARS	bk/gd
	80005	KC-135E	117th ARS	bl/y
	80006	KC-135R	191st ARS	bl/bk
	80008	KC-135R	133rd ARS	bl
	80009	KC-135R	126th ARS	w/bl
	80010	KC-135R	153rd ARS	bk/gd
	80011	KC-135R	22nd ARW	y/bl
	80012	KC-135E	191st ARS	bl/bk
	80013	KC-135E	927th ARW	pr/w
	80014	KC-135E	108th ARS	w/bl
	80015	KC-135R	434th ARW	r/w
	80016	KC-135R	18th Wg	w
	80017	KC-135E	171st ARW	y/bk
	80018	KC-135R	22nd ARW	y/pr
	80020	KC-135E	116th ARS	gn/w
	80021	KC-135R	126th ARS	w/bl
	80023	KC-135R	136th ARS	bl
	80024	KC-135E	171st ARW	y/bk
	80027	KC-135R	319th ARW	y
	80030	KC-135R	106th ARS	w/r
	80032	KC-135R	108th ARW	bl
	80034	KC-135R	319th ARW	bl
	80035	KC-135R	22nd ARW	y/bl
	80036	KC-135R	319th ARW	
	80037	KC-135E	171st ARW	bk/y
	80038	KC-135R	916th ARW	gn
	80040	KC-135E	108th ARW	bl
	80041	KC-135E	927th ARW	pr/w
	80042	KC-135T	319th ARW	y
	80043	KC-135E	191st ARS	bl/bk
	80044	KC-135E	108th ARW	bk/y
	80045	KC-135T	92nd ARW	bl
	80046	KC-135T	92nd ARW	
	80047	KC-135T	19th ARG	y/bl
	80049	KC-135T	92nd ARW	y
	80050	KC-135T	92nd ARW	bk
	80051	KC-135R	507th ARW	bl/y
	80052	KC-135E	452nd AMW	y
	80053	KC-135E	927th ARW	pr/w
	80054	KC-135T	92nd ARW	gn
	80055	KC-135T	92nd ARW	bk
	80056	KC-135R	153rd ARS	bk/gd
	80057	KC-135E	108th ARS	w/bl
	80058	KC-135R	507th ARW	bl/y
	80059	KC-135R	153rd ARS	bk/gd

Notes	Type			
	80060	KC-135T	92nd ARW	gn
	80061	KC-135T	319th ARW	r
	80062	KC-135T	92nd ARW	gn
	80063	KC-135R	507th ARW	bl/y
	80064	KC-135E	940th ARW	or/bk
	80065	KC-135T	22nd ARW	
	80066	KC-135R	507th ARW	bl/y
	80067	KC-135E	108th ARS	w/bl
	80068	KC-135E	108th ARS	w/bl
	80069	KC-135T	92nd ARW	y
	80071	KC-135T	22nd ARW	y/bk
	80072	KC-135T	92nd ARW	gn
	80073	KC-135R	106th ARS	w/r
	80074	KC-135T	18th Wg	w
	80075	KC-135R	434th ARW	bl
	80076	KC-135R	434th ARW	r/w
	80077	KC-135T	92nd ARW	bk
	80078	KC-135E	108th ARW	bl
	80079	KC-135R	507th ARW	bl/y
	80080	KC-135E	191st ARW	bl/bk
	80082	KC-135E	116th ARS	gn/w
	80083	KC-135T	121st ARW	bl
	80084	KC-135T	92nd ARW	
	80085	KC-135E	452nd AMW	y
	80086	KC-135T	92nd ARW	gn
	80087	KC-135E	108th ARW	bl
	80088	KC-135T	22nd ARW	y/bk
	80089	KC-135T	319th ARW	w
	80090	KC-135E	940th ARW	or/bk
	80092	KC-135R	133rd ARS	bl
	80093	KC-135R	319th ARW	r
	80094	KC-135T	92nd ARW	bk
	80095	KC-135T	319th ARW	w
	80096	KC-135E	940th ARW	or/bk
	80098	KC-135R	133rd ARS	bl
	80099	KC-135T	92nd ARW	bl
	80100	KC-135R	18th Wg	w
	80102	KC-135R	434th ARW	r/w
	80103	KC-135T	92nd ARW	gn
	80104	KC-135R	136th ARS	bl
	80106	KC-135R	106th ARS	w/r
	80107	KC-135E	191st ARS	bl/bk
	80108	KC-135E	940th ARW	or/bk
	80109	KC-135R	153rd ARS	bk/gd
	80111	KC-135E	108th ARW	bk/y
	80112	KC-135T	92nd ARW	bl
	80113	KC-135R	319th ARW	r
	80114	KC-135R	92nd ARW	bl
	80115	KC-135E	108th ARW	bl
	80116	KC-135E	197th ARS	
	80117	KC-135T	92nd ARW	
	80118	KC-135R	18th Wg	w
	80119	KC-135R	319th ARW	bl
	80120	KC-135R	319th ARW	y
	80121	KC-135R	507th ARW	bl/y
	80122	KC-135R	168th ARS	bl/y
	80123	KC-135R	22nd ARW	y/bl
	80124	KC-135R	22nd ARW	y/bl
	80125	KC-135T	92nd ARW	bl
	80126	KC-135R	22nd ARW	y/bl
	80128	KC-135R	6th AMW	y/bl
	80129	KC-135T	92nd ARW	bl
	80130	KC-135R	126th ARS	w/bl
	FY88			
	86005	EC-137D	88th ABW	
	86008	EC-137D	88th ABW	
	FY59			
	91444	KC-135R	121st ARW	bl
	91445	KC-135E	116th ARS	gn/w
	91446	KC-135R	153rd ARS	bk/gd
	91447	KC-135E	927th ARW	pr/w
	91448	KC-135R	196th ARS	bl/w
	91450	KC-135R	196th ARS	bl/w

Type			Notes
91451	KC-135E	927th ARW	pr/w
91453	KC-135R	121st ARW	bl
91455	KC-135R	153rd ARS	bk/gd
91456	KC-135E	108th ARW	bk/y
91457	KC-135E	171st ARW	bk/y
91458	KC-135R	121st ARW	bl
91459	KC-135R	100th ARW	r/w/bl
91460	KC-135T	92nd ARW	gn
91461	KC-135R	168th ARS	bl/y
91462	KC-135T	319th ARW	
91463	KC-135R	173rd ARS	r/w
91464	KC-135T	92nd ARW	bk
91466	KC-135R	136th ARS	bl
91467	KC-135T	92nd ARW	bl
91468	KC-135R	92nd ARW	bl
91469	KC-135R	916th ARW	gn
91470	KC-135T	92nd ARW	y
91471	KC-135T	92nd ARW	
91472	KC-135R	203rd ARS	y/bk
91473	KC-135R	191st ARS	bl/bk
91474	KC-135T	92nd ARW	y
91475	KC-135R	97th AMW	y/r
91476	KC-135R	319th ARW	
91477	KC-135R	927th ARW	pr/w
91478	KC-135R	153rd ARS	bk/gd
91479	KC-135E	171st ARW	y/bk
91480	KC-135T	92nd ARW	bl
91482	KC-135R	18th Wg	w
91483	KC-135R	121st ARW	bl
91484	KC-135E	171st ARW	bk/y
91485	KC-135E	108th ARW	bl
91486	KC-135R	22nd ARW	y/bl
91487	KC-135E	108th ARS	w/bl
91488	KC-135R	18th Wg	w
91489	KC-135E	191st ARS	bl/bk
91490	KC-135T	92nd ARW	bk
91492	KC-135R	319th ARW	r
91493	KC-135E	132nd ARS	w/gn
91495	KC-135R	173rd ARS	r/w
91496	KC-135E	171st ARW	y/bk
91497	KC-135E	108th ARW	bl
91498	KC-135R	366th Wg	y/gn
91499	KC-135R	196th ARS	bl/w
91500	KC-135R	22nd ARW	
91501	KC-135R	319th ARW	
91502	KC-135R		
91503	KC-135E	108th ARW	bk/y
91504	KC-135T	92nd ARW	bk
91505	KC-135R	196th ARS	bl/w
91506	KC-135E	171st ARW	bk/y
91507	KC-135R	19th ARG	y/bl
91508	KC-135R	319th ARW	r
91509	KC-135R	196th ARS	bl/w
91510	KC-135T	319th ARW	r
91511	KC-135R	22nd ARW	
91512	KC-135R	92nd ARW	gn
91513	KC-135T	92nd ARW	bl
91515	KC-135R	18th Wg	w
91516	KC-135R	196th ARS	bl/w
91517	KC-135R	97th AMW	y/r
91518	C-135K	15th ABW	
91519	KC-135E	171st ARW	y/bk
91520	KC-135T	92nd ARW	bl
91521	KC-135R	168th ARS	bl/y
91522	KC-135R	136th ARS	bl
91523	KC-135T	92nd ARW	bk

Lockheed C-141 Starlifter
62nd AW, McChord AFB,
  Washington (gn):
    4th AS & 8th AS;
164th AW, Memphis, Tennessee ANG:
  155th AS (r);

172nd AW, Jackson Int'l
  Airport, Mississippi ANG:
    183rd AS (bl/gd);
305th AMW, McGuire AFB,
  New Jersey (bl):
    6th AS, 13th AS & 18th AS;
445th AW AFRC, Wright-
  Patterson AFB, Ohio (si):
    89th AS & 356th AS;
452nd AMW AFRC, March ARB,
  California (or/y):
    729th AS & 730th AS;
756th AS/459th AW, AFRC,
  Andrews AFB, Maryland (y/bk)

C-141B/C-141C*

Type			Notes
FY63			
38076	62nd AW		gn
38080*	164th AW		r
38082	62nd AW		gn
38084*	452nd AMW		or/y
38085*	452nd AMW		or/y
FY64			
40611	62nd AW		gn
40614*	172nd AW		bl/gd
40619	305th AMW		bl
40620*	459th AW		y/bk
40622*	172nd AW		bl/gd
40627*	164th AW		r
40632*	172nd AW		bl/gd
40633	62nd AW		gn
40637*	459th AW		y/bk
40638	62nd AW		gn
40640*	172nd AW		bl/gd
40645*	459th AW		y/bk
FY65			
50216*	459th AW		y/bk
50221	62nd AW		gn
50222*	164th AW		r
50225*	452nd AMW		or/y
50226*	459th AW		y/bk
50229*	452nd AMW		or/y
50232*	445th AW		si
50237*	445th AW		si
50240	62nd AW		gn
50245*	452nd AMW		or/y
50248*	452nd AMW		or/y
50249*	445th AW		si
50250*	445th AW		si
50256*	445th AW		si
50258*	445th AW		si
50261*	445th AW		si
50267	62nd AW		gn
50271*	459th AW		y/bk
50273	305th AMW		bl
50279	305th AMW		bl
59401	305th AMW		bl
59409*	445th AW		si
59412*	445th AW		si
59414*	452nd AMW		or/y
FY66			
60130*	172nd AW		bl/gd
60131	305th AMW		bl
60132*	445th AW		si
60133	62nd AW		gn
60134*	445th AW		si
60136*	452nd AMW		or/y
60139*	164th AW		r
60140	62nd AW		gn
60147	62nd AW		gn
60148*	445th AW		si
60151*	452nd AMW		or/y
60152*	452nd AMW		or/y
60157*	164th AW		r

C-141

Notes	Type			Notes	Type		
	60158	62nd AW	gn		67950*	445th AW	si
	60160	62nd AW	gn		67952*	452nd AMW	or/y
	60164*	172nd AW	bl/gd		67953*	445th AW	si
	60165	62nd AW	gn		67954*	445th AW	si
	60166	62nd AW	gn		67955	62nd AW	gn
	60167*	452nd AMW	or/y		67956	305th AMW	bl
	60168	305th AMW	bl		67957*	452nd AMW	or/y
	60169	305th AMW	bl		67959*	445th AW	si
	60171	62nd AW	gn		FY67		
	60174*	459th AW	y/bk		70002	305th AMW	bl
	60175	62nd AW	gn		70003	305th AMW	bl
	60177*	445th AW	si		70004	305th AMW	bl
	60181*	452nd AMW	or/y		70010	305th AMW	bl
	60182*	452nd AMW	or/y		70011	305th AMW	bl
	60183	305th AMW	bl		70012	305th AMW	bl
	60185*	172nd AW	bl/gd		70014	305th AMW	bl
	60190*	172nd AW	bl/gd		70015*	452nd AMW	or/y
	60191*	172nd AW	bl/gd		70019	62nd AW	gn
	60192	305th AMW	bl		70021*	164th AW	r
	60193*	445th AW	si		70024*	164th AW	r
	60196	305th AMW	bl		70027*	459th AW	y/bk
	60201*	452nd AMW	or/y		70029*	164th AW	r
	67944	305th AMW	bl		70031*	445th AW	si
	67947	305th AMW	bl		70166*	459th AW	y/bk
	67948	62nd AW	gn				

Gates C-21A Learjet 40110 is flown by the 86th AW from Ramstein AB, Germany. *Daniel March*

28th BS Rockwell B-1B Lancer 60109 at high speed. *PRM*

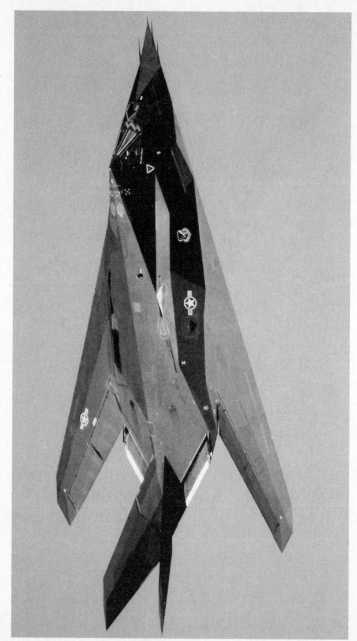

This 49th FW F-117A Nighthawk shows its distinctive shape and paint scheme. *PRM*

Lockheed P-3 Orion
CinCLANT/VP-30, NAS Jacksonville, Florida;
CinCPAC/ETD, MCBH Kaneohe Bay, Hawaii;
CinCUSNFE, NAF Sigonella, Italy;
CNO/VP-30, NAS Jacksonville, Florida;
NAF Keflavik, Iceland;
NASC-FS, Point Mugu, California;
NAWC 23, Dallas/Love Field, Texas;
Navy Research Lab, Patuxent River, Maryland;
NFATS, Patuxent River, Maryland;
NWTSPM, NAS Point Mugu, California;
USNTPS, NAS Point Mugu, California;
VP-1, NAS Whidbey Island, Washington [YB];
VP-4, MCBH Kaneohe Bay, Hawaii [YD];
VP-5, NAS Jacksonville, Florida [LA];
VP-8, NAS Brunswick, Maine [LC];
VP-9, MCBH Kaneohe Bay, Hawaii [PD];
VP-10, NAS Brunswick, Maine [LD];
VP-16, NAS Jacksonville, Florida [LF];
VP-26, NAS Brunswick, Maine [LK];
VP-30, NAS Jacksonville, Florida [LL];
VP-40, NAS Whidbey Island, Washington [QE];
VP-45, NAS Jacksonville, Florida [LN];
VP-46, NAS Whidbey Island, Washington [RC];
VP-47, MCBH Kaneohe Bay, Hawaii [RD];
VP-62, NAS Jacksonville, Florida [LT];
VP-64, NAS Willow Grove, Pennsylvania [LU];
VP-65, NAS Point Mugu, California [PG];
VP-66, NAS Willow Grove, Pennsylvania [LV];
VP-69, NAS Whidbey Island, Washington [PJ];
VP-92, NAS Brunswick, Maine [LY];
VP-94, NAS New Orleans, Louisiana [PZ];
VPU-1, NAS Brunswick, Maine;
VPU-2, MCBH Kaneohe Bay, Hawaii;
VQ-1, NAS Whidbey Island, Washington [PR];
VQ-2, NAF Rota, Spain;
VX-1, NAS Patuxent River, Maryland

Serial	Code	Type	Unit
148883		NP-3D	NFATS
148889		UP-3A	NAWC-AD
149674		NP-3D	NRL
149675		VP-3A	CinCPAC
149676		VP-3A	CNO
150495		UP-3A	NAF Keflavik
150496		VP-3A	CinCUSNFE
150499	[337]	NP-3D	NWTSPM
150511		VP-3A	
150515		VP-3A	VP-30
150521	[341]	NP-3D	NWTSPM
150522	[340]	NP-3D	NWTSPM
150524	[335]	NP-3D	NWTSPM
150526		UP-3A	VQ-1
152141	[408]	P-3A	VP-1
152150		NP-3D	NFATS
152165	[404]	P-3A	VP-1
152739		NP-3B	NAWC-23
153442		NP-3D	NRL
153443		NP-3D	USNTPS
154577		P-3A	VP-1
154587		NP-3D	NRL
154589		NP-3D	NRL
156507	[PR-31]	EP-3E	VQ-1
156509		P-3C	VP-8
156510	[LL-510]	P-3C	VP-30
156511	[PR-32]	EP-3E	VQ-1
156514	[PR-33]	EP-3E	VQ-1
156515	[LY-515]	P-3C	VP-92
156516		P-3C	VP-5
156517	[PR-34]	EP-3E	VQ-1
156518	[LL-518]	P-3C	VP-30
156519	[21]	EP-3E	VQ-2
156520		P-3C	VP-5
156521		P-3C	VP-65
156522	[LL-522]	P-3C	VP-30
156523	[LL-523]	P-3C	VP-30
156525	[LT-527][11]	P-3C	VQ-2
156527		P-3C	VP62
156528	[PR-36]	EP-3E	VQ-1
156529	[24]	EP-3E	VQ-2
156530	[LL-530]	P-3C	VP-30
157310	[LA-310]	P-3C	VP-5
157311		P-3C	VP-45
157312	[LN-312]	P-3C	VP-45
157313	[LC-313]	P-3C	VP-8
157314	[314]	P-3C	VP-8
157315		P-3C	VP-16
157316	[23]	EP-3E	VQ-2
157317		P-3C	VP-92
157318	[PR-35]	EP-3E	VQ-1
157319	[LF-319]	P-3C	VP-16
157321	[LK-321]	P-3C	VP-26
157322	[322]	P-3C	VP-1
157323		P-3C	VP-65
157324	[PD-324]	P-3C	VP-9
157325	[25]	EP-3E	VQ-2
157326	[22]	EP-3E	VQ-2
157327	[PD-327]	P-3C	VP-9
157328	[LL-328]	P-3C	VP-30
157329	[RD-329]	P-3C	VP-47
157330	[330]	P-3C	VP-46
157331	[LL-331]	P-3C	VP-30
158204	[204]	P-3C	NFATS
158205	[QE-205]	P-3C	VP-40
158206	[JA-03]	P-3C	VX-1
158207	[LC-207]	P-3C	VP-8
158208	[YD-208]	P-3C	VP-4
158209	[YD-209]	P-3C	VP-4
158210	[210]	P-3C	VP5
158211	[211]	P-3C	VP-1
158212	[RD-212]	P-3C	VP-47
158214	[LL-214]	P-3C	VP-30
158215	[YD-215]	P-3C	VP-4
158216	[216]	P-3C	VP-46
158218	[RD-218]	P-3C	VP-47
158219	[LN-219]	P-3C	VP-45
158220	[YD-220]	P-3C	VP-4
158221	[RC-221]	P-3C	VP-46
158222	[QE-222]	P-3C	VP-40
158223	[YD-223]	P-3C	VP-4
158224	[LD-224]	P-3C	VP-10
158225	[225]	P-3C	VP-9
158226	[226]	P-3C	VP-47
158227	[227]	NP-3D	NRL
158563	[LA-563]	P-3C	VP-5
158564	[LA-564]	P-3C	VP-5
158565	[LD-565]	P-3C	VP-10
158566	[LA-566]	P-3C	VP-5
158567	[LF-567]	P-3C	VP-16
158568	[LC-568]	P-3C	VP-8
158569	[569]	P-3C	VP-8
158570	[LN-570]	P-3C	VP-45
158571	[LA-571]	P-3C	VP-5
158572	[LA-572]	P-3C	VP-5
158573	[LD-573]	P-3C	VP-10
158574		P-3C	NASC-FS
158912		P-3C	NFATS
158913	[QE-913]	P-3C	VP-40
158914	RC-914]	P-3C	VP-46
158915	[915]	P-3C	VP-46
158916	[LL-916]	P-3C	VP-30
158917	[LC-917]	P-3C	VP-8
158918	[YD-918]	P-3C	VP-4
158919	[LN-919]	P-3C	VP-45

158920	[LF-920]	P-3C	VP-16	161013	[LT-013]	P-3C	VP-62
158921		P-3C	VP-47	161014	[LV-014]	P-3C	VP-66
158922	[RD-922]	P-3C	VP-47	161121		P-3C	VP-5
158923	[923]	P-3C	VP-4	161122	[224]	P-3C	VPU-1
158924	[LF-924]	P-3C	VP-16	161123	[LU-123]	P-3C	VP-64
158925	[925]	P-3C	VP-16	161124	[LA-124]	P-3C	VP-5
158926	[LD-926]	P-3C	VP-10	161125	[LV-125]	P-3C	VP-66
158927	[927]	P-3C	VP-16	161126	[PR-50]	P-3C	VQ-1
158929	[LD-929]	P-3C	VP-10	161127	[127]	P-3C	VP-62
158931		P-3C	VP-5	161128		P-3C	VP-5
158932	[LN-932]	P-3C	VP-45	161129	[LV-129]	P-3C	VP-66
158933	[LN-933]	P-3C	VP-45	161130	[PR-52]	P-3C	VQ-1
158934	[934]	P-3C	VP-1	161131	[LU-131]	P-3C	VP-64
158935	[LL-43]	P-3C	VP-30	161132	[PD-132]	P-3C	VP-9
159318	[LA-318]	P-3C	VP-5	161329	[LU-329]	P-3C	VP-64
159319	[319]	P-3C	VP-8	161330	[030]	P-3C	VP-46
159320	[320]	P-3C	VP-26	161331	[LU-331]	P-3C	VP-64
159321	[RC-321]	P-3C	VP-46	161332	[PG-332]	P-3C	VP-65
159322	[322]	P-3C	VP-26	161333	[PG-333]	P-3C	VP-65
159323	[323]	P-3C	VP-46	161334	[PZ-334]	P-3C	VP-94
159324	[324]	P-3C	VP-46	161335	[PZ-335]	P-3C	VP-94
159326	[PD-326]	P-3C	VP-9	161336	[LY-336]	P-3C	VP-92
159327	[PD-327]	P-3C	VP-9	161337	[PZ-337]	P-3C	VP-94
159328	[RC-328]	P-3C	VP-46	161338	[LA-338]	P-3C	VP-56
159329		P-3C	VP-47	161339	[YD-339]	P-3C	VP-4
159503		P-3C	VP-26	161340	[LC-340]	P-3C	VP-8
159504		P-3C	VPU-2	161404	[LL-404]	P-3C	VP-30
159506	[568]	P-3C	VPU-1	161405	[QE-405]	P-3C	VP-40
159507	[RD-507]	P-3C	VP-47	161406		P-3C	VP-40
159512		P-3C	VP-5	161407	[PG-407]	P-3C	VP-65
159513	[LL-18]	P-3C	VP-30	161408	[PZ-408]	P-3C	VP-94
159514	[LL-514]	P-3C	VP-30	161409		P-3C	VP-664
159884	[LD-884]	P-3C	VP-30	161410		P-3C	NAWC 23
159885	[885]	P-3C	VP-9	161411	[LL-3]	P-3C	VP-30
159886	[09]	P-3C	VQ-2	161412	[PG-412]	P-3C	VP-65
159887		P-3C	NASC-FS	161413	[LL-39]	P-3C	VP-30
159889	[889]	P-3C	VX-1	161414	[LA-414]	P-3C	VP-5
159891	[LN-891]	P-3C	VP-45	161415	[LL-415]	P-3C	VP-30
159894	[LL-40]	P-3C	VP-30	161585		P-3C	VPU-1
160283	[PD-283]	P-3C	VP-9	161586	[LL-11]	P-3C	VP-30
160284	[LL-284]	P-3C	VP-26	161587	[YD-587]	P-3C	VP-4
160286	[286]	P-3C	VP-26	161588		P-3C	VP-30
160287	[LC-287]	P-3C	VP-8	161589	[589]	P-3C	VP-9
160288		P-3C	NASC-FS	161590	[LL-4]	P-3C	VP-30
160290	[290]	P-3C	NFATS	161591	[PZ-591]	P-3C	VP-94
160291	[JA-05]	P-3C	VX-1	161592	[PZ-592]	P-3C	VP-94
160292		P-3C	VPU-2	161593	[LL-593]	P-3C	VP-30
160293	[293]	P-3C	VP-4	161594	[LL-594]	P-3C	VP-30
160610	[RC-610]	P-3C	VP-46	161595	[LV-595]	P-3C	VP-66
160611	[LU-611]	P-3C	VP-64	161596	[LL-596]	P-3C	VP-30
160612		P-3C	VP-1	161763	[763]	P-3C	VP-47
160761	[LU-761]	P-3C	VP-64	161764	[YD-764]	P-3C	VP-4
160762	[LV-762]	P-3C	VP-66	161765	[PG-765]	P-3C	VP-65
160763	[LT-763]	P-3C	VP-62	161766	[PJ-766]	P-3C	VP-69
160764	[764]	P-3C	NRL	161767	[PD-767]	P-3C	VP-9
160765	[765]	P-3C	VP-10	162314	[LY-314]	P-3C	VP-92
160766	[PJ-766]	P-3C	VP-69	162315	[YD-315]	P-3C	VP-1
160767	[767]	P-3C	VP-66	162316		P-3C	VP-45
160768	[PR-51]	P-3C	VQ-1	162317	[YD-317]	P-3C	VP-4
160769	[LK-769]	P-3C	VP-26	162318	[PJ-318]	P-3C	VP-69
160770		P-3C	VP-8	162770		P-3C	NFATS
160999	[LL-999]	P-3C	VP-30	162771	[YD-771]	P-3C	VP-4
161000	[LF-000]	P-3C	VP-16	162772	[772]	P-3C	VP-1
161001	[LU-001]	P-3C	VP-64	162773	[773]	P-3C	VP-40
161002	[002]	P-3C	VP-16	162774	[RD-04]	P-3C	NFATS
161003	[PD-003]	P-3C	VP-9	162775	[QE-775]	P-3C	VP-40
161004	[LK-004]	P-3C	VP-26	162776	[LA-776]	P-3C	VP-5
161005	[LU-005]	P-3C	VP-64	162777	[RD-777]	P-3C	VP-47
161006	[PG-006]	P-3C	VP-65	162778	[LA-778]	P-3C	VP-5
161007	[LU-007]	P-3C	VP-64	162998	[RD-998]	P-3C	VP-47
161008	[LL-008]	P-3C	VP-30	162999	[PJ-999]	P-3C	VP-69
161009	[LL-50]	P-3C	VP-30	163000		P-3C	VP-459
161010	[LL-010]	P-3C	VP-30	163001	[LT-001]	P-3C	VP-62
161011	[LK-011]	P-3C	VP-26	163002	[LT-002]	P-3C	VP-62
161012	[YD-012]	P-3C	VP-4	163003	[PJ-003]	P-3C	VP-69

163004	[PG-004]	P-3C	VP-65
163005	[LT-005]	P-3C	VP-62
163006	[JA-06]	P-3C	VX-1
163289	[LT-289]	P-3C	VP-62
163290	[PJ-290]	P-3C	VP-69
163291	[PG-291]	P-3C	VP-65
163292	[LF-292]	P-3C	VP-16
163293	[LA-293]	P-3C	VP-5
163294	[LY-294]	P-3C	VP-92
163295	[LY-295]	P-3C	VP-92

Boeing E-6 Mercury
Boeing, McConnell AFB, Kansas;
VQ-3 & VQ-4, SCW-1, Tinker AFB, Oklahoma

162782	E-6B	VQ-4
162783	E-6B	VQ-3
162784	E-6B	VQ-3
163918	E-6B	VQ-3
163919	E-6B	VQ-3
163920	E-6B	VQ-3
164386	E-6A	VQ-3
164387	E-6B	VQ-3
164388	E-6A	VQ-4
164404	E-6A	VQ-4
164405	E-6A	VQ-4
164406	E-6B	VQ-3
164407	E-6A	VQ-4
164408	E-6A	VQ-4
164409	E-6B	VQ-4
164410	E-6A	VQ-4

McDonnell Douglas C-9B Skytrain II/DC-9-32*
VMR-1, Cherry Point MCAS, North Carolina;
VR-46, Atlanta, Georgia [JS];
VR-52, Willow Grove NAS, Pennsylvania [JT];
VR-56, Norfolk NAS, Virginia [JU];
VR-57, North Island NAS, California [RX];
VR-58, Jacksonville NAS, Florida [JV];
VR-59, NAS Fort Worth JRB, Texas [RY];
VR-61, Whidbey Island NAS, Washington [RS];

159113	[RX]	VR-57
159114	[JS]	VR-46
159115	[RX]	VR-57
159116	[RX]	VR-57
159117	[JU]	VR-56
159118	[JU]	VR-56
159119	[JU]	VR-56
159120	[JU]	VR-56
160046		VMR-1
160047		VMR-1
160048	[JV]	VR-58
160049	[JV]	VR-58
160050	[JV]	VR-58
160051	[JS]	VR-46
161266	[JS]	VR-46
161529	[JS]	VR-46
161530	[RY]	VR-59
162753	[JT]	VR-52
162754	[JT]	VR-52
163036*	[JT]	VR-52
163208*	[RY]	VR-59
163511*	[JS]	VR-46
163512*	[RX]	VR-57
163513*	[JV]	VR-58
164605*	[RS]	VR-61
164606*	[RS]	VR-61
164607*	[RS]	VR-61
164608*	[RS]	VR-61

Grumman C-20D Gulfstream III/
C-20G Gulfstream IV*
VR-1, NAF Washington, Maryland;
VR-48, NAF Washington, Maryland [JR];
VR-51, MCBH Kaneohe Bay, Hawaii [RG]

163691		VR-1
163692		VR-1
165093*	[JR]	VR-48
165094*	[JR]	VR-48
165151*	[RG]	VR-51
165152*	[RG]	VR-51
165153*		

Boeing C-40A Clipper
VR-59, NAS Fort Worth JRB, Texas [RY]

165829	[RY]	VR-59
165830	[RY]	VR-59
165831	[RY]	VR-59
165832		Boeing
165833		Boeing
165834		Boeing
165835		Boeing
165836		Boeing

Lockheed C-130 Hercules
NAWC-AD, NAS Patuxent River, Maryland;
VR-53, NAF Washington, Maryland [WV];
VR-54, New Orleans NAS, Louisiana [CW];
VR-55, Moffett Field, California [RU];
VR-62, Brunswick NAS, Maine [JW];
VMGR-152, Futenma MCAS, Japan [QD];
VMGR-234, NAS Fort Worth, Texas [QH];
VMGR-252, Cherry Point MCAS,
    North Carolina [BH];
VMGRT-253, Cherry Point MCAS,
    North Carolina [GR];
VMGR-352, MCAS Miramar, California [QB];
VMGR-452, Stewart Field, New York [NY]

147572	[QB]	KC-130F	VMGR-352
147573	[QD]	KC-130F	VMGR-152
148246	[GR]	KC-130F	VMGRT-253
148247	[QD]	KC-130F	VMGR-152
148248	[QD]	KC-130F	VMGR-152
148249	[GR]	KC-130F	VMGRT-253
148890	[GR]	KC-130F	VMGRT-253
148891	[BH]	KC-130F	VMGR-252
148893	[QD]	KC-130F	VMGR-152
148894	[BH]	KC-130F	VMGR-252
148895	[BH]	KC-130F	VMGR-252
148896	[BH]	KC-130F	VMGR-252
148897	[BH]	KC-130F	VMGR-252
148898	[BH]	KC-130F	VMGR-252
148899	[BH]	KC-130F	VMGR-252
149788	[BH]	KC-130F	VMGR-252
149789	[BH]	KC-130F	VMGR-252
149791	[QB]	KC-130F	VMGR-352
149792	[QB]	KC-130F	VMGR-352
149795	[QB]	KC-130F	VMGR-352
149796	[QB]	KC-130F	VMGR-352
149798	[QB]	KC-130F	VMGR-352
149799	[QD]	KC-130F	VMGR-152
149800	[QB]	KC-130F	VMGR-352
149803	[GR]	KC-130F	VMGRT-253
149806		KC-130F	NAWC-AD
149807	[QD]	KC-130F	VMGR-152
149808	[BH]	KC-130F	VMGR-252
149811	[GR]	KC-130F	VMGRT-253
149812	[QD]	KC-130F	VMGR-152
149815	[QB]	KC-130F	VMGR-352
149816	[QD]	KC-130F	VMGR-152
150684	[GR]	KC-130F	VMGRT-253
150686	[BH]	KC-130F	VMGR-252
150687	[GR]	KC-130F	VMGRT-253
150688	[GR]	KC-130F	VMGRT-253
150689	[QB]	KC-130F	VMGR-352
150690	[QD]	KC-130F	VMGR-152
151891		TC-130G	Blue Angels
160013	[QD]	KC-130R	VMGR-152
160014	[QD]	KC-130R	VMGR-152
160015	[QB]	KC-130R	VMGR-352
160016	[QB]	KC-130R	VMGR-352

USN/USMC

160017	[QB]	KC-130R	VMGR-352
160018	[QD]	KC-130R	VMGR-152
160019	[QD]	KC-130R	VMGR-152
160020	[QD]	KC-130R	VMGR-152
160022	[QB]	KC-130R	VMGR-352
160240	[QB]	KC-130R	VMGR-352
160625	[BH]	KC-130R	VMGR-252
160626	[BH]	KC-130R	VMGR-252
160627	[BH]	KC-130R	VMGR-252
160628	[BH]	KC-130R	VMGR-252
162308	[QH]	KC-130T	VMGR-234
162309	[QH]	KC-130T	VMGR-234
162310	[QH]	KC-130T	VMGR-234
162311	[QH]	KC-130T	VMGR-234
162785	[QH]	KC-130T	VMGR-234
162786	[QH]	KC-130T	VMGR-234
163022	[QH]	KC-130T	VMGR-234
163023	[QH]	KC-130T	VMGR-234
163310	[QH]	KC-130T	VMGR-234
163311	[NY]	KC-130T	VMGR-452
163591	[NY]	KC-130T	VMGR-452
163592	[NY]	KC-130T	VMGR-452
164105	[NY]	KC-130T	VMGR-452
164106	[NY]	KC-130T	VMGR-452
164180	[NY]	KC-130T	VMGR-452
164181	[NY]	KC-130T	VMGR-452
164441	[NY]	KC-130T	VMGR-452
164442	[NY]	KC-130T	VMGR-452
164597	[NY]	KC-130T-30	VMGR-452
164598	[QH]	KC-130T-30	VMGR-234
164762		C-130T	NAWC-AD
164763		C-130T	NAWC-AD
164993	[CW]	C-130T	VR-54
164994	[WV]	C-130T	VR-53

164995	[CW]	C-130T	VR-54
164996	[WV]	C-130T	VR-53
164997	[WV]	C-130T	VR-53
164998	[WV]	C-130T	VR-53
164999	[QH]	KC-130T	VMGR-234
165000	[QH]	KC-130T	VMGR-234
165158	[CW]	C-130T	VR-54
165159	[CW]	C-130T	VR-54
165160	[CW]	C-130T	VR-54
165161	[RU]	C-130T	VR-55
165162	[QH]	KC-130T	VMGR-234
165163	[QH]	KC-130T	VMGR-234
165313	[JW]	C-130T	VR-62
165314	[JW]	C-130T	VR-62
165315	[NY]	KC-130T	VMGR-452
165316	[NY]	KC-130T	VMGR-452
165348	[JW]	C-130T	VR-62
165349	[JW]	C-130T	VR-62
165350	[RU]	C-130T	VR-55
165351	[RU]	C-130T	VR-55
165352	[NY]	KC-130T	VMGR-452
165353	[NY]	KC-130T	VMGR-452
165378	[RU]	C-130T	VR-55
165379	[RU]	C-130T	VR-55
165735	[BH]	KC-130J	VMGR-252
165736	[BH]	KC-130J	VMGR-252
165737		KC-130J	
165738		KC-130J	
165739		KC-130J	
165809		KC-130J	
165810		KC-130J	

US-based US Coast Guard Aircraft

Grumman C-20B Gulfstream III
USCG, Washington DC
01

Lockheed HC-130H Hercules
USCGS Barbers Point, Hawaii;
USCGS Clearwater, Florida;
USCGS Elizabeth City, North Carolina;
USCGS Kodiak, Alaska;
USCGS Sacramento, California

1500	Elizabeth City
1501	Elizabeth City
1502	Elizabeth City
1503	Elizabeth City
1504	Elizabeth City
1601	Sacramento
1602	Sacramento
1603	Elizabeth City
1700	Kodiak
1701	Barbers Point

1702	Kodiak
1703	Barbers Point
1704	Sacramento
1705	Barbers Point
1706	Clearwater
1707	Kodiak
1708	Clearwater
1709	Kodiak
1710	Kodiak
1711	Barbers Point
1712	Elizabeth City
1713	Clearwater
1714	Barbers Point
1715	Kodiak
1716	Sacramento
1717	Kodiak
1718	Clearwater
1719	Elizabeth City
1720	Clearwater
1790	Sacramento

US Government Aircraft

BAe 125-800A (C-29A)
Federal Aviation Administration, Oklahoma

N94	(88-0269)
N95	(88-0270)
N96	(88-0271)
N97	(88-0272)
N98	(88-0273)
N99	(88-0274)

Gates LearJet 35A
Phoenix Aviation/Flight International/
  US Navy, Naples
N20DK
N50FN
N88JA
N118FN

Military Aviation Sites on the Internet

The list below is not intended to be a complete list of military aviation sites on the Internet. The sites listed cover Museums, Locations, Air Forces, Companies and Organisations that are mentioned elsewhere in 'Military Aircraft Markings'. Sites listed are in English or contain sufficient English to be reasonably easily understood. Each site address is believed to be correct at the time of going to press. Additions are welcome, via the usual address found at the front of the book, or via e-mail to hjcurtis@ntlworld.com.

Name of site	Internet Dial (all prefixed 'http;//')
No 2 Sqn	www.rafmarham.co.uk/organisation/2squadron/2squadron.htm
No 4 Regiment Army Air Corps	www.4regimentaac.co.uk/
No 5 Sqn	www.5squadron.fsnet.co.uk
No 6 Flt	www.shawbury.raf.mod.uk/6fltaac.htm
No 8 Sqn	www.users.globalnet.co.uk/~8sqnwad/
No 9 Sqn	www.rafmarham.co.uk/organisation/9squadron/9sqn_front.htm
No 13 Sqn	www.rafmarham.co.uk/organisation/13squadron/13squadron.htm
No 15 Sqn	www.xvsquadron.co.uk/
No 23 Sqn	www.users.globalnet.co.uk/~23sqnwad/
No 31 Sqn	www.rafmarham.co.uk/organisation/31squadron/31sqn.htm
No 39(1 PRU) Sqn	www.rafmarham.co.uk/organisation/39squadron/39squadron2.htm
No 42(R) Sqn	www.kinloss.raf.mod.uk/opswing/ops42r.htm
No 45(R) Sqn	www.cranwell.raf.mod.uk/3fts/45sqn/45sqn.htm
No 55(R) Sqn	www.cranwell.raf.mod.uk/3fts/55sqn/55sqn.htm
No 56 Sqn	www.56firebirds.raf.mod.uk/
No 120 Sqn	www.kinloss.raf.mod.uk/opswing/ops120.htm
No 201 Sqn	www.kinloss.raf.mod.uk/opswing/ops201.htm
No 206 Sqn	www.kinloss.raf.mod.uk/opswing/ops206.htm
Aberdeen, Dundee and St Andrews UAS	dialspace.dial.pipex.com/town/way/gba87/adstauas/
The Army Air Corps	www.army.mod.uk/armyaircorps/index.htm
Blue Eagles Home Page	www.deltaweb.co.uk/eagles/
Defence Helicopter Flying School	www.shawbury.raf.mod.uk/dhfs.htm
ETPS	www.etps.dera.gov.uk/
Liverpool University Air Squadron	www.sn63.dial.pipex.com/
Manchester & Salford Universities Air Sqn	www.masuas.dial.pipex.com/
Ministry of Defence	www.mod.uk/
Oxford University Air Sqn	users.ox.ac.uk/~ouairsqn/
QinetiQ	www.qinetiq.com/
RAF Benson	www.raf.mod.uk/rafbenson/index.htm
RAF Brize Norton	www.rafbrizenorton.com/
RAF Church Fenton (unofficial)	www.rafchurchfenton.org.uk/
RAF College Cranwell	www.cranwell.raf.mod.uk/
RAF Cosford	www.raf.mod.uk/cosford/
RAF Kinloss	www.kinloss.raf.mod.uk/
RAF Leuchars	www.leuchars.raf.mod.uk/
RAF Lossiemouth	www.raflossiemouth.co.uk/
RAF Lyneham	www.lyneham.raf.mod.uk/
RAF Marham	www.rafmarham.co.uk/
RAF Northolt	www.northolt.com/
RAF Northolt (unofficial)	www.fly.to/Northolt/
RAF Odiham	www.rafodiham.co.uk/
RAF St Athan	ourworld.compuserve.com/homepages/st_athan/
RAF Shawbury	www.shawbury.raf.mod.uk/
RAF Valley	www.rafvalley.org/
RAF Waddington	www.raf-waddington.com/
Red Arrows	www.raf.mod.uk/reds/redhome.html
Royal Air Force	www.raf.mod.uk/
Royal Auxiliary Air Force	www.rauxaf.mod.uk/
SAOEU	www.saoeu.org/
Universities of Glasgow & Strathclyde Air Squadron	www.ugsas.fsnet.co.uk/
The University of Birmingham Air Squadron	www.sn61.dial.pipex.com/
University of London Air Sqn	www.raf.mod.uk/ulas

Military Aviation Internet

Name of site	Internet Dial (all prefixed 'http://')
MILITARY SITES – US	
Air Combat Command	www.acc.af.mil/
Air Force Flight Test Center (Edwards AFB)	www.edwards.af.mil/
Air Force Reserve Command	www.afrc.af.mil/
Air National Guard	www.ang.af.mil/
AMARC - up to date list of aircraft	www.dm.af.mil/amarc/inventory.htm
Aviano Air Base	www.aviano.af.mil/
Holloman Air Force Base	www.holloman.af.mil/
Hurricane Hunters Home Page (53rd WRS)	www.hurricanehunters.com/
Liberty Wing Home Page (48th FW)	www.lakenheath.af.mil/
NASA	www.nasa.gov/
Nellis Air Force Base	www.nellis.af.mil/
Spangdahlem Air Base	www.spangdahlem.af.mil/
Travis Air Force Base	www.travis.af.mil/
The Thunderbirds	www.nellis.af.mil/thunderbirds/
USAF	www.af.mil/
USAF Europe	www.usafe.af.mil/
USAF World Wide Web Sites	www.af.mil/sites/
US Army	www.army.mil/
US Marine Corps	www.usmc.mil/
US Navy	www.navy.mil/
US Navy Patrol Squadrons (unofficial)	www.vpnavy.com/
Whiteman Air Force Base	www.whiteman.af.mil/
MILITARY SITES – ELSEWHERE	
301 Sqn Klu	www.301sqn.com/
315 Sqn Klu	www.geocities.com/Pentagon/Quarters/8440/
Armée de l'Air	www.defense.gouv.fr/air/
Armée de l'Air (unofficial)	www.mygale.org/06/airmil/index.shtml
Aeronautica Militare	www.aeronautica.difesa.it
Austrian Armed Forces (in German)	www.bmlv.gv.at/
Belgian Air Force	www.mil.be/baf/eng/index_e.htm
East European Air Forces (unofficial)	mm.iit.uni-miskolc.hu/Data/Winx/
Finnish Defence Force	www.mil.fi/english/
Forca Aerea Portuguesa	www.emfa.pt/
Frecce Tricolori	users.iol.it/gromeo/
German Marine	www.bundeswehr.de/bundeswehr/marine/index.html
Indian Air Force	www.bharat-rakshak.com/IAF/
Israeli Defence Force/Air Force	www.idf.il/
Japan Air Self Defence Force	www.jda.go.jp/jasdf/indexe.htm
Luftforsvaret	www.mil.no/luftforsvaret/
Luftwaffe	www.bundeswehr.de/bundeswehr/luftwaffe/ index.html
NATO	www.nato.int/
Royal Australian Air Force	www.adfa.oz.au/DOD/RAAF/
Royal Danish Air Force (in Danish)	www.ftk.dk/
Royal Netherlands AF	www.mindef.nl/english/rnlaf1.htm
Royal New Zealand AF	www.airforce.mil.nz/
Royal Thai Air Force	www.rtaf.mi.th
Singapore Air Force	www.mindef.gov.sg/rsaf/
South African AF Site (unofficial)	www.geocities.com/dwingrin/saaf.htm
Spanish Air Force	www.aire.org/
Swedish Air Force	www2.mil.se/
Swedish Military Aviation (unofficial)	www.canit.se/%7Egriffon/aviation/
Swiss Armed Forces	www.vbs.admin.ch/internet/e/armee/
Turkish General Staff (Armed Forces)	www.tsk.mil.tr/
AIRCRAFT & AERO ENGINE MANUFACTURERS	
BAE Systems	www.baesystems.com/
Bell Helicopter Textron	www.bellhelicopter.textron.com/index.html
Boeing	www.boeing.com/
Bombardier	www.bombardier.com/
Britten-Norman	www.britten-norman.com/
CFM International	www.cfm56.com/
Dassault	www.dassault-aviation.com/
EADS	www.eads.net/
Embraer	www.embraer.com/
Fairchild Dornier	www.fairchilddornier.com/
Fokker	www.fokker.com/
General Electric	www.ge.com/
Gulfstream Aerospace	www.gulfstream.com/
Kaman Aerospace	www.kaman.com/
LET	www.let.cz/

Name of site	Internet Dial (all prefixed 'http;//')
Lockheed Martin	www.lockheedmartin.com/
Lockheed Martin Aeronautics	www.lmaeronautics.com/palmdale/index.html
Raytheon	www.raytheon.com/rac/
Rolls-Royce	www.rolls-royce.com/
SAAB	www.saab.se/
Sikorsky	www.sikorsky.com/
Westland	www.gkn-whl.co.uk/

UK AVIATION MUSEUMS

Aviation Museums in Great Britain	www.rdg.ac.uk/AcaDepts/sn/wsn1/dept/av/gb.html
Bournemouth Aviation Museum	www.aviation-museum.co.uk/
Brooklands Museum	www.motor-software.co.uk/brooklands/
City of Norwich Aviation Museum	www.cnam.co.uk/
de Havilland Aircraft Heritage Centre	www.hertsmuseums.org.uk/dehavilland/index.htm
Flambards Village Theme Park	www.flambards.co.uk/
Gatwick Aviation Museum	www.gatwick-aviation-museum.co.uk/
The Helicopter Museum	www.helicoptermuseum.co.uk/
Imperial War Museum, Duxford	www.iwm.org.uk/duxford/
Imperial War Museum, Duxford (unofficial)	dspace.dial.pipex.com/town/square/rcy85/
The Jet Age Museum	www.jetagemuseum.org/
Lincs Aviation Heritage Centre	freespace.virgin.net/nick.tasker/ekirkby.htm
Midland Air Museum	www.midlandairmuseum.org.uk/
Museum of Berkshire Aviation	fly.to/MuseumofBerkshireAviation/
Museum of Flight, East Fortune	www.nms.ac.uk/flight/main.htm
Museum of Science & Industry, Manchester	www.msim.org.uk/
Newark Air Museum	www.newarkairmuseum.co.uk/
North East Aircraft Museum	members.tripod.com/~BDaugherty/neam.html
RAF Manston Spitfire & Hurricane Memorial	www.spitfire-museum.com/
RAF Museum, Hendon	www.rafmuseum.org.uk/
Science Museum, South Kensington	www.sciencemuseum.org.uk/
Yorkshire Air Museum, Elvington	www.yorkshireairmuseum.co.uk

AVIATION SOCIETIES

Air Britain	www.air-britain.com/
Air North	www.airnorth.demon.co.uk/
Cleveland Aviation Society	homepage.ntlworld.com/phillip.charlton/cashome.html
East London Aviation Society	www.westrowops.co.uk/newsletter/elas.htm
Friends of Leeming Aviation Group	www.crakehal.demon.co.uk/aviation/flag.htm
Gilze-Rijen Aviation Society	www.gras-spotters.nl/
Royal Aeronautical Society	www.raes.org.uk/
St Athan Aviation Group	www.westrowops.co.uk/newsletter/stamu.htm
Scramble (Dutch Aviation Society)	www.scramble.nl/
Solent Aviation Society	www.solent-aviation-society.co.uk/
Spitfire Society	www.spitfiresociety.demon.co.uk/
Ulster Aviation Society	www.d-n-a.net/users/dnetrAzQ/

OPERATORS OF HISTORIC AIRCRAFT

Battle of Britain Memorial Flight	www.bbmf.co.uk/
Catalina Online	www.catalina.org.uk/
Classic Jets (UK)	www.classicjets.co.uk/
Delta Jets	www.deltajets.ik.com/
Kennet Aircraft	www.airplane.demon.co.uk/
Old Flying Machine Company	www.ofmc.co.uk/
The Fighter Collection	www.avnet.co.uk/tfc/
The Real Aeroplane Company	www.realaero.com/
The Vulcan Operating Company	www.tvoc.co.uk/

SITES RELATING TO SPECIFIC TYPES OF MILITARY AIRCRAFT

The 655 Maintenance & Preservation Society	www.jetman.dircon.co.uk/xm655/
The Avro Shackleton Page	www.home.aone.net.au/shack_one/
B-24 Liberator	www.b24bestweb.com/
Buccaneer Supporter's Club	www.buccaneerclub.co.uk/
EE Canberra	www.netcomuk.co.uk/~lesb/canberra.html
English Electric Lightning - Vertical Reality	www.aviation-picture-hangar.co.uk/Lightning.html
The Eurofighter site	www.eurofighter.org/
The ex FRADU Canberra Site	www.fradu-hunters.co.uk/canberra/
The ex FRADU Hunter Site	www.fradu-hunters.co.uk/
F-4 Phantom II Society	www.f4phantom.org/
F-16: The Complete Reference	www.f-16.net/
F-86 Web Page	www.f-86.tripod.com
F-105 Thunderchief	www.geocities.com/Pentagon/7002/

Military Aviation Internet

Name of site	Internet Dial (all prefixed 'http://')
The Gripen	www.gripen.com/
International F-104 Society	home.hetnet.nl/~hluijkx/ifs/ifs.html
K5083 - Home Page (Hawker Hurricane)	www3.mistral.co.uk/k5083/
Lockheed C-130 Hercules	hometown.aol.com/SamC130/
Lockheed SR-71 Blackbird	www.wvi.com/~lelandh/sr-71~1.htm
The MiG-21 Page	www.topedge.com/panels/aircraft/sites/kraft/mig.htm
P-3 Orion Research Group	home.wxs.nl/~p3orin/
P-51 Mustang	www.p51mustang.com/
Scramble on the Web - SAAB Viggen Database	www.scramble.nl/viggen.htm
Swiss F-18 Hornet site (unofficial)	www.geocities.com/CapeCanaveral/Lab/6063/
Thunder & Lightnings (Postwar British Aircraft)	www.thunder-and-lightnings.co.uk/
Vulcan 558 Club	www.vulcan558club.demon.co.uk/
Vulcan Restoration Trust	www.XL426.com

MISCELLANEOUS

Aerodata	dspace.dial.pipex.com/aerodata/
Aeroflight	www.netlink.co.uk/users/aeroflt/
The 'AirNet' Web Site	fly.to/AirNet/
Air-Scene UK	www.f4aviation.co.uk
AirSpeed	www.netmontage.co.uk/airspeed/
Chinese Military Aviation	www.concentric.net/~Jetfight/
David Hastings' Military Aviation Page	users.ox.ac.uk/~daveh/Military/
Dutch Spotters On-line	www.dutchspotters.com/
Farnborough Movements & Photographs	www.geocities.com/CapeCanaveral/Hangar/1937/
Military Aircraft Database	www.csd.uwo.ca/~pettypi/elevon/gustin_military/
Military Aviation	www.crakehal.demon.co.uk/aviation/aviation.htm
Military Aviation Review/MAP	www.mar.co.uk/
Polish Aviation Site	aviation.pol.pl/
Russian Aviation Page	aeroweb.lucia.it/~agretch/RAP.html
Scramble on the Web - Air Show Reports	www.scramble.nl/airshows.htm
The Spotter's Nest	www.spotters.it/
UK Military Aircraft Serials Resource Centre	www.serials.uk.com
UK Military Spotting	www.thunder-and-lightnings.co.uk/spotting/

Tornado F3 ZG731 carries the AWC/F3OEU markings on its tail. *Daniel March*

Still retaining its former small ships Flight markings, this Westland Wasp HAS1 XT781 is now privately owned at Cranfield *PRM*

Distinctively painted former Swiss Air Force Hunter F58 J-4015/HB-RVS. *PRM*

The last RAF VC10 K2 ZA142 refuelling a pair of Tornado F3s. *Daniel March*

New EHI-101 Merlin HC3 ZJ 122 is flown by No 28 Squadron from RAF Benson. *Daniel March*